Emergency Department Compliance Manual

2006 Edition

Emergency Department Compliance Manual provides everything you need to stay in compliance with complex emergency department regulations, including such topics as: legal compliance questions and answers: find the legal answers you need in seconds; Joint Commission survey questions and answers: get inside guidance from collegues who have been there; hospital accreditation standard analysis: learn about Joint Commission standards as they apply to the emergency department; and reference materials for emergency department compliance. The *Manual* offers all the tools you need to comply with emergency department-related regulations, laws, and accreditation standards.

Highlights of the 2006 Edition

New and updated legal and regulatory information affecting your Emergency Department, including:

- Benefits of compliance, keeping track of HIPAA complaints, obtaining a National Provider Identifier, and the Medicare Claims Appeals Process;

- Commentary on patient safety in the Joint Commission Survey;

- Updated section on hospital accreditation standards;

- New forms, policies, and other reference materials to faciliate compliance including:

  — Patient Identification Policy

  — Guidelines for Inter- and Intra-Hospital Transport of Critically Ill Patients

  — Pain Management: Medication Administration Record

  — X-Ray Release Form

  — Emergency Department Input/Throughput/Output Model of Patient Flow Diagram

5/06

For questions concerning this shipment, billing, or other customer service matters, call our Customer Service Department at 1-800-234-1660.

For toll-free ordering, please call 1-800-638-8437.

a Wolters Kluwer business

Emergency Department Compliance Manual
2006 Edition

Consulting Editor
Rusty McNew, RN, MA, CPHQ

Contributors
Denise Casaubon, RN, BSS
Kathleen Gilbert
Ann H. Nevers, JD, LLM Health Law

ASPEN
PUBLISHERS

76 Ninth Avenue, New York, NY 10011
www.aspenpublishers.com

This publication is designed to provide accurate and authoritative information in regard to the subject matter covered. It is sold with the understanding that the publisher is not engaged in rendering legal, accounting, or other professional services. If legal advice or other professional assistance is required, the services of a competent professional person should be sought.

—From a *Declaration of Principles* jointly adopted
by a Committee of the American Bar Association
and a Committee of Publishers and Associations

© 2006 Aspen Publishers, Inc.
a Wolters Kluwer business
www.aspenpublishers.com

Printed in the United States of America

ISBN 0-7355-5330-0

1 2 3 4 5 6 7 8 9 0

About Aspen Publishers

Aspen Publishers, headquartered in New York City, is a leading information provider for attorneys, business professionals, and law students. Written by preeminent authorities, our products consist of analytical and practical information covering both U.S. and international topics. We publish in the full range of formats, including updated manuals, books, periodicals, CDs, and online products.

Our proprietary content is complemented by 2,500 legal databases, containing over 11 million documents, available through our Loislaw division. Aspen Publishers also offers a wide range of topical legal and business databases linked to Loislaw's primary material. Our mission is to provide accurate, timely, and authoritative content in easily accessible formats, supported by unmatched customer care.

To order any Aspen Publishers title, go to *www.aspenpublishers.com* or call 1-800-638-8437.

To reinstate your manual update service, call 1-800-638-8437.

For more information on Loislaw products, go to *www.loislaw.com* or call 1-800-364-2512.

For Customer Care issues, e-mail CustomerCare@aspenpublishers.com; call 1-800-234-1660; or fax 1-800-901-9075.

Aspen Publishers
a Wolters Kluwer business

SUBSCRIPTION NOTICE

This Aspen Publishers product is updated on a periodic basis with supplements to reflect important changes in the subject matter. If you purchased this product directly from Aspen Publishers, we have already recorded your subscription for the update service.

If, however, you purchased this product from a bookstore and wish to receive future updates and revised or related volumes billed separately with a 30-day examination review, please contact our Customer Service Department at 1-800-234-1660, or send your name, company name (if applicable), address, and the title of the product to:

Aspen Publishers
7201 McKinney Circle
Frederick, MD 21704

Editorial Board

Contents

Acknowledgments

Developing and revising the *Emergency Department Compliance Manual* is a unique project, requiring the participation of many individuals. We are especially in debt to Consulting Editor Rusty McNew, Tenet Health System, who shares his expertise and creativity regarding strategies for preparing for Joint Commission surveys, as well as many sample materials from his organization. We also are immensely grateful to all Editorial Board members and contributors who aided in compiling examples of compliance documentation. Finally, we applaud the group of professionals who graciously consented to interviews about their recent Joint Commission survey experiences. Their candid comments bring a personal and practical section to the manual.

Introduction

Emergency department (ED) compliance issues can be overwhelming. Federal laws, state laws, local laws, liability concerns, and Joint Commission on Accreditation of Healthcare Organizations (Joint Commission) accreditation requirements affect nearly all aspects of patient care and departmental management. Leaders must balance their compliance obligations against patient care concerns, management time, and limited resources. The 2006 edition of this manual is designed to assist ED managers in finding that balance by providing urgently needed up-to-date information in a comprehensive, easy-to-use compliance tool that can be used to improve the care delivered to patients and meet various external requirements.

FEATURES OF THIS MANUAL

Legal Compliance Questions and Answers

This section of the manual provides an easy reference to legal issues commonly encountered in hospital EDs. A list of questions at the front of this section will enable you to quickly locate helpful and current information on a variety of difficult legal areas such as complying with fraud and abuse laws, patients' rights regulations, the Consolidated Omnibus Reconciliation Act (COBRA), negotiating consent requirements, obtaining reimbursement for ED services, avoiding employment law problems, and more. Citations to laws, regulations, and cases are provided for guiding additional research. Appendix 1-A provides a state-by-state summary of laws and regulations regarding exceptions to patient consent under emergency circumstances.

Joint Commission Survey Questions and Answers

This section contains valuable advice from staff members at hospitals that have recently and successfully navigated a Joint Commission survey. Interviewees provide frank and detailed information on what surveyors did and didn't look for, how they prepared staff for the survey, and how they demonstrated participation in performance improvement activities. This section is organized by topic, to allow you to readily compare the experiences of hospitals across the country.

Hospital Accreditation Standards Analysis

This section condenses applicable Joint Commission standards and elements of performance that are surveyed on the ED. Many standards are scored specifically in the ED while others are scored as a composite of the organization. This matrix allows ED managers to quickly find the standard, element of performance and understand how it is applicable to the ED.

Communication between the ED manager and the organization is a key component in the continuous Joint commission readiness. ED managers are encouraged to be in the communication loop on all activities that impact all applicable standards.

- *Comment:* This column describes the relationship between ED and hospital responsibility for demonstrating compliance with the standard. It also indicates what the standard assesses.

- *Evidence:* This column lists the types of evidence that might be used to show compliance with the standard. Special emphasis is paid to documents that are developed or maintained in the ED.

- *Staff questions:* This column lists questions that the Joint Commission surveyor might ask the ED director, nurse manager, ED staff members, and others to assess compliance with the standard.

Reference Materials for Emergency Department Compliance

This section of the manual provides documentation that hospitals across the country have recently used to show compliance with Joint Commission standards, as well as documentation used to meet legal requirements discussed in Legal Compliance Questions and Answers.

CMS and Joint Commission Standards Checklist

This tool allows customers to cross reference the Medicare Conditions of Participation to the Joint Commission Standards, and also provides a place for them to note any deviations in their own state law requirements. This checklist will simplify compliance efforts by highlighting duplications and inconsistencies in the many standards that emergency departments must follow.

PART 1

Legal Compliance Questions and Answers

INTRODUCTION TO COMPLIANCE

The emphasis on establishing corporate compliance programs for hospitals and other health care facilities is the direct result of the government's aggressive efforts to enforce legislative provisions governing health care fraud and abuse. Corporate compliance programs have been imposed on numerous providers by the government as part of settlements following fraud and abuse investigations, and many health care organizations have voluntarily implemented such programs to protect themselves from sanctions under fraud and abuse laws. As a result, compliance efforts have been closely linked with the subject of fraud and abuse legislation, even though an effective compliance program is much broader in scope and covers many other types of legislative requirements and prohibitions. In fact, compliance efforts should be directed at establishing a culture within a hospital that promotes prevention, detection, and resolution of all instances of conduct that do not conform to all federal and state laws, private payer health program requirements, as well as the hospital's ethical and business policies. [Department of Health and Human Services, Office of Inspector General, Compliance Program Guidance for Hospitals, Feb. 23, 1998]

Compliance recommendations should include a Code of Conduct that creates a culture of compliance and regular review of the effectiveness of the compliance program. Compliance effectiveness review can focus on the compliance officer role, adequacy of corporate policies, adequacy of open communication, regular training and education, internal monitoring and audits, response to detected deficiencies, and enforcement of disciplinary standards. [Department of Health and Human Services, Office of Inspector General, Supplemental Compliance Program Guidance for Hospitals, 70 Fed. Reg. 4858 (Jan. 27, 2005)]

What are the benefits of compliance?

Voluntary compliance can be a good way to demonstrate good faith efforts to comply with all relevant laws and regulations that impact hospital activities. Voluntary implementation of Compliance Program Guidance (CPG) recommendations can help the hospital demonstrate commitment to responsible corporate conduct, increases the chance to finding and correcting illegal or unethical behavior at an earlier point in time, and reduces subsequent financial loss to the hospital and government agencies. [Department of Health and Human Services, Office of Inspector General, Supplemental Compliance Program Guidance for Hospitals, 70 Fed. Reg. 4858 (Jan. 27, 2005)]

What types of activities are governed by health care fraud and abuse legislation?

Both at the state and federal levels, statutory fraud and abuse prohibitions apply to the following categories of health care provider activities:

- false claims or other fraudulent billing activities
- bribes or kickbacks, including a complex array of discounts, rebates, profit-sharing agreements, or other business relationships
- illegal referrals, prohibiting physicians or other types of health care providers from referring patients for health care services to entities in which the physician has a financial interest

What are the fraud and abuse issues that are of particular concern to a hospital emergency department (ED)?

As the above list indicates, the broad language of many of the fraud and abuse provisions in federal law and numerous state statutes makes these provisions applicable to a very wide range of potentially illegal activities. Several areas of activity are of particular concern to physicians practicing in a hospital ED, especially if the physicians are part of an emergency department staffing organization that contracts with a hospital to provide services in its ED. Some of the areas of risk for fraud and abuse liability include

- Procedural coding. The importance of accurate coding in avoiding fraud and abuse liability is significant for all health care providers. Emergency physicians are ultimately responsible for the coding and billing that is done on their behalf in a hospital ED and should periodically review the way their services are coded and billed. Billing practices which raise concerns include improper coding, upcoding, unbundling (billing separately for services), billing for medically unnecessary services or non-covered services, duplicate billing, billing for services not documented, or filing fraudulent cost reports. Recent hospital compliance program guidance (CPG) also focuses on areas of risk that may be underappreciated in industry such as: outpatient coding, admissions and discharges, supplemental payments, and use of information technology.
- Reassignment. When providing emergency services as an employee or a contracting physician, an emergency physician may assign the right to set and collect fees for his or her services but only within the limits of federal and state law. Payment may be made to a hospital where emergency physician services are provided if there is a contractual arrangement between the facility and the physician under which the hospital bills for the physician's services. In these cases, the emergency physician should retain the right to review what is billed and collected on his or her behalf.
- Teaching physician billing. A probe launched in 1996 by the Department of Health and Human Services and the Office of the Inspector General (HHS and OIG) focused on Part B reimbursement to hospitals or faculty physicians for the services of attending physicians in cases where patients were actually treated by residents acting under the supervision of an attending physician. Emergency physicians that practice at teaching hospitals must make sure that they comply with current teaching physician billing rules. [Refer to Services Provided by Teaching Physicians and Residents, under Reimbursement in this Part.]
- Gain sharing and other financial arrangements with hospitals. Potential violations of the antikickback statute can occur in financial arrangements between hospitals and hospital-based physicians that require physicians to pay more than the fair market value for services provided by the hospitals (for example, billing services, personnel, utilities) or compensate physicians for less than the fair market value of goods and services that they provide to hospitals. An OIG Management Advisory Report issued in 1991 lists a number of arrangements between hospital-based physicians and hospitals that would be suspect under the antikickback statute, including

  1. payment by a group of ED physicians to a hospital of half of its cash receipts exceeding $600,000 per year
  2. payment by a physician group of 50 percent of their gross receipts to a hospital's endowment fund

14

3. an agreement by a physician group to purchase equipment and donate the equipment to the hospital at the termination of the contract, where the hospital has the unrestricted right to terminate the contract at any time
4. payment by a physician group to a hospital of 33 percent of all its profits above a set amount, to cover the facilities capital improvements, equipment, and other departmental expenditures [OIG Management Advisory Report: Financial Arrangements between Hospitals and Hospital-Based Physicians, OEI-09-89-00330, Jan. 31, 1991]

The OIG has also issued a special advisory bulletin stating that gainsharing arrangements between hospitals and physicians are prohibited by federal law and are subject to civil monetary penalties. [Office of Inspector General Special Advisory Bulletin, "Gainsharing Arrangements and CMPs for Hospital Payments to Physicians to Reduce or Limit Services to Beneficiaries," issued July 1999, available on the Internet at *http://www.oig.hhs.gov/fraud/docs/alertsandbulletins/gainsh.htm*] Gainsharing typically describes an arrangement where a hospital gives a physician a percentage share of any reduction in the hospital's costs for patient care attributable in part to the physician's efforts. For example, in an advisory opinion, the OIG found that a joint arrangement in which an ambulance company would purchase a helicopter and the hospital would provide a helipad and crew at no cost raised concerns under the antikickback statute; however, there was minimal risk of abuse because the arrangement (1) involved emergency services only, (2) did not involve steering to the hospital, (3) was overseen by a regional counsel, and (4) had a positive impact on quality of care. The OIG indicated that it would not impose sanctions on such an arrangement. [OIG Advisory Opinion No. 03-14]

Emergency medicine groups are encouraged to develop compliance programs of their own to protect against fraud and abuse liability in their contractual arrangements with hospitals. [See American College of Emergency Physicians, Strategic Plan and Environmental Assessment, 1999-2000]

- Quality Emergency Care: The HHS/OIG and the Department of Justice have successfully enforced the federal fraud and abuse laws by investigating and prosecuting nursing homes under the Civil False Claims Act for billing for inadequate patient care. The charges in these cases typically allege that the care provided to nursing home residents failed to meet federal and state requirements relating to the quality of care. In the 2005 supplemental compliance guidance, the OIG has indicated that it has authority to exclude providers from federal programs for providing substandard care. [Department of Health and Human Services, Office of Inspector General, Supplemental Compliance Program Guidance for Hospitals, 70 Fed. Reg. 4858 (Jan. 27, 2005)]
- Referrals: The Stark self referral law and antikickback statutes prohibit certain referrals. The Stark law prohibits payment for designated health services (DHS) if the referral is from a physician with whom the hospital has a prohibited relationship. The antikickback statute prohibits direct or indirect payments to induce referrals. However, safe harbors can be met which protect the provider under the statute. Areas of concern under the antikickback statute include: joint ventures, physician compensation, relationships with other health care entities, recruiting arrangements, discounts, medical staff credentialing (based on referrals), and malpractice insurance subsidies.
- Ambulance restocking arrangements: Agreements between hospitals and ambulance suppliers under which hospitals restock drugs and medical supplies used during emergency runs at no charge could technically violate the antikickback statute if

this practice is intended to induce ambulance personnel to steer patients to a particular hospital. However, if all the hospitals within a geographic area served by the same EMS council participate in ambulance restocking programs, it is unlikely that free ambulance restocking could influence the referral process. A safe harbor to the antikickback statute was finalized by HHS/OIG in December 2001 [66 Fed. Reg. 62,979 (2001)] To be covered by the safe harbor, a restocking arrangement must meet four general conditions relating to the appropriate billing of federal health care programs, documentation requirements, safeguards relating to referrals, and compliance with other applicable laws. In addition, each of the three safe harbor categories involves a set of specific conditions providers must meet. An earlier, proposed version of the safe harbor would have protected certain restocking arrangements where the ambulance provider pays the facility fair market value for replenished drugs or supplies used in connection with the transport or where free or discounted restocking is provided by the hospital under the oversight of an EMS council or similar organization. The final rule is more lenient, however, eliminating requirements involving monitoring by an oversight entity and easing certain restrictions involving billing.

Since publishing the final rule, the OIG has also issued advisory opinions regarding ambulance restocking arrangements. The first (OIG Advisory Opinion No. 02-2, issued April 4, 2002) involved a non-profit ambulance company that serves several counties and uses each ambulance at least three times a week on runs to two non-profit hospitals. After emergency runs the hospitals restock certain drugs and supplies for free under county and state protocols. Neither the hospitals nor the ambulance company bill for the restocked drugs or supplies, and the arrangement is not based on the volume or value of referrals. The OIG found that the arrangement satisfies the criteria for the general replenishing safe harbor. In another opinion (OIG Advisory Opinion No. 02-3, issued April 4, 2002), the OIG likewise found an arrangement would meet the criteria for the general replenishing safe harbor where a quasi-governmental agency composed of representatives of EMS providers, hospitals, and medical directors proposed a formal regional ambulance restocking program in which participating hospitals would restock all ambulances uniformly with the drugs and supplies used in treating emergency patients. Ambulance providers would not be charged, and hospitals would bill Medicare or other parties only to the extent allowed under the payor's rules and regulations. Recent advisory opinions have reviewed whether state or city owned ambulance services can bill insurers for reimbursement of services without collecting copayments from taxpayers, and the OIG has found that it was acceptable to consider the resident taxes as a copayment and that failure to collect copayments with each service would not violate antikickback provisions. However, this did not apply when the government contracted with a private ambulance supplier to provide services. [See the following OIG Advisory Opinions: 02-8 (June 19, 2002), 02-15 (Oct. 7, 2002), 03-09 (Apr. 25, 2003), 04-02 (Mar. 8, 2004), 04-10 (Aug. 11, 2004), 04-12 (Sept. 28, 2004), 04-13 (Oct. 12, 2004), 04-14 (Nov. 4, 2004), 05-07 (Feb. 25, 2005)]

What other types of legal issues are implicated in a comprehensive hospital compliance program?

The OIG's Model Compliance Guidance for Hospitals sets forth the basic elements of an effective hospital compliance program and lists a number of risk areas that are of particular concern to hospitals. While many of these risk areas focus on practices that could implicate fraud and abuse laws, other legal issues that should be addressed in an effective compliance program include

- medical records documentation practices
- patient confidentiality
- patient dumping and EMTALA compliance
- employment, licensure, and staffing issues
- environmental compliance issues
- informed consent issues
- quality of care issues
- antitrust issues
- tax exempt status issues [Department of Health and Human Services, Office of Inspector General, Compliance Program Guidance for Hospitals, Feb. 23, 1998]

In January 2005 supplemental compliance program guidance (CPG) set forth new compliance recommendations and risk areas for hospitals. These voluntary guidelines focus on the following risk areas:

- accuracy of claims information
- compliance with referral and antikickback statutes
- gainsharing arrangements that may reduce or limit services
- EMTALA compliance
- substandard care
- relationship with federal program beneficiaries, i.e., gifts, cost sharing waivers, or free transportation
- HIPAA privacy and security
- excess billing of Medicare or Medicaid recipients, and
- other issues such as discounts to uninsured, preventative care, and professional courtesy billing waivers. [Department of Health and Human Services, Office of Inspector General, Supplemental Compliance Program Guidance for Hospitals, 70 Fed. Reg. 4858 (Jan. 27, 2005)]

Can the emergency room physician rent office space from the hospital?

The OIG has issued a special fraud alert in regard to physician rental of office space from a person or entity to which the physician might refer because of the concerns that the rental may induce referrals. Emergency room physicians renting space from the hospital would be in a position to refer patients to the hospital as inpatients. Therefore, care needs to be taken in establishing rental agreements. If the OIG were to review the rental agreement it would look at the appropriateness of the agreement, the amount paid for rent, and time and space considerations. While not required, complying with the elements of the space rental safe harbor can provide protection because then the agreement will be considered appropriate. To comply with the safe harbor, the agreement must be (1) in writing and signed (2) must cover all the premises rented and include all the terms of the rental agreement, (3) the rental must be for specific time intervals, (4) the term of the rental agreement must exceed one year, (5) the charge for rent must be set in advance based on fair market value, and (6) the space rented must not exceed the area needed for business purposes. If the emergency room physician was to rent space from any other entity that the physician was in a position to make referrals to, the same provisions would apply. [OIG Special Fraud Alert, *Rental of Space in Physicians Offices by Persons or Entities to Which Physicians Refer* (Feb. 3, 2000) & 64 Fed. Reg. 63,518 (Nov. 19, 1999)]

Can emergency room physicians participate in a joint venture with the hospital?

One of the original safe harbors set forth by the OIG was for joint ventures in which the physician provided personal services when opportunities to make referrals were limited and the contract was based on fair market value for the services. [56 Fed. Reg. 35,952 (July 29, 1991)] Since then the OIG has issued special fraud alerts in regards to certain types of joint ventures. The OIG has expressed concern that there may be opportunities for referrals in joint ventures where the investor is in a position to make a referral, when the joint venture business structure is a "shell" with an ongoing business entity, or when the physician investment is small or based on amounts borrowed from the entity the physician is in a position to refer to. [59 Fed. Reg. 65,372 (Dec. 19, 1994)]

More recently the OIG has expressed concern with joint ventures in which the owner expands into a related line of business that depends upon referrals from the owner's existing business by contracting with an existing business competitor to manage the services on behalf of the owner. For safe harbor protection, the arrangement would need to be an arm's length transaction based on fair market value. Factors which would make the joint venture suspect include a joint venture which involves: (1) a new line of business, (2) a captive referral base, (3) little or no bona fide business risk on the part of the owner, (4) status of manager or supplier as a competitor, and (5) the manager or supplier's remuneration impacted by referrals. [OIG Special Advisory Bulletin: Contractual Joint Ventures (Apr. 23, 2003) available at *http://www.oig.hhs.gov*]

Can a hospital provide complimentary non-emergency local transport?

In a letter in regard to complimentary transport, the OIG indicated that a hospital can provide non-emergency complimentary transportation for patients and family members to and from the hospital or ambulatory care center when the transportation is valued at less that $10 per trip and less than $50 per year. The hospital transportation must comply with certain criteria; therefore, the program must have been in place prior to August 30, 2002, it must be offered uniformly without charge, the transportation can only be to and from the hospital and in the hospital service area, the cost of the transport cannot be claimed on federal cost reports, and the transportation cannot be ambulance transportation. [Department of Health and Human Services, Office of Inspector General, Supplemental Compliance Program Guidance for Hospitals, 70 Fed. Reg. 4858 (Jan. 27, 2005)]

How do compliance guidelines for ambulance suppliers impact the ED?

In March 2003 the OIG issued final compliance program guidance (CPG) for ambulance suppliers who interact frequently with the emergency ED. The guidance sets forth voluntary provisions to assist ambulance suppliers to comply with fraud and abuse standards. Areas of concern for ambulance suppliers include: improper transportation, medically unnecessary trips, trips claimed but not provided, misrepresentation of destinations, false documentation, billing individual services when group transport was provided, upcoding basic life support to advanced life support, and payment kickbacks. Other risk areas include: transportation calls when someone has already died, multiple-patient transports, situations where multiple ambulances respond, and billing amounts that exceed usual charges. The ED personnel may be the ones who assist in identifying whether ambulance transport is necessary, the level of care needed during transport, and whether life support is needed and at what level. A physician certification statement (PCS) should indicate whether the ambulance service is medically necessary. Safe harbors generally available for fraud and abuse are also available for ambulance suppliers. [Final Compliance Program Guidance for Ambulance Suppliers (Mar. 24, 2003) available on the Internet at *http://www.oig.hhs.gov/fraud/ complianceguidance.html*]

How do compliance guidelines for pharmacy manufacturers impact the ED?

In April 2003 the OIG issued voluntary compliance guidance for pharmacy manufacturers and identified three areas of risk: (1) data integrity, (2) kickbacks and illegal remuneration, and (3) compliance with drug sample laws. The concerns with data integrity relate to manufacturers' ability to manipulate average wholesale price (AWP) for drugs. Kickback concerns with purchasers such as an ED include product discounts, providing product support such as billing at no charge, educational grants to attend seminars about the manufacturers' product, research funding for product research, and reimbursement such as rebates and payments to convert to the manufacturers' drug. Kickback concerns with physicians include switching arrangements to encourage switching patients to the manufacturers' brand, consulting and advisory payments which must be for fair market value, payment for research, business courtesies such as entertainment and gifts, and educational and research grants such as for continuing medical education (CME) especially when it relates to the manufacturers' drug product. Drug sample concerns include concerns with compliance with the Prescription Drug Marketing Act (PDMA), which prohibits the sale or billing for drug samples provided by drug manufacturers. [Final Compliance Program Guidance for Pharmaceutical Manufacturers (Apr. 28, 2003), available on the Internet at *http://www.oig.hhs.gov/fraud/ complianceguidance.html*]

PATIENTS' RIGHTS

Beginning in 2000, patients' rights issues came to the forefront, as legislators on the federal and state levels enacted new laws to ensure the safety and self-determination of patients, following headlines concerning medical errors and managed care mistreatment in the popular press. Federal agencies responded as well, most notably by incorporating patients' rights guarantees in the Medicare Conditions of Participation, and issuing final regulations setting out standards for the privacy of patient health care information as required by the Health Insurance Portability and Accountability Act (HIPAA). Congress has continued to debate the scope and content of a series of proposed patients' rights bills with various provisions. In the meantime, current patient right provisions require the hospital to inform patients of their rights, and to establish processes for the prompt resolution of patient grievances including specific times, procedures, and decisions. The ED can participate with other hospital departments to establish these processes. Patients have the right to participate in their plan of care and be informed of decisions; they also have the right to privacy and safety in an environment free of abuse or harassment. (42 C.F.R. § 482.13)

Patients' right to be free of restraint and seclusion include specific ordering, documentation, and time requirements for restraint and seclusion as part of the Medicare patients' rights provisions. JCAHO includes patient rights in its 2005 hospital accreditation standards focusing on patient rights to: respect, be involved in treatment decisions, wishes of the patient in regard to life decisions, be informed of the outcome of care including unanticipated outcomes, confidentiality, privacy, security, to access protective and advocacy services, to be protected in human research, to receive information about care and treatment, to access and receive health information, to make decisions based on patient needs, and to be free from mental, physical, sexual and verbal abuse, neglect or exploitation. [*2005 Hospital Accreditation Program Standards*]

Patient confidentiality, while of great importance, is often difficult to ensure in the ED setting, where the numbers of patients and urgency of care may make it difficult to safeguard patient information closely. However, it is crucial to do so, more than ever, as discussed below.

Consent to treatment is a basic concept that is second nature to health care providers. It is a more complex concept than it first appears, however, and can give rise to a variety of questions, such as what constitutes valid consent, whether consent must be in writing, and who can consent if the patient is not able. Finally, EDs are governed by a number of antidiscrimination laws that require hospitals to provide care to the public in a nondiscriminatory manner. ED administrators should review policies and staff conduct to determine whether patients are being discriminated against on the basis of race, national origin, gender, or disability. Federal and state laws prohibiting discrimination may create affirmative duties for EDs, such as providing foreign language or sign language interpreters or modifying the physical premises to increase accessibility for individuals with disabilities. This section discusses all of these patients' rights issues.

Restraint and Seclusion

Do any federal regulations address the use of restraints and seclusion?

In 2000, the Medicare Conditions of Participation were amended to incorporate a patients' bill of rights, which set standards for the use of restraint and seclusion of hospital patients. These standards must be met by hospitals that receive Medicare or Medicaid reimbursement. The regulations establish patients' right to be free from both physical restraints and drugs that are used as a restraint that are not medically necessary or are used as a means of coercion, discipline, convenience, or retaliation by staff. The standards distinguish between the use of restraint for medical and surgical care from the use of restraint or seclusion for behavior management, setting out separate criteria for each. [42 C.F.R. § 482.13]

What constitutes a restraint?

Under the regulations, a restraint is any manual method, physical device, mechanical device, material, or equipment attached or adjacent to the patient's body that he or she cannot easily remove, if it restricts freedom of movement or access to one's body. A drug constitutes a restraint if it is a medication used to control behavior or to restrict the patient's freedom of movement and is not a standard treatment for the patient's medical or psychiatric condition. [42 C.F.R. § 482.13]

According to the Centers for Medicare and Medicaid Services (CMS) guidance, what constitutes a restraint depends on whether the object or technique is being used for the purpose of limiting patient movement and access to their body. According to the guidance, devices that serve multiple purposes, such as a gerichair or side rails, constitute a restraint when they have the effect of restricting a patient's movement and cannot be easily removed by the patient. A drug qualifies as a restraint if it is used to restrict a patient's freedom of movement in medical post-surgical situations and is not a standard treatment for the patient's medical or psychiatric condition. Tucking a patient's sheets in so tightly that he or she cannot move is another example of a physical restraint under the standards. [HCFA, Interpretive Guidelines, Hospital Conditions of Participation for Patients' Rights, May 2000]. However, the use of restraints for the purposes of law enforcement (for example, if a prisoner is in handcuffs and needs treatment) is not governed by the restraint regulations because in such cases the restraint is not related to the provision of health care.

How do the patients' rights standards limit the use of restraints for medical and surgical care?

The standards, which have generated much controversy in the hospital community

- limit restraint use to those situations in which less restrictive interventions have been determined to be ineffective to protect the patient or others from harm
- require the order of a physician or qualified licensed independent practitioner
- prohibit the use of standing or PRN (as needed) orders for restraints
- require consultation with the patient's treating physician as soon as possible (if the physician did not personally write the order)
- necessitate a written amendment of the patient's plan of care mandate that restraints be implemented in the least restrictive manner possible and in accordance with safe and appropriate restraining techniques
- require the withdrawal of restraints at the earliest possible time
- establish that restraint use must be continually assessed, monitored, and reevaluated
- impose ongoing staff training requirements [42 C.F.R. § 482.13]

What documentation is necessary with regard to restraint orders and evaluations?

The guidance states that the rationale that a patient might fall is an inadequate basis for using a restraint. Each individual patient's history of falls, medical condition, and symptoms must be evaluated on a case by case basis. According to the guidelines, restraints are not a substitute for adequate staffing and monitoring. The guidelines emphasize the importance of documentation of: continual reevaluation of patients in restraints, the rationale for ordering a restraint, the rationale for the time frame for the order, and that other less restricting alternatives were considered. Consistency with hospital policy and reliance on current standards of safety and technique are also factors in evaluating whether restraint use is appropriate. [HCFA, Interpretive Guidelines, Hospital Conditions of Participation for Patients' Rights, May 2000]

What are the procedures that must be followed for ordering, evaluating, and documenting the use of restraints or seclusion for behavior management?

Seclusion and restraints for behavior management can only be used in emergency situations if needed to ensure the patient's or others' physical safety when less restrictive interventions have been determined to be ineffective. According to the guidelines, an emergency is a situation where the patient's behavior is violent and aggressive and poses an immediate and serious danger to the safety of the patient or others.

Like restraints for medical or surgical care, seclusion and restraints for behavior management can only be used in accordance with the order of a physician or other authorized licensed independent practitioner. Standing orders and PRN orders are prohibited. The patient's treating physician must be consulted as soon as possible, unless that individual ordered the restraint or seclusion. The restraint or seclusion triggers a written modification of the patient's plan of care, must be implemented in the least restrictive manner possible, must be applied in accordance with safe appropriate restraining techniques, and must be ended at the earliest possible time. The condition of the patient must be continually assessed, monitored, and reevaluated. Staff must have ongoing education in the safe use of seclusion and restraint, as well as alternatives for handling behavior that would traditionally have been treated through the use of restraint or seclusion.

Unlike restraints for medical or surgical care, there are specific timelines for the duration of orders and reevaluation of patients under restraint or in seclusion for behavior management. A physician or other licensed independent practitioner (where permitted by state law) must evaluate in person the need for restraint or seclusion within one hour of initiation. Written orders are limited to 4 hours for adults, 2 hours for patients ages 9 to 17, and 1 hour for patients under age 9. Orders may only be renewed up to a total of 24 hours, at which time a second face to face evaluation by a physician or other licensed independent practitioner is required. In the event that a patient who is restrained for aggressiveness or violence quickly recovers and is released before the physician or licensed independent practitioner arrives to perform the assessment, the physician or practitioner must still see the patient face to face to perform the assessment. [42 C.F.R. § 482.13, CMS Conditions for Participation, Hospital COPs for Patients' Rights Question and Answers (Oct. 10, 2001), available on the Internet at *http://www.cms.hhs.gov/cop/2b1.asp*]

Further, seclusion may not be used simultaneously with restraint for behavior modification unless the patient is continually monitored face to face by an assigned staff member or continually monitored by staff in close proximity to the patient using both video and audio equipment. [42 C.F.R. § 482.13]

Documentation is crucial to demonstrating compliance, particularly with respect to changes in the patient's behavior, attempts to use other interventions first, the rationale for using restraint or seclusion, the patient's response, compliance with hospital policy, and the removal of the restraint or seclusion.

Confidentiality of ED Records

What rules of confidentiality apply to ED records?

General rules establishing the confidentiality of patient information apply to the information gathered and compiled in an ED record. These rules are frequently elaborated in state statutes or regulations. A few states simply specify that the medical record is confidential and impose a general obligation on hospitals to develop an appropriate policy for record confidentiality without further statutory or regulatory guidance. Enactments in other states similarly embody the principle of confidentiality and the patient's right of access. In Connecticut, for example, a statutory Patient's Bill of Rights provides that patients are entitled to confidential treatment of personal and medical records. [Conn. Gen. Stat. § 19a-550(b)(9)] Patients may approve or refuse their release to any individual outside the facility, except in the case of the patient's transfer to another health care institution or as required by law or a third party payment contract. Numerous other statutes provide that medical records are confidential and may be disclosed only with the patient's consent or as provided in the statutes. Note that while the general rule establishes that the medical record is a confidential document, numerous exceptions allow disclosure or impose mandatory reporting of patient information under specific circumstances.

In addition to state laws, in December 2000 the Department of Health and Human Services issued final regulations that set out standards for the privacy of individually identifiable patient health information that required compliance by April 2003. [65 Fed. Reg. 82,462, available on the Internet at *http://www.hhs.gov/ocr/hipaa/finalreg.html*]. The rules apply to all communications regarding medical records that have been maintained by health care providers or plans, whether electronic, written, or oral. The rules generally provide that a health care provider may not disclose health information that identifies the patient unless authorized by the patient or is specifically allowed under the regulations. State law is generally preempted to the extent it conflicts with the federal privacy standards, but state laws that are more stringent (i.e., provide greater privacy protections) will take precedence over the federal regulations.

What does patient consent for disclosure consist of under the federal privacy rule?

The initial privacy standards finalized in 2000 required a patient's written consent before using or disclosing the patient's personal health information (PHI) to carry out treatment, payment, or health care operations. However, criticism from the health care community focused on the administrative burden and expense as well as the obstacle the rule created to patient quick access to health care services.

In response to these concerns, in March 2002 HHS published proposed changes to the privacy rule. According to HHS, the revisions were designed to continue to protect patients' privacy, yet eliminate the obstacles to patients' getting needed care and treatment. Under the proposed changes, the requirement for written consent is eliminated, although it is still an option. Providers must, however, make a good faith effort to obtain a written acknowledgement that the patient received a copy of the provider's notice of privacy practice at the time of the first service, except in emergency situations. The proposed modifications retain the patient's right to request restrictions and authorization requirements.

The proposed rule was finalized August 14, 2002. The final rule clarified the need for individual written consent to use health information for marketing purposes, and requires notice of privacy protections to all patients even though consent to use health information for regular health care is optional. The intent of the rule is not to limit common health care communications as long as reasonable means are used to protect confidentiality. For example, the ED can continue to use sign in sheets and call names of people in the waiting room without violating the rule. When person health information (PHI) is released as appropriately authorized, only the minimum necessary information should be disclosed. Hospitals can establish criteria upon which disclosure will be made. The final rule also clarifies that parents acting as the personal representative of minor children have the right to access medical records of the minor children, but determination of when a child is emancipated and what disclosure is permissible is governed by state law. [67 Fed. Reg. 53,181 (Aug. 14, 2002)]

Whom does the Health Insurance Portability and Accountability Act (HIPAA) privacy rule apply to?

Health Insurance Portability and Accountability Act (HIPAA) applies to health care providers, such as a hospital unit, that bill for health care services electronically.

Three questions can be asked to determine if HIPAA applies:

(1) Does the organization bill for a covered service, i.e., health care services?
(2) Is the transaction covered, i.e., is the organization submitting a bill or claim or storing health data?
(3) Is the covered transaction billed electronically?

If the answers to the questions are yes, then the organization is considered a "covered entity" and HIPAA applies. Privacy protections became effective April 2003. Each organization must designate a Privacy Officer who is responsible for meeting regulatory requirements on behalf of the facility. The ED should coordinate compliance efforts with the hospital Privacy Officer.

Who can be a business associate under HIPAA?

A business associate is a person or entity that performs activities on behalf of a covered entity using personal health information. For example, a business associate with the ED could include a billing manager, claims or utilization review or administration, practice manager, an accountant, lawyer, or consultant, or someone involved in data analysis, accreditation, or financial review. These business associates need access to personal health information to perform their activities on behalf of the hospital. A covered entity must have a contract with a business associate requiring the business associate to protect the privacy of the health information, describe the use of the health information and requiring protections to limit disclosure of personal health information. As of April 2004 all contracts must include the required business associate language. Sample contract language is available on the Internet at *http://www.hhs.gov/ocr/hipaa/contractprov.html*.

Situations in which an entity is exempted from the business associate include: disclosures by a covered entity to a health care provider to treat the patient such as disclosure from the emergency room physician to a specialist on-call or to a laboratory, disclosures to a health plan sponsor or insurer such as information required for payment purposes, incidental access to information such as the evening janitor, other entities that participate in an organized health care arrangement (OHCA), disclosures for research purposes. An ED may give patient payment information to an ambulance service provider that transported the patient to the hospital in order for the ambulance provider to bill for its treatment services. [*OCR Guidance Explaining Significant Aspects of the Privacy Rule* (Dec. 4, 2002)]

What are the HIPAA requirements for data privacy?

HIPAA protects individually identifiable health information used by covered entities through the following requirements:

Privacy Notice—The organization should provide patients with notice of their privacy rights and the organizations privacy practices. The organization must make a good faith effort to obtain the patient's written acknowledgement of the notice. Consent for use of health information for routine health care delivery such as treatment, payment, and health care operations is optional.

Privacy Officer—The Privacy Officer is to develop and implement privacy policies and procedures and train all staff on privacy requirements. The organization is to limit data use to the minimum necessary use or disclosure for which there is authorization.

Marketing Use—A covered entity must obtain a patient's prior written authorization to use health information for marketing purposes unless there is a face to face encounter or communication involving a promotional gift of nominal value. Marketing includes selling lists of patients to a third party, thus precluded use of a patient list by a third party without patient consent. Marketing does not include discussion of treatment options, products or services with a patient.

FDA Use—The organization allows disclosure of information to the Food and Drug Administration (FDA) for reporting purposes.

Incidental Data Use—Health providers can use data as part of treatment and decision making without violating privacy rules. For example, hospitals can keep charts at the bedside, doctors can talk to patients in semi-private rooms, and doctors and nurses can confer at nursing stations without violating the rule.

Authorization—Patients are required to grant permission in advance for non routine use of data or disclosure.

Parents and Minors—The rule clarifies that state law governs parents' access to health information in regards to their minor children.

Limited Data Set—Limited data that does not include identifiable information can be disclosed for research, public health, and health care operations if there is an agreement to ensure data security and privacy. [*Standards of Privacy of Individually Identifiable Health Information*, 45 C.F.R. §§ 160 & 164, *Modifications to the Standards for Privacy of Individually Identifiable Health Information—Final Rule*, DHHS Fact Sheet (Aug. 9, 2002)]

Are there situations where patient health information may be disclosed for other purposes?

The final rule provides that special authorization is not required for specific purposes where there is an "overriding public interest," such as disclosures to public health authorities that are authorized or required by law to collect information for public health purposes (for example, reporting of disease or injury, reporting deaths, investigating the occurrence and cause of injury and disease, and monitoring adverse outcomes related to food, drugs, biological products, and dietary supplements), disclosures for purposes of research, legal proceedings, or law enforcement, or to report abuse or neglect.

Who keeps track of HIPAA complaints?

The Office of E-Health Standards and Services (OESS) has a HIPAA information tracking system (HITS) to store HIPAA complaint and investigation information. Disclosure of complaint information will be limited to the following needs: CMS in order to reach CMS goals, other state or federal agencies for HIPAA enforcement, members of Congress based on inquiry, Department of Justice (DOJ) for litigation, CMS contractors who administer health benefits, and federal agencies investigating fraud and abuse. [70 Fed. Reg. 38,944 (July 7, 2005)]

How will HIPAA be enforced?

In 2005, a proposed enforcement rule was issued that recommended the following:

- a health care entity be considered a person subject to enforcement,
- in an investigation there is a responsibility to provide records, cooperate and permit access to information,
- an entity is prohibited from retaliating against someone who files a privacy complaint,
- when multiple organizations are involved and found to have violated the rule, joint and several liability will occur,
- fines are limited to $100 per violation and $25,000 for identical violations,
- the number of violations will be determined by the facts and circumstances of the situation,
- factors that will be considered in setting a penalty include the nature of the violations, the circumstances, culpability, history of prior offenses, and the financial condition of the entity,
- an entity may raise affirmative defenses to the alleged violation including no knowledge of the violation, reasonable cause for the violation which is then corrected quickly, and that the violation was punishable as a wrongful disclosure of individually identifiable health information, and
- hearing and appeal rights are set forth. [HIPAA Administrative Simplification Enforcement Proposed Rule, 70 Fed. Reg. 20,224 (Apr. 18, 2005)]

How do HIPAA disclosure clarifications impact the ED?

HIPAA rule clarifications have clarified that ambulance providers may report to health care providers on the status of transported patients as part of the health care treatment. ED personnel may leave a message at the home or on an answering machine for a patient, but should disclose as little information as possible.

Personal health information (PHI) may be disclosed to someone who can assist in notifying the family of the patient's location or condition either with patient approval, or in an emergency when it is in the best interest of the patient. For example, the ED could notify the Red Cross, police, or other emergency response personnel of the patient's location and condition. Similarly, the ED may disclose relevant information to the family or friends of a patient, even when the patient cannot signify approval because of incapacity, when it would be in the best interest of the patient to do so.

The hospital may inform callers and visitors of a patient's location and condition in the ED, and the patient's phone number and room can be released as part of a patient directory, even if the ED directory is separate from the rest of the hospital. Disclosure may also be made to law enforcement to comply with a court order, to report a violent crime, etc. [OCR HIPAA FAQ available at *http://www.hhs.gov/ocr/hipaa/*]

What are some examples of reporting requirements that could apply to health care professionals working in an ED?

Legislative reporting provisions, both state and federal, that allow or mandate the disclosure of patient information without the patient's consent frequently apply to health care professionals who treat patients in an ED. These provisions cover a variety of situations, including cases of suspected child abuse or neglect, abuse of adults and injuries to disabled persons, drug abuse, communicable diseases, and disclosure of patient information to law enforcement officials. For further discussion of reporting requirements that apply to these issues, see "Responsibilities Relating to Crimes outside the ED."

Under what circumstances does the duty to report communicable diseases typically arise?

All states have enacted communicable disease reporting laws, which variously require hospitals and practitioners to inform public health authorities of cases of infectious, venereal, or sexually transmitted diseases. The statutes usually list the particular diseases that must be reported and direct practitioners to give local public health officials the patient's name, age, sex, address, and identifying information, as well as the details of the illness. [*See, e.g.*, Ala. Code §§ 22-11A-1 through 22-11A-73] The health department may have the authority to request patient records for purposes of conducting epidemiological investigations. [*See, e.g.*, Fla. Stat. § 395.3025(5)] Only the information required by the statute should be disclosed.

A few states have laws authorizing hospitals to disclose confidential information when emergency medical personnel come into contact with a patient suffering from a reportable condition. [*See, e.g.*, Fla. Stat. § 395.1025] The procedures for notifying emergency personnel vary among the states, with some statutes allowing the hospital to directly notify the person at risk and others requiring the hospital to notify authorities at the state board of health, who then contact the emergency personnel. In either case, the hospital is usually precluded from revealing the name of the afflicted patient.

What types of rules govern the disclosure of human immunodeficiency virus (HIV) or acquired immune deficiency syndrome (AIDS) related information?

Many confidentiality statutes allow the release of HIV- or AIDS-related information without the patient's consent to medical technicians who provide emergency care to an HIV-positive patient. The statutes vary, however, in the purpose for such disclosure. Some link disclosure to the health of the patient, others indicate a concern for the safety of the emergency workers, and many reflect an ambiguous balance between the two concerns. In some states, for example, confidential HIV-related information may be released to medical personnel in a "medical emergency" to the "extent necessary to protect the health or life of the named party." [*See, e.g.*, Colo. Rev. Stat. § 25-4-1404(1)(c)] The Hawaii law defines "medical emergency" as any disease-related situation that threatens life or limb. [Haw. Rev. Stat. § 325-101] Other states authorize disclosure to health care providers rendering medical care when knowledge of HIV test results is necessary to provide appropriate emergency care or treatment to the patient. [Del. Code Ann. tit. 16, § 1203(a)(4)] Both types of laws demonstrate concern for the patient's treatment.

Other laws reflect a concern for the safety of rescue workers. Illinois allows release of the identity of the subject of an HIV test to "[a]ny health care provider or employee of a health facility" involved in an accidental contact with the blood or bodily fluids of an individual that could transmit HIV according to a physician's medical judgment. [410 Ill. Comp. Stat. Ann. § 305/9]

A few states impose an affirmative duty on an attending physician or health care facility to respond to inquiries by emergency rescuers as to contact with a patient later diagnosed with a contagious disease or virus including HIV. The rescuers entitled to receive such information include paid or volunteer firefighters, emergency medical technicians, rescue squad personnel, and law enforcement officers. The notification must occur within two days after confirmation of the patient's diagnosis. The information must be communicated in a manner that protects the confidentiality of both the patient and rescuer. [*See, e.g.*, Mich. Comp. Laws § 333.20191]

Are there reporting requirements that apply to diagnoses of drug abuse?

Some states require health care professionals to report diagnoses of drug abuse. In New Jersey, for example, the law requires health care practitioners to report the names of drug-dependent persons within 24 hours after determining that the person uses a controlled dangerous substance for purposes other than treatment of sickness or injury as prescribed and administered under the law. [N.J. Stat. § 24:21-39] In Texas, health care providers treating a patient for an overdose of a controlled substance must report the case at once to the state Department of Health. [Tex. Health & Safety Code § 161.042]

Is there a duty to report certain types of patient information to law enforcement authorities?

The new federal privacy regulations do not impose a duty on hospitals to furnish law enforcement authorities with patient information, but provide that limited information may be disclosed without patient consent in order to locate or identify a suspect, fugitive, or missing person, or regarding a victim of a crime who cannot agree to disclosure because of incapacity. A hospital may also disclose patient information if it believes that the disclosure is necessary for authorities to apprehend a participant in a violent crime or an escapee from custody. [42 C.F.R. § 164.512]

State law varies widely as to a hospital's duty to report certain kinds of patient-related information, such as cases involving gunshot or knife wounds [*see, e.g.,* Cal. Penal Code § 11161 and Tex. Health & Safety Code § 161.041], or disorders affecting a motorist's ability to drive safely to law enforcement authorities. In states having these types of reporting statutes, a patient's consent is not required in order to release the record. In fact, under some statutes, hospitals may be guilty of criminal misdemeanor if they fail to report certain cases. For further discussion of these reporting requirements, see "Responsibilities Relating to Crimes outside the ED."

As a general rule, however, hospitals should not release medical records or other patient information to law enforcement personnel without the patient's authorization. In the absence of statutory authority or legal process, a police agency has no authority to examine an ED record or other medical record. If a law enforcement official does provide the facility with a valid court order or subpoena, the hospital, upon the advice of counsel, may provide the information requested.

What specific confidentiality concerns arise with respect to patient information collected in an ED?

Specific confidentiality concerns arise with respect to patient information that is collected in an ED because of the physical setting in which treatment is delivered, the urgent nature of the treatment, and the high patient volume. In particular, the use of status boards to record the progress of patients through ED procedures, the prescription drug abuser lists that many EDs keep on 3 × 5 file card systems, and the physical layout of examination rooms can generate unique difficulties in protecting patient privacy.

A specific privacy concern that arises in the ED is the filming of patients for television productions. The telecast of several documentaries including footage of actual emergency room patients raised concerns with the Joint Commission on Accreditation of Healthcare Organizations (Joint Commission) that patient privacy was being violated. As a result, it issued a standards clarification for patient rights and informed consent when videotaping or filming patients in a hospital ED. The standard clarification states that

- it is appropriate to film or videotape patient care activities in the ED if patients or surrogate decision makers give informed consent
- if the patient is unable to give informed consent and no surrogate decision maker is available, patient care activities in the ED may be filmed as long as it is in accordance with a policy that requires a patient's informed consent before the film is used for any purpose

- the film or video must remain in the physical possession of the hospital and not released to anyone for any purpose until such informed consent is obtained
- if the patient does not give informed consent for the use of the film, then the relevant footage must be removed or the video destroyed
- the hospital must post a notice to the community it serves (in the public areas of the hospital) informing the public that filming or videotaping may be occurring while emergency services are being delivered [Joint Commission: Comprehensive Accreditation Manual for Hospitals 2005, RI 2.5]

The CMS (formerly HCFA) guidance interpreting the federal regulations also states that video or other electronic monitoring or recording methods should not be used during the examination of a patient without his or her consent. [CMS, Interpretive Guidelines, Hospital Conditions of Participation for Patients' Rights, May 2000]

Why does the use of status boards present confidentiality concerns?

Many EDs use a status board to track the progress of patients seeking care in the ED. A status board typically consists of a write-on/wipe-off or other erasable board that shows information including patient names, complaints or diagnoses, and room numbers. These boards, when placed in view of patients and visitors, present a serious breach of confidentiality concern. For example, although ED staff might not consider tracking diagnostic tests on the status board a confidentiality problem, a status board that says, "John Smith, curtain 3, shortness of breath, HIV test ordered" is a clear violation of patient privacy if other patients and visitors can read the information. The Joint Commission has repeatedly cited status boards as a patient privacy problem. Alternatives that better safeguard patient confidentiality include

- using patient numbers rather than names. Many EDs find this method cumbersome.
- omitting medically sensitive information such as complaints, diagnoses, and diagnostic tests from the board. Simply including the patient's name and room or curtain number is not likely to violate confidentiality.
- implementing a computerized "status board" that requires staff members to log on to obtain patient information. If this method is adopted, the computer terminal must either be placed where access is strictly limited to ED staff, or the system should automatically "log off" after staff use, so that patient information is not readily visible.

What confidentiality concerns arise with the use of drug abuser lists?

Another ED practice that can raise confidentiality concerns is the establishment of a prescription drug abuser list that is compiled to alert department personnel of the identity of patients who have been diagnosed as drug abusers and who fraudulently seek treatment at the ED to obtain more drugs. These lists are often compiled on a 3 × 5 card file system, and are not always stored in a secure location.

These abuser lists raise significant liability risks not only under general confidentiality rules but also under federal legislation governing alcohol and drug abuse patient records. In particular, provisions in the Public Health Service Act state that records of the "identity, diagnosis, prognosis, or treatment" of any patient maintained in connection with these programs are confidential and may not be disclosed except for certain purposes and under certain circumstances. [42 U.S.C. § 290dd-2] The regulations define "patient" as any individual who has requested or received a diagnosis or treatment for drug abuse at a federally assisted program. [42 C.F.R. § 2.11] An earlier court has ruled that a person who enters a hospital ED for immediate treatment of conditions arising from a drug overdose is a "patient" under the regulations because that individual clearly "applied for treatment or diagnosis of drug abuse." [*United States v. Eide*, 875 F.2d 1429 (9th Cir. 1989)] The court further ruled that the ED qualified as a "program" because it provides diagnoses, treatment, and referrals and because many drug users enter the hospital through the ED as the first step to further drug treatment. However, a more recent case found that an ED was not a "program" and indicated that there were two ways an ED could be considered a "program" (1) when the primary function of the ED is to provide treatment for drug and alcohol abuse, and (2) when the ED held itself out to the community as providing drug and alcohol abuse treatment services. The later court decision was based on federal regulations stating that the regulation was not intended to apply to emergency department personnel who refer a patient for drug treatment unless the primary purpose of the staff is to provide drug and alcohol treatment. [*Center for Legal Advocacy v. Denver Health and Hosp. Auth.*, 320 F.3d 1107 (10th Cir. 2003) and 42 C.F.R. § 2.12(e)(1)]

Are there any special confidentiality concerns with regard to minors and their parents?

Under the federal privacy rule, a person's right to control his or her health information is based on the person's right under state law to control the health care itself. Because a parent usually has authority to make health care decisions about his or her minor child, a parent or legal guardian is generally the child's personal representative under the privacy rule and has the right to obtain the minor child's health information. Even where a child receives emergency medical care in the ED without a parent's consent, normally the parent would still be the child's representative and can get all information about the child's treatment and condition.

There are exceptions, however, where a parent might not be the minor child's "personal representative" with regard to certain health information about the child being treated in an ED. Such situations include

- when state law does not require parental consent before a minor can obtain a particular health care service (e.g., treatment for an STD or for sexual assault) and the minor consents to the health care service, the parent is not considered the minor's representative under the privacy rule, and information regarding that treatment can only be disclosed with the minor's consent
- when a parent agrees that the minor and the physician may have a confidential relationship, the parent does not have access to the health information related to that relationship. For example, if an ED physician asks the parent of a 16-year-old if the physician may speak with the child confidentially about a medical condition and the parent agrees, the parent has no right to information regarding that conversation unless the minor child consents to disclosure.
- when a physician believes in his or her professional judgment that the minor child has been or may be subjected to abuse or neglect, or that treating the parent as the child's

representative could endanger the child, the physician may choose not to treat the parent as the minor's representative

However, the standards of the federal privacy rule do not preempt state laws that specifically address disclosure of a minor's health information to a parent, whether the state law authorizes or prohibits the disclosure. Thus, for example, if an ED physician believes that disclosing information about a minor would endanger the minor, but a state law requires disclosure to a parent, the physician may comply with the state law without violating the privacy rule. [Complete Privacy Rule Text (Oct. 10, 2002) available on the Internet at *http://www.hhs.gov/ocr/combinedregtext.pdf*]

What other measures should ED personnel follow to ensure patient privacy and confidentiality?

ED personnel should ensure that patients are treated in separate rooms or that the beds are separated by curtains or screens. During oral communications among themselves and with patients and their family members, ED personnel should reasonably safeguard patient health information. Although overheard communications are unavoidable in a busy emergency room, where it may be necessary for ED personnel to speak loudly in order to ensure appropriate treatment, ED personnel should take reasonable precautions to minimize the chance of inadvertent disclosures to others who may be nearby. Examples of this would include speaking apart, speaking quietly when discussing a patient's condition with family members in a waiting room or other public area, and by avoiding using patients' names in public hallways and elevators. [Complete Privacy Rule Text (Oct. 10, 2002) available on the Internet at *http://www.hhs.gov/ocr/combinedregtext.pdf*] ED personnel should also be aware of the hospital's confidentiality policy and be aware of the specific ways the policy is put into practice in the ED.

What is the difference between data privacy and security?

Data privacy focuses on who can access personal health information (PHI), and it focuses on all patient information. The data privacy requirements include data safeguards to protect patient privacy and prevent unintentional disclosure or use of information. As part of complying with data privacy standards, some of the security standards may have been met.

Security requirements cover electronic personal health information (EPHI) only and focus on administrative, physical, and technical safeguards to protect confidentiality, data integrity, and available access to data by those who need it.

What are the HIPAA requirements for data security?

HIPAA data security requirements focus on the security of electronic personal health information (EPHI) for covered entities by setting required and addressable standards. If a standard is required, policies and procedures should be put in place to meet the standards. It the standard is addressable, the organization should implement the standard if it is reasonable. If it is not reasonable, the organization should (1) document the reasons for its decision not to implement the standard, and (2) implement an equivalent measure that is reasonable and appropriate unless in light of the assessment the standard can be met without implementation of the specification or the alternative. To determine whether a standard is reasonable, the organization should look at factors such as how probable and critical the data security risk is, the costs of security, and the size and complexity of the covered entity. Organizations should balance risk and capabilities to determine when to implement programs. [45 C.F.R. § 164.306]

Implementation of data security standards is required by all covered entities except small health plans by April 20, 2005. A hospital ED would be considered a covered entity. Small health plan data security implementation is required by April 20, 2006. [*Security Standards Final Rule*, 68 Fed. Reg. 8334 (Feb. 20, 2003)]

What administrative, physical, and technical safeguards are involved in data security?

Required administrative safeguards for data security include having a security management process, assigning security responsibilities, isolating health care clearinghouse functions, setting up security incident response and reporting, and implementing plans for data back-up, disaster recovery, and emergency mode operation. The program should be regularly evaluated and contracts should include appropriate data security provisions. Administrative safeguards that are addressable include workforce security issues such as clearance and authorization for personnel, access authorization, security awareness and training, and testing and revising procedures.

Required physical safeguards include workstation use and security, and device and media control of disposal and reuse of equipment. Addressable standards include contingency operations and security plans, access control and validation procedures, maintenance records, accountability, and data backup and storage plans.

Required technical safeguards include access control through unique user identifiers with emergency access procedures and authentication of the person accessing the data. Addressable technical standards include automatic logoff, encryption, audit controls, and transmission security. [45 C.F.R. §§ 164.308, 164.310, 163.312]

Who must obtain a National Provider Identifier (NPI)?

In order to improve electronic transactions, CMS requires all health care providers who are covered entities to obtain and use a National Provider Identifier (NPI). Applications for the NPI begin May 23, 2005 and the provider identifier must be in place by May 23, 2007 for all providers except small health plans who have until May 23, 2008. A NPI application can be completed online at *https://nppes.cms.hhs.gov*

Consent to Treatment

Is patient consent always necessary for medical treatment?

The general legal principle is that patient consent to medical treatment is necessary. There are some situations, however, when patient consent is not required, for example

- in an emergency
- when the patient is not able to give consent due to minority

- when the patient is not able to give consent due to mental incapacity
- when the law designates a substitute decision maker, such as in the case of abused children
- when a court permits treatment without consent, such as in the case of taking a blood sample pursuant to a search warrant. In many of these situations, "substituted consent" of a decision maker other than the patient, such as the next of kin, a guardian, or a court, is required.

What is informed consent?

While patients presenting at the ED often require urgent medical treatment, in many cases there is time to obtain patient consent before initiating treatment. The consent obtained must be "informed consent;" that is, the patient must understand the procedure and its inherent risks and benefits and voluntarily give consent.

What information must be disclosed to the patient to obtain informed consent?

The law of informed consent has been shaped by years of court cases, with each state forming its own response regarding what information must be disclosed to the patient. Generally, however, the list includes:

- diagnosis
- nature and purpose of the proposed treatment
- risks and consequences of the proposed treatment
- probability that the proposed treatment will be successful
- feasible treatment alternatives
- prognosis if the proposed treatment is not given

The applicability of each of the items on the list may shift from case to case, depending on the particular facts. Nevertheless, the list has value as a disclosure checklist for the practitioner.

For hospitals, including EDs, the importance of obtaining informed consent to medical treatment has been reiterated by the federal government's adoption of a patients' rights Condition of Participation, the requirements of which hospitals must meet to be approved for, or to continue participation in, the Medicare and Medicaid programs. [*See, e.g.,* 42 C.F.R. § 482.13] Among other requirements, the rule contains a standard on patients' rights requiring hospitals to establish policies and procedures directed at protecting the patient's right to participate in the development and implementation of his or her plan of care. The standard expressly provides that patients or their representatives (as allowed under state law) have the right to make informed decisions regarding their care, be informed of their health status, be involved in care planning and treatment, and be able to request or refuse treatment.

Do all states use the same method to determine whether the consent was informed?

There are two different standards that states use to define informed consent: the professional community standard and the reasonable patient standard. The first is a physician-based standard, while the second is a patient-based standard. It is important for ED staff to learn which standard applies in the state in which they practice.

The professional community standard focuses on the physician and states that a physician's duty to disclose information is limited to the information that a reasonable medical practitioner would disclose under the same or similar circumstances.

The reasonable patient standard focuses on the patient and states that the physician must disclose all information material to the patient's decision to accept the proposed treatment. This is considered the more modern standard. Some states have adopted this standard through legislation. In Pennsylvania, for example, state law requires physicians to inform a patient of the nature of the proposed treatment, its risks, and the alternatives that a reasonable patient would consider material to the decision about whether to undergo treatment. [40 Pa. Cons. Stat. § 1303.504] Similarly, the Alaska Supreme court focused on the reasonable patient standard when a physician recommended that a patient go to the emergency room for treatment. The court ordered the lower court to determine whether the physician had disclosed enough information for a reasonable patient to determine whether to seek treatment. The physician had disclosed that the emergency room would probably take x-rays and insert a nasogastric tube for this person with abdominal pain; however, it was claimed that he failed to disclose the seriousness of the situation, the risk she faced, and the need to seek immediate attention. [*Marsingill v. O'Malley*, 58 P.3d 495 (Ala. 2002)]

Does the failure to disclose relevant information to a patient automatically result in liability?

Even when relevant information is not disclosed, there is no liability unless a court is convinced that the patient, if given the information that should have been disclosed, would have chosen a different course of treatment and avoided physical injury. This link between the nondisclosure and the patient's injury is called proximate cause or causation.

Under the reasonable patient standard, the patient must prove that the specific danger that was not disclosed was material (important) to the patient's decision. Some courts measure this by determining what a reasonable person would find material to his or her decision, while other courts require the information to be tailored to the needs of the particular circumstances of the patient in the case at hand.

Is a signed consent form sufficient evidence of informed consent?

Simply requiring the patient to sign a form does not satisfy informed consent requirements, as the form serves merely as evidence of the informed consent process. For example, a general consent form, worded to permit a physician to perform whatever procedures are in the patient's best interest, is invalid because it does not illustrate that the patient made an informed decision after receiving adequate information. On the other hand, it is important to document consent or the lack of consent. While not legally conclusive, a well-written, properly executed consent form is strong evidence that informed consent was given.

A legally effective consent form must

- be signed voluntarily
- show that the procedure performed was the one to which consent was given

- show that the consenting person understood the nature of the procedure, the risks involved, and the probable consequences

Some state statutes create a presumption that a written informed consent is valid. For example, in Ohio, a consent is considered valid if it (1) sets forth the nature of the procedures, (2) the person making the consent acknowledges disclosure and that all questions were answered and (3) is signed by the patient or his legal representative. To overcome this presumption of validity, a claimant must show by a preponderance of the evidence that the consent was not in good faith, was fraudulent, or made by someone who didn't understand English. [Ohio Rev. Code § 2317.54] Other states place the burden of proof on the plaintiff to show that the medical provider did not supply appropriate information in obtaining the consent or did not inform the patient of the common risks and alternatives. [See Tenn. Code Ann. § 29-26-118 requiring appropriate information and Alaska Stat. 09.55.556 requiring discussion of risks and alternatives, and Utah Code Ann. § 78-14-5 requiring substantial and significant risks] Note that generally, however, a patient does not need to be informed of every remote risk.

Other state statutes provide defenses to medical malpractice based on failure to obtain informed consent. These defenses include: the fact that the risks not disclosed were remote, a statement by the patient that he would continue treatment regardless of risk, the fact that consent was not possible, or health care provider judgment and discretion that full disclosure would adversely impact the patient. [Alaska Stat. § 09.55.556]

Is consent required in a medical emergency?

A true medical emergency may obviate the need for consent. The two factors necessary to trigger the emergency care doctrine are the patient's incapacity to consent and the need for immediate treatment. When immediate treatment is required to preserve life or prevent a serious impairment to health and it is impossible to obtain the patient's consent or that of someone authorized to consent on the patient's behalf, the physician may perform the required procedure without liability. Consent is implied by law as a matter of public policy because the physician's inaction in an emergency might result in greater harm to the patient.

Some states have enacted laws that formalize this emergency exception to the informed consent requirement. In Pennsylvania, for example, the physician's duty to obtain informed consent does not apply in emergencies. [40 Pa. Cons. Stat. § 1303.504]

What if the patient is able to consent but the need for quick action does not permit full disclosure?

This situation may occur in the ED when, for example, a patient presents with a heart attack in progress, a snake bite, or a severe allergic reaction. These situations do not meet the strict parameters of the emergency doctrine because the patient may be competent and able to consent to treatment. The situation is exigent, however, and the physician may not have time to provide full disclosure of all possible treatment alternatives.

Some states have enacted laws recognizing an exception to the consent requirement in such circumstances. In Alaska, for example, failure to obtain consent is permissible when "under the circumstances, consent by or on behalf of the patient was not possible." [Alaska Stat. § 09.55.556]

In states that have not recognized this exception in either case law or statute, the physician will have to make a reasonable medical decision, communicate with the patient as much as possible while not delaying necessary treatment, and document the circumstances and his or her reasons for proceeding. One view is that the patient's coming to the ED in need of immediate treatment implies the patient's consent. Another view is that treatment in such circumstances is simply a logical and necessary extension of the emergency doctrine.

How serious must the patient's condition be to render care without consent?

The patient's condition must be so serious that the initiation of treatment cannot be delayed until consent is obtained or the patient would suffer death or serious permanent impairment. This is a medical judgment. In cases in which delay would not materially increase the hazards, although it is clear that the medical treatment in question will be needed in the near term, failure to obtain consent cannot be excused on the grounds that an emergency existed. Courts have ruled that no consent was needed in the following cases:

- A 17-year-old boy's elbow was crushed beyond repair, and three physicians agreed that amputation was necessary to protect his life. The patient was unconscious from anesthetic administered to allow suturing of a profusely bleeding head wound and his family could not be contacted. [*Jackovach v. Yocum,* 237 N.W. 444 (Iowa 1931)]
- A 15-year-old boy's foot was run over by a train. A physician and four surgeons agreed that it was necessary to amputate the foot to save the patient's life. Although there was evidence at trial that it was possible to save the foot, the court ruled that it was inconceivable that the patient's parents would have refused to consent to the amputation under the circumstances. [*Luka v. Lowrie,* 136 N.W. 1106 (Mich. 1912)]
- A physician amputated a patient's gangrenous lower leg without obtaining informed consent. The court ruled that the physician was not liable because the patient's condition constituted a life-threatening emergency. [*Stafford v. Louisiana State Univ.,* 448 So. 2d 852 (La. Ct. App. 1984)]

What should ED staff do to comply with consent requirements in an emergency?

As with all questions of fact, it is important that the need for haste in rendering treatment be documented fully and carefully. Whenever possible, the health care provider should seek confirmation that an immediate threat to life or health exists. Hospitals should insist that staff engage in such consultation as time and circumstances permit. Findings supporting the existence of an emergency should be noted on the patient's record, with particular emphasis on the nature of the threat, its immediacy, and its magnitude. The initialing of such notations by consultant physicians is advisable from an evidentiary standpoint; at the least, the consulting physicians' names should be recorded.

The attending physician should be particularly wary of proceeding when a difference of opinion surfaces about the need for immediate treatment. Unfortunately, such disagreements do arise from time to time, forcing providers to choose between a conservative course safeguarding their legal position and the professional and ethical imperative to attempt to preserve life and health. See **Appendix 1-A** for a state-by-state description of consent to emergency medical treatment.

Can health care providers rely on the emergency doctrine if a patient representative is available?

The emergency doctrine contemplates not only that a medical situation require immediate treatment but also that the provider be unable to consult with next of kin or others recognized by the law as capable of giving consent on the patient's behalf. The search for such proxy authorization must extend as far as available time reasonably allows. State law often defines who may act on the patient's behalf. If these persons are not available, or if trying to contact them would be impractical given the urgency of the situation, then treatment can be rendered without consent under the emergency doctrine.

What is administrative consent?

The attempt to locate next of kin frequently falls to the hospital's administrative officials, which explains in part the significance of the so-called administrative consent to emergency care. The administration's approval serves three basic purposes:

1. documenting that the fullest possible attempt was made to secure a proxy consent
2. showing that someone with experience in emergency health care situations concurred with the physician's judgment that immediate care was needed (in fact, it might be used to provide additional proof that the hospital took all reasonable steps to ensure adequate medical consultation)
3. preventing the hospital from later instituting any internal disciplinary action against the physician for proceeding without consent

Administrative consent may be spelled out in a hospital policy or procedure and should be followed so that it protects both the institution and the practitioner. What must be recognized, however, is that the administration of a hospital has no special power to grant a legally effective consent; that must come from the patient, from a duly empowered representative, or from the circumstances. Administrative consent serves essentially an evidentiary function. Its significance and the procedures for its issuance should be clearly communicated to all members of the administrative and medical staffs.

What if the patient representative refuses to consent to treatment a provider considers essential to save the patient's life?

Where the circumstances clearly dictate immediate medical treatment but the person empowered to speak for the patient forbids it, the provider may not be absolutely bound by that decision. Assuming the necessity of treatment can be proved, the provider probably will not be held liable for proceeding. Such an approach is risky, however. It is much safer to secure a court order authorizing the treatment if there is time to do so. Some hospital administrations have set up channels for seeking court orders authorizing the provision of treatment when consent cannot be obtained in the regular manner. The court's power in this regard may be set forth by statute. Such procedures are often used for providing treatment to minors when their parents cannot be located to give consent or, more rarely, when the parents are available but refuse consent.

A New York case illustrates the use of a court order to avoid liability. A patient was unconscious and unable to either refuse or consent to needed surgical treatment. His wife refused to authorize treatment. A court authorized treatment, finding that the patient would die without surgery. The court pointed out that physicians should not be exposed to liability for either an unauthorized procedure if they render needed treatment or malpractice if they do not. By authorizing the treatment, the court insulated the physician from liability. [*Collins v. Davis*, 254 N.Y.S.2d 666 (Sup. Ct. 1964)]

What kind of treatment is authorized in an emergency?

Authorized treatment during an emergency when there is no patient consent is limited to whatever is reasonable under the circumstances. Reasonable treatment is dictated by the patient's condition. While exploratory surgery may be indicated for a patient who has sustained extensive abdominal injuries in a car accident, the surgeon is not justified in performing elective surgery that is not necessary to treat the emergency situation. Whatever treatment is necessary to alleviate the threat of death or serious permanent injury would be considered reasonable.

Can minors consent to medical treatment?

Generally, minors cannot consent to treatment. In most cases, the health care provider must secure the consent of the minor's parent or other person standing *in loco parentis* (in the place of the parents). There are several exceptions to this rule, however, including emergency situations, emancipated minors, and state laws that allow minors to consent to treatment for various conditions, such as sexual assault, sexually transmitted diseases (STDs), drug or alcohol abuse, and pregnancy-related care. See **Appendix 1-A** for a state-by-state description of when a minor can consent to emergency medical treatment.

What if there is a medical emergency and the parents cannot be located?

Parental consent is implied when there is a need for immediate action necessary to preserve a life or prevent permanent bodily harm, which is the definition of a true emergency.

Most states have statutes specifically addressing consent to emergency medical and surgical treatment of minors. A North Carolina statute, for example, authorizes medical treatment without parental consent if the minor's life or health is in jeopardy or if delaying treatment to seek consent would create a threat of serious injury to the minor. Surgical treatment under such circumstances requires consultation with another surgeon or physician, except in rural areas where consultation may not be promptly available. [N.C. Gen. Stat. §§ 90-21.1 through 90-21.4] Arizona and New Mexico have laws providing that consent may be given on behalf of a minor by anyone standing *in loco parentis* to the minor when an emergency exists and the parents cannot be located. [Ariz. Rev. Stat. § 44-133; N.M. Stat. Ann. § 24-10-2]

What is an emancipated minor?

Most states recognize the concept of the emancipated minor, that is, one who, although below the chronological age of majority, has assumed the lifestyle and responsibilities of an adult. Emancipation is generally accomplished by marriage and/or cessation of dependency on parental support. Having a separate home and independent means of financial support are key factors in assessing emancipation. In many states, a minor is automatically emancipated upon becoming a parent. Whether a minor is emancipated is a factual question that depends on the circumstances of the particular case.

Most states have statutes that allow married and emancipated minors to give effective consent to medical and surgical treatment. Many of these statutes also provide that parents of minors have the power to consent to care of their children. A Delaware statute states that consent for treatment of any minor by any licensed medical, surgical, dental, or osteopathic practitioner or any hospital or public clinic, and to hospitalization and other reasonably necessary care, may be given by

- a parent or guardian
- a married minor or, if the married minor is unable to give consent by reason of physical disability, then by his or her spouse
- a minor of the age 18 years or more
- a parent of a minor for his or her child
- a minor or any person professing to be temporary custodian of the minor at the request of a parent or guardian, for the examination and treatment of (i) any laceration, fracture, or other traumatic injury or (ii) any symptom, disease, or pathology that may reasonably be expected to threaten the health or life of such minor; provided that the consent given shall be effective only after reasonable efforts shall have been made to obtain the consent of the parent or guardian [Del. Code Ann. tit. 13, § 707]

What is mental competency?

For consent purposes, competency is an ability to understand the nature and consequences of the treatment to which one is asked to consent. Mental incompetency is not limited to patients who have been legally declared incompetent. It also includes patients who, in the opinion of the treating physician, are either permanently or temporarily unable to give consent. Permanent inability to give consent may apply to patients who suffer from mental retardation or senility. Temporary inability to give consent may result from head injury, alcohol, or drugs.

Who can consent to treatment if the person is mentally incompetent?

If a person has been declared legally incompetent, and a legal guardian or conservator has been appointed, that person's consent must be obtained. The guardian or conservator should be asked to provide proof of legal authority to make medical decisions for the patient.

In many cases, the person has not been declared legally incompetent, but in the physician's medical judgment the person is either permanently or temporarily incompetent to provide consent to treatment. Whenever possible, a hospital or other provider contemplating treatment of a person arguably incompetent should try to obtain substituted consent from the person's next of kin or a court order authorizing the proposed treatment. If the next of kin refuses to consent, it may still be possible to obtain a court order allowing the treatment.

In some cases the patient, while competent, may have executed an advance directive (such as a durable power of attorney) relating to the provision of medical care if the person is incapacitated. Such a document may grant agents full power and authority to make health care decisions on behalf of the person who executed the document to the same extent as that person would make if he or she were competent.

In emergency situations, when death or serious harm is imminent, general rules regarding emergency treatment will protect the provider who acts reasonably and in good faith. See **Appendix 1-A** for a state-by-state description of capacity and consent to emergency medical treatment.

Who can refuse treatment when a person is mentally incompetent?

In light of legal battles over treatment refusal and the right to withdraw life support, a number of states have passed statutes that give surrogate decision makers the right to determine if treatment may be refused or withheld. These surrogate decision makers are typically the next of kin and can refuse treatment even if it will result in death. Statutes frequently specify that the person must be terminally ill or in a persistent vegetative state (PVS) in order for support to be withheld. Some statutes provide guidelines on how the decision will be made. The primary approaches to surrogate decision making include: (1) substituted judgment in which the surrogate makes the decision the person would make if competent and able to do so, (2) clear and convincing evidence standard in which the surrogate must set forth proof that the person wished to have life support terminated, and (3) the best interests of the patient standard in which objective criteria are used to determine if refusal or termination of life sustaining treatment is in the best interest of the person.

Some states also provide for the physician to make the decision. This typically occurs when no surrogate is available, no guardian has been appointed, and there is no advanced directive. The physician may be authorized to make the decision independently or may be required to obtain the consensus of a second physician. When a state has this kind of statute, the physician would be authorized to withhold treatment without court order. For example, the Utah statute requires the physician to obtain the written consent of another physician as well as the legal guardian or spouse, parent, or adult child to terminate a life-sustaining procedure. [Utah Code Ann. § 72-2-1107]

Have any courts applied mental incompetency analysis to intoxicated patients?

A Rhode Island case illustrates how incompetency to consent may be applied in an emergency when an intoxicated patient refuses medically necessary treatment. A patient arrived at the ED complaining of head, eye, back, and rib pain after a car accident in which he was not wearing a seat belt. He had consumed the equivalent of 16 alcoholic drinks and his blood alcohol level was 0.233, well above the state's legal limit for driving (0.10). The patient learned that a physician planned to perform a peritoneal lavage to check for abdominal bleeding. The patient refused to consent to the procedure. The physician explained to the patient that he was not in a position to appreciate his injuries and that the physician was following standard hospital procedure. The patient attempted to get up and began yelling and struggling with the physician. A security guard arrived, and the patient was restrained and administered anesthesia. The procedure was performed and the patient sued, arguing that he did not consent. The hospital defended that it properly administered emergency treatment to a patient who was not competent to refuse consent in accordance with hospital protocol and medical professional practice guidelines.

The highest court in Rhode Island considered whether intoxication could be presented to a jury as evidence of incompetence to consent. To consent to treatment, a patient should be able to reasonably understand his or her condition, the nature and effect of the proposed treatment, and the risks of pursuing and not pursuing the treatment. Determining whether a patient is in a mental condition to understand the risks and consequences of treatment includes an assessment of the effect of intoxication, the court ruled. Cautioning that intoxication does not make every patient incapable of informed consent, the court held that a particular patient's capacity is for the jury to assess. In this case, the jury should consider testimony that the hospital complied with the standards of the American College of Surgeons, the effects of a 0.233 blood alcohol content, the practices of physicians in similar situations, and hospital protocol for treating intoxicated patients injured in serious accidents. [*Miller v. Rhode Island Hosp.*, 625 A.2d 778 (R.I. 1993)]

Can a mental health patient give valid consent to treatment?

It is a medical judgment whether a patient is able to understand the information necessary for informed consent and make a rational decision regarding that information. There is no presumption of inability to give valid consent merely because the patient is a mental health patient. The medical determination of whether a patient is competent to consent to treatment should be well documented in the medical record. For additional discussion, see "What is mental competency?" For sample documentation, see **Part 4**.

What is an advance directive?

An advance directive is a witnessed, written (and in some states oral) statement voluntarily executed by a person who is mentally competent. An advance directive may appoint an agent who will render health care decisions on behalf of the patient and may indicate the type of treatment or withholding of treatment the patient wishes in the event he or she is unable to make such decisions when treatment is necessary. Advance directives include living wills and durable powers of attorney for health care. For sample documentation, see **Part 4**.

How do advance directives apply in emergency situations?

Several state laws include provisions that address the effect of an advance directive in an emergency situation. This usually arises in the case of a seriously or terminally ill patient who has executed an advance directive. Generally, when emergency medical services personnel are called, they initiate cardiopulmonary resuscitation (CPR) when necessary; however, this may be altered by an advance directive.

In Arkansas, for example, the EMS Do Not Resuscitate Act refers to a standardized card, form, necklace, or bracelet of uniform size and design used to indicate that the patient has executed an advance directive specifically addressing cardiopulmonary resuscitation or that the patient's attending physician has issued an EMS DNR order for the patient and has documented the grounds in the patient's medical record. Such identification authorizes qualified EMS personnel to withhold cardiopulmonary resuscitation in the event of a cardiac or respiratory arrest. [Ark. Code Ann. § 20-13-901]

The following is an example of how the advance directive would work in this situation. The caregiver of a seriously ill patient calls 911 when the patient begins to go into crisis. The EMS team arrives prepared to administer CPR if the patient's condition warrants it. Because the patient has previously executed an advance directive specifically prohibiting CPR, and the caregiver has approved documentation to that effect and presents it to the EMS team, CPR is not administered. The EMS team is still authorized to provide other types of support to ensure the patient's safety and comfort, including intravenous fluids, oxygen, nutrition, or hydration, and can transport the patient to a health care facility. In the absence of proper documentation regarding the advance directive, the EMS personnel would have begun CPR if the patient's condition warranted it, regardless of the caregiver's statements.

Should advance directives be followed in the ED?

If the attending physician is aware of the advance directive, it should be followed. According to the patients' rights Condition of Participation required by CMS, hospitals must take measures to protect a patient's right to have hospital staff and practitioners comply with advance directives in providing care to patients. [42 C.F.R. § 482.13] This regulation also specifies that a patient has a right to formulate advance directives, and therefore if the patient is competent upon arriving in the ED and requests assistance in drafting an advance directive, the hospital should be prepared to offer such assistance. If, however, the patient's condition and the circumstances do not allow for providing such assistance (i.e., the patient arrives at the ED unconscious with life-threatening medical condition), necessary treatment should not be delayed to permit extensive investigation into whether the patient has executed a legitimate advance directive.

What if a patient refuses to consent to treatment in the ED?

A competent adult patient who has been informed of the consequences of such a decision has the right to refuse to consent to treatment. To provide treatment in the face of refusal to consent would constitute battery. Courts have specifically recognized that the emergency treatment exception cannot override the refusal of treatment by a patient who is capable of providing consent, even if the attending physician is persuaded that, without treatment, the patient's life is threatened. [*See, e.g., Shine v. Vega*, 709 N.E.2d 58 (Mass. 1999)] Nor can a physician, after a patient's refusal, wait until the patient's condition worsens or until the patient lapses into unconsciousness and then commence treatment, basing such action on the existence of an emergency or the patient's lack of competence.

If the patient refuses care in the face of pressing need, this may be evidence of incompetence. The attending physician must make a medical judgment of whether the patient is competent. This assessment must be fully documented and medically supportable.

If the patient is not competent, there may be a patient representative who is authorized to consent to treatment. However, if a patient is not capable of giving consent and a relative refuses to consent to treatment that the provider considers essential to the patient's life or health, the provider should seek a court order authorizing such treatment.

Can a suicidal patient give a valid refusal of treatment?

As discussed under Mental Competency, above, certain patients lack the competency to consent to or refuse treatment. When patients are brought to the ED after a suicide attempt and refuse to consent to life-saving care, many clinicians deem the individual incompetent to refuse care on the basis of the suicide attempt alone and provide necessary emergency treatment despite their refusal. A risk assessment supports this view, as a wrongful treatment or false imprisonment suit poses a lesser risk of hospital liability than a wrongful death suit. Some courts have upheld the right of suicidal patients to refuse care, however, especially if those patients are terminally ill. Thus, ED leaders should consider requiring a competency evaluation, where time allows, before overriding these patients' refusals. If the patient is found competent, the refusal to accept treatment should be honored. For sample documentation, see **Part 4: 4-44**.

How should refusal of consent be documented?

Refusal of consent should be documented in the medical record, along with documentation that the consequences of the person's refusal to consent were explained to the patient and the physician's assessment that the patient was competent at the time of the refusal.

It is also good policy to obtain a signed release form that exculpates the hospital and its employees and staff from liability for any consequences flowing from the refusal. It should contain the information stated above. If the patient refuses to sign a release form, a note reflecting that should be added to the medical record.

Antidiscrimination Laws

What laws prohibit race, national origin, and gender discrimination?

A number of laws provide overlapping prohibitions against discrimination in hospitals. Public hospitals are subject to the federal Constitution, including the Equal Protection clause of the 14th Amendment. This clause prohibits state action (applied by some courts to include hospital care) from being used to deny individuals equal protection of the laws—making race and gender unlawful criteria for restricting or denying public hospital care.

Receipt of federal funding triggers a number of nondiscrimination provisions. Under Title VI of the Civil Rights Act of 1965, institutions that receive federal assistance (including Medicare, Medicaid, and Hill-Burton funds) must not discriminate on the basis of race, color, or national origin. [42 U.S.C. §§ 2000d through 2000d-7] Title II of the Civil Rights Act of 1964, which prohibits race, color, religion, and national origin discrimination, has also been applied to hospitals, as both public and private hospitals come within the definition of "public accommodation." [42 U.S.C. §§ 2000a through 2000a-6] Hospitals that receive Hill-Burton funds are prohibited from discriminating on the basis of race, color, national origin, creed, or any other grounds unrelated to the patient's need for the service or the availability of the needed service, presumably including gender. [42 C.F.R. § 124.603]

Finally, many states have enacted laws that preclude institutions serving the public from discriminating on the basis of race, ethnic background, and gender. Provisions specifically barring hospitals from discriminating on these grounds are incorporated in many hospital licensure laws.

What should hospitals do to avoid race, national origin, and gender discrimination suits?

Hospital admitting policies should be reviewed for compliance with antidiscrimination laws. Although it is not likely that policies explicitly condone disparate treatment of minorities, policies may disparately affect patients in protected minority groups in violation of antidiscrimination laws. For example, a policy automatically excluding all pregnant women from a drug detoxification program constituted discrimination on the basis of sex if the facility had the capacity to safely treat some pregnant women, a New York court has ruled. [*Elaine W. v. Joint Diseases N. Gen. Hosp. Inc.*, 613 N.E.2d 523 (N.Y. 1993)] Policies that limit Medicaid patients to a certain number of beds may also discriminatorily affect minority groups.

What federal laws govern discrimination on the basis of handicap or disability?

There are two major federal statutes that prohibit discrimination on the basis of handicap or disability. Under the Rehabilitation Act of 1973, individuals cannot be excluded from participating in or receiving the benefits of a federally financed program or activity (including Medicare, Medicaid, and Hill-Burton) solely because they have handicaps. [29 U.S.C. § 794(a)]

Title III of the Americans with Disabilities Act (ADA) of 1990 prohibits places of public accommodation from discriminating against individuals with disabilities in the provision of goods and services. Hospitals are specifically included within the definition of "public accommodation." Unlike the Rehabilitation Act, the ADA does not require receipt of federal funds to apply. [42 U.S.C. §§ 12182 through 12189]

What are an ED's legal duties toward disabled patients?

Under the ADA and the Rehabilitation Act, hospitals may not offer unequal services to individuals with disabilities. This prohibition requires not only that hospitals make non-discriminatory treatment and admitting decisions, but also that hospitals accommodate disabled patients so that the services offered to disabled patients are equal to those offered to nondisabled patients. For example, hospitals may make the exchange of information between staff and deaf patients "equal" by providing sign language interpreters for deaf patients and their families so that they may participate in their health care to the same extent as a nondisabled individual. Other accommodations that may be necessary for disabled individuals to make comparable use of ED services include posted signs, Braille materials, a policy addressing service animals in the ED, and improved physical accessibility of hospital facilities.

Patients with Limited English Proficiency (LEP)

Emergency departments are frequently involved with patients and families who speak no English at all, or if they have some ability, their comprehension level in English makes communications difficult. This communication barrier makes obtaining informed consent difficult and makes active decision making by the family nearly impossible. In response to federal constitutional provisions, antidiscrimination laws, and court decisions, HHS's Office of Civil Rights (OCR) has issued requirements over the past 30 years on these issues, but hospitals have been very slow to adopt them, which has resulted in substantial compliance issues. In 2000, the OIG issued guidelines that outline the requirements for hospitals and their departments, including emergency services. [Title VI of the Civil Rights Act of 1964: Policy Guidance on the Prohibition against National Origin Discrimination as It Affects Persons with Limited English Proficiency. 65 Fed. Reg. 52,762–52,774 (Aug. 30, 2000)] The guidelines were subsequently modified and republished in 2002. [67 Fed. Reg. 4968 (Feb. 1, 2002)] Revised guidelines were published in 2003. [68 Fed. Reg. 47,311 (Aug. 8, 2003)]

Under the new federal guidelines, do hospitals have a responsibility to provide foreign language interpreters?

The 2003 OCR policy guidance focuses on the need to take reasonable steps to ensure meaningful access to programs and activities by LEP persons. Hospitals are expected to establish meaningful communication with "Limited English Proficient" (LEP) patients when reasonable based on a balancing of the need to make services accessible without creating an undue burden on small or nonprofit organizations. The guidelines, which apply to hospitals that receive federal funds such as Medicare and Medicaid, do not have the force of law or regulation, but should be closely considered, because they set forth the criteria that investigators will rely on when investigating claims of national origin discrimination based on failure to provide no cost interpretive services, and also suggest "safe harbors" that can be used to ensure that OCR will not find a facility in violation. The guidelines are clear that failure to comply with a safe harbor does not indicate non-compliance with the guidelines.

The 2003 guidelines focused on four factors to consider in determining the organization's LEP responsibility. These are: (1) The number or proportion of LEP persons eligible or likely to be served by the program or organization. The greater the number or percentage of LEP persons served, the greater the need for services. (2) The frequency with which the LEP individual comes into contact with the program. For these purposes, an organization can differentiate a language such as Spanish, which may be encountered frequently, from another language that is used less frequently. (3) The nature and importance of the program to people's lives. For example, emergency surgery and consent would be important with a high need for services, while consent for elective surgery might be delayed without a negative impact. (4) The resources available and costs involved to implement a program. Each organization will then determine the appropriate mix of LEP services through oral interpreters and written translated materials that is necessary under the four-factor test.

The need for translation of both written documents and oral communications must be assessed. The OCR outlined safe harbor guidelines to help a hospital determine when documents need to be translated into other languages. The safe harbor requires that

- The HHS recipient provides written translation of vital documents to each LEP group with five percent or 1,000 individuals, whichever is less, or
- When less than 50 individuals in a language group meet the five-percent standard the organization does not need to translate the vital document, but should provide written notice in the LEP person's primary language of the right to oral interpretation of materials free of cost.

A vital document is one such as an intake form, consent form, or test; non-vital documents include general information. [68 Fed. Reg. 47,311 (Aug. 8, 2003)]

How should notice be provided to LEP persons?

An organization has flexibility to determine how to provide notice to LEP persons based on the four-factor test. Methods of providing notice include, but are not limited to:

- posting and maintaining signs in regularly encountered languages other than English in waiting rooms, reception areas and other initial points of entry. These signs should inform applicants and beneficiaries of their right to free language assistance services and invite them to identify themselves as needing such services. [General information is available in other languages on the Internet at *http://www.lep.gov*]
- using telephone and voice menu services with multiple languages
- translation of application forms and instructional, informational, and other written materials into appropriate non-English languages by competent translators
- inclusion of statements about the services available and the right to free language assistance services, in appropriate non-English languages, in brochures, booklets, outreach and recruitment information, and other materials that are routinely disseminated to the public, and
- through community outreach with non-English spots on television or radio or presentations at schools and churches.

May a hospital depend on the use of family as interpreters?

The guidance encourages a hospital or the care provider to determine the competence of an interpreter. Options for hospitals in regard to interpreters include:

- hiring bilingual staff
- hiring staff interpreters
- contracting with an outside interpreter service
- using telephone interpreters
- using community volunteers
- using family or friends.

When using family members, the provider should be aware of conflicts of interest that may arise or limits of ability that impact translation. For example, in the ED language assistance should not result in delay of medical emergency treatment. A family member may serve as a good interpreter in the ED. Extra caution should be taken when using a minor to interpret and in using a family member to interpret when there is a concern about possible abuse.

A recent study of medical errors and interpreters found that family and staff interpreters had a higher interpretation error rate than professional interpreters. These errors included omission of words or phrases (52 percent), addition of terms (8 percent), substitution with different phrases (13 percent), editorialization by adding their own view (10 percent), and false fluency—using a word or phrase that did not exist (16 percent). Sixty-three percent of the translation errors had medical consequences. For example, one interpreter told a family to begin topical steroids in four days when the physician said to start it immediately and administer it for four days. [Flores G., Laws M.B., Mayon S.J., et al., *Errors in Medical Interpretation and their potential clinical consequences in pediatric encounters*, Pediatrics, 2003 (111:6-14)] Thus, care should be taken in using family or staff interpreters who have not been trained.

In a non-emergency situation if the caregiver determines that the family member is unable to continue translating because of the technical medical terminology, the exam should be delayed while arrangements are made for another interpreter. This may be as simple as a locating a bilingual staff member or calling a telephone interpreter. [68 Fed. Reg. 47,311 (Aug. 8, 2003)]

How should hospital employees be made aware of the hospital's language assistance policies and procedures?

Over the years, OCR has observed that hospitals often develop effective language assistance policies and procedures but that employees are unaware of the policies, or do not know how to, or otherwise fail to, provide available assistance. Effective training is one means of ensuring that there is not a gap between a hospital's written policies and procedures, and the actual practices of employees who are in the front lines interacting with LEP persons.

It is important that this training be part of the orientation for new ED and other hospital employees and that all employees in client contact positions be trained properly. Given the high turnover rate among some employees, hospitals may find it useful to maintain a training registry that records the names and dates of employees' training.

What are the elements of an effective LEP plan?

An effective LEP plan should include the following components: (1) identification of LEP individuals who are in need of services, (2) language assistance measures, which are made available to staff who know how to obtain such services, (3) staff training, (4) notice to LEP persons that services are available and free of charge in the language the LEP person will understand, and (5) monitoring and updating the LEP plan to regularly determine if changes have occurred that would warrant a program change.

What monitoring or quality improvement programs should be utilized?

It is crucial for a hospital to monitor its language assistance program on a regular basis to assess the current LEP makeup of its service area, the frequency of contact with the language group, the importance of the activity to the LEP person, the available hospital resources, the assistance needed to meet the needs of the LEP person, whether staff members know of the LEP plan, and sources for assistance and whether they are still current and viable. One element of such an assessment is for a hospital to seek feedback from clients and advocates. OCR has stated that compliance with Title VI is most likely when a hospital continuously monitors its program, makes modifications where necessary, and periodically trains employees in implementation of the policies and procedures.

How will OCR enforce compliance with the LEP requirements of Title VI?

OCR's goal is to encourage voluntary compliance with the guidance policy in a way that balances the need for services with the costs of compliance. The guidelines are intended to encourage organizations to take reasonable steps to ensure meaningful access for LEP persons through use of the four-factor analysis. [68 Fed. Reg. 47,311 (Aug. 8, 2003)]

Have state laws addressed the issue of non-English-speaking patients?

Some states have enacted laws requiring hospitals to provide foreign language interpreters. A law in Massachusetts, for example, requires hospitals to provide emergency services in all emergency rooms to non-English speaking patients [105 Mass. Regs. 130.1103]. Hospitals in that state must designate a coordinator of interpreter services and notify ED patients of their right to an interpreter and may not use underage family members as interpreters.

How have courts and government investigators viewed the ED's duty to accommodate deaf and hard of hearing ED patients?

There have been a number of lawsuits brought by patients against hospitals for failing to provide sign language interpreters in the ED. The federal Department of Justice has prosecuted a number of these claims as well. Hospitals have set forth a number of arguments in defending charges of discrimination, contending that

- the patient suffered no adverse medical consequences
- a relative of the patient was available to provide translation services
- effective communication was established through writing notes, or with the help of a hospital staff member with limited sign language (i.e., finger spelling) skills
- the hospital had a contract with an interpreter service, but an interpreter was not available promptly

These arguments have been largely unsuccessful. Courts and investigating agencies have typically reasoned that the hospital cannot escape liability for disability discrimination by showing that adequate communication was established so that the patient received the care he or she needed. Rather, courts and the government have found that the ADA protects not only a deaf patient's right to receive the same medical care as hearing patients, but that the deaf patient be able to participate in his or her care to the same extent as hearing patients. Where hospitals have relied on relatives for translation services, courts have criticized the hospital for relying on an interpreter who may not understand medical terminology and compromising the patient's right to confidential medical care. Further, entering into a contract for translation services does not satisfy the hospital's duty; the services must be available and present when needed in connection with emergency care. [*See, e.g., Negron v. Snoqualmie Valley Hosp.*, 936 P.2d 55 (Wash. Ct. App. 1997); *Naiman v. New York Univ.*, 95 Civ. 6469 (LMM) (S.D.N.Y. May 13, 1997)]

In 2000, the Justice Department issued a publication entitled "Sign Language Pictograms for Hospital Communication" to 1000 hospitals and hospital associations. This publication was developed in connection with a settlement against 32 hospitals throughout Connecticut that faced allegations under the ADA that they failed to communicate with deaf and hard of hearing patients. The publication consists of illustrations of sign language phrases with captions written in English. For more information, call the Department's toll free ADA information line at 1-800-514-0301. In 2003, the Justice Department issued communication recommendations for hospitals focusing on patients who were deaf or hard of hearing and recommended use of sign language, oral interpreters, cued speech interpreters, or computer-assisted real-time transcription. Interpreters are especially recommended when discussing medication conditions, tests, or treatment; obtaining informed consent; during ongoing physician communication; and when providing follow-up instructions. TTY devices are required at public pay phones for the emergency room and recovery area as well as other waiting areas. Visual alarms should be used to notify people of fire or safety concerns. [*Communicating with People Who Are Deaf or Hard of Hearing in Hospital Settings*, DOJ (Oct. 2003)]

Must a health care provider obtain authorization to disclose personal health information to an interpreter?

When an interpreter helps a covered entity with language services and provides services that are part of the health care operations, then personal health information can be disclosed under the privacy rule as long as the interpreter is part of the workforce as an employee, contract interpreter or volunteer. If the interpretive services are arranged by contract, then the organization should be sure the contract meets the requirements of a business associate contract. [45 C.F.R. § 160.103] If a family member is used to interpret, then the agreement of the individual patient should be obtained prior to using the service. [45 C.F.R § 164.510 and DHHS FAQ on Sharing PHI with Interpreters (Mar. 8, 2005)]

Patients with HIV or AIDS

Do disability discrimination laws apply to patients with HIV or AIDS?

The ADA protects all individuals who are human immunodeficiency virus (HIV)-positive, even those individuals who are outwardly asymptomatic, the United States Supreme Court has ruled. An individual who was HIV-positive, but not exhibiting the infection's most serious symptoms, went to a dentist for an examination. When the dentist discovered a cavity, he informed the patient that he would not fill her cavity in his office and offered to treat her in the hospital. Although he agreed to charge his regular fee, the patient would be responsible for paying the hospital for the cost of using its facilities. The patient sued the dentist under the ADA. The Supreme Court ruled that the patient's HIV infection was a disability under the ADA. Stating that it was a "misnomer" to refer to HIV as asymptomatic in its early stages, the Court determined that HIV is a physical impairment from the moment of infection because of the immediacy with which the virus begins to damage the infected person's white blood cells and the severity of the disease. Further, HIV infection substantially limits reproduction, which is no less important than activities such as working and learning, which are listed as major life activities in the Rehabilitation Act's regulations defining disability, the Court reasoned. Thus, the Court affirmed that HIV infection is a disability under the ADA. [*Bragdon v. Abbott*, 524 U.S. 624 (U.S. 1998)]

Can EDs be liable for discrimination for exercising special precautions when treating patients with HIV or AIDS?

Courts have ruled that hospitals implementing blood and body fluid precautions when treating patients with HIV and acquired immunodeficiency syndrome (AIDS) are not liable under disability discrimination statutes. [*Doe v. District of Columbia Comm'n on Human Rights*, 624 A.2d 440 (D.C. 1993); *Syracuse Community Health Ctr. v. Wendi A. M.*, 604 N.Y.S.2d 406 (App. Div. 1993), *aff'd*, 659 N.E.2d 760 (N.Y. 1995)] EDs should treat all patients with similar conditions in accordance with hospital practice and procedure, however, and protocols should be based on prevailing medical knowledge. [*North Shore Univ. Hosp. v. Rosa*, 657 N.E.2d 483 (N.Y. App. Div. 1995)]

Treatment must not be delayed, however, or the hospital is at risk for liability under the Consolidated Omnibus Budget Reconciliation Act (COBRA). A federal court in Kansas ruled that a patient who was asked to undergo an HIV test before being treated in a hospital ED can sue under COBRA. The patient sought treatment for abdominal pain, later diagnosed as acute appendicitis. Before he was evaluated and admitted for surgery, however, a physician inquired into the patient's sexual orientation, and upon learning that the patient was homosexual, required him to consent to an HIV test and await the results before being treated. The patient later sued the hospital and the physician, claiming that he did not receive the appropriate medical screening exam required under COBRA, because he was treated differently than similarly situated patients. Rejecting the hospital's argument that COBRA did not apply because there was no proof that treatment was delayed due to an economic motive, the court allowed the claim to proceed. [*Blake v. Richardson*, No. 98-2576-JWL (D. Kan. Apr. 2, 1999)]

Breach of confidentiality is also a concern when special precautions are used for treating patients with infectious diseases. For a discussion of this issue, see "Under what circumstances does the duty to report communicable diseases typically arise?" under ED Records and Confidentiality.

Can hospitals and health care providers be liable for refusing to treat patients with HIV or AIDS?

Hospitals may be held liable for discrimination for refusing to treat or admit patients known or suspected to have HIV or AIDS. For example, an on-call admitting physician and a hospital violated the ADA when the physician refused to admit an HIV-positive man, a federal trial court in Ohio has ruled. The HIV-positive man was traveling when he had a severe allergic reaction to a new prescription medication. He sought treatment in the ED at the nearest hospital, where the attending physician determined that the reaction should be further treated. When the physician requested approval for admission, however, the hospital's on-call admitting physician expressed concern over whether the patient had progressed from HIV-positive to full-blown AIDS status, and he denied admission. Because the patient required prompt medical care, the attending physician arranged for admission at another hospital. The patient sued the hospital and the admitting physician. [*Howe v. Hull*, 873 F. Supp. 72 (N.D. Ohio 1994)]

The court ruled that both the hospital and the admitting physician were liable for discrimination under the ADA. The court found that the admitting physician could be personally liable, because he had the authority and discretion to admit the patient to the hospital and because his decision was not the implementation of an institutional policy at the hospital. The court ruled that the decision not to admit the patient was discriminatory, finding that the patient had been denied the opportunity to receive medical treatment and that the patient's HIV status was the motivating factor in the admitting physician's refusal to admit the patient to the hospital.

Does transferring the care of an HIV-positive patient constitute disability discrimination?

Transferring an HIV-positive patient to another physician or hospital may not constitute disability discrimination under certain circumstances, if the treatment is beyond the provider's expertise or the provider does not have the resources to properly treat the patient. In one case, for example, a Massachusetts federal trial court ruled that an obstetrician who transferred a pregnant HIV-positive patient to another hospital better able to treat her did not violate the Rehabilitation act or a state disability discrimination statute. [*Lesley v. Chie*, 81 F. Supp. 2d 217 (D. Mass. 2000), *aff'd*, 250 F.3d 47 (1st Cir. 2001)] There the physician transferred the patient to a hospital with more expertise because the hospital where he practiced did not have an AZT program in place, he had never prescribed AZT, and he did not know how to manage its side effects.

Are there confidentiality concerns related to the treatment of patients with HIV or AIDS?

Many states have enacted laws specifically addressing the confidentiality of medical information concerning AIDS, reflecting the importance of protecting the type of medical information from disclosure. These laws prohibit disclosure of HIV status without patient consent, although all of the laws contain statutory exceptions to this blanket prohibition. [*See, e.g.,* Fla. Stat. Ann. § 381.004 and Haw. Rev. Stat. § 325-101] Several states also have general medical confidentiality statutes protecting HIV- or AIDS-related information. Protection of HIV-related information may be available through statutes establishing patient-physician privilege. [*See, e.g.,* N.Y. C.P.L.R. 4504(a)] For a more detailed discussion of this issue, see above section, Patients' Rights, Confidentiality of ED Records.

In addition to statutory privileges, if confidential information is improperly revealed, the person could sue for invasion of privacy, defamation, or intentional infliction of emotional distress. In one case, for example, a hospital and physician were found liable for defamation when a newspaper printed the picture of an HIV-positive patient who was being treated at the hospital. [*Anderson v. Strong Mem'l Hosp.*, 531 N.Y.S.2d 735 (Sup. Ct. 1988), *aff'd*, 542 N.Y.S.2d 96 (App. Div. 1989)]

What are the reporting requirements for patients who are HIV-positive or have AIDS?

Laws in all 50 states require the names of people with AIDS to be reported to state or local health departments. In addition, all states have been required to report AIDS cases to the federal CDC since 1983. The reporting requirement is usually imposed on the physician who initially diagnoses AIDS, although it may apply to other health care providers, such as laboratories.

The majority of states also require some sort of HIV case reporting. Name-based reporting for individuals infected with HIV is a contentious issue, however. In order to allay concerns about patient confidentiality, some states report using unique-identifier codes or initials. At least 40 states require some sort of HIV case reporting. Because the reporting requirements differ among states, each hospital should check the requirements of its state law.

What does DHHS recommend when there is a non-occupational exposure to HIV?

The Department of Health and Human Services (DHHS) recommends antiretroviral drugs to prevent HIV infection after unanticipated exposure through sex or injection drug exposure. For those who seek care within 72 hours of exposure and there is substantial risk of transmission, a 28-day course of highly active antiretroviral therapy (HAART) is recommended. The drug therapy should begin as soon as possible after exposure. When the person seeks care more than 72 hours after exposure and there is substantial risk of transmission, no recommendation is made. Each physician should evaluate the risk and care on a case-by-case basis. When the benefits of drug treatment outweigh the risks and exposure is high, then non-occupational post exposure prophylaxis (nPEP) may be considered. When there is little risk of exposure and care is sought more than 72 hours after exposure, nPEP is not recommended. Further, the DHHS recommends counseling to reduce risk. [*Antiretroviral post-exposure prophylaxis after sexual, injection-drug use, or other non-occupational exposure to HIV in the U.S.*, DHHS Recommendations 54 MMWR RR02 (1/20/05)]

CONTENT OF THE ED RECORD

The importance of properly charting patient information and the difficulties that arise in accurately recording this information are highlighted when medical services are delivered in an ED. In the ED, the limitations on time and space, the numbers of patients that are seen, and the urgency of medical intervention often make it difficult to properly document all significant findings. The following section discusses legal requirements governing the content of the ED record.

What types of information should an ED record contain?

Many ED record forms are only one page in length, sometimes double sided, and do not provide much space to record information. Even with these space limitations, however, a complete ED record should contain the following types of information:

- patient identification, including demographic information
- means and time of arrival (although in practice, it is the patient's time of registration with the department that is usually recorded)
- consent signature
- patient's vital signs
- history of illness or injury
- diagnosis
- reports of procedures, tests, and results
- medical orders and follow-up instructions
- patient's condition on discharge or transfer

For sample documentation, see **Part 4**.

Are there specific legal requirements that govern the content of an ED record?

Legal requirements governing the content of the patient records compiled in hospital EDs are found in state and federal statutes and regulations. In jurisdictions in which there are no state regulations spelling out the content of ED records, the general provisions relating to the content of medical records apply. Frequently, these provisions simply state that the content of a medical record must be adequate, accurate, and complete. The medical record documentation will provide the basis for proper billing that complies with fraud and abuse standards and billing coding requirements.

How does federal law govern the content of an ED record?

At the federal level, the enactment of COBRA significantly increased the importance of establishing complete and accurate emergency care records. Under this statute, any hospital with an ED must provide for an appropriate medical screening examination (MSE) to any individual who comes to the department and requests treatment for a medical condition, or at the request of someone acting on that individual's behalf. A hospital cannot delay an MSE, further medical examination, or treatment to inquire about the individual's method of payment or insurance status. Although the law contains no specific requirements for documentation of medical screening, a hospital should carefully document this type of patient care to defend against charges that it violated the law. The ED should create and retain a record of each medical screening it conducts. If the medical screening indicates that the individual does not have an emergency condition, the hospital will have satisfied its obligations under the law. For evidence purposes, however, its records should demonstrate that the screening was conducted and that such a conclusion was reached.

Proper documentation is particularly important if the individual refuses to consent to the screening or refuses to undergo recommended further treatment. The ED record should include written informed consent when an individual has refused an examination, treatment, or transfer. The law also prohibits transferring an individual who has not been stabilized unless certain consent and medical certification requirements are met. Documentation on the stabilization of a patient's condition or a transfer, therefore, should be accurate and complete in order to prove that the hospital complied with its duties under the law. The documentation should indicate the status of the individual's condition and the treatment provided to achieve stabilization. In the event of a transfer, the record should include a statement by medical personnel that within reasonable medical probability, no material deterioration of the patient's emergency medical condition will result from the transfer or will occur during the transfer process. The transferring hospital must send a copy of all medical records relating to the emergency condition that are available at the time of the transfer, including observations of signs or symptoms, preliminary diagnosis, treatment provided, results of any tests, the informed consent to transfer, the physician's certification, and the name and address of any on-call physician who refused or failed to appear within a reasonable time to provide necessary stabilizing treatment. Failure to do so may not only generate liability under COBRA, but also generate common law liability for the hospital. In a ruling by a federal appeals court, for example, a patient's widow was allowed to sue a hospital for negligence under state law, claiming that its ED failed to forward an X-ray of the patient's chest to the hospital where the patient was transferred. [*Dickey v. Baptist Mem'l Hosp.*, 146 F.3d 262 (5th Cir. 1998)] For a more detailed discussion of ED obligations under COBRA, see "Duty To Treat Patients Regardless of Ability To Pay" in this section. [Note that Medicare regulations on the conditions of participation formerly distinguished between ED records and medical records, but no longer do so.]

How does state law govern the content of an ED record?

Some state laws and regulations specify the information to be recorded in ED records. In Wisconsin, for example, regulations specify that the ED patient record must contain

- patient identification
- a history of disease or injury

- physical findings
- laboratory and X-ray reports if any
- diagnosis
- record of treatment
- disposition of the case
- authentication
- appropriate notations regarding time of the patient's arrival, time of physician notification, time of treatments (including administration of medications), and time of patient discharge or transfer from the service [Wis. Admin. Code § 124.24]

Similarly, Maine details the content of the ED record, specifying that in addition to the types of information listed above, the record must contain documentation of notification of appropriate authorities in suspected medicolegal cases. [Code of Me. Rules § 10-144-112] In Oklahoma, regulations require that an emergency medical record contain documentation if a patient leaves AMA. [Okla. Admin. Code § 310:667-19-11] Connecticut requires documentation of the reasons for transfer or discharge in the medical record. [Conn. Gen. Stat. § 19a-535]

STAFFING ISSUES

EDs encounter unique staffing issues arising from the necessity of providing 24-hour emergency services every day. State hospital licensure laws govern ED staffing, and on-call staffing requirements vary from state to state. Staffing and compensation requirements under federal laws may also raise legal concerns. For example, EDs are subject to COBRA requirements related to the availability of on-call physicians, as well as fair labor standards pertaining to payment for on-call hours. In addition, federal antidiscrimination law may come into play if ED employees are dissatisfied with an ED's grooming or dress code policies. The nature of providing emergency services may also generate special liability and employment issues, such as refusal to treat an HIV-positive patient, employee substance abuse, failure to respond to a call, and drug ordering by nonphysicians. The following questions and answers discuss state and federal laws, as well as judicial decisions relevant to these ED staffing issues.

On-Call Staffing

Are hospitals required to staff the ED with on-call physicians and other employees at all times?

Hospital licensure laws generally require an ED to provide 24-hour services with adequate professional and ancillary staff coverage, including on-call staff, to ensure that all persons are treated within a reasonable length of time, depending on the priority of need for treatment. In some states, the hospital licensure law simply requires that the ED provide 24-hour staff coverage and have at least one physician on call at all times. [*See, e.g.,* Va. Code Ann. § 32.1-127, 12 Va. Admin. Code § 5-410-280] In many states, however, the hospital licensure regulations contain more detailed ED staffing requirements. In Rhode Island, for example, the ED must be staffed on a 24-hour basis by a physician or physicians with more than two years of practice following full licensure or, in hospitals that have an approved residency program, by residents with more than two years of training in specialties of medicine or surgery. [R.I. Code R. § 23-17-24] In Illinois and New Jersey, the ED must have a physician specialist on call and able to arrive within minutes for each major clinical service provided by the hospital. [Ill. Admin. Code tit. 77, § 250.710 ("within minutes")] In Wisconsin, if an on-call physician is unable to reach a patient within 15 minutes, he or she must provide specific instructions to the emergency staff on duty if emergency measures are necessary. [Wis. Admin. Code § 124.24] Many states also require that one registered nurse be on duty in the ED at all times and that ancillary departments, including laboratory, X-ray, and pharmacy, be staffed or provide on-call services at all times. [*See, e.g.,* Ill. Admin. Code tit. 77, § 250.710]

Although not as specific as some state law requirements regarding the availability and response time of on-call physicians, federal requirements under EMTALA (see extensive discussion of this statute later in Part I of this manual) specify that hospitals must maintain a list of on-call physicians who can provide treatment necessary to stabilize a patient with an emergency medical condition. [42 C.F.R. § 489.20(r)(2)] CMS does not require that a hospital's medical staff provide on-call coverage 24 hours a day, 365 days a year. CMS guidance has stated that if there comes a particular time that a hospital does not have on-call coverage for a particular specialty, that hospital lacks capacity to treat patients needing that specialty service and it is therefore appropriate to transfer the patient because the medical benefits of transfer outweigh the risks. [HHS/CMS Program Memorandum to Associate Regional Administrators, *On-Call Requirements-EMTALA,* June 13, 2002] It is desirable, but not mandatory, that when certain specialties are not available full-time, then EMS staff should be advised of times when certain specialties are not available to minimize transfer due to lack of complete on-call coverage. [*EMTALA Final Rule,* 68 Fed. Reg. 53,222 (Sept. 9, 2003)]

Can two hospitals in the same geographic area share on-call coverage so that together they provide full coverage in a particular specialty?

Federal law allows physicians to provide simultaneous on-call coverage at more than one hospital in order to maximize patient access to care; however, when a physician is providing simultaneous on-call coverage at several hospitals, all hospitals involved must be aware of the on-call schedule as each hospital independently has an obligation under EMTALA, and must have policies and procedures to follow when an on-call physician is not available to respond. Policies may include procedures for back-up on-call physicians or the implementation of an appropriate transfer under EMTALA, or any other policies that will meet the needs of emergency patients. [CMS Memorandum to Associate Regional Administrators, *On-Call Requirements-EMTALA,* #S&C-02-35 June 13, 2002; *EMTALA Final Rule,* 68 Fed. Reg. 53,222 (Sept. 9, 2003)]

How frequently is a hospital's medical staff of on-call physicians expected to provide on-call coverage?

Federal law does not set requirements on how frequently a hospital's on-call physician staff is expected to provide on-call coverage. Hospitals are expected to provide services based upon the availability of physicians required to be on-call. CMS has recognized that physician practice demands, conferences, and vacations must be incorporated into the availability of staff, and that some hospitals have limited financial means to maintain on-call coverage all the time. CMS acknowledges that hospitals have flexibility to comply with EMTALA obligations by maintaining a level of on-call coverage that is within their capability. [CMS Memorandum to Associate Regional Administrators, *On-Call Requirements-EMTALA*, #S&C-02-34, June 13, 2002] CMS requires no specific ratio for how many days a hospital must provide on-call physicians based upon the number of physicians on staff for a particular specialty. Rather, on-call coverage should be provided within reason depending on the number of physicians in a specialty. In determining whether a hospital is in compliance CMS has indicated that it will consider the facts of each individual case, including such relevant factors as the number of physicians on staff, other demands on these physicians, the frequency with which the hospital's patients typically require services of on-call physicians, and the provisions the hospital has made for situations in which a physician in the specialty is not available or the on-call physician is unable to respond. The hospital has flexibility to comply within its capability. [*EMTALA Final Rule,* 68 Fed. Reg. 53,222 (Sept. 9, 2003)]

Can senior medical staff be exempted from on-call activities?

The EMTALA final rule makes it clear that exemption of senior medical staff from on-call activities does not necessarily violate EMTALA. The hospital is required to keep an on-call list in a way that "best meets the needs of the hospital's patients." Exemption of senior medical staff based on years of service or age does not violate EMATLA as long as it does not adversely impact patient care. The hospital has flexibility in utilizing its ED personnel. [*EMTALA Final Rule,* 68 Fed. Reg. 53,222 (Sept. 9, 2003)]

What federal law affects payment for on-call hours?

The Fair Labor Standards Act (FLSA), a federal statute governing wage and hour issues, may affect the rate at which employees covered under the Act (or nonexempt employees) are paid for on-call hours. [29 U.S.C. §§ 201 through 219] Most employees are nonexempt and protected under the FLSA. Employers must compensate any nonexempt employee required to work in excess of 40 hours per week at an overtime rate of at least one and one-half times the employee's regular rate. Hospitals, however, may enter agreements with employees to establish an alternative work period of 14 consecutive days and to pay the overtime for hours worked in excess of 80 hours during that period. Even under this option, the employee must be paid overtime rates for hours worked in excess of eight in any one day.

Federal regulations interpreting FLSA requirements address whether employers must pay nonexempt employees for time spent on call. If the health care employer requires an employee to remain on call either at the institution or so close to it that the employee cannot effectively use the time for his or her own purposes, then the time spent on call must be compensated as working time. For example, when a hospital employee returns home after a normal shift with the understanding that he or she is expected to return to the hospital in the event of an emergency, the time spent at home is normally not compensable. If, however, the conditions placed on the employee's activities are so restrictive that the employee cannot use the time effectively for personal pursuits, then such time on call is compensable. [29 C.F.R. § 553.221]

How have courts determined whether on-call time constitutes working time under the FLSA?

Courts have also focused on whether restrictions placed on the employee during on-call hours prevented the employee from using the time for his or her own purposes. A Colorado appeals court, for example, ruled that four physician assistants (PAs) employed by a multiple-site state correctional facility were entitled to overtime compensation for time spent on call. The PAs each worked 40 hours per week and also rotated through on-call time, during which they would provide emergency medical services after regular working hours. The state paid the PAs one and one-half times their regular rate for hours when they were physically present at a facility on a call, but it did not compensate them for time spent waiting for calls. The PAs argued they should be paid for all on-call hours because the employer required a 20-minute response time to any of seven sites located within an 8-mile radius, and so they could not use the on-call time for personal pursuits. The appeals court agreed, concluding that the short response time, high volume of calls, number of facilities, and geographical radius between facilities placed severe restrictions on the PAs' activities during on-call hours. The court found that the time was used predominantly for the employer's benefit and therefore was working time. [*Casserly v. State*, 844 P.2d 1275 (Colo. Ct. App. 1992)]

Similarly, a federal trial court in Georgia has held that, under the FLSA, hospital respiratory therapists who were required to respond to pages during their 30-minute lunch period were entitled to be paid for that break. The therapists wore pagers on their lunch break and were required to respond to a page by calling in immediately. The test for whether a break is compensable is whether the employees are subject to limitations on their personal freedom that inure to the benefit of the employer, the court stated. In this case, such criteria have been met, the court concluded, because the hospital benefited from its requirement that therapists respond to pagers, and the therapists' use of their time during lunch breaks was significantly limited by this requirement. [*Hoffman v. St. Joseph Hosp.*, Civ. No. 1:97-CV-0753-RLV (N.D. Ga. Apr. 14, 1998)]

On the other hand, some courts have held on-call time noncompensable. A federal trial court in Kansas, for example, ruled that hospital emergency medical technicians who work a 24-hour on-call shift during which they must remain within city limits were not entitled to compensation for on-call time. Under the hospital's procedures, the on-duty crew would respond to an emergency call, and the on-call crew would be notified to maintain a heightened sense of readiness. If another emergency call came in while the on-duty crew was responding to the prior emergency, the on-call crew was required to report to the hospital in five minutes. The court reasoned that this notification system provided the technicians with a warning that lessened the restrictive nature of the five-minute call-back requirement. [*Burnison v. Memorial Hosp.*, 820 F. Supp. 549 (D. Kan. 1993); *see also, Sletten v. First Care Med. Servs.*, Civil No. 98-2446 (D. Minn. 2000)]

Similarly, emergency medical technicians with a seven-minute response time did not qualify for compensated time because they were able to pursue personal pursuits at home and were thus not considered working while on call. The entire rural town was within the seven-minute response time, there was less than a 50 percent chance the technicians would be called in, and the hospital credited the employees for two hours' work each time they responded at a rate of one and a half their regular salary. Thus, the employees were paid for three hours' work each time they responded even if the actual response was much shorter. If the call took more than two hours, they were compensated for actual time worked. The court found that the FLSA did not require a different arrangement. [*Dinges v. Sacred Heart St. Mary's Hosps.,* 164 F.3d 1056 (7th Cir. 1999)]

Courts have focused on whether someone is "engaged to wait" which would require compensation because other activities are restricted, or whether they are "waiting to be engaged" which time allows them to pursue other personal activities. When an operating nurse was on call with a pager and required to return the call within 5 minutes and report to work within 30 minutes, the court found that she was "waiting to be engaged" because she could pursue other activities at home or in the community during this time so that the on-call time was not compensable [*Huskey v. Trujillo,* 302 F.3d 1307 (Fed. Cir. 2002)] Some courts have looked at several factors to determine whether on-call time should be compensable which include: whether there is an on-premises living requirement, whether there are excessive geographic restrictions on the employees' movement, whether the frequency of the calls was unduly restrictive, whether the fixed time limit to respond was unduly restrictive, whether call time could be traded, whether a pager could ease restrictions, and whether the person could engage in personal activities. [*Owens v. Local No. 169,* 971 F.2d 351 (9th Cir. 1992)]

What may a hospital ED do to ensure that its policy of payment for on-call employees does not violate the FLSA?

To avoid a potential violation of FLSA's wage and hour provisions, hospitals may wish to make a written request to the Wage and Hour Administrator for an interpretation of the FLSA as applied to the particular facts of the employer's policy of payment for on-call time spent on and off premises.

What happens if a physician doesn't respond to a call?

The ED staff must carefully document what time the physician was called, the information presented to the physician, and the physician's response, including any requests for additional information and the nursing response. When a physician refuses to come in, the nurse attending the patient must follow procedures for appealing to department or hospital leadership and/or calling in an alternate physician. If staff members with concerns about a patient fail to advocate for that patient, the hospital may ultimately be held liable for a bad outcome. For example, Maryland's highest court sustained a verdict against both a hospital and a physician in a case in which a patient was brought to the hospital after he was struck by a car and the physician failed to respond to a call for assistance in the ED. Upon the patient's arrival in the ED, he was not personally attended to by a physician although he was in shock, as indicated by dangerously low blood pressure. There was telephone contact between an ED nurse and the physician who was providing on-call coverage, but the physician failed to come to the hospital until the patient was near death. The court found that the physician's failure to respond was clearly not reasonable care because the physician knew that wounds sustained as a result of a car accident could have been serious internal injuries that should be evaluated and treated by a physician. The court also held that the negligence of the nurse, who failed to contact the on-call physician after the patient's condition had worsened, did not relieve the physician of liability. Relying on the doctrine of respondeat superior, the court ruled that the hospital was liable for the nurse's negligence. [*Thomas v. Corso*, 288 A.2d 379 (Md. 1972)] A federal court in Missouri has also recognized the duty of physicians to respond to call, holding a general surgeon, who attended an out-of-town medical conference while on call without notifying the hospital, liable to a patient whose treatment was delayed as a result. [*Millard v. Corrado*, 14 S.W.3d 42 (E.D. Mo. 1999); but *see Anderson v. Houser*, 523 S.E.2d 342 (Ga. Ct. App. 1999), *cert. denied*, No. S00C0414 (Ga. Mar. 3, 2000) (no liability for on call physician who was out of town because no doctor-patient relationship existed)]

A physician's failure to respond to a call also has ramifications under EMTALA, the federal statute discussed extensively later in Part I of this manual. Under that statute, the physician may be cited and fined up to $50,000 per violation. If CMS (the Centers for Medicare and Medicaid Services) finds that the violation was gross and flagrant or repeated, the physician is subject to exclusion from Medicare and Medicaid. [42 U.S.C. § 395dd(d)(1)] If the hospital's attempts to call in an alternate physician fail and the patient must be transferred, the physician's refusal to respond and the steps taken to find another provider must be carefully documented, and the EMTALA transfer requirements closely followed.

Failure to respond to call may also trigger investigation or disciplinary proceedings under hospital rules or medical staff bylaws, or by the state medical board. Failure to respond to call may also constitute a breach of the physician's contract with the hospital. Internal reporting requirements and procedures should be closely followed.

Can an on-call physician be held liable to a patient if the physician is not actually called?

Some courts have determined that there is no duty on an on-call attending physician without a showing that the doctor accepted the patient, consulted with a physician about the patient, or was actually summoned for consultation for treatment, unless the on-call agreement between the hospital and the physician provides otherwise. [*Rivera v. Prince George's Cty. Health Dept.*, 649 A.2d 1212 (Md. Ct. Spec. App. 1994), *cert. denied*, 656 A.2d 772 (Md. 1995)] The Virginia Supreme Court recently adopted this reasoning in a case in which a child was brought to a teaching hospital's ED with chicken pox lesions in her mouth and was lethargic and not eating or drinking. Residents did not contact the on-call physician, who was not physically present in the emergency room, but was available to answer any questions from the treating residents. The residents treated the child for dehydration and released her the next morning with instructions to see her pediatrician. The child saw the pediatrician, but developed a serious respiratory condition and later died. In the malpractice suit that followed, the state Supreme Court agreed with the trial court that there was no physician-patient relationship between the child and the on-call physician, and therefore the physician owed the child no duty of care. The high court noted that the physician-patient relationship is a consensual relationship that exists if a patient entrusts her treatment to the physician and the physician accepts the case. Here there was no indication that the physician agreed to accept responsibility for the child's care. She had no direct contact with or consultation concerning the child, and there was no evidence that she assumed responsibility by contract with the hospital or by hospital policy. [*Prosise v. Foster*, 544 S.E.2d 331 (Va. 2001)].

One court, however, has taken a contrary position. The North Carolina Supreme Court held that an on-call attending physician had a common law duty to supervise residents who provided medical care to patients, even though the relationship did not fit traditional notions of the doctor-patient relationship, because of the increasingly complex modern delivery of health care. [*Mozingo v. Pitt County Mem'l Hosp.*, 415 S.E.2d 341 (N.C. 1992)]

Does a telephone consultation with an on-call physician create a physician-patient relationship that could result in liability?

A physician on call with an OB/GYN practice group spoke with a person by phone, the court found that this was not sufficient evidence that a physician-patient relationship had been established, nor was there evidence that the physician had acted negligently. The claim against the on-call physician was dismissed. [*Webb v. Nash Hosps. Inc.*, 133 N.C. App. 636 (N.C. Ct. App. 1999)]

Similarly, a court found that when a transferring hospital physician speaks with a physician at the hospital accepting transfer, the physician at the receiving hospital does not have an established physician-patient relationship to form a duty of care until care is rendered at the receiving hospital. [*Sterling v. John Hopkins Hosp.*, 145 Md. App. 161 (Ct. App. Md. 2001), *cert. denied*, 808 A.2d 808 (2002)]

What does developing an on-call schedule entail?

EMTALA final regulations require each hospital to maintain an on-call list of physicians that "best meets the needs of the hospital's patients who are receiving services" under EMTALA based on the hospital resources "including the availability of on-call physicians." Hospitals must have policies and procedures in place that specify response to situations where a particular specialty is not available or cannot respond due to circumstances beyond the physician's control. Final regulations were effective November 10, 2003. [42 C.F.R. § 489.24(j)]

Although COBRA requires a hospital to establish an on-call schedule for the specialties offered at the facility, the federal law and its implementing regulations do not require 24-hour coverage in all specialties offered. For example, a hospital with only one or two neurosurgeons on staff is required to have an on-call schedule for neurosurgery, but would not be required to have continuous on-call coverage for that specialty. Generally, on-call specialty coverage should be proportionate to care generally available at the hospital. However, when the sub-specialist is called and there is a disagreement about the need to come in, the specialist should defer to the ED physician's judgment. The hospital should ensure that the specialist or sub-specialist has the privileges needed to provide care while on-call. [*EMTALA Final Rule,* 68 Fed. Reg. 53,222 (Sept. 9, 2003)]

To safeguard patients, backup procedures should be in place in the event that an on-call physician becomes unavailable. The on-call lists should be posted and accessible to attending physicians, residents, and nurses, who should be trained on how to use the lists and backup procedures. When planning the on-call schedule, careful consideration should be given to how many backup physicians are necessary in light of the patient load, physician specialties, proportion of patients who present needing care in a particular specialty, whether the physicians take call at more than one facility, whether physician contracts or medical staff bylaws set forth requirements for on-call hours, whether state law requires 24-hour coverage for certain specialties, the physical health of on-call staff, the availability of nearby hospitals for transfer, and other relevant factors.

Joint Commission standards regarding the assessment of community and patient needs should also be considered with respect to the development of an on-call schedule. The Joint Commission standards require leaders to continually evaluate the relationship between patient needs and departmental resources. [For guidance on evaluating patient needs, refer to **Part 3**, under the headings Management of Human Resources and Leadership.]

What can the ED do to ensure adequate specialty call coverage?

Traditionally, on-call panels of physicians have been based on ethical responsibilities of physicians who voluntarily agree to be on-call or legal responsibilities established through medical staff bylaws. However, as the number of uninsured, underinsured, and out-of-plan patients in the ED have increased; as reimbursement has not been available for all ED services; as liability remains high for the ED professional; and as EMTALA rules have eased requirements of mandatory specialty on-call backup, adequate on-call coverage has become a serious problem. The growth of specialty hospitals has also reduced on-call specialty coverage, while EMS providers are left to determine whether specialty hospital care is appropriate based on presenting symptoms. [*ACEP Policy Statement: Specialty Hospitals* #400340 (Oct. 2004)]

An ACEP study released in September 2004 found that two-thirds of emergency departments reported shortages of on-call specialists such as neurosurgery, orthopedics, and obstetrics specialists, and one-third of ED directors spent more time placing calls to medical specialties to consult and admit patients. Sixteen percent of hospitals reported that specialists were negotiating for fewer on-call hours. This has led to adverse effects such as delayed treatment, more transfers, and reduced access to specialty care. Further, patient frustration has increased with longer waiting times and more transfers. [*On-call specialist coverage in U.S. Emergency Departments*, ACEP Survey of Emergency Department Directors (Sept. 2004)]

While some hospitals have bylaws that require call panel participation as a condition of affiliation, mandating call can result in physicians choosing to practice at hospitals without mandates. Recommendations are to include policy changes on a global scale to encourage funding for emergency room safety net care while finding ways to limit liability for those who render care in good faith. On a hospital level, ACEP sets forth an EA program (established by Emergency and Acute Care Medical Corporation (EACMC) in California) as a best practice model to ensure adequate ED call coverage. This program based in California uses compensation agreements to improve on-call panel coverage. EA programs compensate on-call physicians at a fixed rate per RVU (relative value unit) for treatment of unassigned patients. Each hospital negotiates the RVU rate with medical staff. Other options include compensation to the doctors for their availability combined with a fee-for-service reimbursement for care rendered. The guaranteed reimbursement encourages physician participation with call panels. The hospital assumes financial responsibility for any billing shortfall, but can offset this by reducing length of stay in the ED and hospital. [*Ensuring Adequate On-Call Backup in the ED*, ACEP News Release 2005]

The Role of Nonphysicians in the ED

What happens when nonphysicians in the ED transmit medical orders for other health care staff to follow?

The term "transmit orders" refers to orders written by a nonphysician (such as a PA) that convey the original intentions of a physician, who usually is also the nonphysician's supervisor. Supervising physicians may communicate these orders to nonphysician providers through any of several means, including conveying the order in person, over the phone, or by written protocols or standing orders. Other health care personnel, including nurses, must comply with transmit orders when the order is clearly made under the direction, direct or indirect, of a supervising physician. In one case, for example, a state nurses' association challenged a law allowing PAs to transmit orders from a physician, but the state supreme court upheld the law, reasoning that medical orders transmitted by a PA (under supervision of a physician) are in fact physician's orders and thus should be honored by nurses. [*Washington State Nurses Ass'n v. Board of Med. Exam'rs*, 605 P.2d 1269 (Wash. 1980)]

What is a standing order?

A standing order is a medical order written for use by nurses and other nonphysicians when a physician is not present. Another term often interchanged with "standing orders" is "protocols," which can be defined as a detailed template for treatment of a very specific medical problem. In most states, standing orders and protocols are a legal and convenient way for drugs and treatment to be given on a physician's order but within the discretion of the nurse or other nonphysician health care provider. Standing orders are commonly used in EDs, particularly as a mechanism for authorizing a nonphysician to prescribe medication or administer drugs to a patient in the physician's absence. Registered nurses and other appropriate personnel are generally allowed to transcribe oral orders of a physician or authorized nonphysician prescriber for the purpose of administering drugs to ED patients.

When might a standing order regarding a patient's medication treatment trigger potential legal problems?

A PA or nurse practitioner who has prescribing authority under a state practice statute might prescribe drugs in accordance with a hospital protocol but neglect to follow the prescribing requirements enumerated in the state practice statute. In that case, the PA or nurse practitioner would be subject to charges of exceeding his or her scope of practice. Similarly, complications arising as a result of a drug administered to a patient by a nonphysician who followed a standing order may give rise to claims that the nonphysician exceeded the scope of his or her legal authority in administering the drug or that the nonphysician's actions constituted practicing medicine without a license.

What should an ED do to ensure that nonphysician patient care does not give rise to legal liability?

- Review relevant state practice acts, as well as hospital licensure laws, to make sure that standing orders are in compliance with these statutes, particularly regarding requirements for documentation of physician oversight (i.e., countersignatures).
- Monitor the use of standing orders to determine whether the quantity and the scope of patient care being rendered without individual physicians' orders are appropriate.
- Assess whether patients are being discharged after nonphysicians alone provide care under standing orders. Implement a mechanism for "catching" these cases and ensuring an appropriate level of physician involvement prior to discharge.
- Educate ED staff members regarding the special legal risks associated with nonphysician drug ordering and the importance of following state scope of practice acts.

What factors impact ED overcrowding?

ED overcrowding occurs as a result of a number of factors. The number of ED visits has increased 20 percent over 10 years ending in 2001, while the number of EDs nationwide decreased by 15 percent. This has led to higher patient volumes and waiting times in EDs that have remained open. Average patient time spent in the ED is three hours. [*New Data Show Upward Trend in Emergency Department Visits*, ACEP Press Release (June 4, 2003)] A study of the impact of final EMTALA regulations in regard to on-call specialty coverage found that two-thirds of ED directors had shortages of on-call specialists in neurosurgery, orthopedics, and obstetrics with the more flexible EMTALA final regulations. This resulted in delayed treatment, increased transfers, and reduced access to specialty care. [*Two-Thirds of Emergency Department Directors Report On-call specialty coverage problems*, ACEP Press Release (Sept. 28, 2004)]

Some reasons for overcrowding are hospital specific, such as high volume of patients, lack of space, or delays in test results. Other reasons relate to the ED's ability to transfer patients to an inpatient bed once it has been decided to admit them. This leads to an increasing number of patients being "boarded" in the ED. There is especially inpatient demand for critical care and telemetry units. [*Hospital Emergency Departments: Crowding Conditions Among Hospitals and Communities* (GAO-03-460)] Other factors that impact overcrowding include staffing shortages and saturation of primary care networks with more patients with chronic diseases and more elderly patients accessing the ED. [*ED Overcrowding:* JCAHO News Release (Feb. 2003)]

What recommendations are in place for ED overcrowding?

A publication released in November 2004 entitled *Managing Patient Flow: Strategies and Solutions for Addressing Hospital Overcrowding* (available at *http://www.jcrinc.com*) focuses on the use of JCAHO leadership, emergency management, care planning, and staffing standards to mitigate the impact of overcrowding and improve patient flow.

Hospitals are already trying to address overcrowding through actions that expand the capacity of the ED or increase the efficiency of inpatient transfer. Overall, community-wide resources are needed to resolve overcrowding. [*Hospital Emergency Departments: Crowding Conditions Among Hospitals and Communities* (GAO-03-460)]

Are there mandatory staffing ratios in the ED?

Some states have enacted statutes that require state agencies to establish minimum staffing ratios. For example, the California code requires the state to establish staffing ratios based on the licensure of the nurse as well as the type of hospital unit. For the ED, the state agency should consider regularly scheduled staff as well as additional nurses needed to care for critically ill persons. Other factors to consider in establishing staffing ratios include: patient care needs, illness, severity, use of equipment or technology, and complexity of clinical judgment. The hospital should also have policies and procedure for training and orientation of employees including orientation for temporary workers. [Cal. Health & Safety Code § 1276.4] Be sure to check with requirements in your state in setting minimum staffing standards.

California also allows the EMT who was caring for the patient prior to ED admission to remain and assist when there is a "patient crisis." Specifically, small and rural hospitals can use EMTs to provide patient care if they have completed hospital ED training, demonstrate competency annually, work according to protocols, and follow procedures for supervision. Hospitals and ambulance set up a contractual agreement for EMT services prior to ED use of EMTs. The hospital must provide for a process for care if the EMT is called off-site for an emergency. [Cal. Health & Safety Code § 1797.195]

Can the ED require mandatory overtime to meet staffing needs?

Some states have set limits on the amount of overtime an employer may require. For example, Maine limits overtime an employee can work to eighty hours in a consecutive two-week period. By agreement, the maximum overtime hours can be lowered. The Maine statute specifically addresses staffing for nurses indicating that a nurse cannot be disciplined for refusing to work more than twelve consecutive hours. If the nurse is mandated to work over twelve consecutive hours, then the nurse must be given ten hours off duty immediately afterward. A nurse can be disciplined for refusing mandatory overtime in the case of an unforeseen emergency when overtime is the last resort to protect patient safety. [26 Me. Rev. Stat. Ann. § 603]

The Maryland statute prohibits mandatory overtime for nurses beyond regularly scheduled shifts, while allowing the nurse to voluntarily agree to work more hours. However, the statute has a number of exceptions that allow a nurse to work mandatory overtime when: (1) there is an emergency situation that was not reasonably anticipated, (2) the emergency is not recurrent or due to lack of employer planning, (3) the employer makes good faith efforts to obtain voluntary workers, (4) the nurse has the skills and expertise to do the work, (5) the standard of care requires continuity of care, (6) the employer informs the nurse of the need for mandatory overtime, and (7) other general overtime requirements are satisfied. The statute further allows overtime when the employment includes an on-call rotation or community based care. The statute further limits liability for care to the regularly scheduled work hours of the nurse as long as she notifies another nurse of the patient status and effectively transfers care of the patient at the completion of the work shift. [Md. Labor & Empl. Code Ann. § 3-421] Similarly, Washington prohibits mandatory overtime for health care employees, while allowing employees to accept voluntary shifts. However, overtime can be required when "unforeseeable emergent circumstances" occur. [Rev. Code Wash. § 49.28.140]

Other states have taken a different view by exempting health care workers or hospital employees providing medical services from state overtime requirements. [*See, e.g.*, Mass. Gen. Laws ch. 151, § 1A] Because state laws differ, it is important to check local laws before implementing mandatory overtime.

How do fair pay regulations impact overtime?

Fair pay regulations effective August 23, 2004, require that workers who earn less than $23,660 a year or less than $455 a week be guaranteed overtime pay for hours worked. The regulations also clarify that first responders such as EMTs, paramedics, and ambulance personnel are not exempt from the FLSA because their primary duty is not management and therefore must be paid overtime when hours exceed forty in a week. Nurses may qualify for the learned profession exemption to overtime provisions if the compensation, salary, or fee is over $455 a week; if the nurse's primary duty required advanced knowledge that is predominantly intellectual in character and consists if discretion in judgment; if the advanced knowledge is in a field of science or learning; and if the advanced knowledge is customarily acquired by a prolonged course of intellectual instruction. Registered nurses (RNs) will generally meet the learned profession exemption and earn over $455 a week. However, licensed practical nurses (LPNs) generally do not meet the learned profession exemption because an advanced degree is not necessary for entry into the profession. [*Final Rule*, 69 Fed. Reg. 22,260 (Apr. 23, 2004); 29 C.F.R. § 541.301(e)]

What does JCAHO recommend to improve staffing effectiveness?

JCAHO has recognized that there is an evolving nursing crisis with patient acuity rising and the number of nurses falling. JCAHO recommends creation of an organizational culture to encourage staff retention by empowering staff, transforming work, setting competent staffing levels, establishing zero tolerance policies for verbal abuse, and encouraging diversity. It also recommends that the nursing educational infrastructure be bolstered and that federal monies be used to create financial incentives for hospitals to invest in nursing care. [*Health Care at the Crossroads: Strategies for Addressing the Evolving Nursing Crisis* (Sept. 20, 2002)]

2005 JCAHO hospital accreditation standards for leadership include requirements that leadership define qualified and competence of staff, that the number of staff needed for competent care be reviewed, and that staffing be integrated into a patient safety program. [*2005 Hospital Accreditation Program Standards*]

Dress Codes

What legal claim might be triggered by an ED's grooming or dress code policies?

Grooming standards and dress codes have triggered lawsuits by employees claiming that the employer's policy violates Title VII's prohibition of gender discrimination. For a discussion of gender discrimination prohibitions in the context of claims by patients, rather than staff, see "What laws prohibit race, national origin, and gender discrimination?" under Antidiscrimination Laws.

How have courts responded to suits based on alleged discriminatory grooming or dress code policies?

Numerous courts have upheld the employer's right to enforce a dress code. In one case, a federal appeals court upheld a county ambulance department's grooming policy for male emergency medical technicians (EMTs) prohibiting mustaches, beards, and hair of certain lengths. The policy was not arbitrary, the court ruled, finding its purposes were to promote esprit de corps among EMTs, establish a uniform and professional image for EMTs, and minimize the possibility that the EMTs' hair would interfere with the performance of their jobs. [*Hottinger v. Pope County*, 971 F.2d 127 (8th Cir. 1992)]

Dress codes will be subjected to a different standard of scrutiny, however, in instances in which male and female employees who perform the same functions are expected to conform to two entirely different dress codes. Several courts have held that Title VII requires that similarly situated employees be treated in an equal manner with respect to dress code requirements. A state appeals court in Michigan, for example, ruled that a hospital's dress code requirements illegally discriminated on the basis of sex. The court rejected the hospital's argument that its policy of requiring female technologists to wear white or pastel-colored uniforms, while male technologists wore white lab coats over their street clothes, was justified because patients are used to seeing males dressed like physicians and females dressed like nurses. [*Michigan Dep't. of Civil Rights v. Sparrow Hosp.*, 326 N.W.2d 519 (Mich. Ct. App. 1982)]

Can a dress code ban employees from wearing union insignia?

As a general rule, the National Labor Relations Act (NLRA) gives employees the right to wear union insignia without fear of retaliation. Companies have implemented dress codes that restrict buttons or union insignia when (1) the ban is needed to ensure productivity, (2) the ban is needed to reduce conflict in the workplace and maintain discipline, (3) the ban is needed to ensure the safety of the workers by preventing accidents or avoiding violence, and (4) the ban is needed to ensure good employee customer relations or other business goals. Courts have upheld some of these dress codes. Some courts have looked at whether the ban is specific to prohibit union items, or is a general ban such as a "no pin" policy. There is a balancing between labor laws that allow insignia showing support of the union and business goals that may necessitate limits on certain types of dress, buttons or insignia.

In a recent district court case, a carpenter who worked at a hospital which had a "no pin" policy except for professional pins or hospital service awards wore a button to work that said "union yes." He was asked to remove the button as violating company policy. He refused and continued to wear the button. When the issue went to court the court determined that wearing the button was permissible free speech. It then looked at the amount of public contact the employee had and found that his public contact was not meaningful or regular since the carpenter frequently worked in empty rooms to complete his work. The court then looked at whether the button interrupted hospital function. The court found that the only disruption came from the enforcement of the dress code and issued judgment for the carpenter. The company was required to allow certain employees to wear union insignia. [*Communications Workers of Am. v. Ector County Hosp. Dist.*, 241 F. Supp. 2d 617 (241 F. Supp. 2d 617 (W.D. Tex. 2002), *aff'd*, 392 F.3d 733 (5th Cir. 2004)] Because this area of the law is evolving and varies from state to state it is important to consult with legal counsel in establishing a policy.

Refusal to Treat Patients

Can a hospital discharge an ED employee who refuses to treat a patient with HIV or AIDS?

In most cases, if the ED is following proper infection control techniques and properly educates the employee, but the employee continues to refuse to care for an HIV-positive patient, the hospital can impose discipline, including termination. In one case, for example, a pregnant home care nurse sued for pregnancy discrimination under Title VII after she was discharged for her refusal to treat an AIDS-infected patient. The nurse declined to care for the patient, even with universal precautions, because she feared the accompanying opportunistic infections often present in AIDS patients (in this case, cryptococcal meningitis) would harm the fetus. The court noted that the hospital had a policy requiring all nurses to treat AIDS patients or be subject to termination and that this policy applied to nonpregnant as well as pregnant nurses. The court therefore dismissed the suit, reasoning that the nurse could not establish that the hospital's policy affected pregnant employees more harshly than other classifications of employees. Although the primary focus of the court's analysis was on the standard for establishing a valid claim of pregnancy discrimination, the case also reflects the court's tacit approval of a hospital policy allowing termination of employees who refuse to treat patients with HIV or AIDS. [*Armstrong v. Flowers Hosp.*, 812 F. Supp. 1183 (M.D. Ala. 1993), *aff'd*, 33 F.3d 1308 (11th Cir. 1994)]

Under certain circumstances, however, the health care employer cannot discharge an employee for refusing to care for HIV-infected patients. For example, if an employee has a reasonable good-faith belief that a hospital's failure to follow proper infection control procedures poses an immediate and grave danger to his or her health, the employee falls within the protection of the Occupational Safety and Health Act. [29 U.S.C. §§ 651 through 678] Occupational Safety and Health Administration (OSHA) regulations allow an employee in this situation to refuse to work, and they also provide that the employee cannot be discharged for such refusal. [29 C.F.R. § 1977.12]

Hospitals also may not have the option to discharge employees for refusal to care for patients with HIV or AIDS in circumstances in which the employment relationship is governed by a collective bargaining agreement. If there is such an agreement, the hospital must follow any contract requirements and procedures for discipline, which may or may not preclude employee discharge for certain charges. In addition, employees may be protected under provisions of the National Labor Relations Act (NLRA), which protect employees engaged in concerted activity for material aid and protection. [29 U.S.C. §§ 141 through 187]

What should an ED do upon learning that an employee refuses to treat a patient with HIV or AIDS?

If proper infection control procedures are being enforced in the ED and an employee refuses to treat a patient with HIV or AIDS, a supervisor or other ED staff member should first ensure that the employee is properly educated about how the virus is transmitted and how employees can protect themselves using universal precautions. The employee may also benefit from education about any professional ethical obligations that may be relevant to providing medical care to patients infected with HIV or AIDS, as well as legal liability issues arising under disability discrimination statutes such as the ADA. For a more detailed discussion, see "Can hospitals and health care providers be liable for refusing to treat patients with HIV or AIDS?" under Antidiscrimination Laws.

The hospital or other health care employer should not discipline an ED employee for refusing to care for patients with HIV or AIDS before investigating whether the employee has legitimate reasons for such refusal. An employee who is undergoing chemotherapy, for example, may have a diminished immune system that would make the employee more susceptible to the secondary infections an HIV-positive patient may be experiencing. Reasons for refusing to care for patients with HIV or AIDS should be evaluated on a case-by-case basis in light of the most current medical information, and if such an evaluation indicates that the employee's health concern is legitimate, the employer should try to reasonably accommodate the health care worker.

Can a health care provider refuse to treat a patient on moral or religious grounds?

Refusal to treat on moral or religious grounds often arises when a procedure such as abortion or sterilization is anticipated or in the context of prescriptions such as contraception where the health care provider may have strong moral views. There has been increasing movement among state legislatures to pass what are known as "conscience clauses" that give health care providers the right to refuse to participate in care because of their moral or ethical values. For example, Missouri law focuses specifically on abortion and gives physicians, nurses, midwives, and hospitals the right to refuse to provide abortions and prevents an employer from discriminating against the employee for refusal to participate unless the refusal creates an undue hardship for the employer. [Mo. Rev. Stat. §§ 188.105, 197.032] Similarly, federal law would require a facility to make reasonable accommodation when an employee objects to treatment on religious grounds as long as the accommodation is not an undue burden to the organization.

Pharmacy refusals to fill prescriptions have risen as more pharmacists have relied on conscience clauses to refuse to fill prescriptions on moral grounds. The American Pharmacy Association has supported policies that allow pharmacists the right to choose not to fill prescriptions they find morally or ethically objectionable, but supports systems to ensure that patient needs are met. The American Medical Association (AMA) passed a resolution in June 2005 restating patient's right to access medical care and noting the need for pharmacists to fill valid prescriptions or refer to a pharmacy that would dispense the medication prescribed. Some states have responded by passing laws requiring pharmacists to fill prescriptions in good faith. [*See, for example,* 225 I.L.C.S. 85/30 or Cal.

Bus. & Prof. Code § 4052 that requires pharmacists to dispense emergency contraception drug therapy]

Staff Substance Abuse

What are some legal concerns for hospital EDs arising from staff substance abuse?

The problem of employee substance abuse among health care professionals may give rise to a number of legal concerns for the ED. If a patient is harmed by an impaired health care provider, both the hospital and the provider may be held liable for the patient's injuries because the physician's negligence may be imputed to the hospital. The hospital may also be subject to direct liability for negligent monitoring of its medical staff member and failing to protect the patient.

What should an ED do when it becomes aware of a staff member with a substance abuse problem?

A first step for the ED would be to informally persuade the impaired practitioner to seek help and to refer him or her to the hospital's employee assistance program or in-house rehabilitation program, if one exists. In the absence of such a program, the ED should refer the employee to an external professional treatment program. Next, the ED should report the impaired practitioner to the chief of the appropriate clinical service, the chief of staff, or a supervisor. Then, if required, the hospital must report that practitioner to the appropriate state licensing body. In some states, state law may insulate impaired practitioners from disciplinary action, including peer review and medical board reporting, unless the impairment becomes habitual or poses a danger to patients.

Participating in a rehabilitation program should be required of any employee or medical staff member who voluntarily admits to having a substance abuse problem or whose substance test results are positive. Employees and medical staff members who successfully complete treatment should be provided with an opportunity to continue working in the ED under an agreement that provides for unannounced testing for a reasonable period after return to work. If an employee is unable or unwilling to rehabilitate, the hospital may have no other option than termination. [*See, e.g.,* American Hospital Association, *Management Advisory, Substance Abuse Policies of Health Care Institutions* (Jan. 1992)]

All communications should be kept strictly confidential to comply with the ADA and with state laws governing medical information and peer review because impaired physicians may have protected status under these statutes. As soon as a potentially impaired practitioner is discovered, ED managers should consult with the hospital's human resources department and medical staff committee for assistance in complying with disability discrimination, confidentiality, and other federal and state laws.

Disabled Workers

What are an ED's legal duties regarding disabled workers?

Under Title I of the Americans with Disabilities Act (ADA), the disabled hospital employee can request reasonable accommodation. The manager should first determine whether the employee has a disability that interferes with a major life function. A doctor's report may be requested in order to confirm the disability, but should be kept confidential. If a disability exists, then the employer determines what constitutes a reasonable accommodation, but this does not mean the employee gets everything he or she asks for. Further, if the accommodation creates an undue burden on the company because of time, money, expense, scheduling, etc., then the manager should document this and can refuse the accommodation.

When the disabled worker is a physician or nurse contracting to provide services, the court may still allow a disability claim under Title III protections for the general public. At least one appeals court has found that a contracted medical doctor was an individual who could sue under the public accommodation law. [*Menkowitz v. Pottstown Mem'l Med. Ctr.*, 154 F.3d 113 (3d Cir. 1998)]

What are an ED's legal duties regarding workers with HIV or other bloodborne infections?

The Supreme Court has held that a disabled worker can be denied a position that would pose a direct threat to the worker's health and safety or pose a significant risk to others. In this case, a worker with a serious chronic illness (hepatitis C) was denied a position in an oil refinery that would harm his health. Similarly, a business may deny employment to a worker who would pose a direct threat to the health and safety of others. [*Chevron USA v. Echazabal*, 122 S. Ct. 2045 (2002)] When a dental hygienist posed a threat of safety to patients, it was not discriminatory to offer her a desk job at half pay. [*Waddell v. Valley Forge Dental*, 276 F.3d 1275 (11th Cir. 2001)] When an emergency room physician was exposed to hepatitis C and subsequently tested positive, she took a two-year break from work but continued to attend staff meetings. The virus went into remission and she requested to return to work. She was given three conditions to return to work: (1) obtain a physician's medical release, (2) attend a refresher in emergency medicine, and (3) submit to weekly blood samples. She was assigned to the emergency room schedule but declined to return to work and sued, claiming disability discrimination and harassment. The court found that the requirements to return to work were reasonable and that subsequent failure of the hospital to offer her an interim contract related to the fact that she had not come in to work, so there was no basis for a disability discrimination or harassment claim. [*Gowesky v. Singing River Hosp.*, 321 F.3d 503 (5th Cir. 2003)]

A policy statement by the American College of Emergency Physicians (ACEP) focuses on ensuring access to emergency care while preventing exposure and transmission of bloodborne infections. The general principles it adopts are that

- appropriate care should be given to all patients who seek emergency care regardless of risk of HIV or other bloodborne infections,
- mandatory testing for HIV, HBV, or HCV should not be required prior to receiving emergency services,
- infection control guidelines should be followed in the emergency room,
- health care workers with potential exposure should have immediate evaluation and prophylaxis,
- when health care workers are infected and can't perform their duties they should be eligible for disability insurance coverage. [ACEP Policy Statement #400293 (Apr. 2004)]

OCCUPATIONAL SAFETY

There are occupational safety concerns in all areas of the hospital, including the ED. The bloodborne pathogens standard is of particular concern in the ED because of the likelihood of exposure to blood and other body fluids. Other occupational safety concerns include airborne hazards, smoking, ergonomic hazards, emergency response planning, and clearance in aisles and passageways. Each of these areas is discussed in the following section. For sample documentation, see **Part 4**.

The Occupational Safety and Health Administration (OSHA) and the Joint Commission have formed a successful partnership to promote safety and health for health care workers. The joint program, initiated in 1996, was originally developed as a three-year venture, but has recently been extended in recognition of the benefits gained from the partnership. OSHA and the Joint Commission have worked together to help hospitals and other health care facilities understand how to meet the requirements of both the federal agency and the accreditation organization. As part of that effort, OSHA and the Joint Commission have jointly developed training materials and publications for health care facilities, and provided specific examples in Joint Commission accreditation manuals to illustrate how compliance with OSHA standards also satisfies Joint Commission standards. In addition, the partnership has enabled OSHA and the Joint Commission to minimize duplicative compliance activities.

Bloodborne Pathogens

What is OSHA's bloodborne pathogens standard?

The OSHA bloodborne pathogens standard applies primarily (although not exclusively) to the health care industry and is particularly applicable to the ED, where health care workers are exposed to potentially contaminated body fluids. The standard's requirements extend to anyone who may come into contact with blood or potentially infectious material in performing his or her job duties; in essence, this means reasonably anticipated skin, eye membrane, or other parenteral contact with blood or other infectious materials. The standard requires employers to implement an exposure control plan to minimize employees' exposure to bloodborne pathogens. The plan must contain the following key provisions:

- engineering and work practice controls
- personal protective equipment (PPE)
- disposal of waste and cleaning of workplace
- employer-provided hepatitis B vaccinations
- postexposure evaluation
- notice of hazards to employees
- recordkeeping [29 C.F.R. § 1910.1030]

In November 2000, Congress passed the Needlestick Safety and Prevention Act, which revised the bloodborne pathogens standard, requiring employers to select safer needle devices as they become available and to involve employees in identifying and choosing the devices. The updated standard also requires employers to maintain a log of injuries from contaminated sharps.

Hospital EDs must participate in hospital-wide efforts to develop and implement policies and procedures aimed at satisfying these requirements.

What is an exposure control plan, and does it apply to the ED?

Hospitals must develop written exposure control plans that identify employees at risk of exposure to blood and the methods to be used to protect and train these workers. This exposure control plan must be accessible to employees and must be updated annually or whenever job task additions or changes affect employee exposure to bloodborne pathogens. The new revisions to the bloodborne pathogens standard require that hospitals review their exposure control plans annually to reflect changes in technology that will help eliminate or reduce exposure to bloodborne pathogens. That review must include documentation of the hospital's consideration and implementation of appropriate and effective safer medical devices. In doing so, the hospital must solicit input from non-managerial health care workers in identifying, evaluating, and selecting safer devices and must document that solicitation in the exposure control plan. Because ED employees are considered to be at risk of exposure to blood, the exposure control plan applies to ED employees. [29 C.F.R. § 1910.1030(c)] For sample documentation, see **Part 4: 4-126 through 4-137**.

What kinds of equipment or engineering controls must be used in the ED to help prevent the spread of bloodborne pathogens?

Hospitals must implement engineering controls, such as puncture-resistant containers for used needles, self-sheathing needles, protective shields, biosafety cabinets, and safer medical devices such as sharps with engineered sharps injury protections and needleless systems. The standard requires employers to regularly inspect and repair engineering controls. [29 C.F.R. §§ 1910.1030(b) & (d)]

What are the handwashing requirements?

Handwashing must be performed as soon as feasible after exposure to blood or other potentially infectious materials and after removal of gloves or other personal protective equipment. [29 C.F.R. §§ 1910.1030(d)(2)(iii) through (vi)] For more information, see Centers for Disease Control and Prevention, *Guideline for Infection Control in Health Care Personnel (1998)*, and Centers for Disease Control and Prevention, *Guidelines for Isolation Precautions in Hospitals, Infection Control and Hospital Epidemiology*, 17:53 (1996).

What kinds of work practices are prohibited in the ED to prevent the spread of bloodborne pathogens?

Employees are prohibited from eating, drinking, and storing food in areas where there is potential for exposure to bloodborne pathogens or where blood, body fluids, or both are stored (e.g., refrigerators and cabinets, medication carts, etc.). [29 C.F.R. §§ 1910.1030(d)(2)(ix) & (x)] Employees are also prohibited from suctioning blood or other body fluids by mouth. [29 C.F.R. § 1910.1030(d)(2)(xii)] For more information, see Centers for Disease Control and Prevention, *Guideline for Infection Control in Health Care Personnel (1998)*.

What are ACEP recommendations in regard to bloodborne infections?

The American College of Emergency Physicians (ACEP) has made recommendations in regard to HIV, hepatitis B, and hepatitis C.

The HIV recommendations are to

- Recommend an HIV test for patients at risk for the disease,
- If clinically appropriate, discuss HIV testing and prophylaxis with victims of sexual assault.
- Use sound physician judgment to inform about HIV risk, balancing the patient need for confidentiality and privacy with the need for a third party to know they may be at risk for HIV.
- Use rapid HIV tests on a patient when health care workers are exposed to blood/body fluids.
- Mandatory HIV testing should not be a condition of employment for health care workers, and disclosure is only recommended when HIV status impacts job performance.
- Health care workers who are HIV-positive should not be precluded from medical service based on HIV status, should not required to inform patients of HIV status unless the patient is at risk of exposure because of contact with the health care worker's blood or body fluids, and are not required to obtained special consent before delivery of emergency services.
- Unless the practitioner has been implicated in provider-to-patient HIV transmission, the health care worker who is HIV positive should not be banned from patient care activities including invasive procedures.
- Decisions to restrict the practice of a HIV-positive worker should be based on objective standards and not HIV status.

The hepatitis B recommendations are

- All emergency health care workers who may be exposed to blood should receive a hepatitis B vaccine unless contraindicated and should be tested to ensure positive immunity after the vaccine.
- The CDC recommendations for health care workers who are HBsAg and/or HbeAg should be followed. HbeAg workers should routinely double glove and should not perform activities that would risk HBV transmission despite use of appropriate infection control techniques.
- If clinically appropriate, hepatitis B testing and prophylaxis should be discussed with victims of sexual assault.

The hepatitis C recommendations are

- Mandatory HCV testing should not be a condition of employment for workers.
- HCV infection should not bar the worker from patient care, including invasive procedures, unless the practitioner has been implicated in a provider-to-patient HCV transmission.

- Decisions to restrict the practice of a HCV-infected health care worker should be based on objective standards and not on HCV status. [ACEP Policy Statement #400293 (Apr. 2004)]

What are the OSHA requirements for handling sharps in the ED?

Employees are prohibited from shearing, breaking, recapping, removing, or bending contaminated needles and other sharps; from picking up potentially contaminated glassware by hand; and from reaching by hand into a container that may contain contaminated reusable sharps. [29 C.F.R. §§ 1910.1030(d)(2) (vii), d(4)(ii)(D) & (E)] For related information, see U.S. Department of Health and Human Services, *Selecting, Evaluating, and Using Sharps Disposal Containers*, NIOSH Pub. No. 97-111 (1998).

Do any other federal agencies address infection control practices in hospitals?

Detailed recommendations on work-practice infection controls relevant to hospital are also specified in guidelines issued by the Centers for Disease Control and Prevention (CDC). [*See* CDC, *Guidelines for Isolation Precautions in Hospitals, Infection Control and Hospital Epidemiology*, 17:53 (1996)]

Do any state laws address bloodborne pathogen exposure through needle safety?

States have begun to enact additional requirements in an effort to reduce health care worker exposure to bloodborne pathogens. Legislation in California, for example, requires the state Occupational Safety and Health Standards Board to revise the state's bloodborne pathogen standard by adopting an emergency regulation aimed at compelling health care facilities to use safer needles and syringes. The statute provides that sharps prevention technology is required in all cases except where the employer or other appropriate party can demonstrate circumstances in which the technology interferes with a medical procedure or does not promote employee or patient safety. The statute requires the revised standard to specifically delineate the circumstances falling within the exception, and to include circumstances where the technology is medically contraindicated or not more effective than alternative measures used by the employer to prevent exposure incidents.

The statute also provides that the new standard contain the following requirements: Written exposure control plans must include an effective procedure for identifying and selecting sharps prevention technology. Written exposure control plans must be updated when necessary to reflect progress in implementing the sharps prevention technology. Information concerning exposure incidents must be recorded in a sharps injury log, including, but not limited to, the type and brand of device involved in the incident. [Cal. Lab. Code § 144.7. *See also* Tenn. Code Ann. § 50-3-203 (requiring state departments of labor and health to jointly develop standards nearly identical to those required by the California legislation)]

OSHA required states that operate their own OSHA-approved state programs to adopt the new federal bloodborne pathogens standard, or a more stringent amendment to their existing standards, by October 18, 2001. [OSHA National News Release, *"Prevention is the Best Medicine"—OSHA Announces Outreach Effort on Needlestick Prevention* (May 9, 2001), available on the Internet at *www.osha.gov*]

Is the hospital required to provide personal protective equipment in the ED?

The hospital must provide, at no cost to the employee, personal protective equipment (PPE) when engineering and work practice controls cannot fully protect an employee from occupational exposure. [29 C.F.R.§ 1910.1030(d)(2)(i)] Employers must also repair, replace, launder, and dispose of personal protective equipment at no cost to the employee. [29 C.F.R. §§ 1910.1030(d)(3)(iv) through (viii)]

What kinds of items are considered personal protective equipment?

The OSHA standard contains a comprehensive list of such equipment, which includes gloves, gowns, laboratory coats, masks, eyeglasses, surgical caps, shoe covers, and resuscitation devices. The type and characteristics of the PPE that must be offered to the employee will depend on the task and degree of exposure anticipated. The standard also contains specific details regarding the adequacy of certain items of protective equipment; for example, it specifically requires the disposal of torn, cracked, or punctured gloves because their function as a barrier may be compromised. [29 C.F.R. § 1910.1030(d)(3)(i)] Hands must be washed after the removal of gloves used as PPE, whether or not the gloves are visibly contaminated. [29 C.F.R. § 1910.1030(d)(3)(ix)(C)]

Do employees always have to wear personal protective equipment?

A limited exemption applies when the employee refuses to wear the equipment because its use "would have prevented the delivery of health care or public safety services or would have posed an increased hazard to the safety of the worker or a co-worker." An example of such an occasion would be an unanticipated emergency in which a patient suddenly begins bleeding and workers lack time to delay treatment to put on gloves, masks, or gowns. OSHA may determine that an employee's decision not to wear PPE does not fall within this limited exemption, however, and fine the employer for violating the standard. [29 C.F.R. § 1910.1030(d)(3)(ii)]

Are there any guidelines on latex sensitivity?

Sensitivity to latex products, or latex allergy, develops in some individuals exposed to natural rubber latex—a plant substance that is used extensively to manufacture latex gloves. Allergic reactions to latex range from skin disease to asthma and anaphylaxis that can result in chronic illness and other disabilities; there is no treatment for these problems other than complete avoidance of latex.

OSHA's sister agency, the National Institute for Occupational Safety and Health (NIOSH) has issued guidance regarding prevention of latex-related health problems in the workplace. [National Institute for Occupational Health and Safety, *NIOSH Alert: Preventing Allergic Reactions to Natural Rubber Latex in the Workplace*, DHHS Pub. No. 97-135 (June 1997), available on the Internet at *www.cdc.gov/niosh/latexalt.html*] NIOSH recommends that hospitals implement policies and procedures to require, or at least encourage, appropriate engineering and work practice controls to reduce the risk of allergic reactions to latex. Such controls include the use of nonlatex gloves for activities that are not likely to involve contact with infectious materials, and where latex gloves are necessary for handling infectious materials, use of reduced protein, powder-free gloves to minimize worker exposure to allergy-causing proteins. Other controls include good housekeeping practice to remove latex-containing dust in latex-contaminated areas, and training materials/ education programs about latex sensitivity.

What measures must be taken to clean the work site and dispose of contaminated waste?

Requirements for cleaning the work site and disposing of contaminated waste include

- implementing a written plan that describes the method and frequency of cleaning ensuring regular inspection and decontamination of reusable garbage bins, pails, and laundry carts that hold potentially contaminated medical waste
- ensuring that blood specimens and other potentially infectious materials are placed in properly labeled containers that will prevent leakage during handling, storage, and transport
- requiring employees who have contact with potentially contaminated laundry to wear appropriate personal protective equipment such as gloves and gowns [29 C.F.R. § 1910.1030(d)(4)] For sample documentation, see **Part 4: 4-126 through 4-137.**

How should disposal of contaminated needles and blood tube holders for phlebotomy take place?

In a Safety and Health Information Bulletin (SHIB), OSHA sets forth advisory guidelines with the best practice for disposal of contaminated needles and blood tube holders. The best practice is to use a share with engineered sharps injury protection (SESIP), such as a safety needle attached to the blood tube holder. After a single use, the blood tube holder and needle assembly should be disposed of in a sharps container. Reuse of the needle will seldom be appropriate. [*Disposal of Contaminated Needles and Blood Tube Holders Used for Phlebotomy*, SHIB 10-15-03]

Must hospitals give employees free hepatitis B vaccines?

Employers must give all employees who have occupational exposure the option to receive a free hepatitis B vaccine and must educate them about the benefits of obtaining a vaccination. The vaccination must be made available to the employee within 10 days after initial assignment to a job task with potential exposure to bloodborne pathogens. It is the employee's choice whether to receive the hepatitis B vaccine, but an employee who chooses not to be vaccinated must sign a waiver form. [29 C.F.R. § 1910.1030(f)]

Employers are allowed to delay offering the vaccine to collateral first-aid providers, defined as employees whose primary jobs are not the rendering of first aid, until after these employees have rendered assistance in a situation presenting a risk of exposure to blood or another potentially infectious body fluid.

If the employee must travel to another location to obtain the vaccination, the employer must pay for the entire travel cost. The employer cannot require the employee to pay for the vaccine and later be reimbursed if reimbursement is contingent on the employee remaining employed at the employer for a specific length of time. Nor can the employer require that the employee's health insurer pay for the vaccine unless the employer pays the entire premium for the coverage and there is no deductible, copayment, or other expense to the employee.

Must hospitals provide an employee post-exposure evaluation following an exposure incident?

Employers must conduct post-exposure evaluations of employees who are exposed on the job. As part of that evaluation, which is to be provided at no cost to the employee, the employer must make available to the employee a confidential medical examination, including a blood test if the employee consents; post-exposure preventive treatment; and counseling. For more information, see Centers for Disease Control and Prevention, *Guideline for Infection Control in Health Care Personnel (1998)*.

The employer must also document the circumstances surrounding the employee's exposure and, if possible, identify the source individual. If an identifiable source individual exists, the employer must test that individual's blood for hepatitis B and HIV, provided that the individual consents. The employer must inform the exposed employee of the source individual's test results but also must be careful not to violate state or local AIDS confidentiality laws by disclosing the identity of the source individual along with those results.

The employer must provide the employee with a copy of the written medical evaluation within 15 days after completion of the evaluation. Aside from information regarding whether the employee should receive a hepatitis B vaccine, all other information (including blood test results) in this report must be kept confidential, even from the employer, to encourage the employee to participate in the medical examination process and to obtain follow-up care. [29 C.F.R. § 1910.1030(f)]

What must employers do to communicate the hazards of bloodborne pathogens to employees?

Employers are required to communicate the hazards of bloodborne pathogens to employees through employee training and education and proper placement of written warnings and labels. Employers must provide training when the employee is first assigned to a job in which there is occupational exposure and then provide additional training on an annual basis, or any time changes in work tasks affect the employee's risk of exposure.

Employers must affix labels to containers of regulated waste. Employers either must affix a biohazard symbol on all transport, storage, and waste containers that hold substances contaminated with blood or other potentially infected body fluids or must place such materials in red bags or containers. In addition, employers are required to appropriately label all contaminated equipment or partially contaminated equipment. [29 C.F.R. § 1910.1030(g)]

What kinds of records must employers keep regarding occupational exposure?

Employers must maintain medical records for each employee with occupational exposure for the duration of the employee's employment plus 30 years. The records must be kept confidential by the employer during this period, and the employer may not disclose contents of the records without the employee's express written consent. The standard also requires employers to maintain training records for a period of three years from the date of training but does not require that they be kept confidential. [29 C.F.R. § 1910.1030(h)]

Additionally, under the new bloodborne pathogens standard employers must also maintain a sharps injury log. The log must be maintained in a way to ensure employee privacy and will contain, at a minimum, information regarding the type and brand of device involved in the incident, if known; the location of the incident; and a description of the incident.

What will OSHA compliance officers look for with respect to bloodborne pathogens?

OSHA compliance officers likely follow an OSHA instruction document developed specifically for their use in enforcing OSHA's bloodborne pathogens standard. [U.S. Department of Labor, OSHA Instruction CPL 2-2.69, Enforcement Procedures for the Occupational Exposure to Bloodborne Pathogens (2001), available on the Internet at *www.osha.gov*] Although the OSHA standard has not been revised since 1991, the Instruction replaces and updates some of OSHA's practical recommendations and sample documentation pertinent to compliance with the standard. For example, appendices to the guidance document provide an Internet resource list, as well as references to current CDC guidelines and updated sample policies and procedures. The new enforcement procedures do not carry the force of law or regulation, but EDs are nonetheless well advised to become familiar with the Instruction, because it will direct compliance officers during hospital inspections.

Airborne Hazards

Are airborne pathogens a concern in the ED?

The risk of tuberculosis (TB) infection, which is an airborne transmissible disease, is the major airborne pathogen transmission concern in the ED. OSHA has shown active interest in the area of TB prevention in health care settings, emphasizing this in introductory comments to both its proposed TB prevention standard (discussed next) and an updated respiratory protection standard [29 C.F.R. § 1910.134] that TB remains a serious health risk, particularly because some outbreaks have involved drug-resistant strains of the disease.

What are the OSHA requirements regarding prevention of the spread of TB in the health care workplace?

For several years, OSHA has relied on the Centers for Disease Control and Prevention (CDC) for guidance on how to respond to the threat of TB transmission in the workplace.

In 1996, for example, in response to the CDC's revision of its guidelines for preventing the transmission of TB in health care settings, OSHA issued a compliance directive incorporating CDC recommendations and providing enforcement guidance to protect workers against hazards posed by TB. [*Enforcement Procedures and Scheduling for Occupational Exposure to Tuberculosis*, OSHA Instr. CPL 2-106 (Feb. 9, 1996)]

In 1997, OSHA proposed a new TB standard based on CDC recommendations. [*Occupational Exposure to Tuberculosis*, 62 Fed. Reg. 54,160 (1997)] The proposed standard required all covered health care employers, regardless of degree of risk, to develop written exposure control and remedial action plans, use engineering controls to protect the work environment, offer free TB skin testing to employees, undertake periodic medical surveillance, and provide employees with TB awareness training. The standard provided detailed recommendations as to appropriate procedures, work practices, and engineering controls.

In 2003, OSHA proposed to terminate rulemaking in regard to tuberculosis based on the reduced number of tuberculosis cases nationwide, steps that had already been taken to prevent transmission of the disease, and the difficulty of identifying those infected. OSHA noted that the greatest risk of transmission was for those with undiagnosed and unsuspected tuberculosis and the rule could do little to eliminate this risk. OSHA will continue to use the general-duty clause or other respiratory protection standards for enforcement. [*Occupational Exposure to Tuberculosis, proposed rule; Termination of rulemaking respiratory protection for M. Tuberculosis; Final Rule; Revocation*, 68 Fed. Reg. 75,767 (Dec. 31, 2003)] New enforcement policy under the code focuses on detailed medical evaluation, fitness testing, written program, training, and recordkeeping. [*Tuberculosis and respiratory protection, Enforcement Policy Memorandum* (July 30, 2004) effective July 2, 2004)]

Ergonomic Hazards

Why should ED leaders consider the impact of ergonomic hazards?

Ergonomic hazards are of particular relevance to hospital EDs where health care workers may be repeatedly lifting patients. Where there is a mismatch between the physical requirements of the job and the physical capacity of the worker, musculoskeletal disorders can result. In a controversial study on musculoskeletal disorders, NIOSH found evidence that work-related lifting and awkward postures are associated with low back disorders. Such disorders are very common in the health care industry overall, where workers' job duties include lifting patients.

Is there an OSHA standard addressing ergonomic hazards at the workplace?

In April 2002, however, OSHA announced a comprehensive plan designed to reduce ergonomic injuries through a combination of industry-targeted guidelines, enforcement measures, workplace outreach, and research. OSHA has begun to develop industry- and task-specific guidelines to reduce and prevent musculoskeletal disorders, starting with guidelines applicable to nursing homes.

In 2003, nursing home guidelines were released that focus on processes to protect employees, identification of problems and solutions in lifting and repositioning, solutions for other high-risk activities, and employee training. OSHA identified risks and solutions related to patient transfer and repositions as well as other activities such as bending to make a bed, collecting waste, pushing heavy carts, removing items from deep carts, and lifting and carrying supplies. While written with the nursing home industry in mind, the guidelines include many activities that take place within the ED and can serve as a reference for solutions to prevent injuries for the identified activities.

It is important to note that even in the absence of a general ergonomics standard, the Department of Labor can issue citations in this area under the general duty clause of the OSH Act. [*See, e.g., Secretary of Labor v. Pepperidge Farm Inc.*, OSHRC Dkt. No. 89-0265 (Apr. 26, 1997) (upholding OSHA's issuance of lifting-hazard violations under the general duty clause); *Secretary of Labor v. Beverly Enterprises, Inc.*, OSHRC Dkt. Nos. 91-3344, 92-0238, 92-0819, 92-1257, 93-724 (Oct. 27, 2000)]. That clause provides that any hazardous working condition not covered by a specific regulation or standard may be cited as a violation and a penalty issued. [29 U.S.C. § 654(a)(1)] OSHA has cautioned that it will vigorously enforce the general-duty clause and will prosecute violators.

Smoking

Does federal law require hospitals to ban smoking in the ED?

There is no federal law that specifically provides the legal authority to ban smoking in the ED. It may be argued, however, that the Occupational Safety and Health Act's general-duty clause, which requires employers to provide a safe working environment, provides support for a smoking ban.

Do state laws address smoking in EDs?

Many state laws do provide such authority. Maryland state law, for example, states that there will be no smoking in any area of the hospital. The exceptions to this broad prohibition do not apply to the ED. [Md. Code Ann., Health-Gen. § 24-205] Virginia law specifies that smoking is prohibited in hospital EDs. [Va. Code Ann. § 15.2-2801] Other state laws may more generally prohibit smoking in publicly owned buildings or buildings with public access [*See, e.g.*, Hawaii Rev. Stat. § 328K-2].

Passageways and Exits

What are OSHA's requirements regarding aisles and passageways?

OSHA regulations mandate that aisles and passageways must be kept clear, in good repair, and free from obstruction across or in aisles. In addition, permanent aisles and passageways must be appropriately marked. [29 C.F.R. § 1910.22(b)] In the ED, these regulations prohibit the blockage of passageways by, for example, supplies or patient gurneys.

Are there regulatory requirements for exits?

Regulatory rules effective December 2002 require the hospital to comply with either OSHA exit, emergency action plan, and fire prevention plans or the National Fire Protection Association's Standard (NFPA) 101, Life Safety Code, 2000 Edition. Companies that comply with NFPA 101 are deemed to be OSHA compliant. This approach is intended to increase flexibility of compliance while protecting the safety and health of employees through performance-oriented objectives. Compliance standards focus on design and construction, maintenance and operational safety requirements, and employee warning of the need to escape. For example, OSHA allows fire doors to remain open as long as they can close in an emergency. Exit heights and widths are set forth and any objects projecting into the exit route must allow the exit to meet minimum width requirements. Exits must not require employees to travel toward high hazard areas and exit signs should have "exit" written overhead, while nonexit doors should have a sign such as "not an exit." [67 Fed. Reg. 67,950 (Nov. 7, 2002)]

What are the 2003 Life Safety Code requirements that impact the ED?

The 2003 Life Safety Code spells out compliance requirements for new and existing hospitals. The code clarifies the speed at which people must be able to exit the health care facility; requires aisles, corridors, and ramps to be clear; establishes minimum door widths; and requires effective notification of employees of the emergency. Sprinkler systems should be in place as spelled out by the guidelines. Waiting areas must have access to an exit corridor with walls sufficiently thick to form a barrier to limit smoke. Every facility should have written copies of a fire protection plan, conduct fire drills, and train employees for emergency response. Smoking should be prohibited when combustible gases or oxygen are in use or stored. [Life Safety Code, NFPA 101 (2003 ed.)]

SECURITY IN THE ED

Security in the ED is a growing concern due to increased incidents of violence in EDs. The factors contributing to increased violence are many and include increased gang activity, drug abuse, alcohol abuse, and mental illness. Circumstances of hospital violence differ from circumstances of workplace violence in general, often resulting from patients and occasionally from their family members who feel frustrated, vulnerable, and out of control. Several studies indicate that violence against hospital workers often takes place during times of high activity and interaction with patients, such as at meal times and during visiting hours and patient transportation. Assaults may occur when service is denied, when a patient is involuntarily admitted, or when hospital personnel attempt to set limits on eating, drinking, or tobacco or alcohol use. (DHHS (NIOSH) Publication No. 2002-101 (Apr. 2002), available on the Internet at *www.cdc.gov/niosh/2002-101.html*).

Although anyone working in a hospital may become a victim of violence, nurses and aides who have the most direct contact with patients are at higher risk. Emergency response personnel and health care providers are also at increased risk of violence, which may occur anywhere in a hospital, but is most frequent in the ED and in waiting rooms, as well as psychiatric wards and geriatric units. It is the responsibility of the hospital to ensure the safety of employees, patients, and visitors to the ED. Other factors which increase the risk of violence include working directly with volatile people such as those under the influence of drugs and alcohol or with psychotic diagnosis, working when understaffed, transporting patients, working in a situation where patients wait a long time for service in crowded waiting rooms, working in situations where staff are alone or with inadequate security, staff training that is inadequate in crisis intervention, working areas where there is access to firearms, failing to restrict public movement through the area, and working in poorly lit areas such as parking lots, rooms, or corridors.

Major areas of concern addressed in this section include legal consequences of violence in the ED, security measures the hospital must undertake, training for ED and security personnel, the use of restraints, reporting of crimes that occur outside the ED, handling of criminal evidence, and administering tests at the request of law enforcement officers.

Legal Consequences of Violence

Can a hospital be liable for violence that occurs in the ED?

A hospital may be liable to employees, patients, and visitors for assaults that occur in the ED. As an employer, a hospital has a duty to provide a safe working environment for its employees. Like all facilities open to the public, the hospital has a duty to provide a safe environment to those it invites onto its premises.

Hospital liability will depend on whether the hospital reasonably could have anticipated (foreseen, in legal terms) the assault on the employee, patient, or visitor, yet failed to take action to prevent the assault. Proper planning, security policies, and staff training should substantially reduce the risks of liability and provide a safer environment for employees, patients, and visitors.

Foreseeability of a risk may depend to some extent on the location of the ED. In high-crime areas, for example, where gang violence is commonplace, a hospital may be negligent for failing to recognize and take precautions against the possibility of violence stemming from retribution against a gang member who is being treated in the ED.

What are some of the potential legal consequences if there is an episode of violence in the workplace?

Depending on the circumstances, ED violence could lead to

- OSHA citations
- penalties for violation of state law
- workers' compensation claims by injured employees
- negligence claims by injured patients or visitors
- assault and battery or false imprisonment claims by persons who are wrongfully restrained

Federal Law Regarding Violence in the ED

Has OSHA issued any regulations regarding prevention of workplace violence against health care workers?

OSHA has issued voluntary guidelines for preventing workplace violence against health care workers. While the guidelines do not carry the legal effect of regulations, health care employers can expect agency investigators to look to the guidelines to determine whether the employer's violence prevention program meets OSHA standards. [*Guidelines for Preventing Workplace Violence for Health Care and Social Service Workers*, OSHA 3148 (1998), available on the Internet at *www.osha.gov*]

How can OSHA use the general-duty clause to issue citations for workplace violence?

Although there are no OSHA regulations regarding workplace violence, OSHA can invoke the general-duty clause in issuing citations. The general-duty clause is a "catch-all" provision that provides that any hazardous working condition not covered by a specific regulation or standard may be cited as a violation and a penalty may be issued. [29 U.S.C. § 654(a)(1)] According to OSHA instructions to field offices, a general-duty clause citation should be issued only in the absence of a specific standard if a hazard is recognized that poses a serious threat to worker safety or health and is capable of being corrected. Four elements are necessary to use the general-duty clause in an enforcement action for workplace violence in the ED.

1. The ED failed to keep the premises free of a hazard.
2. It was a recognized hazard.
3. The hazard caused death or serious harm.
4. There was a feasible and useful method to correct the hazard.

What do OSHA's voluntary guidelines for preventing workplace violence against health care workers say?

The guidelines contain detailed recommendations for developing an effective violence prevention program, identifying the four main components of a program as

1. management commitment and employee involvement
2. worksite analysis
3. hazard prevention and control
4. safety and health training

Minimum requirements for an effective workplace violence prevention plan include a zero-tolerance policy for workplace violence, assurance that employees reporting violence will not suffer reprisal, and a comprehensive plan for maintaining security. The guidelines outline specific methods of preventing violence in the health care workplace, such as arranging furniture to prevent entrapment of staff, instituting visitor sign-in procedures, and establishing a system to identify patients with a history of assaultive behavior.

[*Guidelines for Preventing Workplace Violence for Health Care and Social Service Workers*, OSHA 3148 (1998), available on the Internet at *www.osha.gov*]

What can ED staff do to prevent violence?

ED staff can be trained to watch for signals that warn of potential violence such as verbal anger or frustration, body language such as threatening gestures, signs of drug or alcohol use, or the presence of a weapon. Each encounter should be evaluated for the potential for violence and staff should avoid being isolated with a potentially violent person and keep an open path to exit from the room for safety reasons. Staff should be familiar with the warning signs of potential violence: pacing and restlessness, clenched fists, increasingly loud speech, and excessive insistence, threats, or cursing. Staff members may be able to diffuse anger and potential violence by remaining calm and caring, by acknowledging the person's feelings, by avoiding aggressive behavior such as rapid movement, moving close to the person, touching the person, or speaking loudly. Staff should avoid making threats or giving orders to a potentially volatile person. If the situation cannot be diffused, then the staff should remove themselves from the situation, call security for help, and report any incidents to management. Training slides and handouts are available on the OSHA Internet site at *http://www.osha.gov*. (DHHS (NIOSH) Pub. No. 2002-101 (Apr. 2002), available on the Internet at *www.cdc.gov/niosh/2002-101.html*).[OSHA E-Tools Emergency Department]

The ED should have a violence checklist in place that includes the following:

- A workplace violence prevention plan to train staff to recognize and diffuse violent situations,
- ED doors that exit out, so that people from the street can only access the ED through the waiting area,
- ED access that is controlled by a receptionist who buzzes people in through a secure door.

Why should EDs follow OSHA's voluntary guidelines?

There are several reasons to follow OSHA's voluntary workplace violence prevention guidelines for health care workers, including

- protection of employees, patients, visitors, and vendors
- reduction in workers' compensation and insurance claims
- insurance premium savings
- compliance with Joint Commission standards
- proof of compliance with OSHA's general-duty clause (and avoidance of OSHA fines and litigation)
- increased employee attendance
- increased employee morale

Are there OSHA reporting obligations when violence occurs in the ED?

OSHA regulations require the entry on the Injury and Illness Log (OSHA 300) of any injury that requires more than first aid, is a lost-time injury, requires modified duty, or causes loss of consciousness. [29 C.F.R. § 1904.9] Injuries resulting from assaults, which are otherwise recordable, must also be entered on the log. (This applies to establishments required to keep OSHA logs.) A fatality or catastrophe resulting in the hospitalization of three or more employees must be reported to OSHA within eight hours. [29 C.F.R. § 1904.39]

Are there other federal guidelines for preventing violence in hospitals?

The National Institute for Occupational Safety and Health (NIOSH) has also issued voluntary guidelines outlining prevention strategies for hospitals. NIOSH recommends that employers develop a safety and health program that includes management commitment, employee participation, hazard identification, safety and health training, and hazard prevention, control, and reporting, and that employers evaluate their program periodically. Although risk factors for violence are specific for each hospital and its work scenarios, employers can follow general prevention strategies:

1. Environmental designs
   - Develop emergency signaling, alarms, and monitoring systems.
   - Install security devices such as metal detectors to prevent armed persons from entering the hospital.
   - Install other security devices such as cameras and good lighting in hallways.
   - Provide security escorts to the parking lots at night.
   - Design waiting areas to accommodate and assist visitors and patients who may have a delay in service.
   - Design the triage area and other public areas to minimize the risk of assault.
     - Provide staff restrooms and emergency exits.
     - Install enclosed nurses' stations.
     - Install deep service counters or bullet-resistant and shatterproof glass enclosures in reception areas.
     - Arrange furniture and other objects to minimize their use as weapons.
2. Administrative controls
   - Design staffing patterns to prevent personnel from working alone and to minimize patient waiting time.
   - Restrict the movement of the public in hospitals by card-controlled access.
   - Develop a system for alerting security personnel when violence is threatened.
3. Behavior modifications
   - Provide all workers with training in recognizing and managing assaults, resolving conflicts, and maintaining hazard awareness. [*Violence: Occupational Hazards in Hospitals*, DHHS (NIOSH) Pub. No. 2002-101 (Apr. 2002), available on the Internet at *www.cdc.gov/niosh/2002-101.html*]

State Law Regarding Violence in the ED

Do state laws address violence in the ED?

Several state laws addressing violence in the ED have been enacted as legislative responses to the perceived increase of violence in hospital EDs. Hospital administrators should be familiar with laws in their state. ED managers should ensure that individuals responsible for hospital-wide violence prevention are familiar with the unique problems and risks of the ED.

What is an example of a state law governing violence in hospitals?

California law provides an example. In that state, hospitals are required to "conduct a security and safety assessment and to develop a security plan with measures to protect personnel, patients, and visitors from aggressive or violent behavior. The security and safety assessment must examine trends of aggressive or violent behavior at the facility . . . . Hospitals are required to track incidents of aggressive or violent behavior as part of the quality assessment and improvement program and for the purpose of developing a security plan to deter and manage further aggressive or violent acts of a similar nature."

By law, the security plan must include (but is not limited to) security considerations relating to the following:

- physical layout
- staffing
- security personnel availability
- policy and training related to appropriate responses to violent acts

California law also specifies that the person or hospital committee members who develop the security plan must be familiar with all of the following:

- "the role of security in hospital operations
- hospital organization
- protective measures, including alarms and access control
- the handling of disturbed patients, visitors, and employees
- identification of factors predicting aggressive and violent behavior
- hospital safety and emergency preparedness
- the rudiments of documenting and reporting crimes, including not disturbing a crime scene" [Cal. Health & Safety Code § 1257.7]

Are there state law reporting obligations when violence occurs in the ED?

State law may also require reporting of violent incidents in the ED. Under California law, for example, any act of assault or battery that results in injury or involves the use of a firearm or other dangerous weapon against any on-duty hospital personnel must be reported to the local law enforcement agency within 72 hours of the incident. [Cal. Health & Safety Code § 1257.7]

Security Measures

What security measures are required in the ED?

Necessary security measures vary from facility to facility and also vary as the social and environmental circumstances around the facility change. Ongoing data regarding violent incidents in the ED, the hospital, and the surrounding areas should be monitored to ensure proper response to changing circumstances. Proper security measures may range from adequate lighting and proper personnel identification to armed security guards and metal detectors.

State law may mandate certain security measures in hospital EDs. For example, Massachusetts law requires that proper identification be worn by all persons, including ED personnel, who observe or treat hospital patients. [Mass. Gen. Laws ch. 111, § 70E] California law requires adequate security personnel. [Cal. Health & Safety Code § 1257.7] State law varies widely and should be consulted to discover particular requirements in each jurisdiction.

How much authority can a hospital security guard assume?

The three basic types of private security officers and their scopes of authority are as follows:

1. *Private citizens* are hired to perform as security officers at the hospital. They have no more authority than a private citizen.
2. *Security officers* have special police or special deputy commissions that grant them more authority than a private citizen but less than that of regular police or deputies. Because these officers generally do not have good-faith immunity, they may be liable for false arrest if they arrest a person who did not commit an offense.
3. *Off-duty police officers or deputies* may moonlight as hospital security guards. State law governs whether these officers retain their authority, powers, and protections while privately employed. In some states these officers retain their authority, while in others they do not. In some states off-duty police officers are required to be armed.

Hospitals should be aware that the scope of authority varies from jurisdiction to jurisdiction. Hospital policies should clearly delineate the security guard's scope of authority. Security guards should also receive adequate training to allow them to perform their duties.

Can hospitals prohibit weapons in the ED?

The hospital can prohibit weapons, dangerous devices, and contraband in the ED and should post a notice to that effect in a conspicuous place. Patients and visitors can be instructed to check all weapons with hospital security. Those not complying can be denied access to the ED. If visitors become disruptive, local authorities may be contacted. Patients admitted through the ED may have weapons confiscated and stored in the hospital security department until they are discharged.

A number of states have passed concealed carry weapons laws that allow a gunowner to obtain a permit to carry a concealed weapon. States differ in terms of where a concealed weapon may be carried. Some allow the weapon anywhere once the person has a permit, while others prohibit concealed weapons in certain locations such as a school, hospital, or government building. For example, in Missouri, a person must be 23 years old to obtain the permit and submit to fingerprinting and background checks as well as safety training to carry the concealed weapon. Missouri prohibits concealed weapons in certain public locations including hospitals accessible to the public. [Mo. Rev. Stat. § 571.101] Some local cities and counties also have weapons laws that may impact whether weapons can be prohibited in the ED. It is important to check local laws for the specific jurisdiction.

Are there legal ramifications regarding the use of metal detectors?

The hospital is responsible for the safety of staff, patients, and visitors to the ED. As part of an effort to provide a safe environment, metal detectors may be used to protect against weapons being brought into the ED. All persons entering the ED can be subjected to a metal detector search as a condition of entering the property. Those refusing the search can be denied entry to the ED.

What should security do in response to an unruly visitor?

Unruly visitors or visitors who refuse to cooperate or follow hospital policies can be escorted from the premises. If the visitor refuses to leave, he or she should be informed that the hospital is private property and he or she may be subject to arrest.

What kind of security training should ED staff receive?

Necessary training may be mandated by state law, which should be incorporated into hospital and ED policies. In California, for example, the law requires all hospital employees who are regularly assigned to the ED to receive "security education and training related to the following topics:

- general safety measures
- personal safety measures
- the assault cycle
- factors predicting aggression and violence
- obtaining patient history from a patient with violent behavior
- characteristics of aggressive and violent patients and victims
- verbal and physical maneuvers to diffuse and avoid violent behavior
- strategies to avoid physical harm
- restraining techniques
- appropriate use of medications as chemical restraints
- any resources available to employees for coping with incidents of violence, for example, critical incident stress debriefing or employee assistance programs."

The law also requires members of the medical staff of hospitals and all other practitioners, including nurse practitioners, PAs, and other personnel who are regularly assigned to the ED, to receive the same training as hospital employees, or at least training identified in the security plan as sufficient. [Cal. Health & Safety Code § 1257.8]

90

Are there staffing and training requirements for security personnel?

State law may determine staffing and training requirements. California law, for example, states that hospitals must have sufficient personnel to provide security pursuant to the security plan. Persons regularly assigned to provide hospital security must be trained regarding the role of security in hospital operations, including the identification of factors predicting aggressive and violent behavior and management of violent disturbances. [Cal. Health & Safety Code § 1257.7]

What security considerations apply when a patient is in custody?

When an ED patient is a prisoner, the hospital and staff must balance the need to provide quality care and protect the patient's safety against the security of staff members and other patients. The care of patients in custody should be provided in accordance with written procedures, by properly trained staff, and in cooperation with law enforcement officials. Considerations include

- whether the patient is permitted to have a family member present
- whether knowing the details of the patient's criminal record or circumstances of custody would influence the staff's ability to provide care
- whether staff members are permitted to refuse to participate in the care of the prisoner
- whether handcuffs and other restraining devices are consistent with or can be removed for needed treatment
- whether law enforcement officers may be present during emergency treatment
- whether compliance with life safety precautions is followed
- whether forensic personnel (i.e., the custodial officer) is oriented to life safety requirements

Responsibilities Relating to Crimes Outside the ED

What types of crimes are EDs responsible for reporting?

State law governs reporting requirements, and, thus, what must be reported varies. However, most states require reporting of sexual abuse, child abuse and/or neglect, abuse of disabled and elderly adults, and other violent crimes, such as gunshot wounds.

What is the ED's responsibility regarding child abuse?

Every state has a mandatory reporting law that obliges health care providers who have reason to believe that a child has been abused to report their findings to a designated state agency, such as a child welfare bureau. If the provider making the diagnosis is a member of a hospital staff, the report may be channeled through the administrator's office.

Many states also authorize hospitals or, alternatively, attending physicians to retain a child in their custody without parental consent irrespective of whether the child requires further medical attention. A decision to take a child into protective custody must be based on a determination that returning the child to the custody of the parents or guardian would present an imminent danger to the child's health or life. Procedures set forth in these statutes require prompt notification of appropriate state officials. Certain states also impose a time limitation on protective custody. Provision must be made for a hearing to determine whether the child should be permanently or temporarily removed from the parents or guardian.

In addition, some states have enacted legislation calling for the creation of multidisciplinary teams in the community and in hospitals to identify and assist victims of child abuse.

What are the consequences of failing to diagnose or report child abuse?

A failure to exercise reasonable care in diagnosing child abuse or laxity in complying with the mandatory reporting laws may result in liability for an errant physician or hospital. This was illustrated in a California case in which a physician in the ED of a hospital treated an 11-month-old child with a fractured leg, a fractured skull, and multiple bruises about the body. The child's mother gave no explanation for the injuries. Three months later the child was taken by her mother to another hospital with puncture wounds on her leg and back, severe bites on her face, and a mutilated hand. A physician at the second hospital diagnosed the child's condition as battered child syndrome, and the child was placed in foster care. A suit was brought on behalf of the child against the first physician and hospital for negligently failing to diagnose the child abuse syndrome and to report the child battery pursuant to California's mandatory reporting laws. The California Supreme Court held that the health care providers would be liable if the child's most recent injuries were a proximate result of the first physician's failure to diagnose child abuse and to report the matter to appropriate officials. [*Landeros v. Flood*, 551 P.2d 389 (Cal. 1976)]

What are the consequences of reporting child abuse when it later turns out there was no child abuse?

Many state laws provide immunity from liability for individuals who report suspected child abuse in good faith. In a 1985 Michigan case, a court reviewed a physician's liability for reporting child abuse when it was later proven that the charges were not true. The child instead had a disease that caused the bones to be brittle and easily broken. The court held that the parents could not recover for erroneous abuse charges because the physician was acting in good faith and was therefore entitled to statutory immunity. [*Awkermann v. Tri County Ortho*, 373 N.W.2d 204 (Mich. Ct. App. 1985) *see also, Howe v. Andereck*, 882 So. 2d 240 (Miss. Ct. App. 2004) and *Casbohm v. Metrohealth Med. Ctr.*, 746 N.E.2d 661 (Ohio Ct. App. 2000)]

What is the ED's responsibility regarding sexual abuse?

State law, particularly hospital licensing provisions, may require hospitals to provide treatment for persons who have been sexually abused. Hospital licensure acts that do not specify that care must be provided to victims of sexual assault might imply that facilities with EDs are obliged to care for such individuals. In the absence of explicit or implicit statutory requirements, hospitals that maintain emergency care facilities should have clearly established procedures for managing a person who has been sexually abused. Further, because of the potential for liability, it would be inadvisable to deny hospitalization or medical services to an individual on the grounds that the person's complaint involved a sexual assault.

It is not uncommon to find local hospital consortia cooperating in the development of guidelines for treating victims of sexual assault. Some hospitals have rape crisis units staffed by specially trained physicians, nurses, psychologists and social workers who provide the medical and psychosocial support a patient needs following an assault.

The American College of Emergency Physicians (ACEP) policy statement on sexual assault recommends that the ED work with local government authorities and establish a plan to address the needs of the sexually assaulted patient including medical, psychological, safety, and legal needs. This would include psychological counseling, pregnancy testing and counseling, treatment for sexually transmitted diseases, and evidentiary exams to collect criminal evidence. The department can establish patient care criteria and prepare staff through ongoing training and education. [ACEP, *Policy Statement: Management of the Patient with the Complaint of Sexual Assault* (#400130) (Oct. 2002)]

What are examples of state laws requiring treatment of sexually abused patients?

Hospital administrators in states with specific statutory requirements regarding the treatment of persons who have been sexually abused should review these provisions carefully in drafting hospital policy. Florida, for example, has a statute that sets forth the types of services that hospitals with EDs should have available in treating victims of sexual assault. These include gynecological and psychological care, as well as medical examinations and procedures required by police officials for the collection of evidence necessary in the prosecution of assailants. [Fla. Stat. ch. 395.1021]

Illinois also has legislation requiring hospitals to provide emergency care for victims of rape. Under that law, hospitals must provide appropriate medical examinations; laboratory tests; medication; blood tests; oral and written information concerning the possibility of infection, sexually transmitted disease, and pregnancy; oral and written information concerning medications and medical procedures; and counseling. [410 Ill. Comp. Stat. Ann. § 70/5]

Are there concerns about evidence in sexual abuse cases?

Physical evidence relating to the sexual abuse is important in pursuing criminal charges against the perpetrator. To ensure that the evidence is preserved in a legally proper manner, the ED must follow certain procedures, which should be specified in ED policies for treating persons who have been sexually abused. A number of groups, including many local prosecutors' offices, willingly provide rape evidence kits along with instructions and training programs on their use.

What is the ED's responsibility for reporting abuse of disabled or elderly patients?

Many states have enacted laws mandating the reporting of abuse, neglect, or exploitation of disabled adults or elderly persons. The laws vary widely. Some laws define "elderly" and "disabled" as well as the terms "abuse" and "neglect," while others do not. The laws also vary regarding who has a reporting obligation and to whom the abuse must be reported. It is therefore important that ED personnel be familiar with the requirements of their own jurisdictions.

What is an example of an abuse reporting law that applies to disabled and elderly patients?

Florida has a broad reporting law. In that state, a health professional who knows, or has reasonable cause to suspect, that a vulnerable adult has been or is being abused, neglected, or exploited must immediately report that knowledge or suspicion to the central abuse registry and tracking system on the statewide toll-free number.

A report of abuse in Florida must contain, to the extent possible, specific information regarding the vulnerable adult, the person's family members, the alleged perpetrator, the caregiver, and the person reporting. The report must also contain a description of the injuries; actions taken by the reporter, if any, such as notification of the criminal justice agency; and any other information that might establish abuse, neglect, or exploitation. [Fla. Stat. ch. 415.1034]

Does the ED have responsibility for reporting special types of wounds?

States generally require the reporting of gunshot wounds. Texas, for example, has a mandatory reporting law that requires that such a case be reported immediately to the law enforcement authority of the municipality or county by the hospital administration or by a physician who treats, or is requested to treat, a bullet or gunshot wound. [Tex. Health & Safety Code § 161.041]

In Florida, the reporting obligation applies to, among others, physicians, nurses, and any employee of a hospital who knowingly treats, or receives a request to treat, a person suffering from a gunshot wound or life-threatening injury indicating an act of violence. The health care provider is required to report to the sheriff's department of the county. Anyone willfully failing to report the treatment or treatment request is guilty of a misdemeanor. [Fla. Stat. ch. 790.24]

A Colorado law obligating physicians to report gunshot wounds to law enforcement officials was interpreted by that state's highest court. In a case where a sheriff's officer asked a female physician assistant to photograph a female victim's bullet wounds to the buttock and thighs, the victim's husband, on trial for the incident, claimed that the photographs violated his wife's physician-patient privilege. The Colorado Supreme Court found that the reporting statute nullified that privilege. The statute clearly stated that in cases where the physician has a reporting obligation, the physician-patient privilege is abrogated with regard to testimony about the information received from the physician's observations of the patient. Because the incident involved gunshot wounds, and the photographs were obtained through the PA's observation of the wounds, rather than through communication with the patient, the court found the privilege did not apply. [*People v. Covington*, 19 P.3d 15 (Colo. 2001), *cert. denied*, 2002 Colo. LEXIS 226 (Colo. March 18, 2002)]

Because state laws vary, it is important that ED personnel know the scope of the reporting requirements in their particular jurisdiction. Failure to report could lead to penalties. On the other hand, disclosure of conditions that are not required by law might violate the patient's privacy rights. Strict adherence to state reporting requirements is therefore necessary and should be incorporated into ED policies and procedures.

What does "maintaining the chain of custody" mean?

When a person is arrested and tried for a crime, various types of evidence are presented in an effort to prove the person's guilt or innocence. Maintaining the chain of custody means that there is continual tracking and documentation of evidence from the time it is collected until it is presented in the courtroom. The goal of maintaining the chain of custody is to prevent tampering with evidence, which would deprive the accused of a fair trial.

In the ED, the issue of chain of custody arises when physical evidence is gathered from, for example, a rape victim. The protocol to be followed must have the prior approval of the police, district attorney, public defender, courts, medical examiner, hospital, and laboratory. That protocol should be reviewed before the evidence is collected to prevent invalidating specimens by inappropriate handling. The protocol should be followed and documented. All specimens must be appropriately labeled and should be signed for by each person handling the specimen thereafter.

The chain of custody issue may also arise with various types of contraband brought into the ED, such as a weapon or illegal drugs. There should be an established policy for handling contraband, which should include maintaining the chain of custody in the event that there is future prosecution in which the contraband will be used as evidence. For example, if a patient presents at the ED with gunshot wounds and is in possession of a gun, the ED staff should follow the established policy in handling the weapon. This generally involves contacting security and releasing the gun to a security officer who locks the weapon in a safe. All steps are documented. It could be that the person is properly licensed to carry a gun and is in fact a police officer. It could be that the person was committing armed robbery and the weapon will be used in prosecuting the case.

Abandonment in the ED

What considerations surround elderly abandonment at the ED?

Policies and procedures that direct the staff how to act in the event of elderly patient abandonment at the ED should be carefully reviewed because these vulnerable individuals trigger special concerns.

According to the American College of Emergency Physicians (ACEP), EDs are used as a safety net not only for medical emergencies, but also for social emergencies faced by individuals and institutions responsible for the care of elderly individuals. ACEP cites a number of factors contributing to the problem of elderly abandonment, including rising health care costs, two career families, cutbacks in government support, and lack of coverage for long-term services needed by the elderly population.

If an elderly patient is brought to the ED for emergency care, but does not have an emergency medical condition, the hospital is not obligated to admit that individual. Where the patient cannot care for him or herself, however, and the person who brought the patient to the hospital will not assume responsibility, the hospital must attempt to make alternate arrangements, by contacting the patient's relatives and social services, for example. In addition, because elderly abandonment constitutes abuse or neglect under many state laws, ED staff will be required by law to file a report with the appropriate authorities to trigger an investigation, likely Adult Protective Services.

Transfer agreements with long-term care facilities will reduce the possibility that a patient transferred to the hospital for emergency care may not be readmitted to the long-term care facility when the emergency medical condition is stabilized. If the long-term care facility should refuse to readmit a stable patient, because the facility can no longer provide the level of care now needed by the resident, hospital and long-term care facility administration should be consulted as to how to develop a safe discharge plan.

Insurance coverage is a significant issue for abandoned patients, as payers will not likely cover the cost of acute care where it is not medically necessary, simply because the patient has been abandoned at an acute care facility. Insurers may prove helpful in these cases, however, as case managers or care coordinators may have the necessary resources to arrange for alternate site care at an appropriate level.

Practical considerations include identifying how and when hospital administration must be notified, what information (if any) may be released to the media and whether staff is properly trained to handle these patients.

What should hospitals consider when designing policies regarding the treatment and custody of abandoned infants?

In the last few years, in the wake of publicity surrounding high profile cases of infants who were abandoned in public places, a number of state legislatures proposed legislation aimed at discouraging abandonment by allowing unwanted newborns to be safely left at hospitals. Where this legislation has been enacted, hospitals must review newborn abandonment policies and revise them to comply with these new laws. In Florida, for example, hospitals with emergency services must admit and provide all necessary services and care to any infant who appears three days old or younger. The hospital has implied consent to perform necessary services and care. The parent who expresses an intent to leave a newborn and not return has "the absolute right to remain anonymous and leave at any time." The parent may not be pursued or followed, unless the parent seeks to reclaim the newborn. After receiving the infant, the hospital must immediately contact a local licensed child placement agency or the statewide central abuse hotline to transfer custody. [Fla. Stat. § 383.50.]

Whether hospitals are required by law to accept abandoned infants, or seek to do so voluntarily, the policies and procedures for treatment and custody of these infants must be carefully outlined. The following should be considered:

- Where may infants be "abandoned"?
- How will individuals know where to leave an unwanted infant?
- What steps will the hospital take to prevent abandoned infants from going unnoticed, or from being harmed or abducted?

- When the infant is discovered, who will be notified?
- Who will assume responsibility for notifying authorities?
- What age children will the hospital accept?
- If the parent brings the child into the hospital, what steps are taken to protect the parent's anonymity? To ascertain the parent's identity?
- What staff training is necessary?
- Does voluntarily accepting abandoned babies create an increased risk of liability for the hospital or for treating staff? Is additional insurance necessary?
- What happens if the parent returns and seeks custody of the child?
- What if another individual arrives and claims custody?
- What information may be released to the media?
- How and when must administration be notified?
- May hospital employees attempt to adopt babies abandoned at the facility?

Administering Tests at Request of Law Enforcement Without Patient Consent

If ED personnel perform test procedures on criminal suspects at a police officer's request, can the suspect later sue?

A successful lawsuit against medical personnel for performing a police ordered test would be a rarity. Some states have statutes providing immunity to physicians, nurses, and employers in such situations. Under an Illinois statute, for example, a hospital and its staff were judged immune from civil liability in connection with a patient's lawsuit alleging that hospital staff grabbed her arm and forcibly drew her blood without her consent after she was arrested on hospital premises for driving under the influence of alcohol. The patient arrived at the hospital following a traffic accident in which another driver had been injured, although the patient had sustained no injuries. Although she declined any treatment, she was detained by emergency room staff until a police officer arrived, placed the patient under arrest, and in accordance with the state vehicle code, advised her that she must submit to a blood alcohol test. Despite the patient's refusal, a hospital physician and nurse grabbed the patient's arm and drew blood from her against her will. The court found that the actions of the hospital and its staff were authorized under another state vehicle code provision which provides that persons authorized to withdraw blood or collect urine cannot be sued civilly for damages, unless they act in a "willful or wanton manner." Grabbing the patient's arm to withdraw blood simply did not rise to the level of "willful and wanton" conduct, the court concluded. [*Ruppel v. Ramseyer*, 33 F. Supp. 2d 720 (C.D. Ill. 1999)]

Note that the Illinois statute, as well as many others, refers only to drawing blood and collecting urine, leaving unanswered the question of what liability might attend more risky, more seriously invasive, or inherently unpleasant tests or procedures such as the pumping out of the subject's stomach or the surgical removal of a bullet for the purpose of ballistics tests.

Can the police order a blood test without the subject's consent?

This situation most often arises when the police want to know the subject's blood alcohol level. The blood must be drawn and tested quickly or the evidence will be destroyed. If the police want the subject's blood tested for another reason, for example, to discover the subject's blood type while in the course of a rape investigation, they can wait until a search warrant is issued, as the evidence will not be destroyed.

The United States Supreme Court has ruled that police may legally order a blood test without the subject's consent if five conditions are satisfied.

1. The suspect has been formally arrested.
2. The blood test is reasonably likely to produce evidence in the forthcoming criminal prosecution.
3. The delay involved in obtaining a search warrant would lead to destruction of the evidence.
4. The test chosen is a reasonable one (e.g., there are no medical or religious reasons for not carrying out the test).
5. The test is performed in a reasonable manner (e.g., the blood is taken by a qualified health care professional using accepted medical techniques in a hospital environment). [*Schmerber v. California*, 384 U.S. 757 (1966)]

Courts continue to define when a police officer can seek a blood test without a warrant. In reviewing the basis for obtaining a blood test, the Tenth Circuit noted that the officer should obtain a warrant for a blood test since a blood test is considered a search protected by the Fourth Amendment unless the officer has probable cause for the blood test and exigent circumstances exist. Exigent circumstances are determined by looking at state law and the importance of the evidence and severity of the offense. Preservation of evidence alone would not necessarily justify a warrantless blood test. [*Marshall v. Columbia Lea Reg'l Hosp.*, 345 F.3d 1157 (10th Cir. 2003)]

Assuming these conditions are met and that the police are therefore acting within their authority, any hospital or health professional could conduct the blood test under police request without fear of liability for battery. In a New Hampshire case, a person refused to have an alcohol blood test administered by the state trooper. When he came into the hospital, the doctor ordered a routine blood test and the results were subsequently given to the trooper. The court found the test admissible in court. While state law prohibited a trooper from administering a test upon refusal, it did not preclude obtaining other blood test results. [*State v. Nickerson*, 780 A.2d 1257 (N.H. 2001)]

What should ED staff do when a police officer asks for a blood test on a patient?

To ensure that the procedure is performed within the parameters discussed in the previous question and answer, ED staff should require the police officer to sign a form attesting that the first three conditions are met. For maximum protection, the provider can supply his or her own determination about the final two conditions. The subject should be asked to sign a consent form, even when it appears that the five conditions for police authority have been met.

Two additional points should be noted. First, the test should not be performed if the subject offers physical resistance because this would tend to make the test procedure unreasonable, defeating the fourth of the listed conditions. Second, the hospital or health professional has no legal duty to obey the police request to perform the test. Thus, cooperation can be withheld if it is not clear that the five conditions are met or if the provider wishes not to participate for any other reason.

What about other kinds of tests to which the suspect does not consent?

In cases in which the invasion of the body is significant and in which time would allow the police to obtain a search warrant, the provider should insist that this be done before acceding to the police request. Although the pressure may be strong to follow police orders without question, there is no reason why health professionals or institutions should be subjected to even a slight risk of tort liability when a court order that would avoid this could be secured. In no event should hospital personnel use physical force to compel a subject to undergo a test.

For example, a state hospital set up a program to test maternity patients' urine for evidence of cocaine use. The Supreme Court found that this was an unreasonable search in violation of the Fourth Amendment if the patient did not consent to the urine test. Even though the goal of the program was to reduce drug use, the immediate outcome of the program was to provide evidence for law enforcement. The interest in deterring drug use did not justify a search without a warrant or without consent. Law enforcement did not demonstrate a special need to justify the tests. [*Ferguson v. City of Charleston*, 532 U.S. 67 (2001)]

DUTY TO TREAT PATIENTS REGARDLESS OF ABILITY TO PAY

Legal complications may arise when a hospital conditions admission on a patient's ability to pay for medical services, especially when a patient seeks emergency care. Federal legislation not only precludes such restrictive admission policies but also sets forth specific circumstances when a hospital must provide care without regard to ability to pay. Failure to provide uncompensated care can also lead to the loss of tax-exempt status.

State statutes and judicial decisions also limit the use of a patient's ability to pay as a criterion for denying hospitalization and medical services. Some legislation includes criminal sanctions for those who prohibit admission to a hospital when patients are unable to demonstrate an ability to pay for their care.

EMTALA

What are COBRA and EMTALA?

These two acronyms refer to the same federal law. Hospitals that participate in the Medicare program are subject to the emergency care requirements enacted in the Emergency Medical Treatment and Active Labor Act (EMTALA), as part of the Consolidated Omnibus Budget Reconciliation Act of 1986 (COBRA). [42 U.S.C. § 1395dd] An amendment to the Medicare statute, the law sets forth parameters regarding the treatment and transfer of all emergency patients, whether or not they are eligible for Medicare. EMTALA, sometimes called the "antidumping" law, was enacted largely out of legislative concern that hospital emergency departments (EDs) were turning away or transferring patients who could not pay for treatment but needed emergency medical care. Because EMTALA has detailed requirements, and because violations may lead to serious administrative consequences as well as liability, hospitals should review their ED procedures for compliance with this important federal law. For sample documentation relating to EMTALA, see **Part 4** under Continuum of Care.

What does EMTALA require hospitals to do?

Under EMTALA, a hospital must examine all individuals who come to the ED seeking treatment. The hospital must provide an appropriate medical screening examination (MSE) to determine if an emergency medical condition exists or if the patient is in active labor. If the patient does have an emergency medical condition or is in active labor, the hospital must stabilize the patient before discharge. The hospital may transfer the patient only upon the signed certification of a physician that the benefits of transfer outweigh the risks. [42 U.S.C. § 1395dd] Each of these requirements is discussed in detail in the questions and answers that follow.

To which patients does EMTALA apply?

Although EMTALA is a Medicare law, it is not limited to Medicare patients. Every patient who comes to the hospital for acute care is protected by EMTALA. The courts have interpreted the wording "any individual" to mean that EMTALA can apply to any patient who comes to the ED, whether they are denied treatment or not and whether they pay for care or not. EMTALA was designed to remedy economic discrimination by hospitals that deny care or transfer indigent and uninsured patients in unstable medical conditions and to extend protection to any individual who enters a hospital's ED. Most federal appeals courts have applied EMTALA's language to allow any patient to challenge his or her emergency treatment under EMTALA, whether alleging economic discrimination or not. The U.S. Supreme Court settled the question when it ruled that a charge of financial discrimination is immaterial to an EMTALA lawsuit. [*Roberts v. Galen of Virginia*, 525 U.S. 249 (1999)]. "Any individual," then, includes not only the indigent, but also all patients, including minors, illegal aliens, private patients, managed care patients, and psychiatric patients.

Note that when an individual comes to the dedicated ED requesting examination and treatment but the condition is clearly not an emergency, the hospital is only required to perform sufficient screening to determine that the condition is not an emergency. [42 C.F.R. § 489.24(c)]

What does "comes to the emergency department" mean?

EMTALA's provisions apply to patients who "come to the emergency department" and request examination or treatment for a medical condition. The Centers for Medicare and Medicaid Services' final regulations on EMTALA take a broad view of the meaning of this phrase—beyond its common sense meaning. The patient does not have to formally enter the ED. According to final regulations, "comes to" the ED means one of the following has occurred.

A person comes to the hospital's "dedicated emergency department" and requests examination or treatment. A dedicated ED is defined as "any department or facility of the hospital" whether on- or off-campus, which meets one of the following requirements:

- state licensure as an emergency room or ED,
- advertising or holding out to the public as a place that provides emergency care on an urgent basis without a prior appointment, or
- a patient sample demonstrates that one-third of outpatient visits for the treatment of emergency medical conditions took place on an urgent basis without prior appointment.

In the absence of a request, a request will be presumed if a reasonable layperson observer would believe that based on the person's appearance or behavior, the person needs a medical exam or treatment for a medical condition.

A person presents to hospital property and requests an exam or treatment for what may be an emergency medical condition. When no request is made, the reasonable layperson observer standard would apply to presume a request. Hospital property refers to the hospital main campus defined in 42 C.F.R. § 413.65(b), including the parking lot, sidewalks, and driveway, but excludes other buildings not part of the hospital such as physician offices, rural health centers, skilled nursing facilities, or non-medical facilities such as a restaurant or shop.

When a person is in a ground or air ambulance enroute to the hospital, i.e., not on hospital grounds, the hospital owns the ambulance, and transport is to examine and treat the person in the hospital's ED, then the person is considered to have come to the dedicated ED. However, if a hospital-owned ambulance is operated under community protocols that require transport to the nearest facility, the person is considered to have come to the facility to which he or she is transported. If the hospital-owned ambulance is under the direction of a non-employed or non-affiliated physician, the person being transported is not presumed to have come to the hospital.

When a person is in a ground or air ambulance on hospital property for treatment at the hospital's dedicated ED, then the person is considered to have come to the dedicated ED. Even if the ED indicates it is on diversionary status and does not have the staff or facilities to accept any further emergency patients, the person will be considered to have come to the ED if the ambulance staff ignores the comments and brings the person to hospital property. However, if the ambulance transports the person elsewhere because of the diversionary status, then the person is considered to have come to the facility to which he or she transported. [42 C.F.R. § 489.24]

Thus, the final rule excludes off-campus hospital departments that do not routinely provide emergency care from the scope of "coming to the emergency room," and clarifies that a hospital would not have an EMTALA obligation with respect to persons presenting to those departments. A hospital should, however, have appropriate protocols in place for dealing with persons who come to off-campus non-emergency facilities to seek emergency care. [EMTALA Final Rule, 68 Fed. Reg. 53,222 (Sept. 9, 2003)]

Does this also apply to a hospital's helipad?

Where a local EMS system or private ambulance uses the hospital's helipad for the sole purpose of meeting a helicopter not owned by the hospital for transport to another facility,

CMS will not apply the "comes to" rule to require EMTALA compliance by the hospital that owns the helipad.

If the ambulance or flight crew, however, requests assistance in the medical management of the patient, the hospital with the helipad becomes obligated to initiate EMTALA procedures for MSE and for any further transfer compliance. [42 C.F.R. § 413.65, 42 C.F.R. § 489.24]

What happens when a patient is close to the ED, but off hospital property, and needs emergency care?

Under the final regulations, property means the entire main hospital campus, including the parking lot, sidewalk, and driveway. The hospital campus is defined as the physical area immediately adjacent to the main buildings, as well as other areas and structures that are not contiguous but are within 250 yards of the main buildings. The final regulations clarify that an EMTALA obligation arises when someone presents elsewhere on hospital property, not the dedicated ED, and requests treatment for an *emergency* medical condition. Hospital property specifically excluded other buildings such as physician offices, rural health centers, skilled nursing facilities, or non-medical areas like a restaurant or shop. No EMTALA obligation arises for treatment requests in these other areas. [*EMTALA Final Rule*, 68 Fed. Reg. 53,222 (Sept. 9, 2003)]

As a practical matter, those in areas not designated as hospital property can determine whether emergency care can be provided in that location or whether the person should be referred to the ED. Hospital planning should consider the following issues:

- establishing the geographical boundaries of hospital responsibility
- under what circumstances EMS will be called
- under what circumstances hospital personnel will transport the patient
- what personnel will be contacted and called to assist with transport
- who will cover for those personnel if they are called away from patient care areas
- what equipment must be kept available for patient transfer
- to what part of the hospital will the patient be transported
- whether additional insurance is necessary

Are there any limits on when patients in ambulances have "come to" the ED?

As stated above, an individual in an ambulance that is owned and operated by the hospital is normally considered to have "come to" the emergency room of that hospital. Final rules issued by CMS in 2003, however, make an exception in the case of hospital-owned ambulances operating under community-wide EMS protocols. Under the proposed rules, the rule on hospital-owned ambulances does not apply if the ambulance is operating under a community-wide EMS protocol that requires it to transport the individual to a hospital other than the hospital that owns the ambulance. In such a case, the individual is considered to have come to the ED of the hospital to which the individual is transported. [68 Fed. Reg. 53,222 (codified at 42 C.F.R. Part 489)]

An individual in a non-hospital-owned ambulance off hospital property is not normally considered to have come to the ED, even if a member of the ambulance staff contacts the hospital asking to transport a patient to the facility. The hospital may deny access if it is in diversionary status, i.e., it does not have the staff or facilities to accept any additional emergency patients. The capacity of a facility to receive emergency care patients means the ability of the hospital to accommodate the individual patient, including numbers and availability of qualified staff, beds, and equipment, as well as the hospital's past practices of accommodating patients beyond its occupancy limits. [42 C.F.R. § 489.24(b)] However, if the ambulance staff disregards the hospital's instructions, and brings the patient to the facility, the patient has come to the ED and EMTALA applies.

One federal appeals court has ruled, however, that a hospital may not divert a non-hospital-owned ambulance that has contacted the hospital's ED and is enroute to that hospital with a patient unless the hospital is in diversionary status. While transporting a heart attack victim to a Honolulu hospital, ambulance personnel radioed the hospital to advise of their imminent arrival. The ED physician redirected the ambulance to another hospital that was farther away, and the patient died soon after arrival at the other hospital. The trial court dismissed an EMTALA suit because the patient had never "come to" the hospital's emergency room as required by EMTALA, but the appeals court disagreed, finding that "comes to" could mean either physical arrival or the act of traveling to the hospital. Although the patient was in a non-hospital-owned ambulance, the court cited HHS regulations providing that if non-hospital-owned ambulance personnel contact a hospital to advise of their approach with a patient, the hospital may deny access if it is on diversionary status. The court concluded that a hospital may not prevent a non-hospital-owned ambulance from coming to the hospital unless it has a valid treatment-related reason for doing so. [*Arrington v. Wong*, 237 F.3d 1066 (9th Cir. 2001)]

Does EMTALA extend to telephone requests for emergency treatment?

Not ordinarily, unless the patient is on hospital property; however, a telephone call requesting emergency treatment may trigger EMTALA if the call is from a medical facility requesting specialized care from the hospital, such as those provided in a burn unit or trauma unit. Under federal regulations, a hospital with specialized services cannot refuse a telephone request for a transfer. Specifically, the regulations provide that a hospital that has specialized capabilities or facilities may not refuse to accept from a referring hospital an appropriate transfer of an individual who requires such capabilities or facilities if the receiving hospital has the capacity to treat the individual. [42 C.F.R. § 489.24(e) & (f)]. Even a hospital that does not hold itself out as having specialized units may be subject to these regulations; CMS's application of the rule makes it clear that if the requested destination hospital has services and physicians available that are better able to meet a patient's medical needs than the transferring facility, the requested hospital is considered to have specialized capabilities and must accept the transfer.

One federal appeals court has ruled that a telephone request for admission to the ED does not trigger EMTALA. In that case, a seriously injured child was brought to a hospital ED. The general practitioner on duty called an orthopedist at another hospital to request transfer. The orthopedist agreed to treat the patient, but an administrator at the second hospital determined that the patient was not insured and refused the transfer. The patient was treated at a third facility, after a delay of approximately seven hours. The patient's parents sued the second hospital under EMTALA. The hospital defended that EMTALA did not apply because the patient had not come to its facility requesting care. The federal appeals court agreed that the patient was not entitled to sue. Although the patient did request treatment from the second hospital, the patient did not come to that facility, the court emphasized. Equating a telephonic request for treatment with the "comes to" clause would render the clause meaningless, according to the court. [*Miller v. Medical Ctr.*, 22 F.3d 626 (5th Cir. 1994)] This decision, however, did not consider the application of the provisions of EMTALA that require hospitals with specialized capabilities to accept transfers. As such, it is not a reliable indicator of how the law will be enforced, either by CMS or by the courts.

What should a hospital do if a patient will not consent to care?

EMTALA requires not only that a patient come to the ED but also that the patient, or someone acting on the patient's behalf, request an examination or treatment for a medical condition. If a patient withdraws his or her request for treatment, the hospital will not be liable under EMTALA. A hospital satisfies EMTALA if it offers medical examination or treatment and informs the patient of the risks and benefits of the examination or treatment but the patient refuses to consent.

The statute does require hospitals to take "all reasonable steps" to obtain written informed consent to refuse the examination or treatment, however. The medical record should document the exam and treatment refused, and the refusal should outline the risks and benefits of treatment. [42 U.S.C. § 1395dd(b)(2), 42 C.F.R. § 489.24(d)] HCFA explained in its November 1999 Special Advisory Bulletin:

If an individual chooses to withdraw his or her request for examination or treatment at the presenting hospital, and if the hospital is aware that the individual intends to leave prior to the screening examination, a hospital should take the following steps:

- Offer the individual further medical examination and treatment within the staff and facilities available at the hospital as may be required to identify and stabilize an emergency medical condition;
- Inform the individual of the benefits of such examination and treatment, and of the risks of withdrawal prior to receiving such examination and treatment; and
- Take all reasonable steps to secure the individual's written informed consent to refuse such examination and treatment.

The medical record should indicate that the person was informed of the risks and benefits of the examination or treatment or both, if applicable, that was refused, and should contain a specific description of the risks and benefits discussed. It is not sufficient to merely state "risks and benefits explained to patient," or to simply note that the family consented. The record should contain the signature of the refusing individual or person acting on the individual's behalf, or should reflect the reasonable efforts made by the hospital to obtain a written refusal. Adequate documentation is vital because there must be no indication that a patient was coerced into refusing care. Numerous hospitals have been cited for failure to obtain written refusals of care when patients leave the ED prior to screening. If an individual leaves without notifying hospital personnel, the hospital should, at a minimum, document the fact that the person had been there, what time the hospital discovered that the patient had left, and should retain all triage notes and additional records, if any. However, the burden rests with the hospital to show that it has taken appropriate steps to discourage an individual from leaving the hospital without evaluation.

[OIG/HCFA Special Advisory Bulletin on the Patient Anti-Dumping Statute, OIG and HCFA, HHS, 64 Fed. Reg. 61,353 (Nov. 10, 1999)]

May hospital staff seek authorization for payment from a patient's managed care organization (MCO) or insurer before the patient has received a medical screening evaluation (MSE)?

The CMS final rule in 2003 that clarified that hospitals may not seek prior authorization for payment before screening a patient for an emergency medical condition and stabilizing the patient was subsequently adopted in the final rule. However, an emergency physician may contact a patient's regular-care physician for advice based on patient medical history, provided the consultation does not delay screening and stabilization services. Once stabilizing treatment has begun, the hospital may then contact the plan for payment authorization. [68 Fed. Reg. 53,222 (codified at 42 C.F.R. § 489.24)]

How should ED staff respond to patient inquiries regarding the cost of care or eligibility for insurance coverage?

An HCFA (now CMS) advisory bulletin outlines suggested practices to minimize the likelihood that a hospital will violate EMTALA. The advisory suggests that when a patient inquires about financial liability for emergency services, the question should be answered by a staff member who has been well trained in EMTALA compliance. The staff member must clearly inform the patient that notwithstanding the patient's ability to pay, the hospital stands ready and willing to provide a medical screening examination and stabilizing treatment, if necessary. Any patient with a potentially emergency medical condition should be encouraged by hospital staff to remain until after screening. Staff efforts must be fully documented, because "the burden rests with the hospital to show that it has taken appropriate steps to discourage an individual from leaving the hospital without evaluation." [OIG/HCFA Special Advisory Bulletin on the Patient Anti-Dumping Statute, OIG and HCFA, HHS, 64 Fed. Reg. 61,353 (Nov. 10, 1999)]

What is an MSE under EMTALA?

Under EMTALA, if a patient comes to the ED and the patient or someone acting on his or her behalf requests an examination or treatment for a medical condition, the hospital must provide for an appropriate MSE within the capability of its ED, including ancillary services routinely available to the ED, to determine whether an emergency medical condition exists. A hospital cannot delay an MSE, further medical examination, or treatment to inquire about the individual's method of payment or insurance status. [42 U.S.C. §§ 1395dd(a) & (h)]

Where can the MSE take place?

According to guidelines for CMS investigators, the MSE may take place in an area of the hospital other than the ED as long as the MSE takes place in a contiguous part of the facility or on part of the hospital campus operating under the hospital's provider number. Specifically, the MSE may be provided in another hospital department or in a hospital-owned physician office on hospital grounds. Hospitals are cautioned that patients with similar conditions must be provided an MSE in the same manner. That is, patients should not be directed to different parts on the hospital campus based on who their physician is or what managed care plan they are enrolled in. Referring a patient to a managed care physician's office, even if the office is on campus, violates EMTALA because the referral is for insurance purposes rather than for medical benefit. If the MSE is not conducted in the ED, a valid medical reason should support the movement of the patient. Further, qualified medical personnel should accompany the patient on any movements between areas on the hospital campus. [HCFA Site Review Guidelines, State Operations Manual, COBRA Investigations, A406]

Regulations issued in 2003 clarify that EMTALA does not apply to hospital outpatient facilities except the dedicated ED. Therefore, the movement of patients between these locations and the ED does not constitute a transfer under the statute. Movement of a patient to a satellite that is not a hospital department, however, qualifies as a transfer, which triggers a host of regulatory requirements, discussed later in this section. Thus, ED staff must be familiar with the status of each location to which a patient might be moved, to determine whether the movement is a transfer to which EMTALA restrictions and requirements apply. [68 Fed. Reg. 53,222 (Sept. 9, 2003), codified at 42 C.F.R. §§ 409 through 413, 419, 424, 489, 498, & 1003]

How does a court decide whether an MSE meets EMTALA's standards?

Courts have generally held that EMTALA does not allow patients to sue for negligent screening or screening that fails to properly identify an emergency condition. Instead, courts defining "appropriate screening" have typically required hospitals to follow the same screening procedures for similarly situated patients. In other words, courts will examine whether a patient received an MSE consistent with that provided to other individuals with the same complaints or symptoms, as well as whether the MSE was consistent with hospital protocols. [*See, e.g., Correa v. Hospital San Francisco*, 69 F.3d 1184 (1st Cir. 1995), *cert. denied sub nom. Hospital San Francisco v. Gonzalez*, 517 U.S. 1136 (1996) (hospital liable for delaying screening exam in violation if its own procedures); *Bloomer v. Norman Reg. Hosp.*, No. 99-6074 (10th Cir. July 12, 2000) (adequacy of MSE will be judged by hospital compliance with its own screening procedures); *Nolen v. Boca Raton Cmty. Hosp.*, 373 F.3d 1151 (11th Cir. 2004) (hospital provided the same screening it would with another other patient and was not required to have written screening procedures in place)]

What happens if hospital personnel mistakenly overlook a patient's symptoms?

The courts have generally held that, if the MSE performed on a particular patient is consistent with MSEs performed on similar patients and complied with hospital standards, the hospital will only face EMTALA liability for failure to stabilize if staff discovered an emergency medical condition. In other words, the negligent failure to diagnose an emergency condition does not generally constitute an EMTALA violation; the patient must sue under state malpractice law instead. The Eighth Circuit, for example, has held that what constitutes an appropriate MSE depends on the patient's condition as perceived by the treating ED providers, even if that perception is negligent. A patient came to an ED after a fall, complaining of chest pain and a popping noise in his chest. After physicians ordered a spinal X-ray, but no chest X-rays, the patient was discharged. Two days later, the patient went to another hospital where it was discovered that he had a broken vertebra, sternum, and rib. The patient sued the first hospital under COBRA, charging that it did not provide an appropriate MSE. The hospital acknowledged that a chest X-ray should be ordered for patients complaining of popping noises in the chest but defended that the patient stated a negligence claim, not an EMTALA claim. The court ruled in favor of the hospital because EMTALA does not create a malpractice cause of action. The court ruled that a patient arguing that an MSE was not appropriate must show that the screening constituted disparate treatment.

In this case, the patient argued that he received nonuniform treatment because the hospital admitted that a patient complaining of popping noises in the chest would be X-rayed. The court rejected this argument, explaining that a physician is required to screen patients only for the conditions that the physician perceives the patient to have. Finding that the physician, either through inadvertence or inattention, did not perceive the patient to have popping noises in the chest or chest pain, the court ruled that the patient was treated no differently from any other patient perceived to have the same condition. [*Summers v. Baptist Med. Ctr. Arkadelphia*, 91 F.3d 1132 (8th Cir. 1996)] Allegations of failure to diagnose or treat a person are actionable under state medical malpractice law, not EMTALA. EMTALA does not create a federal cause of action for medical malpractice in emergency rooms. [*Vickers v. Nash Gen. Hosp.*, 78 F.3d 139 (4th Cir. 1996); *Reynolds v. Maine General Health*, 218 F.3d 78 (1st Cir. 2000)]

The Ninth Circuit joined the Eighth Circuit and several others in a recent ruling that a hospital does not violate EMTALA when it fails to diagnose the cause of a patient's emergency condition, but treats the symptoms it identifies and concludes that the patient has been stabilized. In that case, the patient presented in the ER and was diagnosed with acute psychosis, but was not found to have an emergency medical (as opposed to a psychiatric) condition. After his discharge he died of a heart attack caused by psychotic delirium, which was in turn caused by drug toxicity. The patient's family sued for the hospital's failure to provide adequate screening under EMTALA. The appeals court agreed with the trial court that the hospital followed its own screening guidelines, and there was no evidence that the screening was so substandard that it violated EMTALA, or that the patient was treated differently from any other patient presenting similar symptoms in the ED. [*Jackson v. East Bay Hosp.*, 246 F.3d 1248 (9th Cir. 2001); *see also, Bryant v. Adventis Health Sys. West*, 289 F.3d 1162 (9th Cir. 2002); *Hunt v. Lincoln County Mem'l Hosp.*, 317 F.3d 891 (8th Cir. 2003)]

Is triage an appropriate MSE?

Many hospital EDs have instituted a triage system, in which patients are screened to determine the order in which they should be examined. Because the purpose of triage differs from the purpose of an MSE under EMTALA (that is, to determine whether an emergency medical condition exists), triage screening does not necessarily satisfy

EMTALA requirements. Note, however, that a federal appeals circuit found that the failure of an ED to follow its triage classifications may give rise to a cause of action for EMTALA. This case involved patient who presented to the ED with chest pain, arm and wrist pain. The hospital triage classification system required a Level 2 triage with a complaint of chest pain, but the doctor triaged the patient at a lower level. The case was to go to trial to determine if the patient had complained of chest pain in the ED. [*Cruz-Queipoetal, et al. v. Hospital Espanol Auxilio Mutuo De Puerto Rico*, No. 04-2375 (1st Cir. July 27, 2005)]

Hospitals must not, after triage, delay an appropriate MSE to obtain financial information from the patient. Hospitals that seek health maintenance organization (HMO) authorization for payment immediately after triage, for example, are in violation of COBRA if the authorization process delays the MSE. Further, triage is often performed by a nurse or physician assistant rather than by a physician, which also raises EMTALA concerns, as discussed below in "Who must perform the MSE?"

Why is dual staffing a problem with respect to the MSE requirement?

As noted above, courts in a variety of jurisdictions have ruled that an "appropriate MSE" is one that is uniformly performed on patients with similar conditions. In a dual staffing system, staff members are assigned to patients depending on the mode of reimbursement, for example, whether the patient is covered by Medicaid or by an HMO. Some managed care companies have "hospitalists," physicians who work solely in the hospital to attend patients under the managed care plan. The managed care plan may dictate that its physician be the only physician to attend to the ED patient. This staffing approach seems inconsistent with the "uniform screening" standard established by the courts, and may expose the hospital to possible EMTALA violations. HCFA (now CMS) has expressed concerns regarding whether dual staffing systems can provide truly consistent treatment of patients in different tracks. A special advisory bulletin stated that dual staffing would not "necessarily constitute a per se violation" of EMTALA, but cautions that certain practices would constitute a violation. For example, a violation would occur if either the managed care or nonmanaged care track were understaffed or overcrowded and patients on one "side" experienced a delay in screening or stabilizing treatment, even though a physician in the alternative track was available to see the patients; if quality oversight plans differ between the two "sides;" or if the protocols for transfer differ between the two sides. [*OIG/ HCFA Special Advisory Bulletin on the Patient Anti-Dumping Statute*, OIG and HCFA, HHS, 64 Fed. Reg. 61,353 (Nov. 10, 1999)] Because dual staffing may inherently create a discrimination in treatment among patients with similar conditions by providing a "separate but equal" track, it is essential that clear and well-detailed criteria and operational practices be enacted in the ED in order to minimize, if not eliminate, any discrepancies between the two tracks. [M.M. Moy, *The EMTALA Answer Book*, 2005 ed. (Aspen Publishers 2005)]

How do EMTALA MSE requirements apply to patients in managed care plans?

In its guidance for COBRA investigators, HCFA (now CMS) has specifically stated, "A managed health care plan (e.g., HMO, PPO) cannot deny a hospital permission to treat its enrollees. It may only state what it will or will not pay for. Regardless of whether a hospital will be paid, it is obligated to provide the services specified in [COBRA]." [HCFA Site Review Guidelines, State Operations Manual, COBRA Investigations, A407]

In addition, the Office of Inspector General (OIG) and HCFA (now CMS) have issued a Special Advisory Bulletin addressing hospitals' responsibility to provide emergency treatment to patients enrolled in managed care, Medicare, and Medicaid plans. The bulletin notes that hospitals routinely seek prior authorization for care for patients in managed care plans, cites the "inherent problems" in seeking prior authorization, and cautions that this practice may improperly influence patients to leave the hospital without receiving an appropriate medical screening examination. The bulletin advises that, "no contract between a hospital and a managed care plan can excuse the hospital from its anti-dumping statute obligations. Once a managed care enrollee comes to a hospital that offers emergency services, the hospital must provide the services . . . without regard for the patient's insurance status or any prior authorization requirement." With regard to Medicare and Medicaid managed care plans, the advisory bulletin notes that the Balanced Budget Act of 1997 requires the federal health plans to pay for emergency services based on a prudent layperson standard. That law also prohibits Medicare and Medicaid from requiring prior authorization for emergency services, including those needed to evaluate or stabilize an emergency medical condition.

Finally, the bulletin outlines suggested practices to minimize the likelihood that a hospital will violate EMTALA. The advisory suggests that hospitals not request prior authorization before screening or stabilization. Nor should staff members ask patients to complete a financial responsibility form or advanced beneficiary notification form before screening. Hospitals should ensure that only qualified medical personnel perform medical screening examinations. Either a physician or a hospital staff member approved by the facility's governing body to perform certain medical functions constitutes qualified medical personnel. When a patient inquires about financial liability for emergency services, the question should be answered by a staff member who has been well trained in EMTALA compliance. The staff member must clearly inform the patient that "notwithstanding the patient's ability to pay, the hospital stands ready and willing to provide a medical screening examination and stabilizing treatment, if necessary." Any patient with a potentially emergency medical condition should be encouraged by hospital staff to remain until after screening. Finally, when a patient chooses to withdraw a request for examination or treatment, a staff member must offer further medical examination and treatment necessary to identify and stabilize an emergency medical condition, inform the patient of the risks and benefits of leaving prior to treatment, and take all reasonable steps to secure the patient's written informed consent to refuse treatment, with full documentation in the medial record. [*OIG/HCFA Special Advisory Bulletin on the Patient Anti-Dumping Statute*, OIG and HCFA, HHS, 64 Fed. Reg. 61,353]

Does a hospital have to provide an MSE to patients who use the ED for routine follow-up?

Some EDs see patients for routine suture removal, follow-up vaccinations, lab work, series of injections, and the like. A hospital could argue that such a patient has not come to the ED seeking examination or treatment and so does not come within EMTALA's medical screening requirement. Hospitals may also decide that an appropriate screening examination satisfying EMTALA requirements for these patients constitutes a cursory visual inspection of the patient and asking whether the patient has any complaints. This issue has not been resolved in the courts. Consideration should be given to how these patients should be entered in the central log, how their status and disposition will be documented, and whether it would be appropriate for them to sign a waiver stating that they are not seeking care for an emergency medical condition.

Who must perform the MSE?

The qualifications for who may perform an MSE are not outlined in the federal regulations. Under EMTALA's regulations, the MSE must be conducted by qualified individuals. Hospital bylaws or rules and regulations must identify which individuals are qualified to perform screening examinations. The decision may not be made on an informal or ad hoc basis [42 C.F.R. §§ 489.24(a) & 482.55] In many hospitals, for example, MSEs of women in labor are performed by experienced registered nurses, advanced practice nurses, or nurse midwives. Where nonphysicians perform the MSE, these individuals must be properly trained, acting under a protocol that clearly delineates the circumstances under which they must consult a physician, and within their permissible scope of practice under both state law and facility privileges. While the MSE should never be referred to as "triage," this is particularly important where nurses or other nonphysicians are performing the MSE.

It is not likely that CMS will completely defer to hospitals to determine who may perform the MSE. Rather, the issue of who is a qualified individual may be questioned under EMTALA, even if a hospital follows its own bylaws and rules. For example, HCFA (now CMS) has cited hospitals that allow nurses to perform MSEs for violating EMTALA. When looking at a hospital's policies on non-physician screening, however, CMS most often finds that a hospital policy has not been complied with, such as instances where non-physicians have exceeded their permissible scope of practice or licensure. CMS has, for example, cited a hospital for a physician assistant who was licensed under state law to see persons over the age of 12, but saw babies and young children in the ED. CMS looks closely at the ED's written policies and may request personnel files to document that all criteria for personnel are met and documented. Lapsed certifications, lack of current copies of licenses, or lack of privileges have resulted in citations on this basis. [M.M. Moy, *The EMTALA Answer Book*, 2005 ed. (Aspen Publishers 2005)]

Requiring physicians, rather than nurses or physician assistants, to screen patients for emergency medical conditions provides the greatest assurance that the person conducting the MSE possesses sufficient training and expertise to be qualified under EMTALA.

Have any courts addressed personnel requirements for MSEs?

At least one federal appeals court has refused to evaluate whether a hospital's policy for allowing nurses to conduct MSEs violates EMTALA. The Tenth Circuit has ruled that a hospital that discharged a patient with chest pain after being examined and treated by a nurse did not violate EMTALA's screening requirement. The patient went to the ED at the instruction of her personal physician, who had called ahead to prescribe a pain shot for her chest pains. A nurse examined the patient, determined that the patient did not suffer an emergency medical condition, administered the prescribed pain shot, and discharged the patient. The patient died that night after a heart attack. The patient's husband sued, claiming that the hospital violated EMTALA by failing to comply with its own policy that requires a physician to examine patients with "life-threatening symptoms of chest pain." The hospital countered that the policy did not apply because the nurse determined that the patient's symptoms were not life-threatening. Rather, the facility complied with a second applicable policy, which allows nursing personnel to evaluate patients with conditions with low complexity and low possibility of morbidity, the hospital argued. Reading the two policies in combination, the court determined that hospital policy requires evaluation by a physician for a patient complaining of chest pain only if nursing personnel determines the patient has life-threatening symptoms. The court refused to assess the adequacy of the hospital's policies under EMTALA. Courts may determine only whether a hospital followed its own policies, the Tenth Circuit concluded, not whether the policies themselves constitute an appropriate screening policy under EMTALA. [*Cunningham v. Fredonia Reg'l Hosp.*, No. 95-3350 (10th Cir. Oct. 11, 1996) (unpublished)]

Unlike the courts, CMS has not been reluctant to subjectively evaluate a hospital's policies and its relative adequacy in individual cases, and has issued citations to hospitals on non-physician screening issues. Thus, it is probably more valuable to look to CMS standards than to court decisions in guiding ED practices regarding personnel requirements for MSEs.

How should hospitals meet the MSE requirements when a community protocol to perform screening of exposed individuals exists?

As a result of the widespread fears in the fall of 2001 about potential bioterrorism, and in particular, the exposure of numerous individuals to anthrax, CMS issued a program memorandum to its regional administrators, clarifying hospitals' EMTALA obligations when staff encounter situations related to the actual or potential exposure to a biological agent. CMS acknowledged that in certain circumstances, referral of a potentially exposed patient prior to the actual MSE would be appropriate. Specifically, there could be cases in which state or local governments have developed community response plans that designate specific entities, such as hospitals or public health facilities, with responsibility for handling certain categories of patient in bioterrorism situations. The transfer or referral of these patients in accordance with such a community plan would not violate the hospital's EMTALA obligations. If, for example, a potentially exposed patient presented at an undesignated hospital, after questioning the patient and determining that the patient falls into the category for which the community has a specified screening site, that hospital could refer the patient to the designated community facility without violating EMTALA. [CMS Memorandum to Regional Administrators, *Question and Answer Relating to Bioterrorism and EMTALA*, Ref. S&C-02-04, Nov. 8, 2001] The 2003 final rule clarified that EMTALA does not apply to a dedicated ED located in an emergency area during a national emergency. [68 Fed. Reg. 53,222 (Sept. 9, 2003), codified at 42 C.F.R. § 489.24]

What is an emergency medical condition under EMTALA?

Under the regulations, an emergency medical condition is a "medical condition manifesting itself by acute symptoms (including severe pain, psychiatric disturbances, and/or symptoms of substance abuse)" of sufficient severity such that the absence of immediate medical attention could reasonably be expected to result in

- "placing the health of the individual (or, with respect to a pregnant woman, the health of the woman or her unborn child) in serious jeopardy"
- "serious impairment to bodily functions"
- "serious dysfunction of any bodily organ or part"

In the case of a woman having contractions, an emergency also exists when there is "inadequate time to effect a safe transfer to another hospital" before she delivers or when "that transfer may pose a threat to the health or safety of the woman or the unborn child." [42 C.F.R. § 489.24(b)]

When does a patient with psychiatric symptoms have an emergency medical condition under EMTALA?

Under COBRA interpretive guidance, a patient is considered to have an emergency medical condition if he or she expresses suicidal or homicidal thoughts or gestures, or is determined to be dangerous to self or others. [HCFA Site Review Guidelines, State Operations Manual, COBRA Investigations, A406]

What must a hospital do when a patient has an emergency medical condition?

If the MSE reveals an emergency medical condition, the hospital must either stabilize the patient or arrange for an appropriate transfer in accordance with EMTALA. The requirements for stabilization and transfer are discussed below.

What if the hospital does not discover an emergency medical condition?

The requirements of EMTALA do not apply unless an emergency medical condition exists. Therefore, hospitals are not obligated to provide screening services beyond those needed to determine that there is no emergency. Once an appropriate medical screening examination has been performed, if no emergency medical condition is revealed, the hospital may properly refer an individual to an outpatient clinic for nonemergency care. This was illustrated by a Tenth Circuit case in which a hospital was not liable for discharging a high-risk pregnancy patient after a nonreactive stress test. A nurse at a hospital's obstetrics department administered the test, which indicated no fetal movement, and consulted with a physician. The nurse then instructed the patient, expecting twins, to return to the hospital the next morning for another stress test. When the patient returned the next morning, test results indicated no movement or breathing in either fetus. One twin was stillborn, and the other was born with brain damage. The patient and her family sued the hospital, arguing that discharging her after the first stress test in an unstabilized, emergency condition violated EMTALA. The hospital asserted that EMTALA does not impose liability if a hospital lacks actual knowledge that an emergency exists.

The court agreed that the hospital was not liable. Following the Fourth, Sixth, and D.C. Circuits, the court ruled that the stabilization requirement of EMTALA is triggered only if a hospital determines that a patient has an emergency medical condition. In this case, the patient did not meet the statute's definition of emergency because she did not exhibit severe "acute symptoms." Because the hospital did not have actual knowledge of an emergency condition, the court ruled in favor of the hospital. [*Urban v. King*, 43 F.3d 523 (10th Cir. 1994)]

Similarly, when a family claimed that EMTALA screening and stabilization was violated when a man died from deep vein thrombosis after release from the hospital, the court disagreed. The man had come into the ED for leg and foot fractures, had two surgeries for the fractures and was released from the hospital where he then died. The family contended that a family history of coagulation problems required evaluation of deep vein thrombosis prior to hospital discharge. The court found that EMTALA focused on emergency room stabilization and treatment which the man received before being transferred to the hospital as an inpatient for the surgeries. His admission to the hospital demonstrated adequate EMTALA screening and stabilization. A failure to diagnose the DVT might be actionable as a state medical malpractice claim, but the EMTALA claim was dismissed. [*Reynolds v. Maine General Health*, 218 F.3d 78 (1st Cir. 2000)]

What if no emergency psychiatric condition is discovered upon screening but the patient later harms himself or herself?

Just as with patients who present with medical conditions, a hospital's duty under EMTALA to a patient with a psychiatric condition is to provide an appropriate medical screening, which generally means that the MSE is performed uniformly for patients with identical symptoms, and in accordance with hospital standards. If that MSE nonetheless fails to identify an emergency medical condition and the patient who is discharged later harms himself or herself, the likelihood of hospital liability under EMTALA is low. A medical malpractice claim remains a possibility, however.

A federal district court in North Carolina illustrated this when it held that a hospital's duty to provide stabilizing treatment under EMTALA does not arise unless the hospital has actual knowledge of the emergency medical condition. A patient came to a hospital emergency room suffering from depression and anxiety, and after a physical exam, blood tests, review of his medical history, and a psychiatric evaluation which resulted in a seven-page report by a psychiatric social worker, it was determined he had bipolar disorder and had not been taking his medication. Because it was determined that the patient did not present a threat to himself or others, he was discharged with instructions to go to a mental health facility and return to the hospital if he felt worse. Three days later, unable to obtain an appointment at the mental health facility, the patient committed suicide, and his survivors sued the hospital under EMTALA, claiming the hospital failed to stabilize the patient before discharging him. The federal district court held that the hospital had no duty to provide stabilizing treatment, because the plain language of EMTALA requires that the hospital staff have actual knowledge of the emergency medical condition in order to trigger a duty to stabilize. Even assuming that the patient had an emergency medical condition, there was no evidence that the hospital had actual knowledge of it; to the contrary, hospital records indicated that the patient was not suffering from an emergency medical condition and was stable. The court pointed to case law holding that EMTALA does not impose any duty on a hospital requiring that screening result in a correct diagnosis. Therefore, whether this diagnosis was correct was not an issue in a suit under EMTALA, although it might be addressed in a suit for malpractice under state law. [*Pettyjohn v. Mission St. Joseph's Health Sys.*, No. 1:99cv171-C (W.D.N.C. Jan. 8, 2001 (unpublished), *aff'd*, 21 Fed. Appx. 193 (4th Cir. 2001); *Thomas v. Christ Hosp. and Med. Ctr.*, 328 F.3d 890 (7th Cir. 2003), in which the court said that whether the person, who subsequently harmed herself, was stabilized as required under EMTALA was a question of fact]

What does "stabilize" mean under EMTALA?

According to the regulations, "to stabilize" means to provide such medical treatment of the emergency medical "condition necessary to assure, within reasonable medical probability, that no material deterioration of the condition is likely to result from or occur during the transfer of the individual from a facility or that . . . (in the case of a woman in labor) the woman has delivered the child and the placenta." [42 C.F.R. § 489.24(b)]

CMS guidance to COBRA investigators has elaborated on this definition, distinguishing between patients stable for discharge and patients stable for transfer.

A patient is stable for discharge "when, within reasonable clinical confidence, it is determined that the patient has reached the point when his/her continued care, including diagnostic work-up and/or treatment, could be reasonably performed as an outpatient or later as an inpatient, provided the patient is given a plan for appropriate follow-up care with the discharge instructions."

A patient is stable for transfer when the treating physician has determined with reasonable clinical confidence, that the patient is expected to leave the hospital and be received at the second facility, with no material deterioration in his/her medical condition; and the treating physician reasonably believes the receiving facility has the capability to manage the patient's medical condition and any reasonably foreseeable complication of that condition. [HCFA Site Review Guidelines, State Operations Manual, COBRA Investigations, A407]

When is a psychiatric patient stable under COBRA?

A patient may only be transferred to another facility without following COBRA procedures or discharged for follow-up care if he or she is stable. HCFA (now CMS) has developed a two-part definition of "stable" for patients with psychiatric conditions, which has one meaning that applies to transfer eligibility, and another for discharge eligibility. For purposes of *transferring* a psychiatric patient from one facility to a second facility, the patient is considered to be stable "when he/she is protected and prevented from injuring himself/herself or others." Chemical or physical restraints may stabilize a psychiatric patient for a period of time so that the presenting emergency medical condition is removed; however, the underlying medical condition may persist and if left untreated may exacerbate the emergency medical condition. Thus, care should be taken in determining whether a patient is truly stable. [HCFA Site Review Guidelines, State Operations Manual, COBRA Investigations, A407]

It must be noted, however, that the use of both chemical and physical restraints are limited by the Medicare Conditions of Participation, as described under Patient Rights, above.

How does the stabilization requirement apply when treatment is medically futile?

A controversial case has addressed the tension between the duty to stabilize and physician reluctance to provide medically futile treatment. EMTALA requires a hospital to resuscitate an anencephalic infant, according to a federal appeals court in Virginia. Shortly after an infant was born missing a substantial portion of her brain, a hospital recommended that the infant's mother authorize a do not resuscitate (DNR) order because aggressive treatment would serve no therapeutic or palliative purpose. The mother refused to authorize a DNR order and transferred the infant to a nearby nursing home. The infant was subsequently readmitted to the hospital three times for respiratory assistance. The hospital sought a court declaration that it was not required to provide treatment other than warmth, nutrition, and hydration should the infant be hospitalized for respiratory distress again. The hospital argued that EMTALA did not require treatment beyond this standard of care and that Virginia physicians could refuse to administer medically and ethically inappropriate treatment.

The court rejected those arguments and ruled that the hospital's refusal to resuscitate the infant would violate EMTALA. The court noted that the statute plainly requires the hospital to prevent the infant's condition from deteriorating. Respiratory distress, not anencephaly, was the condition requiring emergency treatment, the court ruled, reasoning that the hospital must resuscitate the infant as it would any other patient in respiratory distress. Neither the statute nor its legislative history created an exception for treatment beyond the standard of care, the court held. The court also concluded that EMTALA overrides state law regarding a physician's right to refuse to administer treatment and ruled that the hospital would violate the statute if it refused to resuscitate the infant in the future. [*In re Baby "K,"* 16 F.3d 590 (4th Cir. 1994), *cert. denied,* 513 U.S. 825 (1994)]

Does the stabilization requirement apply to areas of the hospital other than the ED?

This has been one of the most hotly debated issues related to EMTALA. While at least one early court case found that EMTALA applied to patients admitted to the hospital, the final rule has taken an opposing position. The final rule clarifies that when a person is admitted to the hospital for stabilization of an emergency medical condition, then the ED EMTALA responsibility has been fulfilled. Inpatient admission means the person is received for inpatient care and occupies a bed, even if the person is subsequently discharged or transferred before occupying a bed overnight. When individuals are already patients of the hospital, with an established relationship that includes previously arranged medical appointments, they are not considered to have "come to the hospital" for reasons that would be covered under EMTALA. [68 Fed. Reg. 53,222 (codified at 42 C.F.R. § 489.24)]

When may a hospital transfer a patient in an emergency medical condition?

An individual in an emergency medical condition who has not been stabilized can be transferred only if one of the following conditions is met.

- The transfer is appropriate as outlined below.
- The individual (or a legally responsible person acting on the individual's behalf), after being informed of the hospital's obligations and of the risk of transfer, requests

transfer in writing, indicating the reasons for the request and that risks of transfer are known, may then transfer to another facility.

- A physician (or other qualified person in consultation with a physician when a physician is not physically present) "has signed a certification that, based on the information available at the time of transfer, the medical benefits reasonably expected from the provision of medical treatment at another medical facility outweigh the increased risks to the individual or, in the case of labor, to the woman or unborn child, from effecting the transfer." The certification should include a summary or risks and benefits of the transfer.
- If a physician is not physically present in the ED, a qualified medical person has signed a certification after consultation with a physician who subsequently countersigns the certification. [42 C.F.R. § 489.24(e)]

A transfer is appropriate if:

- The transferring hospital provides medical treatment within its capacity that minimizes the risks to the individual's health or the health of the unborn child, in case of labor.
- The receiving facility has available space and qualified personnel to treat the individual and has agreed to accept the transfer and to provide treatment.
- The transferring hospital sends to the receiving facility all medical records (or copies) related to the emergency condition, available at transfer, including observations of signs or symptoms, preliminary diagnosis, and treatment provided; results of any tests and the informed consent to transfer or the physician's certification; and the name and address of any on-call physician who has refused or failed to appear within a reasonable time to provide necessary stabilizing treatment.
- The transfer is effected through qualified personnel and transportation equipment, including the use of necessary and medically appropriate life support measures.
- The transfer meets any other requirements the Secretary of DHHS finds necessary to the health and safety of the individual. [42 C.F.R. § 489.24(e)]

What considerations apply when a hospital seeks to transfer or discharge a psychiatric patient?

As with all patients, EMTALA procedures must be followed when a patient with a psychiatric condition is transferred (i.e., either the patient is stable or a physician has certified that the benefits of transfer outweigh the risks, the patient has consented to transfer, the receiving hospital has agreed, etc.). (See the previous questions and answers.) The level of medical support necessary for transfer must also be considered. Use of ambulance transport and escort by qualified medical personnel may protect the patient from harm during transport, as well as shield the transferring hospital from EMTALA exposure. Transport via police car does not likely satisfy EMTALA requirements. Likewise, transport of a patient with suicidal or homicidal ideations by private car is not advised.

What if a patient refuses to consent to a transfer?

If a hospital offers to transfer the individual and informs the individual of the risks and benefits of the transfer but the individual refuses to consent, the hospital will have fulfilled its obligation under EMTALA. The hospital chart must indicate that the patient has been informed of the risks and benefits of the transfer and state the reasons for the person's refusal. The chart must also contain a description of the proposed transfer that was refused by or on behalf of the patient, the risks and benefits of the transfer, and the reasons for the refusal of the transfer. [42 C.F.R. § 489.24(d)]

How do state civil commitment statutes affect a hospital's duty to psychiatric patients?

State civil commitment procedures generally apply when a patient poses a threat to himself or herself, or others, and refuses needed treatment or transfer. Civil commitment statutes vary by state. However, most laws provide

- criteria for involuntary detention or commitment
- a brief initial period of emergency detention for treatment or evaluation
- an opportunity to petition for longer periods of detention
- a procedure for release when the symptoms of mental illness and dangerousness have been alleviated

Because state civil commitment laws and procedures vary, it is important for ED personnel to be aware of the particular requirements in their jurisdiction and be prepared to carry out whatever the law requires.

May hospitals refuse to accept a patient transfer?

A hospital that has specialized capabilities (such as burn units or neonatal intensive care units) cannot refuse to accept an appropriate transfer of an individual who requires such specialized capabilities if the hospital has the capacity to treat the individual. [42 C.F.R. § 489.24(e)] However, EMTALA does not address lateral transfers between hospitals of equal capabilities. Thus, a hospital without specialized units may refuse a transfer without violating EMTALA. This was illustrated by a Sixth Circuit case that held that the mother of a patient who died of injuries resulting from an accidental gunshot wound could not sue the multiple hospitals that refused to accept the patient because the patient had not "come to" any of those hospitals under the meaning of EMTALA. The patient sought treatment at a hospital ED that did not have a surgeon available. The ED physician contacted five other hospitals, all of which refused the patient's transfer. The patient died two hours after he arrived at the ED. His mother sued the hospitals that refused to accept the patient, alleging that they had breached their duty to provide emergency treatment under EMTALA. The appeals court dismissed the claims. The EMTALA duty to provide screening for and stabilization of emergency conditions is triggered only when a patient comes to the ED, the court explained. In this case, the patient was not physically presented to any of the hospitals that refused transfer. Acknowledging that EMTALA requires hospitals with specialized capabilities to accept a transfer if they have the capacity to treat a patient, the court ruled that the lawsuit failed to state this type of claim because the suit did not directly or indirectly allege that any of the hospitals had specialized capabilities or that they had the capacity to treat the patient. [*Fingers v. Jackson-Madison County Gen. Hosp. Dist.*, No. 95-5903 (6th Cir. Nov. 21, 1996) (unpublished)]

The incident that gave rise to this case occurred prior to CMS regulations issued in 1994 that focused on the availability of specific equipment, specialties, services, or levels of care that are not available at the sending hospital to constitute "specialty capabilities" of the receiving hospital. The case did not follow the later regulations in coming to a decision. Thus, if there is a mechanical failure of equipment, no ICU beds available, or an on-call physician is not available due to being currently in surgery or if the hospital does not have a specialist in the needed area of practice, CMS has found that the requested receiving facility must accept the transfer. [M.M. Moy, *The EMTALA Answer Book*, 2005 ed. (Aspen Publishers 2005) citing CMS, State Operations Manual, Tag No. A411]. Under federal law, courts are required to defer to the interpretation of the regulatory agency unless patently in controvention of the law. Using CMS's standards, the availability of the specialist in the above case created an obligation to accept the patient.

What is "reverse dumping" under EMTALA?

Reverse dumping occurs when a hospital emergency room refuses to accept an appropriate transfer of a patient that requires the specialized capabilities the hospital offers. The refusal by a physician to receive a patient needing the care the hospital is equipped to provide is binding on the hospital and can expose the hospital to liability for reverse dumping. In order for a transferring hospital to make a transfer, the consent of the receiving hospital is required when the patient is unstable.

A person was involved in an automobile accident on a highway outside the city and was taken to a small regional hospital outside the city. The man was diagnosed with a life-threatening injury to his abdominal aorta which required surgery the small hospital was not capable of performing. The doctor at the small hospital called to arrange transfer to a city hospital. Doctors at the city hospital refused to accept the transfer even though the city hospital had the capacity and capability of performing the surgery. The court found that the city hospital was bound by the actions of the ED physicians who declined the transfer. [*St. Anthony Hosp. v. United States Dep't of Health & Human Servs.*, 309 F.3d 680 (10th Cir. 2002)]

What is EMTALA's transfer certificate requirement?

EMTALA requires an express written certification for all unstabilized transfers. Physician certification cannot simply be implied from the findings in the medical record and the fact that the patient was transferred. The transfer certificate must meet EMTALA requirements. Although technically, EMTALA requires certification only if a patient has an emergency medical condition that has not been stabilized, the most prudent policy would be for ED staff to fill out certificates for every transfer. The important elements that the certificate must include are: patient condition, risks and benefits of transfer, receiving hospital, mode of transportation, signed consent by the patient or legally responsible person, and certification by the transferring physician.

How has CMS interpreted the transfer certification requirement?

The statement of risks and benefits is often the source of EMTALA citations. CMS does not permit a purely "check in the box" form; at least one handwritten risk and benefit should be entered. ED physicians must be aware that the reason for transfer is not the same as the benefit of transfer. HCFA has cited hospitals for listing benefits merely as "higher level of care," "to PICU," "Trauma Center," and "equipment not available here." CMS expects the statement of benefits to explain specifically what the destination hospital can provide that the transferring hospital cannot. Unlike the examples above, the statement of benefits should identify the exact service, specialty care, level of care, or equipment that the patient needs that is not currently available at the transferring hospital. For example, if the transfer is for an MRI and the transferring hospital has an MRI, the statement of benefits should explain, "Our MRI is down."

CMS also expects the possible risks to be expressly stated if they include death or disability. Failure to list known risks in sufficient detail for the patient to understand may result in citation, possible fines, and potential civil liability for the hospital and the physician. Often physicians simply enter "none" in this section, but CMS has cited this as not entered in good faith. Again, the statement of risks should be handwritten; preprinted risks such as traffic accidents are helpful, but are not sufficient. At the very least, all transfers pose a risk of increased pain from the vibration and jolting involved in a routine ambulance transport, and the best procedure is to note this.

How have courts interpreted physicians' duty to certify transfers?

At least two federal appeals courts interpreting EMTALA have examined whether a physician actually deliberated the risks and benefits of transfer. EMTALA certification must be a true assessment, not merely a signature, according to one of the first cases to arise under the law. The Fifth Circuit ruled that a physician's failure to weigh the medical risks and benefits before transferring a severely hypertensive woman in active labor violated the law. Although the physician had signed the "Physician's Certificate Authorizing Transfer," the court concluded that he had not engaged in a meaningful weighing of the risks and benefits. [*Burditt v. United States Dep't of Health & Human Servs.*, 934 F.2d 1362 (5th Cir. 1991)]

On the other hand, the Ninth Circuit has ruled that a hospital did not violate EMTALA by failing to enumerate the risks and benefits of a patient's transfer on a form if the hospital could show that a physician actually considered the medical risks and benefits. An infant arrived at a hospital ED having seizures. Unable to control the seizures, a physician decided to transfer the infant to a larger hospital with a pediatric intensive care unit. Before transfer, the physician filled out a certification form, checking a box to confirm that the benefits of transfer outweighed the risks to the patient. The physician did not summarize the medical risks and benefits as the form required, however. The infant was transferred but became quadriplegic as a result of the seizures. Her guardian sued the first hospital under EMTALA, relying on the section of the statute requiring the transferring physician to include a written summary of the risks and benefits to the patient. The federal appeals court refused to impose EMTALA liability. Although the hospital violated a "record-keeping" provision of the law, the court acknowledged, the purpose of the statute was satisfied, as evidence demonstrated that the physician deliberated over the risks and benefits before signing the transfer certification form. [*Vargas ex rel. Gallardo v. Del Puerto Hosp.*, 98 F.3d 1202 (9th Cir. 1996)]

What is the hospital's duty under EMTALA with regard to posting signs?

The law requires a hospital to conspicuously post signs specifying the rights of individuals under EMTALA with respect to examination and treatment for emergency medical conditions and women in labor, and to indicate whether or not the hospital participates in the Medicaid program. [42 C.F.R. § 489.20(q)] The signs should be posted in a place likely to be noticed by all persons entering the ED, as well as persons waiting for examination and treatment, and must be clearly readable from the patient's perspective. Signs in general waiting areas must be readable from a distance of 20 feet. Signs must also be posted in all other areas covered by EMTALA, such as obstetrics, psych assessment, and out-patient clinic areas.

CMS has required hospitals investigated for EMTALA violations to post signs advising the public that the hospital is obligated to provide screening for emergency medical conditions without regard to their ability to pay. CMS has also found an EMTALA violation in a hospital that posted signs stating that if an ED visit turned out not to be a true emergency, the patient would be responsible for the bill. This was despite state Medicaid rules that required such posting. CMS surveyors have also cautioned hospitals that signs similar to those stating "Payment for services due at discharge" may violate EMTALA. The rationale is that these signs may discourage patients from remaining in the ED until they have undergone an MSE. While it is not certain that a citation for this type of sign would be upheld, administrators should consider how the usefulness of the sign balances against CMS's concern.

Can managed care organizations be held responsible for EMTALA violations?

Generally, the hospital alone will be fined for violating EMTALA, even where the transfer or referral was at the behest of a patient's managed care plan. A federal trial court in Illinois, for example, refused to apply EMTALA to a utilization review company. The court held that the EMTALA provision creating a patient's right to sue specifically limits its application to instances in which a Medicare-participating hospital violated EMTALA. [*Bangert v. Christian Health Servs.*, No. 92-613 (S.D. Ill. Dec. 17, 1992) (unpublished)] Similarly, HMOs are not subject to liability for failing to satisfy EMTALA's requirements. [*Dearmas v. Av-Med, Inc.*, 814 F. Supp. 1103 (S.D. Fla. 1993)] Managed care organizations may be subject to liability, however, under other federal or state laws, such as the Social Security Act [42 U.S.C. § 1395f, 1395mm], for failing to provide medically necessary services, including emergency services, to enrollees.

What are on-call requirements under EMTALA?

EMTALA requires a hospital to provide emergency screening or treatment. The hospital should have a list of physicians who are on call after the initial exam to stabilize an individual with an emergency medical condition. The capability of a hospital to provide services is based on the skills of specialists who have staff privileges and who are required to provide on-call services. The hospital has discretion to maintain the on-call list in a manner to best meet patient needs. A hospital is not required to have a specialist on call at all times, but should have policies and procedures to follow when a certain specialty is not available. When a specialist is not available, the hospital will lack the capacity to treat patients requiring that specialty and can appropriately transfer the patient. Hospitals are expected to provide services based on the availability of physicians on call. However, if a physician is on call and does not respond as required, there could be EMTALA liability.

In determining whether a hospital has established reasonable on-call coverage, CMS will look at all relevant factors such as the number of physicians on staff, other demands of the physicians, the frequency of patients requiring certain on-call physicians, and provisions the hospital has made when someone of a certain specialty is not available. CMS requirements do not preclude a hospital from exempting senior medical staff from on-call duties based on years of service or age or both as long as patient care is not adversely affected. The hospital must list individual physicians on its on-call list; the name of a physician group is not sufficient. CMS leaves the hospital flexibility to implement an on-call schedule that works well with its community and medical staff. [*CMS Program Memorandum on On-Call Requirements-EMTALA*, S & C 02-34 (June 13, 2002)] Final regulations give hospitals discretion in contracting for on-call specialists. [*EMTALA Final Rule*, 68 Fed. Reg. 53,222 (Sept. 9, 2003)]

Under EMTALA, can a physician be on call at more than one hospital simultaneously?

EMTALA requires an on-call list to be maintained in a manner that best meets the needs of patients. This may include allowing physicians to be on call at more than on hospital simultaneously. Each hospital involved should be aware of the on-call schedule. Medical staff bylaws or policies and procedures should define the requirement of an on-call physician to respond, examine, and treat patients. The policies and procedures should also clarify how it will handle the situation when the primary specialist is not available or the on-call physician can't respond because of unavoidable conditions. This may include a backup call schedule or transfer of the patient. Allowing physicians simultaneous call does not relieve the hospital of its EMTALA obligation.

In determining whether the on-call list meets the needs of patients, CMS. Will look at all relevant factors such as physicians on staff, other demands on the physicians, frequency of services needed, and provisions the hospital has made for situations in which specialty is not available. Thus, a reasonable approach is taken to review of on-call scheduling. [*EMTALA Final Rule*, 68 Fed. Reg. 53,222 (Sept. 9, 2003) and *CMS Program Memorandum on Simultaneous On-Call Responsibilities*, S & C 02-35 (June 13, 2002)]

Can physicians be liable for EMTALA violations?

Courts have ruled that physicians cannot be found liable under EMTALA. However, EMTALA's administrative civil money penalties do apply to physicians. A physician responsible for the examination, treatment, or transfer of an individual (including a physician on call) who negligently violates the law is subject to a civil money penalty of up to $50,000 per violation. If the violation is gross and flagrant or repeated, the physician is subject to exclusion from Medicare and Medicaid. [42 U.S.C. § 1395dd(d)(1)]

Physicians and other individuals should also note that state laws may provide for individual liability. Further, hospitals found liable for EMTALA violations may be able to recover from the individuals who actually committed the violations, including physicians. A federal trial court in Louisiana has held that a hospital may recover damages from the independent staff physician directly responsible for its EMTALA violation. [*McDougal v. Lafourche Hosp. Serv. Dist. No. 3*, No. 92-2006 (E.D. La. May 25, 1993) (unpublished)] However, a federal trial court in Kansas ruled that a jury award could not be apportioned between a hospital and a physician in an EMTALA suit, even though the jury attributed specific percentages of fault to each party. The court did note that the hospital could bring a separate indemnity claim against the physician to recover the damages attributable to his negligence. [*Griffith v. Mt. Carmel Med. Ctr.*, 842 F. Supp. 1359 (D. Kan. 1994)] Another federal court dismissed claims against the physicians and only allowed hospital EMTALA claims to proceed. [*Binkley v. Edward Hosp.*, 2004 U.S. Dist. LEXIS 18838 (N.D. Ill. 2004)]

What are the penalties for a hospital that violates EMTALA?

The government may fine a hospital that negligently violates EMTALA up to $50,000 (or up to $25,000 for hospitals with less than 100 beds) for each violation. Hospitals that fail to substantially meet the EMTALA requirements are also subject to suspension or termination of their Medicare provider agreements. [42 U.S.C. § 1395dd(d)(1), 42 C.F.R. § 489.53] Although many hospitals have been fined, few have been terminated.

In calculating the penalty amount for EMTALA violations, HHS/OIG will also consider "other instances" of patient dumping. In a final rule issued in March 2002, penalties imposed for a violation of EMTALA may reflect other, unrelated instances where an ED failed to provide appropriate emergency medical screening, stabilization, and treatment of persons coming to the ED or to effect an appropriate transfer. [67 Fed. Reg. 11,928 (2002) (codified in 42 C.F.R. Parts 1001, 1003, 1005 and 1008)] The "other instances" that may be considered include anything that is relevant to the hospital's culpability, regardless of whether they resulted in convictions or judicial or administrative decisions, and also regardless of when they occurred, so that HHS/OIG can consider prior events as well as those that occurred after the incident for which penalties are being assessed. Thus, the method of determining civil monetary penalties will impose greater fines on hospitals with multiple abuses rather than treating them like those with a single violation.

Liability is another potential consequence of EMTALA violations, as illustrated by the cases discussed earlier. An individual who suffers personal harm as a direct result of a hospital's violation of the law can sue the hospital for damages. A medical facility that suffers a financial loss as a direct result of a hospital's violation of EMTALA (a transferee hospital, for example) can also sue the hospital for damages. [42 U.S.C. § 1395dd(d)(2)] EMTALA does not, however, permit private parties to sue to terminate a hospital's provider agreement. [*Deberry v. Sherman Hosp. Ass'n*, 775 F. Supp. 1159 (N.D. Ill. 1991)] EMTALA violations may also lead to investigations under Hill-Burton (described below), state laws regarding patient admissions, and Joint Commission on Accreditation of Healthcare Organizations (Joint Commission) accreditation.

How likely is a CMS investigation?

CMS has dedicated significant resources to investigate EMTALA violations. Between 1986 and 1996, $1.45 million in settlements and judgments were levied. In fiscal year 1999 by contrast, 61 settlements resulted in penalties of more than $1.7 million. ED administrators should note that CMS investigation or citation may trigger lawsuits by patients who, after reading press reports of the CMS investigation, believe their care violated EMTALA.

In 2004, Interpretive Guidelines were released by CMS explaining the current approach to EMTALA investigation. CMS will investigate based on complaints of EMTALA violations. The investigation will focus on the initial allegation as well as whether other EMTALA infractions have taken place. The investigation is unannounced and will include the following steps:

- entrance conference
- case selection
- record review
- interviews
- exit conference
- professional team review (M.D. peer review), and
- assessment of compliance or deficiency.

The CMS process provides for sharing information on the findings and giving the hospital a chance to share information on its compliance. [*Interpretive Guidelines—Responsibilities of Medicare Participating Hospitals in Emergency Cases*, SOM—Appendix V (May 21, 2004)]

Hill-Burton

What is Hill-Burton?

The Hospital Survey and Construction Act of 1944, commonly known as the Hill-Burton Act, requires facilities receiving financial assistance under the Act to provide a reasonable volume of services to patients who cannot pay for such care. Under the regulations, a facility must provide uncompensated services at a certain level to comply with Hill-Burton. [42 U.S.C. §§ 291 through 291c-1] The duty to provide uncompensated care lasts 20 years for hospitals that received funds under Title VI. Many hospitals have now satisfied their uncompensated care obligation. Receiving Hill-Burton funds also triggers a community service assurance, which does not expire.

What does Hill-Burton require EDs to do?

The Hill-Burton regulations require facilities under an uncompensated care obligation to provide notice that uncompensated services are available. This is accomplished by notices published in newspapers with a general circulation; notices posted in the admissions area, ED, and business office of the hospital; and notices given to individuals. The posted notices, furnished by DHHS, must be printed in English and Spanish, as well as any other language spoken by more than 10 percent of the population in the hospital's service area. Before care is initiated, individual notice must be given to each person who seeks service, except in the case of an emergency. In an emergency, it should be given to the next of kin or to the patient as soon as it is practical to do so. Notice must be provided before the bill for services is presented. Once the notice is given, the patient must actually request that care be provided. The notice must clearly indicate the eligibility standards and the procedure to follow to apply for care. It should also indicate that providing uncompensated care is a legal obligation of the hospital and that the hospital will make a written determination on a patient's request by a specific date. [42 C.F.R. § 124.504]

What are the consequences of failing to provide Hill-Burton notice?

The ramifications of failing to provide notice can be severe. At least one court has ruled that a hospital's failure to notify a medically indigent ED patient of the potential availability of free or reduced-cost health care under the Hill-Burton Act bars that hospital from later suing to collect its bill. [*Hospital Ctr. v. Cook*, 426 A.2d 526 (N.J. Super. Ct. App. Div. 1981), *see also Cooper Med. Ctr. v. Boyd*, 430 A.2d 261 (N.J. Super. Ct. App. Div. 1981) and *Yale New Haven Hosp. v. Mitchell*, 683 A.2d 1362 (Conn. 1995)] At least one court has limited private action to those who applied for and were improperly denied funds while the uncompensated service fund was in operation, thereby limiting recovery by a widow whose application was denied because the hospital did not have a compensation program in operation believing it had met its quota under the statute. The hospital's failure to operate the program was remedied by prospective program implementation, not by privately compensating the widow. [*White v. Moses Taylor Hosp.*, 841 F. Supp. 629 (M.D. Pa. 1992)] Another court ruled, however, that the U.S. government violated the 1979 Hill-Burton regulations when it refused to give a hospital credit toward its uncompensated care obligation on the grounds that the hospital was in technical violation of the Hill-Burton notice requirements. [*Douglas County d/b/a Douglas County Hosp. v. Bowen*, No. 6-85-1078 (D. Minn. Aug. 3, 1988) (unpublished), *see also Flagstaff Med. Ctr. v. Sullivan*, 962 F.2d 879 (9th Cir. 1992) noting new era of "substantial compliance" rather than "technical violations"]

HHS may disallow all uncompensated services claimed in a year when it finds that the facility was in substantial noncompliance with its assurance. Even if a hospital substantially complies, HHS may disallow claims for uncompensated services that are not documented as uncompensated services. [42 C.F.R. § 124.512(d)] Further, if HHS dismisses a complaint or if there has been no action on the part of the attorney general to ensure compliance within six months from the time the complaint is filed, the individual who filed the complaint may bring an action to effect compliance. [42 C.F.R. § 124.511(a)(4)]

What is the community service assurance?

Hospitals that have received Hill-Burton funds must also satisfy a community service assurance. Unlike the uncompensated care obligation, which expires after a period of years, the community service assurance lasts indefinitely and applies specifically to emergency services. The community service assurance requires the hospital to serve all patients in the "facility's service area without discrimination on the basis of race, color, national origin, creed, or any other grounds unrelated to either the individual's

need for the service or the availability of the service in the facility." [42 C.F.R. § 124.603]
Thus, failure to treat patients based on inability to pay violates Hill-Burton as well as
COBRA.

What are a hospital's duties under the community service assurance?

The Department of Health and Human Services Office for Civil Rights has outlined the
community service assurance to include the following duties:

- Hill-Burton facilities may not deny emergency services to any person residing in
  their service area on the grounds that the person is unable to pay for those services.
- Hill-Burton facilities may not adopt patient admissions policies that have the effect of
  excluding persons on grounds of race, color, national origin, creed, or any other
  grounds unrelated to the patient's need for the service or the availability of the needed
  service.
- Hill-Burton facilities must post notices informing the public of their community service obligations in English and Spanish, as well as any other language that 10 percent
  or more of the households in their service area usually speak. [Office of Civil Rights
  Fact Sheet, *Community Service Assurance under the Hill-Burton Act*, available on the
  Internet at *http://www.hhs.gov/ocr/hburton.html*]

How does Hill-Burton affect a hospital's emergency admissions policies?

The regulations prohibit a facility from denying a person emergency care because of an
inability to pay for care rendered if that person resides in the area (or works in the area
according to Title XVI). However, a patient accepted for care under this provision may be
discharged or transferred to another facility when doing so would not carry a substantial
risk of deterioration in the patient's medical condition. [42 C.F.R. § 124.603(b)]

If a hospital requires preadmission deposits and this policy effectively denies or substantially delays hospitalization or care because the individual cannot pay the deposit, the
hospital has violated Hill-Burton's community service obligation. The facility need not
eliminate the deposit requirement in all cases. Rather, the hospital must establish alternative arrangements so that individuals who do not have the necessary cash when the
services are requested, but who are likely to be able to pay at a later date, are not denied
care. [42 C.F.R. § 124.603(d)(3)]

State Law Duties

Have courts interpreted a hospital's duty to provide emergency care to nonpaying patients?

In nearly every state, a hospital can be liable for refusing to provide emergency treatment to a patient who cannot pay. The extent of a hospital's duty to provide either treatment or admission for care is not unlimited, however. Several states still follow the legal
principle that a hospital does not have a responsibility to admit or treat a person in a

nonemergency situation. Yet, differentiating emergency from nonemergency matters is not a simple task. There is a common point in many court decisions considering this issue: To deny a person treatment or admission solely because he or she cannot pay for services has been seen by some courts as an unlawful, arbitrary action by an institution charged with the responsibility of serving the community. Courts may draw upon a facility's charter, incorporation papers, licensure application, or the state indigency laws in determining a hospital's duty to look beyond a person's ability to pay when it decides whether to treat or admit that individual. [*See, e.g., Williams v. Hospital Auth.*, 168 S.E.2d 336 (Ga. Ct. App. 1969)]

How have state legislatures addressed the duty to provide emergency treatment to indigent patients?

Many states have enacted statutes to address the relationship between a hospital's obligation to provide care and patients' inability to pay for care. Many of the medical indigency statutes establish administrative bodies that promulgate rules and regulations to determine individuals' eligibility for state-funded care. These rules apply to publicly operated facilities as well as to private hospitals that have contracted with Medicaid. [Va. Code Ann. § 32.1-11, Cal. Welf. & Inst. Code § 14000, 35 Pa. Cons. Stat. 449.8]

The duty to provide care without regard to the ability to pay may appear in state hospital licensure laws or implicate licensing status as a penalty. In New York, for example, a hospital's operating certificate can be revoked for failing to provide emergency care. [N.Y. Pub. Health Law § 2806]

Legislative enactments may be similar to EMTALA, specifically stating that no one in need of emergency medical care may be denied hospitalization or treatment on the grounds of an inability to pay for necessary services. ED administrators must be familiar with these types of state statutes, as they may impose duties beyond those created by EMTALA. In Florida, for example, the legislature has enacted a statute similar to EMTALA but with no "comes to the ED" provision, triggering a screening requirement upon a mere request for emergency services. In Florida, hospitals not operating at capacity have a duty to accept and treat patients en route to the hospital for whom ambulance personnel request care. [Fla. Stat. ch. 395.1041]

REIMBURSEMENT

This section addresses several reimbursement issues of concern to EDs. EDs have had difficulty obtaining payment from managed care organizations, and this section discusses federal and state laws intended to remedy this problem, as well as a series of studies examining the impact of the laws. This section also addresses those Medicare reimbursement issues of particular importance to EDs, such as the outpatient prospective payment system, provisions contained in the Balanced Budget Act (BBA) of 1997, teaching physician regulations, reimbursement for interpreting X-rays and electrocardiograms (EKGs), and CMS guidance concerning the use of physician staffing companies. It is important for EDs to understand the legal issues surrounding these reimbursement issues so they can obtain adequate revenue to meet their financial requirements and avoid fraud and abuse allegations.

Payment by Managed Care Organizations

Have state legislatures addressed the tension between managed care plans' restrictive payment policies and the duty to treat under COBRA?

In response to retrospective denials that occur when a managed care payer refuses to pay for treatment because the condition is later revealed to be a nonemergency, more than half of state legislatures have enacted laws requiring payers to cover ED treatment for nonemergency medical conditions under certain circumstances. Maryland was the first state to enact such a law. The Maryland statute requires HMOs to reimburse hospital emergency facilities and providers for medically necessary services rendered to meet federal emergency treatment requirements. The law also prohibits retrospective denials, requiring HMOs to reimburse facilities and providers if the HMO "authorized, directed, referred, or otherwise allowed" an HMO member to use the ED. The law also prohibits preauthorization requirements and defines "emergency services" under a prudent layperson standard. Emergency services are services provided after the sudden onset of sufficiently severe symptoms that a prudent layperson could reasonably expect to result in serious jeopardy of health, serious impairment of bodily function, or serious dysfunction of any bodily organ or part in the absence of immediate medical attention. Other states, such as Arizona, have responded to retrospective denials with a requirement that initial ED screening and stabilizing treatment be covered. [Md. Code Ann., Health-Gen. § 19-712.5; Ariz. Rev. Stat. § 20-2803] A recent study indicated that 47 states have adopted the prudent layperson law and that this standard has not led to increased costs, nor increased ED use. However, disputes still arise between managed care organizations and hospitals over the amount that will be paid. [Hall, Mark. *The Impact and Enforcement of Prudent Layperson Laws*, 43 Annals of Emergency Medicine, 5 (May 2004)]

Has the federal government adopted the prudent layperson standard?

The prudent layperson standard for payment of ED services has also been adopted at the federal level, in certain contexts. The BBA of 1997 adopted prudent layperson language for both Medicare+Choice enrollees and Medicaid managed care participants. Specifically, Medicare+Choice organizations and Medicaid managed care plans must cover emergency services that are needed to evaluate or stabilize an emergency medical condition, defined as a medical condition manifesting itself by acute symptoms of sufficient severity (including severe pain) such that a "prudent layperson, who possesses an average knowledge of health and medicine, could reasonably expect the absence of immediate medical attention to result in (1) placing the health of the individual (or, with respect to a pregnant woman, the health of the woman or her unborn child) in serious jeopardy, (2) serious impairment to bodily functions, or (3) serious dysfunction of any bodily organ or part." [42 U.S.C. §§ 1395w-22 & 1396u-2]

To implement the BBA, the Medicaid program has specifically prohibited Medicaid managed care plans from requiring preauthorization for screening and treatment of conditions that meet the prudent layperson standard for emergencies. The agency has eliminated any confusion regarding whether managed care organizations operating under a

Medicaid "waiver" were subject to COBRA by clarifying that all Medicaid beneficiaries should have access to emergency services whether in a managed care program or not. [*Final Rule*, 67 Fed. Reg. 40,989 (June 12, 2002)]

CMS has clarified coverage of emergency services by Medicaid managed care organizations. In a letter to state Medicaid directors, the agency stated that, "The BBA requires that a Medicaid beneficiary be permitted to obtain emergency services immediately at the nearest provider when the need arises. When the prudent layperson standard is met, no restriction may be placed on access to emergency care. Limits on the number of visits are not allowed." [Timothy M. Westmoreland, Director, Center for Medicaid and State Operations, Letter to State Medicaid Directors, Apr. 18, 2000] These actions were an outgrowth of the Patient Bill of Rights set forth that included coverage of emergency services in situations where a prudent layperson could reasonably expect the absence of care to place their health in serious jeopardy.

Are EDs having difficulty obtaining reimbursement from managed care organizations for emergency services in spite of the enactment of these federal and state laws?

According to several studies published in the March 2000 *Annals of Emergency Medicine*, managed care organizations (MCOs) in many states are not providing reimbursement for emergency procedures and some MCOs are violating laws designed to ensure payment for emergency services. In one study that looked at the impact of two laws in Florida designed to prevent denial of claims for emergency services, the study's authors found that the laws did reduce the number of denied claims but that inappropriate denials persisted. In addition, claims denied due to lack of a medical emergency increased since the laws were enacted. The study's authors concluded that even with the passage of legislation, auditing of emergency claim denials remains necessary. In an analysis of payment claim denials due to lack of a medical emergency in North Carolina by two MCOs, the study's authors found many of the denials met the state's prudent layperson standard. The study again illustrates the need to monitor compliance with the law. [Effect of State Legislation Prohibiting Denial of Emergency Department Patient Claims, *Annals of Emergency Medicine* (Feb. 2000)]

A 2004 study reviewed coverage of ED services in two health plans and found that there was a wide variety of interpretation of the prudent layperson standard. The ED post-service denials comprised one-half of appeals in one plan and one-third in the other. Ninety percent of the claims were overturned and paid on appeal. The appeals typically had the following characteristics: one in five claims related to services for children; a common reason for dispute was diagnosing illness; typical signs and symptoms bringing people to the ED were abdominal pain, cramps, and spasms; and the average cost for services appealed was $1,107.00.

Several state health regulators, including Florida and Washington, have fined MCOs for denying claims for emergency services. Florida has fined at least five HMOs for denying emergency room claims. In Washington, an HMO paid a $10,000 fine for violating the state's prudent layperson law.

Hospitals should note that enforcement of prudent layperson laws is more likely now than it was a few years ago. Hospitals should ascertain whether their billing procedures can track claims in a way that will reveal a pattern of denials for emergency services by a particular payer. If a pattern of inappropriate denials is detected, the hospital should complain to the state attorney general, the state insurance commissioner, or to the state authority that enforces the prudent layperson statute. Hospitals may also want to seek advice from their state or national hospital association. Exchanges of reimbursement information with other hospitals may raise antitrust concerns; accordingly hospitals should be careful not to share reimbursement information with other hospitals. [Disputes over Coverage of Emergency Department Services: A Study of Two Health Maintenance Organizations, *Annals of Emergency Medicine* (Mar. 2004)]

Billing Medicare for ED Services

What is the prospective payment system for hospital outpatient services?

The outpatient prospective payment system is a payment system for hospital outpatient services, including emergency services and urgent care. Payment for hospital outpatient services is made under rates for Ambulatory Payment Classification (APC) groups. CMS has classified outpatient services and procedures into 451 groups that are comparable clinically and use similar resource amounts. CMS has assigned each APC a weight based on the median costs for the services within the APC group. The payment rate is the product of a conversion factor and the APC rate. The prospective payment system applies to nearly all hospitals, including those hospitals that are excluded from the inpatient prospective payment system and community mental health centers, but it does not apply to critical access hospitals and Maryland hospitals. Outpatient PPS went into effect on August 1, 2000, except for the provisions that apply to provider-based facilities owned by hospitals, such as physician office practices; these provisions became effective on October 10, 2000. [65 Fed. Reg. 18,434 (2000), codified at 42 C.F.R. §§ 409 through 413, 419, 424, 489, 498, & 1003]

What services are excluded from the outpatient PPS?

The following services are not paid for under the outpatient prospective payment system:

- services provided by certain providers, including: physicians, nurse practitioners, physician assistants, certified nurse midwives, psychologists, anesthetists, and clinical social workers, which will continue to be paid for under the Medicare fee schedule
- rehabilitation services
- ambulance services
- prosthetics, prosthetic supplies, devices, and implants (except for intraocular lenses), and orthotic devices
- durable medical equipment, except implantable durable medical equipment
- clinical diagnostic laboratory services
- services provided to patients with ESRD that are paid under the ESRD composite rate and drugs and supplies furnished during dialysis
- services and procedures that cannot be safely furnished in an outpatient setting or that require inpatient care

- services provided to persons who are inpatients of a skilled nursing facility and which are covered under the SNF prospective payment system
- services not covered by Medicare, including services that are not medically necessary [42 C.F.R. § 419.22]

How does CMS reimburse physician visits in the ED?

The physician provider manual sets forth use of the ED billing codes 99281 through 99288. The ED billing codes can only be used from the ED, but can be used by any physician who evaluates someone there. The ED codes should be used even if it is determined that the person did not present with an emergency condition. A lower level billing code will simply be used. The ED will typically bill a 99281 to 99288 code, with the code level based on how extensive the evaluation and management services are. If a critical care emergency occurs in the ED, the critical care billing codes (99291 and 99292) can be billed.

If the patient's regular treating physician is asked to come in and evaluate the patient, the regular physician can bill an initial hospital visit (code 99211 or 99223) if the patient is subsequently admitted to the hospital. If the patient is subsequently discharged, the physician will bill using an ED visit code. If the treating physician is contacted by telephone only, there will be no service billing.

Similarly, if another physician is asked to consult, i.e., an on-call specialist is contacted, the specialist or consulting physician can bill for a consultation if the patient is admitted and treatment continues. If the patient is discharged, the evaluation will be billed using an ED code. [*Medicare Processing Manual: Ch. 12 Physician and non-physician services*, 30.6.11 Emergency Department Visits (revised 10-1-03)]

How does CMS reimburse hospital services in the ED?

Hospital ED services are billing using codes 99218 through 99285 depending upon the severity of service. The bill should include the site of the visit and level of intensity. If someone comes to the ED for services, then seen again the same day for a different problem; the bill should be submitted with a GO code. [*Medicare Processing Manual: Ch. 4 Hospital (Including Impatient Hospital Part B and OPPS)*, 160 Payment for Hospital Emergency Services (revised 10-03-03)]

How does CMS reimburse physician observation services?

CMS reimburses physicians' services for observation to the physician who admits the person for hospital observation using codes 99217 through 99220. The physician does not need to have hospital admitting privileges, but does need to have privileges for observation. A medical observation record should be kept that includes the date and time of admission, nursing notes, and progress notes made by the physician while the patient is in observation. This record should be in addition to the ED or outpatient record. If another physician is called in to consult, then the other physician will bill an outpatient consultation code.

If the patient is discharged the same day as the observation, then the initial observation will be billed. On the other hand, if the observation patient is subsequently admitted to the hospital and discharged the second day, the second day will be billed as 99217 hospital observation discharge. It will seldom be necessary to bill for more than two days of observation, but should this situation arise, days more than two days before discharge will be billed with an outpatient visit code.

If the patient is admitted as an inpatient after observation, the physician will bill an initial hospital visit code and cannot bill 99217 hospital observation discharge or an outpatient visit on the date of admission. [*Medicare Processing Manual: Ch. 12 Physician and non-physician services*, 30.6.8 Payment for Hospital Observation Services (revised 10-1-03)]

How does CMS reimburse hospital observation services?

Observation services are outpatient services that are usually included in the APC reimbursement for the ED service or procedure. CMS has clarified that observation services must be billed one of two ways: (1) as packaged services or (2) as a separate APC under APC 339 for the diagnosis of chest pain, asthma, or congestive heart failure that warrant observation. Thus, packaged service billing can take place when observation services are ordered by a physician or approved by an appropriate authority and last less than 48 hours, then CMS will reimburse the observation when billed as revenue code 762. If other ancillary services are provided in connection with the observation, the code 760 for treatment/observation can be billed in connection with ancillary laboratory services. If observation is for a non-covered service and notice of non-coverage has been given to the beneficiary, then the facility can bill for only the services that are covered. On the other hand, separate APC billing (APC 339) for observation can take place when the patient has a diagnosis of chest pain, asthma, or congestive heart failure for a stay of 8-48 hours.

CMS requires observation services to be billed using code G0244. CMS has also adopted two G codes for direct admissions for observation: G0263 and G0264. G0263 is for initial nursing assessment for a direct admission for observation for congestive heart failure, chest pain or asthma. G0264 is for initial nursing assessment for observation of a diagnosis other than congestive heart failure, chest pain, or asthma. G0264 will be paid under APC code 600 for a low-level clinic visit. Effective January 1, 2003 the code G0258 for intravenous infusion during observation stay is deleted. Hospitals bill for intravenous infusion during observation with codes G0244 for observation and Q00811 for infusion therapy other than chemotherapy. [*Program Memorandum Intermediaries*, A-02-129 (Jan. 3, 2003) effective Jan. 1, 2003, and *Medicare Hosp. Manual, Transmittal* 770 (Feb. 23, 2001) effective July 1, 2001, and *Program Memorandum Intermediaries*, Transmittal A-02-129 (Jan. 3, 2003)] In addition to billing the observation code and appropriate diagnosis codes, the hospital bill should include an evaluation and management visit in the ED, clinic, or critical care billed with a 25 modifier; include other diagnostic services; and be submitted on a 13x bill type. [*Medicare Processing Manual: Ch. 4 Hospital (Including Inpatient Hospital Part B and OPPS)*, 290 Payment for Hospital Observation Services (revised 10-03-03)]

How is a hospital reimbursed if an ED patient is admitted to the hospital?

Medicare patients who are seen in the emergency room and then admitted to the hospital will have the cost of emergency care bundled into the payment for their inpatient care. The diagnosis-related group (DRG)-based prospective payment made to the hospital under Part A of Medicare is calculated to include many of the costs of services provided to hospital patients, including the cost of emergency services.

How does Medicare pay for the services of non-physician providers?

Medicare will cover the services of some non-physician providers at a percentage of the physician fee schedule rate. PA services are reimbursed at 80 percent of the lesser of either the actual charge or 85 percent of the physician fee schedule amount. [42 U.S.C. § 1395l(a)(1)(0)] Payment for PA services is only made to the PA's employer, regardless of whether the PA is an employee or independent contractor. A PA's employer must accept assignment, that is, accept the Medicare rate as payment in full, when a PA treats beneficiaries. Medicare will reimburse nurse practitioners and clinical nurse specialists for the services they provide in any geographic area at 80 percent of the lesser of either the actual charge or 85 percent of the physician fee schedule amount. [42 U.S.C. §§ 1395x(s)(2)(K) & 1395l(a)(1)] In addition, Medicare covers payment for certified nurse-midwives' services at no greater than 65 percent of the physician fee schedule amount and pays for the services of certified registered nurse anesthetists. [42 C.F.R. §§ 414.54 & 414.60] CMS will reimburse nurse practitioners (NPs), certified nurse specialists (CNSs), certified nurse midwives (CNMs), and physician assistants (PAs) for evaluation and management services as long as the service is medically necessary and within the scope of services in the state for that practitioner. CMS will not independently reimburse for occupational therapy or physical therapy services. [*Medicare Processing Manual: Ch. 12 Physician and non-physician services*, 30.6.1 Selection of E & M Service (revised 5-14-04)]

How are shared ED visits billed?

If the non-physician provider provides the face-to-face portion of the evaluation and management visit and the physician does not have a face-to-face encounter with the patient but reviewed the medical record, then the non-physician provider should bill for the service. If the physician and non-physician provider both had a face-to-face encounter with the patient, then the evaluation and management service can be billed under either the physician or non-physician provider UPIN/PIN number. [*Medicare Processing Manual: Ch. 12 Physician and non-physician services*, 30.6.1 Selection of E & M Service (revised 5-14-04)]

Can physicians bill Medicare for services provided to hospital patients by members of their staff who cannot bill Medicare directly, such as nurses or therapists?

Unlike its coverage in the outpatient setting, Medicare coverage in a hospital setting does not include services and supplies provided "incident to" a physician's services. In addition, a physician cannot bill Medicare for the supervision of his or her staff. Medicare will only pay for physician services provided in a hospital if the services are personally furnished for an individual beneficiary by a physician; the services contribute directly

132

to the diagnosis or treatment of the patient; and the services ordinarily require performance by a physician. When a physician's staff provides services in a hospital setting, Medicare includes payment for these services in the payment it makes to the hospital. Although a physician cannot seek payment from Medicare or the beneficiary for services provided by his or her staff, a physician may seek payment from the hospital. [42 C.F.R. § 415.102]

However, if the physician assumes the operating costs of the department, for example, through a contractual agreement, then the reimbursement includes:

- payment for physician services, and
- payment for reasonable cost basis for costs such as overhead, supplies, equipment costs, and non-medical personnel, as long as the books are made available as requested to verify costs.

The physician will be treated as being related to the hospital under this kind of agreement. [42 C.F.R. § 415.102(d)]

Can an ED physician bill Medicare for the assistance of a physician assistant (PA) performing an evaluation and management service when the PA is employed by the emergency physician group and not by the hospital?

The physician can bill for the services of the employed PA. The PA should have his or her own provider information number, and claims should be submitted on an assignment basis. When the PA conducts the evaluation and management visit, the service should be billed under the PA provider number. However, if the physician also evaluates the patient in person, then either the physician or PA number may be used for billing. When the physician bills for services of an employee, code 99211 should be used. [*Medicare Processing Manual: Ch. 12 Physician and non-physician services*, 30.6, 30.6.1 Selection of E & M Service (revised 5-14-04) & 110.3 (10-01-03)]

Can a physician staffing company receive Medicare payment for services provided by physicians who have contracted with the company?

CMS has indicated that physician practice management companies, including ED staffing companies, cannot receive payment from Medicare for the services provided by physicians who have contracted with the practice management companies. Direct payments cannot be made to companies that staff hospitals with physicians who have an independent contractor relationship with the companies. Because these physicians are not employees, they do not fit into an existing exception that allows a hospital or clinic to receive payment for the services of a physician employee. In addition, an independent contractor physician who purchases stock in an ED staffing company is not able to reassign his or her Medicare benefits to the company. Shareholders of a corporation are not necessarily employees. Finally, physician practice management companies generally do not qualify under the agency exception because of the method of calculating the physician practice management company's fee. However, a physician may bill for physician he/she employs or for another doctor with whom he has a reciprocal arrangement. [42 U.S.C. § 1395u(b)(6)]

How can physicians in a group practice bill?

Physicians in a group practice can bill as if they were one physician. If they are of the same specialty, only one evaluation and management service should be billed in a day. If the physicians are of different specialties and see the patient for different reasons, more than one evaluation and management code may be billed in a day. [*Medicare Processing Manual: Ch. 12 Physician and non-physician services*, 30.6.5 Physicians in Group Practice (10-01-03)]

How does CMS reimburse telehealth services?

Telehealth services are reimbursable when an expert physician, nurse practitioner, physician assistant, nurse midwife, certified nurse specialist, clinical psychologist, or clinical social worker is needed for consultation, an office visit, individual psychotherapy, or pharmacologic management from a distant site. The initiating site will be eligible if it is in a professional shortage area or demonstration project and not classified as a metropolitan statistical area (MSA). The telehealth services must be interactive unless the services are in Alaska or Hawaii. Reimbursement is at the same rate as if the service were provided in person. [*Medicare Processing Manual: Ch. 12 Physician and non-physician services*, 190 Medicare payment for telehealth services (10-01-03)]

What billing risks can impact claims integrity?

Billing risks that can impact claims integrity and compliance with procedure coding requirements include outpatient coding, admissions and discharge coding, supplemental payments, and use of information technology. Outpatient coding risks include:

- billing an outpatient service code for a service that is considered an inpatient only service,
- billing for medically unnecessary services,
- failure to follow the National Correct Coding Initiative (NCCI)
- using outdated charge description masters (CDMs) resulting in improper claims for ancillary services,
- failure to follow multiple procedure discount rules,
- improper E & M coding and observation service coding.

Admission and discharge coding risks include the need to comply with the "same day rule" to bill services rendered on the same day together unless an exception is met, monitoring of partial hospital payments, abuses with same day discharge and readmissions, the need to keep an up-to-date list of DRGs impacted by Medicare post-acute transfer policy, and excessive transfers between hospitals and adjacent long-term care hospitals.

Supplemental payment risks include improper pass-through costs, non-compliance with DRG outlier rules, improper designation and claims for provider-based entities, and improper claims for clinical trials, organ acquisition, and cardiac rehab. Providers should also ensure that information technology is used to protect data privacy, security, and accuracy of claims. [Department of Health and Human Services, Office of Inspector General, Supplemental Compliance Guidance for Hospitals, Jan. 27, 2005 (70 Fed. Reg. 4858)] Beginning October 1, 2005 CMS will no longer process non-HIPAA compliant electronic Medicare claims.

What is the Medicare claims appeal process?

The Medicare appeal process has been standardized so that there is a similar appeal process for eligibility, enrollment or claims decisions for all Medicare claims (Part D prescription drug appeals begin January 1, 2006). The Medicare beneficiary or their representative (such as a medical provider) can file the claims appeals. The initial claim determination will be made by the fiscal intermediary or carrier. If there is disagreement with the initial decision, then a request for reconsideration can be filed and a Qualified Independent Contractor (QIC) will review the case. The third level of appeal requires filing the appeal with an Administrative Law Judge (ALJ) within 60 days of the notice of reconsideration. The ALJ in the Health and Human Services Office of Medicare Hearings and Appeals (OMHA) will then review and decide the claim. The fourth and last level of appeal is to district court.

Interpreting X-Rays and EKGs

Can only board-certified radiologists provide X-ray interpretations and board-certified cardiologists furnish EKG interpretations?

CMS has stated that nothing in the Medicare Act indicates that special qualifications are needed to interpret an X-ray or EKG. Thus, an ED physician can interpret an X-ray or EKG and bill Medicare for this service. [*Medicare Claims Processing Manual: Ch. 13 Radiology Serves & Other Diagnostic Procedures*, 100.1 (revised 10-02-03)]

Will Medicare pay both ED physicians and specialist physicians to interpret X-rays and EKGs furnished to ED patients?

Generally, Medicare will pay for only one interpretation of an EKG or X-ray furnished to an ED patient. Under unusual circumstances, Medicare will pay for a second interpretation. For example, Medicare will pay for a second interpretation if the first interpretation results in a questionable finding for which the physician performing the initial interpretation believes another physician's expertise is needed. In addition, a second interpretation may be justified when a second interpretation of the results of the procedure results in a changed diagnosis. Medicare will not pay for a second interpretation made for quality control purposes. Medicare requires documentation of the unusual circumstances before it will pay for a second interpretation.

CMS has stated that if a radiologist or cardiologist furnishes a contemporaneous interpretation (a written interpretation or an oral interpretation that will be written later), the emergency physician should not bill for the service. The Medicare carrier should pay only the cardiologist or radiologist. A "contemporaneous" interpretation is an interpretation that occurs at the same time as the diagnosis and treatment of the patient in the ED, not hours or days after the patient is sent home. Medicare has also stated that it will pay for an interpretation furnished by teleradiology as long as the interpretation is used in the diagnosis and treatment of the patient. [*Medicare Claims Processing Manual: Ch. 13 Radiology Serves & Other Diagnostic Procedures*, 100.1 (revised 10-02-03)]

What conditions must an ED meet to receive payment for interpretation of an X-ray or EKG?

Medicare will pay for an interpretation of an X-ray or EKG only if there is a written report prepared for inclusion in the patient's medical record maintained by the hospital. A review of the findings of the procedure without a written report similar to a written report that a specialist in the field would prepare does not qualify for separate payment because it is included in the ED visit payment. For example, notations such as "fx-tibia" or "EKG-normal" would be considered a review of the findings that is included as part of the ED payment and does not qualify for separate payment. According to CMS, an interpretation and report should address the findings, relevant clinical issues, and comparative data (when available). [*Medicare Claims Processing Manual: Ch. 13 Radiology Serves & Other Diagnostic Procedures*, 100.1 (revised 10-02-03)]

Who will Medicare reimburse if both the ED physician and a radiologist or cardiologist submit a claim for the interpretation of an X-ray or EKG?

The Medicare Carrier's Manual instructs carriers to pay the first bill they receive when the carrier receives multiple claims for the same interpretation. Carriers will no longer use physician specialty as the primary factor in deciding which claim to pay. In some cases, Medicare carriers will be required to institute recovery action. For example, if the first claim is from a radiologist, the carrier will pay the radiologist's claim because the carrier does not know that a second claim is forthcoming. However, if a second claim comes from an ED physician and the carrier can determine that this was the interpretation that contributed to the diagnosis and treatment of the patient, the carrier will pay that claim. If the radiologist's claim was for quality control purposes and not because the ED physician required a second interpretation, the Medicare carrier will institute recovery action against the radiologist. [*Medicare Claims Processing Manual: Ch. 13 Radiology Serves & Other Diagnostic Procedures*, 100.1 (revised 10-02-03)]

Services Provided by Teaching Physicians and Residents

When will Medicare reimburse physician services under the physician fee schedule for services furnished in teaching settings?

Regulations revised on October 1, 2004, set Medicare reimbursement for services provided by teaching physicians working with residents. Teaching physicians are physicians, other than another resident, who involve residents in the care of their patients. The regulations require that teaching physicians provide more than general direction to interns and residents to obtain Medicare reimbursement. Teaching physicians must be "present during the key portion of any service or procedure for which payment is sought." [42 C.F.R. § 415.172(a)]

Are there special requirements concerning a physician's presence during high-risk or other complex medical procedures?

For surgery and high-risk or other complex medical procedures, the teaching physician must be present during all critical portions of the procedure and must be immediately available to provide services during the entire service or procedure. Complex and high-risk procedures include interventional radiologic and cardiologic supervision and interpretation, cardiac catheterization, cardiovascular stress test, and transesophageal echocardiography. The regulation does not define the terms "all critical portions" or "immediately available." For endoscopic procedures, the teaching physician must be present during the entire procedure. However, teaching physicians do not need to be present during other diagnostic tests and may bill for test interpretations if they document that they personally performed the tests or reviewed a resident's interpretation with the resident. [42 C.F.R. § 415.172; *Medicare Claims Processing Manual: Ch. 12 Physician/Nonphysician Practioners*, 100.1.2 & 100.1.5 (revised 10-01-03)]

What special requirements must a teaching physician meet to receive Medicare reimbursement for evaluation and management services?

Except for services provided in certain primary care centers, the teaching physician must be physically present during the portion of the service that determines the level of service that will be billed (the "key portion"). The teaching physician must personally document the patient's medical record, either in writing or by a dictated note, indicating his or her presence and participation in the service. CMS has indicated that some reliance on resident documentation is permissible, although the degree of reliance on resident documentation remains somewhat confusing. CMS has stated that if the teaching physician is repeating the key elements of the service previously obtained and documented by the resident, the teaching physician does not need to repeat the documentation. The teaching physician can make brief summary comments that tie into the resident's entry and confirm or revise the key elements. The key elements include the following:

- relevant history of present illness and prior diagnostic tests
- major finding(s) of the physical examination
- assessment, clinical impression, or diagnosis
- plan of care [*Medicare Claims Processing Manual: Ch. 12 Physician/Nonphysician Practitioner*, 100.1 (revised 10-01-03)]

What are the special rules applicable to diagnostic radiology and other diagnostic tests provided by teaching physicians?

Teaching physicians receive full payment for the interpretation of diagnostic radiology and other diagnostic tests if the teaching physician performs the interpretation or reviews the resident's interpretation. CMS has indicated that it will not pay for an interpretation if the documentation is only a countersignature of the resident's interpretation. The teaching physician must document that he or she performed the interpretation or reviewed the resident's interpretation. [42 C.F.R. § 415.180; *Medicare Claims Processing Manual: Ch. 12 Physician/Nonphysician Practitioner*, 100 (revised 10-01-03)]]

EMERGENCY RESPONSE PLANNING

What federal laws require hospitals to implement emergency response plans?

The Homeland Security Act of 2002 established the Department of Homeland Security (DHS) with the intent to coordinate emergency management between a variety of government agencies. It also provides for emergency preparedness and response. [6 U.S.C. § 1] The DHS has released a national response plan focused on a comprehensive approach to manage domestic incidents that integrates best practices from a variety of first responders such as EMS, law enforcement, fire, and health professionals. It focuses on both private citizen and public organization involvement and is available at the DHS website at *www.dhs.gov*. OSHA has also issued a National Emergency Management Plan (NEMP). [OSHA Directive HSO-01-00-001 (Dec. 18, 2003)]

Under Title III of the Superfund Amendments and Reauthorization Act of 1986 (SARA), every state is required to coordinate emergency response activities by establishing local emergency planning committees (LEPCs) responsible for developing community response or contingency plans that contain emergency response procedures and programs for hospitals, police, emergency medical personnel, and other first-responders to emergency circumstances. [42 U.S.C. §§ 11001 through 11050] A hospital designated by an LEPC to handle emergency victims suffering from exposure to hazardous substances must have an Emergency Response Plan, as well as decontamination equipment, personal protective equipment (PPE), and trained personnel. As directed by SARA, OSHA established a comprehensive rule to protect employee health and safety during hazardous waste operations, including emergency responses to the release of hazardous substances. [29 C.F.R. §§ 1910.120] This regulation requires hospitals to plan for emergencies if they expect to use their employees to handle emergencies involving hazardous substances and to ensure that employees are trained by an Emergency Response Plan that is approved by the Joint Commission and meets criteria set out in the regulations.

According to an OSHA informational booklet released in 1997, hospitals in many localities have not been effectively integrated into the community disaster response system required under SARA. The booklet describes in detail the steps that hospitals should take to implement a comprehensive Emergency Response Plan that complies with OSHA regulations. [*Hospitals and Community Emergency Response—What You Need To Know*, OSHA 3152 (Dec. 12, 1997), available on the Internet at *www.osha.gov*] OSHA has also set forth investigative procedures when fatalities and catastrophes occur. [*Fatality/Catastrophe Investigation Procedures*, CPL 02-00-137 (Apr. 14, 2005)]

Has the Joint Commission issued standards for disaster preparedness?

For over 30 years the Joint Commission has required its accredited health care organizations to meet established disaster preparedness standards, but failed to specifically address what should be included. The standards were significantly changed in 2001 to introduce the concept of multijurisdictional and community involvement into the disaster preparedness process. This new emphasis was prophetic of the terrible reality of terrorism and mass destruction of September 11, 2001. The focus of the standards shifted from a very basic approach to emergency preparedness to the concept of integrated emergency management. The Joint Commission now expects that health care organizations will address the four specific phases of disaster planning: (1) mitigation, (2) preparedness, (3) response and (4) recovery. In addition, health care organizations must take an "all-hazards approach" to planning and develop a chain-of-command approach that is common to all hazards determined to pose credible threats to the community. This requires that planning of disaster preparedness start with an analysis of vulnerability to an unconstrained list of extreme events. These new Joint Commission standards for emergency management represent a significant step toward improving not only the health care organization's but the nation's readiness for a chemical and/or biological emergency.

What constitutes an "emergency" according to the Joint Commission?

An emergency is a natural or manmade event that suddenly and significantly

- disrupts the environment of care
- disrupts care and treatment
- changes or increases demands for the organization's services

What are the management activities that must be addressed?

"*Mitigation activities* lessen the severity and impact of a potential emergency." Mitigation begins by identifying potential emergencies (hazards) that may affect the "hospital's operations or the demand for its services, followed by implementing a strategy that supports the perceived areas of vulnerability within the organization."

"*Preparedness activities* build hospital capacity to manage the effects of emergencies, should one occur." Some of the important preparedness steps include

- creating an inventory of resources, including supplies and equipment, that may be needed in an emergency, including prearranged agreements with vendors and health care networks
- maintaining an ongoing planning process
- holding staff orientation and training on basic response actions
- implementing hospital wide rehearsals or drills.

"*Response activities* control the negative effects of emergency situations." These activities are best divided into two categories. The first category includes actions that all staff must take when confronted by an emergency, such as reporting to prearranged locations. The second category includes actions taken by management, such as initiating the plan, assessing the situation, issuing warning and notification announcements, setting objectives and priorities, and serving as a liaison with external groups, such as federal and state agencies of emergency management and public health departments.

"*Recovery actions* begin almost concurrently with response activities and are directed at restoring essential services and resuming normal operations." Depending on the emergency's impact on the organization, this phase may require a large amount of resources and time to complete. Recovery not only includes activities related to the facility, but also loss of revenues, support of staff, dealing with community reaction, and so forth. [*JCAHO Comprehensive Accreditation Manual for Hospitals, EC 4.1 (2005)*]

What are the applicable Joint Commission standards?

The standards are found in Joint Commission Environment of Care standards EC 4.10 that describe emergency management requirements, including assessment of vulnerabilities, determination of the hospital role in a community-wide EMS response, and policies and process to notify staff, external authorities, etc. in the event of emergency conditions.

The Medical Staff standards MS 4.110 provide for disaster privileging of health care providers.

What types of problems need to be considered?

Risks vary by type and intensity at each location, but some of the issues that must be considered include the following:

- Security
  - bomb threats and the resulting need for investigation and evacuation
  - civil disturbances in the ED
  - gang-related activity in the ED or involving a patient
  - community panic that may result in ED patients attempting to leave the hospital at a time or under circumstances that are unadvisable
  - hostage incidents involving staff or patients
  - terrorist attacks, including nuclear, biological, chemical, and traditional explosives and arms
  - VIP patients or visitors
  - employee violence against self, other employees, or patients
  - domestic violence involving a patient or employee
  - theft of drugs, chemicals, or radiological materials
- Weather
  - snowstorms or ice storms
  - earthquakes that may involve damage to the physical structure of the hospital
  - hail or high winds that may involve damage to the physical structure of the hospital
  - hurricanes or tornadoes that may involve damage to the physical structure of the hospital
  - severe cold or heat/humidity
  - severe rainfall or floods that may involve damage to the physical structure of the hospital
  - sinkholes

Any of the above weather events may prevent oncoming staff from getting to work and require on-duty staff to shelter in place, and may result in the disruption of vital services to the hospital.

- Utility system failures
  - central medical vacuum
  - electrical
  - emergency power
  - fuel for heat

- heating/air conditioning
- communications systems, internal or external
- fuel for reserve power
- water supply
- water contamination
- sewage
- fire suppression systems
- oxygen systems
- internal gas leaks
- Other
  - structural compromise
  - internal or external fires or explosions
  - air system contamination
  - internal biohazard spill
  - internal nuclear material incident
  - natural epidemics
  - mass casualty transportation accidents
  - mass casualty external structural incident
  - bioterrorism threat
  - external hazardous material incident
  - external chemical attack
  - internal chemical contamination
  - refugees from metropolitan area disasters
  - transfer patients from another hospital evacuation or disaster
  - need for immediate evacuation

Has the Joint Commission issued any interpretive guidelines to help hospitals in complying with the disaster preparedness standards?

In the December 2001 the Joint Commission newsletter published a special issue of its newsletter providing guidance to health care organizations in preparing for terrorist attacks that may involve nuclear, biological, or chemical incidents. [JCAHO *Perspectives*: Special Edition on Emergency Management Planning (Dec. 2001)] The guidance outlines how to use Joint Commission standards as a starting point to prepare for an emergency, and recommends development of practical emergency management education programs and recognition of common elements among mass casualty emergencies that can help an organization better prepare for such emergencies.

JCAHO has also issued a policy statement focusing on strategies for community-wide emergency preparedness systems. JCAHO recommends that the entire community become involved in preparing for a local response. Key aspects of preparedness should focus on the community health resources that are available to care in the event of an emergency. Community should evaluate their "surge capacity" or ability to care for large numbers of patients at a given time as well as their ability to stand alone providing services for the 48 to 76 hours it may take for back up assistance to arrive. Each system should have strong leadership in preparing the community for an emergency situation. [*Health Care at the Crossroads: Strategies for Creating and Sustaining Community-Wide Emergency*

Preparedness System, JCAHO (Mar. 12, 2003) available on the Internet at *http://www. jcaho.org/about+us/public+policy+initiatives/emergency_preparedness.pdf*]

What kind of testing of Emergency Medical Plans is required by JCAHO?

JCAHO has proposed to revise testing of Emergency Medical Plans under standard EC 4.2 with the goal of accessing preparation and capabilities for an actual emergency. Test should include plausible scenarios based on hazard vulnerability analysis (HVA) and demonstrate effectiveness of capabilities and identify areas of improvement. Measurable performance expectations should be set to work with data analysis and strategies for improvement. Emergency services should be tested once a year and facilities with a role in a community response management program should participate with a community test once a year. [Proposed Revisions to Testing of Emergency Medical Plan (May 13, 2005)]

What other state or federal resources provide guidance for emergency management?

As the medical community learned on September 11, 2001, a large-scale disaster can strike without warning. The attacks on the World Trade Center and the Pentagon, as well as subsequent incidents of anthrax exposure, placed hospitals on the front lines in triaging the injured and diagnosing those infected. In the event of a future mass casualty event, hospital administrators and staff will play a vital role as responders and as sources of accurate information for patients, the public and the medical community. Because of this it is essential that administrators have access to current information on preparing for a variety of disaster related emergencies.

The Federal Emergency Management Agency (FEMA) provides a variety of information on preventing and preparing for disasters, as well as disaster assistance. FEMA has also compiled a list of state emergency managers, available on the Internet at *http:// www.fema.gov*. Another educational resource for disaster preparedness is the American Hospital Association (AHA), which has compiled an overview of the needs of the nation's hospitals related to future mass casualty events and a list of resources for hospital readiness, response and recovery activities (available on the Internet at *www.aha.org*). The AHA has also prepared a Chemical and Bioterrorism Preparedness Checklist that is designed to help hospitals describe and assess their preparedness for chemical and biological incidents. The American Medical Association (AMA) also offers extensive information on disaster preparedness and medical response to bioterrorism (available on the Internet at *http://www.ama-assn.org*). The Department of Homeland Security (DHS) established effective March 1, 2003, plans and prepares for and coordinates emergency response that occurs on a national level (available on the Internet at *http://www.dhs.gov*). Should an incident occur emergency response will be under the direction of the medical director for the emergency medical services (EMS) system and the incident command system (ICS). ACEP recommends that volunteer medical personal work within the established systems as requested by the ICS and that preparation is made to develop a better surge capacity. [*Unsolicited Medical Personnel Volunteering at Disaster Scenes*, ACEP Policy Statements #400320 (June 2002) *and Health Care System Surge Capacity Recognition, Preparedness, and Response* (Aug. 2004)] The Center for Disease Control (CDC) coordinates emergency preparedness and planning in regards to chemical agents and bioterrorism (available on the Internet at *http://www.bt.cdc.gov*).

PATIENT SAFETY

Patient safety is an important component of any hospital unit. JCAHO national patient safety goals for 2006 are: (1) improve the accuracy of patient identification, (2) improve the effectiveness of communication among caregivers, (3) improve the safety of using high alert medications, [(4) eliminate wrong-site, wrong patient, wrong patient surgery has been incorporated into the Universal Protocol for hospitals and (5) improve the safety of using infusion pumps was retired for 2006] (7) reduce the risk of health care associated infections, (8) accurately and completely reconcile medications across the continuum of care, (9) reduce the risk of patient harm from falls. [Note that other goals and numbers omitted are not applicable. [*2006 National Patient Safety Goals* available at *http://www.jcaho.org*]

How can the requirement to improve the accuracy of patient identification be met?

This goal involves two components. First, using at least two patient identifiers when taking blood samples, administering medication or blood products, taking blood and other specimens for clinical testing, or providing any other treatment or procedures. A patient identifier may be the patient's name, assigned identification number, telephone number, or other patient specific identifier. Bar coding that includes two or more patient specific identifiers is acceptable, but room number is not. The term "identifier" refers to methods of identifying the patient, not sources of information. Thus, comparing the name of the patient with the name on a record would be one identifier found in two places. A second identifier might be date of birth, social security number, address, phone number, etc. The second component incorporated in the Universal Protocol is to confirm the correct patient, procedure, and site prior to any surgical or invasive procedure. This requires active communication through an affirmative statement or action that the patient, procedure, and site are correct.

What is required to improve effectiveness of communication among caregivers?

Ineffective communication is the most common cause of sentinel events, while effective communication improves patient safety. The following actions should be taken to ensure effective communication within the organization:

- verify verbal or telephone orders and test results by having the person receiving the order "read-back" the complete order or test result,
- standardize a list of abbreviations that should not be used in the organization,
- measure timeliness of reporting of critical test results and values,
- report all critical test results within time frames established by the laboratory,
- implement a standard approach to "hand-off" communication which includes the opportunity to ask and answer questions.

What are recommendations for telephone orders in the ED?

Telephone orders involve good communication between health care providers. First, there should be a process for taking verbal or telephone orders that require verification of the order by having the person receiving the order read the entire order back to the person giving the order. This involves writing down the complete order, then reading it back, then receiving confirmation that the order is correct. Second, standard abbreviations, acronyms and symbols should be used throughout the organization including a list of abbreviations not to use. A standard list of dangerous abbreviations is available at the Institute for Safe Medication Practices (ISMP) available at their web site at *http:///www.ismp.org*. ACEP recommends that the hospital have a policy in place regarding criteria for dictating and accepting telephone orders and that telephone orders given to ED personnel should be subject to the review and approval of the emergency room physician on duty. Drug Enforcement Administration (DEA) regulations prohibit dispensing controlled substances from ED stocks of patients by telephone order. [*Telephone Orders in the Emergency Department* ACEP Policy Statement #400099]

Other recommendations to reduce error with verbal orders include limiting verbal orders to urgent situations where immediate written or electronic communication is not feasible; establishing policies and procedures that limit use of verbal orders; define the parameters of who may send and receive such orders and how they will be documented; creating a culture where it is acceptable to question verbal orders; defining elements to be included in the verbal order such as name, age, weight, drug name, drug form, strength, dose frequency, route of administration, quantity and duration, indication; verifying the content of the orders by confirming drug names and spelling or providing brand and generic names and indications for use; repeating the entire verbal order to the prescriber; and documenting orders in the medical record where they are cosigned by the prescriber as soon as possible. [Recommendations to Reduce Medication Errors Associated with Verbal Medication Orders and Prescriptions, National Coordinating Council for Medication Error Reporting and Prevention (Adopted Feb. 20, 2001)]

What can be done to avoid medication errors?

Medical error occurs when the wrong medication, wrong dose, or wrong patient occur during medication administration. The Institute of Medicine (IOM) identified medical error as prevalent in its 1999 report titled "To Err Is Human" [*To Err Is Human*, Institute of Medicine (1999)] JCAHO has also noted that medical error is one of the top reasons for sentinel events in JCAHO audits. Medication errors can be caused by a number of factors including poor handwriting, similar sounding or looking drug names, drug abbreviations, misinterpretation of labeling or packaging, miscalculations, lack of knowledge or skill, or incorrect administration. Ways to address specific problems leading to medication errors are listed below.

Sound-alike drugs—Sound-alike drugs such as Celebrex and Celexa and Cerebrex; Xanax and Zantac; or Cytotec and Cytoxan can lead to error. Clear handwriting, exact spelling, and reading back of verbal orders can reduce medical error.

Inadequate patient history—Inadequate patient history can lead to drugs that are contraindicated for comorbid conditions, drug allergies, or wrong form or dose of the medication.

Dose error calculations—To verify dose calculations, the physician can include the clinical pharmacologist in prescription preparation or take drug levels prior to determining dose.

Decimal points—Misplaced decimal points can lead to confusion. A whole number should not have a zero after the decimal point (2 mg NOT 2.0 mg) and a zero should be placed before any number less than 1 mg (0.2 mg. NOT .2 mg).

Inappropriate abbreviations—Abbreviations can be easily misinterpreted and should not be used unless approved by the hospital for use.

Illegal and incomplete orders—Unclear handwriting can lead to confusion. Printing can make things more clear or use of a computer system. All components of the complete medication order should be verified including the name of the drug, dose, route, and frequency of administration.

What are JCAHO standards for medication use?

JCAHO Medication Management Standards focus on reducing process variation, error and misuse through uniform medication processes and practices based on sound medical evidence. These standards require the following:

- Access to patient and medication information such as age, weight, diagnosis, comorbidities, pregnancy status, medication allergies and sensitivities, and current medications,
- Medication availability, selection, storage, and safe management in the hospital setting including management of medications brought into the hospital by families,
- Clear ordering and transcribing policies and processes,
- Safe preparation and dispensing of medications through review of medication orders and correct labeling, including processes to provide medications when the pharmacy is closed and to retrieve recalled or discontinued drugs,
- Safe administration of medication including self-administered medications,
- Monitoring the effects of medications on patients including action and reporting of adverse drug events or medication errors,
- A process to manage high-risk or high-alert medications, and
- Regular evaluation of medication management systems. [Comprehensive Accreditation Manual for Hospitals, Medication Management, JCAHO, effective Jan. 1, 2005]

JCAHO also has recommendations for drugs that look and sound alike. For example, do not store the problem medications by name but in alternative locations. Ensure both generic and brand name of the drug are included on orders to avoid duplication, and determine the purpose for which the medication is prescribed. [*Look-alike, sound-alike drug names*, JCAHO Sentinel Event Alert, Issue 19 (May 2001).] The 2006 safety goal to improve medication safety now requires an annual review and list of look-alike/sound-alike drugs with actions to prevent errors in use of these drugs. [*2006 National Patient Safety Goals* available at *http://www.jcaho.org*]

Medications with the highest risk of injury include insulin, opiates and narcotics, potassium chloride concentrate, anticoagulants, and sodium chloride solutions above 0.9 percent. For medications that require a high concern for safety, the standard focuses on first, removing concentrated electrolytes such as potassium phosphate, sodium chloride above 0.9 percent from patient care areas. This is to avoid inadvertent use in an undiluted form. Second, standardizing and limiting the number of drug concentrations available in the organization. When multiple concentrations of a drug are necessary, such as for infants, special precautions should be taken to avoid dosing errors by specifying actual drug dose, not volume and writing out the dose calculation as part of the order.

The 2006 patient safety goal to reconcile medications across the continuum of care requires that a process be set up to obtain and document a complete list of the patient's current medications upon admission so that medications the organization provides can be compared to the list. A complete list of the patient's medications should be communicated to the next provider of service when the patient is transferred inside or outside the organization. Organizations can prepare for full implementation in January 2006. [*2006 National Patient Safety Goals* available at *http://www.jcaho.org*]

___

What potentially dangerous abbreviations can lead to medication errors?

A major cause of medication error is the use of abbreviations and dose expressions. For example, when using "U" for units, the U may be interpreted as a zero. Similarly the use of a zero after a decimal point such as 2.0 may be misinterpreted as 20 or failing to put a zero before a decimal point such as .2 may be interpreted as 2.

Other examples of confusing abbreviations are:

- **D/C** which could stand for discharge or discontinue,
- **DPT** which could stand for demoral, phenergan, thorazine or the diphtheria, pertussis, tetanus vaccine,
- **MgSO4** or **MSO4** which could be magnesium sulfate or morphine sulphate,
- **Qhs** which could be read every evening or every hour,
- **Sub q** which could be read as subcutaneous or every so often

JCAHO has recommended the following risk reductions strategies: (1) develop a list of unacceptable abbreviations that is shared with all prescribers, (2) develop a policy requiring medical staff to refer to the list, and (3) establish a policy that if an unacceptable abbreviation is used, the prescription order is verified with the prescriber before being filled. [*Medication Errors related to potentially dangerous abbreviations*, JCAHO Sentinel Event Alert, Issue 23 (Sept. 2001); *Please don't sleep through this wake up call*, ISMP Medication Safety Alert, (May 2, 2001); *Eliminating dangerous abbreviations and dose expressions in the print and electronic world*, ISMP Medication Safety Alert, (Feb. 20, 2002) with table of dangerous abbreviations linked to the article. Available on the Internet at *www.ismp.org*]

___

What abbreviations are on the JCAHO "do not use" list?

The following abbreviations are on the JCAHO "do not use" list because of the possibility of confusion.

- **U**—write out the word *unit* to avoid confusion with 0 or cc,
- **IU**—write out "*international unit*" to avoid confusion with I.V. or 10,
- **QD** or **QOD**—write out "*daily*" or "*every other day*",

- **.X**—avoid missing decimal points by writing zero before the decimal, but not after (i.e., do write 0.X or X, but do *not* write .X or X.0)
- **MS** or **MSO4** or **MgSO4**—write out *"morphine sulfate"* or *"magnesium sulfate"* to avoid confusion.

Other abbreviations under consideration for future "do not use" list include: > or < which can be confused with a 7 or L, drug names and apothecary units, @ which can be confused with 2, cc which can be mistaken for u, or ug which can be mistaken for mg.

What can be done to prevent nosocomial infections?

Nosocomial infections can be reduced through infection control strategies in the department. These include things like adequate orientation and training, sound equipment cleaning, good handwashing, use of single-use intravenous flush vials, use of waterless handrubs, raising expectations, and regular training on infection control. [*Infection Control related to sentinel events*, JCAHO Sentinel Event Alert, Issue 28 (Jan. 22, 2003)]

How can patient safety be protected in emergency situations?

In an emergency situation such as during a code in the ED, the "repeat back" method is an acceptable way to verify an order. For example, during a code the physician calls out the medication order and the nurse repeats it back before administering the drug. The code recorder documents the name of the drug, dose, time, route, and rate. This is an acceptable method of documenting and verifying the order.

Since the risk of making a mistake is higher during an emergency, it is recommended that medications be stored in the emergency department in ready to use forms or that other protections against misuse be put in place. If a procedure is performed emergently, then the practitioner should verify the site and location and if possible, take a "time out" to verify that the appropriate site has been selected for the procedure. JCAHO has a protocol to avoid wrong site, wrong procedure, and wrong person surgery through preoperative verification, site identification and marking prior to the procedure, and use of "time out" to verify the appropriateness of the site, procedure and person. [*Universal Protocol for wrong site, wrong procedure, and wrong person surgery* JCAHO (July 1, 2004)]

What is the impact of patient safety legislation?

Federal patient safety legislation was signed into law on July 29, 2005 and encourages voluntary reporting of patient safety data to approved provider or patient safety organizations (PSO). Patient safety data is defined broadly to include data, reports, records, memoranda, analysis, deliberations, work statements, root cause analysis, and quality improvement processes. The law prohibits accrediting bodies from taking action based on patient safety data nor can providers be required to reveal communications with a PSO.

The PSO can only disclose patient safety data when the data is non-identifiable, when there is evidence of wanton or criminal actions that lead to patient harm, as needed to carry out PSO or research activities, and voluntary disclosures can be made for public health surveillance. The Department of Health and Human Services (DHHS) will maintain a patient safety network of databases based on voluntary reporting, develop voluntary national standards to encourage electronic exchange of health care information, and contract with research organizations to study the impact of medical technology on health care. [Patient Safety and Quality Improvement Act (PSQIA), Pub. L. No. 109-41 (July 29, 2005)

APPENDIX 1-A

State Regulation of Consent to Treatment in an Emergency

The following state-by-state analysis provides a detailed summary of state laws and regulations regarding exceptions to patient consent under emergency circumstances. The state laws and regulations are divided into the following three categories:

- **Emergency:** Under this heading laws and regulations are noted that waive or modify the general requirement for patient consent in the event of an emergency. Some states waive consent in an emergency altogether, while others establish that consent in an emergency is implied. Other variations include whether a second opinion is necessary before proceeding with treatment, and whether and when relatives or other individuals must be located and informed.
- **Incapacity:** This analysis addresses statutes and regulations that give general direction to health care providers seeking to treat patients who lack the capacity to consent. Because this concept overlaps with consent in an emergency, the Emergency section also should be consulted.
- **Minors:** This analysis addresses state laws and regulations that contain exceptions allowing physicians to treat minor patients under emergency circumstances without parental consent. Not included in this analysis, however, are emergency exceptions to parental notification/consent under special circumstances such as abortion, suspected child abuse, treatment for venereal disease, HIV testing, and mental health or substance abuse treatment.

Where a category has not been included within the summary for a particular state, the issues covered in that category are not presently governed by statute or regulation. State case law should be consulted in these areas, as well as for assistance in interpreting the summarized statutes and regulations. This analysis should not be construed as legal advice, but as a research tool.

ALABAMA

- **Emergency**: Consent is not required if a person is physically or mentally unable to consent to services and there are no known relatives or legal guardian. Two or more physicians must decide that a delay would increase the risk to the person's life or health. [Ala. Code § 22-8-1]
- **Incapacity:** Consent is not required if a person is physically or mentally unable to consent to services and there are no known relatives or legal guardian. Two or more physicians must decide that a delay would increase the risk to the person's life or health. [Ala. Code § 22-8-1]
- **Minors:** Services may be rendered without parental consent when, in a physician's judgment, an attempt to secure consent would result in a delay that would increase the risk to the minor's life or health. [Ala. Code § 22-8-3]

ALASKA

- **Emergency:** It is a defense that consent by or on behalf of the patient was not possible under the circumstances. [Alaska Stat. § 09.55.556(b)(3)]
- **Incapacity:** Capacity to give informed consent is present when the patient is competent as demonstrated by the ability to assimilate relevant facts, understand any mental limitations, can rationally think about treatment decisions, and can state reasons to object to offered medications. [Alaska Stat. § 47.30.837] A person is considered competent to make decisions, but can authorize an agent to make health decisions for the person if the person later lacks capacity through an advanced directive or can appoint a surrogate decision maker. [Alaska Stat. §§ 13.52.010, 13.52.030, and 13.52.100]
- **Minors:** Minors can consent to their own medical or dental treatment when the minor is living alone and managing his/her own affairs, when the parent or guardian cannot be reached or is unwilling to give or withhold consent, when the minor is the parent of child, or when the care is for pregnancy or venereal disease. The consent is valid if the representations of the minor were relied on in good faith. [Alaska Stat. § 25.20.025] A minor can reach majority at the age of 18 or when married. [Alaska Stat. §§ 25.20.010, 25.20.020]

ARIZONA

- **Emergency:** In a medical emergency where surgical or medical is necessary to save the "life, physical health, eyesight, hearing or member of the person" then the Medical Director of the agency may consent to the treatment if time does not permit obtaining a court order. Upon rendering of treatment, the patient's guardian will be immediately notified. [Ariz. Rev. Stat. § 36-512]
- **Incapacity:** A person with serious mental illness shall be determined to be in need of guardianship or conservatorship if the person's ability to make important decisions is so limited that absence of a person with legal authority to make such decisions creates a serious risk to the person's health, welfare, or safety. [Ariz. Admin. Code § 9-21-206(C)(1)]

- **Minors:** A surgical procedure cannot be performed upon a minor without the written consent of a parent, except when an emergency exists and treatment is necessary, or if the parent cannot be located or contacted after reasonable effort. [Ariz. Rev. Stat. § 36-2271] Any person acting in loco parentis can consent for treatment for a minor when an emergency exists and the parents cannot be located. [Ariz. Rev. Stat. § 44-133].

ARKANSAS

- **Emergency:** When an emergency exists and no one is immediately available who is authorized or capable of consent, consent is implied. Consent may be given by a court where an emergency exists, there has been a protest or refusal of consent, and there is no other person immediately available who is authorized or capable of consent. [Ark. Code Ann. §§ 20-9-603 & 20-9-604] Specific consent for surgery shall be documented prior to the procedure, except in case of emergency. [Ark. Reg. DHFS 603]
- **Incapacity:** A person has an "unsound mind" and is incompetent to consent to treatment where the person is unable to perceive all facts relevant to the condition and proposed treatment in order to make an intelligent decision. An unsound mind may be temporary or intermittent. Whether a person has an unsound mind does not depend on the cause of the incapacity (i.e., whether from natural state, age, shock, anxiety, illness, injury, drugs, sedation, intoxication, or other cause). [Ark. Code Ann. § 20-9-601]

CALIFORNIA

- **Emergency:** A provider is not liable for damages for injury or death in an emergency situation for failure to inform the patient of the possible consequences of a medical procedure. This applies when the patient is unconscious, the provider reasonably believes that there is insufficient time to fully inform the patient, or the patient is legally incapable of consenting and the provider reasonably believes that the procedure should be begun immediately and there is insufficient time to obtain the consent of an authorized person. [Cal. Bus. & Prof. Code § 2397] A provider may give treatment without informed consent in an emergency if it is documented in the patient's record that immediate action is necessary to preserve life, prevent serious bodily harm to the patient or others, or alleviate severe pain. To act without consent, it must be impractical to obtain the required consent and the action taken must be customary among physicians of good standing in similar circumstances. [Cal. Code Regs. tit. 22, §§ 73524(e) (intermediate care facilities), 72528(e) (skilled nursing facilities)]
- **Incapacity:** If the attending physician in a skilled nursing or intermediate care facility orders treatment that requires informed consent, but is unable to obtain consent because the resident lacks capacity and there is no person with legal authority to make decisions for the resident, the physician shall inform the facility, and an interdisciplinary team will oversee the resident's care. [Cal. Health & Safety Code § 1418.8]
- **Minors:** A minor can consent to medical care if 15 or older, is living separately, and manages his/her own finances. The physician can advise the parents or guardian of medical treatment with or without the minor's consent. [Cal. Fam. Code § 6922]

A minor is considered emancipated upon turning 18, when married, or when serving in the military. [Cal. Fam. Code § 7002] A minor can consent to treatment for pregnancy, treatment for a communicable disease, or drug and alcohol counseling if over 12. [Cal. Fam. Code §§ 6925, 6926, 6929]

COLORADO

- **Incapacity:** If a patient's attending physician or the court has determined that the patient lacks the capacity to give informed consent to medical treatment and there is no guardian with medical decision-making authority, agent appointed in a medical power of attorney, or other person with legal authority to consent for the patient, the physician or his or her designee must attempt to locate as many interested persons as practicable (i.e., the patient's spouse, parent, adult child, sibling, or grandchild, or any close friend), and inform them that a proxy decision maker should be selected, and the person selected shall make medical treatment decisions on behalf of the patient. [Colo. Rev. Stat. § 15-18.5-103]

CONNECTICUT

- **Incapacity:** Informed consent must be received from a patient prior to receiving medication for the treatment of psychiatric disabilities. No medical procedure may be performed without the patient's written informed consent or, if the patient has been declared incapable, the written consent of a conservator. [Conn. Gen. Stat. § 17a-543] A power of attorney to make health care decisions for one who can't can be put in place but can not render void any document created with health care instructions. [Conn. Gen. Stat. § 1-54a] By statute, a person can create a document designating a health care agent, attorney-in-fact, or conservator to act in the event of future incapacity or in regards to an anatomical gift. The document must be put in place by someone over 18 and signed and witnessed. [Conn. Gen. Stat. § 19a-575a]
- **Minors:** Parental consent is generally required for treatment of a mentally ill child unless the physician believes treatment is needed to avoid serious harm to the child in which case treatment can be administered while waiting for parental consent. An involuntary patient may receive medications or treatment without consent, but written consent is required for a medical or surgical procedure by the parent, next of kin, or court-appointed doctor. However, if the head of the hospital and physician determine that the child is in a critical emergency measures to protect the child's well-being may be taken without consent. [Conn. Gen. Stat. § 17a-81]

DELAWARE

- **Emergency:** A health care provider is not liable for damages for negligence for lack of an informed consent *State Regulation of Consent to Treatment in an Emergency* App 1-A:3 in an emergency situation. In a negligence claim for lack of informed consent, health care providers can also raise the defense that a person of ordinary intelligence would understand the hazards of the treatment, the injured person indicated that he wanted treatment regardless of the risk or was not interested in receiving information about the risk, or it was reasonable for the health care provider to limit disclosure because it might have an adverse outcome on the person. [Del. Code Ann. tit. 18, § 6852]

- **Incapacity:** Capacity to consent to medical care or treatment includes the ability to understand and make choices, the information upon which consent is based, and the voluntariness of the decision. Consent is not required for emergency treatment defined as action required to preserve the life or bodily integrity of the person. [Code of Del. Regs. 40-601-401]

- **Minors:** A minor age 12 or older who is or may be pregnant or suffering from an infectious disease may give written consent for any diagnostic, preventive, or therapeutic procedure, except abortion. The minor's consent is valid regardless of whether the pregnancy or disease is later confirmed. The physician has the discretion to provide or withhold information concerning treatment from the minor's parents or spouse. If the minor consents to an operation, however, notice of intent to perform the operation shall be given to the minor's parents by telegram sent at the time of diagnosis by the surgeon. The surgeon may proceed without notice if delay would endanger the minor's life or if there is a reasonable probability of irreparable injury. [Del. Code Ann. tit. 13, §§ 708 & 710]

 The following individuals may consent to any diagnostic or therapeutic procedure for a minor by a health care provider: a parent, a married minor, a spouse (if the minor is unable to consent due to physical disability), a minor 18 or older, or a minor parent for his or her child. In the case of a traumatic injury that, if untreated, might reasonably threaten the minor's health or life, a temporary custodian may consent, after reasonable efforts are made to obtain parental consent. [Del. Code Ann. tit. 13, § 707]

DISTRICT OF COLUMBIA

- **Emergency:** In an emergency in which delay in obtaining consent for surgery would create a risk or harm as indicated by the judgment of two physicians, the surgery may be performed without consent of the person if information is provided to the person's parent, guardian, spouse or next of kin to allow them to make a knowing consent prior to the surgical procedure. If there is no person who can be reasonably contacted then the surgery may be performed with the approval of the chief medical officer of the facility. [D.C. Code Ann. § 7-1305.07]

- **Incapacity:** Mental incapacity to make health care decisions shall be certified by two physicians, one a psychiatrist, with a written opinion to be included in the patient's record regarding the cause and nature of the incapacity and its extent and probable duration. The record must show that the patient is incapable of understanding the health care choice, making a decision concerning the particular treatment, or communicating a decision even if capable of making it. A provision also specifies which individuals are authorized to consent for an incapacitated person, in order of authority. [D.C. Code Ann. §§ 21-2204, 21-2210 & 21-2211]

- **Minors:** A health care provider may treat a minor without parental consent when the provider believes that delay would substantially increase the risk to the minor's health or life, or would unduly prolong suffering. A health care provider may render emergency services to any injured minor when the provider believes that giving aid is the only alternative to probable death or serious physical or mental damage. In an emergency where major surgery or any dangerous procedures will be performed, concurrence of another physician shall, if practical, be obtained. [22 D.C. Code Mun. Regs. § 600]

No health care professional is compelled to treat a minor based on the minor's own consent, but may refer the minor. A health care provider may rely upon a minor's representations if the provider acts in good faith. The health care provider has discretion whether to inform the parents of any treatment given or needed in the following situations: (1) severe complications, major surgery, or prolonged hospitalization; (2) the safety and health of the minor patient is in jeopardy; or (3) the minor's physical and mental health and family harmony would benefit. [22 D.C. Code Mun. Regs. § 602]

FLORIDA

- **Emergency:** Any hospital or employee working within a clinical area of the facility and providing patient care, who renders good faith medical care because of an emergency, will not be liable for damages for the medical care except when care is given with reckless disregard for the consequences to the life or health of another. Reckless disregard for consequences is conduct of the health care provider that the health care provider knew or should have known would result in injury to life or health. Factors to consider in determining whether there was reckless disregard include: seriousness of the situation, lack of time to obtain consultation, lack of a prior patient-physician relationship, inability to obtain a proper medical history, and time constraints of co-existing emergencies. [Fla. Stat. § 768.13]

- **Incapacity:** A facility administrator may petition the court to appoint a guardian based upon the opinion of a psychiatrist that a patient is incompetent to consent to treatment. The facility must provide sufficient information so that the guardian can decide whether to consent to treatment, including information that the treatment is essential to the care of the patient and does not present an unreasonable risk of serious, hazardous, or irreversible side effects. [Fla. Stat. § 394.4598] If the patient has not named a surrogate decision maker, the following persons are authorized to consent to health care for the patient, in order of priority: court-appointed guardian; spouse; adult child; parent; adult sibling; adult relative having regular contact with the patient; close friend. [Fla. Stat. § 765.401]

- **Minors:** A physician may render emergency medical care to a minor without parental consent when delay would endanger the health or well-being of the minor and care is rendered in a licensed hospital or college health service. Treatment without parental consent is only permissible when parental consent can not be immediately obtained because the minor's condition renders him incapable or revealing the identity of the parents or guardian or the parents or legal guardian cannot be immediately located at their residence or business. The parents should be given notice of the medical care as soon as possible after care is rendered and the reason for treatment without consent should be documented in the medical record. There is no liability for medical care provided within accepted standards of medical practice. [Fla. Stat. § 743.064]

GEORGIA

- **Emergency:** Consent to medical care is implied in an emergency. An emergency arises when competent medical judgment dictates that treatment is necessary, a person authorized to consent is not readily available, and delay in treatment is reasonably expected to jeopardize the patient's life or health, including potential disfigurement or impaired faculties. [Ga. Code Ann. § 31-9-3; Ga. Comp. R. & Regs. § 360-14.02] A patient is presumed to consent to CPR unless a do not resuscitate order is in place and nothing limits the right of an adult to refuse medical care. [Ga. Code Ann. §§ 31-39-7 & 31-39-9]

  Detailed consent procedures relating to cardiopulmonary resuscitation. [Ga. Code Ann. §§ 31-39-3 through 31-39-9]
- **Incapacity:** The inability of any adult to consent to treatment must be documented in the medical record by a physician who has personally examined the adult and found that the adult either lacks sufficient understanding or capacity to make a responsible decision regarding medical treatment, or lacks the ability to communicate consent decisions. When a person has been found unable to consent to treatment, the following persons may consent on the person's behalf, in order of priority: spouse; guardian; adult child; parent; adult sibling; grandparent. [Ga. Code Ann. § 31-9-2]
- **Minors:** A parent may consent to treatment for a minor, even if the parent is a minor. A married person may consent to treatment even if a minor. A person acting in loco parentis may consent for a minor under his care. Any female may consent to treatment for childbirth, pregnancy, or prevention of pregnancy regardless of age. [Ga. Code Ann. § 31-9-2]

HAWAII

- **Emergency:** Informed consent is not required when obtaining consent for an emergency treatment or surgical procedure is not feasible under the circumstances without adversely affecting the patient's condition. [Haw. Rev. Stat. § 671-3(d)]
- **Incapacity:** Informed consent must be obtained from the patient's guardian if the patient is not competent to give informed consent, before any nonemergency treatment for mental illness. This consent shall be a part of the patient's record. [Haw. Rev. Stat. § 334E-1]
- **Minors:** The consent for medical care by a minor is valid when it is for pregnancy, venereal disease, or family planning. The consent is binding as if the minor was of the age of majority and cannot be later disaffirmed. [Haw. Rev. Stat. § 577A-2]

IDAHO

- **Emergency:** When a medical emergency exists that would endanger the life or health of the person if treatment is delayed or withheld, then the attending physician or dentist may authorize and provide for the care and treatment or procedure as if consent had been given. [Idaho Code § 39-4503(g)]

- **Incapacity:** Any person of ordinary intelligence can consent to his or her own health care. If a person does not have the capacity to consent for medical care for himself, then the law presumes the following may consent in the order of priority listed: legal guardian, living will and durable power of attorney for health care, spouse, parent, relative, competent person responsible for the care of the person. [Idaho Code §§ 39-4502, 39-4503]

- **Minors:** The following may consent to care for a minor in the order of priority listed: legal guardian, living will and durable power of attorney for health care, spouse, parent, relative, competent person responsible for the care of the person. [Idaho Code § 39-4503] A court may authorize medical or surgical care for a child when the parents or legal guardian are not immediately available and cannot be found after reasonable effort and a physician indicates that it is his professional opinion that the life of the child would be greatly endangered without treatment and the parent or guardian refuses or fails consent. The court will make every effort to grant the parents or guardian an immediate informal hearing as long as the hearing does not jeopardize the child's life. Oral authorization by the court is sufficient to allow for treatment of the child. [Idaho Code § 16-1627]

ILLINOIS

- **Incapacity:** Declaration form for mental health treatment. [755 Ill. Comp. Stat. 43/75] Providers may rely on the decision by a surrogate decision maker to the same extent as if the decision had been made by a patient with capacity. [755 Ill. Comp. Stat. 40/30]

- **Minors:** A physician may render services without parental consent when the physician believes that an attempt to obtain consent would result in delay that would increase the risk to the minor's life or health. [410 Ill. Comp. Stat. 210/3(a)]

INDIANA

- **Emergency:** Consent to health care is not required in an emergency. [Ind. Code § 34-18-12-9]

- **Incapacity:** Before providing mental health services, a provider must obtain consent. A patient's legal guardian or other court-appointed representative, health care representative, or attorney-in-fact for health care are authorized to consent on behalf of a mentally incompetent person. [Ind. Code §§ 16-36-1.5-4 through 16-36-1.5-6] Whenever a provider believes that a patient may lack capacity to give informed consent, the provider shall consult with the attorney-in-fact who has the power to act for the patient. [Ind. Code § 30-5-7-3] Consent to medical treatment of an incompetent person is not required in an emergency. A superintendent of a health care facility may consent to treatment of an incompetent patient. If the superintendent and the treating physician determine that a patient is incompetent to consent to treatment that is medically necessary, the superintendent shall obtain a second opinion from a physician independent of the facility. [Ind. Code §§ 16-36-3-3, 16-36-3-4 & 16-36-3-5]

- **Minors:** The following persons may consent to health care for a minor: (1) a guardian; (2) a parent or person in loco parentis, if there is no guardian or the guardian is unavailable or fails to act; (3) an adult sibling, if there is no guardian, or if a parent is not available or declines to act. [Ind. Code § 16-36-1-5]

IOWA

- **Emergency:** A provider may render emergency care without consent when the patient is unable to consent for any reason and there is no legally authorized person reasonably available to consent. [Iowa Code § 147A.10]
- **Incapacity:** A person may prepare a durable power of attorney for another to make health care decisions in their behalf in the event the person is incapable. A health care provider caring for the person or the provider's employee cannot serve as the attorney in fact. [Iowa Code §§ 144B.1 *et seq.*]

KANSAS

- **Minors:** A health care provider may render emergency care in good faith to a minor without first obtaining parental consent. [Kan. Stat. Ann. § 65-2891] A minor sixteen or over may consent to hospital, surgical, or medical treatment procedures when no parent or guardian is immediately available and the consent may not be disaffirmed by the minor. [Kan. Stat. Ann. § 38-123b] A pregnant minor can consent to medical care. A minor can also consent to treatment for venereal disease, drug abuse or addiction. [Kan. Stat. Ann. §§ 38-123, 65-2892 & 65-2892a]

KENTUCKY

- **Emergency:** A provider is not required to obtain consent prior to providing care in an emergency situation. [Ky. Rev. Stat. Ann. § 304.40-320(3)]
- **Minors:** A minor may receive emergency medical services without parental consent when the provider believes that delaying treatment to obtain consent would risk the minor's life or health. [Ky. Rev. Stat. Ann. § 214.185(4)]

LOUISIANA

- **Emergency:** Consent to treatment is implied where an emergency exists, a person authorized to consent is not reasonably available, and a delay in treatment could jeopardize the patient's life or health or result in disfigurement or impaired faculties. [La. Rev. Stat. Ann. § 40:1299.54]
- **Incapacity:** The following may consent, in order of priority, to medical treatment for an adult who is not competent to act: a judicially appointed tutor or curator; an authorized agent for health care; a spouse not judicially separated; an adult child; a parent; a sibling; other relatives. [La. Rev. Stat. Ann. § 40:1299.53]
- **Minors:** Minors may consent to diagnosis and treatment of an illness or disease. Parental or spousal consent is not necessary, but a provider has discretion as to whether to inform a spouse or parent as to treatment given or needed. [La. Rev. Stat. Ann. § 40:1095]

MAINE

- **Incapacity:** A surrogate may make a decision to withhold or withdraw life sustaining treatment for a person who lacks capacity when there is no guardian and the person has a terminal illness or is in a persistent vegetative state (PVS). The priority of family members who can act as surrogate is spelled out. No judicial approval is needed for the surrogate decision to be binding. [Me. Rev. Stat. Ann. tit. 18A, § 5-805]
- **Minors:** A children's home may consent to emergency treatment for a state ward residing in the home. [Me. Rev. Stat. Ann. tit. 22, § 3-B] Treatment for venereal disease, drug and alcohol abuse, or sexual assault evidence can take place without the consent of a parent or guardian. [Me. Rev. Stat. Ann. tit. 32, § 3292]

MARYLAND

- **Emergency:** In an emergency, a health care provider may treat a patient who is incapable of making an informed decision without consent if no person authorized to consent is immediately available, there is a substantial risk of death or serious harm to the patient, and delaying treatment to obtain consent would adversely affect the patient's condition. [Md. Code Ann., Health-Gen. § 5-607]
- **Incapacity:** If a person has been certified to be incapable of making an informed decision and has not appointed a health care agent, a provider may obtain consent for the person's health care from the following, in order of priority: an appointed guardian; a spouse; an adult child; a parent; an adult sibling; a friend or relative who has had regular contact with the person and is familiar with the person's activities, health, and beliefs. [Md. Code Ann., Health-Gen. § 5-605]
- **Minors:** A minor may consent to medical treatment if the minor is married or is a parent, or if the provider believes that the minor's life or health would be adversely affected by delaying treatment to obtain the requisite consent. [Md. Code Ann., Health-Gen. § 20-102]

MASSACHUSETTS

- **Emergency:** No consent is required for medical care in an emergency. A medical emergency includes a condition that is immediately life threatening including severe bleeding, blocked airway, unconsciousness, cardiac arrest, cardiovascular accident, a fracture, extensive burns, severe cuts, severe injury, or any condition where delay in treatment would harm the life, limb, or mental well-being of the patient. [110 Mass. Code Regs., 11.01 & 11.03]
- **Incapacity:** When an attending physician determines that a patient lacks capacity because of mental illness or developmental disability, based upon training or experience in diagnosing or treating similar conditions, the authority of a health care agent, if one has been named, shall begin, and the agent has authority to make any health care decision that the patient could make after receiving all medical information necessary to make informed decisions about his or her health care. [Mass. Gen.

Laws ch. 201D, §§ 5 & 6] If there is no health care proxy, a provider may rely upon the informed consent of responsible parties on behalf of incompetent or incapacitated patients. [Mass. Gen. Laws ch. 201D, § 16]

- **Minors:** A physician or hospital may provide emergency treatment to a minor without parental consent when delay in treatment will endanger the minor's life, limb, or mental well-being. [Mass. Gen. Laws ch. 112, § 12F] A provider may treat a minor in the custody or care of the Department of Social Services (DSS) in an emergency without anyone's Consent. [110 Mass. Code Regs. 11.01 & 11.03; *see* 110 Mass. Code Regs. 11.11 through 11.23 for consent requirements applicable to specific extraordinary medical treatment]

  A provider may treat a minor in the custody of the Department of Youth Services (Medicaid recipient) in an emergency without anyone's consent. [109 Mass. Code Regs. 11.04; *see* 109 Mass. Code Regs. 11.13 through 11.17 & 11.30 for consent requirements applicable to specific extraordinary treatment]

MICHIGAN

- **Emergency:** Emergency medical services personnel may provide treatment to a person who objects to the treatment if they determine that the person's condition makes him or her incapable of competently objecting, unless the objection is expressly based on the person's religious beliefs. [Mich. Comp. Laws § 333.20969]
- **Incapacity:** Written consent of the nearest relative, legal guardian, or person in loco parentis is required for a person needing surgical or medical treatment who is not of sound mind or not in a condition to make his or her own decisions. [Mich. Comp. Laws § 400.66H]
- **Minors:** A court may order that medical services be provided to a child whose health requires it and whose parent has not provided treatment because of legitimate religious beliefs. [Mich. Comp. Laws § 722.634] A minor can consent to substance abuse treatment and the health professional may inform the spouse, parent, guardian or person in loco parentis of treatment given for medical reasons. [Mich. Comp. Laws § 333.6121]

MINNESOTA

- **Incapacity:** A health care facility must attempt to notify the family or designated emergency contact of a patient who enters the facility unconscious, comatose, or unable to communicate, so that the family member may participate in treatment planning, unless the patient has an advance directive to the contrary or has previously named a health care agent. [Minn. Stat. § 144.651, sub. 10(b)] Unless the person specifies otherwise, the appointment of the health care agent is considered a nomination of a guardian of the person. [Minn. Stat. § 145C.07]
- **Minors:** Any minor may receive health services without parental consent when delaying treatment to obtain consent would risk the minor's life or health. [Minn. Stat. § 144.344]

MISSISSIPPI

- **Emergency:** Consent to medical treatment is implied in an emergency if a person authorized to consent has not refused to consent or, if so, there has been a subsequent material and morbid change in the patient's condition and no authorized person is immediately available to consent. An emergency is defined as a situation where any delay caused by an attempt to obtain consent would jeopardize the patient's life or health or would reasonably result in disfigurement or impairment. [Miss. Code Ann. § 41-41-7]
- **Incapacity:** An adult or emancipated minor may execute a power of attorney for health care, which may authorize the agent to make any health care decision the principal could have made while having capacity. Unless otherwise specified, the agent's authority becomes effective upon a determination that the principal lacks capacity and ceases to be effective when the principal has recovered capacity. [Miss. Code Ann. §§ 41-41-205 & 41-41-215]
- **Minors:** The following, in order of priority, may consent to surgical or medical treatment of an unemancipated minor: the minor's guardian; a parent; an adult sibling; a grandparent. If none of the above is reasonably available, an adult who has shown special care and concern for the minor and who is reasonably available may act. [Miss. Code Ann. § 41-41-3]

MISSOURI

- **Emergency:** Consent is implied in an emergency if an authorized person has not refused to consent or, if so, there has been a subsequent material and morbid change in the patient's condition and no authorized person is immediately available and willing to consent. A situation is an emergency if medical treatment is immediately necessary and any delay caused by an attempt to obtain consent would jeopardize the patient's life or health or result in disfigurement or impairment. [Mo. Rev. Stat. § 431.063]
- **Incapacity:** An adult who is incapable of giving informed consent for treatment with any experimental treatment, test, or drug at a teaching hospital for a medical school may be treated with the consent of the following persons, in order of priority: spouse; adult child; parent; sibling; relative by blood or marriage. [Mo. Rev. Stat. § 431.064]
- **Minors:** Any parent may consent to medical treatment for his or her minor child in his or her legal custody. In the absence of an authorized parent at a time when delay may jeopardize the minor's life or health or result in disfigurement or impairment, any adult sibling, grandparent, or any adult standing in loco parentis for a minor may consent. A minor may consent to his own care when legally married, for pregnancy, venereal disease, or drug or substance abuse. [Mo. Rev. Stat. § 431.061] A physician, nurse, or emergency medical technician may render emergency care without compensation to a minor at the scene of an accident without obtaining parental consent. [Mo. Rev. Stat. § 537.037]

MONTANA

- **Emergency:** A health professional can render emergency care, without compensation, when it is believed that the care is the only alternative to death or serious physical or mental damage. [Mont. Code Ann. § 41-1-405]
- **Incapacity:** Anyone eighteen years of age or older may have a written declaration to withhold or withdraw life sustaining treatment. [Mont. Code Ann. § 50-9-103]
- **Minors:** Any minor may consent to emergency care without which the minor's health would be jeopardized. [Mont. Code Ann. § 41-1-402] A minor may consent to emergency psychiatric counseling without parental or spousal consent when that consent cannot be obtained within a reasonable time and there is danger to the life, safety, or property of the minor or others. [Mont. Code Ann. § 41-1-406]

  A health professional does not need parental or spousal consent to provide non-emergency services to a minor for a condition that will endanger the minor's life or health if obtaining consent would delay services. If a minor is mentally or physically incapable of giving consent and has no known relatives or guardian, consent is not required for necessary health services. [Mont. Code Ann. § 41-1-405]

NEBRASKA

- **Emergency:** There is no liability for medical care rendered at the scene of the accident. [Neb. Rev. Stat. § 25-21,186] Emergency care is not required when the person objects to treatment on religious or other grounds. Out-of-hospital care providers are not liable for rendering treatment when the person is unable to give consent. [Neb. Rev. Stat. §§ 71-5193, 71-5195] Signing of written information is not required prior to an initial telehealth consultation in an emergency in which the patient is unable to sign and the legal representative is unavailable. [Neb. Rev. Stat. § 71-8505]
- **Incapacity:** Incapacity means that the person is unable to understand the health care decision and its alternatives or is unable to communicate an informed health care decision. [Neb. Rev. Stat. § 30-3402(7)] A person can designate another competent adult with power of attorney to make health care decisions. [Neb. Rev. Stat. § 30-3403]

NEVADA

- **Emergency:** Consent will be implied if the proposed procedure is reasonably necessary and any delay could reasonably be expected to result in death, disfigurement, impairment, or serious bodily harm, and no authorized person is available to consent. [Nev. Rev. Stat. § 41A.120]
- **Incapacity:** The legal guardian of a person who has been adjudicated mentally incompetent must give written informed consent to a plan of care, treatment or training, or necessary surgical procedure at a mental health facility. [Nev. Rev. Stat. § 433.484]
- **Minors:** A minor may consent to treatment for him or herself or his or her child if the minor is in danger of a serious health hazard if treatment is not provided. Parental consent is not necessary if a minor described above understands the nature and purpose of the treatment and its probable outcome and voluntarily requests it. Before

initiating treatment, the provider must attempt to obtain the minor's consent to communicate with a parent and note such efforts in the record, but may omit such efforts if it would jeopardize necessary treatment. [Nev. Rev. Stat. § 129.030] Any person standing in loco parentis to a minor may consent to emergency treatment of a minor who needs immediate hospitalization or medical attention if a parent cannot be located. [Nev. Rev. Stat. § 129.040]

NEW HAMPSHIRE

- **Emergency:** A health care professional need not obtain consent in rendering emergency treatment to any person who is unable to give consent for any reason, including minority where there is no person available who is legally authorized to consent to the treatment. [N.H. Rev. Stat. Ann. § 153-A:18]
- **Incapacity:** A person may appoint a health care agent who can make decisions on behalf of the person when the person lacks the capacity to do so himself. [N.H. Rev. Stat. Ann. § 137-J:14] A guardian can consent or withhold consent to medical treatment. [N.H. Rev. Stat. Ann. § 464-A:25]
- **Minor:** Any minor 12 years of age or older may consent to treatment for drug dependency. [N.H. Rev. Stat. Ann. § 318-B:12-a]

NEW JERSEY

- **Emergency:** No consent is required for an emergency. [N.J. Stat. Ann. § 26:2H-12.8] If a patient does not give informed consent, the physician will explain the reasons in the medical record. [N.J. Admin. Code § 8:43-G-4.1(a)(7)]
- **Incapacity:** Executive officers of state or county mental or correctional institutions or juvenile facilities may consent to essential medical treatment of incompetent persons confined in or placed by those facilities if there is no known parent or guardian competent to consent to the treatment or if after reasonable notice the parent or guardian refuses or fails to execute written consent or denial to the treatment. [N.J. Stat. Ann. § 30:4-7.2] If the patient is unable to give informed consent, then the consent of the next of kin, or guardian, or by advanced directive should be sought. [N.J. Admin. Code § 8:43G-4.1(a)(7)] If a person lacks capacity the health care representative can make decisions on behalf of the person, even if a legal guardian is appointed, unless the terms of the legal guardian appointment or court decree indicate otherwise. [N.J. Stat. Ann. § 26:2H-61]
- **Minors:** Parental notice is required for treatment of a minor who appears to have been sexually assaulted, unless it is not in the minor's best interests, but emergency care may be provided if the parents cannot be located. [N.J. Stat. Ann. § 9:17A-4]

NEW MEXICO

- **Emergency:** A person who renders care in good faith at the scene of an emergency is immune from liability. [N.M. Stat. Ann. § 24-10-3] A physician may administer a psychotropic medication in order to protect the client from serious harm on an emergency basis. The medical record should include a report explaining the emergency and the reason other less drastic treatment without consent would not work. [N.M. Stat. Ann. § 43-1-15]

- **Incapacity:** Any person regardless of age can consent to care for a sexually transmitted disease or her own pregnancy. [N.M. Stat. Ann. §§ 24-1-9, 24-1-13] If a person is not competent, consent can be obtained from the legal guardian or other person authorized by law. [N.M. Stat. Ann. §§ 24-2B-3, 45-5-209] A surrogate may make a health care decision on behalf of a person who lacks capacity when there is no agent or guardian. Family members are listed as potential surrogates followed by someone with special care for the person. If there is a disagreement among surrogates, the health provider may follow the decision of the majority. N.M. Stat. Ann. § 24-7A-5]

- **Minors:** Anyone standing in loco parentis to a minor may consent to emergency medical attention for the minor if a parent cannot be located with reasonable efforts. [N.M. Stat. Ann. § 24-10-2] An emancipated minor or minor who is married may render consent to medical care which cannot later by disaffirmed. [N.M. Stat. Ann. §§ 24-10-1 & 24-10-2] A minor can consent to an HIV test on himself. [N.M. Stat. Ann. § 24-2B-3]

NEW YORK

- **Emergency:** Informed consent is only required before nonemergency procedures. [N.Y. Comp. Code R. & Regs. tit. 10, § 405.7(b)(9)]

- **Incapacity:** Generally, a person who is not capable of providing informed consent may receive treatment with the consent of close relatives (a parent, spouse, or adult child) or a judicially appointed surrogate (a guardian, conservator, or committee), or by court order. In the absence of one of those surrogates or where those surrogates are willing, a surrogate decision-making committee may consent. [N.Y. Comp. Codes R. & Regs. tit. 14, § 710.1]

- **Minors:** A medical practitioner may render emergency medical attention to a minor without parental consent when an attempt to obtain consent would delay treatment that would increase the risk to the minor's life or health. [N.Y. Pub. Health Law § 2504] A person who is married or pregnant can consent to medical care for herself. [N.Y. Pub. Health Law § 2504]

NORTH CAROLINA

- **Emergency:** Informed consent is only required before non-emergency procedures or treatments. [10A N.C. Admin. Code 13B.3302]

- **Incapacity:** Any adult of sound mind may make an advance instruction regarding mental health treatment, which may include consent to or refusal of mental health treatment when the principal has been determined to be incapable. Such an advance instruction may be combined with a health care power of attorney. [N.C. Gen. Stat. §§ 122C-72 & 122C-77, 32A-16]

- **Minors:** A physician may provide emergency treatment to a minor where: (1) a parent cannot be located or contacted after reasonable effort when the minor needs the treatment; (2) an effort to contact a parent would cause a delay that would seriously worsen the minor's condition or endanger his or her life; (3) the minor's identity is unknown; or (4) the parents refuse to consent, and the need for immediate treatment is so apparent that the delay involved in obtaining a court order would endanger the minor's life or seriously worsen his or her condition, in which case a second medical opinion shall be obtained. [N.C. Gen. Stat. § 90-21.1]

NORTH DAKOTA

- **Incapacity:** Persons who may consent to health care for an incapacitated person are, in the following order of priority: (1) a person to whom the patient has given a durable power of attorney that includes the authority to make health care decisions, unless the court has authorized a guardian to make medical decisions; (2) the appointed guardian; or (3) any persons from the following classes who have maintained significant contacts with the patient: (a) the patient's spouse; (b) children older than age 18; (c) parents, including a stepparent; (d) adult siblings; (e) grandparents; (f) grandchildren older than age 18; (g) close relative or friend older than age 18. [N.D. Cent. Code § 23-12-13]
- **Minors:** Persons who may consent to health care for a minor are, in order of priority, the same as those listed under the Incapacity category. [N.D. Cent. Code 23-12-13] A minor may consent to emergency treatment in a life-threatening situation without parental consent. [N.D. Cent. Code § 14-10-17.1]

OHIO

- **Emergency:** No person is liable for rendering care at the scene of an emergency outside the doctor's office or hospital unless there is willful or wanton misconduct. [Ohio Rev. Code Ann. § 2305.23] No physician or registered nurse advising emergency medical services through communication device or telemetering will be liable unless there is willful or wanton misconduct. [Ohio Rev. Code Ann. § 4765.49]
- **Incapacity:** An adult of sound mind may create a durable power of attorney for health care. The attorney-in-fact can make health care decisions for the principal. [Ohio Rev. Code Ann. §§ 1337.12, 1337.13]
- **Minors:** A minor can consent to an HIV test. [Ohio Rev. Code Ann. § 3701.242]

OKLAHOMA

- **Incapacity:** An attorney-in-fact previously designated by a person may make mental health treatment decisions for the person in the event that the person is certified as incapable of giving informed consent to mental health treatment that is necessary. [Okla. Stat. tit. 43A, §§ 11-104 through 11-107]
- **Minors:** A minor may consent to emergency medical treatment if delaying treatment to obtain parental or spousal consent would endanger his or her life or health; the provider must, however, make a reasonable attempt to inform the minor's parent or spouse. Any spouse of a minor may consent to treatment when the minor is unable to

consent because of physical or mental incapacity. When a minor is incapacitated and has no known relatives, two physicians may agree on the treatment. [Okla. Stat. tit. 63, § 2602]

OREGON

- **Incapacity:** A person of sound mind may appoint a representative to make decisions regarding mental health treatment on his or her behalf in the event that he or she becomes unable to evaluate information or communicate, to the extent that he or she lacks capacity to consent to mental health treatment. [Or. Rev. Stat. §§ 127.700 through 127.705 & 127.712] A health care representative can be appointed to make decisions on behalf of a person who lacks capacity, or the person may set forth advance directives in advance regarding the medical choices he would like made. [Or. Rev. Stat. §§ 127.535, 127.550] A physician may withdraw life sustaining procedures if no surrogate decision maker is available and if certain conditions are met, i.e., a terminal illness, unconsciousness, when no benefit would come from the procedures, etc. [Or. Rev. Stat. § 127.635]
- **Minors:** A minor age 15 or older may consent to medical or surgical treatment without parental consent. [Or. Rev. Stat. § 109.640] When a parent is not available to consent to the emergency medical care for a minor, a judge of the juvenile court can authorize care. [Or. Rev. Stat. § 419B.110]

PENNSYLVANIA

- **Emergency:** In an emergency there is no duty to obtain informed consent. [40 Pa. Stat. § 1303.504, 28 Pa. Code § 103.22]
- **Incapacity:** A person may set forth a durable power of attorney authorizing someone to act on their behalf making medical decisions if needed, or a person can be declared incapacitated and a guardian established. [20 Pa. Cons. Stat. § 5604, 20 Pa. Cons. Stat. § 5512.1]
- **Minors:** Parental consent is not needed for treatment of a minor when an attempt to obtain consent would cause a delay of treatment that would increase the risk to the minor's life or health. [35 Pa. § Stat. § 10104] A parent or legal guardian may confer the power to consent to health care to an adult friend or family member. [11 Pa. § Stat. § 2513]

RHODE ISLAND

- **Emergency:** Informed consent is impliedly waived in connection with emergency services rendered outside a hospital or in connection with EMS training, unless the treatment is inconsistent with the level of the person's training and experience and unless it involved gross negligence or willful misconduct. [R.I. Gen. Laws § 23-17.6-5]
- **Minors:** Any person age 16 or older or who is married may consent to routine emergency or surgical care. [R.I. Gen. Laws § 23-4.6-1]

SOUTH CAROLINA

- **Emergency:** No consent is necessary for treatment of a patient unable to consent if no representative of the patient is available immediately and the delay of trying to locate an authorized person presents a substantial risk of death, serious permanent disfigurement, loss or impairment of a bodily member or organ, or other serious threat to the patient's health. No consent is needed for treatment to relieve suffering if an authorized person is unavailable. [S.C. Code Ann. § 44-66-40]

- **Incapacity:** Health care decisions regarding an adult, or a married or emancipated minor, who is unable to consent, may be made by the following, in order of priority: court-appointed guardian; person named in a durable power of attorney; person given priority to make health care decisions for the patient under another statute; spouse, unless legally separated; parent or adult child; adult sibling, grandparent or adult grandchild; any other relative with a close personal relationship with the patient; person with authority to make health care decisions for the patient under another statute. [S.C. Code Ann. §§ 44-66-20 & 44-66-30] No consent is needed for treatment that is necessary to relieve suffering; restore bodily function; or preserve the life, health, or bodily integrity of a patient unable to consent, where no one authorized to make health care decisions for the patient is available. [S.C. Code Ann. § 44-66-50] The preceding does not apply where the physician knows that the health care is contrary to the patient's religious beliefs. [S.C. Code Ann. § 44-66-60]

- **Minors:** A health care provider may render any necessary health services to a minor without parental consent, with the exception of an operation. An operation may be performed without consent if essential to the child's health or life. [S.C. Code Ann. § 20-7-290] A minor age 16 or older may consent to any health services other than an operation. [S.C. Code Ann. § 20-7-280] A minor parent can consent for care of his/her child. [S.C. Code Ann. § 20-7-300] Non-emergency health care decisions for minors can be made by others in the following order of priority: legal guardian, parent, grandparent or adult sibling, other relatives with a close relationship to the person, authorized designee of the department. [S.C. Code Ann. § 44-26-60]

SOUTH DAKOTA

- **Emergency:** Consent is not required in an emergency. [S.D. Codified Laws § 34-12C-8]

- **Incapacity:** A health care decision may be made by another person for a person who (1) has been declared legally incompetent, (2) has had a guardian appointed, or (3) whose physician has determined that he or she is incapable of giving informed consent. Such a determination by a physician is effective until either the physician or a court later determines that the person is capable of giving informed consent or that the diagnosis is no longer valid. An attending physician may decline to determine a person's capacity for informed consent and a health care provider may, but need not, rely on any such determination. [S.D. Codified Laws § 34-12C-2] The family members of an incapacitated person who has no legal guardian or attorney-in-fact may consent to medical treatment for the person, in the following order of priority: spouse; adult

166

child; parent; adult sibling; grandparent or adult grandchild; aunt or uncle, or adult niece or nephew. [S.D. Codified Laws §§ 34-12C-3 & 34-12C-6]
- **Minors:** A minor may receive emergency medical treatment without parental consent if a parent is not immediately available and delaying treatment to obtain consent would threaten the minor's life or health. [S.D. Codified Laws § 20-9-4.2]

TENNESSEE

- **Minors:** Parental consent is not necessary for emergency medical treatment of a minor in order to save the minor's life or prevent worsening of his or her medical condition, but a reasonable effort must be made to notify the minor's parents before treatment begins. [Tenn. Code Ann. § 63-6-222]

TEXAS

- **Emergency:** Consent for emergency medical care is not required when a person can not communicate because of injury, accident, illness, or when unconscious and suffers from a life-threatening injury or illness. A court may order treatment for a person in an emergency when the person is unable to consent to prevent serious bodily injury or loss of life. [Tex. Health & Safety Code § 773.008] A health care provider's failure to disclose the risks of treatment may not be considered negligent in the case of an emergency. [Tex. Civ. Prac. & Rem. Code § 74.106] In the case of emergency care, there is no obligation to obtain consent from a surrogate decision maker. [Tex. Health & Safety Code Ann. § 313.003]
- **Incapacity:** The following persons, in order of priority, may consent to treatment of a hospital or nursing home patient who is mentally or physically incapable of communicating: the patient's spouse; adult child (with waiver and consent of other adult children); a majority of available adult children; parents; the person the patient identified to act for him or her before becoming incapacitated; nearest living relative; or clergy member. [Tex. Health & Safety Code Ann. § 313.004]
- **Minors:** Consent for emergency care for a minor is not required when there is a life-threatening injury of illness and the parents or guardian are not present. [Tex. Health & Safety Code § 773.008] When a parent is unable to consent for a minor, the following may consent: a grandparent, adult sibling, adult aunt or uncle, an educational institution or adult that has written authority to consent, the court, an adult responsible under juvenile court proceedings, a peace officer who has a minor in custody, and the Texas Youth Commission for a child who has been committed. [Tex. Fam. Code § 32.001]

UTAH

- **Emergency:** Health care providers who render emergency medical care in good faith to a patient have implied consent of the patient where the patient is unable to give his or her consent and where there is no legal representative available to consent to emergency treatment. [Utah Code Ann. § 26-8a-601] A person who is terminally ill may establish an advance directive to withhold life sustaining measures, but an emergency provider is not bound by the directive unless the person who is ill is identified as a person with a directive such as through an identifying bracelet. [Utah Code Ann. § 75-2-1105.5]

- **Incapacity:** A guardian may be appointed to make decisions on behalf of a person who is incapacitated. [Utah Code Ann. § 75-5-303] The following can consent to health care: a parent for a minor child, a married person for a spouse, a person acting in loco parentis for a minor, a person 18 or over for a parent, any person 18 years of age or older, a female of any age in connection with pregnancy and childbirth, or an adult sibling or grandparent in the absence of a parent. [Utah Code Ann. § 78-14-5] When a person has a terminal illness and lacks the capacity to consent, life-sustaining procedures may be withdrawn when the physician has the written concurrence of another physician and the spouse, parent, or adult child. If the family member making the decision is not the legal guardian, the document must have two witnesses as well. [Utah Code Ann. § 72-2-1107]
- **Minor:** Consent for medical treatment for a minor as indicated in the section on incapacity. [Utah Code Ann. § 78-14-5]

VERMONT

- **Emergency:** There is no right of action to recover for medical malpractice based on lack of informed consent in the case of an emergency. Further, in an informed consent suit, it is a defense that consent was not reasonably possible. [Vt. Stat. Ann. tit. 12, § 1909(b) & (c); Vt. Stat. Ann. tit. 18, § 1852]
- **Incapacity:** Adults can designate someone with a durable power of attorney for health care in the event of later incapacity through an advanced directive. [Vt. Stat. Ann. tit. 18, § 5263]

VIRGINIA

- **Emergency:** Consent is not required in an emergency for mental health or drug abuse treatment. Consent for continued treatment that lasts more than 24 hours for care rendered in an emergency should be obtained. If capacity of the person to consent is in question, an independent evaluation should be performed by a qualified professional not participating the person's care. [12 Va. Admin. Code § 35-115-70].
- **Incapacity:** A circuit court may authorize treatment for a mental or physical disorder of a person who is incapable of making an informed decision on his or her own behalf and who has no legal representative, if it is in the person's best interests. The court may not authorize nontherapeutic sterilization, abortion, or psychosurgery; admission to a mental retardation facility or psychiatric hospital; or use of antipsychotic medication for more than 180 days or electroconvulsive therapy for more than 60 days. [Va. Code Ann. § 37.1-134.21; *see also* Va. Health Care Decisions Act, Va. Code Ann. § 54.1-2981 through 54.1-2993 (addresses advance directives, including required procedure for physicians when advance directive is lacking)]

168

- **Minors:** Where a minor has been separated from parental custody, a judge, superintendent of social services, director, or principal executive officer of the agency or institution that has control of the minor's custody, or any person in loco parentis, may authorize necessary surgical or medical treatment. Where that person's consent cannot be obtained within a reasonable time and delay may adversely affect the minor's recovery, consent is implicitly waived, but the minor's own consent is needed if he or she is at least age 14 and physically able to consent. [Va. Code Ann. § 54.1-2969]

WASHINGTON

- **Emergency:** Consent to treatment is implied in a recognized health care emergency if the patient is not competent to give informed consent and a person authorized to consent on his or her behalf is not available. [Wash. Rev. Code § 7.70.050]
- **Incapacity:** Informed consent for an incompetent person may be obtained from, in order of priority: the patient's appointed guardian; the person to whom the patient has given a power of attorney for health care decisions; the patient's spouse; the patient's adult children; the patient's parents; the patient's adult siblings. [Wash. Rev. Code § 7.70.065]
- **Minor:** Health care providers are immune from liability for failure of informed consent if a parent consents to treatment of the minor regardless of whether the parents are married or separated, whether the consenting parent is the custodial parent, and whether or not the parents agree about the issue of consent. [Wash. Rev. Code § 26.09.310]

WEST VIRGINIA

- **Emergency:** No consent is needed for emergency medical services when the person is unable to consent and there is no person reasonably available to consent; however, this does not contravene objections to treatment on the grounds of religion, in a living will, or in a do not resuscitate order when the treating physician is aware of the will or order. [W. Va. Code § 16-4C-17]
- **Incapacity:** When a person is or becomes incapacitated and has no legal guardian or representative under a medical power of attorney, the attending physician shall select a surrogate decision maker who is authorized to make health care decisions for the incapacitated person without a court order. [W. Va. Code § 16-30-7]
- **Minors:** If there is a substantial possibility that a minor will suffer death or serious disability, disfigurement, or suffering as a result of the refusal of a parent to consent to necessary medical treatment, a court may appoint a special guardian to consent to necessary treatment. [W. Va. Code § 49-6B-1]

WISCONSIN

- **Incapacity:** A person age 18 or older and of sound mind may voluntarily execute a power of attorney for health care, which will take effect upon a finding of incapacity by two physicians or by a physician and a psychologist. [Wis. Stat. 155.05] When a court determines that a person is incompetent, it shall appoint a guardian for the person, who may consent to or refuse psychotropic medication on behalf of the person as provided in a court order. If the patient has previously executed a power of attorney for health care, the court may order that it remain in effect and limit the power of the guardian to make those health care decisions for the patient that are not to be made by the health care agent under the terms of the power of attorney. [Wis. Stat. § 880.33]

WYOMING

- **Emergency:** Consent is not required for emergency surgery. [Wyo. Stat. § 35-2-115] Consent is implied/waived where volunteer ambulances or emergency vehicles furnish emergency medical services, unless grossly negligent. Wyo. Stat. § 1-1-120.
- **Incapacity:** When a person is suspected by a law enforcement officer or examiner to be mentally ill, treatment may be given during an emergency detention period if the incompetent person's guardian consents, but that consent is not necessary where treatment is limited to diagnosis or evaluation or where treatment is necessary to prevent immediate serious physical harm. [Wyo. Stat. Ann. § 25-10-109]
- **Minors:** The court may consent to emergency medical or surgical examination or treatment of a minor taken into custody under the Juvenile Justice Act if a qualified physician believes that the minor has a serious physical condition or illness that requires prompt treatment. [Wyo. Stat. Ann. § 14-6-220]

PART 2

Joint Commission Survey Questions and Answers

INTRODUCTION

This section presents first-person accounts of the Joint Commission accreditation process from the point of view of the emergency department. The following interviews describe the staff preparation activities demonstrated by recently surveyed hospitals, their methods of sharing information about critical performance improvement initiatives, and their overall survey experience. In addition, several hospitals share tips on how best to prepare for a Joint Commission visit.

SURVEY FOCUS

Question: What did the Joint Commission survey team focus on when they visited your emergency department?

Answers:

Mary Ellen Palowitch, RN, BSN, CEN, MHA
Clinical Director, Emergency Department
Anne Arundel Medical Center
Annapolis, Maryland

Everything! Tracers—Admissions to the Inpatient Units. Surveyor was concerned about patients waiting in "holding" status (i.e., who were admitted but were waiting in the ED for a bed). Were meds given in a timely manner? Was the patient fed in the ED? (This was in direct response to a patient complaint that she was "starving" when she finally got to the floor). Was appropriate care being given while in the ED—meaning the *same level* of care as in other units of the hospital?

Also, ED through-put; turn-around times; admission back-ups; what was being done to improve ED volume; how bypass status is handled; Triage (discussed use of ESI 5-level triage system); pain assessment, re-assessment, and documentation; code cart checklists; refrigerator temperature logs; OR and PACU through-put and impact on ED; etc.

On the walk-through by a second surveyor two days later, we were asked about how we screen for domestic violence/abuse, what coverage did we have for DV/Abuse patients who needed to be seen and where were the patients interviewed; disaster planning, including whether we had a tent for hazmat, did it have hot water, did the city and county participate in our drills; chaplaincy program and ease of access; mental health patients— where are they located in the ED, are their rooms safe, how are they monitored; can the ED be locked down in an emergency; interdepartmental communications. Our physicians were asked how they handle waiting times and high volume times, discussed new Rapid Medical Evaluation process.

Andy Jones, RN
Director, Emergency Department
Russell County Medical Center
Lebanon, Virginia

Continuity of care between the ED and other areas of the hospital.

Claudia Flanagan, RN
Nurse Manager, Emergency Department
Holy Redeemer Hospital
Meadowbrook, Pennsylvania

Point-of-care testing. Doors being propped open—patient privacy—that was a very big issue. Outdated medications—the surveyors checked dates on insulin in the refrigerator.

Brennan Bryant, RN
Manager, Emergency Services
Baylor Medical Center
Irvine, Texas

The attention was focused on the processes supporting and involved in providing care to emergency department patients rather than observation of care rendered for a particular patient. There were two particular encounters. One related to taking the primary nurse of a chest pain patient and the chart to interview her about the nursing documentation and care provided. The surveyor spent approximately one hour with the staff nurse asking her to explain in detail the care, documentation and "normal process" for chest pain patients. The other encounter related to the Pediatric Crash Cart. One would expect that they check for completeness of crash cart check logs. Instead, the surveyor went to the cart and pulled the references used to care for pediatric patients. Particular interest and focus was placed on drug calculations for peds and whether the Broselow tape was current and if there were references to the Rule of 9s for calculating critical drips—unfortunately we did have a section on drug calcs related to the rule of 9s, but we quickly deleted and re-wrote references to EXCLUDE any such reference. That was it. We expected frequent repeat visits back to the ED over the several day survey process related to the use of the tracer methodology. At our institution, that didn't happen.

Kelly Dawson, RN
Nurse Manager, Emergency Services
Carson Tahoe Regional Medical Center
Carson City, Nevada

Patient ID was very big—two forms of ID, etc. Talked about disaster planning and what we had in place in that regard. Also, patient flow, ED overcrowding and what we've done to alleviate that. And, of course, patient safety.

STAFF EDUCATION AND TRAINING

Question: How have you changed your staff education and training in response to the Joint Commission's new focus on continuous readiness and the tracer methodology?

Answers:

Brennan Bryant, RN
Manager, Emergency Services

Baylor Medical Center
Irvine, Texas

We provided staff with lots of training materials—"Here are the questions you are most likely to be asked and here are the most likely answers." We made sure staff knew that during the survey, they could not look to us [department management] for answers or help. We did reassure them, however, that they could access the usual resources. This helped put staff more at ease with the process.

Kelly Dawson, RN
Nurse Manager, Emergency Services
Carson Tahoe Regional Medical Center
Carson City, Nevada

We did lots of tracers. We found we were not all that far behind in paperwork so that lessened the anxiety. The hospital did a lot of all-employee education: put together a JCAHO readiness handbook; had the QA staff attend ED staff meetings to go over expected topics, etc.

Andy Jones, RN
Director, Emergency Department
Russell County Medical Center
Lebanon, Virginia

We did a lot of staff education on unapproved abbreviations and standardized policies and procedures. Got staff comfortable with the fact that the surveyors wouldn't ask to see hard-copy documentation of policies and procedures but would ask various staff members to talk about putting the policies and procedures *into the day-to-day delivery of patient care* and then compare the individual responses.

Mary Ellen Palowitch, RN, BSN, CEN, MHA
Clinical Director, Emergency Department
Anne Arundel Medical Center
Annapolis, Maryland

We had an unannounced survey about two years ago and after that we started perpetual readiness rounds and tracer practice rounds, so we already had that level of staff training in place prior to our 2005 survey. We volunteered for unannounced visits so everyone knows he or she has to stay ready.

PERFORMANCE IMPROVEMENT

Question: How did you demonstrate performance improvement for the surveyors?

Answers:

Kelly Dawson, RN
Nurse Manager, Emergency Services

Carson Tahoe Regional Medical Center
Carson City, Nevada

We were asked what we had done with regard to certain projects, e.g., additional CNA and ED tech coverage; staffing changes that had been implemented to accommodate heavy times, etc.

Claudia Flanagan, RN
Nurse Manager, Emergency Department
Holy Redeemer Hospital
Meadowbrook, Pennsylvania

We have several measures in place that were discussed with the surveyors. For example, EKGs must be done within ten minutes of presentation and shown to a physician; any patient presenting with stroke-like symptoms must be evaluated immediately; our new pneumonia pathway and protocol requires chest x-ray and antibiotic administration within one hour.

Andy Jones, RN
Director, Emergency Department
Russell County Medical Center
Lebanon, Virginia

They were looking for what we *did* with the PI data rather than for the data itself. We were asked to demonstrate what we did with the information we learned; how it was shared with other areas of the hospital; how it impacted the quality of care, not only in the ED but throughout the hospital.

Brennan Bryant, RN
Manager, Emergency Services
Baylor Medical Center
Irvine, Texas

The two measures we demonstrated were Accuracy of 5-level Triage and Pain Scores at Discharge. These were done via retrospective chart audit. No one asked to see a PI manual or for specifics related to PI projects.

Mary Ellen Palowitch, RN, BSN, CEN, MHA
Clinical Director, Emergency Department
Anne Arundel Medical Center
Annapolis, Maryland

The first surveyor spoke at length about specific ED throughput issues and what we had in place to improve lab and x-ray report turnaround. At the leadership interview, I presented to all three surveyors the ED throughput project that had been implemented a year prior to this survey. Data on process and performance improvements was shared, including our comprehensive team approach.

PATIENT SAFETY

Question: Was there an apparent emphasis on the National Patient Safety Goals (NPSGs) and patient safety in general? How did the focus on the NPSGs affect your ED policies and procedures; e.g., improve communications; improve medication safety; decrease infection rate.

Answers:

Claudia Flanagan, RN
Nurse Manager, Emergency Department
Holy Redeemer Hospital
Meadowbrook, Pennsylvania

Yes. Patient safety was given a lot of attention. We looked at communication issues throughout the hospital (not just the ED). Patient falls—we're looking at every patient's fall potential—trying to identify those patients at risk and take preventive measures. For example, our pharmacy distributed a list identifying and highlighting those medications that put a patient at increased risk of falling.

Brennan Bryant, RN
Manager, Emergency Services
Baylor Medical Center
Irvine, Texas

Patient safety—yes. Previously, we wouldn't have expected the surveyors to do such a detailed analysis of the cart contents, the references located within or to support its use. In relation to NPSG, monitoring that occurred related to read back of verbal orders occurred outside the department and in tandem with other tracers. There was not a follow along to ensure that two patient identifiers were used—there were a couple of staff questioned about how and when they identify patients.

Mary Ellen Palowitch, RN, BSN, CEN, MHA
Clinical Director, Emergency Department
Anne Arundel Medical Center
Annapolis, Maryland

Definitely! Lots of emphasis on patient ID and procedures to ensure patient safety. Also, acceptable abbreviations and Do Not Use abbreviation lists.

Kelly Dawson, RN
Nurse Manager, Emergency Services
Carson Tahoe Regional Medical Center
Carson City, Nevada

This was huge! But it wasn't difficult for us. Rather than being asked to list what we had done toward the NPSGs, the surveyors approached this as "real-person care"—"The patient in Room 4, how do you know who he is? What was done to confirm his ID?" Very much a case study approach that seemed to make the staff more comfortable.

Andy Jones, RN
Director, Emergency Department
Russell County Medical Center
Lebanon, Virginia

Yes. A big push on that. Mostly through watch and observe. The surveyor would follow a staff member into a patient's room to see if identification measures were taken—e.g., saying the patient's name, checking the patient's wristband, asking for the patient's date of birth, etc. Again, they were looking for actions, not just documentation.

SURVEY PREPARATION ADVICE

Question: What advice can you share with other emergency departments that would help them prepare for a Joint Commission site visit?

Answers:

Mary Ellen Palowitch, RN, BSN, CEN, MHA
Clinical Director, Emergency Department
Anne Arundel Medical Center
Annapolis, Maryland

The biggest thing, by far, is to ensure you are providing the same level of care to patients who have been admitted but are being held in the ED waiting for a bed as they'd receive in any other unit of the hospital. We've improved our procedures in this regard so admitting orders are started in the ED as soon as the patient goes into holding. We enter consults and orders for all tests, even initiate discharge planning. We give meds as prescribed and make sure the patient is fed if appropriate—rather than letting those things wait until the patient is up on the floor.

Perpetual readiness rounds and tracer methodology practice involving a wide variety of staff have helped us a lot. That's what they're looking for when they come—they did 20 tracers during their survey! You have to be ready for that.

Andy Jones, RN
Director, Emergency Department
Russell County Medical Center
Lebanon, Virginia

You need to know what's going on with other parts of the hospital outside of the ED—other PI initiatives, other policies, core measures, etc., and understand how they all impact the ED.

Kelly Dawson, RN
Nurse Manager, Emergency Services
Carson Tahoe Regional Medical Center
Carson City, Nevada

Keep in mind that JCAHO is not out to flunk you! I think we were less nervous about this last survey because we were all confident that we were prepared for it, that we are providing good patient care.

One comment that the surveyor made during the exit interview is the grounds for this advice—be as warm and welcoming to the survey team as possible. The surveyors actually mentioned how welcomed they had felt with everyone on our staff. Obviously, if everyone runs when JCAHO show up—if staff flees in terror—the surveyors are much less comfortable and much more suspicious that things aren't what they should be. When staff appears friendly and open, the surveyors are more at ease and more confident about the care being delivered and the people delivering it.

We're getting ready to move to a new hospital and know we will be undergoing another survey soon after that. However, we really feel that we will be ready for it because we have everything in place to get through that.

Brennan Bryant, RN
Manager, Emergency Services
Baylor Medical Center
Irvine, Texas

Concentrate your preparatory efforts on front line staff so that they're equipped for and comfortable with their expected roles during the survey. Provide them with education and reference materials—"cheat sheets"—at every meeting, every opportunity you get.

In 2006, the unannounced surveys will challenge us to remain in a constant state of readiness—therefore, processes must be defined, adjusted and most importantly COMMUNICATED to front line staff. We can suppose unannounced visits will be similar to the last tracer visits, but we can't be sure.

PART 3

Hospital Accreditation Standards Analysis

INTRODUCTION

Part 3 of the Emergency Department Compliance Manual analyzes the standards in the Comprehensive Accrediation Manual for Hospitals: The Official Handbook (CAMH) published by the Joint Commission on Accreditation of Healthcare Organizations (Joint Commission) and updated quarterly. Part 3 was prepared based on the new standards published on JCAHO's web site, *www.jcaho.org,* effective January 1, 2006. The web site contains a cross reference for readers to compare the 2005 to the 2006 standards.

The information in Part 3 is presented in a chart format for easy reference. The chart format contains four columns: Standard, Comments, Evidence, and Staff Questions.

- The **Standard** column designates those particular Joint Commission standards that uniquely apply to the Emergency Department.

- The **Comments** column provides a brief explanation of each standard and special considerations for the Emergency Department.

- The **Evidence** column outlines specific types of evidence that may be used to show Emergency Department compliance with the standard. The types of evidence suggested include both written documentation review and physical inspection.

- The **Staff Questions** column lists detailed questions to use in preparing staff for the Joint Commission survey.

ETHICS, RIGHTS, AND RESPONSIBILITIES

Standard	Comments	Evidence	Staff Questions
RI.1.10 RI.1.30	ED policies, procedures, and performance must be in compliance with the organization's ethical code, and staff members must be well informed about the content and application of the code to ensure business is conducted in an ethical manner. Care and treatment of patients must be delivered based on patient need regardless of the organization's financial implication. Areas of particular impact in the ED include admission, transfer, and discharge of patients. In addition, leadership must show evidence of uniform performance of patient care process (moderate sedation, restraint use, assessing patients in comparable settings, etc.) throughout the organization to ensure all patients receive a comparable level of care. Lastly, staff needs to be prepared to discuss the circumstances and the hospital's policy when a staff member requests not to perform patient care, while still ensuring that the patient's needs will be met. Excuses from care include cultural, ethical, and/or religious reasons. *Note:* In an emergency situation, when other accommodations cannot be made, the staff member may need to perform assigned duties so that the patient is not negatively affected by the delivery of care.	• Patient and staff interviews • General open medical records will be reviewed during the ED tour but closed records may also be reviewed. • Organization policies and procedures supporting ethical business and patient care practices (e.g., code of ethics, governing body and medical staff bylaws, hospital compliance organizationwide policies and procedures, conflict of interest policies and procedures, staff rights/exclusion from patient care, plan for provision of patient care specific to ED) • Organizationwide marketing material that accurately represents the organization • Ability to demonstrate decisions are based on identified patient care needs as per organizationwide policy • Pre-employment processes re: staff rights to assess whether the job duties would conflict with the person's cultural values, religious beliefs	• How does your organization ensure adherence to ethical care and business practices? What is an example of ethical business practices that would be discouraged in the ED? • Does your organization have a written code of ethics? Describe how you were informed about it. Can you show me a copy? What is the purpose of the code of ethics? • What ethical issues pertain to admission, transfer, discharge, billing, and marketing? Have you had any of these issues arise in the last year? If so, what happened? • What is your policy if a staff member has a relationship with another organization such as a nursing home, home care, hospice, ambulance company, or payer (e.g., ownership, contractual arrangement)? • How do you define a conflict of interest? Can you give me an example of one that has occurred in the ED and what steps were taken? • How and when do you inform patients about the cost of care? • What happens when a staff member refuses to participate in an aspect of the patient care such as blood administration for religious or cultural reasons? What do you do to ensure that the patient's care is not impacted?

184

Standard	Comments	Evidence	Staff Questions
RI.1.40	Care is based on the patient's needs and not on any insurance payment. Policies must address how to resolve denial-of-care conflicts over care, services, or payment. Needs of patients should take precedence over denial-of-care conflicts: when care or services are subject to internal or external review that results in a denial of care or payment, treatment and discharge decisions must be made in response to the care needed by the patient, regardless of the recommendations of the review entity. ED leaders and staff should be aware of special utilization review issues pertinent to the ED.	• Organization polices addressing resolving denial of care conflicts re: payment. • Code of ethics policy, enforcement • Organization description of the hospitals' relationship to external entities conducting the utilization review • ED procedures addressing potential disagreement with external organizations' recommendations for treatment and/or discharge • Interviews with ED leaders and staff regarding utilization review criteria that are likely to affect care decisions in the ED • Case management practices in the ED if any. • Documentation of data collected for external utilization review process relevant to the ED • ED Performance Improvement (PI) activities that incorporate information from external utilization review, managed care issues • ED denials data	• How has managed care affected your department? • Does your organization or insurance companies require you to deny care in certain situations? • Describe an instance when care was denied to a patient and explain why. • Do you ever deny emergent care to a patient based on what their insurance of HMO says? • How does the ED Staff interact with the patient's insurance company, HMO, etc. while in the ED?

Standard	Comments	Evidence	Staff Questions

RI.2.10 RI.2.20 RI.2.40 RI.2.50 RI.2.60	These standards require that the organization address ethical issues in patient care. Patients' rights to treatment or service are protected, in compliance with applicable law and regulation. Patients/surrogate decision makers must be involved in all aspects of care and be informed of the following patient rights: right to privacy, civil rights, to effectively communicate with hospital caregivers, informed consent, consent for recordings/filming that is not related to patient care, knowledge of professionals providing care, ability to refuse care/treatment, access to protective/advocacy services, confidentiality, security, pain management, end of life care, complaint resolution, receiving care in a safe environment that fosters patient dignity and a positive image, and being knowledgeable about the outcomes of care. Additionally, organizations must respect patient rights to their cultural, spiritual/pastoral care, psychosocial, and personal values, beliefs, and preferences. Patients must be informed of the organization's advance directive policy and procedure. Patients or authorized family members also have the right to access, amend, and receive an accounting of disclosures regarding their health information. The physician surveyor usually performs the emergency department (ED) visit. Ensure that you have a fully interdisciplinary team for the interview. The surveyor will be applying tracer methodology where care is traced through the system to evaluate how different departments and disciplines work together to provide optimal patient care and outcomes. The surveyor may request to interview ED representatives such as the ED physician, registered nurse (RN), respiratory therapist and other clinical support services as warranted. Many of the issues are covered in more detail in subsequent standards.	• Interviews with patients, family, and staff
		 • The patients/surrogate decision maker is informed within a timeframe specified by the organization, of the name of the licensed independent practitioner (physician) primarily responsible for care, as well as the name of the licensed independent practitioner(s) performing any treatment/services.
		 • Open and closed medical records
		 • Organizationwide policies
		   - all patient rights policies and procedures
		   - copy of patient rights and responsibilities handouts
		   - organization informed consent policy, forms
		   - accessing pastoral care services
		   - pastoral care telephone number readily accessible
		   - organization HIPAA policies, procedures
		   - organization consent for recording or filming for purposes other than the identification, care and treatment of the patient.
		   - A separate consent is needed if the intent is to use the recording/filming externally. If the recording/filming is used internally, the consent may be part of a general consent to treat or another form if a statement is included in the form regarding the use of the recording/filming.
		 • Staff orientation and continuing education materials on patient rights/organizational ethics, training records
		 • Organization consent forms for patient care designed and written in terms, language the patient can understand
		 • Examples of executed consent forms
		 • Organizationwide ethics committee or functioning of ethics resolution process
		 • Patient and family education committee or process
		 • Evidence of how the ED distributes information to patients on their rights.
		 • Evidence that the organization informed consent process for high-risk medications procedures, blood administration and anesthesia including moderate sedation includes the following elements: nature of
			• Describe how staff learns about patient rights and responsibilities.
			 • Have you participated in any recent in-service on this topic?
			 • How do you communicate to other care givers that the patient has an advance directive?
			 • What types of procedures do you obtain informed consent for?
			 • How is patient understanding and consent documented?
			 • What elements are included in the informed consent process?
			 • What is the role of the nurse re: informed consent?
			 • What is the role of the physician re: informed consent?
			 • What about moderate sedation and blood and blood product administration?
			 • Who obtains informed consent for invasive radiology procedures off-hours and weekends?
			 • Show me your consent forms for various procedures, tests, treatments, or patient types.
			 • When would you not obtain informed consent for these situations?
			 • Do you have a consent form for recording or filming patients or their care when the purpose is not for medical care, treatment or services (e.g., use for PI or education)?
			 • What is your policy regarding videotaping of ED activities? In the event videotaping is allowed, what procedures are followed?
			 • Describe your policy and procedure for using surrogate decision makers for consent.
			 • What mechanism do you have in place for obtaining informed consent from patients with limited English proficiency? How do you know that the patients understand?
			 • What is the procedure staff follow when the organization cannot provide the care a patient requests? Can you discuss an example of such an incident and how staff responded?

Standard	Comments	Evidence	Staff Questions
		proposed care, treatment, services, medications interventions or procedures, etc.; potential benefits, risks, side effects, including potential problems related to recovery; likelihood of achieving patient care goals; reasonable alternatives; relevant risks, benefits, and side effects related to alternatives, including possible risks of not receiving care; and limitations on the confidentiality of information learned from or about the patient, when indicated. • Documentation of pastoral care in the medical record. • Organization written copy of patients' rights and responsibilities appropriate to patient's language, age, and understanding for common patient populations available/ posted in department. Signage is updated to include the right to a safe environment and the right to pain assessment and management.	• Do you have a medical review process? • Are medical records reviewed for compliance with patient rights policies and procedures? Who performs the review? How often? • Who or what resources can staff access if there is an ethical issue regarding a patient's care? • Do you use pastoral care services? When would you access pastoral care services? • How would you access these services? Would this service be documented in the chart? • Describe your procedures for informing patients of their rights. • Are these rights posted? What happens if the patient requests a written copy of the rights? • How do you communicate these rights if the patient speaks another language, cannot read, or is hearing or sight impaired? • Describe your process for allowing patients to access, request amendment, and receive an accounting of disclosure regarding his/her health information.

187

Standard	Comments	Evidence	Staff Questions

RI.2.30
RI.2.70
	This standard addresses patients being actively involved in making all decisions about their care, and resolving any dilemmas that may arise (e.g., controversy over end of life decision making, pain management). If the patient cannot make health care decisions, a surrogate decision maker is identified, as allowed by law and regulations. The legally responsible representative would then approve care decisions. The family should be as involved in the care as permitted by law and with the permission of the patient/surrogate decision maker. ED staff must know how to determine the appropriate surrogate decision maker. Durable power of attorney, living wills/ advance directives, and information supplied by extended care facilities, are often sources of this information.	• Interviews with staff, patients, and families
		• Open and closed records
		• Organization policies related to the following:
		  - guardianship
		  - family/surrogate decision makers' involvement in care decisions
		  - access to legal counsel regarding care decisions
		  - patient and family education (e.g., brochure or handouts on ethics process)
		  - specifically resolving conflicts in care decisions/ethical dilemmas
		• ED staff orientation and continuing education
			• When authorized, does the family or surrogate engage in the patient's care decisions? Where is this documented?
			• How do you include the patient in the decision regarding his/her care? Where is this documented?
			• What is the policy when the patient does not have the mental or physical capacity to make care decisions?
			• How do you determine who is the next of kin?
			• How do you determine who the legal surrogate decision-maker is?
			• Please describe how conflicts in care (e.g., end-of-life decisions) are resolved.
			• Can you recall a situation that required an ethics consultation? How/who do you contact for an ethics consultation?
			• Where would this conflict and resolution be documented?
			• Is there an organizationwide or ED specific committee and/or individual responsible for coordinating the ethics consultation process?
			• How do you inform patients, families, and staff about your ethics resolution process?
			• Give me an example of an ethical dilemma re: patient care that occurred in the last 12 months.
			• Do you receive education on ethical issues that may occur in the ED and who to call if an issue arises?

Standard	Comments	Evidence	Staff Questions

RI.2.80	The organization has a mechanism to address end-of-life decision making, specifically related to advance directives, organ donation, and resuscitative services. Adults are given written information about their rights to accept or refuse care, including resuscitative services and life-sustaining treatment.
	
	Each adult patient must be asked if he/she has an advance directive. This inquiry must be documented within the medical record. The patient has the right to modify his/her advance directive at any time. Whether a patient has a directive or not does not hamper his/her ability to receive care. In the absence of an actual advance directive, and in accord with applicable state law, the patient's wishes may be documented within the patient's chart, when feasible.
	
	The physician and/or RN determine if an ED patient arrives with an advance directive through the assessment process and according to policy/procedure. Procedures should ensure thorough communication of the patient's wishes, and there should be a mechanism to assist or refer the patient for help with formulating advance directives upon request. In the ED, processes are implemented for clinicians and the healthcare representative to honor the patient's advance directive according to policy/procedure, meeting applicable laws and regulations. In addition, the organization documents and follows the patient's wishes with respect to organ donation, to meet the intent of the law. If the organization cannot meet the patient's wishes re: end of life measures the patient is notified.
		• Patient and clinical staff interviews
		• Demonstration that the staff caring for a patient are aware of the existence of an advance directive.
		• Open and closed medical records
		• Organization policies and procedures, including:
		  - advance directives
		  - forgoing or withdrawing life-sustaining treatment
		  - organization Do Not Resuscitate (DNR)
		  - organization care at the end of life
		  - organization patient and family educational handouts available related to patient rights (e.g., patient rights and responsibilities, advance directives.
		• Staff education re: patient and family sensitivity to end of life issues.
			• Describe how you inquire about patients' advance directive status.
			• What are the legal requirements for your organization related to advance directives?
			• What is your procedure if the patient comes into the ED with an advance directive?
			• Are armbands used in this community to signify that the patient is a DNR?
			• Is a patient's advance directive information communicated to the members of the care team? To other departments?
			• What happens if the patient travels to radiology for a procedure and he/she is a DNR? How is that communicated?
			• Are advance directive educational materials are distributed to patients?
			• Describe your procedure for assisting patients who do not have an advance directive but wish to create one. How is one created?
			• If the advance directive is not with the patient, for example it has been left at home, do you attempt to document its substance in the patient's medical record and notify all patient caregivers? Where is this documented? Do you document the patient's wishes concerning organ donation? How is this communicated with the inpatient care providers when the patient is admitted? How often do you ask the patient of their advance directive that was left at home?
			• Describe your policies and procedures for resuscitative services.
			• What training is provided to staff regarding end-of-life care ethical and legal issues?

189

Standard	Comments	Evidence	Staff Questions
RI.2.90	It is essential that the patient is informed regarding the outcomes of care, including unanticipated outcomes. The Licensed Independent Practitioner (LIP) or his/her designee must inform the patient, and when appropriate, family regarding any unanticipated outcome related to a JCAHO sentinel event to the patient if the patient does not already know of the event or if further discussion is warrented. The LIP must advise the patient if he or she has been harmed by the care provided, i.e., if medical errors were made, and what treatment is being administered to manage the patient's condition.	• Patient, family, staff interviews • Organization policies and procedures on communication of outcomes to patients, if available • Open and closed medical records • Staff orientation and continuing education	• What is the ED policy and/or practice regarding communications with patients and/or authorized family members regarding unanticipated outcomes of care? • Do you inform the patient/ authorized family member about unanticipated outcomes of care that relate to sentinel events considered reviewable by the JCAHO? • Can you name examples of sentinel events as given by the Joint Commission? • What information is given to patients or their families regarding outcomes of treatments or procedures when those outcomes differ significantly from the anticipated outcomes? • Who informs the patient of the unanticipated outcome? • How is this documented? • Is this trended for the organization? Whose role is that?
RI.2.100	The organization must demonstrate how it ensures effective communication with its patients.	• Organization policy and procedure on communicating with patients • Organization mechanisms/ resources exist for ensuring patients receive information in an understandable format regarding care and services • Organization signs or information notifying patients that communication assistance is available if needed • Organization call list for interpreters/translators • Organization advocacy services or patient care service representatives available to assist with meeting patients' special communication needs • Organization resources to overcome communication barriers for vision, speech, hearing, language, and cognitive impairments • Patient access to areas where they can have private telephone conversations based on their needs and care provided	• What barriers have you had regarding communication to patients in the ED? • How have you overcome these barriers to communication with the patients you serve in the ED? • How do you communicate with patients who are deaf or speak another language? • When do you access interpretive services? How do you know if the interpretive service person is compentent to translate? • How do you access interpretive/translation services? • What are the prominent languages spoken in the ED other than English? • What percentage of the patients seen has limited English proficiency? Has the organization offered classes in that language? • Have there been issues related to limited English proficiency in the ED? What PI activities have occurred in regards to this?

Standard	Comments	Evidence	Staff Questions
RI.2.120	The organization has a mechanism to resolve patient and family complaints.	• Organization and ED specific complaint resolution policy and procedure, including a statement that patients are free to complain and make suggestions for improvement without retaliation (i.e., coercion, discrimination, reprisal, or unreasonable interruption of care) • Organization example of complaint resolution form • Any state required signage • Education material informing patients, families, and staff about the organization's complaint resolution process, including a patient's right to file a complaint with the state • Complaints resolution process demonstrating how complaints are received, reviewed, and when feasible, resolved • Examples of how the organization has responded to complaints, incorporating suggestions into its PI program • Process for reporting complaints to committees, the governing board (mandated per the CMS Conditions of Participation) and any state required reporting. • Patient satisfaction data, surveys, results (e.g., complaint tracking)	• How are patients and families made aware of their right to complain? • What type and volume of complaints do you receive in the ED? • What type of complaints do you receive? Are these fed into the PI process? • What is your role in resolving complaints? • What improvements have been made based on complaints in the ED? • What is your mechanism to resolve patient and family complaints? • What do you do if you cannot resolve a patient complaint? • How does this link to the patient grievance process?

Standard	Comments	Evidence	Staff Questions
RI.2.130 through RI.2.140	The organization is responsible for establishing and maintaining methods of ensuring patient rights to privacy (auditory and visual), security and confidentiality of information. The environment of care safeguards patient dignity and promotes a positive self image.	• Staff, patient, family interviews • Open and closed medical records • Relevant Organization and ED specific policies and procedures, to include those related to HIPAA and Safety • Safety and security program and strategies implemented • Reviewing ED operations for compliance with organizationwide policies • Ensuring patient security regarding patient valuables • Design of the environment • Staff orientation and continuing education, documentation • Performance improvement (PI) studies concerning privacy, confidentiality, security • Patient and family education materials distributed on patient rights, including patient safety, privacy, security, and confidentiality • Patient satisfaction data *Site inspections/observations* • Appropriate placement of stretchers in interview areas and examination areas • Use of curtains and partitions without compromising monitoring of patient condition and safety • Patient covered during treatment • Patient names and clinical information not displayed on patient tracking boards • Patient surveys/comment boxes • Patient communication boards do not have identifiers such as name/room number associated with a treatment such as an X-ray, lab, etc. • Patient records are secure with no visible information to other patients/family.	• Describe the mechanisms you use to ensure privacy for patients during triage, assessment, examination, and treatment. • How do you ensure privacy at triage, registration and the discharge area? • How do you keep written patient information confidential? • Are all areas where patients receive care secure? How are they secure? • If hallways are used as treatment areas, how do you minimize the privacy and confidentiality issues? What are you doing to minimize or eliminate your space constraints (numbering treatment areas, use of curtains, etc.)? Are renovations planned to increase the space to treat patients? • What procedure do you follow to secure patient valuables and other possessions? • What is your policy for allowing family members to accompany patients in the ED?
RI.2.150	Organizations must ensure patients have freedom from mental, physical, verbal, sexual abuse, neglect, and exploitation.	• Mechanism to protect patients from abuse, neglect, exploitation from an individual (e.g., staff, students, volunteers, patients visitors, family) • Organization policies and procedures • Interviews with staff • Open and closed charts • Education records of staff attending in-services on abuse and neglect	• How are allegations of observed or suspected cases of abuse managed in the ED? • What resources are available to staff in assisting with suspected or actual cases of abuse? • What do you do if the patient alleges he was abused while a patient in the ED?

192

Standard	Comments	Evidence	Staff Questions
RI.2.160	Policies and procedures should address the care of ED patients to define when pain should be screened, assessed, and reassessed, and to provide for communication to patients about effective pain relief.	• Organization and ED department specific pain policy and procedure including pain assessment and management • Examples of pain scales used (e.g., 0-10) for when patients are verbal, as well as nonresponsive/nonverbal (e.g., FLACC) • Patient and clinical staff interviews • Open and closed medical records • Clinical staff education related to pain assessment and management including nurses, respiratory therapist, EKG technicians, patient care assistants, nurses aides, etc. • Patient education on pain management using medications and other pain management techniques • PI data related to pain management	• Describe how patients' pain is screened/assessed upon arrival in the ED, and whether and how it is reassessed at any time. • What is the difference between screening for pain and assessing for pain in the ED? • How do you screen/assess pain in the patient who is nonverbal? • How do you screen/assess pain in the infant? • How do you screen/assess pain in the neonate? • How often do you reassess for pain in the ED? • What are the primary medications you administer for pain management? • How are you competent to administer and monitor the effects of these medications? • How do you reassess for the effectiveness for pain management interventions such as medication administration? Oral medication? IV medication? • In what timeframe do you reassess post medication intervention? • Where is this documented? • How do you ensure effective management of pain for patients? • Are there any educational programs for clinical staff regarding pain assessment and treatment? • Describe how the patient is educated about pain management in the ED.

Standard	Comments	Evidence	Staff Questions
RI.2.170	The ED is responsible for implementing the organization's policies and procedures for the patient population needing protective services (e.g., guardianship, advocacy services, conservatorship, and child/adult protective services). Procedures exist to help patients' families and courts determine a patient's need for special protective services due to the following evidence.	• Organization policies and procedures, forms (see sample documentation section) • Staff interviews (see sample staff questions) • Open and closed medical records • Staff orientation and continuing education documentation • Organization educational material supplied to patients/families on protective services/resources (e.g., lists of state client advocacy groups, posting of legal patient rights, etc.) • Signage	• Describe how you protect the rights of victims of domestic abuse, child abuse, or neglect • What training have you had to determine a patient's special needs for protective services? Have you had this for elder abuse, domestic abuse, child abuse? • Did this training include education to sensitivity care? • What resources are available to certain patient populations needing protective services? Can you show me examples? • What steps do you take to ensure safety of patients while they are in the ED? • What are some of the signs and symptoms for child, elder and domestic abuse? How do you screen for these? • How do you contact Social Services/Work if needed? What about off-hours and weekends? • Do you have a list of community resources available to patients/family? Is this available in a handout for patients?

Standard	Comments	Evidence	Staff Questions
RI.2.180	These standards assess how the rights of patients asked to participate in any research/investigational study/clinical trial are protected. All research projects are reviewed in relation to guidelines prior to being used in the organization. There is a requirement added to address confidentiality and inclusion of research information in the medical record. The ED is a key area in which to initiate research projects, trials, and studies. ED staff must ensure that the patient and family receive all information necessary for full understanding of the project.	• Organization policy on investigational drugs, clinical trials, research • Staff, patient, and family interviews • Open and closed medical records—copies of all information given to the research participant are contained within the medical record or research file, along with evidence of informed consent • Evidence that the research protocol was reviewed and approved per the organization's policy prior to implementing the study • Patients are informed of any risks, benefits and alternatives associated with the research to assist with their decision to participate or refuse • Executed organization consent forms and relevant discussions include the following documentation: the name of the person providing the information to the participant, his/her right to privacy, confidentiality, safety, and the date the form was signed • Patients are given information related to other treatments and may refuse the research without any ramification • List of current research projects in the ED • Staff education to research projects as warranted • Involvement of Pharmacy and Therapeutics Committee when an investigational drug is used • Approval by ED medical staff of educational materials distributed to patients on investigational drugs. Patients are told the extent of how their personal health information will be kept in confidence • Staff membership or input on institutional review board (IRB)or body assigned to approve research projects	• How do you know what research is ongoing in the ED? How are you educated to this research? • What body reviews investigational drugs, protocols? • Does the ED medical staff have knowledge of this research? • Who obtains consent for patients participating in research projects? Where will this be documented? What is the physician involvement? • What information is given to patients participating in investigational studies or clinical trials? • What happens when a patient refuses to participate in a research project/clinical trial? Where is this documented? • If investigational drugs are administered or dispensed in the ED, how is staff educated on the drugs? How is pharmacy involved? Is there literature on the research available to staff? How is the principal investigator involved? • Give me an example of research that has occurred in the ED within the last 12 months. What was your role? • What would happen if there were a research-related injury?

195

Standard	Comments	Evidence	Staff Questions
RI.3.10	Patients and authorized families are informed on their responsibilities and role in the treatment process, specifically, their role in helping to facilitate the safe delivery of care. The JCAHO outlines the essential responsibilities, such as: • providing information to assist the staff in gathering a complete medical information (e.g., history, indicating changes in health status, perceived risks in care, indicating care expectations) • asking questions to staff, clarifying information provided (including expressing concerns, and understanding expectations) • following instructions/treatment plan, working with staff to adjust their plan of care to meet specific needs/limitations, accepting outcomes if not following treatment plan • acting according to the hospital's regulations—with consideration and respect for others in the ED, other care areas, meeting financial obligations, etc.	• Organization policy and procedure defining process for reviewing responsibilities • Documentation of education about patient responsibilities in care/treatment • Organization handout/ brochure/posting of patient responsibilities in treatment and waiting areas • Evidence of medical staff involvement in pre-printed handouts or education protocols • Evidence of involving patients/ authorized family in patient safety (e.g., implementation of the SpeakUP program sponsored by the JCAHO) • Patient and staff interviews	• Are patients informed of their role and responsibilities in the treatment process? How do you inform patients of their responsibilites? • Do you have any booklet or handout indicating patient responsibilities to orient your patient/authorized family to the ED? Is this documented anywhere? • Describe your procedure for informing patients and their families, when appropriate, on their responsibilities for care (e.g., their role in patient safety, the assessment process, use of medications, medical equipment, pain management, use of SpeakUP campaign). Can you show me this?

PROVISION OF CARE

Standard	Comments	Evidence	Staff Questions

PC.1.10	This standard concerns the organization evaluating the needs of its patients, accepting only those patients when it can provide the appropriate level of care to meet those needs.	• Policies
		• Plan for provision of patient care and services specific to the ED
		  - Triage screening/assessment
		  - Triage protocols
		  - Assessment and reassessment of patient
		  - Procedures defining assessment requirements
		  - Admitting
		  - Transfer internal and external
		  - Referral
		  - Accessing other services, providers, staff, as needed for appropriate level of patients' care
		• On-call physician list
		• Evidence of the application of the criteria that define the information needed to match the patient to the appropriate care setting (e.g., intensive care unit admission, and discharge criteria)
		• Admissions criteria defined, including exclusionary statements indicating information needed for referral to a more appropriate service or setting; defining patient populations not served by the organization
		• Criteria for discharge, transfer of patients from the ED
		• Criteria for placement on established Clinical Practice Guidelines or protocols
		• Referrals to outside clinics
		• Referral and transfer agreements
		• Leadership and staff interviews
		• Observation of patient entry to ED, flow-through waiting, triage area, and transfer
		• Handouts for community resources
		• Open and closed medical record reviews
		• PI studies on appropriateness of admissions, transfers, and discharges
			• What type of patients do you treat in this ED?
			• How do you know patients receive the care needed in the appropriate setting? Where is this kept in a policy and procedure?
			• Describe the patient's initial experience on entering the ED.
			• What information do you obtain during patient screening to determine what care and services the patient needs?
			• What is the range of care you provide? Patient visits per day/annual?
			• Is this a trauma, burn etc. referral center?
			• Do you treat OB patients in the ED or do they go straight to the OB department?
			• Do you treat pediatrics in the ED? What about infants?
			• Do you have sufficient staff and equipment to provide services to meet the needs of your patient population?
			• Where are patients referred when needed care cannot be provided? How do you access these services? What about off hours and weekends?
			• How are patients transported to another organization?
			• How do you access the services of other departments within your organization?
			• What types of patients do you accept from other hospitals? What is this process?
			• What criteria determine whether a patient is admitted for treatment?
			• How are patients selected for transfer or referral to another setting?

Standard	Comments	Evidence	Staff Questions

PC.2.20 PC.2.120 PC.2.130 (references PC.870 as it relates to assessing patients end-of-life care needs)	ED assessment and reassessment policies and procedures must be defined in writing. These standards concern performing a thorough initial assessment and reassessment in specified timeframes of the patient's care needs. The information collected on patient's entry into the ED may indicate the need for further assessments. Triage, used to determine the order in which patients will be treated, does not meet the criteria of patient assessment. Assessment includes physical, psychological, social assessments, including patients' age-specific needs/ information (infant, child, adolescent). Data and information is also gathered during the initial assessment, *as appropriate* regarding: nutrition/ hydration status, functional ability, and any special needs such as cultural, religious, spiritual, end-of-life care issues, etc. Patients requiring further assessments for rehabilitation and/or nutritional services are referred to the appropriate care provider and/or setting, as needed.	• Open and closed records indicating patient assessments for physical, psychological, social status, and further assessments (when indicated)
		 • Staff interviews
		 • Policies and procedures:
		   - triage
		   - scope of assessment, reassessment and care for the ED patient approved by a licensed independent practitioner with appropriate clinical privileges
		   - assessment and reassessment policies and procedures specific to type, age of patient, and condition
		   - scope of assessment/ reassessment by each discipline, criteria defined for when an additional assessment is needed (e.g., nutrition, functional)
		 • Organization medical staff bylaws, rules and regulations defining the medical staff's documentation requirements ED for physicians
		 • Clinical practice guidelines, algorithms for assessment
		 • Organization translation services available for performing assessments
		 • Observation of staff screening, assessing, reassessing within their scope of practice,
		   - nutrition screen
		   - pain screen
		   - functional screen
		   - abuse screen
		   - discharge screen according to applicable law and regulation
		 • Evidence that initial assessments are performed as defined by the organization
		 • Evidence a nursing assessment is performed by a registered nurse, if applicable
		 • Staff records indicating staff have special skills to care for specific patient populations
		   - orientation
		   - job descriptions
		   - continuing education
		 • Protocols and clinical practice guidelines
			• Describe how you developed the triage protocols and the scope of assessment and care for patients in need of emergency care. Who approved these for the ED? Did you have input?
			 • Do L&D nurses perform medical screening exams? Do they have documented competencies?
			 • How long does it take to perform the triage screen from the time the patient enters the ED?
			 • How long until each patient is triaged?
			 • How long from the time of the triage until the initial screening and assessment is completed?
			 • Have you implemented any improvements to decrease throughput time?
			 • What objective screening indicators do you use for pain, abuse, functional, nutrition, and discharge planning?
			 • What is the difference between a "screening" and "assessment"?
			 • Was there an opportunity to involve authorized family members in gathering this information?
			 • Where do you have in writing the data and information collected in the ED? Please show me the form.
			 • When do you reassess the patient?
			 • Describe the assessment processes for infants, children, and adolescent patients. Show me the forms used for pediatrics.
			 • When would you reassess the patient?
			 • When would you document developmental age, length or height, head circumference, weight, and immunization status for patients? Do you collect these for all pediatrics?
			 • How do you ensure that staff are properly trained in performing population (age-specific) assessments?
			 • What is the process for responding to a pediatric code?

198

Standard	Comments	Evidence	Staff Questions
		• Initial ED and inpatient Assessment Tool • Performance Improvement Data • Evidence of ED physician examination. Inpatient history and physical, nursing assessment, and other ancillary screens	• How are you competent to care for neonate, infants, pediatrics, adolescents, and geriatrics? • What information do you assess regarding end-of-life, spiritual, and cultural variables? • Do ED physicians perform inpatient H&PS in the ED? How are the initial screens (nutrition, pain, abuse, discharge planning, functional) reported to the physician if needed? • What happens when a patient is admitted as an inpatient but stays in the ED because there is no bed? Do you perform an inpatient initial nursing assessment?

PC.2.150	These standards concern reassessment of patients to meet their continuing care needs. The ED assessment and reassessment policies meet applicable law and regulatory requirements.
	The standards concern special issues for reassessment intervals and criteria for the ED, depending on type of patient, condition, care received, and procedure performed.
		• ED policies, procedures that include reassessment practices
		• Assessment/reassessment forms
		• Compliance with organization medical staff bylaws, rules, and regulations
		• Open and closed records—demonstration of follow-up care being arranged for further assessments of patient's care needs (e.g., referral to primary care physician, community resource)
		• Policies, procedures, standards of care, for example
		  - clinical care for certain patient types, significant changes in patient condition
		  - care given, procedures performed
		  - clinical practice guidelines, algorithms
			• When are patients reassessed? What are the timeframes per level of care? What is the scope of the reassessment? Please show me the assessment and reassessment for the respiratory therapist who works in the ED.
			• Who can reassess the patient? RN, LUN/LPN, aide?
			• What data/information is included in a reassessment?
			• What procedures do you follow if there is a significant change in patient's condition and care needs?
			• How often does respiratory therapy reassess patients in the ED?

Standard	Comments	Evidence	Staff Questions
PC.3.10	Standard concerns the identification of victims of abuse using established criteria set by the organization. Examples of abuse include: - physical assault - rape or other sexual molestation - domestic abuse - abuse/neglect of children and elders Staff must be educated in screening for abuse and neglect, and know how to refer these cases appropriately.	• Organization and ED specific policies regarding abuse screening, use of criteria, and reporting mechanisms • Policy on assigning responsibilities for collecting, safeguarding, and releasing evidentiary material(s) • PI Studies re: Victim of Abuse • Staff interviews • Open and closed medical records • Staff records indicating attendance at mandatory orientation, continuing education sessions • ED assessment tools designed to document domestic, child, elder, physical abuse, rape, sexual molestation • Organization list of community agencies that provide assistance for victims of abuse • Staff knowledge of criteria for screening abuse or neglect; ability to discuss reporting mechanisms, timeframes for reporting as per policy • Evidence that all cases of abuse or neglect are immediately reported in compliance with the organization's policy	• What types of abuse do you care for in this ED? • What training have you received to assist you in identifying victims of abuse? • Can you describe your screening mechanism for identifying victims of abuse (e.g., elder, child, physical, domestic, sexual, adult violence)? Who performs further assessments, if needed? • If a child is a potential victim of abuse, who do you report this to? How soon? • Who reports? Where is this documented? • What are examples of criteria used to assess elder abuse? adult violence? child abuse? • Have you cared for a patient who you have suspected of being a victim of abuse? • What did you do after you suspected the abuse? • How was medical staff involved? • Where are the telephone numbers for reporting abuse as mandated by local and state laws? • How do you safeguard any evidence collected in the assessment process? • Do you perform sexual assault nurse examinations? • How often do you receive education on abuse? • What do you do if the patient states he/she was abused while in the ED?
PC.3.120 - PC.3.130	These standards (PC.3.120) are required for hospitals that after alcohol and/or addiction to substance abuse programs. Standards (PC.3.130) apply to hospitals treating patients for behavioural or emotional issues. The ED must ensure its patient population includes appropriate assessments for this population in order to optimize the care to patients with these high-risk needs.	• Medical staff bylaws or rules and regulations	• Do you offer substance abuse or behavioral health treatment in this hospital? • How is the ED linked to this inpatient treatment program? • What communication process is in place? • What is the process for transferring these patients? • Can I speak with the person responsible for these programs?

Standard	Comments	Evidence	Staff Questions
PC.3.230	Standards concern performing tests in a timely manner to determine patient's health care or treatment needs. Diagnostic tests and procedures require an order. Clinical information regarding the reason for the test is submitted with the order based on organizational policy and applicable law and regulation. Testing that requires clinical interpretation must have appropriate information supplied with the order. This guides the person responsible for interpreting the results.	• Interview with staff, physicians, radiology department, radiology physicians • Organizational and ED specific policies regarding testing and reporting procedures, protocols • Clinical pathways, inclusion of testing/reporting requirements • Access to testing, time frames • Laboratory and radiology reports • Open and closed medical records indicating diagnostic test and procedures were performed as ordered within timeframe established by the organization • Diagnostic study request filled out completely • Order with evidence of appropriate pertinent information required by policy • Radiology "overread" PI data • Diagnostic testing turnaround time PI data and activities	• How does the ED ensure that the required clinical information is submitted with requests for diagnostic tests? What information would you give to the radiology department when ordering a radiograph for a long bone fracture? • What is the most common laboratory procedure that you perform in the ED? What is the turnaround time for this test both routine and stat? • If there is 24-hour radiologist coverage, how do the residents, when applicable, learn to read X-rays? Do you have an overread or discordance program? • What are main radiographs taken in the ED? Do the ED physicians read these test results? What happens if they are overread the next day by radiologist and the reading is not the same as the ED physicians?

Standard	Comments	Evidence	Staff Questions

PC.4.10
PC.5.10
PC.5.50
	These standards concern the integration of assessments to assign priorities to care needs and make a plan of care. There must be evidence that care is planned with patient participation, and with the clinical staff working together as a team. The plan of care for a patient must be monitored and modified, as needed, to ensure that clinicians are achieving established goals/outcomes. In the ED, the focus is on meeting patients' emergent and urgent care needs, while also planning for any continuous needs. ED clinicians often participate in planning for a patient's continuous care needs by admitting, transferring, or discharging a patient to another care provider in the community. Staff understanding the use of the JCAHO tracer methodology will assist with demonstrating compliance with these standards.	• Policies and procedures documentation forms
		  - assessment
		  - triage
		  - care planning
		  - admission, transfer, discharge
		  - ED scope of services
		• Criteria for requests for consultation of specialists
		• Evidence that care decisions are based on the assessment of patient needs
		• Use of at least two patient identifiers (neither being the patient room number) whenever taking blood samples, administering medications, blood products or performing procedures or treatments
		• When applicable, the patient's plan of care incorporates mechanisms to limit the use of restraints
		• Open and closed records
		• Assignment of severity categories, triage classifications to patients (e.g. level 1, acute, to level 5, nonacute)
		• Guidelines for assessment and care of different types of patients and patients with specific conditions, disorders, injuries, for example
		  - geriatric
		  - adult
		  - pediatric
		  - infant
		  - neonate
		  - pregnant
		  - with cognitive impairment
		  - with disabilities
		  - with infectious disease (e.g., tuberculosis)
		  - victims of abuse (pediatric, adult female, adult male); domestic, child, elder abuse
		  - behavioral health, substance abuse disorders
		• Policies and procedures for ancillary and support services (including hours of availability of services, turnaround time expectations, reporting mechanism to ED)
		• Guidelines, operational policies and procedures involving specific types of care, diagnoses, and procedures, for example:
		  - care protocols
		  - decision algorithms
		  - clinical practice guidelines, criteria for implementation
		  - preprinted orders
		  - physician orders
		  - moderate sedation
		  - trauma resuscitation
			• Describe how various disciplines in the ED collaborate to prioritize specific patient care needs. Give me an example of the above.
			• How are patients and when appropriate, families, involved with planning for care?
			• Have appropriate resources been allocated to the ED to meet its patient care goals?
			• What is your procedure for documenting when assessed clinical problems are not addressed?
			• Do you develop a plan of care for each patient?
			• When is this plan evaluated for success?
			• Are other disciplines involved in the plan?
			• Are these needs prioritized?
			• How do you evaluate if the patients care goals have been met?
			• What practice standards, protocols, and clinical practice guidelines do you use?
			• How were you educated about these guidelines?
			• If a patient has been placed in restraints do you include this in their place of care?
			• How do you access chaplain services, social services, and rehabilitation services?
			• How do you arrange for equipment to be sent home with the patient?
			• Who educates the patient on use of the equipment?
			• If a patient cannot ambulate home and has no family to transport him or her, what do you do?
			• What performance improvement activities have you conducted to ensure patient care was delivered in the appropriate timeframe?
			• What two patient identifiers do you use in the ED? When do you use them? What is the process for a patient who has no ID and is unable to give demographic information?
			• What do you do when the patient has not met a goal that was initiated for his care and he is being discharged home?

Standard	Comments	Evidence	Staff Questions
		- emergency (stat) operating room cases - observation bed - behavioral health transfer - care of prisoners (forensic patients) • Job descriptions, competencies of staff, continuing education outlining responsibilities for assessments and care planning	

Standard	Comments	Evidence	Staff Questions

PC.5.60	The continuum of care is essential to the provision of optimal care and services to patients. Providers in the ED must coordinate care with others in the continuum to ensure a smooth transition through the continuum to meet patient needs.	• Staff, interviews
		• Referral and transfer agreements
		• Open and closed records (plan of care, progress notes and related sections)
		• Organizationwide medical staff bylaws
		• Departmental policies and procedures including timeframes to meet patient needs:
		  - transfer
		  - referral
		  - discharge process
		  - follow-up process
		  - call back system
		  - ancillary studies (e.g., turnaround times, recalls, and rereads)
		• Communication, documentation with other departments, services, external resources (e.g., home care, social work, primary care physician, case managers)
		• Information management (e.g., computer, software) support for continuous care processes
		• Meeting minutes reflecting discussions of continuum of care issues, review of cases/chart reviews/focus on timely provision of services to meet patient needs
		Minutes contain the topic, findings, conclusions, actions, and responsibility.
		• PI projects involving admission, care planning, transfer, referrals, discharge processes
		• Process to resolve any issues involving internal/external resources (duplication/conflicts)
			• Describe how you provide patients seamless, coordinated care.
			• What processes ensure effective communication by care providers in various settings?
			• When is this documented?
			• Describe the procedure for transferring a patient to another department or organization.
			• Describe the process for discharging a patient. Does the ED nurse go with the critical patient to radiology or other areas of the hospital?
			• How is the patient transported to radiology, OR, MRI?
			• Who is responsible for responding to codes in the ED, MRI, and radiology?
			• Who oversees the patient's care in the ED?
			• How do you communicate the patient's status, (hand-off) treatments, and medications to a receiving unit when the patient is transferred? Where is this documented?
			• Describe your procedure for notifying and recalling patients who need additional studies (i.e., radiology, laboratory or EKG). Do you document this in the patient's medical record?
			• How do you obtain any needed external resources?
			• What timeframe expectations have you defined in the department to ensure you meet patient needs (triage, turnaround for studies, reassessing vitals, etc.)?
			• Do you have any contracted services that deliver care in the ED?

Standard	Comments	Evidence	Staff Questions
PC.6.10	Assessing patient and family, when appropriate, education needs is critical to ensure a favorable outcome for the patient. Staff should consider cultural, religious, emotional, and language barriers, readiness to learn (motivation level), physical and cognitive limitations. Patient education varies depending on the patient's diagnosis, condition, assessed needs, as well as the organization's services that it provides. When appropriate to the needs of the patient, educational topics include: the plan of care, health practices and safety measures, safe and correct use of medications, diets, oral health, nutritional care, safe mechanisms to use medical equipment or supplies, pain management, self care (hygiene/grooming), and habilitation/rehabilitation techniques.	• Staff interview • Patient interviews—patients indicate receiving sufficient information to make care decisions, and be able to meet their ongoing needs • Open and closed records • Observation of patients • Policies, procedures implemented related to patient education, self-care, assessments of educational needs • Evidence of barriers to learning being identified • Evidence of patient and family involvement in care, and the education being provided to the patient/authorized family to meet patient needs • Organizations may want to show evidence of the implementation of the JCAHO's SPEAK UP campaign-signage and/or brochures will demonstrate an organization's commitment to educating patients/families about important patient safety topics • Documentation that patient was educated regarding topics: 　- Pain management options offered during treatment/ method for treating pain, risk for pain, use of pain scales, importance of effective pain management, understanding pain, how to assess/reassess pain, follow-up for management of pain at home 　- When to contact a physician or health care provider in the event pain symptoms worsen, fever, nausea occur 　- Medication usage (e.g., medication handouts) 　- Nutrition counseling, oral health and Drug-Food Interactions (e.g., evidence of literature/brochures regarding diet) as warranted 　- Medical equipment (e.g., crutches) 　- Rehabilitative techniques 　- Continuing care needs, plan of care	• How do you get the patients involved in care or services before they are discharged to meet their continuing care needs? • How do you know that the patient understands the education staff provides? Where is this documented? • What actions do you take if you know there are barriers preventing understanding? How do you make accommodations for limitations identified? Can you describe a challenging case that was successfully managed? • Show me a record that demonstrates you have assessed for barriers to learning. • What provisions do you make if the patient is deaf or has a language barrier? • Show me evidence that you educated patients on the safe and effective use of medications prescribed for the patient. • Who performs the patient's education? • In reviewing a chart, indicate evidence of instructions provided regarding medical equipment, special diet needs, pain management, self-care, and/or any rehabilitative techniques offered to the patient/family (if applicable). How do you know the patient understood the instructions?

Standard	Comments	Evidence	Staff Questions
PC.6.30	There are methods to educate and train patients that are based on their abilities, and as appropriate to the care and services provided by the organization. An organization must assess a patient's preferred method of learning (e.g., verbal, demonstration, written) and readiness to learn. The ED must demonstrate education is provided using strategies to meet patient's identified needs, preferences, abilities, attempting to overcome any identified barriers, when feasible. Interdisciplinary collaborative education among caregivers is expected, as appropriate. Understanding a patient's comprehension of education provided is essential.	• Organizationwide policies, procedures, and plans related to patient education demonstrating collaborative efforts by caregivers • Open and closed records demonstrating education provided based on patient's abilities • Clinical practice guidelines incorporating patient and family education and other preprinted education handouts • Patient interviews • Evidence that the content of teaching material is understandable • Staff education and teaching material regarding teaching methods based on various ages, learning styles, evaluating if patients understand education being provided, etc. • Demonstration of medical staff involvement in the development of patient education material.	• What role does clinical staff play in developing and implementing patient and family education? Is the medical staff involved? • What grade level do you use for instructional material? Is the material available in the ED? • How is the patient's education communicated to the appropriate caregivers? • Who approves all education material? • Do you have an interdisciplinary Patient and Family Education Committee or other group supporting this function? What is the link to the inpatient setting? • Can you describe a case that would depict how you would demonstrate compliance with providing collaborative, interdisciplinary education? • Does your organization have an interdisciplinary patient and family education form for inpatients? Do you use this when a patient is admitted or remains in the ED due to bed availability? Where does the ED document educational activities? • How do you determine a patient's preference for learning? • How do you adopt teaching methods based on a patient's assessed educational needs? • Has the organization supported any programs to assist clinical staff in learning patient teaching techniques? • How do you know a patient understands the education delivered? • How is teaching different for the adolescent than for the adult?

Standard	Comments	Evidence	Staff Questions

PC.7.10	As it applies to the ED, there should be a mechanism to provide appropriate food and nutrition products to meet any patients' nutritional needs while in the department. Diet or snack physician orders may need to be modified based on the patient's diagnosis, condition, and any special cultural/religious/ethnic preferences. Food and nutrition products must be stored and prepared under appropriate conditions in the ED. All meals must be ordered by a physician and noted on the patient's order sheet.	These standards concern the following issues:
		• Organizationwide and ED policy and procedures regarding the provision of food and nutrition products, meeting special preferences for food, and management of storing patient's personal food items
		• Staff and patient interviews
		• Open and closed records
		• Ordering food and nutrition (order sheets)
		• Nutritional Services Dept. policies re: the ED
		• Provision of food products in an efficient, effective manner
		• Monitoring of response to nutrition care
		• Standardization of nutrition care
		• Inspection of refrigerators:
		  - Temperature logs
		  - Cleanliness
		  - Separation of food from nonfood and patient from staff food
		  - Date on food
		• Inspection of ice machines for calcium, rust, and lime deposits
		• Inspection of ED nutrition room, drawers, sink, and cabinets
			• What is the ED policy on provision of meals/snacks for patients?
			• How does the ED oversee management of food and nutritional issues?
			• How are food and nutrition supplements ordered or prescribed, stored, and distributed in the ED or observation beds?
			• Who monitors the refrigerators where patient food is stored? What is the correct temperature to store patient meals/snacks?
			• Who cleans the patient refrigerators?
			• Is an order needed for each patient meal?

Standard	Comments	Evidence	Staff Questions

PC.8.10	The ED must assess patients for indications of pain, conduct further assessments (e.g., use pain scale, assess quality of pain), as needed, and treat patients with the goal of obtaining maximum pain relief. If the patient's pain cannot be managed, the patient is referred for further treatment to meet their ongoing care needs.	• Organizational and department-specific policies regarding pain assessment that includes criteria for following-up on pain
		• Staff interviews
		  - Evidence of staff knowledge regarding pain management
		  - Indications that staff encourage patients to self-report their pain
		• Documentation of a further comprehensive assessment if pain is identified, appropriate to the patient's condition, diagnosis, and scope of services provided
		• Pain signage if any
		• Documentation of pain management process in open and closed records—assessing pain on admission, reassessments, pain consults/referrals, flow sheets
		• Clinical practice guidelines or protocols
		• Documentation of staff orientation and ongoing education to pain management
		• Patient and family, when appropriate, education materials
		• Pain assessment system or tools allowing documentation of each pain site
		• Pain surveys, including assessing patient satisfaction with pain management within the ED
		• Use of pain management procedures, interventions
		• Pain scales (for use with verbal, nonverbal, age appropriate, for cognitively impaired) available for staff to use to assess pain
		• Neonatal and pediatric pain scales.
		• Evidence of medical staff involvement in pain policy and scale.
			• Please describe your pain screening/assessment protocol (for children, adults, cognitively impaired patients, elderly patients).
			• How were you trained in pain management?
			• How do you record pain screening/assessment and reassessment findings?
			• How do you educate the patient to pain management?
			• How do you measure a patient's response to pain management interventions? Where is this documented?
			• What do you do if a patient is not responding to pain management interventions during their stay? At discharge?
			• How do other disciplines participate in the pain management process?
			• Where do other disciplines document their treatments given when pain is a factor?
			• How is pain assessed for cognitively impaired individuals?
			• How do you assess pain in children?

Standard	Comments	Evidence	Staff Questions
PC.8.70	This standard applies to all dying patients, ensuring that appropriate, palliative measures be implemented for patients to receive optimal care and treatment at the end of their life. Patients' end of life care needs must be met in an environment supporting patient comfort and dignity.	• Organizationwide policy and procedures on caring for patients end-of-life care needs • Staff education programs implemented on end-of-life care • Open and closed medical records • Patient and staff interviews • Examples of physical and psychological measures used to provide patient comfort (e.g., bereavement group, ethics consult, palliative measures, visits with clergy, spiritual advisers) • Discussions with staff regarding cases that provide evidence of their meeting patient/family end-of-life care needs (e.g., cultural, psychosocial, religious, ethnic)	• How have you (clinical staff) been educated to meet the end-of-life care needs of your patients? • When appropriate, how have you supported families of dying patients? • How do you ensure that patients die comfortably, privately, and with dignity? • Is there any patient in the department that is dying right now? Can you show me evidence of how you have met their end-of-life care needs? • What are examples of measures you implement to meet a patient's end of life care needs? • How do you ensure that the patient's and family's psychosocial, emotional, and spiritual needs are identified and addressed? • How has non-licensed staff been educated?
PC.9.30	This standard addresses an organizationwide system for resuscitation services. The ED should not only have sufficient department-appropriate equipment and processes, but also demonstrate compliance with organizational standards.	• Staff training and orientation documentation • CPR forms • PI documentation and data • Policies, procedures, processes, and protocols • Equipment to meet needs of patient population in the ED (pediatric versus adult) • Evidence of medical staff approval of emergency medication, supplies and location of crash carts • Site inspection • Interviews with staff • Open and closed record review • Crash cart logs	• What is the ED's role in the hospital's resuscitation services? • What is the procedure for responding to a code? • How are staff trained? What is required for the ED: NRP, NALS, BCLS, and ACLS? • What indicators have been developed to monitor resuscitation activities for performance improvement? • Show me the pediatric dosing sheet/tool, etc. used to calculate emergency medications? • Are these indicators both process and outcome driven? • What have you improved related to resuscitations in the ED? • Are the criteria approved by the medical staff? • Do you respond to codes outside of the ED? • Do you participate in organizationwide PI for CPRs? • Have you been educated in the crash cart in the ED? Where is this documented? • What competencies are in place to determine licensed staff members are competent to find drugs and supplies as well as operate the defibrillators?

Standard	Comments	Evidence	Staff Questions
PC.11.10 through PC.11.100	Restraint and Seclusion standards. These standards apply to ED patients where restraints are used for medical/ surgical purposes; primary reason for use is to support and promote medical healing.		
PC.11.30 PC.12.60 PC.12.70 PC.12.90 PC.12.100 PC.12.110 PC.12.130 PC.12.140	These standards are for ED patients in a non-behavioral health care setting in which restraint or seclusion is used for behavioral health reasons—due to emotional or behavioral disorders that may lead to injury against the patient or others. These patients are often in the ED to be stabilized, and may be awaiting admission to an inpatient psychiatric unit or to be transferred to a psychiatric facility.		

Standard	Comments	Evidence	Staff Questions

PC.11.10 through PC.11.100	These standards address the use of restraints and seclusion in the ED for other than behavioral health care reasons (e.g., used to promote healing). ED managers are cautioned that the revised Medicare Conditions of Participation provide more specific restrictions (i.e., a physician or other licensed independent practitioner must evaluate the patient within one hour of the initiation of restraint or seclusion), which must be followed by hospitals that receive Medicare funds for behavioral health-related restrains only. Consequently, the JCAHO standards may change and should be monitored closely. For updates, check the Joint Commission's Web site at *www.jcaho.org*. Organizations also need to ensure compliance with their state standards, and any other accrediting standards (e.g., AOA) pertinent to their organization.	*Interviews with staff*
		• Organzationwide policies and procedures in compliance with applicable laws and regulations approved by the medical staff, nursing leadership, and others, as indicated
		• Open and closed medical records, with particular emphasis on dated and timed, patient-specific orders and qualification of the practitioner entering the order, clinical justifications, attempts at less restrictive alternatives, and assessment and monitoring of patients
		• Observation of patient care
		• Staff training materials, inservice/orientation records, and competencies
		• PI data and resulting improvements
		  - organizations should have aggregate, baseline performance measures established prior to instituting targeted monitoring of restraint and seclusion usage
		• External benchmarks for restraint use, if available
		• Awareness of staffing needs in relationship to restraint alternatives
		• Orders written, renewed according to policy regarding assessing the patient, applying restraints, criteria for monitoring/reassessing needs, criteria for discontinuing the use
		• Regulatory requirements met per the JCAHO standards include:
		  - Restraints used with an order from the LIP which must be in the record within 24 hours of the initiation of restraints (within 1 hour to meet CMS requirements)
		  - Restraint use may be initiated by an RN if the LIP is not available and he/she has completed an appropriate assessment, used alternatives, least restrictive measure
		  - The LIP must be immediately notified if restraints use is because of a significant change in the patient's condition, otherwise the JCAHO standards allow for the LIP to be notified within 12 hours of use (organizations must be in compliance with the most stringent of their applicable laws/regulations—CMS
			• What is the organization's/ hospital's philosophy regarding restraining patients?
			• What is the difference between a non-behavioral and a behavioral restraint?
			• Give me an example
			• What are some examples of restraint alternatives used in the ED?
			• What are the criteria for placing a patient in restraints?
			• What are the criteria for removing restraints?
			• How is this communicated to the patient?
			• Who may order restraints?
			• May restraints be initiated before an order is given, and if so, how soon after restraints are initiated must an order be obtained?
			• What staff members may participate in the application/ use of restraints and/or in assessing or monitoring patients in restraints or seclusion? How were they trained? Were they trained on each type of restraint device used in the ED?
			• Do you have annual competency assessments related to restraint use for employees?
			• How long is an order for restraints valid?
			• How often is a patient in restraints monitored?
			• What do you monitor for the patient in restraints?
			• What steps do you take to try to avoid restraint use for a particular patient?
			• How do you protect the safety and dignity of patients in restraints in the ED?
			• How do you document restraint use?
			• How do you identify those patients who may be at risk for needing restraints during your assessment process?
			• Due to the potential risks in this setting, what strategies have been implemented to prevent the use of restraints, when feasible? Do you perform a trial release for patients in restraints?
			• Do you have a PI process for reviewing restraint usage in the ED organization? What does your PI data reflect? What preventive approaches,

Standard	Comments	Evidence	Staff Questions
		requires notification within 1 hour of use) - Continued use of restraints beyond 24 hours is authorized by an LIP renewal or new order if clinically justified and after the LIP has examined the patient. - The LIP must examine the patient at least every 24 hours to re-evaluate the need (clinical justification) for restraints/ order - Evidence of when restraints have been applied, removed, or reapplied - No standing orders or PRN allowed - When feasible, patient and when appropriate, family, are informed as soon as possible regarding restraint use	new alternatives, and process improvements have been attempted? Have your efforts resulted in improvements? • When would you communicate with the patient and/or, when appropriate, family regarding the potential for restraint use or if restraints have been applied? • What restraint education is given to the patient and family when appropriate? • Do you use PRN orders for restraints? (Not allowed by CMS or JCAHO) • Do you use protocols for restraints (not allowed by CMS)?

Standard	Comments	Evidence	Staff Questions
PC.11.30 PC.12.30 PC.12.60 PC.12.70 PC.12.90 PC.12.100 PC.12.110 PC.12.130 PC.12.140	JCAHO standards used for restraint use in the non-behavioral health care settings where restraints are applied for behavioral health reasons. ED staff should be familiar with these standards, as well as applicable laws and regulations pertinent to this patient population. Those standards apply to the ED when the patient is assessing, stabilizing, treating or awaiting transfer to a psychiatric hospital or unit.	• Organizationwide policy and procedure requirements for patients restrained for behavioral reasons in non-behavioral health care settings; use must be for managing a patient's emergent needs, when nonphysical alternatives are ineffective • Documentation forms • Open and closed records indicate the following: - Reason for use indicates the patient's behavior may result in harm to the patient, staff, or others - Restraint order (written or verbal) required by an LIP within 1 hour of restraint initiation if the LIP determines restraints should be continued - The LIP must come to the unit within the following time frames to physically evaluate the patient's emergent needs: within 4 hours of restraint use for patients 18 years or older; within 2 hours for all others under the age of 17 (within 1 hour for hospitals with Medicare Deemed status - CMS requirement) - When the LIP agrees with the use of restraints, evidence of time-limited orders and renewals according to policy: - 4 hour order for patients 18 years or older - 2 hour order ages 9-17 - 1 hour under 9 years - If restraints were applied urgently, and removed prior to an order by an LIP, the LIP must evaluate the patient in person within 24 hours of the initiation of the restraint/seclusion • Interviews with the medical staff and other clinicians to indicate the following procedures are followed: - Informing patients of the behaviors necessary to allow for the discontinuation of restraints - Discontinued restraints prior to the order expiring if the patient meets the discontinuation criteria. - Reapplying restraints within the timeframe of original order if the efforts to discontinue use failed, and the patient is at risk for injuring himself or others. - Providing continued monitoring by a trained staff member during restraint use. For the first hour of restraint usage, continuous in-person monitoring is required. Following that hour, continuous monitoring through audio and video is allowed if the patient's condition permits, and the patient/authorized family member agrees.	• Describe how procedures are different for those patients restrained for behavioral health or emotional disorders as opposed to restraints for medical purposes. • How are you trained in the ED to differentiate the restraint procedures for medical surgical patients versus patients with medical surgical needs? • What are your criteria used to discontinue a behavioral health patient from restraints? • For patients restrained emergently due to behavioral health reasons, how soon is an order from the LIP obtained? • How soon does the LIP need to physically evaluate the patient from the time restraints were initiated? What are the time limits for orders for this population? For monitoring requirements initiated?

Standard	Comments	Evidence	Staff Questions

PC.13.20	The following standard focuses on planning for operative or other procedures, and/or the administration of moderate or deep sedation or anesthesia.
	This includes general, spinal or other major regional sedation, and sedation (with or without analgesia) where you would normally expect for the patient to have a loss of protective reflexes. The JCAHO standards related to operative/other procedures would include any procedure (e.g., MRI, cat scan) where sedation/anesthesia is being administered.
	The extent to which these standards may be applicable to the ED depends on the level of emergency services offered by the organization.
	The ED's provision of moderate or deep sedation and anesthesia services should be consistent with organizationwide policies and procedures.
	The organization/department needs to demonstrate that clinicians have the skills and available resources to recover patients who have the potential of reaching various stages of sedation/anesthesia to reduce the potential for any adverse events.
	Those clinicians involved with the administration of sedation/anesthesia, should be knowledgeable regarding the four levels of sedation and anesthesia defined in the Comprehensive Accreditation Manual (CAMH): minimal sedation (anxiolysis); moderate sedation/analgesia (conscious sedation); deep sedation/analgesia; anesthesia.
		• Scope of care in the ED with evidence of qualified staff available to manage patients at whatever level of sedation or anesthesia the patient reaches
		• Staffing plan in the ED to match level of services provided
		• Compliance with the following policies and procedures, if applicable to your ED:
		  - moderate sedation
		  - deep sedation
		  - limitations on surgery/procedures and general anesthesia in the ED
		• ED policies for assessment, procedures, tools, guidelines for emergency procedures (e.g., physical status, risk assessment, diagnostic data), patient classification levels concerning specific operative or other procedures performed in ED, airway assessment
		• Credential files of the medical staff /LIP with ED specific sedation/anesthesia privileges to meet all levels of sedation/anesthesia that the LIP may provide to patients
		• Job descriptions, competencies, of team members involved with administering moderate or deep sedation or anesthesia - file demonstrate appropriate qualifications for position/services performed
		• Nurses may not administer anesthesia as specified in policy and procedure
		• Evidence of a registered nurse that oversees perioperative nursing care
		• Resuscitation materials, crash carts (age-appropriate, if applicable) and other necessary equipment for the sedation/anesthesia indicating up-to-date preventive maintenance, stocked with appropriate supplies, accessible for staff involved with procedures/sedation
		Equipment to meet the scope of services in the ED (e.g., administer intravenous fluids, drugs, blood products, and monitor the patient's physiological status)
		• Implementation of organizationwide patient safety measures, such as the use of two patient-specific identifiers when identifying patients prior to administering a medication, or performing the procedure
		• Evidence of the use of anesthesia
			• What types of sedation and/or anesthesia do you give in the ED?
			• How do you know the physician is priviliged to administer anesthesia in the ED?
			• Do you administer moderate/deep sedation? If so, who oversees the care of the patient? Describe your policies.
			• Does the patient receive pre-procedural education?
			• Who decides the type of sedation (moderate or deep) for each patient?
			• Describe your staffing arrangement when providing moderate sedation in the ED.
			• Who completes/is responsible for the pre-anesthesia risk assessment? (This should be the LIP.)
			• What steps are involved in the pre-anesthesia risk assessment?
			• Do you have separate policies and procedures for pediatric assessment?
			• How is the pediatric preanesthesia risk assessment different?
			• Who performs the immediate anesthesia reassessment? What does this include?
			• How are you competent/qualified to perform or assist with sedation and/or anesthesia in the ED?
			• Who approves anesthesia policies and procedures for the ED?
			• Do you provide obstetric or emergency operative services? If so, how long does it take to initiate anesthesia once the need for it has been identified? More than 30 minutes?
			• Show me in an applicable record, where anesthesia or sedation services were planned.
			• Do you perform a "time out" prior to an invasive procedure in the ED? What does "time out" mean in the ED?
			• How do you care for a patient who has just received moderate sedation? What do you document?
			• What performance improvement data is collected in the organization/

214

Standard	Comments	Evidence	Staff Questions

		risk assessment guidelines according to patient type (e.g., pediatric, diabetic)
		• A determination that the planned anesthesia is suitable for the patient based on a preanesthesia risk assessment performed by a LIP
		• Medication inventory (inspection for any medications considered for sedation or anesthesia care)
		• PI studies showing an effort to monitor practice versus policy regarding operative and other procedures and a focus on optimizing patient outcomes (e.g., minimizing complications resulting from sedation/anesthesia, assessing the appropriateness of anesthesia/sedation plans, monitoring activities, etc.)
		• Open and closed medical records demonstrating implementation of policy(ies) for *moderate/deep sedation or anesthesia*
		• These processes must occur as indicated in the Joint Commission's elements of performance:
		  - Determining patient acuity (e.g., assignment of ASA class)
		  - Providing education to patient/family (when appropriate) on the procedure, services to be rendered
		  - Evidence of implementing the national patient safety goals:
		    (1) Marking the surgical site and involve the patient
		    (2) Use of time out procedure to verify/confirm the correct patient, procedure and site
		  - Pre-sedation/pre-anesthesia assessment completed
		  - Plan of care completed by LIP or LIP confirms agreement with a plan for services being rendered
		  - Re-evaluation/assessment is conducted by an LIP with appropriate qualifications, immediately prior to the induction of moderate or deep sedation or anesthesia. Re-evaluation should include pulse, respirations, blood pressure, and airway.
			ED regarding assessment and planning procedures involving sedation or anesthesia services?
			• How do you know which physicians have the credentials to perform procedures in your area? How is this list updated?

Standard	Comments	Evidence	Staff Questions
PC.13.30	This standard concerns demonstrating that appropriate policies, procedures, and processes exist for monitoring patients during operative and other procedures. Appropriate processes to ensure patient safety must be in place whenever sedation or anesthesia is being administered.	• Organzationwide policies, procedures, protocols for administration, monitoring, and documenting, for sedation/anesthesia services • Organizationwide policies, protocols that indicate the number and qualifications of staff needed to perform and monitor according to patient type, type of sedation/anesthesia, type of procedure • Medical record review of monitoring processes • Documentation in the medical record indicating the procedure and/or administration of sedation/anesthesia for each patient, evidence of appropriate monitoring procedures (e.g., flow sheets) • Required equipment necessary for monitoring patients • Evidence of appropriate methods/techniques implemented to monitor patients • Evidence of staff competencies, training to monitor patients appropriately, based on service rendered.	• Who is responsible for monitoring the patient during anesthesia? • What do you measure during procedure? • What equipment is used during the monitoring phase? • Where are the policies and procedures, guidelines and protocols for sedation and anesthesia? • What forms do you use to document the monitoring? • If applicable, what methods are used to continuously monitor patients' oxygenation, ventilation, and circulation levels? • How are you competent to monitor the patient who is receiving moderate sedation? • What is your role vs. the physician's role? • How do you know a LIP can administer moderate sedation or perform an invasive procedure in the ED? • Do you ever get pulled away from the bedside while monitoring intraprocedure?

Standard	Comments	Evidence	Staff Questions
PC.13.40	This standard concerns post procedure monitoring of patients including physiological and mental status, pathological conditions, IV fluids and drugs administered, impairments and functional status, pain intensity and quality and response to treatment, and unusual events or complications and their management. A licensed independent practitioner (LIP) must discharge the patient from the area using criteria approved by the medical staff leaders. If criteria is used, the LIP must still write an order to use the criteria for discharge.	• Interviews with staff • Organizationwide policies and procedures regarding post-operative/procedure monitoring, criteria for post-anesthesia discharge including documentation guidelines (to include monitoring for physiological, mental status, pain level) • Organizationwide policies and procedures for ensuring patient safety at discharge post procedure, sedation/anesthesia (e.g., discharged by LIP in the care of a responsible adult. • Open and closed records, evidence of appropriate post-procedure monitoring and discharge from ED • Staff personnel records/medical staff files indicating staff qualifications, documentation of training, continuing education • Medical staff bylaws regarding the qualifications for the LIP that can deliver moderate sedation and deep sedation • Immediate access to physician delineation of privileges for procedures including moderate sedation. • Patient care checklists, assessment/monitoring tools, flow sheets, scoring sheets, risk assessment/patient classifications • PI studies, medical record review data, and any corrective action plans • Patient discharge instructions that include where to return in the event of nausea, pain or respiratory distress • Interviews with applicable members of the interdisciplinary team, demonstrating proficiency in evaluating the patient, performing the procedure, monitoring and recovering the patient from sedation/anesthesia based on the standards and organizational policy • Policy and procedure that notes a RN is responsible to monitor the patient during anesthesia including moderate sedation.	• Please describe your process for monitoring patients following the procedure performed in the ED. • What do you monitor? (Physiological or mental status? Pain level?) • Where is this documented? • What are the criteria for discharging patients who have received sedation or anesthesia from this area? • Do you use protocols/criteria to discharge a patient who has had sedation anesthesia? If so, did medical staff approve the protocols/criteria? • Can the patient who receives moderate sedation in the ED be discharged home alone? Can he/she drive an automobile home? • Does the physician write a post-procedure note? • How is the patient "discharged" from the recovery phase of moderate sedation? • Does this require an order?

Standard	Comments	Evidence	Staff Questions

PC.15.10	This standard requires that the organization's established follow-up process provide for continuing care to meet patients' needs. Follow-up planning should identify the patient's physical, emotional, symptom management, and social needs following discharge or transfer.	• Patient, leader, staff interviews
		• Call back policies, procedures
		• Lists of private and community resources given to patients/families
		• Open and closed records documenting the patient's continuing care needs following discharge
		• Organizationwide policies and procedures:
		  - Discharge planning
		  - Patient and family education, discharge instructions, handouts
		  - Diagnostic testing, follow-up procedure
		• List of Medicare-certified home health agencies as required by CMS
			• What is your role in the discharge planning process? What is the physician's role?
			• How do you ensure that the patient receives necessary follow-up care or diagnostic testing?
			• When do you tell/inform the patient they are being transferred either out of the hospital or to an inpatient room? Can you show me the procedure?
			• Describe the procedure you follow if the patient lacks a primary caregiver or social support services.
			• How are social services/social work within your hospital involved?
			• Do you phone patients following discharges to assess their clinical needs and satisfaction with care?
			• If yes, do you use a survey tool? Who makes the calls? How long after discharge are the calls made?
			• Is this conducted seven days a week?
			• How do you use the data collected?
			• How do you reassess and evaluate the services used by patients after they move to another level of care?
			• What do you do if a patient cannot read discharge instructions?
			• Do you ever need to access a social worker for patient care needs in the ED? What is the process for accessing the social worker?
			• Can you give me an example of an instance where you contacted the social worker for a patient's care need?

Standard	Comments	Evidence	Staff Questions

PC.15.20	This standard requires that referral, transfer, discontinuation of services, or discharge of patient to another level of care, health professional, or setting is based on the patient's needs and the organization's capability to provide the care needed.
	The organization must inform the patient/authorized family member in a timely manner about the discharge plan and/or transfer to another facility or level of care.
	All patients must receive education about other available resources, and how to obtain further care, services and treatment to meet his/her identified needs.
	Under the federal "Emergency Medical Treatment and Active Labor Act" (EMTALA), organizations are prohibited from discharging or transferring a patient in an emergency condition for financial reasons (42 U.S.C. § 1395dd).
	This standard also concerns discharge planning.
	Discharge planning should be initiated early in the treatment process, based on requirements of the plan of care or other written guidelines.
	Improved discharge planning within an organization may assist the ED in facilitating the flow of patients to appropriate care settings.
	The goal is to reduce ED waiting times and improve patient satisfaction.
		• Interviews with patients, leaders, and staff
		• Policies and procedures:
		  - Triage protocols
		  - Assessment (continuing care needs identified—both physical and psychosocial)
		  - Criteria for admission, referral, transfer to the inpatient setting, transfer to another facility, discontinuation of services, discharge
		  - Transfer
		  - Referral
		  - Discharge planning
		  - Follow-up
		  - Call back
		• Open and closed records (including triage assessment, reassessments, ongoing charting, necessary documentation such as discharge instructions, transfer forms, etc.)
		• Referral and transfer agreements
		• Evidence of patient/authorized family education regarding the reason for transfer or discharge, including:
		  - Alternatives to transfer, if applicable
		  - Anticipated need for continuing care following discharge, and how to obtain these services, if applicable
		• Evidence of arrangements made to meet a patient's needs following discharge
		• Evidence of referrals to private and community groups, consultation notes
		• Case management program, if applicable, to facilitate patient flow through the organization, ED
		• PI projects (re: discharge planning) demonstrating ED participation
		• List of Medicare-certified home health agencies as required by CMS, as well as other external resource agencies
			• What are the ED criteria for referral? Transfer? Discontinuation of services? Discharge?
			• Describe when a transfer can take place. Under what circumstances? During transfer, how do you know who is responsible for the patient?
			• What information must be documented in the medical record prior to transfer? What information must be provided to patients/authorized family members?
			• What is the organization's mechanism for referrals to other care institutions and providers?
			• Do you ever transfer ICU patients to the ED when it is very busy? Are standards in place for this practice? How are staff competent to take care of these patients when this happens?
			• Do you collect data to measure improvement with the organizations internet transfer process?
			• What happens when the patient activity increases in the ED but nurse staffing remains the same?
			• When ED staff anticipates some level of continuing care after a patient's discharge, what is the procedure for keeping the patient informed of the care process?
			• Describe the types of information that is provided to the patient regarding continuing care.
			• What community resources do you promote prior to discharge and include in your discharge instructions? Where is this documented?
			• How are you trained to identify and assist patients for whom discharge planning is essential?
			• Please describe the discharge planning for this patient.
			• Do you have a social worker you work with? How are they contacted after hours and on weekends?
			• What is the role of the social worker in the ED?
			• What are the components of an ED discharge plan?
			• What patient care instructions does the patient leave the ED with prior to being discharged?

Standard	Comments	Evidence	Staff Questions
PC.15.30	This standard requires that appropriate information be exchanged when patients are transferred or discharged.	• Open and closed records (e.g., review of transfer forms) • Medical record review results • Use of fax machines, networked personal computers to assist with the flow of patient information among providers and various health care settings	• Describe the flow of clinical information when patients are transferred or discharged. • What type of information management support do you have for the exchange of clinical patient information? • Describe how treatment records are made available to providers performing follow-up care. • How do you document that you have notified and exchanged information to other areas transferring or receiving patients? • Is there evidence demonstrating the following information is shared with other providers to meet a patient's continuing care needs: reason for transfer or discharge; physical and psychosocial status; summary of care, treatment, services, progress towards goals, and community resources or referrals provided to the patient? • Do you communicate directly when handling after-care from the ED to another area in the hospital or an external facility? • Where do you document the "hand-off" communication to the next provider?

Standard	Comments	Evidence	Staff Questions
PC.16.10 PC.16.20 PC.16.30 PC.16.40 PC.16.50 PC.16.60	These standards concern waived testing or "point of care" testing. Organizationwide and department-specific standards must be consistent in outlining how to meet these standards. The policy must review the following topics: - how the results of each waived test are to be used in patient care areas, that is definitively or only as a screen - identification of the staff members to perform the test, and supervise the testing - that staff performing the tests are oriented and trained with the organizationwide policy, and pass a competency regarding the testing process on a regular basis defined by the organization The standards pertain to CLIA '88 legislation. The Food and Drug Administration (FDA) allows certain tests to be performed by individuals other than laboratory staff as long as manufacturer instructions are followed.	• Staff interviews, knowledge regarding how the organization defines the use of waived tests, who performs the test, training, education and competency completed, QC • Organization and ED policies, procedures, and resources are up-to-date, readily available to staff regarding waived testing: - list of waived tests performed in the ED - organizationwide and ED specific policies - specimen procedures (collecting, identifying, labeling, preserving) - how waived testing results are used (screening, diagnoses, making care decisions) - current test instructions - system for ensuring quality of testing equipment, supplies (e.g., instrument calibration) - scope of staff responsibilities in ED for testing - up-to-date checklist of waived testing/lab testing - documentation of test results - quality control methodologies • Performance improvement activities • Staff records supplying the following information: - job descriptions identifying staff assigned waived testing responsibilities - competencies evaluating staff proficiency in test methodologies - attendance records for orientation, continuing education training for staff performing tests - role of the pathology/laboratory in the development and approval of all waived tests and procedures • Site inspection • Examination of storage areas for waived testing supplies • Observation of staff performing quality control checks as indicated by policy and procedure • Evidence that waived tests are being used according to organizational policy (as a screen or definitively). • Logs or audits of quality control records, instrument problems, test results	• What waived testing is performed in the ED? • How do you use the results of waived testing? • Can you define how waived testing is evaluated (definitive or for screening purposes only)? • How are you trained to perform particular waived testing (e.g., use of glucometers)? • Are you trained on each test in the ED? • How often are your waived testing competencies evaluated? • Who monitors your performance? • Can you demonstrate quality control activities for the test? • Who is responsible for performing waived testing? How many CLIA license do you have in the organization for waived testing? • Who is responsible for overseeing waived testing for the organization? What is their role? • Describe the procedures you follow when performing waived testing activities. • If the waive test is used for screening purposes, do you complete a confirmatory test? • Where are your policies and procedures for point of care or waived testing? • Where are your quality control and test records stored? • Do physicians perform their own waived testing? Is care based on these test results? Do the physicians go though the same waived testing competencies training as the nurses go through? • Where are the reference ranges for each specific waived test in the medical record (conducted in ED)?

MEDICATION MANAGEMENT

Standard	Comments	Evidence	Staff Questions
MM.1.10	This standard concerns using patient information to safely prepare and dispense medications. To assist with the safe provision of medications, the organization defines in policy the health care providers that must have access to *a minimum amount of patient-specific information* that includes: age, sex, current medications, diagnoses, co-morbidities, concurrently occurring conditions, relevant laboratory values, allergies and past sensitivities. When applicable to the patient, the health care providers also have height, weight, pregnancy/lactation status, and any other information defined by the organization.	• Policies related to gathering/using patient information for ensuring safe medication practices • Staff and patient interviews • Interview with pharmacy staff • Open and closed medical records, medication profiles • Information support systems • Automated dispensing machine if used	• What patient-specific health information is available for those health care professionals involved with medication usage processes in the organization? ED? Who collects this data? What is the minimal information required to process a medication order? • Who determines if the patient is pregnant and what medications she can be administered? What about nursing mothers? • Who has access to this information? • How do you assess the patient for herbal, vitamin and over-the-counter drug use? • When do you need to document the following: weight and height? pregnancy and lactation?

Standard	Comments	Evidence	Staff Questions
MM.2.10 MM.2.20 MM.2.30 MM.2.40	Policies and procedures need to be consistent with the organization's policies regarding selecting, procuring, storing, and securing all medications, including those medications brought in by patients/authorized family. There is an emphasis on medication orders being readable/legible and transcribed correctly. This standard also concerns improving the safety of using high-alert medications as indicated in the national patient safety goals. JCAHO expects that organizations implement the following two actions to improve patient safety when using high-alert medications: (1) remove concentrated electrolytes from patient care units; (2) standardize and minimize the number of drug concentrations available. The Joint Commission defines medication as any substance (excluding food and devices) used to diagnose, treat, or prevent an abnormal condition.	• The ED must be aware of the organization's policies regarding selecting, procuring, storing medications based on applicable law and regulations, including: - Annual appraisal of ED floor stock by medical staff - List of sound-alike and look-alike drugs - physician input ED for selecting drugs used in the formulary - List of medical staff approved medications, criteria used (minimum criteria includes indications for use, effectiveness, risk, cost, patient response) - Multidisciplinary group deciding on which emergency medications/supplies will be stored in the organization and ED - Obtaining medications in emergency conditions - Using approved medications properly and safely storing/stocking medications in the ED under appropriate conditions (e.g., temperature control) and in compliance with applicable law/regulations - Will observe if organization licensed staff has access to medications - Regularly inspecting the medication storage areas of the ED to ensure laws, regulations, policies are enforced based on policy. Also reviewing area for patient safety concerns (e.g., separating look-alike, sound-alike drugs) - Managing medications patients bring to the ED from home • Clinical staff interviews • Evidence of pharmacy oversight in department, such as required inspections based on applicable law and regulation • Open and closed records • Physician knowledge and participation in recommending and placing drugs on the formulary • ED medical director involved in the development of the formulary or medication list, criteria for selection • Formulary or drug list available in the ED *Site inspection* • Tour of medication areas • Tour medication preparation areas	• Where are medications stored in the department, and who is responsible for them? What medications in the ED are look-alike and sound-alike? Are medications provided to the ED using a unit dose system? - How do you ensure that unlicensed individuals cannot obtain them? Does this include 16 fluids? • How are drugs selected for the organization? For the ED? What criteria are used? Where is your formulary or the organization's list of approved medications? • Describe the procedure for procuring drugs that are not on the formulary/drug list. • When you add a new drug in the ED, do you test/monitor to see if the drug is safe? • How do you ensure that emergency medications are always available, controlled, and secured? • What drugs are kept in the ED? Did the ED medical director approve of this list? • Are crash carts checked per policy? How are outdated carts inspected? Who decides what is contained in the crash carts? What is the process for replenishing crash carts? Where are crash cart locks kept? Are crash carts in the ED stocked the same as in other areas of the hospital? Are crash cart locks kept in the ED? • How often does the pharmacy inspect your medications and stock levels in the ED? How do staff in the ED know the medications are within date? • Where are syringes stored? Are these locked? • Where are concentrated electrolytes kept? What special precautions have been taken to prevent accidental rapid IV infusion? How does staff obtain them when needed? Has pharmacy approved concentrated electrolytes being kept in the ED? • Does the process for maintaining concentrated

Standard	Comments	Evidence	Staff Questions
		• Inspection of ED logs, charts, accurate inventory and storage of approved medications, security mechanisms in effect • Prescriptive and non-prescriptive medications are stored in locked containers in a room, cart, or under continuous supervision, based on organizational policy • Procedures involving controlled substances to meet applicable state and federal laws, organizational policy; practices enforced to prevent misuse of medications, proper storage and replacement of inventory after use • Standardized drug concentrations limited • Department inventory accurate—evidence of no expired, damaged, contaminated medications, or storing of concentrated electrolytes such as concentrated potassium	electrolytes in the ED have approval from the Joint Commission? • What procedures are in place for minimizing the diversion of controlled substances? How often do you count narcotics? Where are the narcotic keys kept? Do you ever keep these keys in a drawer? Do you have an automated dispensing machine? When do you run the discrepancy and reconciliation report? • What is your procedure if a patient brings medications in from home? • How has the department prepared for emergencies/ disasters re: medication replenishment? • Are all medications dispensed in a ready to use form to minimize medication errors (e.g., use of unit-dose distribution system)? • What about liquid (P.O.) actetaminophen for children? Is this provided to the ED in a unit does form? • Who examines crash cart to determine enforcement of policy and procedure on emergency medications/ crash carts? • If applicable, will check to see if daily inspections or per policy are performed on crash carts in the ED; will want to see no missing shifts/days; keep only one month's checklists on the crash cart. File the others in the manager's office and available as requested. • Who inspects for location of security locks/seals to see if they are kept secured/ controlled, and how emergency drugs/supplies are restocked after use? • Are all emergency travel boxes secured with a sequentially numbered lock? How often are these checked? • Does pharmacy check the crash carts on a monthly basis?

Standard	Comments	Evidence	Staff Questions
MM.3.10 MM.3.20	These standards concern the processes for ordering or prescribing medications based on the patient's diagnosis/condition, and assesses if orders are legible and transcribed correctly.	• Applicable policies and procedures relating to ordering and procuring medications that meet applicable law and regulation • Required elements of an order including reason for order (e.g., diagnosis, condition, specific indication-for-use) • Use of generic versus brand names • Special precautions when ordering, ordering for specific patient populations • Management of incomplete or unclear orders (includes legibility issues, range orders, rewrites) • Use of an approved "Do Not Use" list of abbreviations, symbols, acronyms, • Evidence of a read-back process for verbal or telephone orders including steps to minimize the use of verbal/telephone orders • Processes implemented for the following type of orders: PRN, standing, hold, automatic stop, resume, titrating, taper, range, use of compounded drug, drug mixtures, use for medication-related devices, investigational medications, herbal products, medications at discharge, standardized orders • An indication for each PRN medication is documented • Open and closed charts indicating orders are written according to policies, required elements of order documented, justification for order documented, transcribed correctly. Evidence of weight-based dosing for pediatric patients • Clinical staff interviews	• What are the requirements for a complete order? What do you do if you are a physician? • What abbreviations or symbols cannot be used in your organization/the ED? • What is your procedure if you cannot read an order in the chart? • Describe your process for rewriting previous orders. • Do you have standard order sets or guidelines? Who updates them? • Do you have any PI projects or activities related to improving the medication ordering/transcribing process over the past year (e.g., limiting verbal/telephone orders, improving legibility, implementing national patient safety goals, improving completeness of orders, etc.)? • Have you minimized the use of verbal orders in the ED? • When do you use weight based dosing for pediatrics in the ED? • Do you use generic or brand names when ordering drugs in the ED? • Where do you store your floor stock? Are there any drugs that sound alike or look alike that are stored next to each other? • Tell me about weight-based dosing for pediatrics seen in the ED • Do you use resume orders in the ED?

Standard	Comments	Evidence	Staff Questions

MM.4.10
MM.4.20
MM.4.30
MM.4.40
	The focus of these standards is on the control of preparation and dispensing of drugs, medication dose system, and process for reviewing medication/ prescription orders.	• Interviews with clinical staff
		• Policies and procedures:
		  - process for preparation and dispensing medications in the ED
		  - process for preparing and mixing medications (process for compounding additive mixing sterile medications, intravenous admixtures, or other drugs) in the ED when the pharmacy may be closed, when there is an emergency, or the stability of the product is limited
		  - labeling procedures for meeting applicable law, regulation, including the elements of performance in standard MM.4.30
		• Employee files indicating appropriate staff were trained to use the proper procedures for preparing hazardous medications as indicated by policy and procedure
		• PI studies involving medication usage related to preparing and dispensing medications
		Site inspection
		• Medications in the department are appropriately labeled, including prepared medications that are not being used immediately for patient care
		• When preparing hazardous medications:
		  - Observation of staff using procedures, appropriate equipment, and materials to comply with the organization's policy, procedure, and relevant law/regulations
		  - Preparation area(s) that is clean, organized, and functional to ensure patient and staff safety
		• Appropriate dispensing procedures to meet law, regulation, organizational policy that ensures timeliness, use of unit-dose or ready-to-administer format when dispensing
			• What medications do you label when you prepare them? What if you are preparing them for more then one patient? Do you label IV bags in the ED? Do you use a unit dose system?
			• How are you trained to prepare any hazardous medications used in the ED?
			• What techniques do you use when preparing medications?
			• Describe how you control medication preparation and dispensing processes.
			• Do you have a 24-hour pharmacy?
			• Do you compound medications in the ED?
			• Who reviews medications for drug-food or drug-drug interactions?

Standard	Comments	Evidence	Staff Questions
MM.4.50	Standard MM.4.50 is applicable to organizations with pharmacy services that do not have 24-hour coverage. The organization must ensure there is a mechanism in place to obtain medications to meet patient needs when the pharmacy is closed.	• Approved policy and procedures in compliance with applicable law and regulatory bodies regarding the following: - after-hours access by qualified, trained, non-pharmacy healthcare professionals to limited approved medications within the pharmacy. Medical staff must approve the removal process from the pharmacy after hours, if applicable - use of night cabinets, closets, automated medication storage/distribution systems, and after-hours drug carts used to decrease the need for non-pharmacy staff to enter the pharmacy. • Storage inspection schedules and documentation, logs • Quality Control and performance improvement studies, outcomes, and action plans to reduce the incidence of non-pharmacy staff entering the pharmacy; and to reduce possible errors from allowing after-hour access. Pharmacy and Therapeutics Committee must review and approve the data and actions to improve. • Use of work process controls (e.g., bar coding, verification checks by a second individual, pharmacy oversight of logs) that would prevent possible errors during after-hour access • Evidence that only trained, competent designated health professionals (may be dependent based on state law) are able to perform this function • Evidence that the organizational arranges for a qualified pharmacist to be available on-call or at another location to support staff questions, or provide those medications not available within the limited, approved supply	• Do you have a 24-hour staffed pharmacy? • If not, how do you remove medication from the pharmacy? • How do you obtain medications that need to be administered during the ED visit that are not available in the ED and the pharmacy is closed? • If a non-pharmacy clinician enters pharmacy after hours, does pharmacy check the order against the patient's medication profile the next morning? • Does the non-pharmacy clinician leave a sample of the medication he/she removed from the pharmacy? • Do you use a night cabinet or automated dispenser for obtaining medications after the pharmacy is closed? • What are the main drugs you access after the pharmacy has closed? • Is data related to after-hours pharmacy access reported to the multidisciplinary group overseeing medication management in the organization (P&T Committee)? • Is this data too noted by drugs removed? • Who has access to the pharmacy after hours? • Is anyone from the ED allowed in the pharmacy after hours? If yes, who, and what type of training and competency validation did the pharmacy give the staff member? • What special procedures does the staff member need to follow? • Have you been successful in limiting the use of accessing the pharmacy after hours?

227

Standard	Comments	Evidence	Staff Questions
MM.4.70 MM.4.80	• These standards concern the organization having a mechanism to manage medication recalls, the discontinuation of medications, and the process for managing unused or expired medications. The organization must comply with applicable laws and regulations with regard to these processes.	• Policy regarding the following: - Organizational medication recall /discontinuation procedures, including the notification process - Management of all unused, discontinued, recalled and/or expired medications; process for controlling and accounting for all unused medications returned to pharmacy • Examples of incidence when the organization has informed health care professionals ordering, dispensing, and/or administering recalled or discontinued medications; the process also includes notifying patients who may have received the medications. • Staff interviews, pharmacy interviews	• How are you informed if a medication is recalled or discontinued by the manufacturer or the FDA for safety reasons? • Describe how the ED manages unused, expired or returned medications. What is the pharmacy's involvement? • What do you do with unused or expired medications?

Standard	Comments	Evidence	Staff Questions

MM.5.10 MM.5.20	These standards concern ensuring organizations having mechanisms for the safe and accurate administration of medications. This includes patients self-administering drugs in the ED.	• Policy defining the staff member's qualifications to administer based on the following parameters: medication, medication class, or route of administration
		• Mechanisms for self-administration of medications
		• Clinical staff interviews
		• Patient interviews, observations
		• Policies and procedures
		  - medication administration
		  - patient identification procedures
		• Verifying staff using the following mechanisms prior to administration of the selected medication:
		  - identifying patients prior to drug administration
		  - ensuring the patient receives the correct medication by comparing the medication order/prescription with two patient's specific identifiers (e.g., name, medical record number, birth date), excluding patient location. The two patient specific identifiers selected should be consistently used throughout the ED (e.g., name and medical record number).
		  - validating that the correct patient receives their intended medication as ordered/ prescribed by verifying the medication order/label
		  - visually confirming the medication has not expired
		  - observing the medication for any visual evidence that the medication is stable
		  - checking that there are no contra-indications for administering the medication
		  - validating that the medication is being given accurately according to the order (re: proper time, dosage, and route)
		  - instructing the patient/ authorized family member regarding any potentially significant adverse reactions or concerns about administering a new medication
		  - communicating any medication usage concerns with the LIP or other prescriber, and appropriate clinical staff
			• How do you validate the medication orders and identify patients prior to giving medications?
			• What is your procedure if you cannot read the physician's handwriting?
			• Do you allow a patient to self-administer his/her own medications in the organization? If yes, describe the procedure you follow for this process to occur.
			• How do you validate that the patient can safely self-administer medication?
			• Do you have an alternative medication administration system?
			• Describe safety measures that you implement prior to administering a patient's medication(s).
			  - verify correct medicine based on product label and MD order
			  - visual exam of no particles, discoloration, and within date
			  - verify no contraindication
			  - verify proper time, dose, and route
			  - patient education
			  - address concerns with proscribing/ordering medical order

Standard	Comments	Evidence	Staff Questions

MM.6.10
MM.6.20
	Organizations must have mechanisms to monitor the effects of medication(s) on patients to assess the appropriateness of the medication, ensure patient safety, and decrease the potential for adverse events and medication errors.	• Open and closed charts (i.e., flow sheets, progress notes, areas in the chart to demonstrate evidence of medications being monitored by members of the clinical team)
		• Evidence that clinicians gather information regarding a patient's own perception about the effects of the medication, including side effects, outcomes, use of lab results, medication profile
		• Documentation that the organization monitors the patient's initial response to the first dose(s) of a medication new to a patient while he or she is being cared for prior to discharge
		• Discharge instructions to teach patients/authorized family members regarding side effects, food-drug interactions
		• Policies:
		  - food-drug interaction reporting
		  - ADR follow-up reporting
		  - medication error reporting process
		  - monitoring of medication effects
			• Describe your process for monitoring the effects of the medication on the patient.
			• Where do you document patient's response to their prescribed medication, including any issues? Do you document a patient's response to a new medication administered prior to discharge? Give me an example.
			• When assessing the effects of medication, do you evaluate the patient's perception of effectiveness, comparison with lab results, clinical response to the intervention, and the medication profile?

Standard	Comments	Evidence	Staff Questions
MM.7.10 MM.7.40	The ED needs a process identified for the management of high-risk or high-alert drugs and investigational medications.	• Staff interviews—interviews pharmacy staff responsible for the ED • Policies and procedures: - Adverse Drug Events - Medication errors - Investigational Medications - Sentinel Event • List of high-risk or high-alert medications defined by the organization/ED based on patterns/trends/external literature, etc. (e.g., investigational drugs, controlled medications, concentrated electrolytes, new medications or non-FDA approved medications, psychotherapeutic medications, look-alike, sound-alike medications, etc.) • Segregate look-alike, sound-alike drugs • Evidence of use of sentinel event alerts, other external databases (ISMP, USP) to minimize risks related to the administration of high-risk/high-alert drugs • Documentation of safe control and administration of investigational drugs • Evidence of PI studies, strategies to reduce the risk of medication errors, adverse events, enhance patient safety • Evidence of action taken when an actual or potential adverse drug event or medication error occurs • Compliance with internal and external reporting requirements for actual or potential adverse drug events • Inspection of medication refrigerators, crash carts and other storage locations.	• What is the process for adverse drug reaction (ADR) and medication error reporting? • How do you minimize the incidents of adverse events? • Where would you report (internally) medication errors or adverse drug reactions? • What processes have you implemented to protect the safety of patients receiving high-alert or high-risk medications? • What safety mechanisms do you implement for patients receiving investigational drugs? • What are your high-alert/high-risk drugs in the ED? • Describe the process for the management of high-alert, high-risk medications in the ED specific to procuring storing, ordering, preparing, dispensing, administering, and monitoring. • Do you segregate look-alike, sound-alike drugs? • When an investigational drug is used, does the pharmacy control storage, dispensing, labeling, and distribution of the investigational medication? • Who reviews and approves any investigational medication used in the ED? • Who supervises and monitors investigational medications being used in the ED?

231

Standard	Comments	Evidence	Staff Questions

MM.8.10	The organization oversees and evaluates its performance of medication usage for the following practices such as: ordering (LIP order), procuring (how the medications get to the ED from the pharmacy), dispensing, preparing, administering, monitoring effects of medications.	• ED and/or organizationwide performance improvement activities concerning medication usage (i.e., ADR, medication errors, Drug Utilization Effectiveness (DUE) studies, pain management, etc.)
		• Open and closed record review, for example
		  - monitoring after medications are administered (e.g., IV fluid for low blood pressure, pain medication)
		  - contra-indications, adverse effects noted
		  - weight, height, allergies, etc.
		  - effectiveness of pain medication is evaluated post-administration
		• Observation of medication pass
		• Evidence of staff inservices on medication safety
		• Minutes that reflect ED participation in collecting and reporting data related to ADR, ADE, medication errors, pain management, etc.
		• FMEA for high-risk medication processes
		• P&T minutes available re: ED data
			• What safety mechanisms have been implemented to improve the management of medications in the organization? ED?
			• What is your role in medication safety?
			• How are you competent to administer drugs new to the organization?
			• What are the risk points in the medication management process in the ED? Has the pharmacy performed a Failure Mode Effects Analysis (FMEA)? If so can you describe the outcome of the FMEA? How have you worked on processes to reduce risks?
			• What external reference databases have been used to assist with improving the organization's performance with medication management?
			• What type of literature do you read as an ED manager to keep abreast of medication safety initiatives?
			• What type of data is collected internally to track and trend performance to oversee medication management?
			• Can you demonstrate improvement over time following PI strategies you have implemented?

232

IMPROVING ORGANIZATION PERFORMANCE

Standard	Comments	Evidence	Staff Questions

PI.1.10	The organization is responsible for collecting data to monitor its performance with important processes. The ED staff must demonstrate compliance with organizationwide and department-specific data collection activities for high priority and required areas, where applicable. Data collection assists with determining priorities, if strategies implemented have led to improvement, and with monitoring the stability of existing processes. Leaders and staff need to demonstrate their ongoing efforts to continuously improve performance within the ED and the organization. The PI focus is on high-risk, high volume, problem-prone processes and functions, and sentinel events. Data collection must also include areas targeted for further study and performance improvement efforts. The organization must consider collecting data in the following areas: staff opinions and needs; staff perceptions of risks to patients and suggestions for improving patient safety; staff willingness to report unanticipated adverse events; and perceptions of care, treatment and services delivered to patients. The organization must also consider collecting data on patient perception of care/services rendered. Data must be collected to determine patient needs and expectations, how well their needs/expectations are being met, how the organization can improve safety, and the effectiveness of pain management, when pertinent.	• Staff interviews, PI team interviews
		• Plans, strategies for data collection
		• Data collection tools used (e.g., surveys, flow sheets)
		• Measurement and improvement committee reports, minutes (e.g., aggregate, comparative data collected)
		• Participation in a reference database
		• Hospital and ED performance improvement plans, reports based on data collected, meeting minutes
		• Graphs interpreting ED data collected, other trend analysis
		• Documentation illustrating the periodic evaluation of common ED procedures including patient throughput
		• Use of data collection tools to measure the functions of important processes and services such as:
		  - operative and invasive procedures
		  - medication usages
		  - quality control
		  - incident reports
		  - reports of unanticipated adverse events and/or outcomes
		  - infection control indicators
		  - sentinel events
		  - waiting times
		  - appropriateness of procedures
		  - appropriateness/effectiveness of pain management
		  - medical record documentation
		  - blood
		  - blood products
		  - restraint use
		  - seclusion use
		  - resuscitation and outcomes
		  - utilization management
		  - infection control
		  - perception of care delivered to patients
		  - research, when applicable
		  - staff and patient opinions and needs, views on perceived risks to patients and opportunities for improving patient safety
		  - staff willingness to report medical/health care errors
		  - staffing effectiveness if applicable
		• Patient safety initiatives
			• What are you measuring as part of ED improvement activities?
			• How have you used the data to make improvements, and enhance care, services, and/or outcomes?
			• Are your improvement efforts consistent with the priorities established by leadership?
			• Is performance improvement an ongoing activity in your organization? In the ED?
			• How do you select and prioritize performance improvement processes? Is there criteria to guide this prioritization process?
			• Who is responsible for collecting data? Where are the data reported and how will data be used?
			• Do you use external comparative data (e.g., state, peer review organization, comparisons with other organizations)?
			• Is the ED included in the aggregated organization data?
			• Describe a disease process/chief complaint for which data has been measured. What did you do with the data?
			• How do you measure the quality of invasive and noninvasive procedures performed in the ED that place the patient at risk?
			• What sampling methodology do you use for studies?
			• Can you demonstrate if performance improvement is sustained over time?
			• What have you done with patient satisfaction/perception data?
			• Do you collect moderate sedation data? Medication management, blood and blood products, restraint, rescusitation, risk management, UM, QC, IC surveillance, autopsies, and/or OPO? What improvements have you made based on the data?
			• How are you measuring compliance with the national patient safety goals?

Standard	Comments	Evidence	Staff Questions
PI.2.10 through PI.2.20	These standards focus on the organization's assessment, aggregation, and analysis of collected data. Data is aggregated at established intervals based on the process being reviewed. ED leaders, in collaboration with staff, need to be prepared to discuss the analysis and use of data collected, especially where undesirable trends are identified. It is important to demonstrate that the ED assesses its performance over time and when available, with external sources that gather comparative information. Statistical analysis is helpful in comparing the organization's performance with historical trends, as well as against other organizations, and in assessing common or special cause variations. Further analysis of the following incidents is mandated: • confirmed transfusion reactions, • serious adverse drug events, • significant medication errors, • major discrepancies between preoperative and post operative diagnoses, • adverse events or patterns of adverse events during moderate or deep sedation and anesthesia use, • hazardous conditions, • sentinel events, and • staffing effectiveness issues.	• Staff and PI team member interviews • ED and hospital PI plan, policies and procedures, including incident reporting procedures, risk reduction plans, strategies, and the management of sentinel events • Data collected, aggregated, and analyzed to demonstrate current performance levels, patterns, and trends • Use of statistical analysis, assessment techniques, e.g., run charts, control charts, and other graphic displays of data. • Use of external comparative data, when available • Follow-up action concerning opportunities for improvement for documents that reflect poor performance, major discrepancies, undesirable patterns, and other problematic issues (e.g., anesthesia, medication usage and errors and hazardous conditions, transfusion practices, staffing effectiveness) • Documentation of data collected regarding X-ray, electrocardiogram (EKG), other variances, and their follow-up • Use of material from external sources such as recent scientific, clinical and management literature, including relevant Joint Commission *Sentinel Event Alerts*	• How is data transformed into meaningful information used by the organization? • Can you describe techniques you use to analyze data collected for established PI priorities? Do you print data using graphs? • How is statistical analysis applied? What statistical quality control methods do you use to analyze data collected? How do you identify a need for a more intensive assessment? • Have you seen any trends in the data? • When trends are unfavorable, what have you done to correct them? • How do priorities change based on data collection activities? • Does the organization participate in a reference database (e.g., trauma registry)? • How does the ED partner with other departments regarding PI projects? • How are PI activities communicated to staff? • What is the staff's role in ED PI activities? • Are you measuring staffing effectiveness in the ED?

Standard	Comments	Evidence	Staff Questions
PI.2.30 PI.3.10 PI.3.20	These standards require organization leaders to implement an organizationwide patient safety program that includes processes for identifying, reporting, reducing, and managing risks to patient safety, including sentinel events. The organization must use data collected to identify changes that will improve performance, outcomes, and promote patient safety. The goal of the program is to proactively identify potential patient safety risks, prevent adverse occurrences, and sentinel events. The ED team needs to demonstrate the department's role in prioritizing patient safety, and implementing strategies to reduce risks. Modifications made to improve care processes/services/outcomes are assessed to confirm they accomplish expected results and maintain improvements. If goals/targets are not met, the organization must implement an action plan to redesign/modify the process to reach performance expectations. Each organization must demonstrate that at least one high-risk process is analyzed (failure modes effectiveness) annually with the implementation of a corresponding strategy and action plan. The process selected must be described, indicating failure modes in the process, and how the failure modes or breakdowns could result in impacting patient care and services. The potential failure modes are then prioritized and analyzed for causes. The organization then redesigns the processes with the greatest risk for adversely influencing care and services. Pilot testing and/or implementing the redesigned process, and monitoring its effectiveness is essential.	• Interviews with leaders, staff • Plans, policies, and procedures related to risk management, patient safety, environment of care, and sentinel event management • Organizationwide patient safety improvement activities that include ED representation • Documentation of patient safety program education attended by ED leaders (e.g., seminars, visits to other organizations, consultants, training programs) • Organizational evaluations of patient safety programs • Allocation of human and other resources to patient safety improvement activities • The organization conducts a failure mode and effects analysis (FMEA) at least annually for a high risk process • Evidence of implementation of the organization's sentinel event policy and reporting process • Documentation of procedures for immediate response to unanticipated adverse events/health care errors • Documented mechanisms for responding to various occurrences (e.g., root cause analysis of a sentinel event) • Reports on incidents of medical/health care errors, and actions taken to improve patient safety	• What risks are involved with your job? What have you done to minimize those risks and prevent health care errors? • Do you feel comfortable reporting incidents? Has the organization worked to create a blame-free environment? • What do you do when you discover that a medical/health care error has been made in the ED? • What is a sentinel event? Does your definition of a sentinel event include "near misses" or "close calls"? • How would you report a sentinel event? • Is a root cause analysis performed when an incident is defined as a sentinel event? • Have you participated in a root cause analysis? • What was your role? • What were your findings, actions, and improvements? What is your role in conducting a root cause analysis? • How do you review and respond to information and recommendations the Joint Commission provides about sentinel events? • What risk-reduction strategy has the organization implemented within the past year to promote patient safety, and reduce risk? How are you measuring your efforts to reduce risk in care processes?

LEADERSHIP

Standard	Comments	Evidence	Staff Questions
LD.1.10 LD.1.20 LD.2.10	The following standards are related to the organization identifying how it is governed and will not be a focus in an ED visit. The governance of an organization has the following responsibilities: -Establishing how it is governed, membership, and defining its responsibilities in writing -Overseeing the organization's reporting structure for planning, operations, and management with clear lines of responsibility and accountability within departments and between departments and administration -Ensuring the medical staff is involved with governance -Making sure the organization complies with law and regulation -Appointing an individual(s) or designee(s) to be responsible for operating the organization according to the authority granted by governance. -Providing mechanisms for conflict resolution -Promoting performance improvement	• Governing body bylaws, rules and regulations • Minutes of senior leadership/governance meetings • Evidence of licensure, inspection results • Organizational chart(s)	• How is the medical staff involved with governance? • How do senior leaders/governance support performance improvement in the ED? • Who is in charge of your organization's operations? • Does ED nursing report to the CNO? • What reports go to the GB meetings? • Is there any feedback to the ED from the GB re: these reports?
LD.2.20	The ED must demonstrate effective leadership ultimately responsible for care, service, and meeting or exceeding its goals in assisting the organization to meet its mission.	• Interviews with leaders and staff. An organizational chart indicating leadership to oversee the operations of the department, program, service, site • Evidence that the ED is operating effectively, efficiently, and coordinating care and services • The ED is directed or managed by one or more individuals with appropriate education and experience and/or is a licensed independent practitioner with appropriate clinical privileges • Evidence of the responsibilities of ED director/manager defined in job description • ED scope of services/goals defined • ED director/manager personnel file, credentialing file (if physician) • Medical staff bylaws, rules, and regulations regarding ED	*To staff* • How do leaders support you and include you in proving the processes and jobs you perform in the organization? • How is patient care integrated throughout the hospital? *To directors/managers* • Do you have your qualifications and responsibilities defined in writing? • How do you coordinate and integrate the ED's services with other departments, services, and with the hospital's primary function? • How do you get the staff involved improving care and processes? • How do you report ED issues to the governing board?

236

Standard	Comments	Evidence	Staff Questions
LD.2.50 LD.3.10	The organization must show evidence of short-term and long-term planning, including its annual operating budget, and long-term capital expenditure plan approved by governance. The ED leaders must show participation in these activities.	• Leadership interviews • Meeting minutes demonstrating ED leaders' participation in organizationwide planning activities • Documents indicating that ED planning issues, such as space allocation, equipment needs, are addressed at the organization level (such as at budget meetings) • Department budgets approved by leadership • Plans demonstrating that ED leadership has planned for the provision of care, services, and treatment needs of the population served either directly or through contracts, consultations, or other agreements • PI data	• Describe your participation in strategic and operational planning. • What is the process for requesting additional resources and capital, such as space or staff? • How does the Emergency Department participate in the organizationwide budget process? • How is staff involved when developing your budget? • Describe the organization's process for overseeing your budget in the ED. • What types of care and services are provided in the ED? How have you planned for providing patient care and services? • Are anesthesia services available if surgery or obstetrical services are provided? • What new services are you planning to implement—short-term (less than 1 year), long-term (more than 1 year)? • What data have you collected on measuring patient outcomes?

Standard	Comments	Evidence	Staff Questions
LD.3.15	An important responsibility for leaders is planning for situations to reduce excessive patient volumes in the ED, and improve the department's efficiencies. Leaders must recognize the causes for ED overcrowding (e.g., limited beds, increased demands on ancillary services, staffing shortages, increased patient demands due to limited availability of other EDs and alternative providers) and take action to better serve its community and improve outcomes. This means leaders must assess and improve patient flow issues within the hospital, including but limited to organization in the ED	• Plans for assessing and alleviating patient care volumes/demands in the ED to reduce overcrowding, and to prevent adverse outcomes. The plans must address the following elements of performance: - delivering care to patients ("holds") in temporary locations that must be outside the ED in approved patient care areas - working with other organizations, such as extended care facilities, home health agencies, crisis programs, and other acute care organizations to expedite discharges from the ED - collecting PI data to monitor the capacity of support services, and patient care/treatment areas receiving ED patients - gathering PI data to assess the effectiveness of the plan to reduce the effects of overcrowding - incorporating strategies to improve the flow of care in the ED, enhance throughput, and incorporate these activities in the organizationwide PI program/activities - implementing mechanisms to reduce/eliminate diversions by working with community resources such as the EMS, air ambulances, fire department, etc. - reporting of these PI activities to the organizationwide PI committee, medical staff, and the governing board. • Patient flow process charts, data: temporary beds, transfers internally • Minutes reflecting hospital leadership participation in patient flow activities • PI indicators: (1) Supply of bed space (2) Patient care process data (3) Patient safety data (4) Support/ancillary services data Criteria for initiating diversion	• How has leadership planned for excessive patient volumes in the ED? Has the organization evaluated the plan for its effectiveness? Is the plan incorporated in the organizationwide performance improvement activities? • What strategies have been implemented to mitigate situations resulting in ED overcrowding? Have you included external entities? Has the medical staff been involved? • Where do you care for patients requiring admission when there are no available beds? • Describe how you have overcome any treatment delays. What disciplines are on your PI team that are addressing overcrowding? • Has the data been reported to the organizationwide PI Committee? How is the governing board involved in this process? What have you done to identify and improve patient flow processes? What departments have been involved in identifying those processes? What data is collected re: patient flow processes? Where is this data reported? Has this been reported to the governing board? On what schedule is this data reported? What criteria guides the decision to place the ED and hospital on diversion?

Standard	Comments	Evidence	Staff Questions

LD.3.20	This standard measures uniformity of care across services. ED compliance will likely be measured here. The organization needs to demonstrate that no matter where the patient enters the system, he or she will be provided the same standard of care or comparable care.
	
	Leaders of the department must ensure the following issues are considered when planning for care and services: scope of services; staff needs, including their developmental/educational needs; recruitment and retention efforts required; the needs and expectations of patients and family (when authorized); resources for providing care and services; and the need for measuring care processes and outcomes of care and services provided.
		• ED enforcement of organizationwide policies and procedures (e.g., restraint and seclusion, moderate sedation, advance directives)
		• ED implementation and support for organizationwide plans (e.g., PI, HR, IC plans) consistent with the mission, values, and goals
		• Application of organizationwide quality control policies and procedures approved by administration (e.g., glucometers)
		• Treatment protocols consistent with those implemented in other departments of organization
		• Enforcement of medical staff bylaws, privileging requirements
		• ED participation in organizationwide PI projects, committees (e.g., patient and family education, ethics) to ensure uniform care, interdisciplinary participation in planning Interdisciplinary participation in reducing ED wait times
		• Staffing plans related to staff qualifications
		• Evidence that all sites providing emergency services in an organization provide a comparable level of care and services
			• How do leaders and staff ensure one standard level of patient care across the organization?
			• Where do you keep your standards of care in the ED?
			• What happens if a patient is admitted but they have no inpatient bed to transfer to? Do you initiate inpatient documentation forms?
			• Are all medical specialties available to the ED 24 hours per day?
			• Do all RNs providing care in the ED have the same orientation, certifications (e.g., ACLS, PALS, NRP, and trauma care)?
			• Does the ED provide the same level of care as other hospital services with respect to:
			  - restraints
			  - moderate sedation
			  - patient education
			  - waived testing
			• Describe how you know that the consulting physician has the credentials to provide the care that your patient may need.

239

Standard	Comments	Evidence	Staff Questions

LD.3.30
LD.3.50
LD.3.140
	This standard evaluates:
	• the timeliness and availability of services needed in relationship to the ED
	• whether the services meet patient needs
		• ED scope of services, timeliness of services provided
		• Evidence of essential services (e.g., radiology, dietetic, nuclear medicine, nursing care, lab, pharmaceutical, rehab department, respiratory) being provided as stated in intent of standard, as well as at least one acute clinical service (e.g., Medicine, OB/GYN, pediatrics, surgery, CAPU, substance abuse)
		• Services provided directly by the ED and/or through referral, agreement, consultation, and/or contractual arrangements are provided safely and effectively
		• Contractual agreements for care rendered in the ED must have an annual evaluation submitted to the governing boards
		• Evidence of a plan approved by leaders defining the care or appropriate referral of patients with behavioral health and/or substance abuse issues when an organization does not provide psychiatric or substance abuse services
		• Evidence the ED is involved with outside vendors used by the Emergency Department
		• Patient and family satisfaction surveys
		• Patient "treatment flow" charts, clinical pathways
		• Open and closed chart review indicating that services are provided within time frame established by organization
		• Tools used to measure patient waiting time
		For laboratory services
		• Evidence that an organization has access to pathology, clinical laboratory services, and consultations to meet patients' health care needs
		• Meeting minutes on discussion of laboratory services, staff satisfaction with lab test selection, results, reporting mechanisms, approval of reference lab
		• Clinical pathways that include time frames for required testing
		• Listing of available diagnostic tests
		• Process for lab or radiology testing on off-shifts
		• Procedure for requesting diagnostic tests
		Site inspection
		• Design of waiting, triage room
		• Patient flow through the ED at time of inspection
			• Describe how you ensure that patients' needs are being met in a timely fashion.
			• How have you used patient satisfaction data to improve patient services in the Emergency Department?
			• What aspects of timeliness of care do you measure to improve care?
			• Do you measure any of the following waiting times?
			  - for triage
			  - for the patient to be seen by a physician
			  - for obtaining a consult from another service
			  - for admitting a patient
			  - for diagnostic studies
			• How do you request a consult from another service area?
			• How does the ED coordinate services with other organizations and departments?
			• How do you coordinate services within the ED?
			• Who interprets X-rays after hours? How is the interpretation documented? Who follows up on unexpected results?
			• Describe your relationship with the emergency medical service (EMS). Are you satisfied with its services?
			• How do you ensure that patients with abnormal lab results receive appropriate follow-up?
			To the department director
			• What services are contracted for in the ED?
			• Regarding contracts, contractual relationships or consultative arrangements:
			  - Does leadership approve those services provided to patients by consultation, contractual arrangements or any other type of affiliation/agreement?
			  - Do you measure left without being seen times?
			  - Did the medical staff have feedback in the selection process?
			  - Are the agreements/contracts defined in writing?
			  - Do the services provided meet JCAHO standards?
			  - Does the organization evaluate that the terms of the contract/agreement and that performance expectation are met?

Standard	Comments	Evidence	Staff Questions
			- Where is this recorded? - Is there evidence that the organization assumes ultimate responsibility for the services provided? Has the Governing Board approved theses contracts? • How do you educate contract staff and measure their competency? • If the organization does not provide primary care to patients with behavioral health and/or substance abuse issues, does the organization have a plan for patient care or the appropriate patient referral? Is there evidence that the plan is followed? *Medical staff* • Do the laboratory services provided by your organization meet the needs of your department? • Are laboratory services/ pathology results sent on a timely basis? Are you confident in the results?
LD.3.60	ED leaders must communicate effectively throughout the organization.	• Mission and goals posted within the department as evidence of communication to staff • Communication and educational materials and memos distributing information to staff • Minutes of meetings discussing mission/goals/timely information • Orientation materials on mission, staff orientation attendance records • Educational bulletin boards posting examples of activities supporting the organization's mission and strategic plans • Observation of department director interfacing with staff	*To staff* • How do you communicate with other departments, programs, with leadership? • What is the organization's mission, vision, strategic goals? How was this communicated to you? • How does the organization foster communication with external organizations? with patients and families, as appropriate? • Describe how leaders communicate the organization's mission, goals, plans, policies, etc. • How does your department's performance contribute to the organization's mission and strategic plan? • What information has been communicated to you regarding patient safety activities within the ED and hospital?

Standard	Comments	Evidence	Staff Questions
LD.3.70 LD.3.80 LD.3.90	Leadership has the following responsibilities that include: • ensuring that the staff hired to deliver care and services have the required credentials, experience, and skill based on the organization's mission, scope of services, equipment used, and the health status of staff as required by external regulatory bodies • implementing an effective staffing plan to provide for patient safety, positive outcomes, and to meet the mission, goals of the department/organization • developing and enforcing organizationwide and ED policies and procedures • providing adequate resources for the department to operate (e.g., space, equipment, technology)	• Interviews with leaders and staff • Emergency Department staffing plan relates to volume of patients seen • Evidence that LIPs, PAs, and Advance Practice Registered Nurses (APRNs) (who are not LIPs) have the privileges according to the medical staff bylaws/rules regulations approved by the governing body • Evidence that leaders provide for adequate space, equipment, and other resources • Updated department policies and procedures developed, reviewed, and approved by department leaders • Meeting minutes from medical staff, governing body, interdisciplinary care, and performance improvement committees • Documents demonstrating request for resources (e.g., staff, equipment, supplies, budget) • Job descriptions and competencies for care providers who are not licensed independent practitioners, and for contracted personnel • Staff orientation materials and attendance records • Staffing plans • HR file review	*To staff* • Is this department adequately staffed? • Are the facilities, equipment, and supplies in the ED adequate for you to do your job? *To the department director* • How do you create an environment to help the ED staff meet the established goals of the department? • What are the job duties of an RN (or other nonlicensed independent practitioner)? • How do you know if he or she is competent? • Who trains the nonprofessional staff? • Can staff work prior to completing the initial hospital orientation? • Can you show me an orientation checklist of a new hire employee? • What competencies are required for RNs in this ED? • How do you define competencies? • How do you know if the agency nurses are competent to take care of patients in this ED? • How do you know what care, treatment, and services a resident and medical student can provide? *To the medical director* • Can you demonstrate that there is adequate physician coverage in the ED? • How many physicians (i.e., attending and residents) are in the department at any time? • Do you post a list of on-call physicians? • Are all medical specialties available in the ED 24 hours/day? • What privileges do medical staff members have? • Who defines the qualifications? • How is the clinical competency of ED staff physicians documented? • If applicable, what can a medical student do in the ED? • How do you know a medical student is competent? • How do you communicate with the Graduate Medical Education program Director re: students and residents? • If applicable, who supervises residents? • What are your policies on staff supervision?

Standard	Comments	Evidence	Staff Questions

LD.3.110	The ED follows the organization's policy and procedure for procuring and donating organs and other tissues. Organizations that would be involved with the organ donation process must have an affiliation agreement with an appropriate Organ Procurement Organization (OPO) for tissue and solid organ procurement. The organization must have evidence of an agreement with at least one tissue bank and one eye bank, when applicable.	• Organ and tissue procurement and donation policy naming the OPO affiliation, indicating important processes such as determining medical suitability, potential donor notification, consent process
		• Documentation indicating timely notification of the OPO of patients who have died or whose death is imminent (for federally administered programs, notification completed according to the respective agency policy and procedure)
		• An organ procurement representative, or a designated requester (employee trained in the notification process) must complete the notification process. Documentation indicates if the patient or authorized family accepts or declines the opportunity to donate
		• Records maintained of the potential donors whose names have been sent to the OPO, tissue or eye bank
		• Collaboration with the OPO and/or tissue/eye bank for the following:
		  - HR files re: education to OPO
		  - Gathering and reviewing performance improvement data/projects regarding the identification of potential donors
		  - Educating staff who interact with the family re: being sensitive to the psychosocial and cultural issues of families of potential donors
		  - Maintaining the potential donor through the donation process
		  - Staff, patient, and family interviews, if appropriate
		• Conversion rate data
		  - percent OPO notifies of impending or actual deaths
		  - OPO notification divided by the number of harvests (organ & tissues)
			• Discuss the organization's mechanism to address procurement and donation of organs and tissues.
			• Who is responsible for determining medical suitability for donation?
			• Who is involved in the family approach? Where is the family approach documented?
			• What type of education did you receive about organ and tissue donations? Who is your OPO?
			• Are any members of the ED staff trained to perform the role of the designated "regulator"?
			• Who educated the staff?
			• Who do you notify when organs or tissue become available?
			• What steps do you take to procure organs and tissues from potential donors?
			• What steps do you take to ensure sensitivity of donation, religious, spiritual, and psychosocial needs at the time of donation for the family?
			• How do you collaborate with the OPO regarding improving the organ and tissue donation process?
			• What data do you have that reflects the number of deaths vs. number of telephone calls to the OPO?
			• What data do you have re: the number of calls vs. number of donations?
			• What PI data do you collect to track, trend and improve OPO notification and conversion rates?
			• Do any of the nurses or other staff in the ED approach the family re: donation? If yes, were they trained by the OPO as a designated "requestor"?

Standard	Comments	Evidence	Staff Questions
LD.3.120	These standards measure whether the education the hospital provides is planned and supports the coordination of patient education activities in all settings to assist in meeting the organization's mission. Education must be relevant to the patient's unique set of circumstances and characteristics. Leadership provides resources for patient education activities appropriate to the patient population served.	• Patient education plan supporting coordinated patient education activities, establishing educational objectives • Open and closed medical records • Review of flow sheets, progress notes, discharge instructions, handouts, etc. • Interviews with patients, staff, and families • Direct observation of patient education occurring • Patient and family education plan, policy, procedure, patient educational flow sheet, and performance improvement activities • Evidence of education material for patients and families (e.g., brochures, handouts, videos, closed circuit television education channel, education display rack, bulletin boards, poster projects) • Physician involvement in educating • Committee minutes, budgets • Evidence of ED participation in the patient and family education process	*To leaders* • Does the organization have a plan for the provision of patient education activities? • How has the organization improved its processes to achieve educational objectives? • How are medical staff involved in the development and approval of patient educational literature? *To staff* • Has the ED developed or implemented any innovative patient teaching materials or programs? • Do you have a Patient and Family Education Committee or a similar group that coordinates activities across health settings? • What type of patient and family education activities do you provide to improve outcomes, promote self-care? • What information is assessed on admission concerning patient education needs? • How do you assess the patient's readiness, ability, motivation and preferences to learning? Do you assessary patient barriers to education? • What do you do with this information? • What education have you received about teaching techniques? Have you had a competency in educating your patients/families? • How do you assess and address cultural or language barriers to learning? • Where is this documented? • Who do you share this information with? • How are your patients educated on medication? Food and drug interactions? Medical equipment? How to obtain further treatment? Where is this documented? *To patient* • What education have you received or do you expect to receive regarding your care? • Was your family included in the education process, if authorized? • Were you referred to any community education resources? • Were you informed where to seek additional treatment, if needed?

Standard	Comments	Evidence	Staff Questions
			• What were you told about your medications? • Were you asked about your pain? Were you instructed on the importance of reporting your pain?
LD.3.150	The ED staff complies with organization requirements when patients are in custody or other legal restrictions. The patient's plan of care and clinical decisions are coordinated for the following topics: use of restraint and seclusion for non-clinical purposes, disciplinary restrictions, length of stay, restriction of rights, and discharge planning.	• Policy and procedure on treating prisoners and other restricted patients • Documentation of treatment of patients in custody or under other restriction • Orientation material (on important organization policy and procedures) provided to guards monitoring prisoners that enter the organization	• Describe training staff receive in caring for prisoners or for patients with legal restrictions. • What is the procedure you follow if a patient is brought in wearing handcuffs? When can you remove handcuffs? How do you know that the handcuffs are not impairing blood circulation? • How would you respond if a police officer asked you to restrain a patient or put a patient in seclusion? • How do you address the restrictions on the rights of the patient in police custody? • How do you ensure the patient in custody receives discharge and follow-up care? • Do you separate a prisoner from other patients? • How do you communicate after caring for a prisoner? • Who is authorized to remove handcuffs/ankle cuffs from patients? • What is the difference between handcuffs and restraints? • Do you inform the prisoner of his follow-up care?

Standard	Comments	Evidence	Staff Questions
LD.4.10	Leadership must implement a plan for performance improvement that establishes performance expectations, and oversees processes for improving the organization's governance, management, clinical and support activities.	• Plan for improvement, evidence of its implementation and that leaders understand the approach to and method of PI used in the organization • Performance expectations for improving care and processes established • Minutes of meetings, strategic plans, goals indicating leadership participates in PI, and that processes are managed using PI • Examples of PI projects/ processes indicating the appropriate individuals and professionals from relevant programs, services, sites, or departments collaborate in organizationwide PI activities. • Documentation of performance improvement and patient safety improvement education attended by ED leaders (e.g., seminars, visits to other organizations, consultants, training programs, focus groups) • Evidence of collaboration between nursing, physician, and other staff in the ED • Communication of PI and patient safety improvement projects and assignments, storyboards • Allocation of human and other resources to performance and patient safety improvement activities	• Can you name some examples of performance improvement objectives established organizationwide and in the ED? • Does the organization have a PI plan? If yes, describe the plan and how it relates to the ED. • Do you have any PI activities related to patient flow? • How has leadership participated in PI to manage and improve important care/ service processes in the ED? • Is PI an ongoing activity in your organization? Department? How are appropriate individuals involved in the PI process? Is PI a collaborative process involving various disciplines, fostering interdisciplinary/ interdepartmental PI activities? Do you include other disciplines in these activities? • Do you report your PI activities to an organizationwide PI Committee?

Standard	Comments	Evidence	Staff Questions
LD.4.20	Leadership must plan new or modified services/processes by having staff work together to design or redesign them. The design of the organizationwide care and services is appropriate to the population served and their expectations, and considers the following topics: needs and expectations of population served and staff; any results of PI studies; potential risks to patients; use of current knowledge/best practices; information about sentinel events, when available; testing (pilot) and analysis to determine proposed design or redesign is an improvement. Department leaders must participate in this process by collaborating with staff and other stakeholders in this service.	• Use of data collected concerning ED patients' needs (e.g., patient and staff satisfaction surveys, community focus group sessions), as well as data and results from PI activities, including risks to patients • Planning documents involving the ED demonstrating process or service design based on patient needs and consideration of the mission, human resources, best practices, practice guidelines, material (sentinel event alerts, when applicable) resources, and pilot testing/analysis • PI projects showing participation of various departments/ services/programs in planning and improving patient care processes, services, outcomes and patient safety • Staff and leadership interviews	• How do you know the services provided in the ED are suitable for the organization? • How are community needs determined and considered in your planning process? • What have you done to make improvements based on patient satisfaction, patient safety, staff opinion surveys, and/or results of PI activities? • Have you expanded to ED or renovated any parts? • Describe how the ED participates in organizationwide planning. How has staff been involved in the design or redesign of services/processes? • Does the ED have representatives participating in organizationwide committees or projects (e.g., Ethics, Strategic Planning, Performance Improvement, Patient and Family Education, etc.)? • What is your improvement model (managers)? • Do you pilot a project prior to implementing throughout the ED? • How are staff involved in PR?
LD.4.40	Leadership must implement an effective patient safety program with the goal of ensuring coordinated patient care, where system/process risks and failures are eliminated or reduced. The patient safety processes must be integrated across the organization proactively and in response to any identified risks or failures, including sentinel events. The ED director should be prepared to demonstrate department contribution.	• Interviews with leaders, staff • Evidence of an organizationwide, integrated patient safety program led by one or more qualified individuals or an interdisciplinary team, with ED participation in patient safety activities • Plans, policies and procedures developed in collaboration with various disciplines, departments defining the scope of the patient safety program, the range of incidents reported/reviewed, response to unanticipated adverse events, including sentinel events, and the process for implementing proactive strategies to reduce risks. • Staff participation in orientation and continuing education programs that include patient safety topics • Staff knowledgeable about internal/external reporting mechanism for system or process failures • Internal communication and education regarding the patient safety program using bulletin boards, suggestion boxes, flyers,	• How has the ED participated in the organizationwide patient safety program? • Was the ED addressed in the evaluation? • Have you implemented a medication reconcilliation process? • Walk me through the process of notifying the physician of a critical test result. • Has leadership evaluated the patient safety program over the past year and reported efforts made to reduce or eliminate risks/ failures to governance/ senior leaders? • What has been the most challenging National Patient Safety Goal to implement? What strategies did you use to overcome this challenge? • Do you collect data on the National Patient Safety Goals? • When is this reported? • How do you identify patients who come to the ED and are

247

Standard	Comments	Evidence	Staff Questions
		posters, staff meetings, communication logs • Participation in interdepartmental patient safety PI projects. Patient care flow charts and other documents illustrating how patient safety is coordinated among departments • Implementation of standards of care that include processes to reduce risk/errors • Documentation of measurement/analysis of performance of high-risk processes that affect patient safety • Evidence of an annual report to the governing body on system/process failures and measures taken to improve patient safety is required that notes the ED patient safety status	unable to give their name or birthdate? • Can you name the National Patient Safety Goals (NPSGs) and what you have implemented in the ED to make these a success? • Who is your patient safety officer? What is his/her role? • What do you do if you observe or hear of a system failure that impacts patient safety?
LD.4.50 LD.4.60 LD.4.70	These standards require organization leaders to establish PI priorities for improving systems and processes that are high volume, high risk, or problem prone, and that would lead to improved outcomes. Leaders must indicate how they alter priorities based on internal/external events. There must be evidence of resources provided for PI and patient safety. Leadership evaluates the PI and patient safety program to monitor its effectiveness.	• Interviews with leaders, staff • Performance improvement initiatives, priority planning, matrixes, lists, assessment tools • Orientation, continuing leadership/staff education (e.g., seminars, visits to other organizations, consultations with specialists, training programs, fairs, focus groups) related to PI and patient safety • Department, leadership, and organizational evaluations of PI and patient safety improvement programs, staffing effectiveness; staff surveys on opportunities for improvement with the adjustment of priorities, as indicated • Evidence of sufficient resources (e.g., staff, technology, IS equipment, time) allocated for PI and patient safety in the organization and in the ED • Organizationwide performance and patient safety improvement activities that include ED participation	• What resources are committed to improving the performance of care, services and patient safety? • How does leadership prioritize PI projects? When are priorities adjusted? • Are the ED priorities consistent with the mission of the organization? • What have you improved in the ED over the past year? • How is staff involved in PI projects and ideas? How do you ensure the ED staff has sufficient time to participate in PI and safety improvement? • How do you communicate the data from PI activities to staff? • How do you involve staff in PI activities? • What education is provided to staff regarding the organizationwide PI and patient safety program? What were you taught? • What activities have led to improvement in performance and patient safety? • How do leaders assess the effectiveness of the PI and patient safety program? • How often do you evaluate the PI Plan?

Standard	Comments	Evidence	Staff Questions
LD.5.10 LD.5.20 LD.5.30 LD.5.40 LD.5.50	Leaders consider the use of clinical practice guidelines for improving processes. When used, leaders identify criteria for their selection and implementation. The leaders review and approve the guidelines selected. The organization evaluates the use of the guidelines as part of its performance improvement program. This is an organizationwide standard with which ED leaders may be asked to show participation.	• Interviews with leaders and staff • Minutes of meetings documenting ED participation in discussions of clinical practice guideline evaluation and use • Examples of guideline use or modification for performance improvement, including results • Guidelines developed based on sources such as the Agency for Healthcare Research and Quality, National Guideline Clearinghouse, and other professional organizations • Staff training materials Policy addressing the development, approval, and monitoring process for Clinical Practice Guidelines? • Policy that guides the development and monitoring of CPGs	• What is an example of a clinical practice guideline used in the ED? If none is used, have you considered using any to design or improve processes? *For organizations using a clinical practice guideline* • Was a literature search completed prior to initiating the tool? • Why was it adopted? • How was it selected? • Who reviewed and approved the use of the guideline? • What data do you collect re: the guideline? • Is the data physician specific? • Have any modifications been made to improve its effectiveness? • What have you learned from any variations in care identified? • How are staff trained regarding this guideline? • Have outcomes improved as a result of its use? • What criteria are used to prioritize future clinical practice guidelines?

249

MANAGEMENT OF THE ENVIRONMENT OF CARE

Standard	Comments	Evidence	Staff Questions
EC.1.10 EC.1.20	These standards relate to the organization developing, implementing and monitoring a safety management plan for the protection of patients, staff, and others visiting the organization. The safety management program must include proactive risk reduction strategies. Leadership must appoint a person(s) to oversee the safety management program as well as an individual(s) to intervene under conditions that endanger life, health, or that may damage equipment, grounds, or facilities. Safety tours or environmental inspections must be performed in the ED at least every six months to comply with the standards. The surveyor will tour the ED to assess ongoing proactive risk reduction monitoring and strategies to detect environmental hazards, unsafe practices, and other deficiencies.	• Leadership and staff interviews • Evidence of a written plan and its implementation to manage a safe environment of care for patients, staff, and others • Organization and ED-specific safety policies and procedures accessible to staff that are enforced, reviewed as needed, minimally every three years. ED-specific safety policies and procedures should be reviewed by an oversight body (e.g., organizations, safety committee, or group in charge of the safety function, safety officer) • ED participation in organization's safety committee or function • Examples of involvement with safety/environment of care: PI projects, performance measures, meeting minutes, agendas, action plan, attendance lists, response to ED safety surveillance rounds • Evidence of an organizationwide proactive risk assessment and implementation of strategies (e.g., work procedures, and controls, surveys, etc.) to reduce identified risks to improve patient safety and the environment of care. Communication with local law enforcement to gather data specific to the geographic area the hospital serves. • Notification and response to product safety recalls, when applicable • Communication/reporting of trends in occupational illness, personnel injuries to the IC Department *Site inspection* • Tour of department, surrounding grounds, and equipment free of hazards, such as exposed electrical wiring • Key near locked doors • Exit signs visible and operational • Outdoor lighting functional with no dead zone areas • Panic button at nurse triage • Ability to lock-down the ED in the event of a threat • Key pad access to treatment areas • Radiograph machine without key left in ignition • House keeping closets locked • O2 cylinders secured • Locked linen chutes • ADA bars in psych unit	• Does your organization have a safety committee or function overseeing the environment of care and patient safety? Is there a person(s) in charge of the committee/function? How does the ED participate in the safety program? • How do you ensure that the environment is safe to take care of patients? • Describe the frequency of any surveillance rounds in the ED. What data is collected? What is done with this data? Where is this data? Where is this data repeated? • How do you contribute to eliminating and minimizing safety risks? • What is the procedure for reporting an incident or threat involving a patient, staff, or visitor? • How do you prevent patient falls? • What is the policy on allowing equipment (e.g., stretchers, portable X-ray equipment) in hallways? • How do you know the equipment in the ED is safe to use? • Describe the safety risks you encounter during your job and how you minimize them to protect yourself, reduce or prevent errors, and/or improve outcomes of care. • What activities have been implemented to increase worker safety? • What incident trends have been noted in the ED? • How are you notified of product safety recalls? • Describe the process for distribution, enforcement, monitoring, and review of the ED and organizational safety policies.

Standard	Comments	Evidence	Staff Questions
		• No electrical cords in Pedi and psych • No hanging cords in Pedi unit • No electric hospital beds in psych • Helicopter pad secure. Staff competent to access helicopter pad.	
EC.1.30	The standard concerns enforcement of the organization's policy to prohibit smoking in the ED. There are no medical exceptions that can be made in outpatient areas. The department should monitor compliance with the policy and ensure strategies are implemented to reduce violations.	• Organizational policy on smoking in all building(s) under the organization's control with the requirement that smoking is strictly prohibited in all organization-based outpatient programs to include the ED • Process enforced to monitor compliance with the organization's smoking policy and procedure. Results discussed in EOC or PI Committees. • Orientation and continuing education material on efforts to communicate, enforce the nonsmoking policy • Patient and family education materials on smoking cessation including its harmful affects on care, passive smoke inhalation, potential fire risks, smoking cessation programs, etc. • No smoking signs posted, as appropriate	• Describe how patients, families, visitors, and staff learn about the organization's smoking policy. • What do you do if an ED patient violates the no smoking policy? • If you observe someone smoking in the building, what is the procedure to follow? • Take me to where your ED staff smoke.

Standard	Comments	Evidence	Staff Questions

EC.2.10	These standards relate to monitoring and compliance with the organizationwide security plan assessed by the surveyor during the ED walkthrough. There is an individual assigned by leadership to oversee the performance of the security management program organizationwide.	• Implementation of organizationwide security plan and related policies, procedures
		• Organizational proactive risk assessment of the organization/ department for security issues (consider the influence of environmental factors and services rendered). This is usually done by partnering with local law enforcement agencies
		• Mechanisms implemented to reduce and prevent security threats and/or incidents
		• Staff knowledge of the following policies and procedures:
		  - security incidents, including those related to civil disturbances, handling VIPs, the media, and staffing during disasters
		  - identification/ID badge/ visitor control
		  - managing patient property
		  - responding to an infant, pediatric abduction
		  - workplace violence
		  - patients with weapons
		  - metal detector use, if applicable
		  - care of prisoner guidelines
		  - vehicular access to ED
		  - access to and egress from sensitive areas secured
		  - method for reporting security incidents
		  - method for reporting missing patient/family property
		• Security orientation, continuing education materials, education schedules, staff files
		• PI projects, measurement of performance standards, action plans in response to security trends
		Site inspection
		• Evidence of the security of the ED environment, equipment, supplies, information
		• Staff wearing ID badges
		• Patients with identification bands
		• Panic buttons for staff at triage
		• Locked doors in ED to prevent public access to appropriate areas
		• ED accessible to emergency vehicles; unauthorized cars addressed
		• Staff entrance doors locked at night
		• Panic alarms at triage
		• ED well lit
		• Telephone numbers for security and police posted
			• How do you ensure the physical and personal security of patients, visitors, and staff in the ED?
			• Do you think there is enough security coverage?
			• Did you receive a security orientation? Do you receive continuing education on security?
			• Whom do you call if a patient or visitor threatens violence?
			• Describe what you do if a patient has a weapon.
			• Who is responsible for the metal detector, and how was that person trained?
			• How do you identify a staff member in the ED?
			• What do you do when you see someone without an ID badge?
			• How do you file a security incident report?
			• What are your most common security incidents?
			• Can you describe a security improvement in the ED?
			• Give me an example of a process for reducing security risks.
			• How responsive is security when you call? Where is their number posted?
			• Describe the procedure you use when a patient's belongings are missing.
			• How would you manage the care of a VIP? What about the media inquiring about the VIP? Where would the media park? Who would speak to the media for the hospital? What patient information would you disclose to the media?
			• How would you respond if there was an abduction announcement called for an infant or pediatric patient? How many infant abduction drills do you have in a year? Has the "infant" ever made it outside the door?
			• What training have you had for the management of a patient exhibiting physically aggressive behaviors?

Standard	Comments	Evidence	Staff Questions

EC.3.10	These standards measure the department's ongoing monitoring of risk and compliance with the organization's hazardous waste plan. Because the ED is a high-volume area for certain hazardous materials, staff should pay particular attention to policies and procedures related to organization and any ED specific requirement minimizing risks related to their use and disposal.	• Hazardous materials and waste plan, policies, procedures, communication
		• Staff and leadership interviews
		• MSDS inventory list identifying hazardous materials and waste used, stored, and/or generated based on criteria that meets applicable law and regulation such as the EPA, OSHA. Evidence of inventory continuously updated. If an electronic MSDS inventory is used staff may be asked to access
		• Approved processes implemented concerning the following aspects of hazardous materials and waste (includes chemicals, chemotherapeutic materials, radioactive materials, infectious and regulated medical wastes, sharps):
		  - selecting
		  - handling (including precautions to take, protective gear used, and the management of spills, exposures)
		  - storing (adequate space and equipment for safe management of waste; separation of hazardous waste storage and processing areas from other areas of the facility)
		  - transporting
		  - using
		  - disposing (includes monitoring the disposing of hazardous gases and vapors)
		• Staff knowledge of emergency procedures to manage spills and exposures
		• Evidence of permits, licenses, manifests for handling
		• Proper labeling of hazardous materials and waste
		• Material Safety Data Sheets (MSDS) immediately accessible to staff
		• Specific policy on when and how to empty hazardous waste disposal containers
		• Compliance with reporting procedures for hazardous material spills
		• PI projects, measurement of performance standards, action plans in response to hazardous material trends (e.g., ED staff knowledge of what to do in the event of a hazardous material spill, etc.)
		Site inspection
		• Inspection showing proper use, disposal of hazardous materials Hazardous waste shower.
			• Where do you store hazardous materials?
			• What does MSDS stand for?
			• Where is MSDS information located? (Usually asked of a clinician and a housekeeper.)
			• What information is contained in an MSDS?
			• What procedure is followed when a hazardous material is spilled? What would you do for a mercury spill? What would you do for a blood spill? Do you have mercury thermometers in the ED? Do you use Cidex in the ED?
			• How is a hazardous material or waste spill reported?
			• Do you have hazardous material spill kits in the ED? If so, where are these kept?
			• What procedure is followed if someone becomes covered with hazardous material?
			• What procedure do you follow if you encounter an unknown chemical?
			• How do you dispose of contaminated sharps or gauze contaminated with body fluids? Are these kept in a place that is not accessible to children in exam rooms/areas?
			• Do you lock your dirty utility room to keep patients from exposing themselves to hazardous waste? Are these rooms negatively vented? What is the air exchange rate for these rooms?
			• How often is regular trash and biohazardous waste picked up from the dirty utility room? Can you show me the schedule?
			• Do you store gloves underneath wall-mounted sharps containers? Is there a chance that blood or body fluids could fall onto the clean gloves used for patient care?
			• Where do you keep information regarding poisons?
			• What do you do if a patient comes into the ED with chemical contamination? Has this happened? How have you been trained to care for these patients specific to the hazardous waste?
			• Can you show me your Personal Protective Equipment (PPE)? Who replenishes this equipment?

253

Standard	Comments	Evidence	Staff Questions
		• Space for safe handling and storage of hazardous materials and waste • Hazardous materials labeled in accordance with federal, state, and local regulation, in a manner adequate to protect patient, visitor, and staff safety • Hazardous waste containers appropriate to minimize potential harm to patients, staff, and visitors • Hazardous waste containers located appropriately throughout the ED (off the floor) • No biohazardous waste bags on the floor • Flammable liquids stored in fire-resistant cabinets; toxic, corrosive materials segregated and appropriately stored • Poison control number accessible to staff	How often is it checked? • What exam gloves would I use if I had a latex allergy? • What are some examples of hazardous wastes in the ED? Mercury? Cidex? • Do you have a decontamination shower? If so please explain how this works. • Are all hazardous waste storage areas locked? • Are chemicals secured on the cleaning carts? • Is the dirty utility room negatively ventilated to prevent the aerosolize of hazardous waste placed in the room while waiting for transfer out of the ED?

Standard	Comments	Evidence	Staff Questions
EC.4.10 EC.4.20	The organizationwide emergency preparedness plan needs to include the role of the ED. Emergency planning must use a four-phase, "all-hazards" approach that should address mitigation, preparedness, response, and recovery. The Joint Commission requires that the organization participate in two emergency preparedness drills per year (the drills may be in response to an actual emergency or be planned). One drill must involve the community. These drills may be no closer than four months and no more than eight months apart. The practice drill involving the community should include an influx of volunteers/ simulated patients into the ED and should assess communication, coordination, and the effectiveness of the organization's command structure. The type of practice drills selected must be relevant to the priority emergencies identified in the organization's hazard vulnerability analysis. As part of its performance improvement program, organizations need to critique all drills to identify opportunities for improvement.	• Copy of Emergency Management Plan • Evidence of an emergency preparedness plan demonstrating leadership and medical staff's involvement with disaster readiness and emergency management. The plan is implemented when deemed appropriate, and indicates the following: - Organizational procedures for each priority emergency identified: mitigation, preparedness, response, recovery strategies, actions, and responsibilities - Organizational process for activating the emergency response and recovery phase that includes a description of how, when, and by whom the phases are to be activated - how staff and external authorities are notified of the emergency response activation - process for identifying and assigning staff to perform essential staff functions under emergency conditions process for physicians to have emergency privileges - processes for managing the following under emergency conditions: provision of care, treatment, services, staff and family support activities, having necessary supplies, security, and communicating with the media. - evacuation procedures - arrangements of an alternate site identified for patient care which includes preparing for transportation issues, tracking patients, communication between the original care site and alternate facility - procedures for the identification of care providers and other staff during a disaster - cooperative planning with other health care organizations for sharing of information regarding command structures and control centers, resources, assets that could be shared in an emergency, and the names of patients and the deceased for identifying and locating victims - procedure for communicating in the ED during an emergency, with backup internal and external	• How does the ED manage demands in emergency situations (e.g., assigning staff, making space accommodations, ensuring supplies and security)? How many drills do you have a year? • When was the last emergency preparedness drill? • What was your role? • Describe community involvement in the drill. Did you have an influx of patients? • What did you learn from the drill? • How often do you have drills? • Describe any backup communication systems and alternatives to utilities. Do you include the threat of nuclear, biological and terrorism in your disaster drills? • How would you manage patients in need of radioactive or chemical isolation and decontamination? • Describe your evacuation routes. Describe your role in an evacuation. • Are there alternate sites to take patients in the event the ED becomes overcrowded during an emergency? • How are you notified after hours that the emergency plan has been activated? • Who authorizes an evacuation? • What equipment is available for transporting patients in emergencies? • Where are the medical records to go during an evacuation? • What is your procedure for notifying authorities when emergency measures are initiated? • How do you know which physicians have privileges during a disaster? • What is the alternative care site if evacuation is necessary? • Where would you place patients in the event of a surge of patients?

Standard	Comments	Evidence	Staff Questions
		communication systems established - defined roles and responsibility of staff during an emergency, including who they should report to in the organizational command center and/or community's command structure - identification of radioactive, biological, and chemical isolation and decontamination • Examples of the ED's contribution to the plan, policies, role of staff • Evidence the organization's hazard vulnerability analysis to identify potential emergencies and the effects these emergencies may have on the organization's operations and the demand for its services • Evidence of participation in community emergency management planning • Staff and leadership interviews • ED participation in safety and/or emergency (disaster) preparedness committee, minutes of meetings • PI projects, measurement of performance standards, action plans in response to emergency preparedness (e.g., indicator might be using disaster critiques to prepare for future disasters) • Updated disaster call list • On-call list • Inventory of emergency supplies • List of duties to be performed in an emergency • Reports on emergency preparedness drill performance. Note: organizations cannot use tabletop exercises for drills • Emergency supplies accessible, stocked; supplies (including electrical) in working condition • Posting education/procedures for managing emergencies, if available (e.g., Utility Systems Failure Guide, bomb threat procedures, roles and responsibilities of staff in a disaster)	

Standard	Comments	Evidence	Staff Questions
EC.5.10 EC.5.20 EC.5.30 EC.5.40 EC.5.50	The organization has a fire prevention plan addressing fire response, evacuation routes, roles and responsibilities of staff, LIPs, volunteers with respect to the fire's point of origin and with evacuation procedures. Surveyors will look for monitoring and compliance in the ED to determine if the area is fire safe. They will inspect to determine if the fire safety plan is implemented to prevent fire, smoke, and other related hazards, protecting patients, visitors, staff, and property. Fire drills must be conducted on a quarterly basis on all shifts and are to be critiqued for the organization to use for performance improvement purposes. New and existing patient care areas must comply with the Life Safety Code, NFP 101 ^{R} 2000 and applicable laws and regulations. The leaders of the organization oversee the development and maintenance of a Statement of Conditions (SOC).	• Staff and leadership interviews • Organizationwide fire safety plan and evaluation of the plan through fire drills to improve the performance of staff and equipment. Includes an annual assessment of the effectiveness of fire response training. • Implementation of fire response plan and the ED department's role in supporting the plan • PI projects, at least one organizationwide PI measurement, action plans in response to life safety issues, staff knowledge with drills (e.g., responding to fire alarm and duties, containment of smoke and fire, transferring patients to safety, use of the fire extinguisher, and evacuation procedures) • Evidence of scheduled inspections, testing and maintenance of ED fire safety equipment/systems • Purchase and use of nonflammable products in the ED department (e.g., bedding, draperies, curtains) • Compliance with life safety codes, reporting of fire protection deficiencies, failures, and user errors • Evidence of staff participation in quarterly fire drills on all shifts in the ED with at least 50% of the drills being unannounced • The organization should insure that the fires safety system, equipment and components in the department meet the prescriptive requirements as stated in standard EC.5.40 • Implementation of Interim life safety measures (ISLMs) when indicated by policy. ISLMs are implemented as outlined in organizational policy during ED construction and/or when life safety deficiencies exist. This process needs to be overseen by those in charge of overseeing the life safety/safety function within the organization to ensure the elements of performance (e.g., ensuring unobstructed exits, access to emergency services, the operation of the fire alarm system, construction site safe, use of additional fire safety equipment, additional staff training, extra fire drills, etc.) in standard EC.5.50 are met	• What training did you receive during orientation on life safety issues? Give an example of what you learned. • What life safety measures take effect if a construction project causes blocked exits or entrances? • How often do you have fire drills? Are these drills conducted without notice? How often? • How do you know if the fire drill was a success? • Is staff performance and knowledge during drills evaluated? • How do you know all staff in the ED have participated in a fire drill at least annually? • Do you receive feedback from the drill? • What do you do if there is a fire? • Where is the closest fire exit? • Where is the closest fire extinguisher? • What type of extinguisher is it? • What procedures do you follow to contain smoke and fire? • How would I know what to do during a fire if I were a contract worker here only for the day or for six months? • Who is responsible for turning off mechanical gasses including oxygen valves in the event of a fire? Are these gas valves labeled? • How do you evacuate the area during a fire? • Where is the nearest fire alarm? How do you operate it? • How do you know when the alarm is being tested? • What expectations do you have for the ED medical staff, students, contracted workers and volunteers in learning about fire safety? • What is your role and responsibility if you are at the fire's point of origin (away from the fire's point of origin)? • What do you do if you see a ceiling tile that is broken, not correctly in place or missing completely? • Show me in this patient care area two illuminated exit signs.

Standard	Comments	Evidence	Staff Questions
		Site inspection <ul><li>ED department compliance (e.g., hallways unobstructed, fire/smoke doors working properly)</li><li>Portable fire extinguishers properly identified, mounted, and inspected at least monthly, and maintained at least annually</li></ul>	<ul><li>Do you have ongoing education and training on fire safety?</li><li>Do you educate agency staff to the fire safety plan prior to the start of their shift?</li><li>Are the stairwells lighted?</li><li>Can you show me that there is no dust in the electrical closets and mechanical closets?</li><li>Do all fire doors positively latch?</li><li>Do you prop open fire and/or smoke doors</li><li>What can be placed in a hallway? What can block a hallway?</li><li>How do you ensure fire extinguishers are not blocked by equipment?</li><li>How do you ensure emergency shut off valves for mechanical gasses are not blocked?</li><li>Have you had any construction in the ED in the last 3 years? Did you implement ILSM? If not, why not? If so, then show me the documentation for ILSM in the ED.</li></ul>

Standard	Comments	Evidence	Staff Questions
EC.6.10 EC.6.20	The ED must demonstrate monitoring of risk and compliance with the organization's medical equipment management plan. Medical equipment must be maintained, tested, and inspected per policy and procedure. Any specific ED policies and procedures must be consistent with the organizationwide plan. The organization must also demonstrate compliance with the national safety goals as it relates to several equipment management topics—improving the safety of using infusion pumps, and improving the effectiveness of clinical alarm systems. Clinical staff must be familiar with these goals, including what mechanisms the organization has implemented to comply with the goals. Organizations must demonstrate the following strategies have been implemented to promote patient safety: (1) making sure there is free-flow protection on all general-use and PCA intravenous infusion pumps; (2) conduct preventive maintenance and testing of alarm systems according to a schedule; and (3) staff must ensure that alarms can be heard and that they are set correctly.	• Staff and leadership interviews • Organizationwide medical equipment plan, policies (e.g., equipment disruption/failure, availability of backup equipment, how to obtain repair services, safety testing of equipment prior to use, testing of clinical alarms in all areas) • ED department's role in supporting and implementing the equipment management plan • Orientation, continuing education materials and attendance records • Organizationwide current, accurate, and separate inventory of medical equipment (regardless of ownership) based on criteria (function, physical risks, incident history). This is kept in the engineering department. • Equipment properly maintained, carries inspection tags (PM); service logs completed per policy • Documentation of an organizationwide process for equipment recalls, medical device alerts, sentinel events • Organizationwide compliance with the Safe Medical Device Act of 1990 that requires processes for identifying, implementing, monitoring and reporting incidents where a medical device is suspected or attributed to the death, serious injury, or serious illness of an individual Safe Medical Devices Act of 1990 • Organizationwide PI projects, measurement of performance standards, action plans in response to medical equipment management (e.g., staff knowledge of response to equipment failure, preventive maintenance) • Organizationwide inventory (specific to ED) of clinical alarms and evidence alarms are tested according to preventive maintenance schedules • Evidence that the ED can ensure free-flow protection on all general-use and PCA intravenous infusion pumps used in the organization.	• Who uses this piece of equipment? How do you know it is safe to use? How do you operate it? What do you do if it malfunctions? • Who trains staff on using the medical equipment? Where is this documented? • Who trains medical students, nursing students, and physicians? • Who trains staff on new equipment? What is the process for bringing new equipment into the ED? Can CIPs bring their own equipment into the ED? • What is the training process when new equipment is introduced? How are LIPs trained on equipment they use? • How is staff competent to use equipment assessed? • What do you do if this piece of equipment malfunctions? Whom do you inform? How do you document this? • How often is this equipment serviced? How do you know? • What is your policy on safety testing of equipment prior to initial use? • What is your policy on safety testing for contracted equipment? • What is your procedure for checking the infusion pumps? Defibrillator? • Who trained you? • Do you lend equipment to other organizations? What is the process?

Standard	Comments	Evidence	Staff Questions
EC.7.10 EC.7.20 EC.7.30 EC.7.40 EC.7.50	The utility systems plan is an organizationwide plan that promotes a highly functioning, adequately monitored, operational utility system by reducing the risks associated with utility failure.	• Staff and leadership interviews • Organizationwide medical utility management plan, policies (e.g., emergency procedures for responding to utility disruptions or failures); ED department's role in implementing plan • Organizationwide inspection and testing records of preventive maintenance, testing of utilities and their critical components. These standards include critical components of life support, infection control systems for high risk patients, and non-life support utility systems/equipment. The activities must be consistent with the maintenance strategies identified in the organization's utility plan • An organizationwide utility management program that has a current, accurate, and separate inventory of utility equipment, assigns risk using selected criteria, implements strategies to test, and maintain equipment to reduce clinical and physical risks • Organizationwide evidence the organization/plant operations conducts maintenance, testing, and inspections on emergency power systems; see elements of performance for EC.7.40 and EC.7.50 • ED orientation, continuing education materials, attendance records for instructional programs on utilities • Organizationwide PI projects, measurement of performance standards, action plans in response to utilities (e.g., staff knowledge of actions to take in a utility system failure) • Organizationwide documentation in meeting minutes of any utility management issues within the ED • Organzationwide documentation of performance and safety testing of critical components of utility system prior to initial use *Site inspection* • Location of emergency shutoff controls for ED utilities • Labeling of control panels within ED (performed during EC building tour) • Appropriate negative and/or positive ventilation systems/equipment to control air-borne contaminants, when applicable • Appropriate emergency telephone numbers posted for utility failures/disruptions	• What orientation and continuing education have you received on utility management? • What do you do if the power goes out? • Do you perform moderate sedation in the ED? Are there battery-powered lights where moderate sedation occurs in the ED? • How would you turn off the medical gas, if necessary? • What would you do if you learned the water was unsafe for drinking? • How do you report a utility problem, failure, or user error? • Who do you call after-hours for utility problems? • Who examines, maintains, and tests critical operating components in the ED? • Describe clinical interventions that care providers may need to perform if there is a complete power outage. • Who would turn off the main utility (electricity, water, gas, medical gasses) sources on weekends and after-hours? • Do you have elevators in the ED? Who checks them for safety?

Standard	Comments	Evidence	Staff Questions
		• Proper installation of emergency power source adequate to the organization/department, as required by the Life Safety Code occupancy requirements and services provided. Electricity supplied to essential areas (emergency areas, elevators, areas providing life support, etc.) and equipment (e.g., life support systems, air compressors, alarm systems, exit lighting for signs/ routes, communication systems) when normal electricity is interrupted	

Standard	Comments	Evidence	Staff Questions
EC.8.10 EC.8.30	The survey will assess ED compliance with organizationwide policy on environmental considerations related to care.	• Policies with respect to patients rights and ethics, specific to environmental factors such as privacy, security, confidentiality • Organizationwide policies for construction, guidelines used • Door locking policies and procedures (for observation units, bathrooms, forensic patients, etc.) • Documentation of risk assessment related to planned construction or renovation that might compromise patient care in the ED (consider air quality, infection control, utility requirements, noise, vibration, and emergency procedures) *Site inspection* • Appropriate space for emergency services relative to patient population (age, and characteristics) • Adequate lighting for services provided • Area for care is safe, clean, functional to meet the needs of the patients served • Ventilation appropriate with respect to air quality considering temperature, humidity, odor • Use of restraint and seclusion followed with respect to organizational policy, law, regulation, respecting patient dignity. Any locked doors or occupied spaces have mechanisms to provide emergency access. • Reducing or eliminating ED overcrowding and use of equipment, stretchers in hallway • Patient privacy not violated on overhead paging system • Doors closed, curtains used where appropriate • Emergency access to locked rooms, such as bathrooms • Adequate lighting for patient care activities • Rooms for patient/religious advisor discussions available • Environment is safe, clean, and attractive • Ventilation allows for removal of odors, acceptable temperature • Auditory privacy • Environmental infection control risk assessment completed prior to renovation	• Is there enough space in the ED exam rooms to provide services? Manage a code? • Where does triage occur? How is patient confidentiality protected? • How are you sensitive to patients' needs for privacy, respect, and dignity in the triage environment? In the waiting area and treatment rooms? • When appropriate, do you provide patients a snack or meal? • How are conversations at registration, triage and other areas kept confidential? • Describe any projects or initiatives that have been implemented to improve the environment of care in the ED. • Did you have renovations in the ED in the last year? If so, what changes if any to fire exits did you make? • How was infection control affected during the renovation?

Standard	Comments	Evidence	Staff Questions
EC.9.10 EC.9.20 EC.9.30	The ED seeks to monitor and improve environmental conditions. Data is collected, aggregated, assessed, and used to improve the environment of care and patient safety program within the organization. A multidisciplinary organizational process exists to improve the organization's environment of care in the organization.	• The ED staff is aware of the reporting and data collection mechanism established for the following: patients, visitor/other incidents (including security and property incidents); occupational health illness and injuries; hazardous materials and waste spills, exposures, etc.; problems, deficiencies, failures, or user errors related to fire safety, equipment management, and utility systems. • The ED participates in data collection activities to identify deficiencies, opportunities for improvement, and to monitor the overall environment of care. • The ED leadership and staff are aware that an individual(s) is assigned to oversee the major functions of the organization's environment of care • Evidence of organizationwide meetings, reports, evidence of a multidisciplinary performance improvement team/group analyzing environment of care findings, plans for improvement to resolve any identified issues • Organizationwide outcomes, improvement reports, including annual reports of the objectives, scope, performance, and effectiveness for each of the seven required Environment of Care plans. Reports demonstrate that recommendations based on PI activities and monitoring of the environment of care plans have been communicated at least annually to hospital leaders for consideration • Organizationwide environment of care data, environmental safety issues, recommendations for improvement, and measurable outcomes are integrated into the organization's patient safety program *as indicated in the Leadership chapter.*	• Have you participated in any data collection to measure the effectiveness of the environment of care plans in the ED? • What strategies have you implemented to improve the environment of care in your unit? • What communication do you receive from the organization re: EOC monitoring, improvements, actions needed? • How do you monitor the effectiveness of any new environment of care recommendations implemented? • Where do you report this monitoring data? • Describe how you resolve environment of care issues identified in your system and in your service area. What other disciplines have you worked with to improve the environment of care? • Does your organization have a multidisciplinary process for measuring performance, outcomes, resolving environment of care issues in a timely manner? How is the ED represented in the process? How often does the multidisciplinary group meet to make recommendations? • How does IC and engineering work together in the ED? • How are environment of care issues and measurable outcomes integrated with the organization's patient safety program? Communicated to leadership and/or the individual(s) responsible for patient safety, and PI? • Explain how you implemented your disaster plan, measured and reported findings. Did you make improvements?

MANAGEMENT OF HUMAN RESOURCES

Standard	Comments	Evidence	Staff Questions

HR.1.10 HR.1.20	The ED must verify there are sufficient staff within the department who have education, training, licensure, and knowledge consistent with legal requirements to meet the needs of the population served. Employee, contract worker, student*, volunteer* personnel files demonstrate evidence that his/her qualifications correspond with assigned job responsibilities.
	
	 *Note: the requirements pertain to students and volunteers working in the same capacity as staff who provide care and treatment.
		• ED staffing plan and evidence of its implementation
		 • Leadership and staff interviews
		 • Personnel indicating the following:
		   - job descriptions/clinical privileges reflecting state law requirements for licensure, scope of practice
		   - orientation (organizationwide and departmental proof of knowledge gained)
		   - performance evaluations corresponding with job descriptions
		   - defined qualifications and competence of staff making decisions about the use and implementation of restraint and seclusion use
		 • The organization must demonstrate the following according to the organization's policy, and in accord with laws and regulations for applicable individuals providing health care, treatment and services in the organization:
		   - Current licensure, certification, registration, if applicable
		   - Training, experience, and competency for the job assignment
		   - Criminal background check
		   - Compliance with employee health policies of the organization for health screening requirements
		   - Staff supervision of students providing patient care/treatment/services
		 • Organizations must ensure that individuals hired who do not have a license, registration, and/or certification are not providing care that would require licensure/registration/certification by law or regulation.
		 • ED and facility organizational chart
		 • Meeting minutes, reports on PI studies regarding appropriate staffing levels and skills
		 • Contracts, if the ED uses contracted staff
			To staff
			 • What knowledge and abilities do you need to work in this department?
			 • How is your performance evaluated in measurable terms?
			 • What qualifications or competencies do you have related to the use of restraint and/or seclusion?
			 • What percentage of your physicians are Board Certified in Emergency Medicine?
			 • Describe your staffing process and how leadership ensures an adequate number of staff are available for patient care.
			 • Are there nurses in the ED on all shifts?
			 • How many nurses are certified by the Emergency Nurses Association?
			 To leaders
			 • What is your process for defining staff qualifications and responsibilities?
			 • Do all your staff meet the requirements you have for any specialized training for the ED RN (e.g., ACLS, PALS, TNCC, NALS, and CEN)?
			 • How do you match staffing needs with the education level and experience of staff?
			 • How do you monitor and adjust staffing based on patient need?
			 • What process do you use for assigning staff to triage based on their education and experience?
			 • How do you ensure that each staff member has a job description that meets essential job requirements?
			 • What happens if the number of staff is on a particular shift is less than planned?
			 • Tell me about how staff are oriented. How long does this last? Is there a checklist you could show me?

Standard	Comments	Evidence	Staff Questions

HR.1.30	The ED must assess staffing effectiveness using data from at least four indicators—two clinical/service screening indicators and two human resource (HR) screening indicators. At least one clinical/service indicator and one HR indicator must be selected from the JCAHO's recommended list of indicators. The organization must clearly demonstrate its reasoning for selecting its indicators, as well as if direct and indirect caregivers are included in the human resource screening indicators.
	In 2005 only two units in the entire hospital are required to participate in the staffing effectiveness standard. ED leaders should collaborate with the human resources department to determine participation.
		• Data collected from HR screening indicators such as:
		  - overtime
		  - staff vacancy rate, turnover rate
		  - staff satisfaction
		  - understaffing as compared to organization's staffing plan
		  - nursing care hours per patient day
		  - staff injuries on the job
		  - on-call or per diem use
		  - sick time
		• Data collected from clinical/service indicators such as:
		  - patient or family complaints
		  - adverse drug events
		  - patient falls or other injuries
		  - post-operative infections
		  - shock/cardiac arrest
		  - skin breakdown
		  - urinary track infections
		• Reports to organization leaders, at least annually, on the compiling and analysis of data (relative to expected targets, goals, desired performance, external comparisons) related to staffing effectiveness and any actions taken to improve staffing. Organizations must analyze data over time to identify trends using line graphs, run and/or control charts to determine the stability of the process. All indicators must be analyzed in combination using statistical techniques to determine if outcomes may be influenced by staffing.
			To leaders
			• Are you participating in any staffing effectiveness data collection?
			• What is your process for using screening indicators to determine staffing effectiveness?
			• How many screening indicators are analyzed to assess the effectiveness of staff?
			• What is the rationale for selecting those particular screening indicators?
			• What caregivers are included in the human resource screening indicators? Is there a process to analyze screening indicator data over time per measure (e.g., target ranges, trends over time, external comparison data) and then in combination with other screening indicators (i.e., statistical correlation)?
			• Are at least four screening indicators (two HR and two clinical service indicators) used relative to patient outcomes to indicate staffing effectiveness?
			How have staff been involved in the review of data from the screening indicators?
			• What changes have been made based on the staffing effectiveness data?
			• What has been shared with the governing board re: staffing effectiveness?

Standard	Comments	Evidence	Staff Questions

HR.2.10	The standard addresses the organization and department orientation programs. Staff members, students, and volunteers must receive initial job training and information on their responsibilities and their workplace prior to providing care or performing services.	• Staff and leadership interviews
		• Job description, orientation program, verification policies and procedures, etc.
		• Evidence that new hires received orientation for the organization and department
		  - attendance records
		  - training material presented
		  - participation in preceptor program
		• Does the training material presented at orientation include the following topics:
		  - review of mission, strategic goals
		  - organizational, program specific and/or department/ unit policies and procedures
		  - overview of organizationwide policies and procedures relative to safety/environment of care, infection control
		  - specific job duties and responsibilities and/or program/unit specific responsibilities related to safety and infection control
		  - cultural diversity and sensitivity
		  - patient rights and organizational ethics
		  - policy on caring for prisoners/educating forensic staff
		  - pain management for clinical staff
		  - abuse and neglect
		  - moderate sedation, if applicable
		  - error reporting (patient safety)
		  - team dynamics
		  - organ procurement organization
		  - sensitivity toward the dying patient
		  - restraints (if applicable)
		  - patient safety, organizational policy and unit specific
		• Following orientation, evidence that the organization assesses and documents each person's ability to carry out assigned responsibilities safely, proficiently, and in a timely manner upon completion of orientation (initial competency and/or orientation performance evaluation)
		• Policy and procedure on caring for prisoners/educating forensic staff (e.g., correctional officers, guards, and others) with no clinical training or experience on how to interact with patients; procedures for responding to
			• How are you trained to perform this procedure?
			• What specialized training do you have as an ED LPN, LVN, RN, or CNA?
			• How are agency nurses oriented to the ED?
			• Describe how a new member of your department would receive the following:
			  - an orientation to the organization and ED (e.g., specific equipment, procedures, patient safety, environment of care, infection control)
			  - an evaluation determining that he or she is ready to perform responsibilities
			• Do you have volunteers, residents, agency/contract staff and/or students working in the department? If yes, what type of orientation do they receive to the organization and department?
			• How do you orient forensic staff/those caring for prisoners?
			How do you educate staff to care for forensic patients?
			• Describe the orientation topics.
			
			Questions for forensic staff:
			• What is your role with regard to the care of this patient?
			• How are you educated in performing your role?
			• How does the organization know you are competent to perform your role in the ED?
			• Describe any training the organization provided to you (e.g., Environment of Care, safety procedures, etc.).
			• What is the difference between use of administrative (i.e., for law enforcement purposes) and clinical restraint and seclusion?
			• How do you manage restraint and seclusion issues?
			• Who do you approach to discuss issues about the patient/prisoner you are overseeing?
			• How are students and volunteers educated on patient safety in the ED?

Standard	Comments	Evidence	Staff Questions
		incidents/unusual clinical events; channels for communicating with clinicians, security and administration; and the difference between administrative and clinical restraint and seclusion.	
HR.2.20	Staff members, licensed independent practitioners, students, and volunteers (as appropriate) can convey their specific job duties or responsibilities pertaining to safety.	• Staff and leadership interviews • Safety/HR/department plans, policies, and procedures pertaining to ongoing education, inservices, training to enhance staff competencies/performance in risk management, and/or the environment of care • Continuing education plans for staff relative to risk management and safety • Evidence that licensed independent practitioners, students, and volunteers, can describe or demonstrate their roles and responsibilities pertaining to safety management • Ongoing error reporting education • Performance improvement related to patient safety and environmental safety	• What are the risks associated with your job? What actions do you do to eliminate or reduce risks? • How do you report risks associated with your job? • Describe your incident reporting mechanism. Do you report close calls where no harm occurred to the patient but could have? • What is your mechanism to report problems, failures, and user errors? • How does the organization train you about safety topics, precautions to take, the environment of care, and patient safety? • What emergency procedures should be instituted should an incident or failure occur in the environment?

Standard	Comments	Evidence	Staff Questions

HR.2.30	The ED must show evidence of staff that focus on self-improvement and self-learning to improve the competence. The organization must provide ongoing education and training to staff, students and volunteers who render patient care, treatment and services. Staff participates in education and training programs to stay current, confirm with law and regulations, to promote patient safety, and when there are changes in job responsibilities.
	Education and training provided is documented.
		• Staff and leadership interviews
		• Policies and procedures, organizationwide and department specific on education and training
		• Submitting and responding to data collected on ED staff's learning needs
		• Schedule of training programs and evidence of topics covered
		• Documentation of department specific training programs
		• Training tools (journals, self-study guides, audiotapes, videotapes, teleconferences, product demonstration, access to school credits, self-tests, cross-training program descriptions, etc.)
		• Meeting minutes (e.g., medical staff, PI, ED, or governing body) on improving competencies, staff proficiency, through staff development/training
		• Education attendance records indicating staff, student, volunteer (when providing patient care, treatment and/or services) participation in outside seminars, internal classes, and/or other continuing education programs
		• Examples of how data was assessed and used to design education program and activities for staff, volunteers/students
		• Ongoing:
		  - ED specific work-related education
		  - ED specific population/age-related competency
		  - ED specific patient and environmental safety
		  - ED specific infection control
		  - team training
		  - training re: reporting unanticipated
		  - education based on PI data
		  - continuing education records, evidence of meeting requirements for any specialized training and education as per organizational/ED policy and procedure(s)
			To the manager
			• How do you ensure that staff have the skills needed for their jobs?
			• Describe how you identify staff learning needs.
			• How do you prioritize and monitor staff education requirements?
			• What training have you planned for your department within the past year? How do you select training topics?
			• What internal education programs do you have?
			• How do you educate the night shift?
			• Do staff pursue higher education and training?
			• How do you enhance team building and improve the training to staff?
			• How does the organization assist you in training to improve your skills and knowledge?
			
			To staff
			• What type of staff educational activities are available? How often?
			• Do education programs have continuing education unit (CEU) credits?
			• If yes, how many CEU education programs are provided annually?
			• What resources does your organization devote to continuing education (e.g., journals, books, videos, seminars, college credits, etc.)?
			• What was the last training session you attended? Has it helped you to improve patient care?
			• How are you competent to treat different patient groups (e.g., infants, children, adolescents, geriatric, pediatric, abuse victims)?
			• Are you meeting the continuing education requirements for your job based on your organization's policies and procedures?
			• What training have you received relative to team building, team dynamics, and team communication? Patient safety? infection control?
			• Describe training programs designed for your job classification and patient population/programs (e.g., behavioral health, dialysis, etc.).

Standard	Comments	Evidence	Staff Questions
			• Were you taught to report unanticipated outcomes or medical errors?

HR.3.10 HR.3.20	Competence to perform job duties is assessed, evaluated, and maintained. The staff performance evaluations must be completed at least once in the three year accreditation cycle, unless applicable law/regulation requires a shorter timeframe.	• Staff and leadership interviews
		• HR/department policies and procedures on the competency and the performance evaluation process
		• Competence assessments exist for students, and volunteers who work in the same capacity as staff providing patient care/services.
		• Competencies are designed/ implemented based on the following: population served, (age-specific) required by job responsibilities, at orientation, and on an ongoing basis relative to techniques, procedures, technology, equipment or skills needed to provide care or services.
		• The organization must define the timeframe for frequency of competency assessments for each job, and indicate the assessment methods.
		• Individuals who assess competencies must be qualified to conduct the evaluation.
		• Organizations must demonstrate evidence of implementation of the competency assessment program, as well as periodic performance evaluations conducted at timeframes identified by the organization's policy and procedure
		• Performance evaluations are based on the performance expectations identified in the corresponding job descriptions
		• Orientation and ongoing competencies related to the following (as applicable):
		  - (age-specific) population served
		  - restraint and seclusion
		• Meeting minutes (e.g., medical staff, PI, ED, or governing body) on improving competencies, staff proficiency, staffing levels
		• Employee, contracted staff, volunteer records include:
		  - job description, signed
		  - orientation
		  - performance evaluations (blank)
		  - competency program, orientation for specific age groups, as applicable
		  - continuing education, training
		  - job and age-specific (if direct care provider) competencies
		• Mechanisms for measuring age-specific competencies for specific jobs within the ED
		• PI studies, reports, minutes on age-specific competency issues
			• What competencies are required to meet the specific population served in the ED, for example, Level 1 trauma, burn center, infants, pediatrics, geriatrics, and other groups?
			• How often are competencies assessed? Where is this documented?
			• Who assess competencies? How are they competent to do so? Does the competency assessment include observing the individual staff member performing the skills while using critical thinking?
			• If improvement activities determine that a person with performance problems is unable/unwilling to improve, what action will the organization take? Will the organization modify the person's job assignment?
			• How often do you receive a performance evaluation?
			• How often does staff have their performance evaluated?
			• What are the competencies of an ED nurse? Technician?
			• Who assesses your competencies?
			• How are your competencies assessed?
			• What mechanism is used to evaluate how staff meet their defined responsibilities?
			• Do you have age-specific competencies?
			• Do you have population-specific competencies?

MANAGEMENT OF INFORMATION

Standard	Comments	Evidence	Staff Questions
IM.1.10	This standard concerns the hospital having an information management (IM) plan created by assessing the organization's internal and external information needs. Representatives from the ED must demonstrate their participation in having their IM needs assessed so that they are incorporated within the IM planning process. Surveyors may focus on how ED leaders make their department's IM needs known to senior leaders.	• Staff and leadership interviews • Evidence of an Organizationwide Information Management Steering Committee or group that prioritizes projects, requests, needs for the organization, including the ED (based on the organization's mission, goals, scope and complexity of services, patient safety, staffing, performance, method of service delivery, resources, availability of technology, and communication barriers evident among caregivers). • organization IM plan includes planning for ED services • Participation in ongoing IM planning documents, strategic plans, needs assessment surveys, requests to administration • Meeting minutes indicating organization IM planning • PI projects in the ED or organizationwide displaying plans, outcomes to improve the flow of patient information (e.g., plans for or observation of new computer system, charting, scheduling system, information storage and feedback mechanisms) • Evidence that staff have their need for knowledge-based information met by the organization	*To leaders* • How do you participate in IM planning? Are physicians and other clinicians involved in the process? • How has the organization assessed your IM needs? • Can you give an example of how you had an IM need met? • Has the organization performed an assessment of the needs of the department for knowledge-based information to assist with information management planning? • While not required products, has the ED considered automated medication dispensing machines, computerized physicians order entry, electronic medical record documentation? • Do you document AWOB, AMA, Left Without Being Seen (LWBS) in the patient's medical record?

Standard	Comments	Evidence	Staff Questions
IM.2.10 IM.2.20 IM.2.30	The ED should ensure that privacy and confidentiality policy and practices are enforced. Information security practices comply with organization policies and procedures while allowing access to data and information in a timely fashion. To protect confidentiality, staff should limit access to patient and staff information based on need. Systems must be implemented to protect the integrity of the data (e.g., medical record, computer system, stored records). Maintaining the continuity of information is essential for patient care and outcomes.	• Staff, leadership, and patient interviews • Organizationwide policies and procedures consistent with applicable law regarding privacy, confidentiality, and security of information, which includes processes for enforcing and monitoring compliance with the policies • Policies specific to obtaining access to information, release of information, preservation of the medical record, removal of records, destroying records/copies, falsification of records • Information management plans/policies, for protecting the integrity of data (e.g., operation of back-up systems, contingency plans, down-time procedures, data retrieval, measures for protection against emergencies, security systems that include passwords, codes) • Policies, and procedures, specifically focused on meeting HIPAA requirements: disclosure policies, authentication, nonrepudiation, encryption, when warranted, and auditability for patient billing. Requirement enforced to remove personal identifiers when releasing health data and information whenever feasible • Evidence of education regarding information management policies and procedures, and further communication when modifications are made • Staff and Patient Interviews *Site inspections indicating evidence of safeguards protecting the privacy, confidentiality, and security of information* • Technology used to assist with limiting access of the information to authorized individuals delivering care, services, treatment, research, education, and proper management of the organization • Examples of preserving information considered "sensitive" and that requires extraordinary means to preserve patient privacy and confidentiality • Security of any clinical information identifying the patient—evidence that PHI, protected health information, is used for purposes identified or as required by law and not further disclosed without patient authorization	• Describe how you preserve the confidentiality and security of data/information. • Who has access to a patient's medical record? To the computer terminal? • What information do you have access to on the computer? • What do you do if a family member asks to look at a patient's record? • What is your policy on releasing clinical information, copies of the record? Can ambulance personnel review ED patient information? Do you get a consent for the release of information? • How do you manage inquiries regarding patients? • What do you do if the media calls for patient information? • How are you trained on confidentiality and security of information issues? • What special procedures do you have to protect patient information (e.g., staff sign confidentiality statements on hire or when using computer system)? • What measures does the hospital take to protect information being revealed to individuals who do not have permission? What processes protect the data or information from security breaches, harm, or being altered? • Who can you give your computer access code to? • When using and disclosing health information, does the organization remove the personal identifiers as much as possible? • Describe your disclosure of information practices. • How do you ensure that staff with legitimate needs have access to data and information without compromising its integrity? • Do you have communication/white boards in the ED? How do you protect the patient's confidentiality if you use these?

271

Standard	Comments	Evidence	Staff Questions
		• Security of active and inactive records • Computer terminals logged off when not in use • Patient names and diagnoses not recorded on a board visible to visitors and other patients • Protective measures implemented to prevent distribution of sensitive information to public (e.g., limiting access to operating room or procedural schedules, special sign-in logs protecting patient name and information that could be viewed by others, and use of technology to provide additional security measures) • Confidential, sensitive patient information not discussed in areas where it may be overheard by individuals other than the patient • Measures to protect records from damage (e.g., sprinklers, fireproof cabinets)	

Standard	Comments	Evidence	Staff Questions

IM.3.10	This standard covers expectation of the use of standard terminology, definitions, and abbreviations, as well as uniform data collection methodologies. The organization must also have an appropriate system for storing and retrieving data for clinical, service and organization-specific information. The storage of information must be safely secured, yet easily retrievable by authorized users. Policies on retaining data and information must comply with law and regulations.
	As applied to the ED, this standard requires that staff have the knowledge and resources for performing important information management functions. The organization must ensure data/information is well timed, precise, and that there is a uniform method of disseminating complete data among users. This data must be transformed into information that is organized and useful to decision makers. The organization must have mechanisms to ensure that information management policies, and procedures are enforced.
	This standard also concerns ensuring organizations have a standardized list of abbreviations, acronyms, and symbols used throughout the organization, including a list of those abbreviations, acronyms, and symbols NOT to use.
		• Staff interactions, use of data, computer system
		• Organizationwide standardized abbreviations, acronyms, and symbols or a standard approved book that would include any examples from the ED
		• Staff knowledge of a policy and/or list of abbreviations not to be used that are considered risky and problematic (see national patient safety goals)
		• Organizationwide medical and clinical policies: terminology, minimum data sets, data definitions, classification, vocabulary, standardized nomenclature, collection, storage, and retrieval of data, unscheduled downtime, data transformation and dissemination
		• Organizationwide standard data definitions for a medical record, automated data tables/dictionary on computer system
		• Medical record accuracy, use of approved terminology and abbreviations, timeliness and accuracy of data collection and dissemination into usable information
		• Quality control systems to oversee data collection activities that includes consideration for timeliness, accuracy of content, completeness, and discrimination necessary for intended use
		• Organizationwide policy outlining the timeframe for retention of data to comply with law accrediting and regulatory bodies
		• Mechanism for ensuring systems are compatible for accurate transmission and assimilation of data for analysis and reporting
		  - diagnostic study turnaround time
		  - medical record entry accuracy
		• PI data, chart reviews, practices that ensure the accuracy of data and information (e.g., use of standard abbreviations, codes, definitions, turnaround time, chart completion rates)
		• Improving diagnostic test turnaround time for test results to become available to practitioners
		• Education, lecture outlines on IM
		  - confidentiality, security, access
		  - use of computers, software
		  - documenting in medical records
			• Do you have a policy on abbreviations or standard data definitions?
			• What abbreviations have you defined as problematic that staff should not use? Is the use of an unapproved abbreviation considered an incomplete order?
			• During open chart review, can you find any abbreviations that should not be used based on your organization's policy? What do you do when you find these? What does this data reflect? Where is this data reported?
			• How do you ensure that data is collected in a uniform manner?
			• How long are your ED charts retained? Where are they stored?
			• Do you use industry or organizational standards for defining data definitions, capturing data, data display, and transmission?
			• Describe any mechanisms you use to ensure that data is collected in a timely and precise manner.
			• How long does it take the medical record to get from the triage area to the treatment area?
			• What is the expected turnaround time for the following:
			  - radiology reports?
			  - lab tests?
			  - blood tests?
			• Describe your process for notifying physicians of discrepancies in radiology or lab results.
			• What is your procedure for notifying patients of the results of diagnostic studies?
			• What type of IM training have clinical staff received? What elements does the education include? From the ED viewpoint, has there been any specialized education? Have you added any IM systems or support specific to your area?
			• Are medical staff and students trained in IM?
			• How do you assess staff knowledge of IM?
			• What ED indicators are collected to improve systems and processes? How do you ensure consistency when

273

Standard	Comments	Evidence	Staff Questions
		- data collection techniques, ensuring accuracy of collecting data - using data, exchanging information, interpreting data - tools available - PI techniques on using data to support decisions, statistical and nonstatistical analysis methods - access to literature, library services - HIPAA • Personnel files showing IM training provided based on the individual's job requirements, information needs	gathering the data? Have you trended your data? Do you use statistical techniques to interpret the data?
IM.4.10	Information management planning allows for the sharing and exchange of data and information from different resources to support decision making. The following are examples of data being used and aggregated to support important functions: individual care, decision making, management, operations, performance improvement, benchmarking with other organizations, research, infection control, patient safety, educating, and analyzing trends.	• Information management system structure that collects, organizes, analyzes, and assists with interpreting data • Evidence that systems and processes support easy access to the record (by authorized users) to assist with clinical decision making balancing privacy, security, and confidentiality concerns • Documentation illustrating that the ED uses data to make patient care decisions and management decisions, to reduce risks to patients, to look for trends over time, to compare with other organizations, and for performance improvement • Maintenance of control register (e.g., computerized or manual log) • PI data reports, use of aggregate data in system • Minutes of meetings indicating use of data and information • Standardization of the medical record • Interviews with staff members that collect and/or use data to support decision making • Open and closed charts demonstrating the following regarding data and information: recorded accurately, timely, completely, and organized for efficient retrieval of needed data • In the ED, surveyors may focus on the maintenance of the control register that gathers the following information from each ED patient: - ID—name, age, gender - date, time, means of arrival - nature of complaint - disposition - time of departure	• If you have clinical systems, are they linked to your financial, billing system? • How are department clinical systems linked (e.g., food and nutrition with laboratory)? • Do you trend reports on volumes, staffing patterns, billing records, thoughput times? • How do you use comparative data and information in the organization/ED? • Is your medical record standardized? • Do you have any performance measures that you are collecting to ensure data is complete, accurate, timely and/or readily available? • Can you describe your maintenance of the control register? What are the items included in the content? • How do you collect information on patient demographics? • Where do you record that required reports have been made to authorities? • Show me a sample of a report where you aggregate the data and use it for decision making. • Do you have an electronic documentation process? • Do you have plans of going to an electronics format? • Do you have computerized physician order entry? Have you thought of going to this order entry process? • What is considered a complete ED record?

274

Standard	Comments	Evidence	Staff Questions

		• Evidence of participation with reference or external databases
		• Reports demonstrating the integration of data from various sources (e.g., clinical with non-clinical information)
		• Examples of how data was used for
		  - decision making
		  - management
		  - analysis over time
		  - PI
		  - IC
		  - patient safety	

IM.5.10	The standard concerns knowledge-based ("literature") IM needs of staff. This standard mainly addresses staff access to knowledge-based information. A hospital is not required to have an on-site library, but must demonstrate that information may be obtained in a timely manner by sharing services with another hospital or resource.
	An organization must meet staff's needs for resources in print, electronic, on the Internet, audio, and/or in another appropriate format. When an electronic system is unavailable, the organization must have a plan to provide access to knowledge-based information. There must be a mechanism to provide resources to staff at all times, through automation, after-hours access, etc.
		• Staff and leadership interviews
		• Organizationwide systems, resources, literature searches, use of library services
		• Listing of library literature, periodicals, practice guidelines, texts, indexes, abstracts, on-line services, satellite services, research data, audio resources, etc.
		• On-site library services or cooperative/contractual arrangement with another organization
			• Describe resources available to meet your knowledge-based ("literature") IM needs.
			• Do you have access to the Internet? An intranet? Have you had training on this?
			• Does your staff have access to the latest resources available in ED services (e.g., latest standards of care, care planning books, medication references, reference literature, articles, etc.) on all shifts?
			• How would you access these resources?
			• How have you used knowledge-based information to support clinical, management decisions, performance improvement, patient safety, staff and patient/family education and/or for research needs?
			• What procedures do you follow when the hospital's electronic system is unavailable
			  - MSDS
			  - laboratory
			  - a medication ordering

Standard	Comments	Evidence	Staff Questions
IM.6.10 IM.6.20	Each patient must have a medical record to document treatment rendered in inpatient and outpatient settings being surveyed by the hospital accreditation program. The following elements of performance must be met in the ED and organizationwide: • Only authorized staff and individuals make medical record entries. Each entry indicates the author and date. • The organization requires authentication for at least the following elements: history and physical, operative report, consultations, and discharge summary. • The organization must indicate which entries made by non-independent practitioners require countersigning. Dating when countersigning signatures depends on regulations, and the organization's policy. • There are uniform procedures/formats implemented to document patient care and services within the medical record. • The medical record contains a variety of patient specific data and information to address the following: patient identification, reasoning for diagnosis/treatment, plan of care, progress of case, prognosis, outcomes from care delivered, and that supports the continuity of care. • A concise discharge summary (for admissions) or final progress note (for individuals with minor problems or interventions defined by the medical staff) includes at least the following topics: reason for hospitalization, significant findings, procedures performed, condition at discharge, and instructions to patient/authorized family. • Organizational policy and/or bylaws indicate required medical record entries and corresponding timeframes for completion of entries. The timeframes for these processes (History and Physicals, Verbal Orders, Closure of Chart) vary from state to state. • This standard requires organizations to define when a medical record is considered complete, including the timeframe for completeness. To comply, medical records must be completed within 30 days of discharge at the latest. The organization's leaders must report statistics on the medical record delinquency rate at least every three months and include inpatient/outpatient records.	• Compliance with the organization's medical staff bylaws, rules, regulations, policies, and procedures (e.g., authenticating records, leaving against medical advice, verbal orders, transfer of information, release of information, discharge instructions, verbal orders, medical record completion) • ED policies and procedures enforced • Open and closed medical records • Staff and patient interviews • Meeting minutes discussing AMA and LWBS (any potential COBRA/EMTALA issues), risk management issues, PI activities, strategies to improve documentation deficiencies identified, outcomes, etc. • Organizationwide physician profiling: physician chart completion statistics as one element of profile • Ongoing medical record review results of defined ED indicators (e.g., evidence of patient identification, initial entries, appropriate orders, countersigning as indicated, consents, consultations, conclusion at termination of treatment, final disposition, and discharge instructions, etc.) • Evidence of discharge handouts containing instructions for self-care, follow-up care, what to do if symptoms worsen • Referrals to community resources both private and non-private • PI studies to improve documentation	*Medical record review questions* • Describe the organizationwide policy on authenticating a medical record entry. What elements of the chart must be authenticated? • How does the organization define authentication? • Who can document in the medical record? How are you sure that only authorized individuals chart within the medical record? When must entries be countersigned? For nursing students? For residents, midlevel practitioners, midwives, nurse practitioners, physician assistants? • Where is it noted that physician orders are completed by nursing? • Where in the medical record do you document: - time and means of arrival, triage documentation including emergency care provided prior to arrival? - identification data (e.g., name, sex, age, date of birth, race, and authorized representative)? - evidence if patient left without being seen? - assessment, diagnosis, and chief complaint? - informed consent, if applicable? - orders, including medications, tests/results? - response to care? - referrals/consultations with internal, external care providers? - advance directives? - use of standards of care, care paths, standardized charting formats? - conclusions at treatment? - final disposition? - documentation for follow-up care? • What procedure do you follow if the patient does not have an advance directive? What if the patient has an advance directive and it is not in the record? What is the ED's policy on honoring advance directives? • Where is there evidence that you provided data/information for a patient's continuous care needs (e.g., discharge instruction,

Standard	Comments	Evidence	Staff Questions
	• There is a defined process for ongoing, open, medical record review based on indicators selected by the organization such as: timeliness, legibility/readability, quality, consistency, clarity, accuracy, completeness, and authentication, scanning/indexing of images. • Medical records must be retained based on applicable state law and regulations, and according to use. Patient care, research, performance improvement, legal requirements, and educational endeavors may also bear on the length of time a record is retained. • Original medical records are not released unless mandated by federal or state laws, court orders, or subpoenas. • The following information must be documented for patients seeking emergency care: Time and means of arrival, if the patient left against medical advice (AMA) or left without being seen (LWBS), conclusion at termination of treatment, including final disposition, condition, and instructions for follow-care, instructions that a copy of the record is available to the practitioner or medical organization providing follow-up care. IM.6.20 needs to be reviewed in detail regarding the list of items that must be included in a medical record, when applicable.		transfer summary, transfer to another unit within the hospital, progress notes)? • How has the organization improved in timely completion of record entries? Do physicians receive data on their performance with timely completion of records? Is this included in their recredentialing process? • How long are your records maintained? • Does each entry in the record indicate an author and date? • How does the ED participate in the ongoing medical record review process? How often? What clinicians participate in reviewing records? What are examples of indicators reviewed? • Describe any improvements or plans for improvement based on data collected from chart reviews. • Have you identified further needs for education, skills reviews based on the record review? *Other Questions* • What education did the patient receive? • Do you have a patient callback program? Has it helped with the continuity of care? • Describe your policy on releasing emergency records to other practitioners providing follow-up care. • If an ED patient goes to another facility, how do you release the patient's record to that facility? • How long does a record stay in the ED prior to going to medical records? • Describe your policy for when a patient leaves against medical advice. Where would this be documented? • What steps have been taken to reduce the number of patients leaving AMA or LWBS?

Standard	Comments	Evidence	Staff Questions
IM.6.30	The standard requires complete documentation of pre, intra, and postoperative procedures, including those other procedures placing the patient at risk. Included in this standard is any procedure using moderate/deep sedation or anesthesia.	• Documentation for operative procedures contains the following: - provisional diagnosis prior to procedure by the LIP - operative progress note recorded immediately after the procedure while the patient is still in the ED - operative report dictated or written immediately after the procedure - operative report authenticated by surgeon, and available in the chart as soon as possible following the procedure - documentation of the name of the responsible LIP discharging the patient included in post operative documentation	• Tell me about the process for moderate sedation: - is an H&P required? - is an anesthesia assessment needed? -ASA? • Are your discharge criteria from post procedure/ moderate sedation approved by the medical staff? • How do you determine the patient's readiness for discharge? Is an order needed by the physician to discharge? • Do physicians in the ED document post procedure notes?
IM.6.50	It is imperative that clinicians comply with their medical staff bylaws, rules, and regulations stating the organization's verbal order policy. Approved ED staff that accept and record verbal/telephone orders or receive critical test results, must also be familiar with the requirements of the JCAHO's national safety goal regarding improving communication among caregivers. The expectation is that staff use a process to ensure the accuracy of the transcription of verbal/ telephone orders or critical test results that require a verification "read-back" of the complete order or test result by the person receiving the order or test result.	• Compliance with the following: - medical staff bylaws, rules, and regulations - Organizationwide verbal order policy and procedure - state and federal law • Record review of the verbal order indicating the following: date of the order, name of the individual who gave it, received it, implemented it, and authorized it within time specified (timeframe is based on the requirements of the organization, and in compliance with state and federal rules and regulations). • Data collection of the unit's performance with verbal order if a problem was identified • Observation of authorized staff accepting verbal orders according to organizational policy, and the national safety goals	• Please describe your verbal order policy and procedure. Is it different for telephone orders? What are the elements for a valid verbal/ telephone order? • How do you know that an order has been completed? • Who is authorized to accept verbal orders in the department? • Who may transcribe a verbal order? Who may transcribe a telephone order? • Do you review verbal orders during the patients ED visit via a chart check process? • Describe your process for verifying the accuracy of verbal orders. • Do you perform "read-backs" in the ED? • Have you minimized verbal orders in the ED? • What does your data reflect?

Standard	Comments	Evidence	Staff Questions
IM.6.60	This standard refers not only to ED access to patient records, but also to ED contribution to the record in a manner that makes information accessible to staff providing follow-up care. The organization must ensure that all relevant data/information from a patient's record is available when needed for patient care.	• Departmental policies and procedures • Use of a computer patient information system • Manual or automated systems exist to track the location of all data and information within the medical record. There is a mechanism to gather required information, or a synopsis of information within the record to have available for follow-up care • Interviews with staff, leaders • Observation of accessing records (e.g., access to fax machines, computer records)	• Describe your medical record system for assembling clinical information for patient care. • Can you show me how to access this patient's record that is in the department and the one in medical records? What if the records on a patient exist in more than one location? • How quickly can you assemble a record from different settings (e.g., hard copy or screen display)? • Who has access to medical records after hours? • What is the process for obtaining them? • Does the record system alert users when components are stored in other location? • How long are the records kept in the ED after a patient has been discharged, admitted, or transferred? • How long does it take to retrieve medical records?

SURVEILLANCE, PREVENTION, AND CONTROL OF INFECTION

Standard	Comments	Evidence	Staff Questions
IC.1.10	This standard refers to the organization's infection control (IC) program and the selection of a surveillance program based on specific criteria. When creating the IC plan or program, the organization must consider its demographics, patient population, patient care demands/ volumes, staffing, priority initiatives, research data available, and data that can be gathered organizationwide and department-specific. Those concerns considered to be epidemiologically important are targeted for improvement by staff. The aim of the IC program is to reduce risks of infections among licensed independent practitioners, patients, staff, contracted workers, volunteers, students, and visitors, using epidemiological principles. Activities of the IC program must be planned with in conjunction with applicable agencies (e.g., the local health department, external support systems) to prevent/limit infection control issues/outbreaks when applicable. Consideration must be made to also decrease the risk of infection from the environment (contamination through food and water). Organizations should be familiar with the sentinel event alert regarding infection control and prevention, and consider implementing strategies to reduce infection risks as outlined in the alert.	• Interviews with staff • Implementation of organizationwide IC plan, policies, procedures • Committee minutes demonstrating ED membership and/or contributions to the committee/function • Minutes from ED decisionmaking body meetings relating to IC issues • Staff education materials • Any ED-specific IC policies and procedures • Attendee list for IC training • The use of evidence-based information on reducing nosocomial infections, use of sentinel event alert on infection control and prevention	• What is the organization's process for prevention, surveillance, and control of infection (e.g., Universal Precautions, Body Substance Isolation)? • How do you treat a patient who presents a risk of epidemiologically important nosocomial infection? • Describe the organization's infection control training program. How was this implemented in the ED? • Where are the IC policies and procedures kept within the ED? • Where is the Personal Protection Equipment (PPE) kept? • Do minutes from organizationwide IC meetings reflect a continuous IC System that uses data to improve services (clinical), an epidemiological process, and partnering with the hospitalwide IC program? • Who collects IC data? How is it used? • What information do you submit to the local health department? • What types of infections are you working on reducing (e.g., device-related, surgical site, communicable diseases, nosocomial TB, vaccine preventable)? • What is the biggest IC risk in the ED? What have you done to mitigate this risk? • How does the IC practitioner communicate to you as a staff member re: IC issues? • Have you conducted a bioterrorism drill using an infectious disease as the threat? • What IC components do you orient the new employee to in the ED?
IC.7.10	The standard refers to organizationwide management of infection control by a qualified individual.	• Organizationwide IC plan, policies, and procedures • Meeting minutes, plans reflecting qualifications of those overseeing IC/employee health (EH) program • Personnel records of IC/ employee health professionals indicating their qualifications, such as training, experience, and certification or licensure.	• What data are provided to you by the IC department? • Who oversees infection control and employee health? • How do you find out about the activities of the infection control committee? • Who would you notify if staff were exposed to an infectious disease? How would you do this?

Standard	Comments	Evidence	Staff Questions
IC.2.10	The standard addresses organization data collection and surveillance of infection control and employee health issues.	• Observation and interviews with staff to review IC strategies • Implementation of organizationwide and departmental infection control and employee health policies and procedures (must be consistent) • Records of IC and/or Safety Team surveillance rounds, and follow-up activities • ED data collection compliance with organization requirements • Case findings of nosocomial infections, employee health issues, and any corresponding action plan • Records of employees who have contracted significant infections • Ability to demonstrate that surveillance activities are selected based on the organization's demographics and services. • Management representation on organizationwide IC Committees • IC risk assessment	• Describe your process for collecting data on nosocomial infections and employee health issues. • What is a nosocomial infection? • What is a blood borne pathogen? • How do you monitor compliance with infection control procedures? • What infection control issues have you encountered this year? • What IC risk assessment was conducted this year? • How does the IC coordinator know that there are several ED staff calling in sick for the same reason? What does the IC coordinator do with this information?
IC.3.10	Organizations have a responsibility to report relevant nosocomial infections through appropriate internal and external reporting mechanisms (e.g., public health agencies, as appropriate).	• Organizationwide policies and procedures on reporting nosocomial infections internally and to public health agencies, as appropriate • Organizationwide policies on reporting employee illness of epidemiological significance to public health agencies • Evidence of reporting of case findings of demographically significant nosocomial infections within committee minutes/PI reports	• Describe the procedure for reporting information about nosocomial infections. • Describe the procedure for reporting employee health problems. Whom do you contact within the organization? • Who is responsible for informing public health agencies of pertinent cases involving nosocomial infections? • What is the process for reporting a patient with a communicable disease? • Does management support reporting nosocomial infections to local health departments, as appropriate? • How does the organization manage any incidence of unanticipated death or major permanent loss of function associated with health care acquired infection (re: referring to sentinel event alert on infection control)?

Standard	Comments	Evidence	Staff Questions

IC.4.10 IC.5.10	Organizations must implement strategies to prevent, minimize, and contain the risk of nosocomial infections throughout the organization, particularly in patient care settings such as the ED.
	The IC program must include both patient care and employee health services
		• Observation and interviews with staff
		• Organizationwide policies and procedures for IC and employee health
		• Orientation, continuing education material, attendance records for IC training
		• Any PI projects to reduce risks/ control the identified outbreaks of infections where the ED staff participated
		• Minutes of IC discussions, activities displaying evidence that the hospital takes action to prevent or reduce the risk of nosocomial infections in patients, staff, and visitors
		• Evidence the organization uses strategies from knowledge-based resources such as through published in scientific research, accrediting and regulatory standards, APIC, and acceptable practice guidelines (e.g., use of the CDC guidelines for hand hygiene).
		Site inspection
		• Alcohol-based hand sanitizers and/or sinks in readily available locations for patients, visitors, and staff
		• Proper disposal of waste that may transmit infection
		• Gloves, gowns, goggles, shields, and other protective gear worn when contacting blood or body fluid
		• Protective gear stored appropriately and not on side rails
		• Staff demonstrating proper handwashing/hand hygiene techniques
		• Separation of soiled and clean linen
		• Clean room not contaminated
		• Open solution bottles dated as per organizational policy
		• Linen hampers not overfilled
		• Bagged linen not on floors
		• Food refrigerators
		  - free of outdated containers
		  - patient food containers dated
		  - patient and employee food separated
		  - food and nonfood items separated
		  - thermometer in medication
		  - medication refrigerator free from food, clean refrigerator
		• Food/beverages away from possible contamination
		• Needle boxes not more than 2/3rds full, off floor in ED
			• Have you had any outbreak of nosocomial infection identified within the past year? If yes, how did you respond to control the outbreak?
			• Have you implemented the CDC recommendations for handwashing/hygiene techniques?
			• Where are your hand degermers located? How much solution do you use in a month?
			• What strategies are used to reduce nosocomial infections?
			• Describe infection control/ employee health orientation and continuing education programs.
			• Are there any patients who should be immediately removed from the waiting room? Which patients?
			• What precautions do you take when a patient may have TB?
			• Name two work practice controls in the ED.
			• What is the single most important way to prevent the spread of infection?
			• Where does the triage person wash his or her hands?
			• Do you have an annual PPD? Why do you have an annual PPD?
			• What is the procedure to follow in the event of a sharps exposure?
			• Have you been involved in any PI projects targeted at reducing and controlling the risks associated with nosocomial infections?
			• Does anyone from the ED attend the IC Committee meeting? How do you receive information from this committee re: IC issues?

Standard	Comments	Evidence	Staff Questions
IC.6.10 through IC.8.10 IC.9.10	These standards concern organizationwide efforts to reduce the risk of significant nosocomial infection transmission. The emphasis is on automating IC data collection, analysis, and improvement efforts (e.g., computer and software resources). The ED must be aware of at least one strategy used to prevent the spread of infections between patients and staff.	IC.6.10 • Evidence - plan for influx of patients due to infectious disease • Staff knowledge of objectives of IC program, link to PI • Management systems support for the infection control program through staff and data systems • Employee Health lists of staff immunizations, staff needing immunization • ED process for participating in IC program. • Knowledge of data collection efforts, PI studies, monitoring, trending of nosocomial infections rates endemic verses epidemic) • Evidence of a system that is used to improve infection control processes organizationwide improving rates/trends of epidemiologically significant infections. • Management support for IC (e.g., computers, software, data analysis, interpretation, presenting findings)	• How have you planned for an influx of infectious patients? • How would you take care of these patients over time? • What resources in the community are available to you in the event of this influx? • What resources support infection control practices? Management staff? Data systems? • Describe at least one activity in the ED performed to reduce infections between patients and staff. • How are employee health programs integrated with infection control practices? How is the ED linked to this? • How is your ED IC program designed to lower the risks and improve the rates/trends of epidemiologically significant infections?

PART 4

Reference Materials for Emergency Department Compliance

The following forms serve as examples. Hospitals should consult with appropriate advisors before adapting the forms in this Part to suit particular purposes.

285

PATIENT RIGHTS AND ORGANIZATION ETHICS

4-1 Psychiatry Emergency Department: Involuntary Patient Rights

PURPOSE

To define the process of explanation of patient rights.

POLICY

All involuntary patients will be informed of their legal rights.

PROCEDURE

1. The registered nurse (RN) or psychiatric assistant assigned in the psychiatry emergency department will verbally inform the involuntary patient of the following rights:
   - A physician at the psychiatric emergency department has decided to initiate an order of protective custody because of a concern for your mental well-being.
   - This may lead to further hospitalization.
   - You have the right to a reasonable opportunity to contact your attorney.
   - After further evaluation you may be sent home if any of the following apply to you:
     — You are not mentally ill.
     — You are not going to harm yourself or someone else.
     — Emergency detention is not the least-restrictive means by which the necessary restraint may be affected.
   - Anything you say here or during hospitalization may be used in further proceedings.
   - A report of your examination may be forwarded to the court.
2. The RN will be responsible for documenting in the nurses' notes that the patient has been informed of his or her rights.

Source: Adapted from Parkland Memorial Hospital, Dallas, Texas.

4-2 Policy on Emergency Treatment Involving Investigational Drugs, Devices, or Biologics

A. Emergency Treatment Is Not Included in "Research" Data

Federal regulations for the protection of human subjects do not permit research activities to be started without prior IBRA review and approval. These regulations, however, do not limit or interfere with the authority of a physician to provide **emergency medical treatment** for patients, subject to FDA requirements for release and emergency use of an unapproved drug, biologic, or device on a single patient.

When emergency treatment is initiated without prior IBRA review and approval, the patient data **may not be** included as research data in a prior or subsequent IBRA-approved project.

B. FDA Regulation of Emergency Use

The emergency use provision in the FDA regulations is an exemption from prior review and approval by the IBRA of a *single* patient use of a drug, device, or biologic considered to be investigational. The emergency use exemption of an investigational drug, biologic or device is permitted **only** if each of the following conditions exist:

- A life-threatening or severely debilitating situation exists necessitating the use of the investigational drug, biologic or device.
- No standard acceptable alternative treatment is available.
- Because of the immediate need to use the drug, biologic or device, there is not sufficient time to use existing procedures to obtain IRBA approval for the use.

For purposes of this section, the following terms have the following meanings:

"Emergency use" of an investigational drug, biologic or device is defined as the use of an investigational article with a human subject in a life-threatening situation in which no standard acceptable treatment is available and in which there is not sufficient time to obtain approval from the IBRA.

"Life-threatening" means diseases or conditions where the likelihood of death is high unless the course of the disease is interrupted and diseases or conditions with potentially fatal outcomes, where the end point of clinical trial analysis is survival. The criteria for life threatening do not require the condition to be immediately life threatening or to immediately result in death. Rather, the subjects must be in a life-threatening situation requiring intervention before review at a convened meeting of the IBRA is feasible.

"Severely debilitating," means diseases or conditions that cause major irreversible morbidity. Examples of severely debilitating conditions include blindness, loss of arm, leg, hand or foot, loss of hearing, paralysis or stroke.

The FDA regulations do not provide for expedited IRB approval in emergency situations. An IRB must either convene and give "full board" approval of the emergency use or, if the conditions of 21 CFR 56.102(d) are met and it is not possible to convene a quorum within the time available, the use may proceed without any IRB approval.

Some manufacturers will agree to allow the use of the test article, but their policy requires "an IRB approval letter" before the test article will be shipped. If it is not possible to convene a quorum of the IRB within the time available, the IRB may send the sponsor a written statement with the IRB is aware of the proposed use and considers the use to meet the requirements of 21 CFR 56.104(c). Although this is not an "IRB approval," the acknowledgement letter has been acceptable to manufacturers and has allowed the shipment to proceed.

C. Patient Consent in an Emergency

Even in an emergency use situation, the Principal Investigator is required to obtain informed consent to the treatment from the patient or the patient's legally authorized representative (as specified under State law) **unless** both the Principal Investigator and an independent physician certify in writing that **all** of the following conditions exist:

- The patient is confronted by a life-threatening situation necessitating the use of the investigational drug, biologic or device.
- Informed consent cannot be obtained because of an inability to communicate with, or obtain legally effective consent from, the patient.
- Time is not sufficient to obtain consent from the patient's legal representative.
- No alternative method of approved or generally recognized therapy is available that provides an equal or greater likelihood of saving the life of the patient.

If time is not sufficient to obtain the determination by an independent physician, the determination should be obtained within five (5) days after the use of the investigational article. *See* "Model Emergency Use Consent Form."

D. Informing the IBRA of Emergency Use

Principal Investigators are required to submit a written report on the emergency use to the IBRA and to the applicable hospital administration within five (5) working days. However, this notification should not be construed as an IRB approval. If the subject's consent was not obtained to the emergency use, the written report must include a written determination by a non-participating staff physician that the four conditions specified in Section C above are met. The report is reviewed by the Chair to ensure that the emergency use meets the applicable regulations. The Principal Investigator is informed that if he/she anticipates the need to use the investigational article in additional subjects, prior review and approval by the IBRA is required. *See* "Notification of Emergency Use of Investigational Product."

In addition, if an IDE for the device exists, the Principal Investigator must notify the sponsor of the emergency use. If an IDE did not exist, the Principal Investigator must notify the FDA of the emergency use and provide the FDA, with a copy to the IBRA, of a written summary of the conditions constituting the emergency, subject protection measures and results. Subsequent emergency use of the device may not occur unless the physician obtains approval of an IDE for the device and its use, as well as IBRA approval.

Source: New York University Cancer Institute, New York, New York

4-3 Model Emergency Use Consent Form

Physician Name: _____ Dept.: _____

Phone: _____ Fax: _____ E-Mail: _____

Name of investigational drug/biologic/device:

_____

Your consent is requested to use the above-named product in

☐   your care

☐   the care of your child

☐   the care of someone for whom you are the legal representative.

Patient Name: _____

Patient at the following facility: _____

This product has not been approved by the Food and Drug Administration. If you agree to the use of this product, this is what we will do:

The most likely risks of using this drug/biologic/device are

There may be other significant or even life-threatening risks that we do not know about. The possible benefits are

If you do not consent to the use of this product, the alternatives are

If this study involves medications or devices regulated by the Food and Drug Administration (FDA), the FDA and other regulatory agencies, the sponsor of the study and Hospital staff working under the direction of the IBRA may inspect records identifying you as a subject in this investigation. In addition, if your participation in this research is for treatment or diagnostic purposes, the facility in which you are treated may ask you to sign a separate informed consent document for specific procedures or treatment, and that informed consent form may be included in the medical record of that facility. The medical record is maintained by your treating physician or hospital, as applicable, and will be subject to state and federal laws and regulations concerning confidentiality of medical records.

This Hospital and any government agency or sponsor providing the drug will *not* provide special services, free care, or compensation for any injuries resulting from the use of this drug/biologic/device. Treatment for such injuries will be provided under the same financial arrangements as those under which treatment is usually provided.

If you consent to this treatment and later believe that you have suffered any injury as a result of this emergency care, you may contact Dr. _____ at _____ or the IBRA administrative office at ___-___-___. They can review the matter with you, identify other resources that may be available to you, and provide information as to how to proceed.

This emergency treatment **will not** be claimed as research and you **will not** be considered a research subject. Any data regarding your treatment **will not** be included in any report of a research activity.

If you have any questions about the drug/biologic/device or about the rights of those agreeing to have an experimental article used in their medical care, you may contact Dr. _____ at _____ or the IBRA at ___-___-___.

I have read the above explanations and have received answers to any questions I have about treatment with this product. I consent voluntarily to the emergency use of this drug/biologic/device.

_____   _____

Patient's Signature (as applicable)   Date

_____   _____

Legal Representative's Signature (as applicable)   Date

_____   _____

Parent's Signature (as applicable)   Date

_____   _____

Signature of Person Obtaining Consent   Date

4-4 Transfer Decision Matrix

	Incoming for a Higher Level of Care	Incoming for the Same Level of Care	Outgoing to a Higher Level of Care	Outgoing to the Same Level of Care
Definition	Patients who have Emergency Medical Conditions **OR** are **IN** Active Labor. Capability &/or Capacity are not available at referring facility.	Patients who do not have Emergency Medical Conditions **OR** are **Not** in Active Labor	Patients who have Emergency Medical Conditions **OR** are **IN** Active Labor. Capability &/or Capacity are not available.	Patients who do not have Emergency Medical Conditions **OR** are **Not** in Active Labor
Memorandum of Transfer (MOT)	YES, except for patients transferred from Veterans Administration Hospitals and other federal facilities, and nursing homes.	YES, except for patients transferred from Veterans Administration Hospitals and other federal facilities, and nursing homes.	YES, except for patients transferred to Veterans Administration Hospitals and other federal facilities, and nursing homes.	YES, except for patients transferred to Veterans Administration Hospitals and other federal facilities, and nursing homes.
Admission Eligibility	Criteria Does Not Apply	Criteria Applies	Criteria Does Not Apply	Criteria Applies the transfer of a patient may not be predicated upon arbitrary, capricious, or unreasonable discrimination based upon race, religion, national origin, age, sex, physical condition or economic status.
Consent	YES	YES	YES	YES
Role of Physician	Determine clinical capability	Determine clinical capability	Determine clinical capability and patient's stability for transfer. Contact the Transfer Hotline. Arrange for duplication of patient's medical record which shall include: Medical history & physical exam; provisional diagnosis, recorded observation of physical assessment of patient's condition at the time of transfer & treatment provided; results of all diagnostic test, i.e., X-rays films, & reports, laboratory tests; reason for transfer; and any other pertinent information.	Determine clinical capability and patient's stability for transfer Contact the Transfer Hotline. Arrange for duplication of patient's medical record which shall include: Medical history & physical exam; provisional diagnosis, recorded observation of physical assessment of patient's condition at the time of transfer & treatment provided; results of all diagnostic test, i.e., X-rays films, & reports, laboratory tests; reason for transfer; and any other pertinent information.
Role of Administrator	Determine capacity	Determine capacity and admission eligibility	Determine capacity	Determine capacity and admission eligibility
Hotline	YES	YES	YES	YES

Source: Adapted from Parkland Health and Hospital System, Dallas, Texas.

4-5 ED Rape Trauma Syndrome Standard of Care

PURPOSE

To provide quality physical and emotional care to the patient who has been sexually victimized.

STANDARD OF CARE

All patients who present to the ED with rape trauma syndrome will be considered a priority and treated with sensitivity and adherence to Public Health Law, section 2805.

STANDARD I

The nurse will provide the following interventions during the immediate phase of management of a rape trauma victim.

Immediate Phase

All patients presented to the Emergency Department with complaints of sexual abuse will be accompanied to a private room and a Rape Crisis Counselor from VIBES will be called pending patient approval.

- Police will be notified only when consent is given by the patient or when there is a legal obligation on the part of the hospital to do so (see ED Policy Treatment of Victims of Sexual Assault).
- The appropriate physician will be called (see ED Policy Treatment of Victims of Sexual Assault).

STANDARD II

A sensitive interview will be conducted with the patient regarding the sexual assault.

Intermediate Phase

  A. Perform physical assessment of patient as follows:
     1. History of present condition
       a. Time, place, and circumstances of assault
       b. For sexual assault or incest involving child; same as adult, plus interview child and parent/significant other separately
     2. Past medical history
       a. date of LMP
       b. date and time of last consensual intercourse
     3. Physical examination
       a. Assess for physiological stability related to physical injury

    b. Prior to physical exam:
       — establish trust relationship
       — explain all procedures
       — obtain consents for procedures and/or photographs
    c. Assist with collection of evidence and physical examination—see guidelines for use of NYSDOH Sexual Offense Evidence Kit
    d. For sexual assault or incest involving child, assess for signs and symptoms of child abuse (see child abuse)
    e. Assist with diagnostic procedures

B. Psychosocial Intervention

Consider that the patient is going through a traumatic acute phase or may experience a delayed or long-term phase. The possibility of these reactions needs to be discussed with the patient so he/she is prepared.

There may also be feelings of powerlessness related to inability to prevent or control the situation.

C. Interventions
- Offer immediate assistance.
- Develop trust relationship.
- Focus on facts and immediate problem solving.
- Accept all types of responses.
- Assist with problem solving and decision making.
- Offer assistance in calling friends or support.
- Encourage patient to make decisions (e.g. now or in 30 minutes).
- Discuss usual post-traumatic reactions.
- Discuss reactions of significant others.
- Provide available resources for unresolved anger and rejection.
- Arrange for transportation to safe environment.
- Refer to mental health counselor if patient unable to progress with direct problem solving assistance.

For pediatric victims of sexual assault or incest:

1. Notify parent if not with child; consider if child is incest victim.
2. Adult interventions are all applicable but must be modified to accommodate development level of child.
3. Notify proper authorities which may include police and child protective services.
4. Refer family for counseling.

STANDARD III

Evaluation

The victimized patient has just undergone a most traumatic event. The sensitive care that has been provided should result in a positive outcome for the patient at time of discharge. The patient

- exhibits decreased anxiety with relaxed body posture and acceptance of help
- cooperates and participates in verbal dialogue
- makes decisions and follows through with plan

- demonstrates coping reactions that are appropriate for event and is aware of own responses
- accepts offer to call supportive person
- relates appropriate telephone numbers
- accepts and understands reason for referral
- comprehends and repeats types of reactions that may occur Encourage patient to make decisions (e.g., now or in 30 minutes).
- decides to inform others based on usual coping behaviors and cites available referral resources
- leaves ED with escort

For children: as for adult, plus

- child is emotionally secure; parent, significant other or adult advocate is present
- authorities are notified
- child leaves ED to return to safe environment

Source: Adapted from Huntington Hospital, Huntington, New York.

4-6 Consent for Donation of Organs and Tissues

I, _____, being the legal next-of-kin and/or
      NAME OF NEXT-OF-KIN OR AGENT

_____ of _____,
RELATIONSHIP   NAME OF DONOR

(1) In the hope and with the expectation that this contribution will be used for transplantation, or for therapy, medical research or education, I, a person authorized
by State law to make this contribution, do hereby authorize, as the Donor or on
behalf of the Donor, the transplantation, retention, preservation or donation of
the organs and parts described below.

  A)   ☐   Any needed organs or tissues
  B)   ☐   Only the following organs and/or tissues. Check below.
        ☐   Kidney ☐ Heart ☐ Lungs ☐ Liver ☐ Pancreas ☐ Eyes ☐ Corneas
        ☐   Heart valves ☐ Skin ☐ Bone ☐ Other_____
  C)   ☐   Limitations, if any _____
  D)   ☐   The removal of organs and/or tissues for medical research, if not accepted for transplant.

(2) I understand that this authorization includes any examination, test and review of
medical history, including but not limited to, the removal of blood, spleen and
lymph nodes, which may be necessary to assure medical acceptability of the
organ and/or tissue I am donating. It also includes the transfer to the transplant
facility of medical information or records pertaining to the Donor.

(3) This authorization is voluntarily made, without obligation on the part of the donee,
the Hospital, or any person authorized by law to receive this gift, and is motivated
solely by humanitarian instincts without hope of compensation of any kind. I
therefore release any claims that I or my legal representative may have now or
in the future against my physician, his or her associates, the Hospital, its agents or
employees, and any donee or authorized person or organization.

_____   _____
SIGNATURE, LEGAL NEXT-OF-KIN OR AGENT   SIGNATURE OF WITNESS

_____   _____
ADDRESS   SIGNATURE OF WITNESS

_____   _____
CITY, STATE, ZIP, COUNTRY   DATE   TIME

Source: Aspen Publishers, Inc.

4-7 Consent Form for Emergency Contraception

I have requested and wish to be treated with medication containing synthetic progestin in order to attempt to prevent a possible pregnancy.

I have given an accurate medical and sexual history to my health care provider, and have been evaluated by her or him.

It has been explained to me that this medication reduces the risk of pregnancy following a single act of unprotected intercourse. Depending on the exact time in the menstrual cycle, the pregnancy rate following a single act of unprotected intercourse may be 0 to 33 percent. (On average, it is 8 percent.) After taking emergency contraception, the pregnancy rate is 0 to 8 percent. (On average it is 1 percent.) This represents a 75-80 percent reduction in risk of pregnancy for this single act of unprotected intercourse. I understand this medication is not 100 percent effective. It has been explained to me that this medication is thought to work in most cases by preventing or delaying ovulation. If ovulation does occur, the medication may prevent implantation of a fertilized ovum into the uterine lining. This medication will not prevent pregnancies resulting from sexual intercourse occurring after I have taken it. My risk of pregnancy may actually be increased if I have unprotected intercourse in the week following emergency contraception.

I understand that this is not a method of birth control that can be used repeatedly or long-term. My health care provider has explained to me how I can obtain information about and access to methods that can be used for pregnancy prevention from now on. My health care provider has explained to me that there may be some side effects from this medication. These may include nausea, abdominal pain, fatigue, headache, breast tenderness, and dizziness. It is very unlikely that I would have any serious side effects, but I have been told to contact the health clinic if I have severe abdominal, chest or leg pain, or severe headache, or problems with my vision.

If this method fails and I do become pregnant, I understand that there is a theoretical risk that this or any medication I may have taken since conception could harm the developing fetus.

I have agreed to return to the health clinic in three weeks for follow-up.
Signed: _____
Clinician:_____
Date:_____

Source: University of Virginia Student Health, Charlottesville, Virginia.

4-8 Emergency Induced Abortion Certification Form

Name of physician performing the procedure: _____

State License Number: _____

Information on facility where procedure performed:

Name _____

Address _____

Telephone Number _____

Date of Procedure _____

"The patient whom this certification concerns is an unemancipated minor. Based on my good faith clinical judgment, I hereby affirm that the following medical condition(s) necessitated the immediate abortion of my patient's pregnancy without prior parental notice otherwise required by Family Code § 33.002 to avert her death or to avoid a serious risk of substantial and irreversible impairment of a major bodily function. I understand this certification is confidential and may not contain personal or identifying information about my patient, including her name, address, or social security number. I have included a copy of this certification in my patient's medical record as required by law."

List the medical indications supporting the physician's judgment:

_____

_____

_____

_____

_____   _____

Physician's Signature   Date

_____

Physician's Printed Name

Please mail the completed form to the following: _____

Any person other than the intended recipient who receives this document in error is hereby notified that any disclosure, copying, distribution, use or taking of any action in reliance on the contents of this document is strictly prohibited. Please notify the state Department of Health at _____ immediately to arrange for return of this document to the department.

Source: Texas Department of Health, Austin, Texas.

4-9 Organ/Tissue Donation: Identification of Donors and Procedures

APPROVED BY THE DIRECTOR OF NURSING

SIGNATURE: _____   _____

DATE: _____

PURPOSE STATEMENT

The purpose of this Nursing policy is to ensure that the appropriate organ procurement organization is notified for identification of potential organ and tissue donors.

STATEMENT OF RESPONSIBILITIES

Performed by: Unit Coordinator, Nurse Managers
Physician's Order: Not required
Special Education: Not required

POLICY STATEMENT

In order to comply with legislative requirements, all deaths will be considered potential donors. All deaths are reported to the appropriate agencies for the purpose of identifying potential organ/tissue donors. Documentation in the medical record reflects this contact and determination of donor suitability.

GUIDELINES

A. Supporting statements regarding compliance with legislative and legal regulations.
    1. Uniform anatomical gift act. California Health and Safety Code, Section 7150: Any person of sound mind and 18 years of age or older may give all or any part of his body for any purpose specified. The gift to take effect upon death.
    2. Required Request Act. California Health and Safety Code. Section 7184: Each general acute care hospital shall develop a protocol for identifying potential organ and tissue donors. The protocol shall require that any deceased individual next of kin, at or near the time of notification of death, be asked whether the deceased was an organ donor or if the family is a donor family. If not, the family shall be notified of the option to donate organs and tissues.
    3. Omnibus Budget Reconciliation Act, November 1987: This federal law made Medicare and Medicaid reimbursement to acute care hospitals contingent on (1) establishment of written protocol for the identification of potential donors (2) notification of the potential donor's family of the option to approve or decline donation and (3) notification of the organ procurement agency.
    4. California Health and Safety Code, Section 7151.5: Any of the following persons, in order of priority stated, when persons in prior classes are not available at the

time of death, and in the absence of actual notice of opposition by a member of the same or a prior class, may give all or any part of the decedent's body for any purpose specified.

    a. Durable Power of Attorney

    b. Spouse

    c. Either parent

    d. An adult son or daughter

    e. Either grandparent

    f. A guardian or conservator of the person of the decedent at the time of the decedent's death.

    g. Any other person authorized or under obligation to dispose of the body.

5. California Uniform Determination of Death Act (1992) California Health and Safety Code, Section 7180: An individual who has sustained either (1) irreversible cessation of circulatory and respiratory functions, or (2) irreversible cessation of all function of the entire brain, including the brain stem. A determination of death must be made in accordance with accepted medical standards.

6. California Health and Safety Code, Section 7181: When an individual is pronounced dead by determining that the individual has sustained an irreversible cessation of all functions of the entire brain, including the brain stem, there shall be independent confirmation by another physician.

7. California Health and Safety Code, Section 7182 (as refers to above): Neither the physician making the independent confirmation shall participate in the procedures for removing or transplanting a part.

B. Definitions

  1. Brain death

    a. A patient who has suffered complete and irreversible cessation of all functions of the brain, including the brain stem. To be a donor, this patient must be maintained on a ventilator and have an intact circulation. This patient may be an organ and/or tissue donor.

  2. Biological death

    a. A patient who has suffered complete and irreversible cessation of the circulatory system. This patient could not be an organ donor but can still donate some tissues for up to 24 hours after biologic death.

  3. Tissue donation

    a. A biologically dead patient is only able to donate tissues. This may include corneas, bone, skin, ligaments, tendons, dura mater, heart valves, and veins.

C. All cardiopulmonary deaths will be reported to the Inland Eye and Tissue Bank (IETB) at 800-555-6555, Extension 15.

D. All brain deaths will be reported to the Southern California Organ Procurement Center (SCOPC) at 800-555-6112.

E. Consult the organ donation manual for:

  1. Supporting Statements Regarding Compliance with Legislative and Legal Regulations

  2. Definitions

  3. Criteria for identification of potential donor

  4. Consent

  5. Confidentiality

PROCEDURE

1.0 In order to comply with legislation, all deaths, both cardiopulmonary and brain deaths, shall be considered potential donors.

1.1 Call SCOPC (800 555-6112) if the patient has brain death (on ventilator).

1.2 Call IBID (800-555-6555, extension 15) if patient has cardiopulmonary death (off ventilator).

1.2.1 Call within one (1) hour of death.

1.2.2 Have the patient's chart available.

1.2.3 Do not notify a funeral home until patient is dismissed as a potential donor.

1.2.4 Send the body to the hospital morgue.

1.2.5 Notify the Coroner whenever applicable.

2.0 The Potential Organ/Tissue Donor Notification Form is to be completed and attached to all death reports. It should state when the appropriate agency was contacted, and the result. If the donor did not meet requirements due to absolute contraindications, then this will be documented. Do not speak with the family until SCOPC has been contacted and advised.

3.0 Review suitability and discuss potential organ donation with primary physician. SCOPC will not approach family without the physician's knowledge.

4.0 Ascertain that brain death declaration has or will be made. Documentation of brain death declaration must be made by two physicians independently of each other. These declarations must be written in the progress notes with date and time included. It is a legal requirement that these physicians cannot be involved in the procurement or transplant procedures.

5.0 Physician is then to notify family of patient's death. (Please advise, if necessary, that the subject of organ donation is not discussed at the same time they are informed of loved one's death. The family usually cannot assimilate thoughts of organ donation at this time.) Social Services may be contacted at this point, if not already, to support the family in their grieving process.

6.0 ALLOW UNDERSTANDING AND ACCEPTANCE OF DEATH (brain death) BEFORE APPROACHING FAMILY ABOUT ORGAN DONATION.

7.0 Only those trained to perform this kind of conversation should be utilized in approaching the family about donation.

7.1 There is specific information that must be told to the family to comply with informed consent for organ donation.

7.2 The goal in talking with a family is not to achieve consent. Organ donation is not for everyone. The family has a legal right to be given the information to make an informed decision, whether it is yes or no.

8.0 SCOPC/IETB will ensure that there is legal consent.

8.1 Report any case in which brain death appears imminent, such as the following catastrophic head injuries:

8.1.1.1 Head trauma

8.1.1.2 Intracranial bleed

8.1.1.3 Metabolic or primary brain tumor

8.2 Have the patient's chart available.

9.0 SCOPC/IETB will obtain Coroner's consent, if applicable.

10.0 SCOPC/IETB Coordinator will order lab and donor maintenance orders. SCOPC/IETB will contact transplant centers to coordinate surgery schedule. SCOPC will contact the Division of Nursing or the Surgery Department to facilitate Bakersfield Memorial's surgery schedule and availability of Anesthesiologist and support staff.

11.0 It should be determined by the primary nurse or the SCOPC Coordinator what the family intends to do prior to the surgery. Some families make plans for a final goodbye to their loved one. Occasionally, some families want to see the body after the surgery. If the case is a Coroner's case SCOPC will contact the Coroner after the case to inform them of the clamp time, as well as notify them that they may pick up the body.

12.0 All other hospital policies and procedures regarding the care of the body should be followed.

13.0 If the donor is a tissue donor, the following will need to occur:

13.1 The body will need to be cooled in the morgue within approximately four (4) hours after biologic death. For cornea donations, the eyes may be instilled with sterile saline and eyelids closed (may need to tape them shut in some circumstances).

Source: Adapted from Bakersfield Memorial Hospital, Bakersfield, California.

4-10 Emergency Judicial Consent to Treatment for Minors Documentation Form

Date of Treatment: _____ Name of Judge. _____

Note: For the purpose of this form only, a minor is defined as a patient less than 18 years old.

DOCUMENTATION RECORD

Please provide the following information regarding juvenile.

Patient's Last Name: _____

Patient's First Name: _____

Patient's Date of Birth: _____

Patient's Address: _____

Please provide the following information concerning patient's parent, guardian, or legal custodian.

Parent/Guardian/Custodian's Relationship to Patient: _____

Parent/Guardian/Custodian's Name: _____

Parent/Guardian/Custodian's Address: _____

Consent of parent/guardian/legal custodian or other person standing in loco parentis is unobtainable because:

Such person is not a resident of this state.	_____ Yes	_____ No
His or her whereabouts are unknown.	_____ Yes	_____ No
He or she cannot be consulted with promptness reasonable under the circumstances.	_____ Yes	_____ No
He or she refuses to give consent after the recommended care and risks associated with treatment or refusal to authorize treatment have been explained.	_____ Yes	_____ No

Please state the diagnosis of the patient's physical condition and nature of the emergency.

_____

_____

_____

_____

_____

Please state the recommended medical, surgical, and nursing care needed.

_____
_____
_____
_____
_____

Please provide name of nearest known relative if no parent or guardian can be found.

Relative's Relationship to Patient: _____

Relative's Name: _____

Relative's Residence: _____

Please provide name and address of physician petitioning the court for authorization of surgical or medical treatment for the patient.

Physician's Name: _____

Physician's Address: _____

Please provide name and address of the hospital or medical facility petitioning for authorization of surgical or medical treatment for the patient.

Hospital's Name: _____

Hospital's Address: _____

Has patient ever been married? ____ Yes ____ No

PLEASE RETURN TO THE RISK MANAGEMENT DEPARTMENT WITHIN 24 HOURS OF OBTAINING EMERGENCY JUDICIAL CONSENT

Source: Copyright Aspen Publishers, Inc.

4-11 Guideline: Patient Leaving before Exam or against Medical Advice

GUIDELINE PURPOSE

To establish guidelines for documentation of patients who present to the emergency department (ED) and leave before completion of evaluation and treatment.

GUIDELINE STANDARD

This policy is in effect when any person leaves ED before evaluation and discharge is completed by staff. The ED Attending will be notified of any patient who expresses intent to leave before completion of evaluation and treatment.

GUIDELINE ACTIONS

1. Required documentation on the patient chart will include answers to the following:
   - Does the patient seem capable of making decisions (i.e. oriented, unimpaired)?
   - Why is the patient leaving (quote preferable)?
   - Was a nurse or physician notified?
   - Was a phone call made by ED staff if they did not speak with patient before leaving?

   In addition, for patients leaving against medical advice (AMA), documentation will include:
   - A completed AMA form. If patient refuses to sign, state such on form
   - Documentation of potential consequence(s) of leaving explained and verbalized as understood by patient.
   - Documentation of family/friend (if present) involvement in decision.
2. The emergency department clerical staff will forward the pink sheet for all AMA/ LBE patients to Department Manager for QA review.
3. Triage priority I and II patients will receive callbacks from the follow-up nurse to ascertain status and reinforce potential need for treatment. Triage priority III and IV patients will receive callbacks as indicated based on case review.
4. Cases will be reviewed by the emergency department management staff on a quarterly basis.

DEFINITIONS

Leave before exam—Occurs after primary survey, but before evaluation by physician.
Against medical advice—Occurs when the patient leaves against advice of treating physician. Implies discussion between patient and physician after evaluation completed; and that an AMA form may have been completed.

Source: University of Michigan Hospitals and Health Centers, Emergency Department, Ann Arbor, Michigan.

4-12 National Standards for Culturally and Linguistically Appropriate Services (CLAS)

The U.S. Department of Health and Human Services Office of Minority Health (OMH) has developed a set of 14 standards intended to assure cultural competence in health care; i.e., "that all people entering the health care system receive equitable and effective treatment in a culturally and linguistically appropriate manner."

The standards are intended to be inclusive of all cultures and not limited to any particular population group or sets of groups; however, they are especially designed to address the needs of racial, ethnic, and linguistic population groups that experience unequal access to health services. Ultimately, the aim of the standards is to contribute to the elimination of racial and ethnic health disparities and to improve the health of all Americans.

The CLAS standards are primarily directed at health care organizations; however, individual providers are also encouraged to use the standards to make their practices more culturally and linguistically accessible. The principles and activities of culturally and linguistically appropriate services should be integrated throughout an organization and undertaken in partnership with the communities being served.

HOW ARE THE STANDARDS ORGANIZED?

The 14 standards are organized by themes: Culturally Competent Care (Standards 1–3), Language Access Services (Standards 4–7), and Organizational Supports for Cultural Competence (Standards 8–14). Within this framework, there are three types of standards of varying stringency: mandates, guidelines, and recommendations as follows:

- CLAS mandates are current federal requirements for all recipients of federal funds (Standards 4, 5, 6, and 7).
- CLAS guidelines are activities recommended by OMH for adoption as mandates by federal, state, and national accrediting agencies (Standards 1, 2, 3, 8, 9, 10, 11, 12, and 13).
- CLAS recommendations are suggested by OMH for voluntary adoption by health care organizations (Standard 14).

THE 14 STANDARDS

1. Health care organizations should ensure that patients/consumers receive from all staff members effective, understandable, and respectful care that is provided in a manner compatible with their cultural health beliefs and practices and preferred language.
2. Health care organizations should implement strategies to recruit, retain, and promote at all levels of the organization a diverse staff and leadership that are representative of the demographic characteristics of the service area.
3. Health care organizations should ensure that staff at all levels and across all departments receive ongoing education and training in culturally and linguistically appropriate service delivery.
4. Health care organizations must offer and provide language assistance services, including bilingual staff and interpreter services, at no cost to each patient/consumer

with limited English proficiency at all points of contact, in a timely manner during all hours of operation.

5. Health care organizations must provide to patients/consumers in their preferred language both verbal offers and written notices informing them of their right to receive language assistance services.

6. Health care organizations must assure the competence of language assistance provided to limited English proficient patients/consumers by interpreters and bilingual staff. Family and friends should not be used to provide interpretation services (except on request by the patient/consumer).

7. Health care organizations must make available easily understood patient-related materials and post signage in the languages of the commonly encountered groups and/or groups represented in the service area.

8. Health care organizations should develop, implement, and promote a written strategic plan that outlines clear goals, policies, operational plans, and management accountability/oversight mechanisms to provide culturally and linguistically appropriate services.

9. Health care organizations should conduct initial and ongoing organizational self-assessments of CLAS-related activities and are encouraged to integrate cultural and linguistic competence-related measures into their internal audits, performance improvement programs, patient satisfaction assessments, and outcomes-based evaluations.

10. Health care organizations should ensure that data on the individual patient's/consumer's race, ethnicity, and spoken and written language are collected in health records, integrated into the organization's management information systems, and periodically updated.

11. Health care organizations should maintain a current demographic, cultural, and epidemiological profile of the community as well as a needs assessment to accurately plan for and implement services that respond to the cultural and linguistic characteristics of the service area.

12. Health care organizations should develop participatory, collaborative partnerships with communities and utilize a variety of formal and informal mechanisms to facilitate community and patient/consumer involvement in designing and implementing CLAS-related activities.

13. Health care organizations should ensure that conflict and grievance resolution processes are culturally and linguistically sensitive and capable of identifying, preventing, and resolving cross-cultural conflicts or complaints by patients/consumers.

14. Health care organizations are encouraged to regularly make available to the public information about their progress and successful innovations in implementing the CLAS Standards and to provide public notice in their communities about the availability of this information.

The complete report, along with supporting material, is available online at *www.OMHRC. gov/CLAS*.

Source: U.S. Department of Health and Human Services' (HHS) Office of Minority Health (OMH) Web site: *www.omhrc.gov/clas/finalculturalla.htm*.

4-13 Patient Identification Policy

POLICY

Each patient will be properly identified before receiving patient care.

PURPOSE

To define the process of patient identification

PROCEDURE

A. **Patient Identification Requirement.**
   1. Patient Identification using 2 patient identifiers is required prior to the following:
      a. Transportation to Surgery or to any Invasive Procedure area
      b. Surgery or Procedure, in the procedure area
      c. **Each time medication is administered and/or IV fluids administered**
      d. Blood or Blood Product Administration
      e. Blood or specimen collection for any Lab Testing
      f. Any procedure or care for which the patient is new to the care provider (except life-threatening emergencies)
   2. The Patient's Identification is compared to a written source relevant to the care provided, such as, the MAR or written physician order compared to the Identiband for each medication administration. (Positive patient identification is never possible from memory)

B. **Identification Band Placement**
   1. All inpatients, outpatient observations patients, outpatients receiving invasive procedures with sedation or anesthesia, and ECC patients will have an Identification band applied upon arrival.
   2. **A temporary identification band is to be applied upon the patient's arrival if a computer generated ID band is not available. The patient's name and date of birth are to be present on the identification band. The computer generated identification band is to be applied as soon as it is available.**
   3. The Identification band shall be applied to the patient's wrists unless clinical reason prevents this location. Alternate location is ankles. Identification band placement is not acceptable on patient's clothing.
   4. Accuracy of the Identification band at time of placement shall be confirmed by the patient and staff member applying the band. If the patient is unable, confirmation shall be with the person consenting to the care of the patient. If there is no one, a picture ID (eg, Driver's License) may be used for correct identification with verification by two staff members. (If unable to verify identify, refer to Unknown Patient Policy)
   5. If a patient Identification band is removed for any reason, it must be immediately replaced using the above guidelines to assure the band is correct.
   6. Refer to CBU policies on identification of infants born at _____.

7. For select NICU patients who may not be able to have the patient identification band on their person for clinical reasons, the patient's crib may be labeled with the patient's identification. If the child is removed from the crib for any reason, the child must be identified or have a staff member present at all times to verify the identity of the child. In this situation, the staff member must not have responsibility for any other child at the same time.

C. **Checking Patient Identification for patients with Identification Bands**

    1. The acceptable 2 patient identifiers are Patient Name and Date of Birth except:

        a. When Bar Coding technology is provided, the 1st patient identifier is the written review of the Patient Name and the second is the Bar Coded review of the Patient's Financial (FIN) Number (Account Number) to the written source.

        b. _____ Hospital staff will use Patient Name and Medical Record Number if Date of Birth is not present on their data source.

        c. In CBU, NICU, and Nursery, in situations of multiple births when patients have the same last Name and Date of Birth, the two Identifiers will be Patient Name and Medical Record Number or Infant Identification Number.

    2. Checking the Patient's Identification is required even when the patient is known by the staff member as a repeat patient.

    3. Patients who have had their identification band removed are to be re-identified and a new name band applied.

D. **Checking Patient Identification for patients in areas not using Identification Bands**

    a. The patient shall be asked to give Name (first and last) and Date of Birth. The patient's response shall be compared to the written source of information, ie, patient chart, etc.

    b. Minor children and adults unable to identify themselves, or for any reason unable to consent to their own treatment, shall be identified by the parent, guardian or other consenting person present with the patient.

E. **Emergency Situation**

Emergency situations (i.e. a code blue) may require treatment without the patient having a name band.

Non-Compliance

Any staff member not adhering to this policy will be subject to disciplinary action, up to and including discharge from _____ Hospital.

Original Approval By: Original Date:
Revision Number: Replaces Policy Last Dated:
Last Revised/Reviewed By: Review/Revised Date:
Signed Document Held By:

SIGNATURES OF APPROVAL:

Date Signed	Signature	Name	Title
_____	_____		
_____	_____		
_____	_____		

Source: Courtesy of Memorial Hospital & Health System, South Bend, Indiana.

4-14 Identification and Labeling of Patient Specimens Policy

POLICY

It is the policy of _____ to properly and accurately identify all patient specimens (blood, urine and tissue).

PURPOSE

To provide a system for accurate identification and labeling of all patient specimens.

PROCEDURE

1. Collect specimens according to the policy and procedure outlined for specific specimen collection.
2. Obtain a sufficient number of patient labels to affix one label to each specimen.
3. The initials of the person collecting the specimen, the date, time, and source of the specimen ie. Throat, cervix, etc. are to be placed on each label. For Urine Specimens the method of collection will also be written on the label, ie. Voided, CCMS, cath.
4. The patient label will be checked against the patient's arm band, or the staff person will ask the patient to state their name and date of birth while reading the patient label to be placed on the specimen.
5. The specimen will be transported to the lab via designated, approved means.
6. Specimens are to remain with the patient until labeled.
7. The individual drawing/collecting the specimen is expected to label the specimen. Lab personnel may label a specimen they witness the nursing staff draw.
8. Patients admitted and their identity is unknown will be given a number (i.e. trauma patient) until their identity is known. Once name and date of birth are known, those become the identifiers to use.

Original Approval By:
Revision Number:
Last Revised/Reviewed By:
Signed Document Held By:

Original Date:
Replaces Policy Last Dated:
Review/Revised Date:

SIGNATURES OF APPROVAL:

Date Signed	Signature	Name	Title
_____	_____		
_____	_____		
_____	_____		

Source: Courtesy of Memorial Hospital & Health System, South Bend, Indiana.

4-15 Unanticipated Outcomes and Adverse Events—Responding, Disclosure and Action Policy

POLICY

It is the policy of _____ Hospital to maintain honesty and integrity in all organizational functions. Consistent with this policy it is appropriate to disclose events or unanticipated outcomes that might adversely affect a patient's health. Our framework for discussing unanticipated outcomes is premised on strong communication processes, both before and after treatment or procedures.

PURPOSE

The purpose of this policy is to provide guidance for physicians and care givers when a procedural or judgmental decision made during the course of care resulted in an adverse patient outcome.

PROCEDURE

Definition

1. Adverse event—an unintended negative result stemming from a diagnostic test or medical/surgical treatment.
2. Disclosure—communications of information regarding the results of a diagnostic test, medical treatment or surgical intervention.
3. Unanticipated Outcomes—a result that differs significantly from what was anticipated to be the result of a treatment or procedure.

General Principles

1. Events to be disclosed—occurrences where patients are significantly harmed or have the potential to be significantly harmed.
2. To whom disclosure will be made—disclosure should be made (when appropriate) to the patient and the patient's family, significant other, or patient advocate.
3. The timing of disclosure of adverse events should occur as soon as possible after the recognition that an adverse event has occurred. If the patient is not able to comprehend the information, disclosure to the patient advocate should occur depending on the severity of the occurrence and their need to know the information.
4. Disclosing adverse events is primarily a physician responsibility. When there are situations in which it is impractical or unreasonable for the physician to do so, the use of a designee is in order. If the physician is out of town or unavailable, the physician covering will be responsible. If the covering physician is unavailable the Chief of the Department will be contacted. If the physician that is not available is the Chief of the Department, the Chief of Staff will be contacted.

315

The Vice President of Medical Affairs and Risk Manager will have the responsibility to ensure disclosure of information regarding an adverse event (to a patient) if a physician cannot or does not inform the patient in a timely manner.

Responding

1. First and foremost, attend to the patient's medical needs. Obtain medical consultation and make arrangements for follow-up care as may be necessary.
2. If the adverse event is of serious nature, notify the unit manager, risk manager, and the physician as soon as possible.
3. Patient outcomes, including poor outcomes, must be explained to the patient by the physician most knowledgeable of the incident, in substantially the same manner that the physician is expected to explain and then obtain informed consent before medical care is rendered.
4. Determine how the details of the event, the outcome, and the treatment plan occurred and explain to the patient and family. Designate a family contact person.
5. Be accessible for questions. Repeated requests for an explanation of the event is a common reaction when patients and family members are informed of an adverse outcome.
6. If the physician is unable to respond, the case will be directed to a physician partner, covering physician, or consulting physician knowledgeable of the case. The Chief of the Department, the Chief of Staff, the Vice President of Medical Affairs and/or the Administrator-on-call may also be consulted by the Administrative Supervisor, as appropriate.
7. Contact/consult with Risk Management and/or the Vice President of Medical Affairs to collaborate and complete reporting requirements as soon as possible.
8. Share information as soon as possible after the test, treatment, or intervention. NOTE: Sometimes the information can put a patient at risk of harm either due to psychological trauma or exposure to physical harm. (Example—physical abuse). If in the professional judgment of the physician, information should be withheld, the reasons for such should be documented in the medical record by the physician.

A. Information to be Disclosed

The information provided to the patient and authorized immediate family members/ decision makers shall be true and should contain these elements where appropriate. As many of these elements as possible should be in the communications:

1. Describe the incident that happened.
2. Who was involved (by job function, not by name)
3. What the reasonable potential short term and long term consequences are
4. What we have done to reduce or manage the consequences to the patient
5. Signs and symptoms that may indicate complication
6. Appropriate actions the patient or decision-maker shall take if complications occur
7. What plans are there to prevent the same type of incident from recurring

B. What to do in Disclosing an adverse event

1. Honesty—Be honest with the patient and family. Organize a family meeting if several relatives are involved in the patient's care or if treatment decisions are complicated.

2. Empathy—empathize with the patient and family; offer emotional support. Show compassion for the patient's distress and accept responsibility for follow-up and action but do not assign blame, or criticize the care or response of other providers.

3. Apologizing—Saying you're sorry to a patient when an adverse event occurs can be appropriate and can be done without placing blame or criticizing yourself or others. Start by describing the event and the medical response in brief, factual terms. Avoid guessing or contemplating out loud about what happened or why, if unknown. An appropriately, worded show of concern can increase the rapport between the patient and provider.

4. Disclosure regarding the event/outcome does not require an admission of liability or error. It takes time to analyze and determine what occurred. Avoid giving misinformation before all the facts are known. To avoid the appearance of contradictory information, it is important to provide an explanation in a context that allows for further elaboration, as details become available. Until all facts are known about what occurred, what systems are involved, etc., it is advisable to do no more than furnish an explanation regarding the unanticipated outcome.

Documenting Action in the Medical Record by the Physician

1. Documentation should be factual stating that there was a discussion of the unanticipated event. It must also be objective and completed immediately after the discussion occurred.

2. Documentation should be dated, timed, and signed at the time of the entry.

3. Avoid writing in the record any information unrelated to the care of the patient (e.g., "incident report filed" or "notified Risk Management").

4. Do not use the medical record to speculate or air grievances about other care givers, about equipment issues, or administrative processes.

5. Record factual statements of the event in the patient's record and any follow-up needed or done as a result of the event.

6. Do not alter any prior documentation.

7. While an addendum to the record can be made, consider carefully whether this information is relevant to the patient's clinical management. Accepted rationale for an addendum would be for the correction of facts (i.e., persons involved, time of event, sequence of events) and for the addition of facts or clarifying information. If you participated in the care, but were unable to access the record until a later date, you may provide added information. An addendum should not be used to state your opinions, perceptions, or defenses.

Equipment and Medical Device Preservation

When an adverse event involves equipment or medical device, preserve these materials for investigation, do not clean or alter them in any way and contact the Risk Manager. The equipment involved needs to be bagged, tagged, and sequestered by biomedical staff or the Administrative Supervisor or designated RN. (Do not return any involved devices to a manufacturer)

Related Policies and Procedures

1. Patient complaint management.
2. Sentinel event.

Original Approval By: Original Date:
Revision Number: Replaces Policy Last Dated:
Last Revised/Reviewed By: Review/Revised Date:
Signed Document Held By:

SIGNATURES OF APPROVAL:

Date Signed	Signature	Name	Title
_____	_____		
_____	_____		
_____	_____		

Source: Courtesy of Memorial Hospital & Health System, South Bend, Indiana.

4-16 Against Medical Advice Policy and Form

POLICY

_____ Hospital and Health System respects an individual's right to consent and refuse any or all medical treatment. A person refusing a part of treatment may consent to other aspects of medical treatment.

PURPOSE

To outline the process when a patient refuses medical treatment. To make the patient aware of risks when refusing treatment against medical advice.

PROCEDURE

Refusal of Treatment/Leaving the Hospital Against Medical Advice:

1. An adult patient or emancipated minor who is conscious and mentally competent has the right to refuse treatment against medical advice.
2. Upon identification of the patient's desire to refuse medical treatment or to leave the hospital without a physician's order, advise the patient of the need to discuss the situation with the attending physician.
3. Ask the patient the reason for his/her refusal. (Appreciate that action can be taken in response to resolve the patient's reason for refusal). Notify the physician of the patient's refusal of medical treatment or his/her desire to leave against medical advice.

4. Inform the patient of the potential risks associated with his/her refusal as provided by the physician. This information may be provided by the physician and/or hospital staff.
5. Have the patient sign the Refusal of Treatment/Against Medical Advice form.
6. If the patient refuses to sign the Refusal of Treatment/Against Medical Advice form, document the refusal to sign on the form. Two witnesses are necessary.
7. Provide the patient with discharge instructions. Prescriptions may also be provided by the physician. Encourage the patient to obtain medical care.
8. If the patient returns to _____ Hospital for inpatient care, no matter how long he/she is absent the patient is to be re-admitted.
9. If an inpatient or an outpatient changes his/her mind, documentation regarding his/her consent to treatment is to be contained in the patient's medical record.
10. An incompetent or unconscious patient or minor is not legally capable of executing an order to refuse medical treatment against medical advice.
11. In the case of an incompetent patient or minor, and if the patient does not have guardian, or the Health System or Hospital personnel believe that the patient's guardian is not acting in the patient's best interest, a social worker and the Risk Manager should be contacted and substitute guardianship should be sought. This would necessitate a referral either to Adult Protective Services or Child Protective Services.
12. If there is a question as to whether or not the patient is competent the physician should be informed of the concern. A psychiatric evaluation may assist in determining competency. A physician is to determine competency.
13. If the health care professionals have any doubt as to the competency of the patient and the potentiality of the patient doing harm to third parties or self as a result of refusal of medical care/treatment, the patient is delayed/restrained until the physician determines the patients' current competency.
    The need for a 72 hour detention may need to be determined by a licensed physician and initiated if indicated.
14. If a homicide threat is voiced, a health care worker will notify the police. Efforts will then be made to notify the identified person(s) against whom the threat is voiced. (Refer to the Duty to Warn policy.)
15. If the situation is such that personnel are unable to physically restrain the patient, and the patient is considered to be a danger to themselves or others and the patient leaves, the police are to be notified of the situation.

Original Approval By: Original Date:
Revision Number: Replaces Policy Last Dated:
Last Revised/Reviewed By: Review/Revised Date:
Signed Document Held By:

SIGNATURES OF APPROVAL:

Date Signed	Signature	Name	Title
_____	_____		
_____	_____		
_____	_____		

Refusal of Treatment/Against Medical Advice

I have been advised by Dr. _____ of my need for the following treatment: _____

_____

_____

I have been advised that the possible consequences of refusing the advice are _____

_____

_____

I refuse this advice and accept total responsibility for the consequences. I release and hold harmless _____ Hospital, its Directors, Officers, Agents, Employees, Physicians and successors from any liability resulting from my refusal of recommended medical care.

If not signed by patient, why: _____

_____

*Signature of Patient or Individual Authorized to Consent for Health Care for the Patient

*	Time:	Date:
Signature of Witness	Time:	Date:
Signature of Witness	Time:	Date:

Source: Courtesy of Memorial Hospital & Health System, South Bend, Indiana.

PATIENT ASSESSMENT

4-17 Assessment of the Emergency Department Patient

PURPOSE

Establish assessment criteria for all Emergency Department patients.

POLICY

1. All patients presenting to the Emergency Department will be triaged and categorized as either Emergent, Urgent or Non-Urgent.

2. All patients admitted to the Emergency Department will have the following documentation:
   - Chief complaint:
     - Subjective data;
     - Objective data.
   - Physical assessment
   - Assessment of psychological status
   - Vital signs:
     - Initial vital signs shall be obtained on arrival to the ED
     - Additional vital signs shall be obtained depending on patient's condition
     - Patients with unstable vital signs are placed on propack cardiac monitoring machine. Vital signs monitored every 30 minutes.
     - Comfort goal and pain scale upon arrival to treatment room
     - Level I & Level II trauma patients will have vital signs recorded every hour
     - Abnormal vitals will be repeated prior to discharge
     - All other patients every 2 hours
   - Pain will be managed per the nursing policy - Pain Management
   - Allergies and medications
   - Interventions performed and response to interventions
   - History of present illness
   - Pertinent past medical history
   - Response to medication
   - Tetanus status
   - Patient education
   - Reassessment and/or evaluation of expected outcomes prior to discharge
   - Nutritional assessment if clinically indicated

3. In addition, the pediatric patient (<16 years old) shall have the following information documented:
   - Weight
   - Head circumference if clinically indicated for infants 24 months and younger.
   - Activity for age
   - Developmental assessment (DASA)
   - Behavior or LOC
   - Referral to pediatrician or specialist as indicated
   - Height if clinically indicated

- A complete set of vitals will be taken on arrival to ER to include BP, pulse, respiratory rate, and temperature. Repeat vital signs will be taken per ER vital sign protocol.

Source: Courtesy of Parkview Medical Center, Pueblo, Colorado.

4-18 Assessment of the Trauma Patient

POLICY

The trauma patient shall be assessed and treated according to Emergency Nursing Association/Trauma Nurse Care Course criteria.

OBJECTIVES

Upon completion of this chapter/lecture, the learner should be able to:

1. Describe the components of the primary assessment.
2. Correlate life-threatening conditions with the specific component of the primary assessment.
3. Identify interventions to manage life-threatening conditions assessed during the initial assessment.
4. Identify the components of the secondary assessment.
5. Describe how to conduct a complete head-to-toe assessment.

Use the ENA/TNCC criteria to assist the nurse with the complete initial assessment of a trauma patient.

A systematic process or initial assessment of the trauma patient is essential for recognizing lifethreatening conditions, identifying injuries, and for determining priorities of care based on assessment findings. The initial assessment is divided into two phases, primary and secondary assessments. Both phases can be completed within several minutes unless resuscitative measures are required. Within an organized team approach to trauma care, this first step of the nursing process (assessment) is often simultaneously conducted with the identification of nursing diagnoses that require immediate intervention. Utilizing an organized, systematic approach when assessing each trauma patient also helps to ensure that injuries will not be missed and that priorities can be set for each intervention based on the life-threatening potential of each injury.

Adherence to "Standard Precautions" (precautions for care of all patients in hospitals) and "transmission-Based Precautions" for care of patients who are known or suspected of being infected or colonized by certain pathogens transmitted by contact with skin, airborne, or droplet are indicated for use by the trauma team. The team "Standard Precautions" encompasses "Universal Precautions" used to protect against transmission of pathogens from moist body surfaces. Use of lead aprons by the trauma team during radiologic procedures is necessary and can often be initiated prior to the patient's arrival. Initial assessment provides the nurse with subjective and objective data that are analyzed, interpreted, and documented. During this initial encounter with the patient, initiate the health care team's protocol for informing family members of the patient's arrival and condition.

A GUIDE TO INITIAL ASSESSMENT

The following mnemonic may assist nurses during the initial assessment of a trauma patient:

- Primary Assessment
  - A—Airway with simultaneous cervical spine stabilization and/or immobilization
  - B—Breathing
  - C—Circulation
  - D—Disability (neurologic status)
- Secondary Assessment
  - E—Expose/environmental control (remove clothing and keep patient warm)
  - F—Full set of vital signs/five interventions (electrocardiographic monitor, pulse oximeter, urinary catheter, gastric tube, and laboratory studies)/facilitate family presence
  - G—Give comfort measures (verbal reassurance, touch)
  - H—History and Head-to-toe assessment
  - I—Inspect posterior surfaces

PRIMARY ASSESSMENT AND RESUSCITATION

Airway, with simultaneous cervical spine stabilization and/or immobilization, breathing, circulation, and disability (neurologic status) are the A-B-C-Ds of the primary assessment. Remove only those clothes necessary to expose the patient in order to conduct the primary assessment. If any lifethreatening compromises or injuries are determined, implement interventions to correct them immediately. Additional assessment steps are not taken until measures to ensure an adequate airway, effective breathing, and effective circulation have been instituted.

In the presence of potentially life-threatening injuries, begin assessment immediately on the patient's arrival to collect objective assessment information. The extent and timing of obtaining information related to both the injury event and the patient's past medical history depend on the severity of the patient's condition. Subjective information from pre-hospital personnel, family, or the patient at this point of the assessment process is limited to a brief statement composed of the patient's major injuries or chief complaints and the mechanism of injury. A more detailed history is obtained during the secondary assessment.

AIRWAY

Assessment

Inspect the patient's airway while maintaining cervical spine stabilization and/or immobilization. Since partial or total airway obstruction may threaten the patency of the upper airway, observe for the following:

- Vocalization
- Tongue obstructing airway in an unresponsive patient
- Loose teeth or foreign objects
- Bleeding
- Vomitus or other secretions
- Edema

INTERVENTIONS
Airway Patent
- Maintain cervical spine stabilization and/or immobilization
- Any patient whose mechanism of injury, symptoms, or physical findings suggest a spinal injury should be stabilized or remain immobilized.
- If the patient is awake and breathing, he or she may have assumed a position that maximizes the ability to breathe. Before proceeding with cervical spine stabilization, be sure interventions do NOT compromise the patient's breathing status.

Airway Totally Obstructed or Partially Obstructed
- Position the patient
  Position the patient in a supine position. If the patient is not already supine, logroll the patient onto his or her back while maintaining cervical spine stabilization. Remove any head gear, if necessary, to allow access to the airway and cervical spine; removal of such gear should be done carefully and gently to prevent any manipulation of the spine.
- Stabilize the cervical spine
  - If the patient has not been stabilized, manually stabilize the head. Stabilization includes holding the head in a neutral position.
  - If the patient is already in a rigid cervical collar and strapped to a backboard, do NOT remove any devices. Check that the devices are placed appropriately.
  - Complete spinal immobilization with a backboard and straps should be done at the completion of the secondary assessment, depending on the degree of resuscitation required and the availability of team members.
- Open and clear the airway.
  - Techniques to open or clear an obstructed airway during the primary assessment include:
    - Jaw thrust
    - Chin lift
    - Removal of loose objects or foreign debris
    - Suctioning
  - Maintain the cervical spine in a neutral position. Do not hyperextend, flex, or rotate the neck during these maneuvers.
  - Suctioning and other manipulation of the oropharynx must be done gently to prevent stimulation of the gag reflex and subsequent vomiting and/or aspiration.
- Insert an oropharyngeal or nasopharyngeal airway
- Consider endotracheal intubation (oral or nasal route)
  Ventilate the patient with a bag-valve-mask device prior to endotracheal intubation. For patients requiring control of the airway with an endotracheal tube, the decision must be made to use the oral versus the nasal route.
  - Oral endotracheal intubation is done with the patient's cervical spine in a neutral position and without any extension or flexion of the cervical spine. This requires a second person to hold the patient's head in this position.
  - Blind nasotracheal intubation is NOT indicated when the patient is apneic or when there are signs of major midface fractures (e.g. maxillary fractures [LeFort II or III]). Basilar skull fractures or fractures of the frontal sinus or cribriform plate are considered relative contraindications.

324

• The use of neuromuscular blocking agents along or in combination with other drugs administered before intubation is usually dictated by institutional protocols.
• Consider needle or surgical cricothyroidotomy

Ventilate the patient with a bag-valve-mask device prior to these procedures. In rare circumstances, the patient's condition may restrict passage of an endotracheal tube. To establish an airway, a needle cricothyroidotomy may be performed with an over-the-needle catheter placed into the trachea through the cricothyroid membrane. Another method is a surgical cricothyroidotomy. An incision is made in the cricothyroid membrane, and a tube is placed into the trachea. Both of these approaches to a cricothyroidotomy should be performed by skilled physicians. In some settings, advanced life support (ALS) personnel (e.g. flight nurses or advanced practice nurses) may also be trained and qualified to perform cricothyroidotomies.

If there are any life-threatening compromises in airway status, stop and intervene to correct the problem before proceeding to breathing assessment. Examples of life-threatening airway conditions are partial or complete obstruction of the airway from foreign bodies or debris (blood, mucus, vomitus) and/or obstruction by the tongue. Penetrating wounds may cause disruption of the integrity of the airway, and blunt trauma may lead to injury of the larynx and/or other upper airway structures.

Breathing
ASSESSMENT
Life-threatening compromises in breathing may occur with a history of any of the following:
  • Blunt or penetrating injuries of the thorax
  • Patient striking the steering column or wheel
  • Acceleration, deceleration, or a combination of both types of forces (e.g., motor vehicle crashes, falls, crash injuries)

Once the patency of the airway is assured, assess for the following:
  • Spontaneous breathing
  • Chest rise and fall (depth and symmetry)
  • Skin color
  • General respiratory rate
    • Normal
    • Slow
    • Fast
  • Pattern of breathing
    • Regular
    • Irregular
    • Cheyne Stokes
  • Integrity of the soft tissue and bony structures of the chest wall
  • Use of accessory and/or abdominal muscles
  • Bilateral breath sounds
    • Auscultate the lungs bilaterally at the second intercostal space midclavicular line and at the fifth intercostal space at the anterior axillary line.
  • Jugular veins and position of trachea

INTERVENTIONS

Breathing Present: Effective

Administer oxygen via a *nonrebreather mask* at a flow rate sufficient to keep the reservoir bag inflated; during inspiration, usually requires a flow rate of at least 12 liters/minute and may require 15 liters/minute or more.

Breathing Present: Ineffective

When spontaneous breathing is present but ineffective, the following may indicate a life-threatening condition related to breathing:

- Altered mental status (i.e., restless, agitated)
- Cyanosis, especially around the mouth
- Asymmetrical expansion of the chest wall
- Use of accessory and/or abdominal muscles
- Sucking chest wounds
- *Paradoxical* movement of chest wall during inspiration and expiration
- Tracheal shift from the midline position

  To inspect and palpate the anterior neck region (i.e., jugular veins and trachea), remove the anterior portion of the cervical collar. Another team member must hold the patient's head while the collar is being removed and replaced.
- Distended external jugular veins
- Absent or diminished breath sounds
- Auscultate breath sounds to determine if present, diminished, or absent
- Administer oxygen via a nonrebreather mask or assist ventilations with a bag-valve-mask device, as indicated
- Assist with endotracheal intubation as previously described

Breathing Absent

- Ventilate the patient via a bag-valve-mask device with an attached oxygen reservoir system
- Assist with endotracheal intubation; ventilate with oxygen via a bag-valve device attached to an oxygen reservoir system

If there are any life-threatening injuries that compromise breathing, stop and intervene before proceeding to circulation assessment. Examples of life-threatening injuries that may compromise breathing are tension pneumothorax, open pneumothorax, flail chest with pulmonary contusion, and hemothorax. These conditions may require simultaneous assessment and immediate intervention (*e.g., needle throacentesis* or covering an open chest wound).

Circulation
ASSESSMENT

- Palpate a central pulse (e.g., femoral or carotid) initially if there is any question as to whether the patient has adequate circulation.
- Palpate the pulse for quality (i.e., normal, weak, or strong); and rate (i.e., normal, slow, or fast).
- Inspect and palpate the skin for color, temperature, and degree of diaphoresis
- Inspect for any obvious signs of external bleeding
- Auscultate *blood pressure*

- If there are other members of the trauma team available, auscultate the blood pressure. If not, proceed with the primary assessment and auscultate the blood pressure at the beginning of the secondary assessment.

INTERVENTIONS

Circulation: Effective

If the circulation is effective, proceed with assessment and intervene according to interventions for ineffective circulation, as indicated.

Circulation Present: Ineffective

Although the pulse is present, other signs may indicate inadequacy of the circulation such as:

- Tachycardia
- Altered level of consciousness or mental status (e.g., agitated, confused, decreased arousability)
- Uncontrolled external bleeding
- Distended or abnormally flattened external jugular veins
- Pale, cool, diaphoretic skin
- Distant heart sounds

Circulation: Effective or Ineffective

- Control any uncontrolled external bleeding by:
  - Applying direct pressure over the bleeding site
  - Elevating the bleeding extremity
  - Applying pressure over arterial pressure points
  - The use of a tourniquet is rarely indicated; however, if the above interventions do not control the bleeding and operative bleeding control is not readily available, a tourniquet may be the last resort.
- Cannulate two veins with large-bore 14- or 16-gauge catheters, and initiate infusions of *lactated Ringer's solution* or normal saline
  - Use warmed solutions
  - Use plastic bags to facilitate pressurized infusion
  - Use "Y" tubing for possible administration of blood
  - Use rapid infusion device, as indicated
  - Use normal saline (0.9%) in intravenous tubing through which blood is administered
  - Venous cannulation may require a surgical cutdown and/or central venipuncture
  - Consider use of a *pneumatic antishock garment* (PASG) for intra-abdominal and/or pelvic bleeding with hypotension
  - Obtain a blood sample for typing to determine the ABO and Rh group
  - Administer blood, as prescribed

Circulation: Absent

If a patient does not have a pulse, cardiopulmonary resuscitation (CPR) is indicated. However, it is possible to have electrocardiographic activity even when the pulse and blood pressure cannot be auscultated. The term *electromechanical dissociation* (EMD) refers to one example of pulseless electrical activity (PEA), whereby the patient has no pulse but has narrow complexes indicating depolarization of the myocardium with no mechanical contraction. *Pseudo-EMD*, a newer term, describes a patient who has no blood pressure by auscultation, but may have some degree of myocardial muscle contraction, albeit too weak to generate a blood pressure. If there is no palpable carotid pulse:

- Initiate cardiopulmonary resuscitation (CPR)
- Initiate advanced life support measures
- Administer blood, as prescribed
- Prepare for and assist with an emergency thoracotomy, as indicated, in the emergency department or resuscitation area; open thoracotomies should only be done in facilities with the resources to manage post-thoracotomy patients.
- Prepare patient for definitive operative care after thoracotomy, if indicated

If there are any life-threatening conditions compromising circulation, stop and intervene before proceeding to the neurologic assessment. Examples of life-threatening conditions that may compromise circulation are uncontrolled external bleeding, shock because of hemorrhage or massive burns, pericardial tamponade, or direct cardiac injury.

Disability—Brief Neurologic Assessment
ASSESSMENT
After the primary assessment of airway, breathing, and circulation, conduct a brief neurologic assessment to determine the degree of disability (D) as measured by the patient's level f consciousness.

- Determine the patient's level of consciousness by assessing the patient's response to verbal and/or painful stimuli using the *AVPU* mnemonic as follows:
  - A—Speak to the patient. The patient who is alert and responsive is considered **A** for **Alert**.
  - V—The patient who responds to verbal stimuli is considered **V** for **Verbal**.
  - P—Apply a painful stimulus. The patient who does not respond to verbal stimuli, but does respond to a painful stimulus is considered **P** for **Pain**.
  - U—The patient who does not respond to painful stimulus is considered **U** for **Unresponsive**.
- Assess pupils for size, shape, equality, and reactivity to light

Interventions
- If the disability assessment indicated a decreased level of consciousness, conduct further investigation during the secondary focused assessments.
- If the patient is not alert or verbal, continue to monitor for any compromise to airway, breathing, or circulation.
- If the patient demonstrates signs of herniation or neurologic deterioration (e.g. unilateral or bilateral [pupillary] dilation, asymmetric pupillary reactivity, or motor posturing) consider hyperventilation.

SECONDARY ASSESSMENT
After each component of the A-B-C-D of the primary assessment has been addressed and life-saving interventions initiated, start the *secondary assessment*. This assessment is a brief, systematic process to identify **ALL** injuries. **Exposure/environmental control (E)** is necessary to assess the patient adequately. It may be necessary to cut away clothing in certain circumstances. Timing of the removal of clothing will depend on the number of trauma team members available. Once clothing has been removed, it is

important to prevent heat loss by using overhead warmers, warming blankets, and warmed intravenous fluids.

The **F** of the assessment mnemonic stands for a **full set of vital signs/five interventions/ facilitate family presence**.

Prior to initiating the head-to-toe assessment to identify other injuries, obtain a full set of vital signs, including blood pressure, pulse rate, respiratory rate, and temperature. If chest trauma is suspected, auscultate the blood pressure in both arms.

After completing the A-B-C-D-E of the assessment, intervening for life-threatening conditions, and obtaining a complete set of vital signs (F), critical decision-making will determine whether to continue with the secondary assessment or to perform additional interventions. The availability of other trauma members to perform these **five** interventions will influence the decision. If the patient sustained significant trauma and required life-saving interventions during the primary assessment, perform the following interventions before proceeding with the secondary assessment:

- Assign another trauma team member to attach leads and monitor the patient's cardiac rate and rhythm.
- Assign another trauma team member to attach a *pulse oximeter*, if available, to monitor the patient's arterial *oxygen saturation* (SpO2). The normal SpO2 is greater than 95%, meaning hemoglobin is 95% saturated with oxygen. SpO2 readings may not be accurate if the patient has inconsistent blood flow, vasoconstriction, or altered hemoglobins such as *carboxy-hemoglobin*. Even if the patient has only a slight change in SpO2 readings, the change in arterial *partial pressure of oxygen* (PaO2) is significant, especially if the PaO2 changes between 100 and 60 mm Hg. The percent of hemoglobin saturated with oxygen has a relationship to the partial pressure of oxygen as demonstrated by the oxygen-hemoglobin dissociation curve. The curve plateaus when PaO2 levels are high but the SpO2 will not significantly change at these higher ranges since essentially the hemoglobin is 100% saturated; however, at lower ranges of PaO2 where the curve is more sigmoidal-shaped, the changes in SpO2 are extremely significant. For example, a 10 mm Hg drop in PaO2 from 90 to 80 represents only a drop in SpO2 from 96.5% to 94.5%. However, if the PaO2 drops from 50 mm Hg to 40, the drop in SpO2 is from 83.5% to 75%. The clinical significance is that patients who have pulse oximetry readings above 90% could have varying levels of PaO2, and, therefore, pulse oximetry alone should not be used to predict PaO2. Oxygen saturation measurements can also be calculated from an arterial blood sample (SaO2).
- Insert an indwelling urinary catheter to monitor urinary output. Suspected injury to the urethra is a contraindication to catheterization through the urethra. Indications of possible urethral injury are:
  - Blood at the urethral meatus
  - Palpation of a displaced prostate gland during a rectal examination
  - Blood in the scrotum
  - Suspicion of an anterior pelvic fracture
- Insert a gastric tube. In the presence of severe facial fractures, insert the gastric tube through the patient's mouth. Gastric decompression and emptying of gastric contents will reduce the risk of aspiration, reduce the risk of respiratory compromise, reduce the risk of vagal stimulation and bradycardia, and prepare the patient for possible operative intervention. Test gastric contents for blood. The tube must be passed carefully while:
  - Maintaining cervical spine stabilization and/or immobilization

- Minimizing the stimulation of the patient's gag reflex
- Having suction equipment available
- Facilitate laboratory studies
  - Blood typing the highest priority. Depending on the severity of the patient's condition, blood typing studies may also include screening and crossmatching.
  - Frequently ordered studies are blood typing, hematocrit (Hct), hemoglobin (Hgb), *blood urea nitrogen* (BUN), creatinine, blood alcohol, toxicology screen, arterial partial pressure of oxygen (PaO2), arterial *partial pressure of carbon dioxide* (PaCO2), pH, base deficit, lactate, electrolytes, glucose and clotting profile (platelets, *prothrobin time* [PT], partial thromboplastin time [PTT]), and beta human chorionic gonadotropin or urine test for pregnancy.

The **F** of the mnemonic also represents family presence. Facilitate the presence of the family in the treatment area and their involvement in the patient's care.

- Assess the family's desires and needs
- Facilitate and support the family's involvement in the care
- Assign a health care professional to provide explanations about procedures and to be with the family in the emergency department
- Utilize resources to support the family's emotional and spiritual needs, such as a social worker or chaplain

The **G** of the mnemonic is a reminder to the trauma team to give comfort measures. Such measures may include, but are not limited to, consideration of pain management (e.g., pharmacologic analgesia); alternative pain control such as touch, positioning, distraction, relaxation techniques; and general comfort measures such as verbal reassurance, stimuli reduction, listening to the patient, and developing a trusting nurse/patient relationship.

History

The **H** of the mnemonic stands for history which can be obtained from the following:

- Pre-hospital information
  Obtain information from pre-hospital personnel as indicated by the circumstances of the injury event. The mnemonic **MIVT** - which stands for Mechanism of injury, Injuries sustained, Vital signs, and Treatment - can be used as a guide to obtaining pre-hospital information.
  - Mechanism and pattern of injury
  Knowledge of the mechanism of injury and specific injury patterns (e.g., type of motor vehicle impact) will help to predict certain injuries. If the patient was transported by pre-hospital personnel, have them describe pertinent on-scene information to the trauma team. Such information includes the location of the patient on their arrival, length of time since the injury event, and extent of extrication or reasons for extended on-scene time.
  - Injuries suspected
  Ask pre-hospital personnel to describe the patient's general condition, level of consciousness, and apparent injuries.
  - Vital signs
  - Treatment initiated and patient responses
- Patient-generated information

- If the patient is responsive, ask questions in order to evaluate the patient's level of consciousness and for the patient to describe discomforts or other complaints. Elicit patient's description of pain (i.e., location, duration, intensity, and character). If domestic violence I suspected, as appropriate questions while providing comfort and a sense of security. Talking to the patient provides reassurance and emotional support and provides the patient with information regarding upcoming procedures.
- Past medical history
  Gather information from the patient or family regarding:
  - Age
  - Pre-existing medical conditions
  - Current medications
  - Allergies
  - Tetanus immunization history
  - Previous hospitalizations and surgeries
  - Recent use of drugs or alcohol
  - Smoking history
  - Last menstrual period

Head-To-Toe Assessment

The **H** stands for head-to-toe assessment. Information from this assessment is collected primarily through inspection, auscultation, and palpation. In specific circumstances, percussion may be indicated. The patient may focus on the more obvious distracting injury and have a decreased response to other injuries. While systematically moving from the patient's head to the lower extremities and the posterior surface, complete the assessment as described on the following pages.

General Appearance

Note the patient's body position, posture, and any guarding or self-protection movements. Observe for stiffness, rigidity, or flaccidity of muscles. Characteristic positions of limbs (flexion or extension), trunk, or head may indicate specific injuries. Note and document any unusual odors such as alcohol, gasoline, chemicals, vomitus, urine, or feces.

Head and Face

- Soft tissue injuries
  - Inspect for lacerations, abrasions, contusions, avulsions, puncture wounds, impaled objects, *ecchymosis*, and edema
  - Palpate for crackling association with subcutaneous emphysema
  - Palpate for areas of tenderness
- Bony deformities
  - Inspect for exposed bone
  - Inspect for loose teeth or other material in the mouth that may compromise the airway
  - Inspect and palpate for depressions, angulation, or areas of tenderness
  - Inspect and palpate for facial fractures resulting in loss maxillary and/or mandibular or structural integrity

- Observe for asymmetry of facial expressions. Also inspect the area for any exposed tissue that may indicate disruption of the central nervous system (CNS) (i.e., CNS tissue from open wounds).
- Eyes
  - Determine gross visual acuity by asking the patient to identify how many of your fingers you are holding up
  - Inspect for periorbital ecchymosis (*raccoon's eyes*), subconjunctival hemorrhage, and/or edema. Determine whether the patient is wearing contact lenses.
  - Assess pupils for size, shape, equality, and reactivity to light
  - Assess eye muscles by asking the patient to follow your moving finger in six directions to determine *extraocular eye movements* (EOMs)
- Ears
  - Inspect for ecchymosis behind the ear (*Battle's sign*)
  - Inspect for skin avulsion
  - Inspect for unusual drainage, such as blood or clear fluid from the external ear canal. Do **NOT** pack the ear to stop drainage as it may be carebrospinal fluid (CFS).
- Nose
  - Inspect for any unusual drainage, such as flood or clear fluid. Do **NOT** pack the nose to stop clear fluid drainage as it may be CSF. If CSF or drainage is present, notify the physician and do not insert a gastric tube through the nose.
  - Inspect position of nasal septum
- Neck
  - Inspect for signs of penetrating or surface trauma, including presence of impaled objects, ecchymosis, edema, or any open wounds
  - Observe position of trachea and appearance of external jugular veins
  - Palpate trachea to determine position (i.e., midline, deviated)
  - Palpate neck area for signs of subcutaneous emphysema and/or areas of tenderness

Chest

- Inspection
  - Observe breathing for rate, depth, degree of effort required, use of accessory and/or abdominal muscles, and any paradoxical chest wall movement
  - Inspect the anterior and lateral chest walls, including the axillae for lacerations, abrasions, contusions, avulsions, puncture wounds, impaled objects, ecchymosis, edema, and scars
  - Inspect the expansion of the chest and excursion during ventilation
  - Observe for expressions or reactions that may indicate the presence of pain (e.g., facial grimace)
- Auscultation
  - Auscultate lungs for breath sounds and note presence of any adventitious sounds, such as wheezes, rales, or rhonchi
  - Auscultate heart sounds for presence of murmurs, friction rubs, and/or muffled sounds
- Palpation
  - Palpate for signs of subcutaneous emphysema

- Palpate the clavicles, sternum, and the ribs for bony *crepitus* or deformities (e.g., step-off, areas of tenderness)

Abdomen/Flanks
- Inspection
  - Inspect for lacerations, abrasions, contusions, avulsions, puncture wounds, impaled objects, ecchymosis, edema, and scars
  - Observe for evisceration, distension, and scars
- Auscultation
  - Auscultate for presence or absence of bowel sounds. Auscultate before palpating because palpation may change the frequency of bowel sounds.
- Palpation
  - Gently palpate all four quadrants for rigidity, guarding, masses, and areas of tenderness; begin palpating in an area where a patient has not complained of pain or where there is no obvious injury.

Pelvis/Perineum
- Inspect for lacerations, abrasions, contusions, avulsions, puncture wounds, impaled objects, ecchymosis, edema, and scars
- Bony deformities
  - Inspect for exposed bone
  - Palpate for instability and tenderness over the iliac crests and the symphysis pubis
- Inspect for blood at the urethral meatus (more common in males than females because of length of urethra), vagina, and rectum
- Altered neurologic function
  - Inspect penis for *priapism* (persistent abnormal erection)
  - Palpate anal sphincter for presence or absence of tone
- Ensure that an appropriate trauma team member has performed a rectal examination to determine if there is any displacement of the prostate gland in males (this may also be done in the posterior assessment)
- Note pain and/or the urge, but inability, to void

Extremities
- Inspect previously applied splints and to **NOT** remove if applied appropriately and if neurovascular function is intact
- Circulation
  - Inspect color
  - Palpate skin temperature
  - Palpate pulses
    In lower extremities, palpate femoral, popliteal, dorsalis pedis; in upper extremities, palpate the brachial and radial pulses.
- Soft tissue injuries
  - Inspect for bleeding
  - Inspect for lacerations, abrasions, contusions, avulsions, puncture wounds, impaled objects, ecchymosis, edema, angulations, deformity, and any open wounds
- Bony injuries
  - Inspect for angulation, deformity, open wounds with evidence of protruding bone fragments, edema, and ecchymosis

- Note bony crepitus
- Palpate for deformity and areas of tenderness
- Motor function
  - Inspect for spontaneous movement of extremities
  - Determine motor strength and range of motion in all four extremities; use range of motion (ROM)/muscle strength scale 0 - 5.
    5 = complete ROM or active movement against gravity and full resistance
    4 = complete ROM or active movement against gravity and some resistance
    3 = complete ROM or active movement against gravity
    2 = complete ROM or active body part movement with gravity eliminated
    1 = barely detectable contraction
    0 = no detectable contraction
- Sensation
  - Determine patient's ability to sense touch in all four extremities

Inspect Posterior Surfaces

The I of the mnemonic stands for inspection of the patient's posterior surfaces.

- Maintain cervical spine stabilization
- Support extremities with suspected injuries
- *Logroll* patient with the assistance of members of the trauma team. This maneuver keeps the vertebral column in alignment during the turning process. Do not logroll the patient onto his or her side with an injured extremity. Logroll away from you (if possible) to inspect the back, flanks, buttocks, and posterior thighs for lacerations, abrasions, contusions, avulsions, puncture wounds, impaled objects, ecchymosis, edema, or scars.
- Palpate the vertebral column including the costovertebral angles (CVA) for deformity and areas of tenderness
- Palpate all posterior surfaces for deformity and areas of tenderness
- Palpate anal sphincter for presence or absence of tone, if not already done during the assessment of the pelvis and perineum

FOCUSED SURVEY

After the primary and secondary assessments and any simultaneous interventions are completed, a more detailed, focused assessment will be necessary for each area or system injured. This will further direct the priorities of care.

Frequently ordered radiographic studies are of the chest, pelvis, and cervical spine (C-1 through T-1 must be visualized). Follow cervical spine clearance procedures as indicated by individual hospital protocols. These radiographic studies may be performed during any phase of the primary or secondary assessment, depending on the patient's condition and the availability of resources.

PAIN MANAGEMENT

The patient's perception of pain may originate from a number of sources because of injury (e.g., the actual injury, procedures, the environment). Trauma patients will have their pain managed per the nursing policy P-005 - Pain Management.

TETANUS PROPHYLAXIS

Determination of the need for *tetanus prophylaxis* following trauma depends on:

- Condition of the wound
- Patient's past vaccination history
- First determine whether the patient has ever received primary vaccination.

SEVERITY INDICES

The *Glasgow Coma Scale score* and the *Revised Trauma Score* are two scoring systems that measure the acuity and severity of the patient's physiologic response to injury. The Revised Trauma Score may be used by pre-hospital personnel and emergency staff as a triage tool. Changes in both scores will reflect the patient's ongoing response to the injury event. Scores can be calculated using a preprinted source indicating the points for each area. Data from the primary and secondary assessments can be used to determine the severity of the patient's condition and provide a baseline for ongoing evaluation of the patient's responses to the injury event and treatment.

Glasgow Coma Scale

The Glasgow Coma Scale (GCS) score ranges from 3 to 15 and is a measure of the patient's level of consciousness. It is not a measure of total neurologic function. Points on the scale correspond with specific responses in three areas; eye opening, verbal response, and motor response. The patient's **BEST** response in each of three areas if noted. For example, if a patient presents with paralysis of the lower extremities but can move an upper extremity, the BEST motor based on the patient's ability to move the upper extremity.

The patient's eye opening response cannot be measured if the eyes are so swollen that the patient cannot open them. Patients who have been given a drug for neuromuscular blockade cannot be evaluated. Patients who have been intubated or who cannot speak because of maxillofacial trauma cannot be evaluated for verbal response.

Source: Courtesy of Parkview Medical Center, Pueblo, Colorado.

4-19 Triage System

POLICY

It is the policy of Parkview Emergency Department that all patients be seen by the ER physician as soon as possible. Under no circumstances will a medical screening exam be delayed on the basis of insurance or ability to pay.

PURPOSE

To increase the quality of patient care by quickly and accurately prioritizing patients' care needs. All patients will be triaged on arrival (within 5 minutes) and registration will occur after triage is completed.

PROCEDURE

1. Triage Assessment

   All patients presenting to the ED will have a routine triage assessment performed, including a primary and focused secondary assessment.

   The following will be accurately documented:
   - Patient name
   - Date and time of arrival
   - Time of initial contact with triage nurse
   - Age
   - Chief complaint—usually 2-3 quoted words from the patient
   - Brief triage history
   - Allergies
   - Immunization status if less than 18 years old
   - Vital signs: blood pressure does not need to be taken in triage unless:
     1. the patient has more then a 15 minute wait in triage holding/waiting room, or;
     2. the triage nurse needs it to help determine appropriate placement
   - Glasgow Coma Scale per protocol
   - The triage assist will escort patient to room and undress patient and take vital signs. If the triage assist is busy with another patient then the ER tech or nurse will take vital signs.
   - Triage acuity assessment
   - Signature of triage nurse
   - Weight if less than 16 years old
   - Pain will be managed per the nursing pain policy - Pain Management

2. Bed Assignment

   a. Bed assignments of triaged patients are dependent on:
      - Acuity of patient
      - Availability of ER beds
   b. When an ER patient is "Emergent", but no beds are currently available, communication between the ER triage nurse and the ER charge nurse to quickly reassign a lower acuity patient to another site so that "emergent" patients will immediately have a monitored bed to be treated on.
   c. "Urgent and Non-Urgent" patients may be asked to wait in the ER Triage holding area until a bed becomes available. All "holding" patients will be reassessed and monitored by the triage nurse or designated RN.
   d. The nurse will be notified by the charge nurse whenever an emergent patient is placed in the nurse pod.

3. Tracker Board (Electronic tracking system cannot identify the patient with any confidential information.)

   When the triaged patient is assigned a room and bed, the charge nurse or designee will write the patient's location on the EDM Tracker Board. In addition, the following will be recorded on the board:
   a. Patient's last name
   b. Time of placement in treatment room
   c. Initials of nurse assigned to patient
   d. Acuity assignment—assigned by charge nurse

Source: Courtesy of Parkview Medical Center, Pueblo, Colorado.

4-20 Assessment of Patients

Registered nurses (RN) assess and reassess patient needs for nursing care. Each patient's physical, psychological and social status is assessed. The RN analyzes collected data and concludes the initial assessment by prioritizing patient needs and initiating an individualized plan of nursing care. Licensed practical nurses (LPN) and nursing assistants (NA) may participate in data collection. However, the RN retains responsibility for identifying patient care needs, the plan of care and coordination of care through discharge.

Time frames for initial nursing assessments

- Inpatient admissions: The RN will conduct an admission assessment and initiate the plan of care as close to the time of admission as possible, preferably within the shift of the patient's arrival on the unit. The assessment must be completed within 24 hours of admission. Patients admitted the day of a planned procedure, whose initial assessment by a RN is documented in the medical record within 30 days of the planned procedure, will be reassessed by a RN on the day of admission prior to and post procedure. The RN will document significant changes from the original assessment.
- Extended stay/observation: The RN will complete an admission assessment and initiate a plan of care (Standard Care Statement) within four hours of patient's arrival on an observation unit.
- Emergency admissions taken directly to the Operating Room or a procedure area: The RN on the receiving inpatient unit will complete the admission assessment preferably within the shift of patient arrival on the unit, but at least within 24 hours. (Check your state law for more stringent timeframes.)
- Emergency Department: The RN will document an abbreviated initial assessment, to include a review of patient physical and cognitive status. Emergent patients are assessed upon arrival. Urgent and non-urgent patients will have initial assessment within one hour of check in to emergency treatment area.
- Labor and Delivery: The RN will document a triage assessment within one hour of arrival to Labor and Delivery. Following admission the RN continues the admission assessment which must be completed within 24 hours of admission.

Essential elements of initial nursing assessments (Generic)

The RN will document an initial assessment that includes generic and individualized elements specific to patient age, diagnosis and condition.
Essential Elements (Generic)
- reason for admission;
- physical status;
- cognitive status;
- psychosocial status;
- communication status;
- allergies;
- special precautions;

- pain;
- medication use;
- substance abuse;
- domestic violence/neglect/abuse screening communicable disease exposure;
- personal routines and self-care needs;
- nutritional screening;
- spiritual/cultural practices;
- Advance Directives (adults = 18 years);
- educational status;
- financial concerns;
- need for discharge planning;
- belongings inventory and disposition.

Additional assessment requirements for the infant, child, or adolescent patient

The RN will document the following assessments:
- emotional, cognitive, communication, educational, social, and daily activity needs;
- developmental age, length or height, and weight;
- head circumference (age: day 1 up to and including 24 months)
- effect of family or guardian on the patient's condition;
- effect of the patients condition on the family or guardian;
- immunization status;
- weight in kg;
- family or guardian's expectations for involvement in the patient's assessment, initial treatment, and continuing care;
- availability of appropriate child restraint device (car seat)

Note: The educational assessment of school age children is performed by the school teacher with parental permission.

Note: In the NCCC, Social Work performs psychosocial assessments and initiates additional referrals as needed.

Additional assessment requirements for psychiatry and rehabilitation patients

Interdisciplinary assessments are done on a single form in Psychiatry and Rehabilitation, so the registered nurse is not responsible for all required elements in these areas. The required functional status assessment is performed and documented by several disciplines on the rehabilitation unit (nursing, physical, occupational, recreational and speech therapies). Additional assessments performed in psychiatry include assessment of thought process and assessment of risk profile.

Additional assessment requirements for patients who are possible victims of alleged or suspected abuse or neglect

Reference the following patient care management protocols:
- "Suspected Victims of Domestic Violence or Elder Abuse/Neglect";
- "Hospitalized Infant, Toddler, Pre-Schooler, School-Age Child and Adolescent".

Reassessments

The RN performs reassessments throughout the patient's hospitalization. The frequency and content of reassessments are specific to patient condition and are identified in patient care management protocols. Patients are reassessed daily for safety risks, e.g. potential for falls and skin breakdown. Reassessments to determine patient response to care and progress in meeting identified outcome goals are documented at least every 24 hours on general care units, and at least every 12 hours in critical care units. Reassessment is always done following a significant change in patient condition, a change in diagnosis, and at the time of unit transfer.

Source: Courtesy of UNC Health Care, Chapel Hill, North Carolina.

4-21 Suicide Precautions/Constant Precautions/Attempted Suicide

<u>PURPOSE</u>:
To prevent injury to patient by maximizing environmental safety.

<u>LEVEL</u>:
This procedure is instituted by the RN. The LPN and NA may monitor and observe the patient.

<u>SUPPORTIVE DATA</u>:
Suicide Precautions are ordered for patients who have either harmed themselves, verbalized intent to do so, or indicated, in an overt or covert manner, a wish to do so. If the nurse is concerned about the patient's potential for suicide, institute Suicide Precautions then contact the patient's physician for an order and a psychiatric consult. If a psychiatric consult is ordered it should be completed the same day as the request. The psychiatrist will evaluate the patient for suicide potential and may recommend Suicide Precautions or Constant Precautions. **If this procedure is implemented then the <u>Self Harm Behavior</u> protocol must also be implemented.**

Constant Precautions are ordered for patients whose suicide potential appears extremely high (any patient who has just made an attempt or who is believed to be planning an attempt). Outside of the Psychiatry Service and Critical Care units Constant Precautions must be instituted for all patients who are placed on Suicide Precautions (with the exception of forensic patients wherein the guard provides continuous 1:1 safety monitoring).

The nurse will institute Constant Precautions following a suicide attempt or gesture regardless of the severity. The nurse will immediately notify the patient's physician and request an urgent psychiatric consult. The patient's physician must write the order for Suicide or Constant Precautions.

On a psychiatric unit if the RN believes the gesture to be a self-mutilating or self-injurious behavior, Constant Precautions may not be appropriate. In this case, the patient's physician or on call psychiatric resident should be notified immediately and asked to evaluate and/or recommend the appropriate level of observation.

Patients who are at increased risk of suicide are those who:
- are experiencing severe anxiety or agitation
- are depressed and/or psychotic
- have a history of previous suicide attempt
- are experiencing intense feelings of hopelessness or abandonment
- have sleep disturbance
- are actively abusing alcohol or substances
- verbally express suicidal thoughts
- have a family history of suicide
- have a suicide plan, with the intent and means to carry out the plan
- have sustained a recent loss (including death of a loved one, divorce, separation, loss of a job, or financial loss)
- say goodbye with finality (e.g. tell staff "I won't be here when you return")
- are unwilling to make a no-harm/no-suicide contract with staff (i.e. patient is not willing to inform staff if he feels like harming himself).

Times of increased risk of a patient attempting suicide are: at change of shift, early morning hours, night time, weekends, holidays, after visitors leave, after phone calls, after disturbing/distressing news, either shortly after admission, and near or at discharge from the hospital.

CONTENT:

STEPS:	KEY POINTS:
Suicide Precautions:	**NOTE: With the exception of forensic patients,** *all* patients on Suicide Precautions who are not in a Psychiatric or Critical Care unit must be on Constant Precautions.
1. Place the patient in a room, which affords the best observation and protection.	1. On non-psychiatric units, if possible, move the patient to a private room close to the nurses' station.
2. Search the patient's belongings, clothing, luggage, and packages at the time precautions are instituted. Tell the patient of your concern for safety and the reason for the search. Remove all medications and other items considered unsafe, including glass or sharp items, nail polish remover or other alcohol-containing solutions, matches or lighter, and any aerosol spray cans (i.e. hairspray). Similar items belonging to the patient's roommate must also be removed.	2. The patient may be allowed to keep eyeglasses, non-breakable toiletry items, or a cordless electric razor. Patient's belongings not in daily use should be sent home or to the Motel Unit. (Document disposition of belongings on the Valuables/Belongings Inventory and place this in patient's chart.) NOTE: Outside of Psychiatry if Suicide Precautions are instituted at anytime after the admission process, a room search must be ordered by the physician. (See **R**oom Search Procedure.) NOTE: Be aware that cleaning agents used by housekeepers are a potential means of self-harm if ingested and should not be accessible to the patient.
3. Monitor items brought onto the unit by visitors. Remove any item considered unsafe (as above) and return it to the visitor when they leave the unit.	3. Check all bags and packages upon entry to the unit. NOTE: Outside of the Psychiatry Service this pertains to only those items brought to the patient who is on precautions, or to the patient's roommate.
4. Supervise patient when he is using sharp/glass articles, toxic solutions, aerosol sprays, lighter, or razor.	4. Neither the patient nor his roommate may keep these articles in the room. These items must be secured at the nurses' station.

STEPS:

Suicide Precautions:

5. Restrict patients on Suicide Precautions to the unit unless it's absolutely necessary to leave the unit for testing or procedures that cannot be delayed.

6. Stay with the patient while he is taking prescribed medication to make sure he/she swallows the medication.

7. Assess the patient's physical/emotional condition and suicide potential every eight hours.
NOTE: The attending psychiatrist and the patient's attending physician must document the patient's suicide potential in the Progress Notes of the patient's medical record, at least every 24 hours.

8. Make a visual observation of the patient every 15 minutes throughout all shifts and document. Observe for any potentially unsafe behavior.

CONSTANT PRECAUTIONS:

STEPS:

Follow Steps 1 through 7 as above.

9. Keep the patient within sight and within reach at *all times*.

10. Instruct Nutrition and Food Services to use disposable products on trays including plastic flatware. No cans or glassware are permitted.

11. Obtain sitter if need exists for supplemental personnel. Have sitter read these procedures and verbalize to the charge nurse his understanding of the meaning and requirements of Constant Precautions.

12. Obtain a physician's order to take the patient off the unit if the patient wishes to smoke (Required only on non-psychiatric units).

13. Make every attempt to verbally convince the patient to stay if the patient tries to leave the unit or hospital without physician authorization. (Psychiatry Staff see "Elopement" policy and procedure in the *UNC Hospitals/NC Neurosciences Hospital Inpatient Psychiatry Policy and Procedure Manual*).

KEY POINTS:

NOTE: With the exception of forensic patients, *all* patients on Suicide Precautions who are not in a Psychiatric or Critical Care unit must be on Constant Precautions.

5. Maintain a *minimum* staff ratio of 1 to 1 when off the unit.

6. Check to see that patient has swallowed medication. If you have reason to believe the patient may be "cheeking" the medication, ask patient to open his mouth, stick out his tongue, and to touch his tongue to the roof of his mouth while you check for "cheeked" medication.

7. Refer to **Self Harm Behavior protocol.** Ask the patient if he is having thoughts of suicide. If yes, ask him if he has a plan as to how he would do it and ask him to share that plan with you. Ask if he can agree to tell a staff member if he is thinking of harming himself, rather than acting on it. Place on **"Constant Precautions"**, if patient is unable or unwilling to agree to this. **NOTE: The patient's willingness to contract in this way** *does not* **mean the patient can be trusted not to attempt suicide. An unwillingness to make such an agreement may indicate the patient is at risk of suicide.**

8. Stagger the 15-minute checks so that they are not made at predictable times. Checks may not exceed 15-minute intervals. **Observation frequency and supervision of the patient may be intensified at the discretion of the charge nurse. Notify the physician of intensified observations.**

NOTE: With the exception of forensic patients, *all* patients on Suicide Precautions who are not in a Psychiatric or Critical Care unit must be on Constant Precautions.

KEY POINTS:

9. Patients are observed at all times, which include: bathroom and bathing times, procedures, tests off the unit, and when visitors are present.

10. Count flatware before and after use. If anything is found missing from the tray the patient and immediate surroundings must be searched until lost item is accounted for.

11. On non-psychiatric units a sitter is *required*, with the exception of the Critical Care Units. Within the ICU's, patient safety checks will be completed and documented at least every 15 minutes, beginning as soon as the patient is responsive. See below, "Obtaining Sitter for Suicidal Patient on Constant Precautions".

12. The physician must write an order allowing the patient to be escorted by staff to the courtyard that adjoins the ICU Waiting Room to smoke. When off the unit, maintain a *minimum* staff ratio of 1-to-1.

13. Contact Hospital Police immediately at 6-3686 if assistance is needed to prevent patient from leaving. If the patient leaves without authorization, immediately do the following:
    • call Hospital Police with a description of the patient and instructions to return patient to the unit
    • search for the patient and attempt to verbally convince the patient to return to the unit
    • notify the patient's physician
    • notify nursing supervisor

Obtaining Sitter for Suicidal Patient on Constant Precautions:

1. Notify the covering house supervisor that a sitter is needed.

1. When possible, Constant Precautions observations are provided by hospital staff. When the nursing staff cannot provide sufficient hours of care, the charge nurse notifies the covering House Supervisor. Supplemental personnel will be employed only when other options for coverage are exhausted.

2. Complete the Sitter Request form and send to the Nursing Supervisor.

2. If the patient has not yet been admitted the admitting unit is responsible for completing the request form.

3. Instruct supplemental personnel of their duties and responsibilities as described in this procedure.

3. The assigned sitter should be made aware of why the patient requires constant supervision, have read this procedure, and they must verbalize their understanding of these responsibilities to the charge nurse.

ATTEMPTED SUICIDE:

1. Initiate "Constant Precautions" *(see above)*.

1. Remain with the patient while calling for assistance via emergency call light. Provide any emergency care, as situation requires. Initiate constant 1 : 1 supervision assuring patient safety.

2. Notify the patient's physician, the covering nursing supervisor, Risk Management.

2. The covering nursing supervisor will notify the hospital director on call.

3. Document incident in the patient's chart and complete an incident report.

DOCUMENTATION: Document every 15-minute checks of the patient on Suicide Precautions on the Safety Precaution Checklist (obtained from Psychiatry). This should include the specific location (patient room, nursing station, etc.) and the behavior of the patient. For patients on Constant Precautions, document the block of time the patient was observed on the Safety Precaution Checklist. Document RN assessment of physical/emotional condition and suicide potential of patient on Suicide or Constant Precautions each shift in the Progress Notes or Patient Care Record. Document attempted suicide in Progress Notes.

REFERENCES: Busch, KA; Fawcet, J; Jacobs, DG. Clinical correlates of inpatient suicide. **Journal of Clinical Psychiatry** 2003; 64: 14-19.
Cardell, R; Horton-Deutch, S. A model for assessment of inpatient suicide potential. **Archives of Psychiatric Nursing** 1994; 8 (6), 366-372.
Goodwin, FK. Preventing inpatient suicide. **Journal of Clinical Psychiatry** 2003; 64: 12-13.
Shea, SC. **The Practical Art of Suicide Assessment.** 2002. John Wiley & Sons, Inc., Hoboken, New Jersey.

APPROVAL: By: Nursing Procedure Committee

REVISED:

Source: Courtesy of UNC Health Care, Chapel Hill, North Carolina.

4-22 Elder Abuse: ED Guidelines

ASSESSMENT

The American Medical Association recommends that doctors routinely ask geriatric patients about abuse, even if signs are absent. Keeping questions direct and simple and asking in a nonjudgmental or nonthreatening manner increases the likelihood that patients will respond candidly. The patient and the caregiver should be interviewed together and separately to detect disparities offering clues to the diagnosis of abuse. Accurate, objective documentation of the interview is essential. The following questions can be used to elicit information about elder abuse.

- Physical abuse
    - —Are you afraid of anyone at home?
    - —Have you been struck, slapped, or kicked?
    - —Have you been tied down or locked in a room?
    - —Have you been force-fed?
- Psychological abuse
    - —Do you ever feel alone?
    - —Have you been threatened with punishment, deprivation, or institutionalization?
    - —Have you received "the silent treatment"?
    - —Do you receive routine news or information?
    - —What happens when you and your caregiver disagree?
- Sexual abuse: Has anyone touched you in a sexual way without permission?
- Neglect
    - —Do you lack items such as eyeglasses, hearing aids, or false teeth?
    - —Have you been left alone for long periods?
    - —Is your home safe?
    - —Has anyone failed to help you care for yourself when you needed assistance?
- Financial abuse
    - —Is money being stolen from you or used inappropriately?
    - —Have you been forced to sign a power of attorney, will, or another document against your wishes?
    - —Have you been forced to make purchases against your wishes?
    - —Does your caregiver depend on you for financial support?
- Follow-up questions (if abuse is identified)
    - —How long has the abuse been occurring?
    - —Is it an isolated incident?
    - —Why do you think this happens?
    - —When do you think the next episode will occur?
    - —Is the abuser present in the ED?

—Is it safe for you to return home?

—What would you like to see happen?

- Have you ever received help for this problem before?

EMERGENCY DEPARTMENT CARE

Many factors are involved in the management of older persons who have been abused, including immediate care, long-term assessment and care, education, and prevention. Intervention can be a lengthy process, especially in a busy ED. Many hospitals have developed multidisciplinary teams (ie, social workers, physicians, nurses, administrators) to help in these situations. The ultimate goal is to provide the aging adult with a more fulfilling and enjoyable life. Immediate care focuses on treating the physical manifestations of abuse and assuring the safety of the patient. This may include the following:

- admitting the patient to the hospital
- obtaining a court protective order
- placing the patient in a safe home
- permitting return home if the patient is competent and refuses intervention

CONSULTATIONS

- Psychiatry consultation—For patients who are demented, depressed, disoriented, or incompetent
- Geriatrics consultation—For specialized care of the geriatric patient
- Neurology or neurosurgical consultation—For patients with focal neurological findings, or intracerebral bleeding
- Orthopedics consultation—For patients with fractures

Source: Excerpted from Krouse, Laurel, "Elder Abuse," eMedicine Clinical Knowledge Base; June 5, 2001.

4-23 Thrombolytic Guidelines Screen

Date of Service _____   Reviewer _____

Pt Name _____   Data Source _____

Medical Record # _____   Physician #s _____

ASPECT OF CARE: Thrombolytic Therapy in Acute MI

1. Indicator: **Appropriate Patient Selection for Thrombolytic Therapy during MI**

Yes   No   **Data Elements (At least one of the following):**

___   ___   1. Chest pain or symptoms of AMI of at least 30 minutes duration and beginning within 12 hours of presentation to the ED.

___   ___   2. Patient beyond the 12 hour window with ongoing or recurrent symptoms or if patient presented in cardiogenic shock.

___   ___   3. EKG changes consistent with AMI (ST elevation > 1 mv in 2 contiguous leads) or the presence of a LBBB or RBBB pattern on EKG.

___   ___   4. Chest pain and EKG changes persist after administration of SL NTG.

___   ___   5. Age < 75 yrs—decision to administer thrombolytic made on a case by case basis.

2. Indicator: **The management is in compliance with the standard of care:**

___   ___   1. Internist arrival to ED within 30 minutes of patient arrival and/or notification

___   ___   2. Thrombo Panel—Chem 19 (Lytes, BUN, Glucose, Creatinine, liver panel), Cardiac Panel—CBC, PT/PTT, Type & Screen, Time from Admission _____ (mins)

___   ___   3. EKG—12 lead (Time from admission _____)

___   ___   4. ASA 160 mg at the onset of thrombolytic administration

___   ___   5. Two large bore Peripheral IV lines (18 G if possible)

___   ___   6. Time infusion started after patient arrival to hospital

___   ___   7. Heparin infusion—Start at 1000 units/hr (**SK—No bolus**; TPA—Bolus of 5000 u and then infusion) Note: For TPA pts > 80 kg—Bolus of 70 u/kg and infusion at 1200 units/hr.

3. Indicator: **Exclusion Criteria—Absolute Contraindications:**

___   ___   1. Active internal bleeding

___   ___   2. Hx of hemorrhagic CVA, esp within the previous 6 months

___   ___   3. Recent (within 2 months) neurosurgery or trauma to head or spine

___   ___   4. Intracranial neoplasm, AV malformation or aneurism

___   ___   5. Known bleeding diathesis

___   ___   6. Severe, persistent uncontrolled HTN (>200 mm Hg systolic or > 120 mm Hg diastolic) despite analgesics, nitrates and/or beta blockers

4. Indicator: **Exclusion Criteria—Relative Contraindications:**

___   ___   1. Recent major surgery or organ bx (within 10 days)

___   ___   2. Recent (within 10 days) GI or GU bleeding (excluding menses)

___   ___   3. Recent trauma to chest or abdomen (within 10 days)

___   ___   4. Acute pericarditis

___   ___   5. Bacterial endocarditis

___   ___   6. Severe renal or hepatic disease

___   ___   7. Pregnancy

___   ___   8. Diabetic or other hemorrhagic retinopathy

___   ___   9. Septic thrombophlebitis or occluded AV cannula at seriously infected site

___   ___   10. Pts already on oral anticoagulants with a PT of > 15 seconds

___   ___   11. Prolonged CPR (> 5 minutes) or traumatic ED intubation < 10 days

___   ___   12. Puncture of a noncompressible vessel (e.g., Subclavian catheterization)

___   13. Any other reason that would result in a significant bleeding hazard

5. Indicator: **Follow Up Care**

___   ___   1. Continue patient on oral aspirin—160 mg/day

___   ___   2. CK/ISOS, CBC and PTT 6 hrs after infusion complete

___   ___   3. PTT q ___ hrs for duration of Heparin infusion

___   ___   4. EKG every 30 minutes during 2 hours of infusion and in one hour after infusion

___   ___   5. Begin patient on an H2 blocker

___   ___   6. Admission to TCGH

___   ___   7. Transfer to another facility (Timing in hours after ED presentation _____)

6. Indicator: **Adverse Events**

Yes	No	**Data Elements (At least one of the following):**
—	—	1. Bleeding Complications
—	—	2. Reocclusion
—	—	3. Other

Source: Courtesy of Tillamook County General Hospital, Tillamook, Oregon.

4-24 Informed Consent for Thrombolytics

Your doctors have determined that your chest pain is caused by a heart attack. Heart attacks are usually due to blood clots in one or more of the arteries in the heart, which blocks the blood supply of oxygen-rich blood to the heart muscle. This blockage causes pain and may result in permanent damage to your heart, or death. Such heart damage may or may not cause a noticeable impairment in your future ability to perform exertional activities.

There are medications available, called **thrombolytics,** that are sometimes able to dissolve the clot in your artery if administered soon after the onset of symptoms. This stops the heart attack process and reduces the extent of heart muscle damage.

In clinical trials involving many patients in both the United States and Europe, some patients receiving thrombolytics have shown a significant improvement in both heart function and in survival from their heart attacks (as compared to similar groups of patients treated in the same manner but without thrombolytics).

Like any medication, thrombolytics have side effects, usually in the form of **bleeding disturbances,** which may require blood transfusions. More serious adverse reactions, some even resulting in stroke and death, have been uncommon but can occur.

The particular thrombolytic drug will be administered through an intravenous catheter in your arm. It will be necessary to have 2 or 3 sites available for other medications as well. During and following the infusion you will otherwise receive standard and conventional heart attack therapy. If you select not to receive thrombolytic therapy you will still be afforded this same standard medical and nursing care.

PATIENT STATEMENT

By signing below I acknowledge that I have read and understand the nature and consequences of my medical condition and the treatment about to be rendered unto me. I have had the opportunity to ask questions. I understand that there may be untoward side effects ranging from bleeding to stroke to death.

I accept these risks in the hopes that this medication will dissolve the blood clot in the artery of my heart, improve performance of my heart, and reduce the extent of heart damage.

I understand that all standard medical care for the treatment of heart attacks will be afforded me whether I accept or refuse this medication. I further certify that I have no known tumor or growth inside my body and that I have no history of abnormal bleeding in the past.

PATIENT SIGNATURE _____

DATE _____

TIME _____

WITNESS SIGNATURE _____

Source: Courtesy of Twin Cities Community Hospital, Templeton, California.

4-25 Asthma Screening Tool

Who is your asthma doctor? _____

SIGNS AND SYMPTOMS	NO	YES	COMMENTS
How long have you/your child had asthma?			Number of Years _____
Do you smoke or are you exposed to smoke often?	☐	☐	
Do you/your child have pets or are you/your child around pets often?	☐	☐	☐ Dog ☐ Cat ☐ Hamster/Rat ☐ Other: _____
Do you/your child cough or wheeze or does your/your child's chest feel tight during the day?	☐	☐	How often does this happen? ☐ Once a week ☐ Once a day ☐ 2-3 times a day ☐ All day long
Do you/your child cough or wheeze or does your/your child's chest feel tight when you exercise or play?	☐	☐	How often does this happen? ☐ Once a month ☐ Once a week ☐ Once a day ☐ Every time I exercise/play
Do you/your child cough or wheeze or does your/your child's chest feel tight during the night that wakes you up?	☐	☐	How often does this happen? ☐ Once a week ☐ Once a night ☐ 2-3 times per night ☐ All night long
What do you/your child think makes your asthma worse?			☐ Do Not Know ☐ Air pollution ☐ Dust ☐ Molds ☐ Pollen ☐ Pets ☐ Strong Smells ☐ Exercise ☐ Foods ☐ Weather Change ☐ Other: _____
Do you/your child know what to do if you have trouble breathing?	☐	☐	☐ If No, instructions were given to patient ☐ If Yes, instructions were reviewed with patient

MONITORING

	NO	YES	
Do you/your child have a peak flow meter?	☐	☐	How often do you use it? ☐ Every Day ☐ Weekly ☐ Monthly ☐ Never ☐ Only when sick
What was your/your child's highest reading over the past week?			

FUNCTIONALITY

	NO	YES	
Have you/your child missed any school or work because of your asthma over the past month?	☐	☐	How much school or work was missed? ☐ 1 day ☐ 2-3 days ☐ 4-5 days ☐ Over a week
Is there anything you/your child can not do because of your asthma?	☐	☐	If Yes, explain:
Have you/your child seen a doctor or been to a clinic during the past month for your asthma?	☐	☐	How many times during the past month? ☐ Once a month ☐ Twice a month ☐ More than 3 times a month
Have you/your child needed to go to the Emergency Room because of your asthma in the past year?	☐	☐	How many times during the past year? ☐ Once ☐ 2-3 times ☐ 4-5 times ☐ More than 5 times
Have you/your child had to spend the night in the hospital because of your asthma in the past year? (other than the Emergency Room)	☐	☐	How many times during the past year? ☐ Once ☐ 2-3 times ☐ 4-5 times ☐ More than 5 times

MEDICATIONS			
What medication(s) do you/your child take for your asthma and how often do you take them?	☐	☐	List:
Do you/your child use a spacer when you take your medications?	☐	☐	
Do you/your child need medication(s) refill(s)?	☐	☐	If Yes, which medication(s)?
Do you/your child have problems taking your medications?	☐	☐	What type of problems? ☐ Side Effects ☐ Trouble getting child to take the medications ☐ Not taking medications as ordered
Has the cost of your medical care kept you/your child from getting medical care for asthma?	☐	☐	If Yes, explain: ☐ Medicine cost too high ☐ Medical visit cost too high ☐ Other
EDUCATION			
Have you/your child ever attended classes on asthma?	☐	☐	When was the last time you took an asthma class? ☐ Within 6 months ☐ Within 1 year ☐ More than 1 year ago

RECOMMENDATIONS TO THE PROVIDER:

☐ Appointment requested within: ____ days/weeks
☐ Referral to Asthma Education Program
☐ Referral to Social Services

☐ Referral to Child Life Specialist

☐ Referral to Smoking Cessation Program
☐ Other:

Signature/Title of person performing the screening: _____

ID# _____ Date: _____

Source: Courtesy of Parkland Health and Hospital System, Dallas Texas.

4-26 Child Abuse Assessment

POLICY

In accordance with State law, physicians or any other persons having reason to suspect that a child has been abused or neglected are required to report directly to the Division of Youth and Family Services (DYFS), the name and age of the child, address of the parent or guardian, description of the child's condition, type of abuse or neglect to which the child has been subjected, an indication of the seriousness of the situation and whether the child appears in immediate or imminent danger, any other information concerning the circumstances of the abuse or neglect, including any evidence of past abuse or maltreatment. The law also requires that such reports be made only to the DYFS, and not to the County Prosecutor.

The entire _____ Health System will comply fully with the State reporting laws, and will cooperate with the Division of Youth and Family Services in its effort to provide for proper child care. All children under age 18 admitted to _____ Health System will be assessed for abuse and neglect (Assessment Criteria). Any person knowingly violating the provisions of this act, including the failure to report an act of child abuse, having reasonable cause to believe that an act of child abuse has been committed, is subject to criminal liability as a disorderly person.

DEFINITIONS

State Law defines an "abused child" as a child under the age of 18 whose parent, guardian, or other person having custody and control:

1. inflicts or allows to be inflicted upon such child physical injury by other than accidental means that causes or creates a substantial risk of death, serious or protracted disfigurement, protracted impairment of physical or emotional health, or protracted loss or impairment of the function of any bodily organ
2. creates or allows to be created a substantial or ongoing risk of physical injury to such child by other than accidental means that would be likely to cause death or serious protracted disfigurement or protracted loss or impairment of the function of any bodily organ
3. commits or allows to be committed an act of sexual abuse against the child
4. a child whose physical, mental or emotional condition has been impaired or is in imminent danger of becoming impaired as the result of the failure of his parent or guardian, or such other person having his custody and control, to exercise a minimum degree of care (1) in supplying the child with adequate food, clothing, shelter, education, or medical or surgical care though financially able to do so, or through offered financial aid or other reasonable means to do so, or (2) in providing the child with proper supervision or guardianship by unreasonably inflicting or allowing to be inflicted harm, or substantial risk thereof, including the infliction of excessive corporal punishment, or using excessive physical restraint under circumstances that do not indicate that the child's behavior is harmful to himself, others, or property, or by any other act of a similar nature requiring the aid of a court

5. a child who has been willfully abandoned by his parent or guardian or such other person having his custody and control
6. a child who is in an institution and (1) has been so placed inappropriately for a continued period of time with the knowledge that the placement has resulted and may continue to result in harm to the child's mental or physical well being, or (2) has been willfully isolated from ordinary social contact under circumstances which indicate emotional or social deprivation. A child shall not be considered abused pursuant to this subsection if the acts of omissions described occur in a day school.

PROCEDURE

Reporting

1. Any person who has reasonable cause to believe that a child has been abused is legally obligated to immediately report that belief to the Division of Youth and Family Services (DYFS) appropriate for that county. DYFS will request the following information: the name and phone number of the person making the report; the name and address of the child; the name and address of the parent, guardian, or other person having custody and control of the child; the child's age; the nature and possible extent of the child's injuries; and any other information that DYFS believes may be helpful with respect to the child abuse and identity of the abuser.
2. In compliance with the legal obligations to report, _____ Health System has established a procedure for notifying DYFS of suspected cases of child abuse. The assigned designee, i.e., social worker, nurse manager, charge nurse, clinician, or program director shall be the coordinating and liaison department with DYFS during normal hours of operation. After hours, weekends and holidays, the administrator-on-call, the attending physician or nursing supervisor will carry out these functions with DYFS.
3. The parent or guardian of the child must be advised of the report to DYFS. All patients five (5) years of age and older must be informed that the allegation(s) will be reported to DYFS. If this creates a problem for either the child or parent/guardian, associates will explain mandatory reporting. Concerns will be given serious consideration and attention.
4. Upon receipt of such a report, DYFS is obligated to respond and take such action as it believes is necessary to ensure the safety of the child. DYFS may request appropriate assistance from local or state law enforcement officials.

Allegations Regarding Health System Associates (Institutional Abuse)

1. Under no circumstances will any form of physical or verbal abuse by any _____ associate to a patient be tolerated. This includes: hitting, slapping, use of excessive force, verbal put-downs, sarcasm, or belittling comments, etc. Such behavior, or allegations of such behavior, will be investigated thoroughly and may lead to disciplinary action if substantiated.
2. Neglectful behavior occurs whenever an associate is engaged in any behavior other than their current assignment as outlined by the supervisor. Associates will monitor

and observe patients at all times during their assigned shift. Taking care of personal business must be done outside of the workplace or while on assigned break. Any report of neglectful behavior by staff will be investigated thoroughly and may lead to disciplinary action if substantiated.

3. Allegations made during the day shift, Monday through Friday, should be reported to the program director, nurse manager or designee. An Incident Report must immediately be initiated. The patient, any witnesses and the alleged perpetrator will be interviewed by the program director, nurse manager or designee. A determination for further action will then be made after consultation.

4. Allegations made evenings, nights, weekends or holidays will be managed consistently by the nursing supervisor. An Incident Report must immediately be initiated. Whenever physical abuse allegations are made, the appropriate physician(s) will be contacted in order to examine the alleged abuse. The nursing supervisor, in conjunction with the administrator-on-call will make a decision regarding the status of the associate.

5. DYFS Institutional Abuse must be notified immediately of the abuse allegation. DYFS will request the name, address, and other data pertaining to the allegation for all involved, as well as a brief description of the alleged incident. In cases involving allegations made by a patient against another patient, information on all parties involved may be shared with DYFS specific to the present allegation and investigation. DYFS may decide to come to the location to begin the investigation. Note: DYFS may request a medical examination by a physician of its own choice. This will need to be cleared through Administration.

Immunity

Anyone acting pursuant to this act in the making of a report under this act shall have immunity from any liability, civil or criminal, that might otherwise be incurred or imposed. Any such person shall have the same immunity with respect to testimony given in any judicial proceeding resulting from such report. (state law)

Hospital Hold/Protective Custody

The Protective Custody Law allows for the hospital administrator or any physician examining and/or treating a child suspected of being abused or neglected to invoke protective custody, without the consent of parents or guardian, for up to three (3) court days (excludes weekends and holidays), during which time DYFS, upon notification of the custody action, will investigate the circumstances in the home environment leading to the suspected abuse or neglect.

Hospital Hold should be considered as a last resort, due to the restriction of time in which DYFS has to work (3 court days). When necessary to protect the child, DYFS will take steps through the court and/or request an extension of the period of custody.

1. The appropriate DYFS must be notified immediately of the child taken into protective custody.

2. If the hold is invoked by a physician, the hospital administrator or designee, and guest relations must be notified within twenty-four (24) hours.

3. DYFS must serve or attempt to serve written notice upon the parent or guardian that said child has been taken into protective custody. The notice will contain information about the duration and location of the protective custody.
4. The initiation of a Hospital Hold means that a child is in the protective custody of the hospital administrator or examining physician as the protem legal guardian of the child. In a situation where the life or health of a child is in danger, treatment may be provided by the hospital without consent of parent(s) or guardian.
5. Visitation by the parents or guardian of a child in protective custody may occur upon request and in the reasonable discretion of the physician, administrator, or designate from DYFS, provided that the life or health of the child will not be endangered. In some instances, visits will be supervised or suspended pending recommendations from DYFS.
6. Differences between the hospital and DYFS regarding visitation and termination of a Hospital Hold should be resolved by collaboration.

Discharge Disposition

1. The child should be discharged to the parents only upon the approval of DYFS. The parents may arrive alone or accompanied by a DYFS worker.
2. The child may be directed to a foster home or other institution if so ordered by the court or if so arranged between DYFS and the parents.
3. If the child is to be picked up by the parents, DYFS or other court-appointed person, this will be documented in the progress notes of the chart. The child should be released only after proper identification has been seen by the nursing staff and documented in the chart.
4. The discharge instruction sheet will be given to the person to whom the child is released.

Release of Medical Record Information

Medical records resulting from the examination of a child may be released to DYFS upon their request for the purpose of aiding in the determination of whether or not the child has been abused or neglected. Such requests should be referred to the Medical Records Department. If the Medical Records Department is not open, the hospital administrator's designate will supply a copy of the record. A written request for the information and a statement from a DYFS representative that the requested information was received (can be handwritten) must be obtained and forwarded to the Medical Records Department.

In-Service Training

All staff and departments potentially involved in the treatment and referral of child abuse/ neglect cases will be involved in a minimum annual educational program. Staff Development will coordinate these education activities.

REFERENCES

"Child Abuse and Neglect: A Professional's Guide to Identification, Reporting, Investigation and Treatment," the Governor's Task Force on Child Abuse and Neglect, October 1988.
Joint Commission: PE. 1.8 (1996), R1.15 (1996)

Source: Adapted from Kennedy Health System, Voorhees, New Jersey.

4-27 Child Abuse and Neglect Indicators: Physical Abuse, Sexual Abuse, Physical Neglect, Emotional Maltreatment

Type	Physical Indicators	Behavioral Indicators	Emotional Indicators
Physical Abuse	Unexplained bruises and welts: • on head, face, lips, mouth • on torso, back, buttocks, thighs • in various stages of healing • clustered, forming regular patterns • reflecting shape of article used to inflict (electric cord, belt buckle) • on several different surface areas • regularly appear after absence, weekend or vacation	Wary of adult contacts Apprehensive when other children cry Behavior extremes: • aggressiveness • withdrawal Frightened of parents Afraid to go home Reports injury by parents	
Sexual Abuse	Difficulty in walking or sitting Torn, stained or bloody underclothing Pain or itching in genital area Foreign objects in vagina or rectum STD, especially in preteens Pregnancy	Unwilling to change for gym or participate in Physical Education Withdrawal, fantasy, or infantile behavior Bizarre, sophisticated, or unusual sexual behavior or knowledge Poor peer relationships Delinquent or runaway Reports sexual assault by caretaker	Infant & Toddler • Irritability • Feeding difficulty • Sleep disturbances • Altered levels of activity School Age Child • Behavioral problems • Anxieties • Sleep disturbances • Disturbing dreams • Withdrawn attitude Adolescent • Fright and confusion • Guilt feelings • Anger and acting out • Depressive affect
Physical Neglect	Consistent hunger, poor hygiene, inappropriate dress Consistent lack of supervision, especially in dangerous activities or long periods Constant fatigue or listlessness Unattended physical problems or medical needs Abandonment Malnutrition Decayed or painful teeth	Begging, stealing food Extended stays at school (early arrival or late departure) Constantly falling asleep in class Alcohol or drug abuse Delinquency (thefts) States there is no caretaker	
Emotional Maltreatment	Habit disorders (sucking, biting, rocking, etc.) Conduct disorders (anti-social, destructive, etc.) Neurotic traits (sleep disorders, speech disorders, inhibition of play) Psychoneurotic reactions (hysteria, obsession, compulsion, phobias, hypochondria)	Behavior extremes: Overly compliant, passive or aggressive, demanding Overly adaptive behavior • inappropriately adult • inappropriately infant Developmental lags (physical, mental, emotional) Attempted suicide	

Source: Adapted from Kennedy Health System, Voorhees, New Jersey.

4-28 Adult Violence Assessment

DEFINITIONS

For the purpose of this policy, adult violence includes any one of the following types inflicted upon any male or female over the age of 18:

- domestic violence
- sexual abuse
- physical assault
  1. Domestic violence is defined as any use of physical force, the threat of use of physical force, or psychological abuse between family members or significant others.
  2. Sexual abuse is forced, manipulated, or coerced sexual activity; it includes: rape, incest, same-sex assault, acquaintance rape, and marital rape.
  3. Physical assault may include aspects of defined domestic violence; in addition, it may include the use of weapons, and the alleged perpetrator may be known or unknown.

POLICY

In accordance with the following:
  1. Prevention of Domestic Violence Act.
  2. State Sexual Assault law.
  3. State Assault Laws.

This Hospital will follow the outlined procedure.

IDENTIFICATION

Identification of adult violence can be supported by the attached guidelines.

PROCEDURE

Confidentiality

When abuse is suspected, provide the patient with a quiet, private environment to speak with associates and/or medical staff. Attempt to interview the patient privately. At the request of the patient, we will allow family/friend to accompany the patient during the interview process. If the family/friend accompanying the patient will not provide the patient privacy, security shall be called to intervene.

Guidelines for Security Department

The hospital needs to provide a safe environment for the victim of adult abuse throughout the hospital stay. Security may be called on to provide this protection to the patient. Security will:

  1. respond when called by the emergency department, physician, social work department, or nursing unit

2. restrict or monitor visitation, if necessary
3. restrain or escort the perpetrator from the hospital premises
4. provide liaison with local law enforcement personnel if necessary to ensure the safety of victim, family, and/or staff

Security will need the following information:
- the name of the patient
- admitting number
- room number
- reason for assistance
- whether or not a police report has been filed
- familiarity with the Prevention of Domestic Violence Act

Interview/Assessment of Victim of Adult Violence

The following will serve as guidelines for all associates during the interview and assessment phase:
- in patient's own words with a brief summary of circumstances surrounding the incident
- maintain patient's attention to immediacy of situation
- clarify patient's support system availability

Patient Education
- Devise a Safety Plan.
- Provide information for the appropriate resources.

Referrals
- For admitted patients with children who may be at risk, coordinate children's care at relatives/friends or referral to Divisio and Family Services (DYFS).
- As warranted, facilitate police and/or legal counseling referral if patient chooses to pursue these avenues.
- Provide patient with knowledge for appropriate community resources:
  —shelter
  —counseling
  —medical follow-up
  —financial/insurance options

Documentation

Documentation on the medical record is essential. Document all findings and referral actions/plans. The medical record will include the following:

- chief complaint and description of the abusive event or violent situation; the patient's own words should be quoted whenever possible

- the physician's assessment
- complete medical history
- relevant social history
- for physical abuse, a detailed description of injuries, including type, number, size, location, stages of healing, color, resolution, possible causes, and explanations given
  - —when applicable, the location and nature of the injuries should be recorded on a body chart or drawing
  - —an opinion on whether the injuries were adequately explained during the assessment
  - —results of all pertinent laboratory and other diagnostic procedures
  - —imaging studies, if applicable
  - —if the police or prosecutor are called, the name of the investigating officer and any actions taken

Documentation will also be performed on the Care Plan.

Staff Development

Adult violence, including domestic violence, sexual abuse, and physical assault, is a mandatory annual education program for the Emergency Department, Home Care, and Family Health Centers. All other departments potentially involved in the treatment and referral of adult violence are encouraged to participate.

Staff Development will coordinate education activities and provide a Self Learning Module upon request.

REFERENCE

Joint Commission: PE.1.8 (1996), Rl.1.5 (1996)

Source: Adapted from Kennedy Health System, Voorhees, New Jersey.

4-29 Violent Injury or Domestic Violence Report

A. Reporting Party:	Name/Title			Signature of Reporting Party		
	Address			Facility		
	Phone ( )	Date of Report				
B. Report Sent To:	Agency @ Police Department @ Sheriff's Office	Official Contacted		Badge #		
	Phone ( )	Date/Time of Incident		Reason for Report Domestic Violent ☐ Violent Injury ☐		
C. Involved Parties — Victim	Name (Last, First, Middle)	Lang.		Birthdate	Sex	Race
	Address	Phone Home Phone Work				
	Whereabouts of patient after treatment	Phone	Can patient be safely contacted there? Yes ☐ No ☐	Special Instructions		
	Safe Person to Contact	Relationship to Victim		Phone		
	Name and Ages of Children in Home			Were children present during incident? ☐ Yes ☐ No		
	Referral to Domestic Violence Services ☐ Yes ☐ No					
Suspect	Name (Last, First, Middle)	Lang.		Birthdate	Sex	Race
	Address					
	Phone Home	Phone Work		Relationship to Victim		
D. Incident Information	1. Date/Time of Incident	Address of Incident				
	2. Type of injury: ☐ Bruises ☐ Fractures ☐ Choking ☐ Internal Injuries ☐ Lacerations ☐ Gunshot Wound ☐ Stab Wound ☐ Sexual Assault ☐ Other/Specify ☐ Self-inflicted ☐ Assault Against On-Duty Hospital Personnel					
	3. Location of injury: ☐ Face ☐ Neck ☐ Head ☐ Eyes ☐ Extremities ☐ Chest ☐ Upper Back ☐ Lower Back ☐ Ribs ☐ Abdomen ☐ Pelvis ☐ Other/Specify					
	4. Narrative Description. Summarize what the victim or person accompanying the victim said happened:					
	5. Explain known history of similar incident(s) for this victim:					

REPORTING

Reporting Decision Matrix:

	Patient has injury or condition caused by (or suspected to be caused by) DV, whether or not treatment is provided	No current injury or condition caused by DV
Patient admits abuse	Refer and Report	Refer only
Patient denies abuse; abuse suspected.	Refer and Report	Refer only
Patient denies abuse, none suspected	Do not Report	Do not Report

Making a legal report:

- A health practitioner is required to make a report when providing medical services to a patient whom s/he knows or reasonably suspects is suffering from a wound or other physical injury that is the result of assaultive or abusive conduct.
- Reporting is mandated, even if the patient does not want a report to be filed.
- Inform patient that a report to law enforcement will be made.
- Make an immediate telephone report to the law enforcement agency in the jurisdiction where the injury occurred.
- Complete a Violent Injury/Domestic Violence Report and mail to law enforcement agency within 2 work days.
- File a copy of the report in the medical record.

Summary of Resources:

Battered Women's Services (24 hr Hotline) _____

Domestic Violence InfoLine (Recording) _____

United Way InfoLine (General Info) _____

QUICK GUIDE FOR SCREENING AND REPORTING DOMESTIC VIOLENCE
SCREENING

Routinely screen patients. At a minimum, screen as follows:

- Any emergency room visit
- Annual physical exam for women; initial obstetrical visit
- Any presentation of indicators which cause reasonable suspicion (i.e., repeat use of emergency or urgent care service, rape or assault; injuries inadequately explained).

Ask direct questions privately without family members present.

- "Because violence is so common in many women's lives, I've begun to ask about it routinely."
- "Are you in a relationship in which you have been physically hurt or threatened?" If no, "Have you ever been?"
- "Did someone cause these injuries? Who?"

If patient answers "no," but you suspect violence:

- Document clinical signs that may indicate abuse.
- Give patient information about resources and help.
- Decide whether you need to report.

If patient answers "yes," send important messages:

- "You are not alone;" "It is not your fault."
- "No one has to live with violence;" "Help is available."

Document findings in the medical record; use patient's words.

- "The patient states..."
- "She said her boyfriend, Joe Smith, struck her."
- Clearly document all injuries; use a body map.
- Take Polaroid photographs of injuries.

360

Complete a discharge safety assessment and plan:

- "Is it safe to leave with the person who brought you?"
- "Is it safe to go home?" "Do you need access to a shelter?"
- "Do you need to stay with family or friends?"

Refer to Community Domestic Violence Resources
- Written information
- Hotline phone numbers
- Remember, it may be dangerous for the patient to carry these items home. Do not insist that the patient take them.

Source: Copyright Aspen Publishers, Inc.

4-30 Elder Mistreatment Assessment

DEFINITIONS

For the purpose of this policy, elderly patients are those 60 years and above. Elder mistreatment is defined as any behavior that causes fear or intimidation, or harms an older person physically or mentally; misdirected aggression which endangers another person. It includes:
- physical mistreatment
- psychological mistreatment
- financial exploitation
- violation of one's rights
- neglect, both active and passive
- self neglect

POLICY

Every elderly person has the right to be protected from aggression/neglect at the hands of another person. Elderly patients are vulnerable to such mistreatment because of their increased dependency due to age and/or frailty. The goal of intervention is to protect the elderly patient from mistreatment. The rights of the elderly patient should be respected in all care planning, and alternative living arrangements should only be considered after all alternatives available to the patient have been explored, and with the patient's understanding of such consequences. Patients admitted from extended care facilities who are suspected of mistreatment while at a facility will be reported to the Office of the Ombudsman for the Institutionalized Elderly. Other suspected cases of elder mistreatment shall be reported, in accordance with State law, to the Board of Social Services, Adult Protective Service Unit.

PROCEDURE

1. The patient suspected to be a victim of elder mistreatment may present to the Health System's attention via the emergency room admission, at the time of the

admission assessment by the physician and/or nurse, through a patient or family member/significant other's disclosure, or from a community agency.

2. Assessment of the patient should include cognitive status, health status, functional status, living arrangements, financial status, social supports, emotional/psychological status, and stresses in the patient's environment.

3. Any suspected case of elder mistreatment will be referred by any associate to the departmental social worker (i.e., home health, dialysis, acute care, family health services, behavioral health, long term care facility) or designee for assessment.

4. When any associate has suspicion or substantial evidence exists regarding elder mistreatment, referrals will be made to the social worker, who will subsequently refer to the Adult Protective Services (APS) Unit at the appropriate County Board of Social Services or in the case of institutional mistreatment to the Office of the Ombudsman.

5. The social worker or designee will collaborate with the Adult Protective Services Unit and will refer to other community agencies/resources as appropriate to establish ongoing support, care and follow-up.

6. When the evidence is not substantiated, the social worker will assess and intervene if other interventions are needed.

7. Also it is important to recognize the needs of the perpetrator if that person is known. Should the perpetrator ?? the primary caregiver, intervention could include but not be limited to the following:
   - education on the patient's condition, prognosis and needs
   - referral for counseling
   - referral for respite assistance
   - suggestions regarding changed living arrangements

Documentation Procedures for Suspected Abuse

Documentation on the medical record is essential. Document all findings and referral actions/plans. The medical record will include the following:
- chief complaint and description of the abusive event or neglectful situation; the patient's own words should be quoted whenever possible
- the physician's assessment
- complete medical history
- relevant social history
- for physical abuse, a detailed description of injuries, including type, number, size, location, stages of healing, color, resolution, possible causes, and explanations given

   —when applicable, the location and nature of the injuries should be recorded on a body chart or drawing

   —an opinion on whether the injuries were adequately explained during the assessment

   —results of all pertinent laboratory and other diagnostic procedures

   —imaging studies, if applicable

   —if the police or prosecutor are called, the name of the investigating officer and any actions taken

Documentation will also be performed on the Care Plan.

STAFF DEVELOPMENT

Elder Mistreatment is a mandatory educational program for the Emergency Department, Home Care, and Family Health Centers. All other departments potentially involved in the treatment and referral of elder mistreatment are encouraged to participate. Staff Development will coordinate education activities and provide a Self Learning Module upon request.

REFERENCE

Joint Commission: PE.1.8 (1996), RI.1.5 (1996)

Source: Adapted from Kennedy Health System, Voorhees, New Jersey.

4-31 Detection: Indications of Elder Mistreatment Patient Signs and Symptoms

This list represents the most common indicators used to detect abuse and neglect. While the presence of any of these indicators may be caused by a variety of non-abusive factors, the combination of several should cause the professional to suspect mistreatment. *Italicized Behavioral and Emotional Indicators are not limited to any one type of mistreatment.*

Type of Mistreatment	Physical/Situational Indicators	Behavioral Indicators	Emotional Indicators
Physical	Unexplained injuries or explanation inconsistent with medical findings: • fractures • welts • lacerations • punctures • burns: unusual location, type or shape similar to object (i.e., iron, cigarette burn) • bruises: presence of old and new, shape similar to object (i.e., belt marks, fingers) bilateral on upper arms (from holding or shaking), clustered on trunk (from repeated striking)	*Denies problem despite evidence* *"Doctor shopping"* *Failure to seek health care* *Incomparability between history and injury* *Patient is accident prone* *Cries easily, frequently* *Is alcohol dependent and functioning is impaired by drinking* *Has nightmares and difficulty sleeping* *Shakes, trembles and cowers in presence of caregiver (abuser)* *Exhibits distrust of others* *Has suddenly become more dependent on the caregiver, adopting the role of the child*	*Talks about past, and avoids talking about future* *Is difficult to care for because of emotional outbursts* *Exhibits stress related illness (i.e., hypertension, asthmatic attacks, somatized pain)*
Sexual	Torn, stained or bloody underclothing Difficulty in walking or sitting Pain, itching, bruising or bleeding in genital area Unexplained STD or genital infections		
Psychological/ Emotional	Unusual weight gain or loss	*Confusion* *Insomnia, sleep deprivation, or need for excessive sleep* *Change in appetite* *Loss of interest in self, activities or environment*	*Excessive fears* *Ambivalence* *Resignation* *Withdrawal* *Agitation* *Helplessness, hopelessness, depression* *Expresses a desire to die*
Financial/ Material	Disparity between income/assets and lifestyle Unprecedented transfer of assets from an older person to other(s) Extraordinary interest by family member in older person's assets Unexplained disappearance of valuables	Inaccurate, confused, or no knowledge of finances Hoarding money Unexplained or sudden inability to pay bills, purchase food or personal care items Lack of receptivity by older person or family member to any necessary assistance requiring expenditure, when finances are not a problem	Fear or anxiety when discussing finances

Type of Mistreatment	Physical/Situational Indicators	Behavioral Indicators	Emotional Indicators
Neglect	Dehydration Malnutrition Hypo/Hyperthermia Excessive dirt or odor Inadequate or inappropriate clothing Absence of eye glasses, hearing aids, dentures or prostheses Unexpected or unexplained deterioration of health Decubitus ulcers (bedsores) Signs of excess drugging, lack of medication or other misuse	*Apathy, confusion and edema* *Is resistant to taking medication, being bathed, eating or allowing caregiver to provide care* *Decreased alertness, responsiveness and orientation*	*Obsesses, worries or is anxious about his or her own performance (i.e., losing dentures or being incontinent)*

DETECTION: INDICATIONS OF ELDER MISTREATMENT

History	Professional Observations	Risk Factors
Pattern of physician and/or hospital hopping	Patient appears fearful of family member	Family member psychopathology; presence of mental illness, mental retardation, dementia or drug or alcohol abuse
Unexplained delay in seeking treatment	Patient appears reluctant to respond when questioned	Transgenerational violence: family history of violence
Series of missed medical appointments	Patient and family member provide conflicting accounts of incident	Dependency: patient or family member dependent on the other for housing, finances, emotional support, or caregiving
Previous unexplained injuries	Family member is indifferent or angry towards patient and refuses to provide necessary assistance	Isolation: patient does not have the opportunities to relate with people or pursue activities and interests in a manner he or she chooses
Explanation of past injuries inconsistent with medical findings	Family member appears overly concerned with costs of medical care and services	Stress: recent occurrence of stressful life events such as loss of a job, moving, or death of a significant other
Previous reports of similar injuries	Family member seeks to prevent the patient from interacting privately or speaking openly with health care provider Family member appears concerned about a particular patient problem but not the patient's overall health	Living arrangements: patient and family member live together

Source: Adapted from Kennedy Health System, Voorhees, New Jersey.

4-32 Clinical and Behavioral Decision Tree: To Restrain or Not To Restrain

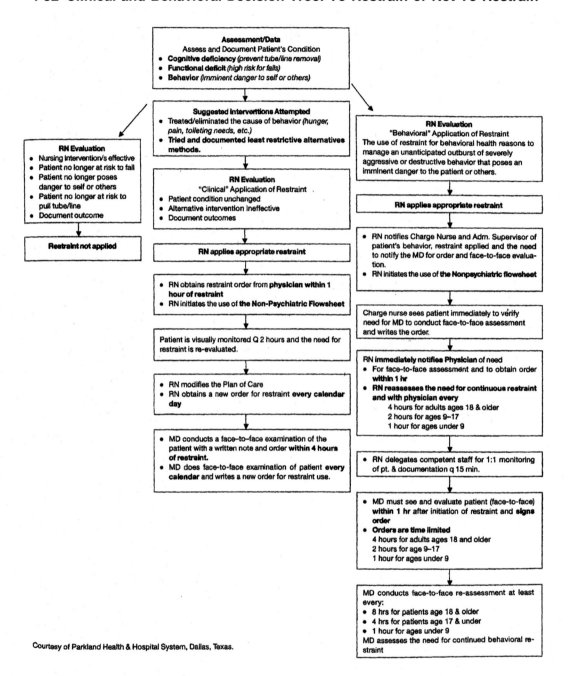

Assessment/Data
Assess and Document Patient's Condition
- **Cognitive deficiency** (prevent tube/line removal)
- **Functional deficit** (high risk for falls)
- **Behavior** (imminent danger to self or others)

Suggested Interventions Attempted
- Treated/eliminated the cause of behavior (hunger, pain, toileting needs, etc.)
- **Tried and documented least restrictive alternatives methods.**

RN Evaluation
- Nursing Intervention/s effective
- Patient no longer at risk to fall
- Patient no longer poses danger to self or others
- Patient no longer at risk to pull tube/line
- Document outcome

Restraint not applied

RN Evaluation
"Clinical" Application of Restraint
- Patient condition unchanged
- Alternative intervention Ineffective
- Document outcomes

RN applies appropriate restraint

- RN obtains restraint order from **physician within 1 hour of restraint**
- RN initiates the use of **the Non-Psychiatric Flowsheet**

Patient is visually monitored Q 2 hours and the need for restraint is re-evaluated.

- RN modifies the Plan of Care
- RN obtains a new order for restraint **every calendar day**

- MD conducts a face–to–face examination of the patient with a written note and order **within 4 hours of restraint.**
- MD does face-to-face examination of patient **every calendar** and writes a new order for restraint use.

RN Evaluation
"Behavioral" Application of Restraint
The use of restraint for behavioral health reasons to manage an unanticipated outburst of severely aggressive or destructive behavior that poses an imminent danger to the patient or others.

RN applies appropriate restraint

- RN notifies Charge Nurse and Adm. Supervisor of patient's behavior, restraint applied and the need to notify the MD for order and face-to-face evaluation.
- RN initiates the use of **the Nonpsychiatric flowsheet**

Charge nurse sees patient immediately to verify need for MD to conduct face-to-face assessment and writes the order.

RN immediately notifies Physician of need
- For face-to-face assessment and to obtain order **within 1 hr**
- **RN reassesses the need for continuous restraint** and with physician every
  4 hours for adults ages 18 & older
  2 hours for ages 9–17
  1 hour for ages under 9

- RN delegates competent staff for 1:1 monitoring of pt. & documentation q 15 min.

- MD must see and evaluate patient (face-to-face) **within 1 hr after initiation of restraint and signs order**
- **Orders are time limited**
  4 hours for adults ages 18 and older
  2 hours for age 9–17
  1 hour for ages under 9

MD conducts face-to-face re-assessment at least every:
- 8 hrs for patients age 18 & older
- 4 hrs for patients age 17 & under
- 1 hour for ages under 9
MD assesses the need for continued behavioral restraint

Courtesy of Parkland Health & Hospital System, Dallas, Texas.

4-33 Pain Screen

Date_____/_____/_____

Resident Name_____ _____ Age_____ Room_____

Diagnosis_____

Physician_____ Nurse_____

Objective: This interview will help to identify the level of pain education and history of the resident to provide optimal resident comfort in the process of easing, controlling and/or diminishing pain. The following documentation may be mutually established with the help of the resident, family members and staff. If the resident is *non*verbal, ask a family member or significant other if they can answer any of the questions. If not, note "not able to obtain from resident or significant other."

Who Answered the following questions:

☐Resident   Family Member (name)_____ Relationship to Resident:_____

RESIDENT INTERVIEW:

1. Do you have pain now?   ☐Yes   ☐No   *Use Pain Rating Scale and indicate level of pain.*

2. Do you ever have pain?   ☐Yes   ☐No   ☐If Yes, how often and where: _____
    _____

3. Are you able to report your pain to the nurse?   ☐Yes   ☐No   ☐If No, why not: _____
    _____

4. Do you feel that it is normal to have pain?   ☐Yes   ☐No   ☐If No, why not: _____
    _____

5. Do you feel that all pain should be treated?   ☐Yes   ☐No   ☐If No, why not: _____
    _____

6. Do you have any cultural or religious beliefs that would influence the management of pain?   ☐Yes   ☐No
    ☐If Yes, please explain: _____
    _____

7. How intense does your pain need to be to be treated?   ☐Rate on a Scale of 1—10_____   Or, explain: _____
    _____

8. How have you treated your pain in the past? (Explain) (medications, other modalities): _____
    _____

9. Have you ever used alcohol to relieve your pain?   ☐Yes   ☐No

10. What drugs, legal or illegal, have you used in the past to relieve your pain?   ☐None   List drugs: _____
    _____

INTERVIEWER OBSERVATIONS:

1. If the resident is not able to describe pain, please check below if there are any current *non*verbal signs of pain:
    ☐Moaning/Yelling   ☐Rocking   ☐Restless Movements   ☐Combative   ☐Grimacing   ☐Guarding   ☐Rubbing Area
    ☐*No Signs of pain*   ☐Other. _____

2. EDUCATION: ☐Resident educated to report pain to the nurse   ☐Family/significant other educated to report signs of
    resident's pain to the nurse   ☐Family/significant other not available at admission to discuss/educate re: pain management

3. OTHER OBSERVATIONS: _____

Source: Best Practices Committee, *HCANJ Pulse Management Guidelines*, 1/05 Revision.
Health Care Association of New Jersey, Hamilton, New Jersey. Reprinted with permission.

4-34 Pain Rating Scale

Date_____/_____/_____

Resident Name_____ Age_____ Room_____

GENERAL INSTRUCTIONS: Choose <u>only one</u> appropriate scale based upon the resident's ability to respond. Identify the scale used and the score for that scale on the bottom of this form. *Any score above 0 requires a Pain Assessment.*

WONG-BAKER SCALE:

Initial Instructions: Explain to the resident that each face is for a person who feels happy because he or she has no pain (hurt) or sad because he or she has some or a lot of pain. **FACE 0** is happy because he or she doesn't hurt at all. **FACE 2** hurts just a little bit **FACE 4** hurts a little more. **FACE 6** hurts even more. **FACE 8** hurts a whole lot. **FACE 10** hurts as much as you can imagine, although you don't have to be crying to feel this bad. Ask the resident to choose the face that best describes how he or she is feeling.

NO HURT	HURTS LITTLE BIT	HURTS LITTLE MORE	HURTS EVEN MORE	HURTS WHOLE LOT	HURTS WORST
0	2	4	6	8	10

NUMERIC SCALE: Choose a number from 0 to 10 that best describes the level of pain.

NO PAIN	MILD PAIN, ANNOYING Pain is present but does not limit activity.	NAGGING PAIN, UNCOMFORTABLE, TROUBLESOME Can do most activities with rest periods.	MISERABLE, DISTRESSING Unable to do some activities because of pain.	INTENSE, DREADFUL, HORRIBLE Unable to do most activities because of pain.	WORST PAIN POSSIBLE, UNBEARABLE Unable to do any activities because of pain.

0 1 2 3 4 5 6 7 8 9 10

FLACC SCALE:

Initial Instructions: The FLACC is a behavior pain assessment scale for use with nonverbal residents who are unable to provide reports of pain. Rate the resident in each of the five measurement categories, add the scores together, and document the total pain score.

	0	1	2
FACE	No particular expression of smile.	Occasional grimace or frown, withdrawn, disinterested.	Frequent to constant frown, clenched jaw, quivering chin.
LEGS	Normal Position or relaxed.	Uneasy, restless, tense.	Kicking, or legs drawn up.
ACTIVITY	Lying quietly, normal position. moves easily.	Squirming, shifting back and forth, tense.	Arched, rigid, or jerking.
CRY	No crying (awake or asleep).	Moans or whimpers, occasional complaint	Crying steadily, screams or sobs, frequent complaints.
CONSOLABILITY	Content, relaxed.	Reassured by occasional touching, hugging, or "talking to." Distractible.	Difficult to console or comfort.

Scale Used: ☐Wong-Baker Score:_____ **Nurse Signature**_____
☐Numerical Score:_____
☐FLACC Score:_____

Source: Best Practices Committee, *HCANJ Pulse Management Guidelines,* 1/05 Revision. Health Care Association of New Jersey, Hamilton, New Jersey. Reprinted with permission.

4-35 Pain Assessment

Date_____/_____/_____

Resident Name_____   _____   Age_____   Room_____

Diagnosis_____

Initial Instructions: (1) Complete SECTION I. If the resident has pain now or has had pain recently, follow the instructions to assess each site of pain. Use another Pain Assessment Form if there are more than 2 sites of pain. (2) Complete SECTION II.

Who Answered the following questions?: (If the resident is nonverbal, ask a family member if they can answer any of the questions. If not, note "not able to obtain from resident or significant other.")

SECTION I—INDICATE THE BEST RESPONSE FOR RESIDENT ASSESSMENT:

1. COMMUNICATION: Is resident alert & oriented? ☐Yes ☐No   Can resident verbalize pain? ☐Yes ☐No
2. PAIN SITE PHYSICAL LOCATION: *Instructions:* Circle the anatomical location on the anatomy charts in SECTION II. *Number the sites of pain from 1-2* and answer the questions for that site. More than 2 sites of pain, use an additional form.

Chest Pain_____   Headache Pain_____

Back Pain: *Upper* Back_____   *Lower* Back_____   *Middle* Back_____   Hip Pain: *Right* Hip_____   *Left* Hip_____

Abdominal Pain: *Upper* Ab_____   *Lower* Ab_____   *Middle* Ab_____   Arm Pain: *Right* Arm_____   *Left* Arm_____

Leg Pain: *Right* Leg_____   *Left* Leg_____   Knee Pain: *Right* Knee_____   *Left* Knee_____

Elbow Pain: *Right* Elbow_____   *Left* Elbow_____   Shoulder Pain: *Right* Shoulder_____   *Left* Shoulder_____

_____Incision Pain (specify):_____

_____Wound Pain (specify):_____

_____Joint Pain (specify):_____

_____Other (specify):_____

PAIN SITE #1 ASSESSMENT:

1. PAIN CHARACTERISTICS: ☐Dull Pain ☐Sharp/Stabbing Pain ☐Pressure ☐Throbbing and Radiating Pain ☐Burning ☐Itching
   ☐Other (specify)_____
   ☐Pain *upon movement* (specify):_____
   ☐Pain *upon touch* (specify):_____
   ☐Other (specify):_____
2. PAIN FREQUENCY AND TIME: ☐Pain is daily ☐Pain is less than daily ☐All Times ☐Intermittent / no pattern
   Time of day_____ Pain Duration_____
3. NON-VERBAL OBSERVATIONS: ☐Anger ☐Agitation, Fidgeting and Restless   ☐Complaining ☐Sighing and/or breathing heavily
   ☐Crying, Moaning and/or Yelling   ☐Depressed, Sad and Worried Look   ☐Wincing and Wrinkled Brow
   ☐Frightened, Guarding and Withdrawn Look   ☐Muscle Rigidity, Resistive, Tense Fingers/Fist
   ☐Other (specify) _____
4. PAIN INTENSITY: Score from Pain Rating Scale: ☐Wong-Baker ☐Numerical ☐FLACC   Scale Score:_____
5. INSPECTION OF PAIN SITE: (specify findings of swelling, redness, heat, etc.) _____
   _____

PAIN SITE #1 ORIGIN AND DIAGNOSIS:

_____

PAIN SITE #2 ASSESSMENT:

1. PAIN CHARACTERISTICS: ☐Dull Pain ☐Sharp/Stabbing Pain ☐Pressure ☐Throbbing and Radiating Pain ☐Burning ☐Itching
   ☐Other (specify)_____
   ☐Pain *upon movement* (specify):_____
   ☐Pain *upon touch* (specify):_____
   ☐Other (specify):_____
2. PAIN FREQUENCY AND TIME: ☐Pain is daily ☐Pain is less than daily ☐All Times ☐Intermittent / no pattern
   Time of day_____ Pain Duration_____
3. NON-VERBAL OBSERVATIONS: ☐Anger ☐Agitation, Fidgeting and Restless   ☐Complaining ☐Sighing and/or breathing heavily
   ☐Crying, Moaning and/or Yelling   ☐Depressed, Sad and Worried Look   ☐Wincing and Wrinkled Brow
   ☐Frightened, Guarding and Withdrawn Look   ☐Muscle Rigidity, Resistive, Tense Fingers/Fist
   ☐Other (specify) _____
4. PAIN INTENSITY: Score from Pain Rating Scale: ☐Wong-Baker ☐Numerical ☐FLACC   Scale Score:_____
5. INSPECTION OF PAIN SITE: (specify findings of swelling, redness, heat, etc.) _____
   _____

PAIN SITE #2 ORIGIN AND DIAGNOSIS:
_____

SECTION II—INDICATE LOCATION OF PAIN:

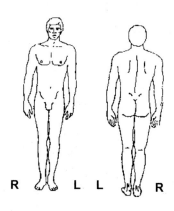

R · L   L · R

PAIN SITE #1 - PAIN MANAGEMENT HISTORY AND RESIDENT GOALS:

1. What causes or increases the pain?_____

2. What medications and other methods have been used to relieve the pain?_____

3. How well have these medications and methods worked?_____

4. What is the resident's goal for pain management? ☐Decrease pain ☐Improved mobility ☐Improved sleep
☐Other: (explain)_____

PAIN SITE #2 - PAIN MANAGEMENT HISTORY AND RESIDENT GOALS:

1. What causes or increases the pain?_____

2. What medications and other methods have been used to relieve the pain?_____

3. How well have these medications and methods worked?_____

4. What is the resident's goal for pain management? ☐Decrease pain ☐Improved mobility ☐Improved sleep
☐Other: (explain)_____

OBSERVATIONS AND/OR COMMENTS:

1. **Accompanying symptoms associated with pain:** (Example: Nausea, Headache) _____

2. **Appetite:** ☐No change ☐Loss of appetite ☐Difficult to sit and eat ☐Other: (explain)_____

3. **Sleeping:** ☐No change ☐Difficult to sleep at night ☐Other: (explain)_____

4. **Physical Activity:** ☐No change ☐Difficult to sit-up/get-up/walk ☐Non-participation in favorite activity
☐Other: (explain)_____

5. **Relationship to others:** ☐No change ☐Decrease in social action ☐Totally withdrawn from friends, family, etc.
☐Other: (explain)_____

6. **Concentration:** ☐No change ☐Loss of concentration ☐Other: _____

7. **Emotions** (complacent, agitated or aggressive behavior, etc.) ☐No change ☐Emotional change (Explain):_____

8. **Personal Hygiene:** ☐No change ☐Unable to wash, dress or perform personal care ☐Other:_____

Note: Information is to be used to formulate the Resident's Pain Treatment Plan. (Care Plan)

RN Signature_____

Source: Best Practices Committee, *HCANJ Pulse Management Guidelines*, 1/05 Revision. Health Care Association of New Jersey, Hamilton, New Jersey. Reprinted with permission.

4-36 Management of Asthma Exacerbations During Pregnancy and Lactation: Emergency Department and Hospital-Based Care*

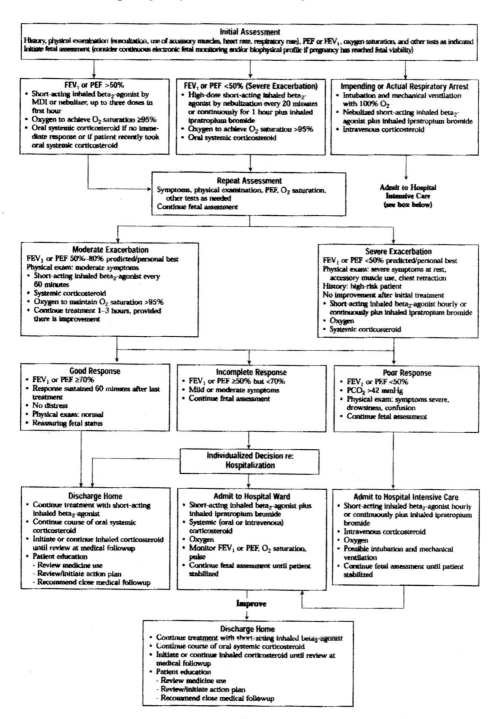

Initial Assessment
History, physical examination (auscultation, use of accessory muscles, heart rate, respiratory rate), PEF or FEV₁, oxygen saturation, and other tests as indicated
Initiate fetal assessment (consider continuous electronic fetal monitoring and/or biophysical profile if pregnancy has reached fetal viability)

FEV₁ or PEF >50%
- Short-acting inhaled beta₂-agonist by MDI or nebulizer, up to three doses in first hour
- Oxygen to achieve O₂ saturation ≥95%
- Oral systemic corticosteroid if no immediate response or if patient recently took oral systemic corticosteroid

FEV₁ or PEF <50% (Severe Exacerbation)
- High-dose short-acting inhaled beta₂-agonist by nebulization every 20 minutes or continuously for 1 hour plus inhaled ipratropium bromide
- Oxygen to achieve O₂ saturation >95%
- Oral systemic corticosteroid

Impending or Actual Respiratory Arrest
- Intubation and mechanical ventilation with 100% O₂
- Nebulized short-acting inhaled beta₂-agonist plus inhaled ipratropium bromide
- Intravenous corticosteroid

Repeat Assessment
Symptoms, physical examination, PEF, O₂ saturation, other tests as needed
Continue fetal assessment

Admit to Hospital Intensive Care
(see box below)

Moderate Exacerbation
FEV₁ or PEF 50%–80% predicted/personal best
Physical exam: moderate symptoms
- Short-acting inhaled beta₂-agonist every 60 minutes
- Systemic corticosteroid
- Oxygen to maintain O₂ saturation >95%
- Continue treatment 1–3 hours, provided there is improvement

Severe Exacerbation
FEV₁ or PEF <50% predicted/personal best
Physical exam: severe symptoms at rest, accessory muscle use, chest retraction
History: high-risk patient
No improvement after initial treatment
- Short-acting inhaled beta₂-agonist hourly or continuously plus inhaled ipratropium bromide
- Oxygen
- Systemic corticosteroid

Good Response
- FEV₁ or PEF ≥70%
- Response sustained 60 minutes after last treatment
- No distress
- Physical exam: normal
- Reassuring fetal status

Incomplete Response
- FEV₁ or PEF ≥50% but <70%
- Mild or moderate symptoms
- Continue fetal assessment

Poor Response
- FEV₁ or PEF <50%
- PCO₂ >42 mmHg
- Physical exam: symptoms severe, drowsiness, confusion
- Continue fetal assessment

Individualized Decision re: Hospitalization

Discharge Home
- Continue treatment with short-acting inhaled beta₂-agonist
- Continue course of oral systemic corticosteroid
- Initiate or continue inhaled corticosteroid until review at medical followup
- Patient education
  - Review medicine use
  - Review/initiate action plan
  - Recommend close medical followup

Admit to Hospital Ward
- Short-acting inhaled beta₂-agonist plus inhaled ipratropium bromide
- Systemic (oral or intravenous) corticosteroid
- Oxygen
- Monitor FEV₁ or PEF, O₂ saturation, pulse
- Continue fetal assessment until patient stabilized

Admit to Hospital Intensive Care
- Short-acting inhaled beta₂-agonist hourly or continuously plus inhaled ipratropium bromide
- Intravenous corticosteroid
- Oxygen
- Possible intubation and mechanical ventilation
- Continue fetal assessment until patient stabilized

Improve

Discharge Home
- Continue treatment with short-acting inhaled beta₂-agonist
- Continue course of oral systemic corticosteroid
- Initiate or continue inhaled corticosteroid until review at medical followup
- Patient education
  - Review medicine use
  - Review/initiate action plan
  - Recommend close medical followup

FEV₁, forced expiratory volume in 1 second; MDI, metered-dose inhaler; PCO₂, carbon dioxide partial pressure; PEF, peak expiratory flow.
*Adapted from EPR-2 1997.

371

Medications and Dosages for Asthma Exacerbations During Pregnancy and Lactation*

Medications	Dosages		
	Adult Dose	Child Dose	
Short-Acting Inhaled Beta₂-Agonists			
Albuterol Nebulizer solution (5.0 mg/mL, 2.5 mg/3mL, 1.25 mg/3mL, 0.63 mg/3 mL)	2.5–5 mg every 20 minutes for 3 doses, then 2.5–10 mg every 1–4 hours as needed, or 10–15 mg/hour continuously	0.15 mg/kg (minimum dose 2.5 mg) every 20 minutes for 3 doses, then 0.15–0.3 mg/kg up to 10 mg every 1–4 hours as needed, or 0.5 mg/kg/hour by continuous nebulization	Only selective beta₂-agonists are recommended. For optimal delivery, dilute aerosols to minimum of 3 mL at gas flow of 6–8 L/min.
MDI (90 mcg/puff)	4–8 puffs every 20 minutes up to 4 hours, then every 1–4 hours as needed	4–8 puffs every 20 minutes for 3 doses, then every 1–4 hours inhalation maneuver; use spacer/holding chamber	As effective as nebulized therapy if patient is able to coordinate.
Bitolterol Nebulizer solution (2 mg/mL)	See albuterol dose.	See albuterol dose; thought to be half as potent as albuterol on a mg basis.	Has not been studied in severe asthma exacerbations. Do not mix with other drugs.
MDI (370 mcg/puff)	See albuterol dose.	See albuterol dose.	Has not been studied in severe asthma exacerbations.
Levalbuterol (R-albuterol) Nebulizer solution (0.63 mg/3 mL, 1.25 mg/3 mL)	1.25–2.5 mg every 20 minutes for 3 doses, then 1.25–5 mg every 1–4 hours as needed, or 5–7.5 mg/hour continuously	0.075 mg/kg (minimum dose 1.25 mg) every 20 minutes for 3 doses, then 0.075–0.15 mg/kg up to 5 mg every 1–4 hours as needed, or 0.25 mg/kg/hour by continuous nebulization	0.63 mg of levalbuterol is equivalent to 1.25 mg of racemic albuterol for both efficacy and side effects.
Pirbuterol MDI (200 mcg/puff)	See albuterol dose.	See albuterol dose; thought to be half as potent as albuterol on a mg basis.	Has not been studied in severe asthma exacerbations.
Systemic (Injected) Beta₂-Agonists			
Epinephrine 1:1000 (1 mg/mL)	0.3–0.5 mg every 20 minutes for 3 doses sq	0.01 mg/kg up to 0.3–0.5 mg every 20 minutes for 3 doses sq	No proven advantage of systemic therapy over aerosol.
Terbutaline (1 mg/mL)	0.25 mg every 20 minutes for 3 doses sq	0.01 mg/kg every 20 minutes for 3 doses, then every 2–6 hours as needed sq	No proven advantage of systemic therapy over aerosol.
Anticholinergics			
Ipratropium bromide Nebulizer solution (0.25 mg/mL)	0.5 mg every 30 minutes for 3 doses, then every 2–4 hours as needed	0.25 mg every 20 minutes for 3 doses, then every 2 to 4 hours	May mix in same nebulizer with albuterol. Should not be used as first-line therapy; should be added to beta₂-agonist therapy.
MDI (18 mcg/puff)	4–8 puffs as needed	4–8 puffs as needed	Dose delivered from MDI is low and has not been studied in asthma exacerbations.
Ipratropium with albuterol Nebulizer solution (Each 3 mL vial contains 0.5 mg ipratropium bromide and 2.5 mg albuterol)	3 mL every 30 minutes for 3 doses, then every 2–4 hours as needed	1.5 mL every 20 minutes for 3 doses, then every 2–4 hours	Contains EDTA to prevent discoloration. This additive does not induce bronchospasm.
MDI (Each puff contains 18 mcg ipratropium bromide and 90 mcg albuterol)	4–8 puffs as needed	4–8 puffs as needed	
Systemic Corticosteroids	(Dosages and comments apply to all three corticosteroids)		
Prednisone **Methylprednisolone** **Prednisolone**	120–180 mg/day in 3 or 4 divided doses for 48 hours, then 60–80 mg/day until PEF reaches 70% of predicted or personal best	1 mg/kg every 6 hours for 48 hours, then 1–2 mg/kg/day (maximum = 60 mg/day) in 2 divided doses until PEF is 70% of predicted or personal best	For outpatient "burst" use 40–60 mg in single or 2 divided doses for adults (children: 1–2 mg/kg/day, maximum 60 mg/day) for 3–10 days.

* Adapted from EPR—Update 2002.
Notes: • The most important determinant of appropriate dosing is the clinician's judgment of the patient's response to therapy.
  • No advantage has been found for higher dose corticosteroids in severe asthma exacerbations, nor is there any advantage for intravenous administration over oral therapy provided gastrointestinal transit time or absorption is not impaired. The usual regimen is to continue the frequent multiple daily dose until the patient achieves an FEV_1 or PEF of 50 percent of predicted or personal best and then lower the dose to twice daily. This usually occurs within 48 hours. Therapy following a hospitalization or emergency department visit may last from 3 to 10 days. If patients are then started on inhaled corticosteroids, studies indicate there is no need to taper the systemic corticosteroid dose. If the followup systemic corticosteroid therapy is to be given once daily, one study indicates that it may be more clinically effective to give the dose in the afternoon at 3 p.m., with no increase in adrenal suppression.[54]

Source: National Asthma Education and Prevention Program Working Group Report on Managing Asthma During Pregnancy: Recommendations for Pharmacologic Treatment Update 2004. U.S. Department of Health and Human Services, National Institutes of Health, National Heart, Lung, and Blood Institute. NIH Publication No. 05-5246. Originally Printed March 2004. Revised January 2005.

4-37 Guidelines for the Inter- and Intra-Hospital Transport of Critically Ill Patients*

These guidelines have been developed by the American College of Critical Care Medicine and the Society of Critical Care Medicine. These guidelines reflect the official opinion of the Society of Critical Care Medicine and do not necessarily reflect, and should not be construed to reflect, the views of certification bodies, regulatory agencies, or other medical review organizations.

The decision to transport a critically ill patient, either within a hospital or to another facility, is based on an assessment of the potential benefits of transport weighed against the potential risks. Critically ill patients are transported to alternate locations to obtain additional care, whether technical, cognitive, or procedural, that is not available at the existing location. Provision of this additional care may require patient transport to a diagnostic department, operating room, or specialized care unit within a hospital, or it may require transfer to another hospital. If a diagnostic test or procedural intervention under consideration is unlikely to alter the management or outcome of that patient, then the need for transport must be questioned. When feasible and safe, diagnostic testing or simple procedures in unstable or potentially unstable patients often can be performed at the bedside in the intensive care unit (1, 2). Financial considerations are not a factor when contemplating moving a critically ill patient.

Critically ill patients are at increased risk of morbidity and mortality during transport (3–17). Risk can be minimized and outcomes improved with careful planning, the use of appropriately qualified personnel, and selection and availability of appropriate equipment (16–37). During transport, there is no hiatus in the monitoring or maintenance of a patient's vital functions. Furthermore, the accompanying personnel and equipment are selected by training to provide for any ongoing or anticipated acute care needs of the patient.

Ideally, all critical care transports, both inter- and intrahospital, are performed by specially trained individuals. Since there will almost certainly be situations when a specialized team is not available for interhospital transport, each referring and tertiary institution must develop contingency plans using locally available resources for those instances when the referring facility cannot perform the transport. A comprehensive and effective interhospital transfer plan can be developed using a systematic approach comprised of four critical elements:

a) A multidisciplinary team of physicians, nurses, respiratory therapists, hospital administration, and the local emergency medical service is formed to plan and coordinate the process;

b) the team conducts a needs assessment of the facility that focuses on patient demographics, transfer volume, transfer patterns, and available resources (personnel, equipment, emergency medical service, communication);

c) with this data, a written standardized transfer plan is developed and implemented; and

*Warren, J., Fromm, R.E., Jr., Orr, R.A., Rotello, L.C., Horst, M., & American College of Critical Care Medicine (2004). Guidelines for the inter- and intrahospital transport of critically ill patients. *Crit Care Med* 32:256-262. Reprinted with permission from Lippincott, Williams & Wilkins.

d) the transfer plan is evaluated and refined regularly using a standard quality improvement process.

This document outlines the minimum recommendations for transport of the critically ill patient. Detailed guidelines targeted to the transport of infants and children have been published by the American Academy of Pediatrics (23). Institutions performing commercial or organized interhospital transports are required to function at and meet a higher standard, as the requirements for organized transport services are considerably more rigorous than the recommendations in this guideline (24, 38–41).

The references for this guideline were obtained from a review of Index Medicus from January 1986 through October 2001 and are categorized according to the degree of evidence-based data employed. The specific category assigned to each reference is noted in the References at the end of this article. The letter *a* denotes a randomized, prospective controlled investigation; *b* denotes a nonrandomized, concurrent, or historical cohort investigation; *c* denotes a peer-reviewed "state-of-the-art" article, review article, editorial, or substantial case series; and *d* denotes a non-peer reviewed opinion such as a textbook statement or official organizational publication. The asterisk symbol will follow a statement of practice standards. This indicates a recommendation by the American College of Critical Care Medicine that is based on expert opinion and is used in circumstances where published supporting data are unavailable.

INTRAHOSPITAL TRANSPORT

Because the transport of critically ill patients to procedures or tests outside the intensive care unit is potentially hazardous, the transport process must be organized and efficient. To provide for this, at least four concerns need to be addressed through written intensive care unit policies and procedures: communication, personnel, equipment, and monitoring.

Pretransport Coordination and Communication

When an alternate team at a receiving location will assume management responsibility for the patient after arrival, continuity of patient care will be ensured by physician-to-physician and/or nurse-to-nurse communication to review patient condition and the treatment plan in operation. This communication occurs each time patient care responsibility is transferred. Before transport, the receiving location confirms that it is ready to receive the patient for immediate procedure or testing. Other members of the healthcare team (e.g., respiratory therapy, hospital security) then are notified as to the timing of the transport and the equipment support that will be needed. The responsible physician is made aware of the transport. Documentation in the medical record includes the indications for transport and patient status throughout the time away from the unit of origin.

Accompanying Personnel

It is strongly recommended that a minimum of two people accompany a critically ill patient.* One of the accompanying personnel is usually a nurse who has completed a competency-based orientation and has met previously described standards for critical care nurses (42, 43). Additional personnel may include a respiratory therapist, registered nurse, or critical care technician as needed. It is strongly recommended that a physician with training in airway management and advanced cardiac life support, and critical care training or equivalent, accompany unstable patients.* When the procedure is anticipated to be lengthy and the receiving location is staffed by appropriately trained personnel, patient care may be transferred to those individuals if acceptable to both parties. This allows for maximum utilization of staff and resources. If care is not transferred, the transport personnel will remain with the patient until returned to the intensive care unit.

Accompanying Equipment

A blood pressure monitor (or standard blood pressure cuff), pulse oximeter, and cardiac monitor/defibrillator accompany every patient without exception.* When available, a memory-capable monitor with the capacity for storing and reproducing patient bedside data will allow review of data collected during the procedure and transport. Equipment for airway management, sized appropriately for each patient, is also transported with each patient, as is an oxygen source of ample supply to provide for projected needs plus a 30-min reserve.

Basic resuscitation drugs, including epinephrine and antiarrhythmic agents, are transported with each patient in the event of sudden cardiac arrest or arrhythmia. A more complete array of pharmacologic agents either accompanies the basic agents or is available from supplies ("crash carts") located along the transport route and at the receiving location. Supplemental medications, such as sedatives and narcotic analgesics, are considered in each specific case. An ample supply of appropriate intravenous fluids and continuous drip medications (regulated by battery-operated infusion pumps) is ensured. All battery-operated equipment is fully charged and capable of functioning for the duration of the transport. If a physician will not be accompanying the patient during transport, protocols must be in place to permit the administration of these medications and fluids by appropriately trained personnel under emergency circumstances.

In many hospitals, pediatric patients share diagnostic and procedural facilities with adult patients. Under these circumstances, a complete set of pediatric resuscitation equipment and medications will accompany infants and children during transport and also will be available in the diagnostic or procedure area.

For practical reasons, bag-valve ventilation is most commonly employed during intrahospital transports. Portable mechanical ventilators are gaining increasing popularity in this arena, as they more reliably administer prescribed minute ventilation and desired oxygen concentrations. In adults and children, a default oxygen concentration of 100% generally is used. However, oxygen concentration must be precisely regulated for neonates and for those patients with congenital heart disease who have single ventricle physiology or are dependent on a right-to-left shunt to maintain systemic blood flow. For patients requiring mechanical ventilation, equipment is optimally available at the receiving location capable of delivering ventilatory support equivalent to that being delivered at the patient's origin. In mechanically ventilated patients, endotracheal tube position is noted and secured before transport, and the adequacy of oxygenation and ventilation is reconfirmed. Occasionally patients may require modes of ventilation or ventilator settings not reproducible at the receiving location or during transportation. Under these circumstances, the origin location must trial alternate modes of mechanical ventilation before transport to ensure acceptability and patient stability with this therapy. If the patient is incapable of being maintained safely with alternate therapy, the risks and benefits of transport are cautiously reexamined. If a transport ventilator is to be employed, it must have alarms to indicate disconnection and excessively high airway pressures and must have a backup battery power supply.*

Monitoring During Transport

All critically ill patients undergoing transport receive the same level of basic physiologic monitoring during transport as they had in the intensive care unit. This includes, at a minimum, continuous electrocardiographic monitoring, continuous pulse oximetry (44), and periodic measurement of blood pressure, pulse rate, and respiratory rate. In addition, selected patients may benefit from capnography, continuous intra-arterial blood pressure, pulmonary artery pressure, or intracranial pressure monitoring. There may be special circumstances that warrant intermittent cardiac output or pulmonary artery occlusion pressure measurements.

INTERHOSPITAL TRANSPORT

Patient outcomes depend to a large degree on the technology and expertise of personnel available within each healthcare facility. When services are needed that exceed available resources, a patient ideally will be transferred to a facility that has the required resources (45). Interhospital patient transfers occur when the benefits to the patient exceed the risks of the transfer. A decision to transfer a patient is the responsibility of the attending physician at the referring institution. Once this decision has been made, the transfer is effected as soon as possible. When needed, resuscitation and stabilization will begin before the transfer (46, 47), realizing that complete stabilization may be possible only at the receiving facility.

In the United States, it is essential for practitioners to be aware of federal and state laws regarding interhospital patient transfers. The Emergency Medical Treatment and Active Labor Act (EMTALA) laws and regulations (updated at intervals from the 1986 COBRA laws and the 1990 OBRA amendment) define in detail the legal responsibilities of the transferring and receiving facilities and practitioners. The American College of Emergency Physicians has published a book (48) that reviews the legal responsibilities of referring institutions as well as the ramifications of noncompliance with the COBRA/EMTALA regulations, and it is an excellent resource for any facility involved in patient transfers. In general, under COBRA/EMTALA, financially motivated transfers are illegal and put both the referring institution and the individual practitioner at risk for serious penalty (49, 50).

Current regulations and good medical practice require that a competent patient, guardian, or the legally authorized representative of an incompetent patient give informed consent before interhospital transfer. The informed consent process includes a discussion of the risks and benefits of transfer. These discussions are documented in the medical record before transfer. A signed consent should be obtained, if possible. If circumstance do not allow for the informed consent process (e.g., life-threatening emergency), then both the indications for transfer and the reason for not obtaining consent are documented in the medical record. The referring physician always writes an order for transfer in the medical record.

Several elements are included in the process of interhospital transfer, and all fall within minimum guidelines, as described subsequently. It is important to recognize that these process elements may frequently, and out of necessity, be implemented simultaneously, especially when stabilization and treatment are needed before transfer. An algorithm has been developed to guide practitioners through the transfer process (Fig. 1).

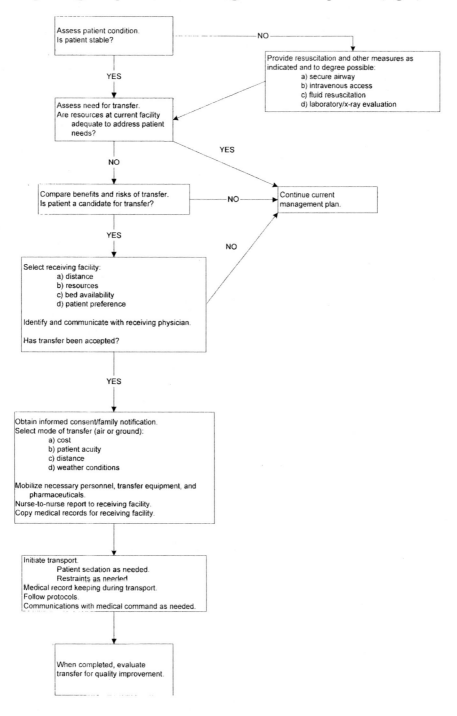

Pretransport Coordination and Communication

The referring physician will identify and contact an admitting physician at the receiving hospital to accept the patient in transfer and confirm before the transfer occurs that appropriate higher level resources are available. The receiving physician is given a full description of the patient's condition. At that time, advice can be requested concerning treatment and stabilization before transport. The appropriateness of transferring a patient from an inpatient setting (critical care unit) to an outpatient setting (e.g., emergency department) at a receiving institution must be cautiously examined. If a physician will not be accompanying the patient during transport (34), the referring and accepting physicians will ensure there is a command physician for the transport team who will assume responsibility for medical treatment during the transport. It may be appropriate for this individual to receive a medical report before the team departs.

In some instances (e.g., when a receiving institution provides the transport team), the receiving physician may determine the mode of transport. However, the mode of transportation (ground or air) usually is determined by the transferring physician, in consultation with the receiving physician, based on the urgency of the medical condition (stability of the patient), time savings anticipated with air transport, weather conditions, medical interventions necessary for ongoing life support during transfer, and the availability of personnel and resources (51, 52). The transport service then will be contacted to confirm its availability, to prepare for anticipated patient needs during transport, and to coordinate the timing of the transport.

A nurse-to-nurse report is given by the referring facility to the appropriate nursing unit at the receiving hospital. Alternatively, the report can be given by a transport team member at the time of arrival. A copy of the medical record, including a patient care summary and all relevant laboratory and radiographic studies, will accompany the patient. The preparation of records should not delay patient transport, however, as these records can be forwarded separately (by facsimile or courier) if and when the urgency of transfer precludes their assemblage beforehand. Under these circumstances, the most critical information is communicated verbally. It is strongly suggested that policies be established within each institution regarding the content of documentation and communication between personnel involved in the transfer.

Accompanying Personnel

It is recommended that a minimum of two people, in addition to the vehicle operators, accompany a critically ill patient during interhospital transport.* When transporting unstable patients, the transport team leader should be a physician or nurse (41, 53, 54), preferably with additional training in transport medicine. For critical but stable patients, the team leader may be a paramedic (41). These individuals provide the essential capabilities of advanced airway management, intravenous therapy, dysrhythmia interpretation and treatment, and basic and advanced cardiac life support. In the absence of a physician team member, there will be a mechanism by which the transport team can communicate with a command physician. If communication of this type becomes impossible, the team will have preauthorization by standing orders to perform acute lifesaving interventions. In the absence of a readily available external transport team, a transport team and vehicle may need to be assembled locally. The development of policies and procedures for such emergencies is strongly recommended.

Minimum Equipment Required

Tables 1 and 2 provide a detailed list of the minimum recommended equipment and pharmaceuticals needed for safe interhospital transport. Emphasis is placed on airway and oxygenation, vital signs monitoring, and the pharmaceutical agents necessary for emergency resuscitation and stabilization as well as maintenance of vital functions. Very short or very long transports may necessitate deviations from the listed items, depending on the severity and nature of illness or injury. Furthermore, advances in knowledge over time will result in periodic review and modification of these lists. All items are checked regularly for expiration of sterility and/or potency, especially when transports are infrequent. Equipment function is verified on a scheduled basis, not at the time of transport when there may be insufficient time to find replacements.

Table 1. Recommended minimum transport equipment

Airway management/oxygenation—adult and pediatric
Adult and pediatric bag-valve systems with oxygen reservoir
Adult and pediatric masks for bag-valve system (multiple sizes as appropriate)
Flexible adaptors to connect bag-valve system to endotracheal/tracheostomy tube
End-tidal carbon dioxide monitors (pediatric and adult)
Infant medium- and high-concentration masks with tubing
MacIntosh laryngoscope blades (#1, #2, #3, #4)
Miller laryngoscope blades (#0, #1, #2)
Endotracheal tube stylets (adult and pediatric)
Magil forceps (adult and pediatric)
Booted hemostat
Cuffed endotracheal tubes (5.0, 5.5, 6.0, 6.5, 7.0, 7.5, 8.0)
Uncuffed endotracheal tubes (2.5, 3.0, 3.5, 4.0, 4.5, 5.0)
Laryngoscope handles (adult and pediatric)
Extra laryngoscope batteries and light bulbs
Nasopharyngeal airways (#26, #30)
Oral airways (#0, #1, #2, #3, #4)
Scalpel with blade for cricothyroidotomy
Needle cricothyroidotomy kit
Water-soluble lubricant
Nasal cannulas (adult and pediatric)
Oxygen tubing
PEEP valve (adjustable)
Adhesive tape
Aerosol medication delivery system (nebulizer)
Alcohol swabs
Arm boards (adult and pediatric)
Arterial line tubing
Bone marrow needle (for pediatric infusion)
Blood pressure cuffs (neonatal, infant, child, adult large and small)
Butterfly needles (23-gauge, 25-gauge)
Communications backup (e.g., cellular telephone)
Defibrillator electrolyte pads or jelly
Dextrostix
ECG monitor/defibrillator (preferably with pressure transducer capabilities)
ECG electrodes (infant, pediatric, adult)
Flashlights with extra batteries
Heimlich valve
Infusion pumps
Intravenous fluid administration tubing (adult and pediatric)
Y-blood administration tubing
Extension tubing
Three-way stopcocks
Intravenous catheters, sizes 14- to 24-gauge

379

Intravenous solutions (plastic bags)
1000 mL, 500 mL of normal saline
1000 mL of Ringers lactate
250 mL of 5% dextrose
Irrigating syringe (60 mL), catheter tip
Kelley clamp
Hypodermic needles, assorted sizes
Hypodermic syringes, assorted sizes
Normal saline for irrigation
Pressure bags for fluid administration
Pulse oximeter with multiple site adhesive or reusable sensors
Salem sump nasogastric tubes, assorted sizes
Soft restraints for upper and lower extremities
Stethoscope
Suction apparatus
Suction catheters (#5, #8, #10, #14, tonsil)
Surgical dressings (sponges, Kling, Kerlix)
Tourniquets for venipuncture/IV access
Trauma scissors
The following are considered as needed:
Transcutaneous pacemaker
Neonatal/pediatric isolette
Spinal immobilization device
Transport ventilator
PEEP, positive end-expiratory pressure; ECG, electrocardiogram; IV, intravenous.

Table 2. Recommended minimum transport medications

Adenosine, 6 mg/2 mL
Albuterol, 2.5 mg/2 mL
Amiodarone, 150 mg/3 mL
Atropine, 1 mg/10 mL
Calcium chloride, 1 g/10 mL
Cetacaine/Hurricane spray
Dextrose 25%, 10 mL
Dextrose 50%, 50 mL
Digoxin, 0.5 mg/2 mL
Diltiazem, 25 mg/5 mL
Diphenhydramine, 50 mg/1 mL
Dopamine, 200 mg/5 mL
Epinephrine, 1 mg/10 mL (1:10,000)
Epinephrine, 1 mg/1 mL (1:1000) multiple-dose vial
Fosphenytoin, 750 mg/10 mL (500 PE mg/10 mL)
Furosemide, 100 mg/10 mL
Glucagon, 1 mg vial (powder)
Heparin, 1000 units/1 mL
Isoproterenol, 1 mg/5 mL
Labetalol, 40 mg/8 mL
Lidocaine, 100 mg/10 mL
Lidocaine, 2 g/10 mL
Mannitol, 50 g/50 mL
Magnesium sulfate, 1 g/2 mL
Methylprednisolone, 125 mg/2 mL
Metoprolol, 5 mg/5 mL
Naloxone, 2 mg/2 mL
Nitroglycerin injection, 50 mg/10 mL
Nitroglycerin tablets, 0.4 mg (bottle)
Nitroprusside, 50 mg/2 mL
Normal saline, 30 mL for injection
Phenobarbital, 65 mg/mL or 130 mg/mL
Potassium chloride, 20 mEq/10 mL
Procainamide, 1000 mg/10 mL
Sodium bicarbonate, 5 mEq/10 mL
Sodium bicarbonate, 50 mEq/50 mL
Sterile water, 30 mL for injection
Terbutaline, 1 mg/1 mL
Verapamil, 5 mg/2 mL

380

The following specialized/controlled medications are added immediately before transport as indicated:
Narcotic analgesics (e.g., morphine, fentanyl) (59)
Sedatives/hypnotics (e.g., lorazepam, midazolam, propofol, etomidate, ketamine) (59)
Neuromuscular blocking agents (e.g. succinylcholine, pancuronium, atracurium, rocuronium) (60)
Prostaglandin E1
Pulmonary surfactant

Monitoring During Transport

All critically ill patients undergoing interhospital transport must have, at a minimum, continuous pulse oximetry, electrocardiographic monitoring, and regular measurement of blood pressure and respiratory rate.* Selected patients, based on clinical status, may benefit from the monitoring of intra-arterial blood pressure (55), central venous pressure, pulmonary artery pressure, intracranial pressure, and/or capnography (56). With mechanically ventilated patients, endotracheal tube position is noted and secured before transport, and the adequacy of oxygenation and ventilation is reconfirmed.

Occasionally, patients may require specialized modes of ventilation not reproducible in the transport setting. Under these circumstances, alternate modes of mechanical ventilation are evaluated before transport to ensure acceptability and patient stability with this therapy. If the patient is incapable of being maintained safely with alternate ventilator therapy, the risks and benefits of transport are cautiously reexamined. Patient status and management during transport are recorded and filed in the patient medical record at the referring facility. Copies are provided to the receiving institution.

Preparing a Patient for Interhospital Transport

There is no evidence to support a "scoop and run" approach to the interhospital transport of critically ill patients. Therefore, referring facilities will, before transport, begin appropriate evaluation and stabilization to the degree possible to ensure patient safety during transport. Unnecessary delays may be experienced if the transport team must perform lengthy or complex procedures to stabilize the patient before the transfer (57). Nonessential testing and procedures will delay transfer and should be avoided. Information and recommendations about this aspect of patient care generally can be requested from the accepting physician at the time of initial contact with the receiving facility.

All critically ill patients need secure intravenous access before transport. If peripheral venous access is unavailable, central venous access is established. If needed, fluid resuscitation and inotropic support are initiated, with all intravenous fluids and medications maintained in plastic (not glass) containers. A patient should not be transported before airway stabilization if it is judged likely that airway intervention will be needed en route (a process made more difficult in a moving vehicle). The airway must be evaluated before transport and secured as indicated by endotracheal tube (or tracheostomy).* Laryngeal mask airways are not an acceptable method of airway management for critically ill patients undergoing transport. For trauma victims, spinal immobilization is maintained during transport unless the absence of significant spinal injury has been reliably verified. A nasogastric tube is inserted in patients with an ileus or intestinal obstruction and in those requiring mechanical ventilation. A Foley catheter is inserted in patients requiring strict fluid management, for transports of extended duration, and for patients receiving diuretics. If indicated, chest decompression with a chest tube is accomplished before transport. A Heimlich valve or vacuum chest drainage system is employed to maintain decompression. Soft wrist and/or leg restraints are applied when agitation could compromise the safety of the patient or transport crew, especially with air transport. If the patient is combative or uncooperative, the use of sedative and/or neuromuscular blocking agents may be indicated. A neuromuscular blocking agent should not be used without sedation and analgesia.

Finally, the patient medical record and relevant laboratory and radiographic studies are copied for the receiving facility. In the United States, a COBRA/EMTALA checklist is strongly suggested to ensure compliance with all federal regulations regarding interhospital patient transfers. Items on this checklist will include documentation of initial medical evaluation and stabilization (to the degree possible), informed consent disclosing benefits and risks of transfer, medical indications for the transfer, and physician-to-physician communication with the names of the accepting physician and the receiving hospital.

REFERENCES

1. Porter JM, Ivatury RR, Kavarana M, et al: The surgical intensive care unit as a cost-efficient substitute for an operating room at a Level I trauma center. *Am Surg* 1999; 65:328–330(c).

2. McCunn M, Mirvis S, Reynolds N, et al: Physician utilization of a portable computed tomography scanner in the intensive care unit. *Crit Care Med* 2000; 28:3808–3813 (b).

3. Waydas C: Intrahospital transport of critically ill patients. *Crit Care* 1999; 3:R83–R89 (c).

4. Blumen IJ, Abernethy MK, Dunne MJ: Flight physiology. Clinical considerations. *Crit Care Clin* 1992; 8:597–618 (c).

5. Olson CM, Jastremski MS, Vilogi JP, et al: Stabilization of patients prior to interhospital transport. *Am J Emerg Med* 1987; 5:33–39 (c).

6. Braman SS, Dunn SM, Amico CA, et al: Complications of intrahospital transport in critically ill patients. *Ann Intern Med* 1987; 107:469–473 (a).

7. Smith I, Fleming S, Cernaiana A: Mishaps during transport from the intensive care unit. *Crit Care Med* 1990; 18:278–281 (b).

8. Insel J, Weissman C, Kemper M, et al: Cardiovascular changes during transport of critically ill and postoperative patients. *Crit Care Med* 1986; 14:539–542 (b).

9. Ehrenwerth J, Sorbo S, Hackel A: Transport of critically ill adults. *Crit Care Med* 1986; 14:543–547 (b).

10. Andrews P, Piper I, Dearden N, et al: Secondary insults during intrahospital transport of head-injured patients. *Lancet* 1990; 335: 327–330 (b).

11. Gentlemen D, Jennett B: Audit of transfer of unconscious head-injured patients to a neurosurgical unit. *Lancet* 1990; 335:330–334 (c).

12. Kanter R, Tompkins J: Adverse events during interhospital transport: Physiologic deterioration associated with pretransport severity of illness. *Pediatrics* 1989; 84:43–48 (b).

13. Katz V, Hansen A: Complications in the emergency transport of pregnant women. *South Med J* 1990; 83:7–9 (c).

14. Martin G, Cogbill T, Landercasper J, et al: Prospective analysis of rural interhospital transfer of injured patients to a referral trauma center. *J Trauma* 1990; 30:1014–1020 (b).

15. Valenzuela T, Criss E, Copass M, et al: Critical care air transportation of the severely injured: Does long distance transport adversely affect survival? *Ann Emerg Med* 1990; 19:169–172 (b).

16. Harrahil M, Bartkus E: Preparing the trauma patient for transfer. *J Emerg Nurs* 1990; 16:25–28 (d).

17. LaPlant G, Gaffney T: Helicopter transport of the patient receiving thrombolytic therapy. *J Emerg Nurs* 1989; 15:196–200 (c).

18. Gore JM: Feasibility and safety of emergency interhospital transport of patients during the early hours of acute myocardial infarction. *Arch Int Med* 1989; 149:353–355 (b).

19. Weg JG, Haas CF: Safe intrahospital transport of critically ill ventilator dependent patients. *Chest* 1989; 96:631–635 (b).

20. Anderson C: Preparing patients for aeromedical transport. *J Emerg Nurs* 1987; 13:229–231 (c).

21. Greco A: Development of an interfacility transport program for critically ill cardiovascular patients. *Clin Issues Crit Care Nurs* 1990; 1:3–12 (c).

22. Hackel, A: Critical care transport. *Int Anesthesiol Clin* 1987; 25:1–137 (c).

23. Task Force on Interhospital Transport: Guidelines for air and ground transport of neonatal and pediatric patients. American Academy of Pediatrics, 1999 (d).

24. American Academy of Pediatrics Committee on Hospital Care: Guidelines for air and ground transportation of pediatric patients. *Pediatrics* 1986; 78:943–950 (c).

25. Fromm RE, Dellinger RP: Transport of critically ill patients. *J Int Care Med* 1992; 7:223–233 (c).

26. Lee G: Transport of the critically ill trauma patient. *Nurs Clin North Am* 1986; 21:741–749 (c).

27. Maxwell B, Miller B: Smooth the way for safe emergency transfers. *RN* 1988; 6:34–37 (d).

28. McCloskey K, King WL, Byron L: Pediatric critical care transport: Is a physician always needed on the team? *Ann Emerg Med* 1989; 18:247–250 (b).

29. Larson D, Mellstrom M: Management of multiple trauma in a rural setting. *Minn Med* 1987; 70:43–45 (c).

30. Blumen I, Gordon R: Taking to the skies. *Emergency* 1989; 21:32–38, 54–55 (c).

31. Kruse D: Interhospital transfer. How to prepare your patient. *Nursing* 1991; 21:41 (c).

32. Runcie CJ, Reeve W, Reidy J, et al: Secondary transport of the critically ill adult. *Clin Intensive Care* 1991; 2:217–225 (c).

33. Venkataraman ST, Orr RA: Intrahospital transport of critically ill patients. *Crit Care Clin* 1992; 8:525–531 (c).

34. McCloskey KA, Johnston C: Critical care interhospital transport: Predictability of the need for a pediatrician. *Pediatr Emerg Care* 1990; 6:89–92 (b).

35. Rubenstein JS, Gomez MA, Rybicki L, et al: Can the need for a physician as part of the pediatric transport team be predicted? A prospective study. *Crit Care Med* 1992; 20:1657–1661 (b).

36. Selevan JS, Fields WW, Chen W, et al: Critical care transport: Outcome evaluation after interfacility transfer and hospitalization. *Ann Emerg Med* 1999; 33:33–43 (b).

37. Warren J, Guntupalli KK: Physiologic monitoring during prehospital and interhospital transport of critically ill patients. *In:* Problems in Critical Care. Kirby RR, Taylor RW, Fromm RE (Eds.). Philadelphia, PA, Lippincott, 1990, pp 459–469 (c).

38. Critical Care Air Ambulance Service. *In:* Resources for Optimal Care of the Injured Patient. Chicago, IL, American College of Surgeons, 1990 (d).

39. Interhospital Transport of Patients. *In:* Resources for Optimal Care of the Injured Patient. Chicago, IL, American College of Surgeons, 1990 (d).

40. American College of Emergency Physicians. Principles of appropriate patient transfer. *Ann Emerg Med* 1990; 19:337–338 (d).

41. Commission on Accreditation of Medical Transport Systems (CAMTS). Accreditation Standards. Fourth Edition. CAMTS, 1999 (d).

42. American Association of Critical Care Nurses: AACN Competence Statements for Differentiating Nursing Practice in Critical Care. Newport Beach, CA, AACN, 1989, pp 2–7 (d).

43. Alspach, JG: Designing a competency-based orientation for critical care nurses. *Heart Lung* 1984; 13:655–662 (c).

44. Meiklejohn BH, Smith G, Elling AE, et al: Arterial oxygen desaturation during post-operative transportation: The influence of operation site. *Anaesthesia* 1987; 421313–1315 (c).

45. Task Force on Guidelines Society of Critical Care Medicine: Guidelines for categorization for services for the critically ill patient. *Crit Care Med* 1991; 19:279–285 (d).

46. Henderson A, Coyne T, Wall D, et al: A survey of interhospital transfer of head-injured patients with inadequately treated life-threatening extracranial injuries. *Aust N Z J Surg* 1992; 62:759–762 (b).

47. Lambert SM, Willett K: Transfer of multiply injured patients for neurosurgical opinion: A study of the adequacy of assessment and resuscitation. *Injury* 1993; 24:333–336 (c).

48. Frew SA: Patient Transfers. How to comply with the law. Dallas, TX, American College of Emergency Physicians, 1990 (d).

49. Dunn JD: Legal aspects of transfers. *In:* Problems in Critical Care. Critical Care Transport. Fromm RE (Ed). Philadelphia, PA, Lippincott, 1990 (d).

50. Public Law 99-272, U. S. Government Printing Office, 42 U. S. Code Service, 135 dd. Washington, DC, Lawyer Cooperative Publishing Company, 1986 (d).

51. Boyd CR, Corse KM, Campbell RC: Emergency intrahospital transport of the major trauma patient: Air versus ground. *J Trauma* 1989; 29:789–793 (b).

52. Werman HA, Falcane RA, Shaner S, et al: Helicopter transport of patients to tertiary care centers after cardiac arrest. *Am J Emerg Med* 1999; 17:130–134 (c).

53. Connolly HV, Fetcho S, Hageman JR: Education of personnel involved in the transport program. *Crit Care Clin* 1992; 8:481–490 (c).

54. Burtnyk S: Secondary transportation of critically ill people—Implications for nurses and the need for specialist training. *Intensive Crit Care Nurs* 1992; 8:234–239 (c).

55. Runcie CJ, Reave WG, Reidy J, et al: Blood pressure measurement during transport. *Anaesthesia* 1990; 45:659–665 (b).

56. Tobias JD, Lynch A, Garrett J: Alterations of end-tidal carbon dioxide during the intrahospital transport of children. *Pediatr Emerg Care* 1996; 12:249–251 (b).

57. Beddingfield FC, Garrison MG, Manning JE, et al: Factors associated with prolongation of transport times of emergency pediatric patients requiring transfer to a tertiary care center. *Pediatr Emerg Care* 1996; 12:416–419 (c).

58. Murray M, Cowen J, DeBlock H, et al: Clinical practice guidelines for sustained neuromuscular blockade in the adult critically ill patient. *Crit Care Med* 2002; 30:142–156 (d).

59. Shapiro BA, Warren J, Egol AB, et al: Practice parameters for intravenous analgesia and sedation for adult patients in the intensive care unit: An executive summary. *Crit Care Med* 1995; 23:1596–1600 (d).

60. Shapiro BA, Warren J, Egol AB, et al: Practice parameters for sustained neuromuscular blockade in the adult critically ill patient: An executive summary. *Crit Care Med* 1995; 23: 1601–1605 (d).

CARE OF PATIENTS

4-38 Definitions for Level of Care Needed

PURPOSE

To clarify the terms used in the ED for the urgency of care needed. To rapidly assess and sort patients so as to expedite the sickest patients back into the ED as fast as possible while expeditiously placing other patients into the appropriate level and order of care.

POLICY

EMERGENT

Sudden onset of a medical condition manifesting itself by acute symptoms of sufficient severity (including severe pain) that the absence of immediate medical attention could reasonably be expected to result in a) the patient's health being placed in serious jeopardy, b) serious impairment to bodily functions, and/or c) serious dysfunction of any bodily organ or part.

PRIORITY 1—EMERGENT: NEED TO BE SEEN IMMEDIATELY, NOTIFY ER PHYSICIAN

Any condition requiring evaluation and/or treatment within a short period of time to prevent disability or physical impairment, not meeting the above requirements. Severe pain possibly indicative of a serious medical problem.

PRIORITY 2—MORE EMERGENT: (Keep in Triage Hold area after Triage OR MOVE TO MEDICAL HOLDING ROOM)

Need to be seen quickly by the ER physician and immediately by the nurse.

PRIORITY 3—SEEN BY ER PHYSICIAN AND NURSE IN A TIMELY MANNER. PATIENTS CAN BE SENT TO ER ADMISSION AFTER TRIAGE AND WAITING ROOM.

LESS URGENT: After Triage can return to Waiting Room to register. Conditions not appearing severe but likely to require IV therapy and/or significant workups.

PRIORITY 4—ERB NON-URGENT

Patients presenting themselves to the ED for primary care.

EXCLUSION CRITERIA: AT THE DISCRETION OF THE TRIAGE NURSE/ CHARGE NURSE

Less than 3 months of age
Greater than 60 years old with a medical complaint
Vaginal complaints
Complaints associated with pregnancy

Source: Courtesy of Parkview Medical Center, Pueblo, Colorado.

4-39 Restraint Record: Alternatives Attempted

Date: _____

Check all that apply (must try alternatives prior to initiating restraints). Alternatives that failed must be documented.

☐ Assisted with toileting q 2 hrs while awake, after meals, and q 4 hrs during the night
☐ Bed exit alarm on
☐ Checked with physician that tube &/or line is still necessary
☐ Cover PEG tube with abdominal binder
☐ Cover peripheral IVs with kerlix or stockinet for protection
☐ Family/sitter staying with patient
☐ Instructed to dangle prior to ambulation, to sit if dizzy and call for help
☐ Moved closer to nursing station
☐ Pain relief/comfort measures
☐ Redirecting focus
☐ Reorientation of patient
☐ Repeated education as to purpose, function & necessity of tube &/or line
☐ Repeated instruction to ask for help when getting out of bed
☐ Routine safety measures *(bed in low position, top rails up as indicated, call light within reach, floor clear, bedside table within reach)*
☐ Verbal de-escalation *(attempt to calm)*
☐ Other:

Physician's order obtained within: ☐ 12 hours for non-emergency **OR** ☐ 1 hour for emergency (severely aggressive/destructive behavior)
☐ Use of restraints, reason for application, behavior required to discontinue restraints discussed with ☐ patient
☐ family Name and relationship: _____
☐ Printed Patient/Family Information educational hand-out given to patient/family
Type of restraint utilized: ☐ Ankle ☐ Vest ☐ Wrist ☐ Other

Date restraint initiated: _____   Time restraint initiated: _____

Initial Boxes	0000	0100	0200	0300	0400	0500	0600	0700	0800	0900	1000	1100	1200	1300	1400	1500	1600	1700	1800	1900	2000	2100	2200	2300
Visual Check Q 10																								
Circ ✓ Q 20																								
Reposition Q 20																								
Release/Exercise Q 20																								
Hygiene/Toilet Q 20																								
Fluids/Food Q 20																								
Reassess Q 40 *(RN only)*																								

Behavior Necessitating Restraints (if for severely aggressive or destructive behavior, Q 15 minute visual checks are required and are to be documented.

_____

Behavior/Circumstances allowing DC

Signature/Title/Initials	Signature/Title/Initials	Signature/Title/Initials	Signature/Title/Initials
Signature/Title/Initials	Signature/Title/Initials	Signature/Title/Initials	Signature/Title/Initials

Source: Courtesy of Parkland Health and Hospital System, Dallas, Texas.

4-40 Care of the Psychiatric Patient

SUBJECT: Psychiatric Patient, Care of
PRIMARY SERVICE: Emergency
EFFECTIVE DATE:
CONTRIBUTING SERVICES: Mental Health Services

PURPOSE

To establish a standard of care for psychiatric and behavioral health patients.

POLICY STATEMENTS

Patients with mental and/or behavioral health problems will be treated with dignity and respect, while ensuring the safety of staff and patients alike.

PROCEDURE

A. Patients who present with psychiatric complaints will be interviewed by the triage nurse to determine patient's need for safety (i.e., harm to self, harm to others).

B. Mental health nursing, social and medical evaluations will be completed through a collaborative effort with physicians, nurses and crisis counselors.

C. Every effort will be made to place patients in a quiet room with family member, if appropriate.

D. Patient will be asked to undress and placed in a gown. Belongings will be searched and kept outside of the room at the discretion of the primary nurse. Primary nurse must have patient seen by the Emergency Physician and order received for seclusion or restraint as soon as possible.

E. The primary nurse will assess patient in terms of safety and determine the need for seclusion or restraints. Restraints or seclusion may be initiated by nurse, cosigned and changed or terminated by the Emergency Department Physician.

F. The Emergency Physician will evaluate patient and determine if crisis counselor is to be called.

G. Voluntary patients are required to sign voluntary admission form after full explanation by R.N. or crisis counselor.

H. Combative patients may need physical constraints to control their behavior. Leather restraints are applied by Security and Emergency Department staff and checked by a nurse every 15 minutes for maintaining circulation within normval limits. Patients in leather restraints are in full view of the nursing staff at all times.

I. Restraints can be the locked seclusion room, chemical restraints (e.g., Haldol, Valium) or leather straps. The goal is to use the least restrictive means to keep patient and personnel safe. Documentation on observation sheet is initiated at the time of restraint application and circulation checks are done every 15 minutes along with patient assessment and offerings of bathroom privileges (may be bedpan), food, liquids.

J. A "Code 6" should be initiated if, in the Emergency Physician or Nurse's judgment, more help is required. (See Code 6 Protocol).

  a. When requesting the Security staff for assistance, it is important that they be advised of the following:

    1. Who the primary nurse is (leadership role in Code 6).
    2. What behavior can be expected of the patient.
    3. What restraints, if any, will be utilized.
    4. What is the predicted time of involvement by the Security staff.

  b. The Security personnel may be requested to assist with observation or continued care of a patient for brief period of time.

K. Should a patient, in restraints, have to be transferred out of the department (i.e., Radiology), then it is necessary for a member of the nursing staff to accompany the patient.

L. A female needs to be in attendance when any care is rendered to a restrained female patient.

M. Should a situation develop where the other patients in the Emergency/Shock Trauma Center (E/STC), the staff, or hospital property may be in jeopardy because of the behavior of a violent patient, the _____ County Police Department may be requested to assist in the patient's management by the Security personnel or the E/STC charge nurse. If the E/STC charge nurse requests the assistance of the police, then the Security Department must be notified.

N. At times, a patient may be restrained at the order of a police officer. This patient is in police custody and the police officer must remain with the patient at all times. Documentation of police custody and restraint must be included in the patient's medical record.

O. Refer to the policy "Application and Removal of Physical Restraints."

P. Transfer of patients to a psych facility/hospital will follow the procedures in interfacility transfers.

Q. The patient who presents for alcohol and drug detoxification will have a mental health, nursing, social and medical evaluation completed through a collaborative effort of physicians, nurses and drug counselors, including but not limited to:

  a. A systematic mental status examination, emphasizing immediate recall and recent and remote memory, as well as any learning impairment that might influence diagnosis and treatment;

  b. A determination of current and past psychiatric disorders.

    c. A determination of the degree of danger the patient presents to self or others, and

    d. A neuropsychological assessment, if indicated by the psychiatric or psychological assessment.

    e. Furthermore, the social assessment of such a patient includes:

      1. The family's history of alcohol and other drug dependence;

      2. The patient's educational level, vocational status, and job performance history;

      3. The patient's social support networks, including family and peer relationships;

      4. The patient's perception of his or her strengths and weaknesses;

      5. The patient's leisure, recreational, and vocational interests and hobbies;

      6. The patient's ability to participate with peers in programs and social activities;

      7. The patient's perception of his or her own dependence;

      8. The patient's daily activity patterns, including those that support, and those that are alternatives to, dependency.

Source: Courtesy of Suburban Hospital, Bethesda, Maryland.

4-41 Dispensing of Medications from the Emergency Department

BACKGROUND

To best serve patient care needs, it is sometimes necessary to dispense medication from the emergency department to allow a patient enough medication until a prescription can be filled. This decision is based so the physician's judgment that such medication is both expedient and necessary.

PURPOSE

To define the policy and procedure by which medications are dispensed to patients who are discharged from the emergency department.

POLICY

1. Medications will be dispensed solely at the physician's discretion.
2. Medication order must be written on the ED chart.
3. Medications should be labeled appropriately, including date, patient name, physician name, type of medication, expiration date, lot number, and instruction for use.

PROCEDURE

1. RN verifies written medication order on ED chart.
2. RN obtains medication from pharmacy and places in *childproof container*. The patient will be given no more than four doses of noncontrolled or two doses of controlled substances.

3. RN fills out self-adhering medication label (see the following example) that includes
   a. patient's name
   b. date
   c. medication name, dosage, and amount
   d. direction for administration
   e. physician's name
   f. expiration date
   g. lot number
4. Prior to peeling off label, *have physician initial* at bottom to indicate that physician
   a. confirms accuracy of order
   b. confirms accuracy of instructions
   c. will adhere signed label to medication container
5. Physician or RN gives medication to the patient, including instructions for use.
6. The back sheet behind the label will serve as the pharmacy log sheet to meet the state's standards of control.
7. Medications are charged to the patient on the ED chart.

THE HOSPITAL EMERGENCY DEPARTMENT

DATE _____

PATIENT NAME _____

DRUG _____

INSTRUCTIONS _____

_____

DR. _____ RN INITIALS _____

Source: Copyright Aspen Publishers, Inc.

4-42 Emergency Contraception (EC)

OBJECTIVE: To develop a consistent method of protecting against pregnancy.

GENERAL GUIDELINES:

These are general guidelines and may not be applicable in all situations. Decisions must be made in the context of the situation and of judgmental parameters existent at the time of decision-making.

Emergency contraception will be offered to all nonpregnant patients whose breast or pubic hair development is Tanner Stage II or beyond, even if they have not begun to menstruate, unless they are reliable users of a hormonal contraceptive.

1. Obtain a gynecologic history.
   a. If the patient is a reliable user of hormonal contraception, EC is not indicated.
   b. If the patient was menstruating normally at the time of sexual intercourse, EC is not indicated.
   c. If the patient may be pregnant, be sure that her pregnancy test is negative before prescribing EC. Pregnancy is a contraindication to EC, not because it can injure the fetus, but because it is not indicated

2. Obtain verbal consent by informing the patient of the availability of EC and its complications and side effects:

    a. Women rarely experience nausea using Plan B as an EC.

    b. The failure rate for EC is not known, but it is thought to be low if used within 72 hours of sexual contact.

        1) The pregnancy rate will increase with increased time between sexual intercourse and the use of EC.

        2) Although EC is generally used up to 72 hours after intercourse, it may be used later after intercourse (up to 120 hours) but its effectiveness is not known.

3. There is no need to split the doses of Plan B by 12 hours. Prescribe both to be taken immediately.

4. Counsel the patient that a pregnancy test should be performed if she misses her period after using EC.

APPROVAL:

Approved by:

Director, Community Health Services

Signature_____

Date _____

Medical Director, CRC

Signature_____

Date _____

Reviewed by: _____

Date: _____

Source: Courtesy of Pinnacle Health Hospitals.

4-43 Procedures Nurses May Initiate Prior to Medical Orders—Pediatrics

POLICY

The nursing staff of the emergency department may initiate any of the following procedures prior to obtaining a medical order if the patient condition warrants. The nurse will follow emergency department/hospital procedures in providing care.

    1. Vital sign frequency
    2. Placement of appropriate monitors
    3. Oxygen therapy
    4. Suctioning—nasopharyngeal
    5. Culture of any unusual drainage
    6. Isolation
    7. Irrigation of nonpatent IVs
    8. Initial consultation of ancillary personnel, e.g., social services, chaplain, child life worker, CPS
    9. Accu-Check for blood glucose
   10. Wound care standard

11. Radiant warmer/isolette for temperature control
12. 12-lead ECG
13. Use of A and D/Vaseline for skin care
14. Medication
    a. Give Tylenol by mouth (when no vomiting is present) in a dose appropriate for weight (10-15 mg/kg) for fever every four hours. When vomiting is present, give Tylenol suppository in a dose appropriate for weight.
    b. Pediaprofen can be given 10 mg/kg if all the following conditions are met:
       i. An appropriate dose of Tylenol has been given.
       ii. It has been one hour since last dose of Tylenol.
       iii. Temperature is 101°F or greater.
15. Bagging child for clean-catch urinalysis (UA) specimen on arrival to triage or ED treatment room with complaints of fever, dehydration, lethargy, poisoning, MVA, abdominal pain
16. Splinting potential fractures
17. Cervical spine immobilization when necessary
18. Placement of oral or nasal airway in appropriate situations
19. Specific gravity on urine
20. Application of ice packs as necessary

Source: Copyright Aspen Publishers, Inc.

4-44 Suicidal Patients in the Emergency Room

EVALUATION

1. Obtain medical clearance.
   - You do not want to be admitting a seriously medically ill patient to the psychiatry ward.
   - Watch for even what was thought to be a minor gesture—acetaminophen, aspirin.
2. Interview.
   - **ID**—Age, sex, psychiatric illness, medical illness, social environment, acute crisis/loss
   - **Intent**—Expression of intent, duration of desire, duration of plan, intensity of thoughts, specific plan, availability of plan, lethality of plan, preparation for death, past attempts
   - **State of mind**—Hopeless, intoxicated (impulsive), manipulative, angry, psychotic. Watch for a calm before the storm—decision to die is made and patient is at peace.
   - **Practicalities**—Do not leave the patient alone. If everything looks okay but your gut feeling is telling you something is wrong—trust that gut feeling and inquire further.
   - **Techniques**
     a. Be nonjudgmental—You are in a position of authority. Someone who is suicidal already has low self-esteem. If you are condescending or judgmental, their self-esteem will probably be made worse. Your approach could make their suicidal intentions stronger.

b. Be calm and supportive. Display confidence in your abilities.

c. Encourage self-disclosure.

SAMPLE QUESTIONS

- What has happened to make life so difficult?
- Are things hopeless?
- Have you recently had a serious loss or crisis (divorce, finances, job, legal)?
- Are you thinking of suicide?
- How long have you been thinking of suicide? frequency, intensity?
- Do you have a suicide plan?
- What preparations have you made to carry out this plan?
- Why do you want to take your life? Make it make sense to me.
- What would suicide solve?
- How much do you want to live?
- How much do you want to die?
- Have you attempted suicide in the past?
- What have you done to try and feel better?
- Have you been using alcohol or drugs?

Source: Gerard P. Clancy, MD, Dean, College of Medicine, University of Oklahoma, Tulsa, Oklahoma.

4-45 Care of Pregnant Trauma Policy and Procedure

SUBJECT: Pregnant Trauma, Care of
PRIMARY SERVICE: Emergency
EFFECTIVE DATE:
CONTRIBUTING SERVICES: Trauma

PURPOSE

To establish guidelines to be used in the treatment of a traumatized pregnant patient.

POLICY

Treatment priorities for a traumatized pregnant patient remain the same as for the non-pregnant patient. Initial management is directed at resuscitation and stabilization of the pregnant patient because the fetus' life is totally dependent on the integrity of the mother's life.

PROCEDURE

1. The traumatized pregnant patient will be triaged in the following manner:
   a. The following trauma patients may be transported to the Hospital for triage:
      1. *Unknown*—not knowing the patient is pregnant.
      2. *Unconscious*—unable to answer questions.

3. *Unviable age of fetus*—less than 25 weeks gestation.

4. *Unstable*—injuries require immediate attention regardless of the fetal gestation age.

5. *Uncertain stability*—further transport may be a risk.

b. The following pregnant trauma patients may be transported directly to an obstetrical/trauma center by appropriate transportation if **all** three conditions are met:

1. Conscious traumatized pregnant patient.

2. Traumatized pregnant patient is considered stable and additional transport time is considered safe.

3. Traumatized pregnant patient's fetus is most likely viable—more than 25 weeks gestation.

c. The trauma surgeon and obstetrician on call will be alerted and respond within 30 minutes of notification, as allowed by the Echelons of Care. If the patient is known to be in the first trimester of the pregnancy, the obstetrician does not need to respond within 30 minutes, but will be contacted at the time of admission and remain a consultant providing service as needed.

2. The following equipment will be gathered and placed in the Trauma Room:

a. Fetal monitor

b. Precipitous delivery tray

c. Incubator

3. All female trauma patients (up to the age of 48) will have a STAT serum pregnancy test performed.

4. Nursing personnel will be required to attend an annual inservice on the use of fetal monitoring equipment.

5. Although needed X-rays of the traumatized pregnant patient must not be withheld, the fetus will be shielded for all radiological procedures unless the shielding interferes with a specific X-ray.

6. Caution will be used in administering medications with the direction of the attending physician and obstetrician.

7. Once the traumatized pregnant patient has been evaluated, a definitive plan of care will be developed by surgeon and obstetrician. The following options will be considered:

a. Stabilize the pregnant patient and transfer to an obstetrical/trauma center as soon as possible for observation and monitoring.

b. If the severity of injuries requires treatment and/or surgery at the Hospital, fetal monitoring and care will be continued as directed by the obstetrician.

c. If the fetus needs to be delivered at the Hospital, there are two options available and are listed below definitive care for the neonate.

1) If the neonate will require neonatal intensive care, notify the Neonatal Unit. They will provide telephone consultation and send a neonatal team to transport the neonate to their facility.

2) If the neonate does not require neonatal intensive care, contact a local hospital with an Obstetrical Service to arrange transfer for the neonate. It will be this hospital's responsibility to transport the neonate to the receiving hospital.

Source: Courtesy of Suburban Hospital, Inc., Bethesda, Maryland.

4-46 Methylprednisolone for Spinal Cord Injury

Responsible Department:	Patient Care Services	Effective Date:	
Contributing Services:	Pharmacy		
New: X	Supersedes:	Dated:	
Review/Renewal Date:		Administration Approval:	

PURPOSE

To identify staff responsibilities in management of the patient receiving high dose methyl-prednisolone for acute spinal cord injury patients. There is evidence that an infusion of methylprednisolone administered within eight hours of injury may delay or avert some of the neurological loss from trauma.

POLICY STATEMENT

Following the methylprednisolone acute spinal cord injury protocol, a loading dose will be given followed by a continuous infusion for 23 hours at a specific designated rate of 12 ml/hour (Bracken, 1992). NOTE: Dose varies according to patient's weight, but the final solution volume is always 276 ml or 12 ml/hr × 23 hours.

PROCEDURE

1. Initial bolus will be prepared by pharmacy, unless the patient is in the emergency department, and is to be delivered over 15 minutes. When the patient is in the emergency department (ED), the initial bolus will be prepared by the ED nurse. The order form will be completed (including the patient's weight) and sent to the pharmacy, who will begin preparing the 23-hour maintenance infusion.
2. When the patient is admitted and the initial bolus is prepared by pharmacy, obtain patient's actual weight (not estimated or stated) and record in Meditech under "administrative data." Dosage is calculated from the patient's weight and when the information is placed into the computer it is accessible to pharmacy.
3. Forty-five minutes after the completion of the initial bolus, begin the 23-hour maintenance infusion.
4. If there is any delay in beginning the 23-hour infusion or if the drug is interrupted (for procedures e.g., MRI), new flow rates must be calculated by the pharmacy, to allow the remaining drug to be administered within the original 24-hour time schedule.
5. The infusion should not be continued beyond 24 hours.
6. Nursing assessment of the patient who is undergoing high dose methylprednisolone should include signs and symptoms of gastrointestinal bleeding, motor and sensory assessment as well as routine neurological assessment.

REFERENCE

Braken, MB et al: Methylprednisolone or nalxone treatment after acute spinal cord injury; 1 year follow-up data: results of second National Acute Spinal Cord Injury Study. *J. Neurosurg* 1992; 76:23-31.

Source: Courtesy of Suburban Hospital, Inc., Bethesda, Maryland.

4-47 Methylprednisolone Acute Spinal Cord Injury Protocol

Wt (Kg)	Loading dose (mg)	*Vol. Solu-Medrol for loading dose (using 1 g vial diluted w/8 ml)	23 hr infusion total dose (mg)	*Vol. Solu-Medrol for 23-hour dose (using 1 g vial diluted w/8 ml)	Mg/hr for 23 hr infusion	Conc. mg/ml (23 hr Infusion)	Vol to withdraw from 23 hr bag (250 ml D5W)	
50	1500	12	6210.0	49.7	270.0	22.5	24	**INSTRUCTIONS**
51	1530	12.2	6334.2	50.7	275.4	23.0	25	
52	1560	12.5	6458.4	51.7	280.8	23.4	26	Prepare loading dose in D5W
53	1590	12.7	6562.5	52.7	285.2	23.9	27	final concentration less than or
54	1620	13.0	6706.8	53.7	291.6	24.3	28	equal to 50 mg/ml
55	1650	13.2	6831.0	54.6	297.0	24.8	29	Prepare 23 hour infusion in D5W
56	1680	13.4	6955.2	55.6	302.4	25.2	30	final volume = 276 ml. (Use a
57	1710	13.7	7079.4	56.6	307.8	25.7	31	250 ml D5W and adjust volume)
58	1740	13.9	7203.6	57.6	313.2	26.1	32	
59	1770	14.2	7327.8	58.6	318.6	26.6	33	Loading dose = 30 mg/kg over
60	1800	14.4	7452.0	59.6	324.0	27.0	34	15 minutes in 50 ml D5W
61	1830	14.6	7576.2	60.6	329.4	27.5	35	
62	1860	14.9	7700.4	61.6	334.8	27.9	36	Continuous dose = 5.4 mg/kg/hr
63	1890	15.1	7824.6	62.6	340.2	28.4	37	over 23 hours in 276 ml D5W
64	1920	15.4	7948.8	63.6	345.6	28.8	38	or 12 ml/hr × 23 hours.
65	1950	15.6	8073.0	64.6	351.0	29.3	39	
66	1980	15.8	8197.2	65.6	356.4	29.7	40	*All dosage calculations for Solu-
67	2010	16.1	8321.4	66.6	361.8	30.2	41	Medrol based on 1 gram vial.
68	2040	16.3	8445.6	67.6	367.2	30.6	42	
69	2070	16.6	8569.8	68.6	372.6	31.1	43	All volumes rounded to nearest
70	2100	16.8	8694.0	69.6	378.0	31.5	44	0.1 ml.
71	2130	17.0	8818.2	70.5	383.4	32.0	45	

Wt (Kg)	Loading dose (mg)	*Vol. Solu-Medrol for loading dose (using 1 g vial diluted w/8 ml)	23 hr infusion total dose (mg)	*Vol. Solu-Medrol for 23-hour dose (using 1 g vial diluted w/8 ml)	Mg/hr for 23 hr infusion	Conc. mg/ml (23 hr Infusion)	Vol to withdraw from 23 hr bag (250 ml D5W)
72	2160	17.3	8942.4	71.5	388.8	32.4	46
73	2190	17.5	9055.6	72.5	394.2	32.9	47
74	2220	17.8	9190.8	73.5	399.5	33.3	48
75	2250	18.0	9315.0	74.5	405.0	33.8	49
76	2280	18.2	9439.2	76.5	410.4	34.7	50
77	2310	18.5	9563.4	75.5	415.8	34.2	51
78	2340	18.7	9687.6	77.5	421.2	35.1	52
79	2370	19.0	9811.8	78.5	426.6	35.6	52
80	2400	19.2	9936.0	79.5	432.0	36.0	53
81	2430	19.4	10050.2	80.5	437.4	36.5	54
82	2460	19.7	10184.4	81.5	442.8	36.9	55
83	2490	19.9	10308.6	82.5	448.2	37.4	56
84	2520	20.2	10432.8	83.5	453.8	37.8	57
85	2550	20.4	10557.0	84.5	459.0	38.3	58
86	2580	20.6	10681.2	85.4	464.4	38.7	59
87	2610	20.9	10805.4	86.4	469.8	39.2	60
88	2640	21.1	10929.6	87.4	475.2	39.6	61
89	2670	21.4	11053.8	88.4	480.6	40.1	62
90	2700	21.6	11178.0	89.4	486.0	40.5	63
91	2730	21.8	11302.2	90.4	491.4	41.0	64
92	2760	22.1	11428.4	91.4	496.8	41.4	65
93	2790	22.3	11550.6	92.4	502.2	41.9	66
94	2820	22.6	11674.8	93.4	507.6	42.3	67
95	2850	22.8	11799.0	94.4	513.0	42.8	68
96	2880	23.0	11923.2	95.4	518.4	43.2	69
97	2910	23.3	12047.4	96.4	523.8	43.7	70
98	2940	23.5	12171.6	97.4	529.2	44.1	71
99	2970	23.8	12295.8	98.4	534.6	44.6	72
100	3000	24.0	12420.0	99.4	540.0	45.0	73

Source: Courtesy of Suburban Hospital, Inc., Bethesda, Maryland.

4-48 The Use of Methylprednisolone in Acute Spinal Cord Injury

DOSAGE AND ADMINISTRATION

Initial bolus

- 30 mg/kg of body weight administered over 15 minutes

45 minute pause

23 hour infusion

- 5.4 mg/kg/hour of body weight

This dosage of and administration of methylprednisolone used in the NASCIS 2 study was a bolus of 30 mg per kilogram of body weight was administered over 15 minutes, followed by a 45 minute pause and then a 23 hour continuous IV infusion of 5.4 mg per kilogram per hour of body weight.

DOSAGE CALCULATIONS

$$\frac{\text{Bolus dose}}{(50 \text{ mg/mL})} \quad = \quad \text{total bolus dose (in mL)}$$

$$\frac{(30 \text{ mg/kg}) \times (\text{patient weight in kg})}{(50 \text{ mg/mL})} = \text{total bolus dose (in mL)}$$

$$\frac{\text{Maintenance dose}}{(5.4 \text{ mg/kg}) \times (\text{patient weight in kg})}{(50 \text{ mg/mL})} = \text{maintenance dose per hour (in mL)}$$

Set the infusion pump to deliver the total bolus dose in 15 minutes, and maintain the intravenous line with normal saline for 45 minutes.

Then set the infusion pump to deliver the maintenance dose over the next 23 hours.

TREATMENT PROTOCOL

- Peripheral vein of at least 3 mm
- Normal saline to keep IV lines open between bolus and maintenance infusion
- Drug infusion continued through surgery whenever possible
- If drug stopped, new flow rates calculated to allow remaining drug to be administered within original time schedule
- Infusion not continued beyond 24 hours

The treatment protocol used during NASCIS 2 should be followed.

A peripheral vein of at least 3 mm was used in most cases; however, a Swann Ganz catheter or central line may have been used.

Intravenous lines were kept open, as necessary, between bolus and maintenance infusion using normal saline.

If drug administration was inadvertently stopped, new flow rates were calculated so that the remaining drug could be administered within the remaining time of the originally planned infusion schedule.

Source: Courtesy of Suburban Hospital, Inc., Bethesda, Maryland.

4-49 Patient Restraint or Seclusion Policy

PURPOSE OF POLICY

To define restraints and seclusion, the appropriate use of restraints or seclusion based on patient behavior, the physician's ordering process, and the care and documentation required for patients for whom restraints or seclusion are used, regardless of where in the hospital the patient is receiving care.

DEFINITION OF RESTRAINTS

A device that restricts the movement of a patient, that is, to prevent the patient from hurting him- or herself or others, knowingly or not.

Category I Restraints

A device that limits the patient's mobility to the extent that the patient will not be able to independently reposition him- or herself or will otherwise be rendered helpless in an emergency. Such devices include four-point leather restraints.

Category II Restraints

Any device not considered by the facility to be a Category I Restraint. Such devices include soft restraints and posey restraints.

DEFINITION OF SECLUSION

Under the direction of a physician or RN, the involuntary confinement of a patient alone in a room in which the patient is physically prevented from leaving.

EXCEPTIONS TO THE RESTRAINT/SECLUSION POLICY

This policy does not apply to

1. mechanisms usually and customarily employed during medical, diagnostic, or surgical procedures that are considered a regular part of such procedures (including but not limited to body restraints during surgery, limb restraints while intubated and ventilated, and arm restraints during intravenous administration)
2. devices used to protect the patient, such as side rails, tabletop chairs, helmets, orthopaedic devices, braces, or wheelchairs
3. devices used to secure patients for transfer, balance, and positioning or for postural support of the patient (e.g., temporarily placing a belt or sheet around the patient when he or she is seated in a chair)
4. situations in which a patient agrees to restraints and a written consent is obtained.

POLICY

When other, less-restrictive, measures have been ineffective, physician-ordered restraints/seclusion can be used only to prevent injury and to prevent disruption of the therapeutic environment.

Physician Orders

A. A physician order is required for any use of a restraint/seclusion.

B. All orders are to include
1. *date and time* that the order was written
2. *type* of restraint to be used
3. the *maximum duration* of restraint/seclusion
4. the *specific rationale* for the restraint/seclusion
5. *special precautions*, if any, to safeguard the patient
6. the physician's *signature*

C. A physician may write an order for restraints/seclusion for a maximum duration of up to, but not more than 24 hours.

D. No "standing," "as needed," or "prn" orders for restraints/seclusion can be given.

E. In emergency situations, an RN may place a patient in an appropriate restraint/ seclusion and obtain a physician order within one hour.

F. If an oral order is obtained, the order must be signed, dated, and timed by the ordering or covering physician within 24 hours.

Nursing Management and Care

A. Explanation to patient/family:
All patients requiring restraint/seclusion must receive an explanation of why restraint is needed and how long it will be used.

B. Care (to be documented):
1. Keep patients who are in seclusion in view *at all times.*
2. *Every 15 minutes*
Patients in (Category I) four-point restraints or seclusion are observed for safety.
3. Unless contraindicated by circumstances as assessed and documented by a physician or registered nurse *every hour* make and document personal contact.
a. Determine if the patient has any special needs that require attention.
b. Check circulation of extremities restrained.
c. Adjust the restraint.
d. Realign the body or massage the extremity restrained, or both.
4. Unless contraindicated by circumstances as assessed and documented by a physician or registered nurse, *every two hours:*
a. Range of motion of restrained limbs is checked.
b. Toileting is offered.
c. Fluids are offered.

       d. The appropriateness of continuing the restraint is assessed, and those factors are documented.

  5. *Meal times/daily hygiene*

       a. Nutrition is offered at meal times.

       b. Hygiene needs are met every 24 hours.

  6. Children younger than 12 years of age may not be placed in four-point restraints.

  7. When applying or repositioning a restraint, the application of force on long bone joints of children should be avoided.

  8. Unless circumstances suggest a medical problem may exist, staff may not disrupt a patient's sleep during the night to implement the clinical procedures described in the Nursing Management and Care section of this policy.

C. Documentation of implementation of restraint/seclusion:

  1. Document the implementation of restraint/seclusion in the patient's medical record.

  2. Include in the documentation the following information:

       a. a description of the specific behavior leading to restraint/seclusion

       b. whether and which less-restrictive techniques were used, such as medication, placing patient near nurses' station, etc.

       c. the readily observable physical condition of the patient

       d. the date and time of the restraint/seclusion

       e. whether the patient was permitted to wear his or her own clothes or other attire

       f. a description of any physical injury to the patient resulting from placement of the patient in restraint/seclusion

D. Release from restraint/seclusion

  1. When a physician clinically determines that a patient is to be released from restraint/seclusion, the physician shall

       a. order the release and write, sign, and date a note indicating the rationale for the release

       b. if orally ordering the release, write, sign, and date the note not later than 24 hours after an oral order to release

  2. When the registered nurse clinically determines that the release of the patient before the maximum period specified on the physician's order is appropriate, the registered nurse shall

       a. order termination of the restraints/seclusion with or without a physician's order, unless the physician's order specifically requires physician concurrence with the termination

       b. document, sign, and date the rationale for the termination of the restraint/seclusion in the patient's record

Source: Adapted from Holy Cross Hospital, Silver Spring, Maryland.

4-50 Psychiatry Emergency Department: Seclusion Safety Guidelines

POLICY

Patients will be placed in locked seclusion rooms to protect themselves and other individuals.

PURPOSE

To provide safety for the patient and other individuals in the psychiatry emergency department.

To provide seclusion guidelines for staff assigned in the psychiatry emergency department.

PROCEDURE

1. Assess the patient's need for seclusion.
2. Assess the need for assistance from the Department of Public Safety (DPS).
3. Ensure seclusion room is a safe environment. It may contain a mattress/blanket if physician determines the items will not be used by the patient in a detrimental manner.
4. Explain to the patient the need for seclusion.
5. Remove the following from the patient:
   - eyeglasses
   - shoes
   - jewelry
   - belts
   - any items that may be potentially dangerous
6. Obtain written physician orders to initiate seclusion procedure, including the estimated length of time for seclusion. Order must be rewritten, if indicated.
7. DPS officers should be used to escort the patient to the toilet or if staff need to enter room for any reason.
8. Patients are **not** to be removed from seclusion without a physician order.
9. Nursing personnel will be responsible for initiating the Checklist for Seclusion Patient, indicating time seclusion initiated, monitored, reevaluated, and discontinued.
10. Nursing personnel will document in nursing notes "Seclusion protocols in place."
11. a. Nursing staff must observe the secluded patient every 15 minutes and document observation(s) per emergency department policy.
    b. Patients in seclusion rooms should be continuously monitored via video-monitoring/intercom systems.

Source: Courtesy of Parkland Memorial Hospital, Dallas, Taxas.

4-51 Psychiatry Emergency Department: Checklist for Seclusion Patients

Patient name: _____ Date: _____

Reason for Seclusion: ☐ Danger to Self ☐ Danger to Others

Time secluded: _____ Time restrained: _____ Type of restraint: _____

Time seclusion discontinued: _____ Time restraints discontinued: _____

Helmet: _____

Code explanation:

		0700-1500	INIT	1500-2300	INIT	2300-0700	INIT
1.	Hitting door						
2.	Yelling	0700	_____	1500	_____	2300	_____
3.	Crying	0715	_____	1515	_____	2315	_____
4.	Cursing	0730	_____	1530	_____	2330	_____
5.	Laughing	0745	_____	1545	_____	2345	_____
6.	Singing	0800	_____	1600	_____	2400	_____
7.	Mumbling	0815	_____	1615	_____	0015	_____
8.	Standing still	0830	_____	1630	_____	0030	_____
9.	Pacing	0845	_____	1645	_____	0045	_____
10.	Sitting	0900	_____	1700	_____	0100	_____
11.	Quiet	0915	_____	1715	_____	0115	_____
12.	Sleeping	0930	_____	1730	_____	0130	_____
13.	Eating meal	0945	_____	1745	_____	0145	_____
14.	Using toilet	1000	_____	1800	_____	0200	_____
15.	Labs drawn	1015	_____	1815	_____	0215	_____
16.	Medicated	1030	_____	1830	_____	0230	_____
17.	Interview	1045	_____	1845	_____	0245	_____
18.	Soiled room	1100	_____	1900	_____	0300	_____
19.	Bathed	1115	_____	1915	_____	0315	_____
20.	Moved to another room	1130	_____	1930	_____	0330	_____
21.	Agitated	1145	_____	1945	_____	0345	_____
22.	Drinking fluids	1200	_____	2000	_____	0400	_____
23.	Fighting staff	1215	_____	2015	_____	0415	_____
24.	Vomiting	1230	_____	2030	_____	0430	_____
25.	Vital signs	1245	_____	2045	_____	0445	_____
26.	Regular resp.	1300	_____	2100	_____	0500	_____
27.	Verbal response	1315	_____	2115	_____	0515	_____
28.	Hitting self	1330	_____	2130	_____	0530	_____
29.	_____	1345	_____	2145	_____	0545	_____
30.	_____	1400	_____	2200	_____	0600	_____
31.	_____	1415	_____	2215	_____	0615	_____
32.	_____	1430	_____	2230	_____	0630	_____
33.	_____	1445	_____	2245	_____	0645	_____

RN Signature: _____ _____ _____

Psychiatric Assistant
Signature: _____ _____ _____

Physician Signature: _____ _____ _____

Shift: _____ _____ _____

Source: Courtesy of Parkland Health and Hospital System, Dallas, Texas.

4-52 Policy and Procedure: Sedation and Anesthesia by Non-Anesthesiologists

I. SUBJECT

Management of Patients Undergoing Procedures Receiving Sedation and Analgesia by Non-anesthesiologists

II. PURPOSE

To provide a uniform hospitalwide standard of care for all patients undergoing Sedation and Analgesia by non-anesthesiologists.

III. DEFINITIONS

Sedation and Analgesia

Sedation and Analgesia is the administration of pharmacologic agents to provide a minimally depressed level of consciousness yet allow the patient to independently and continuously maintain an airway and respond to physical stimulation and verbal commands. The purpose of Sedation and Analgesia is to enhance the patient's comfort during therapeutic and diagnostic procedures.

Note that patients whose only response is reflex withdrawal from a painful stimulus are sedated to a greater degree than encompassed by Sedation and Analgesia. Patients not meeting this definition require Monitored Anesthetic Care (MAC).

Monitored Anesthetic Care involves the presence of an anesthesiologist and encompasses levels of Sedation and Analgesia likely to produce the loss of protective reflexes and failure to maintain a patent airway.

Specifically excluded from governance by this policy are patients on life support on a special care unit, patients under the direct care of the formally organized Department of Anesthesia, patients receiving night-time sleep Sedation, other Sedation given on an inpatient nursing unit, pre-operative Sedation, or narcotics for pain.

IV. RESPONSIBILITY/CRITERIA

It is the responsibility of the physician performing the procedure to manage patients receiving Sedation and Analgesia.

The physician performing the procedure shall determine whether Sedation and Analgesia or Monitored Anesthetic Care (MAC) shall be used during any given procedure.

The physician performing the procedure must: 1) assess the needs of the patient and the demands of the procedure, 2) choose Sedation and Analgesia or Monitored Anesthetic Care, and 3) appropriately monitor the patient.

For Sedation and Analgesia, the physician performing the procedure shall include pertinent history and physical on the record for the procedure. Consideration for NPO status and risk of aspiration shall be given prior to any Sedation and Analgesia procedure.

Nursing support shall be appropriate for the procedure.

Since Sedation and Analgesia may convert unexpectedly to Monitored Anesthetic Care at any time, it is recommended that the Code Blue cart and defibrillator shall be available.

V. SEDATION AND ANALGESIA PROCEDURE

This policy shall be followed in conjunction with unit-specific protocols related to the specific procedure being performed.

1. Procedures requiring Sedation and Analgesia must meet the criteria in Section IV.
2. Sedation and Analgesia may be administered in all patient care areas satisfying the criteria stated in Section IV.
3. Administration of Sedation and Analgesia must be given in the presence of the physician performing the procedure he/she is credentialed to perform;
   a. individuals responsible for patients receiving Sedation and Analgesia shall understand the pharmacology of the agents that are administered, as well as the role of pharmacologic antagonists for opioids and benzodiazepines. Individuals monitoring patients receiving Sedation and Analgesia shall be able to recognize the associated complications. At least one individual capable of establishing a patent airway and positive pressure ventilation, as well as a means for summoning additional assistance, shall be present whenever Sedation and Analgesia is administered;
   b. Credentialing for a procedure assumes this competency;
   c. Anesthesia personnel and a code blue team are available 24 hours a day.
4. Sedation and Analgesia may be administered by appropriately licensed health care personnel who have documented competency in the administration and care of the patient undergoing Sedation and Analgesia;
5. The on-going assessment process will be performed by a registered nurse or the physician performing the procedure. A designated individual other than the physician performing the procedure shall be present to monitor the patient throughout the procedure. This individual may assist with minor, interruptible tasks which do not interfere with such monitoring;
6. All medications given for Sedation and Analgesia during procedures will be written on the physician order sheet and will be signed by the physician according to current Hospital policy;
7. Only medications that are approved in the Hospital formulary will be given. Utilization of these drugs will be according to protocol acceptable to the Pharmacy and Therapeutics Committee;
8. The physician performing the procedure shall be physically available until patient's discharge from the procedure area;
9. The patient is discharged to the appropriate unit or home according to current Hospital policy post procedure;
10. Quality Assessment and Improvement: Monitoring of procedures performed with Sedation and Analgesia will be done according to the Hospital's Quality Assessment and Improvement Process. Summary results will be submitted to the Medical Staff's Anesthesia Department CQI Committee at regularly-defined intervals and the Quality Improvement Council as required.

VI. REQUIRED ELEMENTS

Pre-Assessment will include verification and documentation of:
1. Informed consent;
2. Relevant physician history and physical;
3. Nursing assessment:
   a. allergies to medications;
   b. level of consciousness;
   c. denture status;
   d. baseline vital signs;
   e. NPO status

Equipment needed includes:
1. Pulse oximeter;
2. Blood pressure cuff;
3. Sedation of choice;
4. Narcan - Mazicon;
5. IV access for IV Sedation;
6. Cardiac monitor available;
7. Oxygen setup with mask, nasal cannula and ambu bag available;
8. Suction setup with Yankauer available;
9. Code Blue cart and defibrillator available.

Intra-Procedure Assessment

Patients' ventilatory and oxygenation status and hemodynamic variables shall be recorded at a frequency to be determined by the type and amount of medication administered as well as the length of the procedure and the general condition of the patient. At a minimum, this should be 1) before the beginning of the procedure, 2) after administration of sedative and analgesic agents, 3) on completion of the procedure, 4) during initial recovery, and 5) at the time of discharge. If recording is performed automatically, device alarms should be set to alert the care team to critical changes in patient status.

1. Vital signs (BP, pulse and respirations) shall be measured at regular intervals, not less than Q15 minutes;
2. S_pO_2 will be monitored continuously and recorded Q15 minutes;
   a. equipment to administer supplemental oxygen shall be present when Sedation and Analgesia is administered. If hypoxemia is anticipated or develops during Sedation and Analgesia, supplemental oxygen shall be administered.
3. Monitoring of patient response to verbal and/or tactile stimulation shall be periodic (Q15 minutes);
4. Ventilatory function shall be monitored continually by observation and/or auscultation and recorded Q15 minutes;
5. Electrocardiographic monitoring shall be used in patients with significant cardiovascular disease as well as during procedures in which dysrhythmias are anticipated;
   Items 1-5 may be recorded in the doctor's progress notes, nursing notes, or procedure records.
6. Intravenous sedative and analgesic drugs should be given in small, incremental doses that are titrated to the desired endpoints of Sedation and Analgesia. Sufficient

time must elapse between doses to allow the effect of each dose to be assessed before subsequent drug administration. When drugs are administered by nonintravenous routes (e.g., oral, rectal, intramuscular), allowance should be made for the time required for drug absorption before supplementation is considered.

7. In patients receiving intravenous medications for Sedation and Analgesia, vascular access shall be maintained throughout the procedure and until the patient is no longer at risk for cardiorespiratory depression. In patients who have received Sedation and Analgesia by nonintravenous routes or whose intravenous line has become dislodged or blocked, the physician performing the procedure shall determine the advisability of establishing or reestablishing intravenous access on a case-by-case basis. In all instances, an individual with the skills to establish intravenous access should be immediately available.

8. Specific antagonists shall be available whenever opioid analgesics or benzodiazepines are administered for Sedation and Analgesia. Naloxone and/or flumazenil may be administered to improve spontaneous ventilatory efforts in patients who have received opioids or benzodiazepines, respectively. This may be especially helpful in cases in which airway control and positive pressure ventilation are difficult. Before or concomitantly with pharmacologic reversal, patients who became hypoxemic or apneic during Sedation and Analgesia shall: 1) be encouraged or stimulated to breathe deeply, 2) receive positive pressure ventilation if spontaneous ventilation is inadequate, and 3) receive supplemental oxygen. After pharmacologic reversal, patients shall be observed long enough to ensure that cardiorespiratory depression does not recur.

9. Whenever possible, appropriate medical specialists should be consulted before administration of Sedation and Analgesia to patients with significant underlying conditions. The choice of specialists depends on the nature of the underlying condition and the urgency of the situation. For significantly compromised patients (e.g., severe obstructive pulmonary disease, coronary artery disease, congestive heart failure) or if it appears likely that Sedation and Analgesia to the point of unresponsiveness or general anesthesia will be necessary to obtain adequate conditions, physicians who are not specifically qualified to provide these modalities should consult an anesthesiologist.

Post-Procedure Assessment/Discharge Criteria

After Sedation and Analgesia, patients shall be observed until they are no longer at increased risk for cardiorespiratory depression. Vital signs and respiratory function shall be monitored at designated intervals until patients are suitable for discharge. Discharge criteria should be designed to minimize the risk of central nervous system or cardiorespiratory depression after discharge from observation by trained personnel.

The patient may be discharged from the procedure area to an in-house patient care area when the five-point Aldrete score is > 8 (8 to 10):

Modified Post-Anesthetic Recovery (PAR) score for patients having anesthesia on ambulatory basis:

I.			
Able to move 4 extremities voluntarily or on command	2	
Able to move 2 extremities voluntarily or on command	1	ACTIVITY
Unable to move extremities voluntarily or on command	0	

II.	Able to breathe deeply and cough freely	2	
	Dyspnea, limited breathing or tachypnea	1	RESPIRATION
	Apneic or on mechanical ventilator	0	
III.	BP plus or minus 20% of pre-anesthetic level	2	
	BP plus or minus 20-49% of pre-anesthetic level	1	CIRCULATION
	BP plus or minus 50% of pre-anesthetic level	0	
IV.	Fully awake	2	
	Arousable on calling	1	CONSCIOUSNESS
	Not responding	0	
V.	Able to maintain O_2 saturation > 90% on room air	2	
	Needs O_2 inhalation to maintain O_2 saturation > 90%	1	O_2 SATURATION
	O_2 saturation < 90% even with O_2 supplement	0	

The patient may be discharged from the Hospital when the 10-point Aldrete score is > 18 (18 to 20).

VI.	Dry and clean	2	
	Wet but stationary or marked	1	DRESSING
	Growing area of wetness	0	
VII.	Pain free	2	
	Mild pain handled by oral medication	1	PAIN
	Severe pain requiring parenteral medication	0	
VIII.	Able to stand up and walk straight*	2	
	Vertigo when erect	1	AMBULATION
	Dizziness when supine	0	
IX.	Able to drink fluids	2	
	Nauseated	1	FASTING-FEEDING
	Nausea and vomiting	0	
X.	Has voided	2	
	Unable to void but comfortable	1	URINE OUTPUT
	Unable to void and uncomfortable	0	

*May be substituted by Romberg's test, or picking up 12 clips in one hand.

These standards are acceptable minimum criteria. Unit-specific protocols mandating measures in excess of these are appropriate.

VII. PERFORMANCE IMPROVEMENT (PI)

The PI monitoring tool attached shall be used for monitoring Sedation and Analgesia procedures. The results shall be summarized and submitted to the Medical Staff Anesthesia Department CQI Committee at regularly-defined intervals. Appropriate peer review shall be directed to department chairs for review. PI shall be reported to Quality Improvement Council per reporting schedule as required.

APPENDIX
GUIDE TO DOSAGES FOR SEDATION AND ANALGESIA

Intravenous sedative and analgesic drugs should be given in small, incremental doses that are titrated to the desired endpoints of Sedation and Analgesia. Sufficient time must elapse between doses to allow the effect of each dose to be assessed before subsequent drug administration. When drugs are administered by nonintravenous routes (e.g., oral, rectal, intramuscular), allowance should be made for the time required for drug absorption before supplementation is considered.

ADULT PATIENTS

1.	Diazepam (Valium)	2.5 to 5 mg
2.	Midazolam (Versed)	1 to 2 mg
3.	Morphine Sulfate	1 to 5 mg
4.	Meperidine HCL (Demerol)	25 mg
5.	Sublimaze (Fentanyl)	2 micrograms/kilogram
6.	Naloxone (Narcan)	0.1 to 0.4 mg
7.	Flumazenil (Romazicon)	0.2 mg

PEDIATRIC PATIENTS

1.	Chloral Hydrate	75 mg/kg p.o.
2.	Diazepam (Valium)	0.04 to 0.3 mg/kg
3.	Midazelam (Versed)	0.02 to 0.05 mg/kg
4.	Morphine Sulfate	0.05 to 0.1 mg/kg
5.	Sublimaze (Fentanyl)	1-2 micrograms/kilogram
6.	Naloxone (Narcan)	5 to 10 micrograms/kg Q 3-5 min
7.	Flumazenil (Romazicon)	0.2 mg IV over 15 seconds, repeat Q 1 min., up to 1 mg total dose

Adjustment of the above dosages on a time-weighted basis is the responsibility of the physician performing the procedure.

This guide is not meant to be exhaustive. As new drugs become available and are appropriate for use during Sedation and Analgesia, it will be the responsibility of the physician performing the procedure to incorporate such drugs into practice.

Source: Adapted from Holy Cross Hospital, Silver Spring, Maryland.

4-53 Ketamine: Emergency Applications

PURPOSE

The purpose of an emergency department protocol for ketamine is to define the guidelines for the administration, monitoring, and recovery of patients undergoing sedation with ketamine.

Introduction

Ketamine produces a unique sedative state that is characterized by the following:

- Dissociation: Following administration of ketamine, the patient rapidly passes into a trance. This trance is first characterized by nystagmus and a glassy-eyed stare. The patient's eyes usually remain open, but the patient does not respond. This state is unique to ketamine and is termed dissociation because, while brainstem function is maintained normally, higher cognitive awareness is disconnected from somatic sensory input. Because brainstem function is preserved, normal or slightly enhanced muscle tone is maintained. On occasion, the patient may move or be moved into a position that is self-maintaining.
- Analgesia: Ketamine produces profound somatic analgesia that is adequate for most surgical procedures.
- Amnesia: Ketamine produces a complete lack of recall of events and procedures performed under sedation.
- Maintenance of airway and breathing reflexes: Upper airway reflexes remain intact and active. Airway reflexes are preserved in a manner superior to most other sedative agents. Sonorous respirations are observed frequently and may be managed by repositioning the patient's head and airway. Stimulation of the vocal cords by instrumentation or secretions rarely produces mild laryngospasm. Brief apnea may occur (albeit rarely) when ketamine is administered via rapid IV push.
- Cardiorespiratory stability: Unlike other sedatives, ketamine usually causes cardiac stimulation, not depression. Therefore, it is a preferred agent in patients who are hypotensive but still require sedation.

POLICY

Ketamine may be administered only by a physician specifically credentialed to administer Ketamine. Ketamine may be used for the sedation and analgesia of children and adult patients in the ED. *It is important to understand that Ketamine is an anesthetic agent.* Ketamine is appropriate for painful procedures, such as dressing changes, central line or chest tube placement, cardioversion, rapid sequence intubation, orthopedic manipulation, and emergency surgical procedures. Ketamine is suitable for most age groups provided that the physician supervising its use is versed in its age-related effects and contraindications. (Emergence phenomena are less frequently dramatic in children and elderly patients, and apnea is observed more frequently in children <3 mo.) Ketamine is relatively contraindicated in the following cases:

- Airway instability or tracheal pathology (unless used with endotracheal intubation to provide a higher margin of safety)

411

- High predisposition to laryngospasm or apnea (active pulmonary infection or children <3 mo)
- A full meal within last 3 hours (because of higher aspiration risk)
- Severe cardiovascular disease, such as angina, heart failure, or malignant hypertension (because of cardiostimulant effects of ketamine; however, this is controversial)
- CSF obstructive states (eg, severe head injury, central congenital, or mass lesions; however, this is controversial)
- Intraocular pressure pathology (eg, glaucoma or acute globe injury; however, this is controversial)
- Previous psychotic illness (because of potential activation of psychoses)
- Hyperthyroidism or thyroid medication use (because of potential for severe tachycardia or hypertension)
- Porphyria (because of possibility of triggering a porphyric reaction)

These are relative contraindications, and most are unconfirmed by rigorous methods. In cases necessitating emergency sedation, the benefits of ketamine may outweigh the risks listed above, particularly if substituting other sedative agents brings greater risks. The literature demonstrates that ketamine has a safety profile that outperforms many other sedative agents. This makes it the agent of choice for many potentially difficult emergency situations.

Potential adverse effects

Potential adverse effects of ketamine administration include hypersalivation, muscle hypertonicity, transient clonus, transient stridor, emesis, transient rash, and agitation.

PROCEDURE

Prior to administration of ketamine, chart an initial patient assessment with weight, vital signs, initial oxygen saturation, and baseline level of consciousness. As with all sedative techniques, make resuscitative equipment for advanced airway management readily available and initiate and continue pulse oximetry with audible alarms until the patient meets recovery criteria. (In regions without pulse oximetry, ketamine is not contraindicated and is preferred over sedation with other agents.) If possible, place the patient in a private treatment room to minimize stimulation during the recovery period. During the procedure, ensure that medical staff continuously attends the patient. Once the procedure is complete and the recovery period is well underway, ensure that staff or family members attend the patient until recovery criteria are met.

Some clinicians routinely premedicate all patients with promethazine or a benzodiazepine to reduce postprocedure agitation, though this may greatly prolong the recovery period. Promethazine is used widely in Africa for adult premedication and may have some advantage over the benzodiazepines because of its additional antiemetic effects; however, controlled studies are lacking. Ketamine may be combined with an antisialagogue to reduce its stimulant effect on oral and respiratory secretions. Either glycopyrrolate, in a dose of 0.01 mg/kg (not to exceed 0.2 mg), or atropine, in a dose of 0.01 mg/kg (0.1 mg minimum, not to exceed 0.5 mg), is acceptable. Pretreatment 30 minutes prior to ketamine administration is best; however, both glycopyrrolate and atropine may be mixed in the same syringe as ketamine if time is short.

Some physicians forego the use of an antisialagogue (more often in adults), preferring ketamine-induced hypersalivation to the additional tachycardia caused by atropine or glycopyrrolate.

Ketamine may be dosed via IM injection, IV injection or infusion, intranasal drops, rectal injection, or oral elixir. For children, IM injection is usually the least traumatic method of obtaining effective sedation, and it may be safely performed without routine need for IV access. For adults, continuous IV infusion is usually the safest and most easily titratable to effect.

IM ketamine is usually dosed initially at 4 mg/kg (with a typical range of 2-10 mg/kg, depending on procedural requirements). Analgesia alone is usually obtained with a dose of 1 mg/kg IM. Complete dissociation is usually obtained with a dose of 4-10 mg/kg IM. Onset of action (glazed eyes and nystagmus) usually occurs within 5 minutes and lasts for up to 30 minutes, depending on the dose used. Prior to beginning any painful procedure, test analgesic effect by pricking the patient with a needle. Booster doses of 2-5 mg/kg IM every 10 minutes (without additional antisialagogue) may be administered if initial sedation is inadequate. A 100 mg/mL ketamine solution is preferred for IM administration to reduce the volume of injected solution.

Perform IV infusion of ketamine by mixing ketamine with saline or D5W to make a 1 mg/mL solution (500 mg ketamine in 500 mL fluid). To prevent inadvertent overdosage, the total amount of ketamine mixed can be limited to the maximum safe dosage (3 mg/kg IV). Using a regular nonmicrodrip IV chamber (15 drops/mL), open the IV to flow at a rapid drop rate (about 2 drops/kg/min). Onset of action (glazed eyes and nystagmus) usually occurs within 2 minutes and lasts until 10 minutes after the infusion is terminated. Prior to beginning any painful procedure, test analgesic effect by pricking the patient with a needle. Once sedation is deep enough, turn down the drip to approximately one half of the induction rate (1 drop/kg/min). Stop the drip 10 minutes prior to the end of the procedure.

IV slow bolus injection is the most commonly used alternative to the 2 methods described above. Initially dose ketamine IV bolus at 1 mg/kg (with a typical range of 0.5-2 mg/kg, depending on procedural requirements). Onset of action (glazed eyes and nystagmus) usually occurs within 1 minute. Surgical anesthesia lasts about 15 minutes, with full recovery in about 60 minutes. As above, prior to beginning any painful procedure, test analgesic effect by pricking the patient with a needle. Booster doses of 0.5-1 mg/kg IV every 10 minutes (without additional antisialagogue) may be administered if initial sedation is inadequate. The maximum dose for routine use is 3 mg/kg, except in patients with alcoholism, who may require much more. The more dilute 10-50 mg/mL ketamine solutions are preferred for IV administration. Perform the injection slowly to avoid ketamine-induced apnea (rare).

Recovery guidelines

In many studies, the incidence of unpleasant emergence experiences is less than 1% in adults and children. Unless safer methods of sedation are available, the fear of the ketamine recovery experience should not preclude its use. Indeed, management of this period requires a certain finesse that may separate the physician experienced in ketamine sedation from the novice. Because of the unique effects of dissociation, patients undergoing ketamine sedation experience a sense of semiconscious bodily detachment as they awaken. During this period, imagination can be confused with actual environmental stimuli. Partially conducted stimuli may be interpreted as pleasant or not. Because of this, the physician potentially has much control of the patient's recovery experience and may direct this experience positively by simple and repeated suggestion and by controlling the recovery environment.

By the same mechanism, misinterpreted or noxious stimuli may cause patients to have a frightening recovery. During this period, minimize physical contact, noise, and stimulation and instruct caretakers not to awaken the patient prematurely. Blood pressure monitoring during this period is discouraged by some anesthesiologists who note undue disruption of recovery from cuff stimulation. Recovery reactions are less frequently dramatic in children and patients who are elderly.

For patients who are recovering poorly, administration of any number of sleep-inducing agents during recovery is helpful. Patients at high risk for agitated recovery can be medicated prior to initiation of the procedure. Such agents sedate the active but partially dissociated mind, blunting the confusion between imagination and reality. If such medication is used, promethazine is effective and provides antiemetic effects. Many practitioners in developing countries consider it to be the drug of choice. Lorazepam, droperidol, haloperidol, and midazolam demonstrate efficacy as well. Diazepam has a variable effect in different studies. Note that sedative agents are not essential for smooth recovery. By using reassurance alone, adult patients in one series experienced no unpleasant reactions during recovery from ketamine sedation.

Recovery criteria

Anticipated recovery time is 0.5-2 hours following administration of ketamine. The patient may be discharged from the hospital when all of the following criteria are met:

- At least 30 minutes has passed since the administration of ketamine.
- The patient's level of consciousness has returned to baseline. (Note that the level of consciousness may be depressed normally following the procedure because of fatigue, and a guardian may be able to validate normal behavior for the patient under these circumstances.)
- The patient is able to stand unassisted without falling.

The physician should record the patient's level of consciousness, as well as the patient's ability to stand, at the time of discharge. Discharge a patient in the company of a guardian or other caregiver. The physician should advise the caregiver that the patient may vomit and have mild disequilibrium, and that the patient should not be administered anything by mouth and not be allowed independent ambulation for 2 hours after discharge. Restrict driving for a full day following ketamine administration.

Source: Excerpted from James Li, MD, "Ketamine: Emergency Application," eMedicine Journal. Copyright 2005, eMedicine.com, Inc. Reprinted with permission.

4-54 Pain Management: Rating/Medication Administration Record

Month: _____ Year: _____

Instructions: Complete this form as you would complete a Medication Administration Record (MAR) document specifying the pain site, pain rating, & post treatment pain rating. (see other side for Pain Scale)

Pain Rating Scale used: **W** ONG-BAKER SCALE **N** UMERICAL SCALE **F** LACC SCALE

Medication	Date:	Date:	Date:	Date:	Date:	Date:
	Scale ___ Level ___ Pain Site ___	Scale ___ Level ___ Pain Site ___	Scale ___ Level ___ Pain Site ___	Scale ___ Level ___ Pain Site ___	Scale ___ Level ___ Pain Site ___	Scale ___ Level ___ Pain Site ___
	Time ___ am pm Initial ___	Time ___ am pm Initial ___	Time ___ am pm Initial ___	Time ___ am pm Initial ___	Time ___ am pm Initial ___	Time ___ am pm Initial ___
	RESULTS: Scale ___ Level ___ Time ___ am pm Initial ___	**RESULTS:** Scale ___ Level ___ Time ___ am pm Initial ___	**RESULTS:** Scale ___ Level ___ Time ___ am pm Initial ___	**RESULTS:** Scale ___ Level ___ Time ___ am pm Initial ___	**RESULTS:** Scale ___ Level ___ Time ___ am pm Initial ___	**RESULTS:** Scale ___ Level ___ Time ___ am pm Initial ___

Medication	Date:	Date:	Date:	Date:	Date:	Date:
	Scale ___ Level ___ Pain Site ___	Scale ___ Level ___ Pain Site ___	Scale ___ Level ___ Pain Site ___	Scale ___ Level ___ Pain Site ___	Scale ___ Level ___ Pain Site ___	Scale ___ Level ___ Pain Site ___
	Time ___ am pm Initial ___	Time ___ am pm Initial ___	Time ___ am pm Initial ___	Time ___ am pm Initial ___	Time ___ am pm Initial ___	Time ___ am pm Initial ___
	RESULTS: Scale ___ Level ___ Time ___ am pm Initial ___	**RESULTS:** Scale ___ Level ___ Time ___ am pm Initial ___	**RESULTS:** Scale ___ Level ___ Time ___ am pm Initial ___	**RESULTS:** Scale ___ Level ___ Time ___ am pm Initial ___	**RESULTS:** Scale ___ Level ___ Time ___ am pm Initial ___	**RESULTS:** Scale ___ Level ___ Time ___ am pm Initial ___

Medication	Date:	Date:	Date:	Date:	Date:	Date:
	Scale ___ Level ___ Pain Site ___	Scale ___ Level ___ Pain Site ___	Scale ___ Level ___ Pain Site ___	Scale ___ Level ___ Pain Site ___	Scale ___ Level ___ Pain Site ___	Scale ___ Level ___ Pain Site ___
	Time ___ am pm Initial ___	Time ___ am pm Initial ___	Time ___ am pm Initial ___	Time ___ am pm Initial ___	Time ___ am pm Initial ___	Time ___ am pm Initial ___
	RESULTS: Scale ___ Level ___ Time ___ am pm Initial ___	**RESULTS:** Scale ___ Level ___ Time ___ am pm Initial ___	**RESULTS:** Scale ___ Level ___ Time ___ am pm Initial ___	**RESULTS:** Scale ___ Level ___ Time ___ am pm Initial ___	**RESULTS:** Scale ___ Level ___ Time ___ am pm Initial ___	**RESULTS:** Scale ___ Level ___ Time ___ am pm Initial ___

Resident Name: _____ Room # _____ Doctor: _____

Diagnosis: _____

Side 1 of 2

415

WONG-BAKER SCALE:

Initial Instructions: Explain to the resident that each face is for a person who feels happy because he or she has no pain (hurt) or sad because he or she has some or a lot of pain. **FACE 0** is happy because he or she doesn't hurt at all. **FACE 2** hurts just a little bit. **FACE 4** hurts a little more. **FACE 6** hurts even more. **FACE 8** hurts a whole lot. **FACE 10** hurts as much as you can imagine, although you don't have to be crying to feel this bad. Ask the resident to choose the face that best describes how he or she is feeling.

NO HURT	HURTS LITTLE BIT	HURTS LITTLE MORE	HURTS EVEN MORE	HURTS WHOLE LOT	HURTS WORST
0	2	4	6	8	10

NUMERIC SCALE: Choose a number from 0 to 10 that best describes the level of pain.

NO PAIN	MILD PAIN, ANNOYING Pain is present but does not limit activity.		NAGGING PAIN, UNCOMFORTABLE, TROUBLESOME Can do most activities with rest periods.			MISERABLE, DISTRESSING Unable to do some activities because of pain.		INTENSE, DREADFUL, HORRIBLE Unable to do most activities because of pain.		WORST PAIN POSSIBLE, UNBEARABLE Unable to do any activities because
0	1	2	3	4	5	6	7	8	9	10

FLACC SCALE:

Initial Instructions: The FLACC is a behavior pain assessment scale for use with nonverbal residents who are unable to provide reports of pain. Rate the resident in each of the five measurement categories, add the scores together, and document the total pain score.

	0	1	2
FACE	No particular expression of smile.	Occasional grimace or frown, withdrawn, disinterested.	Frequent to constant frown, clenched jaw, quivering chin.
LEGS	Normal Position or relaxed.	Uneasy, restless, tense.	Kicking, or legs drawn up.
ACTIVITY	Lying quietly, normal position, moves easily.	Squirming, shifting back and forth, tense.	Arched, rigid, or jerking.
CRY	No crying (awake or asleep).	Moans or whimpers, occasional complaint	Crying steadily, screams or sobs, frequent complaints.
CONSOLABILITY	Content, relaxed.	Reassured by occasional touching, hugging, or "talking to." Distractible.	Difficult to console or comfort.

General Instructions:

1. Choose only one appropriate scale based upon the resident's ability to respond.
2. Identify the scale used and the score for that scale on the other side of this form by using the following key:

W ONG-BAKER SCALE

N UMERICAL SCALE

F LACC SCALE

Side 2 of 2
of Pain Management: Rating /
MEDICATION Administration Record

Source: Best Practices Committee, *HCANJ Pain Management Guidelines*, 1/05 Revision. Health Care Association of New Jersey, Hamilton, New Jersey. Reprinted with permission.

4-55 Pain Management: Rating/Treatment Administration Record

Instructions: Complete this form as you would complete a Medication Administration Record (MAR) document specifying the pain site, pain rating, & post treatment pain rating. (see other side for Pain Scale)

Pain Rating Scale used: **W** ONG-BAKER SCALE **N** UMERICAL SCALE **F** LACC SCALE

Treatment

Date:	Date:	Date:	Date:	Date:	Date:
Scale___ Level___ Pain Site___	Scale___ Level___ Pain Site___	Scale___ Level___ Pain Site___	Scale___ Level___ Pain Site___	Scale___ Level___ Pain Site___	Scale___ Level___ Pain Site___
Time___ am pm Initial___	Time___ am pm Initial___	Time___ am pm Initial___	Time___ am pm Initial___	Time___ am pm Initial___	Time___ am pm Initial___
RESULTS: Scale___ Level___ Time___ am pm Initial___	**RESULTS:** Scale___ Level___ Time___ am pm Initial___	**RESULTS:** Scale___ Level___ Time___ am pm Initial___	**RESULTS:** Scale___ Level___ Time___ am pm Initial___	**RESULTS:** Scale___ Level___ Time___ am pm Initial___	**RESULTS:** Scale___ Level___ Time___ am pm Initial___

Treatment

Date:	Date:	Date:	Date:	Date:	Date:
Scale___ Level___ Pain Site___	Scale___ Level___ Pain Site___	Scale___ Level___ Pain Site___	Scale___ Level___ Pain Site___	Scale___ Level___ Pain Site___	Scale___ Level___ Pain Site___
Time___ am pm Initial___	Time___ am pm Initial___	Time___ am pm Initial___	Time___ am pm Initial___	Time___ am pm Initial___	Time___ am pm Initial___
RESULTS: Scale___ Level___ Time___ am pm Initial___	**RESULTS:** Scale___ Level___ Time___ am pm Initial___	**RESULTS:** Scale___ Level___ Time___ am pm Initial___	**RESULTS:** Scale___ Level___ Time___ am pm Initial___	**RESULTS:** Scale___ Level___ Time___ am pm Initial___	**RESULTS:** Scale___ Level___ Time___ am pm Initial___

Treatment

Date:	Date:	Date:	Date:	Date:	Date:
Scale___ Level___ Pain Site___	Scale___ Level___ Pain Site___	Scale___ Level___ Pain Site___	Scale___ Level___ Pain Site___	Scale___ Level___ Pain Site___	Scale___ Level___ Pain Site___
Time___ am pm Initial___	Time___ am pm Initial___	Time___ am pm Initial___	Time___ am pm Initial___	Time___ am pm Initial___	Time___ am pm Initial___
RESULTS: Scale___ Level___ Time___ am pm Initial___	**RESULTS:** Scale___ Level___ Time___ am pm Initial___	**RESULTS:** Scale___ Level___ Time___ am pm Initial___	**RESULTS:** Scale___ Level___ Time___ am pm Initial___	**RESULTS:** Scale___ Level___ Time___ am pm Initial___	**RESULTS:** Scale___ Level___ Time___ am pm Initial___

Resident Name: _____   Room # _____   Doctor: _____

Diagnosis: _____

Side 1 of 2

417

WONG-BAKER SCALE:

Initial Instructions: Explain to the resident that each face is for a person who feels happy because he or she has no pain (hurt) or sad because he or she has some or a lot of pain. **FACE 0** is happy because he or she doesn't hurt at all. **FACE 2** hurts just a little bit. **FACE 4** hurts a little more. **FACE 6** hurts even more. **FACE 8** hurts a whole lot. **FACE 10** hurts as much as you can imagine, although you don't have to be crying to feel this bad. Ask the resident to choose the face that best describes how he or she is feeling.

NO HURT	HURTS LITTLE BIT	HURTS LITTLE MORE	HURTS EVEN MORE	HURTS WHOLE LOT	HURTS WORST
0	2	4	6	8	10

NUMERIC SCALE: Choose a number from 0 to 10 that best describes the level of pain.

NO PAIN		MILD PAIN, ANNOYING Pain is present but does not limit activity.		NAGGING PAIN, UNCOMFORTABLE, TROUBLESOME Can do most activities with rest periods.		MISERABLE, DISTRESSING Unable to do some activities because of pain.		INTENSE, DREADFUL, HORRIBLE Unable to do most activities because of pain.		WORST PAIN POSSIBLE, UNBEARABLE Unable to do any activities because
0	1	2	3	4	5	6	7	8	9	10

FLACC SCALE:

Initial Instructions: The FLACC is a behavior pain assessment scale for use with nonverbal residents who are unable to provide reports of pain. Rate the resident in each of the five measurement categories, add the scores together, and document the total pain score.

	0	1	2
FACE	No particular expression of smile.	Occasional grimace or frown, withdrawn, disinterested.	Frequent to constant frown, clenched jaw, quivering chin.
LEGS	Normal Position or relaxed.	Uneasy, restless, tense.	Kicking, or legs drawn up.
ACTIVITY	Lying quietly, normal position, moves easily.	Squirming, shifting back and forth, tense.	Arched, rigid, or jerking.
CRY	No crying (awake or asleep).	Moans or whimpers, occasional complaint	Crying steadily, screams or sobs, frequent complaints.
CONSOLABILITY	Content, relaxed.	Reassured by occasional touching, hugging, or "talking to." Distractible.	Difficult to console or comfort.

Side 2 of 2
of Pain Management: Rating /
TREATMENT Administration Record

General Instructions:

1. Choose *only one* appropriate scale based upon the resident's ability to respond.
2. Identify the scale used and the score for that scale on the other side of this form by using the following key:

W ONG-BAKER SCALE

N UMERICAL SCALE

F LACC SCALE

Source: Best Practices Committee, *HCANJ Pain Management Guidelines*, 1/05 Revision. Health Care Association of New Jersey, Hamilton, New Jersey. Reprinted with permission.

EDUCATION

4-56 Policy and Procedure: Discharge Instructions

I. PURPOSE

To provide procedures for effective patient discharge and follow up.

II. POLICY

A. All patients will be assessed for medical stability, orientation, readiness to learn and barriers to learning.

B. All patients discharged from the Emergency Department will receive condition-appropriate instructions for home care and appropriate referrals.

III. RESPONSIBILITIES

A. The physician or nurse will verbally instruct patient on specific discharge instructions, including medications.

B. Patient will verbally state understanding or return demonstration of discharge instructions.

C. Patient will sign discharge instruction sheet:
   1. One copy is given to the patient.
   2. One copy is placed in patient's medical record.

D. Appropriate medical follow up referral will be given.

E. Assure that all medications and procedures ordered by the physician have been accomplished. Patient will be observed for at least twenty (20) minutes after receiving any antibiotic, narcotic or any other medications that the Emergency physician states appropriate to observe to insure there are no signs or symptoms of an untoward reaction. Take home medications must be dispensed by the physician.

F. Assure all patients have appropriate transportation arranged upon discharge. This may include arranging transportation through family, friends, ambulance services, taxi vouchers or bus token. The Emergency Services case manager or social worker may be involved in the process as appropriate.

IV. PERSONNEL

Registered Nurses, Licensed Vocational Nurses, Physicians

V. EQUIPMENT/SUPPLIES

Aftercare Instruction Forms

VI. BUSINESS UNIT ADDENDUM

A. Patient to be accompanied to Financial Counselor's Office or have the Financial Counselor come to the bedside if there are financial arrangements or payments to be made.

B. Employees treated for workers' compensation cases may be referred for one follow-up visit to the Urgent Care. Those employees who require follow-up for a wound recheck and a second follow-up visit for suture removal may also be referred to the Urgent Care. The employee should then be referred to Employee Occupational Health Services. Employees requiring more than one follow-up visit are to be referred directly to Employee Occupational Health Services. It is the responsibility of the Employee Occupational Health Nurse to make the appropriate physician referral.

C. Workers' compensation cases are to be referred to the Compensation coverage physician of that particular company, as listed in the Workers' Compensation Rolodex. If the patient has no physician and has undergone procedures, such as suturing for a laceration, care of a simple burn, and I&D of a wound, etc., the patient may be referred back to the Urgent Care for the initial follow-up wound check or suture removal. The Emergency Center physician will determine at the first follow-up visit what action will then be taken.

Source: Courtesy of Scripps Mercy Hospital, San Diego, California.

4-57 Sample Fall Prevention Brochure

Fall Prevention for Family Members and Visitors
Adventist Health
Tillamook County General Hospital

About Caregiving at Home After Discharge

Evaluate:

- Loose rugs or carpeting
- Walkways
- Furniture placement
- Lighting
- Assisting devices such as safety grab bars

Consider:

- Walkers, wheelchairs, canes, etc.
- A communication system (baby monitoring system has worked well).
- A night light in the room and in the hallway.
- An overbed table.
- A raised toilet seat
- Grab bars near the toilet and tub

- Nonskid mats in the tub and elsewhere.
- A lower water temperature
- Hand held shower in the bath area.
- Handrails in the hall

General Information

Patients with certain diagnoses or situations are automatically placed on Fall Precautions. Assessment on admission will help staff determine who is at risk.

Working Together

If there are any concerns or requests you have to make the hospital environment even safer for your loved one, *please* share this with us. Thank You!

FALL PREVENTION

It is very important to all of us that your family member / loved one be safe. Being ill and/or in a different environment can be very confusing. Sometimes we forget that there has been a change in our body functions or that there is weakness where we had strength before. Factors that contribute to falling are weakness, loss of balance, slipping or tripping over equipment. We would like to let you know what WE can do together as a TEAM to keep your loved one safe.

Things that can help prevent your family member from falling:
- Caregivers perform a "Fall Risk Assessment" upon admission.
- If the assessment determines there is a Fall Risk, a magnetic sign will be posted on the outside of the patient room door to notify everyone to keep an eye out to assist as needed.
- The staff may assign a room closer to the nurse's station.
- Generally, two side rails will be up. There is actually more of a potential for injury if the lower side rails are up
- The staff will provide frequent observations and perform "founds."
- Specific devices may be placed, such as a TABS electronic alarm unit that activates when a patient moves a certain distance or attempts to get up. A Fall Mat may be placed on the floor to provide a non-skid surface. A chair wedge may be used which encourages a person to remain comfortably seated.
- Tissues, the phone and other needed items should be kept within reach of the bed or chair.
- The call light or a bell is kept within easy reach at the bedside and in the bathroom to call for assistance.
- Chairs and the bed are kept at the lowest height.
- Eyeglasses or hearing aids should be used to lessen confusion, as appropriate. Never place or store these items in tissue. Ask the nursing staff for a container.
- Lighting must be adequate. A night light is used at bedtime.
- Family or friends are encouraged or may be asked to sit with your family member.

421

- Feel free to do things that help your family member relax, such as watching TV, listening to music, or reading to them.
- Encourage them to ask for pain medicine when needed.
- Provide comfort by changing their position every two hours or giving them back rubs.
- Assist with walking or exercising as appropriate.
- Place a commode chair next to their bed.
- Bring in pictures and familiar articles.
- Keep the area where they walk clear and free from furniture.
- Wear non-skid shoes or slippers that fit well.
- Safety bars are located in the bathrooms and hallways.
- Supportive devices such as gait belts, walkers, hemi walkers, canes and Geri chairs are available.
- Medical equipment should be removed from the room as soon as it is not needed. Inform the nursing staff if you sec extra items.

Patient Restraints

Restraints are used as a last resort. They may actually increase confusion and disorientation.

In general, these measures are used only when treatment depends on them and after weight the benefit of the treatment against the possible harm of the restraint.

Source: Courtesy of Tillamook County General Hospital, Tillamook, Oregon.

CONTINUUM OF CARE

4-58 Pediatric Asthma Continuity Flow Sheet

Chronic Medications: _____ _____ — _____

_____ — _____ _____ _____

Severity Code: (1) Mild Intermittent (2) Mild Persistent (3) Moderate Persistent (4) Severe Persistent

	+ −	Comments	+ −	Comments	+ −	Comments
Date of Visit						
Severity Level Code						
Basic Assessment						
Vital Signs (t/r/p/bp)						
Height/Weight						
Predicted Peak Flow						
Current Peak Flow %						
Personal Best Peak Flow						
O_2 Sat Level						
Signs & Symptoms						
Coughing, wheezing, SOB or chest tightness during the day? (freq.)						
Awakened at night due to asthma symptoms? (freq.)						
How long does your quick relief inhaler last?						
Symptoms while exercising or playing?						
Episodes when asthma symptoms were a lot worse than usual?						
What does pt think caused the symptoms to get worse? (pets/weather change/cig. smoke/molds/pollens/wood stoves/ fireplaces/chemicals/roaches)						
Monitoring						
Has peak flow dropped below 80% of personal best since last visit?						
If yes, what did pt do when this occurred?						
When does pt usually measure peak flow?						
Functionality (Since Last Visit)						
Missed work or school? (freq)						
Reduced your activities? (amt)						
Change in caregiver's work/school due to child's asthma? (amt)						

	+	Comments	+	Comments	+	Comments
	−		−		−	
Any emergency room visits? (Include dates and location)						
Any hospitalizations? (Dates/location)						

Medications

Has pt missed/stopped taking any regular doses of meds for any reason?						
Has pt had trouble filling prescriptions?						
Has asthma medicine caused you any problems? (shakiness, nervousness, bad taste, sore throat, cough, upset stomach)						

Other Medications Being Taken/Alternative Treatments or Remedies (List)

Examination/ Meds/Procedures/ Follow Up	Date:	Examination/ Meds/Procedures/ Follow Up	Date:	Examination/ Meds/Procedures/ Follow Up	Date:

	+	Comments	+	Comments	+	Comments
	−		−		−	

Education

Learning Style Evaluated/Documented						
Signs & Symptoms of Asthma						
Inflammatory nature of asthma						
Avoiding asthma/environmental triggers						
Patient compliance using tools (MDI, Spacer, Nebulizer)						
Can patient demonstrate use of peak flow meter and inhaler with spacer?						
Role of Medications						
Smoking avoidance						

Action Plan

Written Action Plan revised						
Written Action Plan reviewed with Pt						
Date of Last Flu Vaccination						

Referrals

Referral to Asthma Education						
Referral to Psychosocial Services						

	+ −	Comments	+ −	Comments	+	Comments
Referral to Other (list)						
Signatures:						
Nurse/Initials:						
Provider:						

Source: Courtesy of Parkland Health and Hospital System, Dallas, Texas.

4-59 Physician Certification for Transfer of Patient from the Emergency Department

AUTHORIZATION FOR TRANSFER

Directions: This form must be completed by a physician who authorizes transfer to another medical facility of a patient determined by the Emergency Department to have an emergency medical condition or to be in active labor. An emergency medical condition and active labor are defined by the Consolidated Omnibus Budget Reconciliation Act (COBRA) of 1985 (42 U.S.C. § 1395dd) and amended by the Omnibus Budget Reconciliation Act of 1987 and 1989.

SECTION 1 COMPLETE AS INDICATED.

A. ☐ **The patient has been stabilized** such that, within reasonable medical probability, no material deterioration of the patient's condition is likely to result from or occur during the transfer. (A patient in active labor has been stabilized if she has delivered, including the placenta.)

B. ☐ **Patient's condition has NOT been stabilized.**

SECTION 2 COMPLETE AS INDICATED.

A. ☐ **Reason for transfer:**   NOTE: if 1(B) was checked, RISKS AND BENEFITS MUST ALSO BE LISTED BELOW.
REMINDER: If the reason for transfer is because the on-call physician failed or refused to appear within a reasonable period of time, indicate the name and address of the on-call physician on the medical record.

_____
_____
_____

SECTION 3 COMPLETE ONLY IF SECTION 1(B) ABOVE HAS BEEN CHECKED. IF NOT, PROCEED TO SECTION 4.

CHECK ONE OF THE FOLLOWING:

A. ☐ **Patient requests transfer** (or a legally responsible individual acting on the patient's behalf requests the transfer). TRANSFER BY UNSTABILIZED PATIENT on signature page of this form must be completed.

B. ☐ **Medical benefits outweigh risks:** Based on the reasonable risks and benefits to the patient, and based upon the information available at the time of the patient's transfer, the medical benefits reasonably expected from the provision of appropriate medical treatment at another medical facility outweigh the increased risks, if any, to the patient's medical condition [including, in the case of a pregnant woman, the risks to the unborn child(ren)] from effecting the transfer.

SECTION 4 OMIT THIS SECTION IF 3 (A) WAS CHECKED. OTHERWISE, COMPLETE A OR B AS APPROPRIATE.

A. ☐ **Patient consents to the transfer** (or a legally responsible individual acting on the patient's behalf consents to the transfer). TRANSFER CONSENT on signature page of this form must be completed.

B. ☐ **Transfer was offered but refused** by the patient or a legally responsible individual acting on the patient's behalf. TRANSFER REFUSAL on signature page of this form must be completed.

SECTION 5 COMPLETE AS INDICATED.

NOTE: The patient may not be transferred unless each of the following requirements is met:

A. ☐ The receiving facility has available space and qualified personnel for the treatment of the patient.

B. ☐ The receiving facility has agreed to accept transfer and to provide appropriate medical treatment.

    1. Name of the receiving facility _____ _____

                                Please print

    2. Name of individual accepting transfer _____

                                       Please print

C. ☐ The receiving facility will be provided with appropriate medical records of the examination and treatment of the patient.

D. ☐ The patient will be transferred by qualified personnel and transportation equipment as required, including the use of necessary and medically appropriate life support measures.

    1. MEANS OF TRANSPORT

        ☐ Ground ambulance (☐ BLS ☐ ALS) _____

                                Name

        ☐ Air ambulance (☐ BLS ☐ ALS) _____

                                     Name

        ☐ Transport Team_____

                                    Name

        ☐ Private car

        ☐ Other _____

    2. PERSONNEL ACCOMPANYING PATIENT (check all that apply)

        ☐ EMT—A

        ☐ EMT—P

        ☐ Physician

        ☐ Nurse

        ☐ Respiratory Therapist

        ☐ Other _____

I certify that I have answered the above questions based upon the information available to me at the time of the patient's transfer. I further certify that I have made the appropriate disclosures as indicated on this form.

_____   _____

Name of Physician Authorizing Transfer (please print)   Physician Signature

                                             Date _____ Time _____

SIGNATURE PAGE FOR PATIENT'S REQUEST/REFUSAL/CONSENT TO TRANSFER

I. TRANSFER REQUEST BY UNSTABILIZED PATIENT

I acknowledge that my medical condition has been evaluated and explained to me by _____

                                               Name of physician

who has recommended and offered to me further medical examination and treatment and has informed me of the hospital obligation to provide stabilizing treatment. The potential benefits of such further medical examination and treatment as well as the potential risks associated with transfer to another facility have been explained to me and I fully understand them. In spite of this understanding, I refuse to consent to the further medical examination and treatment that has been offered to me, and request transfer to _____.

        Name of receiving facility

_____

Signature of patient or legally responsible
individual signing on patient's behalf

_____   _____
Date and time   *Relationship to patient*

II. TRANSFER CONSENT

I acknowledge that my medical condition has been evaluated and explained to me by _____ who has recommended that I be transferred to the service of Dr. _____ at _____.

Name of receiving facility

The potential benefits of such transfer, the potential risks associated with such transfer, and the probable risks of not being transferred have been explained to me and I fully understand them. With this knowledge and understanding, I agree and consent to be transferred.

_____   _____
Date and time   *Signature of patient or legally responsible*
                                          individual signing on patient's behalf

                                          _____
                                                   Relationship to patient

III. TRANSFER REFUSAL

I acknowledge that my medical condition has been evaluated and explained to me by _____

Name of physician

who has recommended that I be transferred to _____.

Name of receiving facility

The potential benefits of such transfer, the potential risks associated with such transfer, and the probable risks of not being transferred have been explained to me and I fully understand them. Even though the above named physician believes it is in my best interests to be transferred, I refuse to be transferred and I request instead to continue receiving treatment at _____ Hospital.

_____   _____
Date and time   *Signature of patient or legally responsible*
                                          individual signing on patient's behalf

                                          _____
                                                   Relationship to patient

Source: Copyright Aspen Publishers, Inc.

4-60 Process for Conversion of Standing Orders/Protocols

A. REQUIREMENTS FOR 3RD PARTY REIMBURSEMENT REGULATIONS:

- Tests/treatments based on identified clinical rationale specific to the patient. Ordering of any test, procedure or treatment must be "medically necessary."
- Each order must:
    1. be linked to a diagnosis or chief complaint. *Batteries or panels of tests, stand alone rule-out, or standard pre- or post-op orders are not acceptable.*
    2. be entered into the medical record with date & signature of the ordering physician (including ID #)
    3. have documented results of tests or treatments filed in medical record and referred to in the physician progress notes.

Only protocols with the above characteristics, which are developed, approved & formatted identifying medical necessity are acceptable.

B. CURRENT USE OF STANDING ORDERS/PROTOCOLS:

An assessment of standing orders, pre-printed orders & "routine orders" was conducted throughout the hospital. The findings revealed that most of the current "standing order," "preprinted order" & "routine order" systems **would not** meet the requirements for 3rd party reimbursement. Therefore, the Compliance Committee assigned a subcommittee the task of identifying all current "standing orders" and "protocols," develop a process and assist departments convert them to acceptable format. The intent of the subcommittee is to systematically assist with a conversion process and *not interrupt or impede medical care.* Departments will need to write these orders according to the Protocol Order Procedure using one of the following formats:

- the generic protocol order form (*protocols can be transcribed onto the generic form as needed.)*
- protocol orders printed in the approved format

C. STANDING ORDER DEFINITION:

Any pre-existing procedure/protocol or unit specific "understanding" that precipitates a health care worker, other than a physician, to proceed with ordering a test or treatment. This type of "order" in the past may have been based on the patient assessment, unit or department specific guideline, a standard procedure for appointment to a specialty clinic or a chief complaint or diagnosis. Examples of standing orders, include but are not limited to:

1) a blood sugar is performed on all diabetics upon arrival at a clinic;
2) a pregnancy test is automatically ordered on all female patients;
3) a battery of laboratory tests are required for any patient seen in a specialty clinic.

D. PROTOCOL DEFINITION:

Written treatment or testing regimes which are designed & approved by the medical staff based on the patient's presenting signs, symptoms and/or diagnosis. Orders are then transcribed onto an order sheet and initiated. The physician must sign these orders. Examples of protocols include, but are not limited to:

1) administering Tylenol 650 mgs PO if a patient's temperature is greater than 104; and
2) laboratory, radiology testing ordered for clinical practice guideline

Source: Adapted from Parkland Health and Hospital System, Dallas, Texas.

4-61 Protocol Approval Flowchart

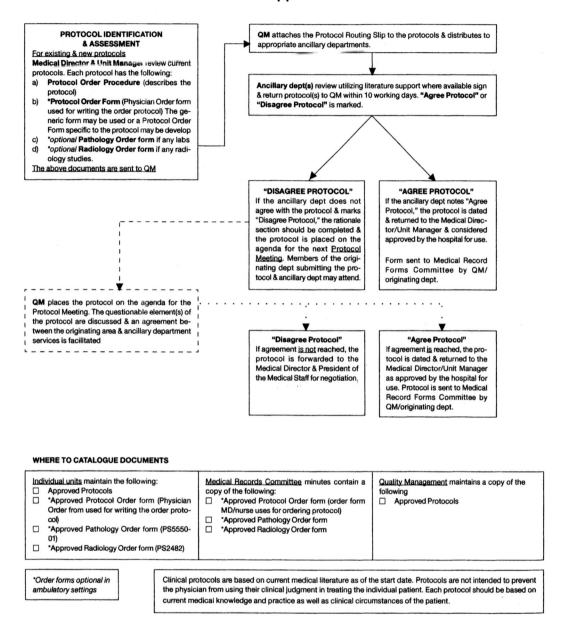

Source: Adapted from Parkland Headlth and Hospital System, Dallas, Texas

4-62 Physical Patient Report Form

Date Report Called: _____

Patient Name: _____

AGE: _____

Physician Calling Report: _____

Presenting Complaint: _____

_____

Order Requests: _____

_____

_____

Patient to be seen by ED physician?:   YES OR NO (circle one)

Patient to by seen by PMD?:   YES OR NO (circle one)

Patient to be admitted?:   Yes OR NO (circle one)

Signature: _____
              (PERSON TAKING REPORT)

Copy to be taken to the Triage Nurse.

Source: Courtesy of Medical Center of Plano, Plano, Texas.

4-63 Emergency Department/Radiology Communication Form

INITIAL IMPRESSION BY E.D. PHYSICIAN

☐ Essentially Normal
   Other Findings:

Date: _____

X-ray Ordered: _____ _____

_____

Chief Complaint: _____

_____

Time: _____
Emergency Physician: _____, MD

RADIOLOGIST'S REVIEW

☐ Agree, No Significant Discrepancy
☐ Disagree with ED physician's
   impression
Diagnosis:

If radiologist disagrees with ED physician's impression:

Notified _____

in ED at _____ on _____
           (Time)   (Date)

☐ Final report dictated.

Radiologist: _____, MD
Date: _____ Time: _____

EMERGENCY DEPARTMENT REVIEW AND FOLLOW-UP

☐ No Significant Discrepancy
☐ Discrepancy, No change in therapy required
☐ Discrepancy, Actions taken:

☐ *Patient notified at* _____ *on* _____ *and advised* _____
                          (Time)   (Date)

_____

☐ Dr. _____ was called at _____ on _____.
                                        (Time)   (Date)
☐ Patient's private physician, Dr. _____ agreed to notify patient.

Completion, Review and Follow-up by: _____, MD
                                        Emergency Department

Anytown Medical Center
Emergency Department/Radiology
   Communication Form

4-64 X-Ray Release Form

I,_____, hereby authorize and request the release of X-rays taken of me to:
(Please Print)

☐ Me (the patient)   Address and Phone: _____

☐ _____   _____
   Name of Relative/Other   _____

☐ _____   _____
   Physician or Hospital

I understand that these X-rays are part of original medical records which belong to the _____. I accept responsibility for their care and prompt return.

Patient's Signature: _____

Signature of Borrower: _____ Date _____

Witnessed By: _____

Films Released (*type and date*) _____

_____

Number of Films Released _____   By _____
                                              Doctor or Technologist

Number of Films Returned _____   Date _____

Recorded By: _____

Source: Copyright © 2005 Medical Insurance Exchange of CA (MIEC), Oakland, California.

IMPROVING ORGANIZATION PERFORMANCE

4-65 Physician Peer/Chart Review

Date of Review: **Patient Medical Record:**   **Treatment Area.**

Yes, = Documentation supports compliance **No** = No documentation to support compliance **NA** = Not Applicable	Yes	No	NA	**Comments** **Document % in completion** *(i.e., 5/10 lab reports initialed)*
A. SYSTEMS REVIEW/NON-CLINICAL				
1. Time Seen by Resident				
1.1 1-60 minutes				
1.2 61-120 minutes				
1.3 >120 minutes				
2. Time Placed in ESD Bed or Stretcher				
2.1 1-60 minutes				
2.2 61-120 minutes				
2.3 >120 minutes				
3. Resident Signature				
4. Faculty Signature				
B. CLINICAL REVIEW				
Neuro				
5. Neuro CC: Neuro Exam Completed				
6. Seizure: Dstix Post Ictal Documented				
7. Head Trauma: GCS Documented				
Respiratory				
8. Asthma: Peak Flow Documented				
9. Pneumonia: Pulse Oximeter Documented				
10. SOB: Pulse Oximeter Documented				
Cardiovascular				
11. Chest Pain Requiring EKG: Read				
GI/GU				
12. Female Lower Abd Pain: Pelvic Exam Completed				
13. Female Dysuria: Pelvic Exam Completed				
14. Abdominal Pain: Rectal Exam				
Endocrine				
15. Diabetes: Dstix Documented				

435

Yes, = Documentation supports compliance **No** = No documentation to support compliance **NA** = Not Applicable	**Yes**	**No**	**NA**	**Comments** **Document % in completion** *(i.e., 5/10 lab reports initialed)*
16. Diabetes: Ketones Measured; Serum or Urine if indicated				
Other				
17. Wounds: Tetanus Assessed				
18. ETOH: Thiamin Administered				
19. Procedure Note Completed				

Source: Courtesy of Parkland Health and Hospital System, Dallas, Texas.

4-66 Mortality Quality Review

Confidential information collected under the protection of the Health Care Quality Improvement Act of 1986

Date of Death: _____

Unit: _____

Service: _____

Please answer all of the following questions to the best of your knowledge:

Yes ☐   No ☐   1. Did this patient expire within 48 hours of receiving **Anesthesia?**
Yes ☐   No ☐   2. Did this patient expire within 48 hours of receiving an **Invasive Procedure?**
Yes ☐   No ☐   3. Based upon the patient's **admission** diagnosis/condition, was this an unexpected death?
Yes ☐   No ☐   4. Were there any unusual occurrences or any Risk/Quality issues which directly or indirectly led to this patient's death?

If the Yes box is # checked, please make additional comments below.

_____
_____
_____
_____

Date: _____

Name: _____

RN

Please route information to the Quality Management Department through Pastoral Care Department.

This information is being collected for Risk and Quality Management Department purposes only.

Do not file in the Medical Record

Source: Courtesy of Parkland Health and Hospital System, Dallas, Texas.

4-67 Nursing Outcome Indicator Tool

Name: _____

MR#: _____

Today's Date: _____

Reviewer: _____

Diagnosis/RN Visit _____

DRG: _____

Name of CPG: _____

Current Unit: _____

Previous

	Open Medical Record Review	Yes	No	N/A	Comment
1	Discharge planning initiated on admission				
2	Pre-discharge orders written: Date & time				
3	D/C Teaching completed: Education plan				
4	D/C Teaching completed: Teaching method				
5	D/C Teaching completed: Eval of learning				
6	D/C Teaching completed: F/U plan				
7	D/C Assessment completed				
8	Appointments: In hand or telephone #/referrals				
9	LOS was increased due to lack of Discharge Planning				
10	Pain assessment/screen/reassessment performed q 4 hrs				
11	MD notified for > level 4 pain post intervention				
12	Non-pharmacological interventions documented: Positioning				
13	Non-pharmacological interventions documented: Ice Pack/Sitz bath				
14	Non-pharmacological interventions documented: Other				
15	Pharmacological interventions documented: Break through pain med				
16	Pharmacological interventions documented: Pre-Procedure med				
17	Pharmacological interventions documented: Timely renewal				
18	Reassessment performed q 60 minutes post pain event				
19	LOS was increased due to lack of Pain Management				
20	Pt.s learning needs assessed/screened on admission/encounter				
21	Barriers to learning documented				
22	Teaching/needs plan; Developed				
23	Teaching plan; Implemented				
24	Teaching plan; Evaluated				
25	Evaluation of learning/understand assessed				

Open Medical Record Review	Yes	No	N/A	Comment
26 LOS was increased due to lack of Patient and Family Education				

Source: Courtesy of Parkland Health and Hospital System, Dallas, Texas.

4-68 ESD Referral Tool
(For QM Department Internal Use Only)

Assessing Issue	Need Medical Record	Referred Out
_____ # Narrative _____ # Complaint Statistics	_____ **Closed** _____ Date _____ Initial	
Date of Incident: _____/_____/_____	Responsibility: _____	
Patient Name: _____	MR #: _____	

I. Location: **II. Origin:**

___ESD	___COPC	___Patient Complaint	___Internal
___Radiology	___Other	___RIR	___Regulatory
___OPC	___Other	___QM Department	___Other

III. Description of Occurrences:

_____
_____
_____

IV. Information Source:

___Medical Record

___Medical Record	Meetings/Referral		
___Management Discussion	Date: *Attendance/Referral:*	Date: *Attendance/Referral:*	Date: *Attendance/Referral:*
___Staffing Pattern	1.	1.	1.
___Policy Procedure	2.	2.	2.
___#	3.	3.	3.
___#	4.	4.	4.
___Other	5.	5.	5.
*Conversation:			
Name: **Date:**			
Name: **Date:**			
Name: **Date:**			

Source: Courtesy of Parkland Health and Hospital System, Dallas, Texas.

4-69 Point of Care Testing Audit

Unit _____   Date _____

HEMATOCRIT

yes   no

Pack test performed and documented every six (6) months.

Minimum spin time posted.

Biomed sticker (electrical safety) on centrifuge.

Centrifuge calibration performed (by Biomed) every six (6) months and labeled on centrifuge (acceptable range 10,000-15,000 rpms).

Centrifuge is free of blood and glass.

Hematocrit tubes current (per expiration date).

Results on chart include: ☐ Time, ☐ Date, ☐ Initials of person performing test.

URINE DIPSTICK TESTING

yes   no

Dipstick bottle current (per expiration date).

Quantimetrix Quality Control bottles current (per expiration date).

+ QC recorded in log when new bottle opened.

− QC recorded in log when new bottle opened.

QC stored in refrigerator. Temperature documented.

Can you link the QC recorded on the log with the bottle on which the QC was performed?

Remedial action documented if problems of errors are identified.

Results on chart include: ☐ Time, ☐ Date, ☐ Initials of person performing test.

GASTROCCULT

yes   no

Slides current (per expiration date).

Developer bottle current (per expiration date).

Results on chart include: ☐ Time, ☐ Date, ☐ Initials of person performing test.

FECAL OCCULT BLOOD

yes   no

Slides current (per expiration date).

Developer bottle current (per expiration date).

Results on chart include: ☐ Time, ☐ Date, ☐ Initials of person performing test.

441

URINE PREGNANCY

yes   no

		QC performed and recorded on every new box opened.
		+ QC (Quantimetrix Level 1) bottle current (per expiration date).
		– QC (Quantimetrix Level 2) bottle current (per expiration date).
		Controls stored in fridge. Temperature documented.
		Remedial action documented if problems of errors are identified.
		Results on chart include: ☐ Time, ☐ Date, ☐ Initials of person performing test.

HEMOCUE HEMOGLOBIN

yes   no

		Low QC bottle current (per expiration date).
		Low QC bottle dated when opened.
		Low QC bottle opened < or equal to 14 days.
		Normal QC bottle current (per expiration date).
		Normal QC bottle dated when opened.
		Normal QC bottle opened < or equal to 14 days.
		QC recorded appropriately and within acceptable limits.
		Control cuvette performed and recorded (within acceptable range).
		QC stored in the fridge. Temperature documented.
		Cuvette bottle current (per expiration date).
		Cuvette bottle dated when opened and used within 90 days after opening.
		Results on chart include: ☐ Time, ☐ Date, ☐ Initials of person performing test.

☐ Unit has up-to-date testing personnel competency documentation.
☐ Unit has retained quality control records for at least 13 years.

Source: Courtesy of Parkland Health and Hospital System, Dallas, Texas.

4-70 Continual Readiness Campaign: ESD Survey Tool

Survey Site/Area:	Date:
Score:	Scored by:

Team members	

MEDICAL RECORDS	MR	YES 2	Part 1	No 0	N/A	NOTES
Consent for treatment present *(RI)* *(Review three charts.)*	1					
	2					
	3					
Additional notes:						
Laboratory test results are reviewed by physician/provider *(PE, TX)* *(Review three charts.)*	1					
	2					
	3					
Additional notes:						
Pain screening is documented *(PE)* *(Review three charts.)* *Pain is rated & documented per scales.*	1					
	2					
	3					
Additional notes:						

Page Score
Highest Possible Score _____   *Score Total _____*

443

MEDICAL RECORDS (continued)	MR	YES 2	Part 1	No 0	N/A	NOTES
Consultation note completed within 2 hours. (CC) (Review three admission charts.)	1					
	2					
	3					
	Additional notes:					
Disposition determined within 6 hours (CC) (Review three admission charts.)	1					
	2					
	3					
	Additional notes:					
Documentation of pt education completed to include (PF) (Review three charts.) • Patient response • Learning style/preferences • Abilities/barriers to learning • Receptiveness to learning	1					
	2					
	3					
	Additional notes:					
Plan of Care documented (TX, CC) (Review three charts.)	1					
	2					
	3					
	Additional notes:					

Page Score
Highest Possible Score _____ **Score Total** _____

444

MEDICAL RECORDS (continued)	MR	YES 2	Part 1	No 0	N/A	NOTES
Physician/provider signature is legible & includes *(IM)* *(Review three charts.)* • *Name, licensure & credential ID #*	1					
	2					
	3					
	Additional notes:					
Nutritional screening completed *(PE)* *(Review three charts.)*	1					
	2					
	3					
	Additional notes:					
Assessment of system functions for normal daily living? *(PE)* *(Review three charts.)* *(Obtain charts for patients age 65 & >)*	1					
	2					
	3					
	Additional notes:					
Discharge instruction planning present *(TX, CC)* *(Review three charts.)*	1					
	2					
	3					
	Additional notes:					

Page Score
Highest Possible Score _____   *Score Total* _____

MEDICAL RECORDS (continued)	MR	YES 2	Part 1	No 0	N/A	NOTES
Restraint medical surgical emergent application *(TX)* *(Review three charts.)*	1					
	2					
• Documentation reflects alternative interventions prior to restraint use.	3					
Mark N/A if restraints have not occurred.	*Additional notes:*					
Restraint medical surgical emergent application *(TX)* *(Review three charts.)*	1					
	2					
Physician Order is	3					
• *secured within 1 hr* • *is time-limited* • *specifies type of restraint* • *does not contain any PRN orders* • *renewed every 24 hrs*	*Additional notes:*					
Mark N/A if restraints have not occurred.						
Review (3) employee competency assessment for documentation of *(HR)*	1					
	2					
• *license/CPR* • *skills/orientation checklist* • *age specific inservices* • *infection control training*	3					
	Additional notes:					

Page Score
Highest Possible Score _____   **Score Total** _____

EMPLOYEE QUESTIONS	Employ	YES 2	Part 1	No 0	N/A	NOTES
What are some basic measures to prevent the spread of infection? *(IC)* *(Ask three employees.)* • Handwashing • Standard precautions • Aseptic technique • Isolation • Special handling of pt equipment • Disinfection & sterilization of equipment	1					
	2					
	3					
	Additional notes:					
What are the measures to prevent the spread of tuberculosis? *(IC)* *(Ask three employees.)* • Obtain PPD skin test by OHS • Remind pt to "cover the cough" • See OHS about a cough lasting for more than 2–3 wks • Think "TB" in a person with classic symptoms (prolonged cough, night sweats, wt loss, coughing up blood)	1					
	2					
	3					
	Additional notes:					
How are HIV, hepatitis B, and hepatitis C spread? *(IC)* *(Ask three employees.)* • Sexual contact • Infecting drug use/sharing needles • Exposure through sharps contaminated w/blood • Rarely by splash of blood to mucous membranes • Remote through blood entering an open cut on the skin	1					
	2					
	3					
	Additional notes:					
*How is an infectious pt handled? *(IC)* *(Ask three employees.)* • Designated area/room • Available equipment • Understanding of contact isolation measures • Early identification & recognition of signs/symptoms of infection • Isolation &/or separation of patient • Advising patient to "cover their cough"	1					
	2					
	3					
	Additional notes:					

*Denotes questions that all staff, all disciplines should know

Page Score
Highest Possible Score _____   **Score Total** _____

EMPLOYEE QUESTIONS (continued)	Employ	YES 2	Part 1	No 0	N/A	NOTES
Where is your PPE located? *(IC)* *(Ask three employees.)* *Specific for each area*	1					
	2					
	3					
	Additional notes:					
What is the process for checking medications for outdates? *(IC)* *(Ask three employees.)*	1					
	2					
	3					
	Additional notes:					
What is "Red Bag Waste"? *(Ask three employees.)* • *Saturated dressings that are dripping, soaked pads likely to ooze or caked dressing likely to flake* • *Filled suction or drainage containers* • *Hospital approved sharps containers with needles, scalpels, broken glass, etc.*	1					
	2					
	3					
	Additional notes:					
Do you ask pt if they have an advanced directive and where would I find evidence that you do so? *(RI)* *(Ask three employees.)*	1					
	2					
	3					
	Additional notes:					

*Denotes questions that all staff, all disciplines should know

Page Score
Highest Possible Score _____   **Score Total** _____

EMPLOYEE QUESTIONS (continued)	Employ	YES 2	Part 1	No 0	N/A	NOTES
*How do you maintain pt confidentiality? (RI) (Ask three employees.) • Employees utilize individual passwords to access pt information • White Boards/Hall Boards should not: List patient's first & last name List patient's diagnosis Identify procedures by pt • Interviews and conversations not overheard • Provide physical privacy by closing doors, drawing curtains, etc.	1					
	2					
	3					
	Additional notes:					
How do you assess for abuse/neglect, where can I find evidence that you do so? (PE) (Ask three employees.) During the history & physical and ongoing • Observation for physical neglect • Observation for suggestive behavior	1					
	2					
	3					
	Additional notes:					
*How would you contact a Language Assistant? (RI) (Ask three employees.) • LA can be reached by pager. • Onsite Spanish interpreters are available during clinic hours. • Interpretation for languages other than Spanish are available using World Wide Interpreter at 800-945-7889. • Sign Language interpreting services can be accessed through social services during normal clinic hours. • LA services shall be documented in medical record • Bilingual providers shall document in medical record that services were provided in primary language	1					
	2					
	3					
	Additional notes:					

*Denotes questions that all staff, all disciplines should know

Page Score
Highest Possible Score _____   **Score Total** _____

EMPLOYEE QUESTIONS (continued)	Employ	YES 2	Part 1	No 0	N/A	NOTES
Do you perform conscious sedation? (TX) (Ask three employees.)	1					
If Moderate/Deep Sedation or Anesthesia	2					
	3					
Identify equipment & documentation tools required for sedation procedures: • pulse oximeter • sphygmomanometer • suction • oxygen • emergency cart with drugs • ambu bag • oral & endotracheal airways • intubation equipment • procedure monitoring form • physician procedure form • defibrillator & EKG monitor must be available on site	Additional notes:					
What do you do for a medical equipment failure? (EC) (Ask three employees.)	1					
	2					
• Equipment shall be removed from the patient.	3					
• Replacement equipment shall be obtained from the appropriate dept. • Malfunctioning equipment & associated supplies, tubing, & sets shall be tagged with a sequestered equipment tag & sent to Engineering/ Bio-Med Mon–Fri. • During non-routine hrs, the tagged equipment shall be placed in locked storage. • A Risk Identification report shall be completed by the involved staff, the report shall include serial, model &/or lot numbers.	Additional notes:					

*Denotes questions that all staff, all disciplines should know

Page Score
Highest Possible Score _____   **Score Total** _____

EMPLOYEE QUESTIONS (continued)	Employ	YES 2	Part 1	No 0	N/A	NOTES
*What steps would you take if there were a fire in your area? (EC) (Ask three employees.) R Rescue C Confine A Alert F Fight	1					
	2					
	3					
	Additional notes:					
*Where is the fire equipment located? (EC) (Ask three employees.) Site Specific • Pull down station and extinguishers	1					
	2					
	3					
	Additional notes:					
*What are your emergency codes? (EC) What is your role in each of these codes? (Ask three employees.) • Code Red—actual fire • Code Red Drill—fire drill • Code Pink —Abduction of infant • Code Yellow—minor or major disaster • Code Yellow Drill—minor or major disaster drill • Code Blue—medical emergency • Code Black—tornado • Code Gray—severe weather • Code Brown—bomb threat Roles listing in department safety manual	1					
	2					
	3					
	Additional notes:					

*Denotes questions that all staff, all disciplines should know

Page Score
Highest Possible Score _____   **Score Total** _____

EMPLOYEE QUESTIONS (continued)	Employ	YES 2	Part 1	No 0	N/A	NOTES
*What is a material safety data sheet? (EC) (Ask three employees.)	1					
	2					
• A specific listing of all chemicals in the department with complete	3					
information/data regarding each of the chemicals: product ID, hazardous ingredients, physical data, fire & explosion hazard, reactivity, health hazard, spill & leak, special protection, special precautions	Additional notes:					
*Where are the material safety data sheets located? (EC) (Ask three employees.)	1					
	2					
Site Specific	3					
	Additional notes:					
*How have you personally been involved in improving the quality of service in your dept or of the hospital as a whole? (IOP) (Ask three employees.)	1					
	2					
	3					
Identify one performance improvement initiative. • What have you done about it? • How have you measured it? • What impact did your interventions have?	Additional notes:					

*Denotes questions that all staff, all disciplines should know

Page Score
Highest Possible Score _____   Score Total _____

EMPLOYEE QUESTIONS (continued)	Employ	YES 2	Part 1	No 0	N/A	NOTES
*What are 3 key points in the hospital's statement? (RI) (Ask three employees.)	1					
	2					
• Provide health related services in a manner that is consistent w/ pt's needs, values and recognized belief system	3					
• Provides services that improve the health of the community • Serves as the primary teaching & research hospital for UTSW • Participates in clinical & health system for the purpose of advancement of medical knowledge & improved health	Additional notes:					
*What is the patient complaint process? (IOP) (Ask three employees.)	1					
	2					
• Complaints should be handled at the level of occurrence whenever possible	3					
• Staff receiving a complaint should listen to the complainant & try to resolve the complaint to the extent she or he is capable • Staff should notify the supervisor • Complaints are documented on the Patient Complaint/Grievance from and a copy forwarded to Division VP	Additional notes:					
*What information is available relative to patient satisfaction with services provided? (IOP) (Ask three employees.)	1					
	2					
	3					
• How do you survey patients to determine if they are satisfied? • What do your results show? • What actions have you taken regarding issues where patients were not satisfied? • What impact did your actions have?	Additional notes:					

*Denotes questions that all staff, all disciplines should know

Page Score
Highest Possible Score _____ **Score Total** _____

EMPLOYEE QUESTIONS (continued)	Employ	YES 2	Part 1	No 0	N/A	NOTES
*How are you competent to do your job? (HR) (Ask three employees.) • Orientation • Education & training • Competencies • Proficiencies	1					
	2					
	3					
	Additional notes:					
What would you do if for ethical reasons you felt you could not care for a patient? (HR) (Ask three employees.) Notify supervisor in advance that this presents a conflict and asked to be reassigned (staff rights procedure).	1					
	2					
	3					
	Additional notes:					
*What have you done to reduce the risk of harm to patients and increased patient safety? (TX) (Ask three employees.) • ID Badges • Pharmacy mixes IV • Removed potentially toxic medications from floor stock (KCl)	1					
	2					
	3					
	Additional notes:					

*Denotes questions that all staff, all disciplines should know

Page Score
Highest Possible Score _____   **Score Total** _____

Signage Present		YES 2	Part 1	No 0	N/A	NOTES
Patient Rights *(RI)* *Posted in English & Spanish*						
IC Please tell the clerk/cover your cough *(IC)* *Posted in Spanish & English*						
Complaint process *(RI)* *Posted in English & Spanish*						

Clinical Environment		YES 2	Part 1	No 0	N/A	NOTES
Correct handwashing technique. *(IC)* *(Observation of three employees' handwashing technique—Recorder or IC Team Member)*	1					
	2					
• Must be performed between pt contacts. • Wash for a minimum of 10 seconds. • Dry with paper towel. • Turn off faucet with paper towel.	3					
	Additional notes:					
Hand assessment identifies compliance *(IC)* *(Assessment of three employees' hands—Recorder or IC Team Member)*	1					
	2					
• Hand jewelry of maximum of two rings, nonornate • Finger nails less than ¼ in. beyond end of nail bed • Nail polish less than 3 days old & unchipped • Staff with direct pt contact—NO ARTIFICIAL NAILS	3					
	Additional notes:					

Page Score
Highest Possible Score _____   *Score Total* _____

Clinical Environment (continued)		YES 2	Part 1	No 0	N/A	NOTES
Food not in medication refrigerator *(IC)* *Check the medication refrigerator in the clinical area.*						
No outdated medications present *(IC)* *Check the medication refrigerator in the clinical area.*						
Medications and syringes are secured? *(TX)*						
Refrigerator temperature log current? *(IC)*						
Opened multi-dose vials are dated *(IC)* • *MDV without preservative may only be used for 24 hr.* • *Manufacturer's expiration dates shall be used.* • *MDV must be inspected for contamination prior to each use, & not used if there is any question of possible contamination.* • *Any MDV used in an emergency may not be reused for other pts.* • *Large volume parenterals (≥ 50 ml) may not be used as a MDV for mixing medications/injectables.*						
Crash cart secured *(EC)*						**Comment if locks that are used are in sequential number order.**
Crash cart log current *(EC)*						

Page Score
Highest Possible Score _____   *Score Total* _____

Clinical Environment (continued)		YES 2	Part 1	No 0	N/A	NOTES
Point of care QM documentation is available and current *Blood glucose monitoring*						
Sharps container present & not more than ¾ full *(EC)*						
Chemicals under sink secured in patient exam rooms *(EC)*						
Check a patient bathroom for an alarm device or bell *(EC)* Hallways are clear. *(EC)* • *Movable items, same side of hallway is acceptable*						
• *Infection control carts may be right outside of infectious patient's room*						
Containers are 18 inches from ceiling. *(EC)*						

Page Score
Highest Possible Score _____   **Score Total** _____

Source: Courtesy of Rusty McNew.

4-71 Continual Readiness Campaign: Scoring Tool

Unit/Area:

Site Surveyed	Average Scores Over Denominator	Site Surveyed	Average Scores Over Denominator
	___/___		___/___
	___/___		___/___
	___/___		___/___
	___/___		___/___
	___/___		___/___
	___/___		___/___
	Total Unit/Area Score:		___/___

Directions:

1. Calculate Highest Possible Score: Count the number of items scored Yes, Part or No and multiply by 2. ***Exclude the items marked NA)***
   (Example: 7 items scored [2 items marked NA excluded] × 2 = 14)
2. Calculate Score Total: Count the number of YES answers & multiply by 2. Count the number of Part answers. Add the 2 totals together.
   (Example: 5 × 2 = 10, + 2 Partials = 12)
3. Calculate Score %. Divide the Score Total by the Highest Possible Score equaling score percentage.
   (Example: 12/14 = 86%)

EXAMPLE SCORING	E/MR	YES 2	Part 1	No 0	N/A	NOTES
Staff						
Correct handwashing technique. (IC) *(Observation of three employees' handwashing technique—Recorder or IC team member)*	1	X				
	2	X				
• *Must be performed between pt contacts.*	3		X			
• *Wash for a minimum of 10 seconds.* • *Dry with paper towel.* • *Turn off faucet with paper towel.*	*Additional notes:*					
Hand assessment identifies compliance (IC) *(Assessment of three employees' hands—Recorder or IC team member)*	1	X				
	2	X				
• *Hand jewelry of maximum of 2 rings, nonornate*	3				X	*EXAMPLE*
• *Finger nails less than ¼ in. beyond end of nail bed* • *Nail polish less than 3 days old and unchipped* • *Staff with direct pt contact—NO ARTIFICIAL NAILS*	*Additional notes:*					
Review three employee competency assessment for documentation of *(HR)*	1	X				
	2		X			
• *License /CPR* • *skills/checklist/orientation*	3				X	
• *age-specific inservices* • *infection control training*	*Additional notes:*					

Improvements	Strengths

Suggested Action Plan

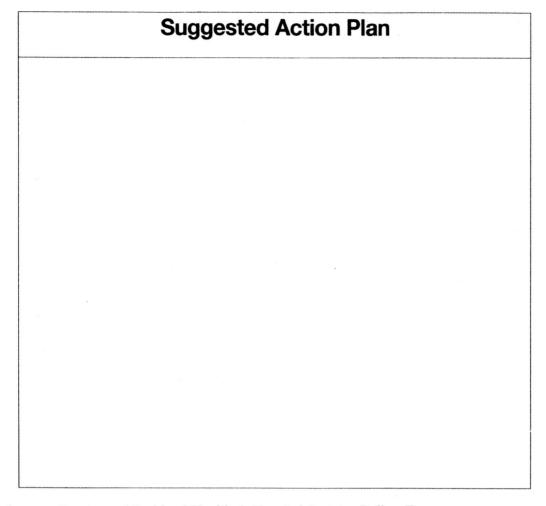

Source: Courtesy of Parkland Health & Hospital System, Dallas, Texas.

4-72 Survey Primer: Emergency Services Visit

During the emergency services visit, the physician surveyor assesses the setting where emergency services are performed. This activity lasts approximately 45 minutes. It is important to note areas maybe surveyed prior to the scheduled visit. Surveyors may jump ahead of the schedule or even return to your area if they have free time.

WHO WILL PARTICIPATE?
- Clinical director or manager emergency services
- Other staff you may designate

WHAT WILL OCCUR?

The visit consists of the following:
- a brief discussion with the director about the volume and scope of services provided and the purpose of the visit

461

- a tour of the area
- a meeting with staff members
- a review of medical records

Conversations with patients and families generally do not occur, but observations about privacy, dignity, and confidentiality are made during the tour of the area.

WHAT DOCUMENTS NEED TO BE AVAILABLE?

Open medical records of patients who are in the area at the time of the visit or who have received services.

SAMPLE QUESTIONS THE SURVEYOR MAY ASK DURING THE VISIT.

1. How does your hospital demonstrate respect for the following patient needs?
   - confidentiality (RI.1.3.1)
   - privacy (RI.1.3.2)
   - security (RI.1.3.3)
   - resolution of complaints (RI.1.3.4)
   - use of pastoral services (RI.1.3.5)
   - communication (RI.1.3.6)
2. Does the environment provide for patients' privacy? (RI.1.3.2)
3. Does the initial patient assessment address physical, psychological, and social status? (PE.1)
4. In the initial assessment, how is the patient's pain identified? (PE.1.4)
5. When warranted by the patient's condition, is there a more comprehensive pain assessment? (PE.1.4)
6. Are there reports of required diagnostic testing? (PE.1.5)
7. Is the assessment process for adolescent patients highly individualized? (PE.5)
8. Have you addressed the special needs of patients who are possible victims of alleged or suspected abuse or neglect? (PE.8)
9. How is physician coverage provided? (TX.1.1)
10. Do storage, distribution, and control of medications reflect policies and procedures? (TX.3)
11. How do policies and procedures support safe medication prescription and ordering? (TX.3.3)
12. How does medication preparation and dispensing adhere to law, regulation, licensure, and professional standards of practice? (TX.3.4)
13. Are medication preparation and dispensing appropriately controlled? (TX.3.5)
14. Is important patient medication information considered when medications are prepared and dispensed? (TX.3.5.3)
15. How does the hospital ensure that emergency medications are consistently available, controlled, and secure? (TX.3.5.5)
16. Describe how you monitor the effects of medications on patients. (TX.3.9)
17. Do you use restraint or seclusion with adequate and appropriate clinical justification? (TX.7.1)
18. Are staff educated and assessed for competence in minimizing the use of restraint and seclusion? (TX.7.1.2)

19. Does staff apply techniques such as redirecting the patient's focus or verbal de-escalation before employing restraint and seclusion? (TX.7.1.4-TX.7.1.4.1)

20. Is restraint and seclusion used pursuant to an order of the licensed independent practitioner primarily responsible for the patient's ongoing care? (TX.7.1.5)

21. If authorized and approved by the patient, is the patient's family promptly notified of the initiation of restraint and seclusion? (TX.7.1.5.1)

22. Is the patient released as soon as he or she meets the behavior criteria? (TX.7.1.12)

23. Are all episodes of restraint and seclusion documented in the patient's medical record? (TX.7.1.14)

24. Is there appropriate equipment available and accessible should patients require resuscitation services? (TX.8)

25. During the entry process, how do you provide patients and families with information about proposed care? (CC.3)

26. How do you provide for coordination among the health professional(s) and service(s) or setting(s) involved in patient care? (CC.5)

27. Describe the process(es) for referral, transfer, or discharge of a patient to another level of care, health professional, or setting. (CC.6)

28. How do you provide for the exchange of appropriate patient care and clinical information when patients are admitted, referred, transferred, or discharged? (CC.7)

29. What aspects of the care provided in this setting do you measure, assess, and improve? (PI.3—PI.5)

30. How does performance in this service relate to your hospital's mission and strategic planning processes? (LD.1. I-LD.1.1.1)

31. Are the services appropriate to the scope and level of care? (LD. 1.3.2)

32. What information is available relative to patient satisfaction with the services provided? (LD.1.3.3.1)

33. Are services available in a timely manner to meet patient needs? (LD.1.3.4-LD.1.3.4.1)

34. Do the leaders collaborate with departmental staff for the development of department budgets? (LD.I.5.2)

35. Are there any issues relating to uniform performance of patient care processes? (LD.1.6)

36. Are the goals and scope of the setting's services defined? (LD.1.7.1)

37. What programs do you have to promote recruitment, retention, development, and recognition of staff members, especially job-related educational programs? (LD.1 .9-LD.I.9.1)

38. Has the hospital considered clinical practice guidelines in the design or improvement of clinical processes? (LD.1.10)

39. If clinical practice guidelines are used, how do hospital leaders identify or set criteria to guide the selection and implementation of the guidelines? (LD.1.10.1)

40. Who is involved in the review and approval of clinical practice guidelines selected prior to implementation? (LD.1.10.2)

41. Describe the process for how clinical practice guidelines are monitored for their effectiveness. (LD.1.10.3)

42. Is there evidence of communication across the hospital? If so, what? (LD.3-LD.3.4; LD.4.3.1-LD.4.3.3)

43. Within this patient care setting, is there evidence of plans and performance standards for the following programs:
    - safety (EC.2.1)
    - security (EC.2.2)
    - hazardous materials and waste (EC.2.3)
    - emergency preparedness (EC.2.4)
    - life safety (EC.2.5)
    - medical equipment (EC.2.6)
    - utilities (EC.2.7)
44. Have staff members been oriented to the environment of care and educated about environment of care issues? Do they perform their responsibilities under the environment of care management plans? (EC.2.8)
45. Do you have regular emergency drills? (EC.2.9.1)
46. Do you have fire drills on a quarterly basis? (EC.2.9.2)
47. Have you performed hazard surveillance surveys in this setting at least every six months? (EC.2.10.1)
48. Has your setting maintained, tested, and inspected life safety elements of the environment of care? Has your hospital documented the required testing of fire alarm, detection, and extinguishing systems? (EC.2.10.2)
49. Have you maintained, tested, and inspected medical equipment in this setting? (EC.2. 10.3)
50. Has your department maintained, tested, and inspected utility systems, including the emergency power system? (EC.2.10.4-EC.2. 10.4.1)
51. Is there adequate privacy to reflect sensitivity to and respect for the patient? (EC.3.3)
52. How do your leaders define the following:
    - the qualifications and responsibilities of staff working in this setting
    - a system to evaluate how well staff responsibilities are met
    - the number of staff needed to fulfill the setting's mission (HR.1-HR.2)
53. How do you monitor and adjust staffing levels based on patient needs? (HR.2)
54. How do you encourage and support staff self-development and learning? (HR.3.1)
55. Do staff members receive an orientation to the department and initial job training and information? (HR.4)
56. Does each staff member participate in ongoing in-service education sessions and other related training to increase his or her knowledge of specific work-related issues? (HR.4.2)
57. How does the department manager determine whether staff are competent to perform assigned duties and, when appropriate, provide care for the special needs and behaviors of specific age groups? (HR.5)
58. Are the information and data you require for patient care provided in an accurate and timely fashion? (IM.5)
59. What types of aggregate data do you have available to emergency services staff of the setting to support patient care and operations decisions? (IM.8)
60. Do you have adequate resources and services available to meet the knowledge-based information needs of the medical staff? (IM.9)
61. Do those who need poison-control information have appropriate access? (IM.9.1)
62. Describe the following:
    - the process for reporting information about infections (IC.3)

- actions you have taken to reduce the risk of or prevent nosocomial infections (IC.4)
- actions you have taken to control outbreaks of identified nosocomial infections (IC.5)

Source: Courtesy of Parkland Health & Hospital System, Dallas, Texas.

4-73 Nursing Outcome Report Action Plan

	Knowledge	Policy	Communication	Documentation	System Process	Performance Practice
1.	D/C Planning Initiated on Admit					
2.	Pre- D/C orders written: Date & Time					
3.	D/C teaching completed: Ed. Plan					
4.	D/C teaching completed: Teaching Method					
5.	D/C teaching completed: Evaluation of learning					
6.	D/C teaching completed: F/U Plan					
7.	D/C assessment completed					
8.	Appointments: In hand or telephone #/referrals					
9.	LOS was increased due to lack of D/C Planning					
10.	Pain assessment/screen/ reassessment performed q 4 hrs					
11.	MD notified for > level 4 pain post intervention					
12.	Nonpharmacological interventions documented: Positioning					
13.	Nonpharmacological interventions documented: Ice pack/ Sitz bath					
14.	Nonpharmacological interventions documented: Other					
15.	Pharmacological interventions documented: Break through pain med.					
16.	Pharmacological interventions documented: Preprocedure med.					
17.	Pharmacological interventions documented: Timely Renewal					

	Knowledge	Policy	Communication	Documentation	System Process	Performance Practice
18.	Reassessment performed q 60 minutes post pain event					
19.	LOS was increased due to lack of Pain Mgmt					
20.	Pts. Learning needs assessed/screened on admit/encounter					
21.	Barriers to learning documented					
22.	Teaching/needs plan: Developed					
23.	Teaching plan: Implemented					
24.	Teaching plan: Evaluated					
25.	Evaluation of learning, understand assessed					
26.	LOS was increased due to lack of Patient & Family Ed.					

Source: Courtesy of Parkland Health and Hospital System, Dallas, Texas.

4-74 Emergency Department Performance Improvement Plan for Physician Assistants

Performance improvement in the emergency department is performed by the medical director, assistant medical director, physician assistant director, or the departmental designee.

A summary of the plan is as follows:

A. The scope of care and aspects of care are reviewed annually and are revised as needed.

B. Chart review: 5 percent of the physician assistant monthly charts will be reviewed using the following sentinels:
- legibility of charts
- timeliness of patient evaluation
- adequate history and physical exam for the severity of the patient complaint
- interpretation of test results
- consideration of differential diagnosis and appropriateness of discharge diagnosis
- discharge instructions
- consultation with attending physicians
- discrepancy between nurse and MD/PA notes are adequately addressed

C. X-ray, EKG, and culture variances are reviewed daily.

D. Focused audits are performed monthly.

E. Departmental referrals and patient complaints are reviewed on an as needed basis.

Aspect of Care — MEDICAL RECORD REVIEW

These indicators are suggested guidelines for review rather than mandatory requirements.

REVIEW FREQUENCY: _____   REVIEW MONTH/YEAR: _____

CASE SELECTION GUIDELINES

Select a random sample of 5 percent of charts and include all emergency physicians in review.

DATE / REVIEWER'S INITIALS / CODE NO.

TOTALS

SENTINEL EVENT

PHYSICIAN CODE													TOTAL #	TOTAL # MET	TOTAL % MET	THRES-HOLDS
DOCUMENTATION																
1. Chart is legible.																90%
2. Time patient seen by MD is noted.																90%
3. Adequate information is documented to identify why high-risk, high-cost or problem-prone tests are ordered, and to provide adequate information for interpretation.																95%
4. Results and interpretation of all ordered tests are documented.																95%
5. Consideration of appropriate differential diagnoses is documented and all considered diagnoses are listed (for seriously ill patients).																98%
6. Time of consultation request and response noted.																96%
7. Discrepancy between nurse and MD notes adequately addressed.																100%
8. Appropriate patient instructions ordered and given.																98%
9. Diagnosis is substantiated by documented results of diagnostic studies and treatment.																100%

Blank Box = Criterion Met   X = Criterion Not Met   G = Non-Applicable Criterion

Remarks: _____

Note: Thresholds do not demonstrate or imply that a problem exists, but merely indicate that a more detailed review should be undertaken.

Source: Courtesy of Suburban Hospital, Inc., Bethesda, Maryland.

4-75 Emergency Department Quality Indicators

PROCEDURE

- ED quality indicators will be addressed for findings, conclusions, actions, and evaluation at the quarterly management of care team meeting.
- The ED monthly report will be used as a guide for discussion by the co-chairs of the team. (The mont will be produced by the executive secretary.)
- The minutes from the team meeting will serve as documentation of the above.
- Quarterly, the indicators will be trended.
- The minutes from the team meeting will serve as documentation of the above.

INDICATORS

1. Mortality and morbidity
2. 72-hr. unplanned readmission
3. 72-hr. unplanned readmission admit
4. Specimen errors
5. Medication errors
6. Patient falls
7. Patient satisfaction
8. Patients residing in the emergency department > 24 hr.

Evaluating Quality Indicators

- Mortality and Morbidity
  Number of Deaths ÷ Total Number of Patients Seen
  Number of Preventable Deaths ÷ Total Number of Deaths
  - 72-hr. Bounceback
  Number of Bouncebacks ÷ Number of Patients Seen
  - 72-hr. Bounceback Death
  Number of Bounceback Deaths ÷ Number of Patients Seen
  - Bounceback Admit
  Number of Bounceback Admits ÷ Number of Patients Seen
  - 72-hr. Bounceback Admit Death
  Number of Bounceback Deaths ÷ Number of Patients Seen
  - Specimen Errors
  Number of Specimen Errors ÷ Number of Patients Seen
  - Medication Errors
  Number of Medication Errors ÷ Number of Patients Seen
  - Patient Falls
  Number of Falls ÷ Number of Patients Seen
- Patient Satisfaction
- Nursing Documentation
- Medical Staff Documentation
  - Invasive Procedures
  Number of Procedures Performed per Criteria ÷ Total Number of Procedures Performed

- Patients Residing in the ED > 24 hr.
  Number of Stays > 24 hr. ÷ Total Number of Patients Seen

Source: Adapted from Parkland Memorial Hospital, Dallas, Texas.

4-76 Conducting an FMEA

Failure Mode Effect and Analysis (FMEA) is similar to a root cause analysis. Both are excellent quality improvement tools. A root cause analysis is used reactively to analyze problems after an occurrence, while the FMEA is a proactive tool used to analyze systems/ processes/behaviors in an attempt to prevent adverse occurrences. FMEA has been used in engineering, aviation and the general business sector for many years however, only recently has it been introduced in health care.

FMEA begins by outlining the current high risk processes/activities in an organization (or within a department). A vulnerability scale is applied by using a weighting system to determine which processes, based on the current practice, have the highest potential for failure/error. Once the priorities are identified, a project management or CQI team is formed to act upon the identified weakness in the safe practice or process. FMEA can also be used when designing new systems.

Joint Commission standards require that health care organizations conduct at least one FMEA annually and incorporate the findings into their Pl program.

CONDUCTING A FAILURE MODE AND EFFECTS ANALYSIS

- Assemble a team. The team may be structured as an organization-wide Patient Safety Committee or developed within each department. Start with high-risk departments.
- Outline the high-risk activities in the organization or department. Identify what the outcome should be.
- Identify potential occurrences, which are at risk for poor patient outcomes or medical errors, i.e. the possible failures that could occur (i.e. the failure mode).
- For each "failure mode," estimate its criticality by
  -severity of the potential effect*
  -probability the failure will occur (based on current procedures, policies, personnel, equip, etc)*
- Calculate the score of each "failure mode" to determine the priority of addressing them with improvement projects. Scores of 8 or above should be addressed first.*
- Conduct an analysis of each potential failure issue using a cause & effect diagram, flow chart, root cause analysis or other appropriate tools.
- Utilizing Pl principles, redesign the process or activity to minimize the risk of that failure mode and protect patients from the failure effects.
- Analyze and test the redesigned process.
- Implement the redesigned process
- Monitor the redesigned process.
- Implement a strategy for maintaining the effectiveness of the redesigned process over time.

*See FMEA tool.

4-77 Failure Mode Analysis Tool

Procedure/Treatment/ Process at risk	Failure Potential	Severity Rating	Probability Rating	*Outcome Score	Action Date	Responsibility	Plan

Probability Score

Frequent = 4

Occasional = 3

Uncommon = 2

Remote (Unlikely) = 1

Severity Score

Catastrophic = 4

Major Permanent = 3

Major Temporary = 2

Minor = 1

Source: Courtesy of Quality Resource Group, LLC, Arlington, Texas.

4-78 Quality Management Patient Complaint/Grievance Committee Flowchart

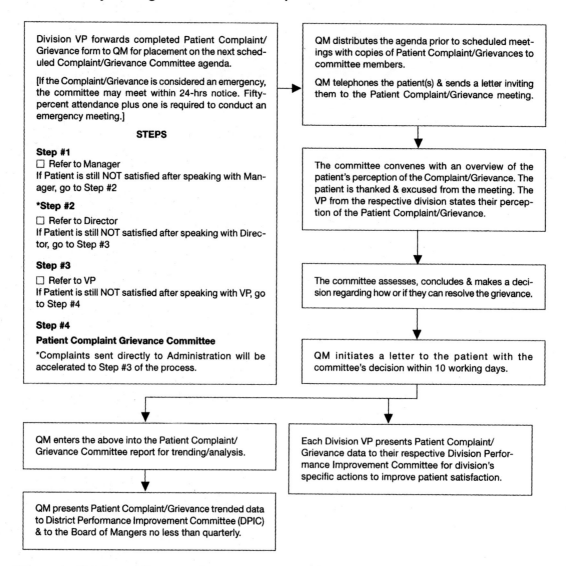

Where to Catalogue Documents

All Grievance Committee documents are maintained in the Quality Management Department

Source: Courtesy of Parkland Health and Hospital System, Dallas, Texas.

4-79 Patient Complaints/Grievance Log

#	Status	Division	Unit	Patient Name	MR #	Incident Date	Referred to	Date Referred	Description	Step #1 Refer to Unit	Step #2 Refer to Director	Step #3 Refer to VP	Step #4 Refer to Grievance Committee/ QM	Comments

Source: Courtesy of Parkland Health and Hospital System, Dallas, Texas.

4-80 Emergency Department Callback Questionnaire

1. Service Date:

   ☐☐ / ☐☐ / ☐☐
   month   day   year

   | Date called: _____ |
   | Time of call: _____ |
   | Nurse calling: _____ |

2. Medical Record Number

   ___ ___ ___ ___ ___ ___

3. Patient age

   ___ ___

4. Time of visit (registration time):
   ___ Day 7 AM–3 PM
   ___ Evening 3 PM–11 PM
   ___ Night 11 PM–7 AM

5. Category:
   ___ emergency   ___ urgent   ___ nonurgent

6. Express Care:
   ___ yes   ___ no

7. The information below was given by: ___ Patient   ___ Family Member   ___ Other

8. Did you (the patient) schedule follow-up care?   ___ YES ___ NO ___ N/A

9. Did you (the patient) fill the prescription?   ___ YES ___ NO ___ N/A

10. Did the nurse introduce him/herself to you (the patient) and/or your family?   ___ YES ___ NO ___ N/A

11. Did the physician introduce him/herself to you (the patient) and/or your family?   ___ YES ___ NO ___ N/A

12. Did you (the patient) receive an ID band?   ___ YES ___ NO ___ N/A

13. Were treatments and procedures explained to you before they were started?   ___ YES ___ NO ___ N/A

14. Were delays in care and treatment explained to you (the patient) and/or your family?   ___ YES ___ NO ___ N/A

15. Did you (the patient) understand the discharge instructions?   ___ YES ___ NO ___ N/A

16. Were you (the patient) satisfied with the care and attention you received?   ___ YES ___ NO ___ N/A

17. How would you (the patient) describe your present condition? ___ Improved   ___ Same   ___ Worse

18. Comments: _____

Source: Courtesy of Kennedy Health System, Voorhees, New Jersey.

4-81 Occurrence Report Form

B.

Date of Occurrence

Time

Location of happening _____

Location assigned or visiting _____

Inpatient ____Outpatient____Visitor_____

Addressograph
Inpatient
Outpatient

C. Complete if visitor or no addressograph:

Name: _____

Last   First   I.

City   State   Zip

(   )

Street Address   Telephone

D. Diagnosis or Chief complaint _____

Service _____ Admission or Visit Date _____

Attending Physician _____

Complete one form per occurrence.

E. Type of Occurance—Complete appropriate occurrence type and then go to Section F.

E1. Treatment/Test/Procedure (*Circle one*)
Invasive/Non-Invasive (*Circle one*)
(*Select one only*)

_____ Delay in Performing   _____ Delay in Obtaining Results

_____ Not Done   _____ Incomplete/Inaccurate documentation

_____ Unordered   _____ Complication during or after

_____ Incorrect Counts   _____ Other _____

____S____N____I

MDR
Was there a faulty medical device or piece of equipment found during this occurrence?
_____ Yes _____ No (select one)

If yes, complete the following:

Equipment Name _____   Serial # _____

Lot # _____ Model #_____   Biomed # _____

Follow malfunctioning Equipment Policy. Send device to Biomed.

Call Risk Management.   Go to F.

E2. Medication/Blood (*Circle One*)   Name of: _____
(*Select One only*)

_____ Incorrect Dose/Route   _____ Incorrect med/unordered

_____ Incorrect Time/date omitted   _____ Reaction

_____ Infiltration   _____ Other _____

If faculty medical device or piece of equipment, complete MDR box above.

Follow Adverse Drug Reaction policy and call pharmacy.

Follow Blood Transfusion policy.   Go to F.

Complete one form per occurence.

E. Type of Occurence — Complete appropriate occurence type and then go to Section F.

E3. Trauma *(Select One)*

_____ Slip   _____ Burn

_____ Slip and Fall   _____ Needlestick

_____ Fall   _____ Other Injury _____

Observed staff _____ Y _____ N   Observed by other _____ Y _____ N

Witnesses: *(Names/Relation to Patient/Visitor)* _____

_____

(Select One)

_____ From bed/Chair/Stretcher   _____ While standing/Walking

_____ In BR   _____ Other _____

(Select One)

Object/Substance contributed to trauma?

_____ Y _____ N _____ Briefly describe _____

(Select One)

Did age or condition contribute to trauma?

_____ Y _____ N _____ Unknown

Outpatients and visitors should be escorted to the Emergency Department for evaluation
and treatment.

Did patient accept offer? _____ Y _____ N.

Call Risk Management Department.   Go to F.

E4. Miscellaneous *(Select one)*

_____ High Risk AWOL   _____ Confidentiality Issues

_____ Verbal Abuse   _____ Property Damage/Loss

_____ Physical Abuse   Briefly describe _____

_____ Other _____

Follow policy regarding AWOL, Abuse or Property Situations.

Was Security contacted? _____ Y _____ N

                                                                   Go to F.

F. Expected Outcome *(Select One)*

_____ Near miss situation. Staff identified   _____ Requires significant medical
before patient involvement.   intervention but likely to recover fully.

_____ Requires no nursing/medical   _____ Requires significant medical
intervention.   intervention, not likely to recover or death.

_____ Requires some medical   _____ Reportable for administrative
intervention but not likely   evaluation
to be admitted or increase L.O.S

                                                                   Go to F.

G. Print Name and ID number or Person Completing Report

Name: _____   ID #: _____

Source: Courtesy of Rusty McNew.

4-82 Creation of a Hospital-Wide Patient Flow Team
Sample Patient Flow Team Structure

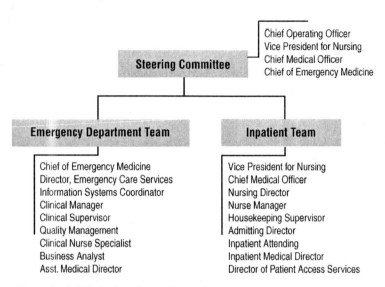

Creation of a Hospital-Wide Patient Flow Team

Creating hospital-wide teams to participate in decisions and guide changes is a critical factor for improving patient flow. Figure shows one model for constructing such teams. In this model, a steering committee of senior hospital leadership is responsible for overseeing all change efforts and provides high visibility for those efforts. Separate teams are created to focus on problems in the Ed and on the inpatient side. Each of these teams has broad representation from departments throughout the hospital including ancillary services, housekeeping, and patient transport. Equally important is ensuring that the ED and inpatient teams include members from each side to the foster an understanding of the problems and issues that each team faces. Teams include both managers front-line staff to encourage the generation of new strategies or initiatives and to engage all levels of employees in the change process.

Source: *Perfecting Patient Flow: America's Safety Net Hospitals and Emergency Department Crowding.* Copyright © 2005 by the National Association of Public Hospitals and Health Systems. **All rights reserved. Reprinted with permission.**

4-83 Emergency Department Input/Throughput/Output Model of Patient Flow

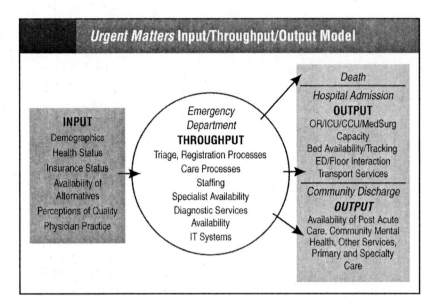

Source: *Perfecting Patient Flow: America's Safety Net Hospitals and Emergency Department Crowding.* Copyright © 2005 by the National Association of Public Hospitals and Health Systems. **All rights reserved. Reprinted with permission.**

4-84 Patient Flow Key Performance Indicators

Factor	Indicator		Reporting Interval
ED Throughput	1. Total ED throughput time — time from patient's arrival in the ED ➤ time of patient disposition*		Weekly
	2. *By treatment path:* Admitted/Fast Track /Other ED Discharged	a. Time from arrival to bed placement — patient arrival in the ED ➤ time the patient is first placed in a bed for exam and treatment	
		b. Time from bed placement to examination — time patient is first placed in a bed ➤ time the patient is first seen by a physician	
		c. Time from disposition decision to departure — time physician issues a discharge or admit order ➤ time patient has left the ED	
Inpatient Flow	3. Time from inpatient bed assignment to bed placement — inpatient bed available and assigned ➤ patient arrives in unit and placed in bed		Weekly
	4. Time of day of discharge — average time of day that inpatients are discharged**		
	5. Bed turnaround time — time that a bed becomes empty ➤ time that the bed is reported as cleaned and available for use by a new patient		
Clinical Processes (Choose one)	6. Time to heart treatment — patient arrival at the ED ➤ time thrombolytic medication is administered or a vessel is opened		Monthly
	7. Time to pain management (fractures/dislocations) — time of arrival ➤ 1st administration of pain management, e.g., medication or ice packs		
Other ED	8. Hours on diversion — if hospitals are allowed to go on diversion, total number of hours on diversion		Monthly
	9. Percent incomplete treatment — percent of patients that leave prior to completion of treatment (left without being seen, against medical advice, or for any other reason before medical treatment is completed)		
	10. Patient Satisfaction — use existing measures of patient satisfaction		

* Disposition is when the physician's orders have been written to admit or discharge the patient and the patient has left the ED.

** Time of discharge is when the physician's discharge orders have been written and the patient has left the hospital.

Source: *Perfecting Patient Flow: America's Safety Net Hospitals and Emergency Department Crowding.* Copyright © 2005 by the National Association of Public Hospitals and Health Systems. **All rights reserved. Reprinted with permission.**

4-85 Medication Discrepancy Tool (MDT)

Medication Discrepancy Tool (MDT)

MDT is designed to facilitate reconciliation of medication regimen across settings and prescribers

✎ **Medication Discrepancy Event Description:** *Complete one form for each discrepancy*

✓ **Causes and Contributing Factors: Check all that apply:**

Italicized text suggests patient's perspective and/or intended meaning

Patient Level _____

1. ☐ Adverse Drug Reaction or side effects

2. ☐ Intolerance

3. ☐ Didn't fill prescription

4. ☐ Didn't need prescription

5. ☐ Money/financial barriers

6. ☐ Intentional non-adherence
   "I was told to take this but I choose not to."

7. ☐ Non-intentional non-adherence (ie:Knowledge deficit)
   "I don't understand how to take this medication."

8. ☐ Performance deficit
   "Maybe someone showed me, but I can't demonstrate to you that I can."

System Level _____

9. ☐ Prescribed with known allergies/intolerances

10. ☐ Conflicting information from different informational sources.

   For example, discharge instructions indicate one thing and pill bottle says another.

11. ☐ Confusion between brand & generic names

12. ☐ Discharge instructions incomplete/inaccurate/illegible.

   Either the patient cannot make out the hand- writing or the information is not written in lay terms.

13. ☐ Duplication.
   Taking multiple drugs with the same action without any rationale.

14. ☐ Incorrect dosage

15. ☐ Incorrect quantity

16. ☐ Incorrect label

17. ☐ Cognitive impairment not recognized

18. ☐ No caregiver/need for assistance not recognized

19. ☐ Sight/dexterity limitations not recognized

✓ **Resolution: Check all that apply:**

☐ Advised to stop taking/start taking/change administration of medications

☐ Discussed potential benefits and harm that may result from non-adherence

☐ Encouraged patient to call PCP/specialist about problem

☐ Encouraged patient to schedule an appointment with PCP/specialist to discuss problem at next visit

☐ Encouraged patient to talk to pharmacist about problem

☐ Addressed performance/knowledge deficit

☐ Provided resource information to facilitate adherence

☐ Other _____

Source: University of Colorado Health Sciences Center, Division of Health Care Policy and Research. Denver, Colorado. Reprinted with permission.

MANAGEMENT OF THE ENVIRONMENT OF CARE

4-86 ESD Fire Drill Quality Control

PURPOSE

To protect patients, staff, and visitors from the hazards of fire
To ensure that the hospital is in compliance with Fire Dept. and JCAHO standards

RESPONSIBILITY:

As delegated by a manager.

FREQUENCY:

Once per shift per quarter.

REPORTED TO:

Area manager/director

TARGETED GOAL:

100%

INITIATIVE TRIGGER:

90%

METHODOLOGY:

1. Audit for documentation of one completed *Department Fire Drill Report* per shift per quarter. Report should be scored as number of yes answers divided by 16.
2. Report % compliance with *Departmental Fire Drill Report* criteria as an average of at least 3 completed drills.
3. Include your interpretation of data as Findings and Conclusions, action plan, and evaluation date.

MEASUREMENT:

Scores on 3 or more completed *Departmental Fire Drill Reports*
_____
3 or more completed Reports

481

REPORTING TIMELINE:
Report completed by the 5th of the last month of the quarter.

Results:

Shift	Score on *Departmental Fire Drill Report*
7 to 3	
3 to 11	
11 to 7	
Other	
% Compliance	

Findings & Conclusions:

Plan of Action:

Note: Code Green Drills are conducted monthly and monitored in a few designated areas by Safety Management. Each area remains accountable for documentation of departmental fire drills.

Source: Courtesy of Parkland Health and Hospital System, Dallas, Texas.

4-87 Department of Emergency Medicine
Hazardous Materials Policy and Procedures

SUBJECT

Treatment of patient contaminated by hazardous materials (HazMat)

POLICY

All patients contaminated by hazardous materials will be properly decontaminated to ensure that all necessary clinical treatment will be provided for the patient and to minimize exposure and contamination risks to staff, visitors, and physical plant.

PURPOSE

Provide direction for the decontamination and treatment of patients received at the hospital who have been contaminated by HazMat. Provide protection for hospital employees, patients, and visitors. Maintain an environmentally safe physical facility.

RESPONSIBILITY

A. The Chair of Emergency Medicine and Director of Nursing shall be responsible for establishing procedures consistent with medical policies.

B. The Employee Safety Office shall be responsible for establishing procedures consistent with OSHA and local requirements.

C. Security staff shall identify possible HazMat patients and assist in properly minimizing exposure risks.

D. ED nurse staff shall properly proceed with decontamination and minimize exposure risks.

E. ED physicians shall properly proceed with medical treatment and minimize exposure risks.

SCOPE

This policy applies to treatment of all HazMat patients regardless of patient acuity or severity of contamination.

PROCEDURES

1.0 Aeromedical Communications Specialists

1.1 Establish a communication link with the transport service and scene command.

1.2 Identify arrival mode.

1.3 Obtain number of patients, medical status, name of contaminant, and ETA.

1.4 Relay information to ED charge nurse.

2.0 ED Charge Nurse

2.1 Document information from dispatch on HazMat check list.

2.2 In conjunction with attending physician, assess prehospital decontamination attempts and assess risk to patient.

2.3 In conjunction with ED attending, determine the need to initiate an EOP response. If an EOP response is required, proceed to Section 4.0.

3.0 ED Attending Physician

3.1 In conjunction with the charge nurse, assess prehospital decontamination attempts and assess risk to patient.

3.2 In conjunction with the charge nurse, determine the need to initiate an EOP response. If an EOP response is required, proceed to Section 4.0.

4.0 Initiating HazMat Response

4.1 ED charge nurse initiates HazMat EOP response by dialing x1111 and informs operator. Request operator to page Medical Toxicologist on call in addition to EOP.

4.2 If the contaminant is determined to be a radioactive material, request operator to page Radiation Safety Office (RSO).

4.3 ED attending physician and charge nurse review and initiate necessary actions outlined on HazMat checklist.

5.0 Patient Arrival

5.1 If by ambulance
   a. RN meets patient at ambulance, assesses acuity, and determines need for resuscitation.
   b. If radiation accident, RSO checks for degree of contamination. Patient goes directly to decontamination treatment area.
   c. Ambulances are to be considered contaminated until they have undergone decon. Security staff restrict access to main care area.

5.2 If walk-in
   a. If patient is ambulatory, then restrict patient from proceeding into any other area of the ED.
   b. Notify charge nurse and HazMat team.
   c. Triage RN assess need for immediate care.
   d. HazMat team can determine classification of the triage RN as a member of the decontamination team or that the patient is to be decontaminated, depending on the substance and the exposure.

6.0 Decon Team Member Roles and Personnel Protective Equipment

6.1 Decon-1 (MD or RN)
   a. Directs procedure, remains outside the "hot area."
   b. Receives only labs or swabs from Decon-2.
   c. Assists as needed.
   d. Obtains supplies from outside personnel.
   e. Assists with removal of patient to clean area when decon is complete.

6.2 Decon-2 (RN or Paramedic Partner)
   a. Assesses patient on arrival and assists in transport to decon treatment area.
   b. Obtains swab samples of eyes, mouth, ears, skin, hair, nares, and wounds if indicated. For radiation contamination patients, swabs are to be obtained by RSO.
   c. Decons patient.
   d. Attempts lab work. ECG if needed.

6.3 Decon-3
   a. Remains outside hot area.
   b. Provides equipment needed for resuscitation or patient care.
   c. Takes and records predecon swabs.
      (The paramedic partner may need to don PPE to assist in patient care. If needed, charge nurse should provide additional personnel outside decon room for equipment.)

6.4 Procedure for PPE
   a. Obtain level B suit.
   b. Obtain self-contained breathing apparatus (SCBA).

    c. Remove jewelry, empty pockets, change into hospital scrubs.
    d. Put on nonsterile surgical gloves.
    e. Step into suit. DO NOT TEAR.
    f. Zip up suit and secure, with all hair covered.
    g. Put on SCBA.
    h. Assistant to tape all exposed areas, zipper.
    i. Put on boots.
    j. Put on second decon suit (heavy) gloves, pull over sleeves.
    k. Assistant to tape edges of gloves and boots.
    l. Tape crotch seam if suit is at all tight.

7.0 Decontamination Procedure

    GOAL: Remove enough of the contaminating material from the patient so that there will no longer be any danger of secondary contamination to those providing medical care. *This should only require 5 to 15 minutes.*

7.1 Identify contaminant class and consult chart to determine appropriate decontamination method/solution.

7.2 For water solubles, contaminated wounds have first priority.
    a. Secure adhesive drape around wound. Irrigate with copious amounts of warm normal saline.
    b. Remove field and dry.
    c. Monitor.
    d. If contamination persists:
        1. Wash with 3% peroxide.
        2. Consider surgical debridement.
        3. Save and monitor all tissue removed.
    e. After wounds are decontaminated, cover and proceed with decontamination of other areas.

7.3 Contaminated nares and mouth
    a. Turn head to side or down as the patient's condition permits.
    b. Rinse with small amounts of water, and suction if needed.
    c. Prevent water from entering the stomach as much as possible.
    d. Insert NG tube, suction, and monitor contents.

7.4 Contaminated eyes
    a. Remove eyeglasses/contact lenses.
    b. Rinse eyes thoroughly with 1000 mL normal saline or water (each eye).

7.5 Contaminated intact skin: If the patient is not injured and can stand, have him or her enter the shower from the contaminated side.
    a. Have patient gently wash with soap and water using a scrub sponge for 3 minutes.
    b. Monitor and repeat as needed.

DO NOT REDDEN OR IRRITATE THE SKIN WITH HARSH RUBBING OR HOT WATER!

7.6 If contamination persists or cannot be monitored, wash with liquid soap and water.

7.7 Contaminated hair
    a. Shampoo hair with mild soap for 3 minutes.
    b. If contamination persists, clip hair off, do NOT shave area.

8.0 Removal of Patient from Decontamination Room to ED Treatment Room

8.1 Place clean plastic on floor for patient exit to clear area.

8.2 Bring clean stretcher to door by Decon-3.

8.3 Decon-3 will extend backboard covered with waterproof sheet from clean to contaminated stretcher. Patient will be transferred along board to clean personnel.

8.4 Board removed by Decon-1 and placed in tent.

8.5 Take postdecon swabs and place in plastic bag labeled with patient's name and medical record number.

8.6 Transfer to care area.

9.0 Team Removal

9.1 Scrub suits before removal.

9.2 Wash gloves.

9.3 Remove SCBA tank and breathe-through mask; pull hood down.

9.4 Unzip suit.

9.5 Remove tape.

9.6 Remove boots.

9.7 Remove outer gloves only.

9.8 Pull suit off, turning inside out.

9.9 Remove mask.

9.10 Remove inner gloves.

9.11 Enter clean zone, shower, and change clothing.

10.0 Room Decontamination

10.1 Employee safety to assess need for decontamination of tent and disposal of materials. Security to keep area secure.

Source: Fred Harchelroad, Jr., "Planning for Hazardous Materials Disasters," *Topics in Emergency Medicine*, Vol. 20:2, Aspen Publishers, Inc., © 1998.

4-88 Cardiopulmonary Resuscitation Emergency Equipment Policy

POLICY

All patient care units and many specialty areas in the hospital, such as clinics, diagnostic procedure areas, physical therapy, recreation therapy, and the cafeteria, have their own resuscitation equipment.

Emergency equipment is specified by the CPR committee and should include
1. locked resuscitative cart with
   - airway equipment (intubation kit(s) and ventilation kit(s) with CO_2 detectors)
   - drug tray
   - miscellaneous supplies and equipment
   - accessory emergency equipment (tracheostomy tray, extension cord)
   - compression board
   - contents book listing emergency equipment and supplies with chart indicating their placement on the cart
   - CPR records for documenting resuscitative efforts
   - emergency equipment checklist with current date and signature indicating completion of the daily review
2. defibrillator (certain areas share this equipment)
3. ECG monitor (certain areas share this equipment)
4. oxygen (wall or cylinder)
5. suction (wall or portable)

RESPONSIBILITY FOR MAINTAINING EQUIPMENT

Equipment Checks

During hours of operation, it is the daily responsibility of each area with resuscitation equipment to check the defibrillator, ECG monitor, and laryngoscope handles and blades for proper functioning; the ventilation kit for expiration date of the CO_2 detector; and the CPR cart for expiration date and integrity of the breakaway lock. Special care units must check all of the above every shift. Resuscitation equipment for recreation therapy and the cafeteria is secured in locked closets and must be checked weekly. Equipment in recreation therapy is checked by the department's staff; equipment in the cafeteria is checked by the peritoneal dialysis nursing staff.
Equipment checks must be documented.

Resuscitative Cart

Resuscitative carts throughout the hospital are equipped in accordance with recommendations of the CPR committee. The integrity of all carts is maintained with a standardized security device, such as a breakaway lock. A CPR cart should be entered only for resuscitative measures. Each cart is labeled with an expiration date and equipped with a locator chart so that it will not need to be opened for purposes of checking expiration dates or educating staff.

The resuscitative cart is exchanged by central sterile services (CSS) Monday through Friday (8 AM to 12 midnight) and by the patient equipment department at all other times and on holidays. Carts are exchanged after each use and whenever the lock is broken. Expired carts will only be exchanged by CSS Monday through Friday, 8 AM to 12 midnight.

All areas in the main hospital are included in the exchange, with the exception of adult/pediatric ICUs, burn center, emergency department, nurseries, operating room, post-anesthesia care, and day-op. Areas outside the main hospital—the ambulatory care center, family practice center, satellite dialysis unit, and clinic—do not exchange carts. Each area excluded from the exchange is responsible for inventorying and restocking the cart after use, as contents expire, and whenever the lock is broken.

Airway Equipment

Intubation kits are supplied/exchanged by central distribution during times specified above. For areas included in the cart exchange, intubation kits will be exchanged with the cart. Areas excluded from the exchange must notify central distribution for an exchange. Laryngoscopes that do not light should be exchanged in central distribution. Ventilation kits are exchanged by respiratory care. Exchanges following codes in the main hospital are automatic. Areas outside the main hospital must notify respiratory care for an exchange after each use. Note: The resuscitation kit is dated to reflect the CO_2 detector's expiration date. Respiratory care should be notified for a replacement kit.

RESUSCITATIVE CART EXCHANGE PROCEDURE

Responsibilities

CSS or the patient equipment department will initiate a cart exchange within 30 minutes of a paged code for all areas in the main hospital included in the exchange. The user department must notify CSS of the need for a cart exchange when an item in the cart expires (as shown by the date on top of the cart) or when a cart's lock is broken.

When a replacement cart is delivered and not needed (after a paged code), it is the responsibility of the user department to see that the delivered cart is returned to CSS following the code. If an occasion should arise when CSS or patient equipment fails to exchange the cart, the user department should initiate the exchange.

CSS maintains a log of all cart exchanges by date, user department, and reason.

For a replacement cart following a paged code, no request is usually needed. CSS or patient equipment will initiate delivery of a replacement cart within 30 minutes. (The user department should initiate a request if the cart is not delivered within 30 minutes or if code is not paged.) The user department must return the used cart to CSS if the cart is not ready for return when the replacement cart is delivered.

For replacement cart due to an outdated item or broken lock, exchanges cannot be accommodated within the 30-minute time frame. The user department should notify CSS/patient equipment of the reason for the requested exchange. Exchanges for expired contents should be scheduled with CSS one week prior to the cart's expiration date.

Note: The cart should not be opened prior to calling CSS for exchange.

Procedure

1. Prior to the exchange, the user department shall do the following:
   a. Remove from exterior of cart the ventilation kit, clipboards, CPR records, emergency equipment checklists, and cart contents book. Note: Areas with portable oxygen and suction should remove the portable suction and the oxygen regulator (leave the oxygen tank on cart).
   b. Clean CPR compression board with approved antimicrobial solution and return to cart. (If the board accompanies the patient during transfer to ICU, it is the responsibility of the user department to retrieve and clean the compression board and to return it to CSS.)
   c. Stamp a miscellaneous charge requisition and a pharmacy charge requisition (located with the drug tray) with the patient's name and the department number, and place them on top of the cart. Note: If the cart is exchanged for reasons other than patient use, stamp a miscellaneous requisition with the user's department number and the reason for the exchange.
2. After receipt of the cart, the user department shall do the following:
   a. Check cart for expiration date and integrity of the lock.
   b. Return to the cart the ventilation kit, clipboards, CPR records, emergency equipment checklists, and cart contents book. Note: Areas requiring portable oxygen and suction should connect the oxygen regulator to the new tank and return the portable suction to the top of the cart.

DEPARTMENTS EXCLUDED FROM THE EXCHANGE

Areas excluded from the exchange are responsible for maintaining their own carts (replacing expired items, inventorying, and restocking the cart after each use and whenever the lock is broken), securing cart with appropriate metal breakaway lock, labeling cart with contents' earliest expiration date, and recording on the emergency equipment checklist in the postcode area.

Cart Locks

Designated representatives for areas excluded from the cart exchange may obtain locks and prongs from CSS (Monday through Friday, day shift). CSS maintains a log of all locks and prongs issued. Locks may be reused by replacing prongs only.

Each department excluded from the cart exchange is accountable each shift for securing and documenting breakaway locks and prongs, reconciling discrepancies, and reporting unresolved discrepancies to the department's manager and risk management.

This card copy is slipped into a plastic sleeve located on top of the code cart. The expiration date is checked when the code cart is checked.

Drugs and Supplies with Expiration Date

Indicate below the item name, drawer number, and expiration date of the next item to expire. Cross out last entry.

Name   Drawer Number   Date

_____

_____

_____

_____

_____

_____

_____

_____

Source: Adapted from the University of North Carolina Hospitals, Chapel Hill, North Carolina.

4-89 Risk Management Process

Adverse Occurrence Reported

Initial investigation data gathered by RM

File details in RM database ← No — Injury/Adverse occurrence (Level IV & V) → Consult with division administration to determine if there is a need for preliminary meeting with MS leadership

Yes

UTSWMC RM notified

Legal counsel notified

*PCRC chair notified

Executive management notified

Joint Commission Sentinel Event

No

Reviewed by department(s) involved

Designated department director reviewer

Designated MD reviewer

No — **RCA required — Yes

No ← Action required

PCRC conducts RCA from involved medical staff department

Yes

- Plan established
- Actions taken
- RM facilities & documents

Peer review referral if appropriate

- PCRC conducts RCA
- Action evaluation plan developed
- RM facilities & documents

Evaluation of action plan

File in RM

Legend
RM—Risk Management
MS—Medical Staff

*PCRC—Patient care review committee
**RCA—Root cause analysis

Courtesy of Rusty McNew.

4-90 Adverse Occurrence/Sentinel Event Procedure

GOAL

Identify and investigate adverse occurrences and sentinel events in order to reduce likelihood of reoccurrence. Following an adverse occurrence or sentinel event, _____ will promptly act to investigate, assess processes and systems involved in order to take corrective actions as appropriate. The focus on the investigation is to evaluate possible factors that led to the occurrence/event in order to make improvements.

PURPOSE

The purpose of this procedure is to
1. clarify risk management, (RM), medical staff department and management responsibilities related to adverse occurrences
2. identify process for reporting, investigating and conducting **a thorough and credible** root cause analysis that maintains quality assurance protection and/or client attorney discovery privilege
3. ensure compliance with OIG, CMS, and Joint Commission regulations/standards related to quality improvement.

DEFINITIONS

- **Adverse occurrence**—Any untoward event that either causes actual injury or has the direct potential to cause injury or loss of function. Adverse occurrences include events that are due to commission or omission.
- **Near miss**—Event that "almost occurred" but was averted that had the potential for having caused injury or loss of function
- **Sentinel event**—An adverse occurrence that causes injury or significant loss of function or death to a patient including, but not limited to
  - unanticipated death or major permanent loss of function, not related to the natural course of the patient's illness or underlying condition
  - suicide of an inpatient
  - infant/child abduction
  - discharge of an infant to the wrong family
  - rape of an inpatient
  - hemolytic transfusion reaction with major blood group incompatibilities
  - surgery on the wrong patient or wrong body part
- **Root cause analysis (RCA)**—Root cause analysis is a process for identifying the basic or causal factors that underlie variation in performance, including the occurrence or possible occurrence of a sentinel event. A root cause analysis focuses primarily on systems and processes, not individual performance. A root cause analysis should develop an action plan that will likely decrease the likelihood of such events in the future, or determines, after analysis, that no such improvement opportunities exist.
  To be thorough, the root cause analysis must consider
  - all pertinent factors associated with the event
  - analysis of the specific systems and processes related to the event
  - a determination of potential improvement processes or systems that will reduce the likelihood of such events in the future
  To be credible, the root cause analysis must
  - include participation by leadership and individuals closely involved in the processes and systems under review

- provide an explanation if the findings in the analysis are deemed "not applicable" or "a known complication"
- include consideration of any relevant literature

- **Department physician reviewer**—A faculty physician appointed by the department chair to review risk management level IV and V and sentinel cases that occur in the specific department. Physician review assists risk management determine whether or not further investigation or referrals are needed or if a root cause analysis group should be convened.

- **Patient care review committee (PCRC)**—A permanent subcommittee of the medical advisory council charged with ensuring that adverse occurrence/sentinel event investigations are thorough and credible and that appropriate actions are taken to reduce the likelihood of reoccurrence. Ad hoc members are appointed as appropriate.

- **Risk management**—Risk management consults with legal services, administration and PCRC to direct investigations, reports occurrences to medical staff and executive management, coordinates and facilitates root cause analysis process, documents and reports as action plans are implemented and follow-up occurs.

RISK IDENTIFICATION REPORTING OF ADVERSE OCCURRENCES/SENTINEL EVENTS

Adverse Occurrences and Sentinel Events shall be reported to the risk management department as soon as the event is known. Reporting may be by the physician, nurse, or any other person with knowledge of the occurrence. The hospital risk identification form shall be completed and submitted within 24 hours of the event. If there is patient injury of a catastrophic nature or a sentinel event identified, risk management should be notified by phone (_____) or pager (_____).

RISK MANAGEMENT PROCESS

1. Screen all risk identification reports regardless of source of information.
2. Categorize according to the severity of the occurrence.
   - Level I—No actual occurrence. No patient or person involved (near miss). Information is entered into a database for aggregate reporting.
   - Level II—Limited or no harm to the patient or persons involved. Limited or no intervention required. Information entered into a database for aggregate reporting.
   - Level III—Moderate adverse occurrence. Intervention required, but not likely to have lasting effect. Not likely to increase a patient's acuity or length of stay. Investigated as necessary to establish above information and entered into RM database for aggregate reporting.
   - Level IV—Moderate adverse occurrence. Increased intervention, transfer to higher level of care (admission to hospital, or transfer to an ICU), or increased length of stay. Investigation actions as appropriate and follow-up to resolution required.

- Level V—Severe adverse occurrence or death. Permanent harm or loss of function. Cause may be unknown. Investigation, actions as appropriate and follow-up to resolution required.
3. Inform hospital legal affairs, executive management, vice president of the involved division and risk management about a sentinel event or a Level IV or V adverse occurrences immediately.
4. Investigate—Level III, IV, and V adverse occurrences Investigation may include any of the following:
   - review of medical record
     - A. initial meeting with division administration to determine if there is need for a preliminary meeting with medical staff leadership
     - B. initial evaluation meeting with chair of PCRC to direct further investigation
     - C. refer to physician reviewer of specific department for clinical evaluation
     - D. refer to nurse or other clinical staff of involved department(s) for review and evaluation
   - review of relevant policies, procedures and standards of care
   - patient care review committee chair call for a root cause analysis (RCA) to be conducted
   - If RCA is to be conducted, PCRC chair will appoint co-chair from involved department
   - when necessary, coordinate and facilitate the completion of a root cause analysis with the patient care review committee and appropriate physicians, nurses and other health care professionals involved in the case. Legal counsel will be invited to attend as appropriate.
   - document findings, conclusions, actions, and evaluation plan
   - prepare a thorough and credible root cause analysis summation within 45 calendar days after a sentinel event has been reported.
   - refer action plan to division performance improvement committee through quality management

REPORTING SENTINEL EVENTS AND LEVEL IV & V ADVERSE OCCURRENCES

- Root cause analysis (RCA) action plans will be reported to respective performance improvement committee within 45 days for follow-up monitoring, as appropriate.
- RCA and action plans will be reported to executive management when designed
- Board of managers shall receive aggregate data on risk occurrences quarterly and information regarding sentinel events and Level IV & V at the next board meeting
- The Joint Commission or other regulatory agencies, upon request, may receive information regarding root cause analysis procedure and documentation regarding action plans for improving care and processes. Due to legal implications, sentinel events are **not** voluntarily reported to Joint Commission.

Approved hospital president, medical staff _____

Source: Courtesy of Rusty McNew.

4-91 Response after a Significant Adverse Occurrence

To swiftly and effectively manage the personal and organizational impacts of a significant adverse occurrence (patient, visitor or employee injury or death related to health care delivery), an interdepartmental, multidisciplinary meeting will be held within a day or two of the occurrence. The purpose of this meeting is to

- provide support to those involved in the occurrence
- obtain information about what happened (chronology of events)
- determine what processes and/or procedures may have impacted the course of events
- direct communication
- determine what additional information, discussion and/or investigation is needed and summarize next steps

When an adverse occurrence is reported to risk management, the risk management staff will validate the type and severity of the occurrence. The risk manager will contact hospital and medical staff leadership to discuss the occurrence and determine what type of response should occur. The following outlines the role and responsibilities of leadership and risk management (before, during, and after the initial response).

Hospital and medical staff leadership shall

- identify persons directly involved with the occurrence and determine who should attend the initial response meeting
- provide support for the purpose of system and process review for improvement purposes and eliminate finger pointing or blame identification/shifting
- designate person(s) to manage communications with the patient and family
- encourage limiting/reducing unit/department discussions regarding the occurrence (rumor control)
- arrange for staff and leadership to meet within a day or two of the occurrence
- participate actively in the initial review, follow-up discussions and, when applicable, a root cause analysis for the development and implementation of action plans
- educate and/or update staff on process improvements

Risk manager will

- Facilitate initial response meeting and promote the completion of follow-up activities
- Document process and system changes and educational efforts
- Report to hospital senior management and legal department as needed
- Ensure that root cause analysis is conducted according to Joint Commission standards

Source: Courtesy of Rusty McNew.

4-92 Workplace Violence: Organizational Assessment

Has the organization done due diligence to prevent and/or detect potential workplace hazards related to violence?

1. Are there policies which define the standards and procedures to be followed by its agents and employees regarding violence or potential for violence?
2. Is there a mechanism for oversight and improving safety for workers, patients & visitors?
3. Has the organization developed a comprehensive compliance program which outlines policy for complying with state and federal laws?
4. Has the organization effectively educated all staff about its procedures related to prevention of violence and criminal activity?
5. Is there a continuing process for monitoring safety and prevention of violence?
6. Is there an effective and relatively easy method for gaining assistance when there is a threat or actual violent incident?
7. Have standards for employee discipline been enforced equally?
8. After an occurrence is there a mechanism to debrief involved staff?
9. Is there a plan for response to potential or actual occurrences? If so, has Sr. Management and the Board approved the plan? Is there at least an aggregate report provided to Sr. Management and the Board to routinely identify and relate risks and improvements?

Source: Courtesy of Parkland Health and Hospital System, Dallas, Texas.

4-93 Emergency Department Safety Assessment Checklist

PHYSICAL ENVIRONMENT

1. Are separate entrances available for ambulatory patients and ambulances?
2. Does the ambulance entrance (if provided) open directly to a nursing station?
3. Does the ambulance entrance stay locked when not in use and how does staff know when to open it? _____ Is there a means for communication from this area to the inside?
4. Is there a means to observe what is going on outside of the ambulance entrance either by direct observation or by CCTV?
5. Is the ambulatory entrance from the outside capable of being locked if a lock-down is ordered?
6. Are areas around the ambulance and ambulatory entrance, including adjacent parking areas well lit?
7. Are there shrubs or other areas where persons considering assaultive behavior could hide? _____ In general, are parking areas for staff, patients and visitors using the ED, especially at night, safe and secure?
8. Is the waiting area staffed by a receptionist and/or triage nurse at all times? _____ Is there a protected area that will make it difficult for a person to grab them or jump over the counter? _____ Is the counter protected by some means (acrylic glazing above counter)? _____ Does the reception area open up to the waiting area?
9. Is a comfortable waiting area provided? _____ Is it clean, are washrooms provided, vending equipment, functional television, informational materials and telephone? _____ Is a separate grieving room provided?
10. Is the triage area separated from the walk-in area? _____ Does the door from the waiting area lock? _____ Does the triage area have an entry into the treatment area?
11. Has an area or room been designated as a safe room for staff or patients if violence erupts? _____ Is this room lockable? _____ Is it centrally located? _____ Is it equipped with a means of communication?
12. Has a room been designated as a seclusion room? _____ Is it specially equipped? _____ How?

OTHER COMMENTS AND OBSERVATIONS

EQUIPMENT

1. Do security personnel carry weapons and if so, what do they carry? _____ Has staff been trained (formal and documented) on their use?
2. Is security staff equipped with portable two-way radios? _____ Do they also carry either a cell phone or does the portable two-way radio have a cell phone?
3. Is Closed Circuit TV available for the ED? _____ Is the quality of the picture good? _____ Does it have storage capacity and for how long? _____ What areas of the ED are covered by the CCTV?
4. Are there any panic alarms in the ED? _____ How do staff request assistance if they need immediate assistance, and is this system effective?
5. Does the facility have a handheld and/or pass through metal detector(s) and have staff been trained in their use?
6. Are outside entryways adequately marked indicating weapons are prohibited?
7. Are weapons collected from visitors and if so, how do they store them?

OTHER COMMENTS AND OBSERVATIONS

STAFF TRAINING

1. Have staff been trained in
   a. access control to the ED?
   b. ED vulnerabilities?
   c. Dealing with emergencies involving violence?
   d. Nonviolent crisis intervention?
   e. Other departmental policies? (list)
2. Is there a system in place that informs forensic staff (law enforcement) of their responsibilities and are these responsibilities provided in writing?
3. Is the ED adequately staffed? _____ Are waiting times documented?
4. Is someone available to periodically check on patients and their family during these waits to communicate and help reduce stress while waiting?
5. Have security personnel received outside formal training or in the process of taking a certification program in security?

OTHER COMMENTS AND OBSERVATIONS

POLICIES AND PROCESSES

1. Assessment policies for victim of domestic and other forms of violence?
2. Workplace violence?
3. Access policy?
4. Visitor (ED) policy?
5. Restraint policy?
6. Hostage plan?
7. Weapons policy? (staff, visitors)
8. Policy on staff debriefing/counseling following violence incident?
9. System for flagging charts and records?
10. Incident reporting (appropriate definition) and analysis system?
11. Emergency procedures? (list)
12. System for conducting periodic security assessments?
13. Forensic policies?
14. Policies for dealing with patient stress?
15. Policies for weapons searches of visitor and patients?

OTHER COMMENTS AND OBSERVATIONS?

Source: Phoenix Area Indian Health Service, Phoenix, Arizona.

4-94 SECURITY RISK ASSESSMENT[*]

Department: Emergency

COMMUNITY RISK (*for Security Risk Occurrence*)			**TOTAL**
Violent crime in area	15	[ ]	
Nonviolent crime	10	[ ]	
Nontypical behavior	5	[X]	
			5

ACCESS FROM OUTSIDE TO INSIDE OF HOSPITAL			
Open to all—no time restrictions	30	[X]	
Open to all—normal hours	25	[ ]	
Restricted to staff—no time restrictions	20	[ ]	
Open to staff only—normal hours	15	[ ]	
Security key restricted	10	[ ]	
Entrance security monitored	5	[ ]	
			30

SECURITY RISK OCCURRENCE PER YEAR: (*Consider patients, staff, and facility*)			
5 or more	20	[ ]	
3 or more	15	[X]	
1 or more	5	[ ]	
None	0	[ ]	
			15

STAFF AVAILABILITY:			
Roaming	25	[ ]	
Central location	20	[X]	
1:3	15	[ ]	
1:2	10	[ ]	
1:1	5	[ ]	
			20

RESOURCE AVAILABILITY:			
No communication or monitoring	20	[ ]	
Telephone communication (Internal or 911)	15	[ ]	
Overhead paging	10	[ ]	
Alarm system/Lifeline/nurse call	5	[X]	
			5

	WORK SHEET TOTAL	75

ACTION:

	105
Administrative review and/or change in policy/Procedure/ practice	↓
	80
	↓
Policy/procedure/security education	
	50
	↓
No change	
	20

[*] Security Risk assessment to be communicated to Environment of Care Committee.

Source: Adopted Courtesy of Tillamook County General Hospital, Tillamook, Oregon.

4-95 Security Presence in the ED

A Security Officer is assigned to the ED during the hours of darkness. Security will be called at the request of the triage nurse, and Security will respond promptly for the following kinds of patients:

- Patients brought in by law enforcement officers.
- Patients requiring restraints.
- Suicidal patients not accompanied by competent relatives or caretakers.
- Intoxicated patients.
- Patients who have exhibited out-of-control behavior in the past.
- Agitated patients at risk for escalation.
- Any patient who has a potential for violence.

Security will check each patient for any weapons or contraband when notified by nursing staff.

- Security will apply sticker to the chart indicating the time they checked the patient for any weapons or contraband.

In addition, Security will be called and will promptly respond when relatives or visitors exhibit behavior, which may escalate into or presents a threat to the staff, patients or other visitors.

Security will accompany patients outside for smoking if, in the opinion of the ED staff or Psych Liaison, not smoking may lead to an escalation of potentially violent behavior.

Source: Courtesy of Parkview Medical Center, Pueblo, Colorado.

4-96 Department Disaster Plan

Usual Hours of Business: 24 hours a day, 7 days a week

POLICY

The Emergency Department shall have a plan, based on the departments internal capabilities, to adequately prepare for any disaster. The plan will be in accordance with the Medical Centers Disaster Manual. Any member of the emergency department staff who becomes aware of a potential disaster will immediately notify the ED physician, charge nurse, ED administrator and ED Hazmat Coordinator.

PROCEDURE

In following the plan, the Hospitals Disaster Manual should be referenced and followed at all times. In the event of a Code Orange, the Emergency Department Disaster Manual will be followed as well. The Emergency Department disaster Manual includes specific instruction for each role to be assumed.

501

NOTIFICATION OF PERSONNEL

During normal business hours, notification will be made via the overhead speaker system, personal pagers or telephone extensions. After hours, home telephone numbers cellular phones or pagers will be used as appropriate to notify employees, the ED Operator will initiate the department recall (the recall list is kept in the department). The Disaster Call List will be followed sequentially in alphabetical order starting with the director.

PUBLIC ADDRESS CODES

A. ABDUCTIONS **(CODE GREEN)**
   Follow the hospital-wide Abduction Procedure in the Disaster Manual.
B. BOMB THREATS **(CODE BLACK)**
   Follow the hospital-wide Bomb Threat procedure in the Disaster Manual.
C. FIRE/EXPLOSION/VISIBLE SMOKE **(CODE RED)**
   Follow the hospital-wide Fire/smoke procedure in the Disaster Manual.
D. **CODE RESPOND**
   Follow the hospital-wide Code Respond procedure in the Disaster Manual.
E. DISASTERS **(CODE ORANGE)**
   Follow the hospital-wide Disaster Response procedure in the Disaster Manual.
F. TORNADO / SEVERE WEATHER **(TORNADO WARNING IS NOW IN EFFECT)**
   Follow the hospital-wide Tornado Threat procedure in the Disaster Manual.
G. WEAPONS AND VIOLENCE
   Follow the Weapons and Violence procedure in the Disaster Manual.
H. HAZARDOUS MATERIAL SPILL
   Follow the hospital-wide procedure for Hazardous Materials/Chemical Spill or Release procedure in the Disaster Manual.
I. BIOTERRORISM
   Follow the hospital-wide procedure of Bioterrorism in the Disaster Manual.

CONTINUATION OF SERVICES

If, by the nature of the event, the Emergency Department must be continued throughout the disaster, the department director or designee shall coordinate these activities. The department director or designee will initiate whatever actions he/she deems necessary for the continuation of services.
   A. STAFF SCHEDULES: Staffing schedules will be made available to account for all Emergency Department staff.
   B. PARKING: Follow the directions for staff parking in the Disaster Manual.
   C. ENTRANCE INTO THE BUILDING: Follow the directions for staff entrance in the Disaster Manual.
   D. ON-DUTY: All personnel will be considered on-duty until such time that the disaster is terminated or with prior approval from the director/designee of Emergency Department.

E. ELEVATOR USAGE
Follow the hospital-wide Disaster Manual for Elevator Location and Security Procedures and Evacuation Procedures and Continuation of Care
ELEVATORS ARE NOT TO BE USED IN THE EVENT OF FIRE OR STRUCTURAL DAMAGE TO THE FACILITY UNLESS CLEARED BY SECURITY OR ADMINISTRATOR-ON-CALL.

F. Evacuation—Follow the directions for Evacuation Procedure in the Disaster Manual.

Source: Courtesy of Parkview Medical Center, Pueblo, Colorado.

4-97 Use of Cellular Telephones and All Two-Way Communication Devices

POLICY SUMMARY/INTENT: To ensure that Electromagnetic Interference (EMI) from cellular telephones and all two-way communication devices does not interrupt proper operation of any medical device within the hospital or patient care buildings.

DEFINITIONS:

EMI: Electromagnetic Interference.

EMI-producing devices Include the following:
Category 1 (High Risk)

1. Cell phones and cell phone like devices (including cell phones with camera capability)
2. 2-way pagers
3. Personal Digital Assistant (PDA); for example, hand-held device that combines computing, telephone/fax, Internet, and networking features; also called palmtops, hand-held computers, and pocket computors with cell phone capabilities that cannot be turned off
4. Analog, digital and personal communication services

Category 2 (Medium Risk)

5. All walkie-talkies or wireless transceiver

Category 3 (Low Risk)

6. Cordless telephones
7. Wireless headsets
8. 1-way pagers
9. Personal Digital Assistant (PDA); for example, handheld device that combines computing, telephone/fax, Internet, and networking features; also called palmtops, hand-held computers, and pocket computers without cell phone capabilities or with cell phone capabilities that can be turned off.
10. All forms of Wireless Network Systems (WANS) including wireless phones

* Note: 1-way pagers do not transmit and therefore, do not produce EMI
AFFECTED DEPARTMENTS/SERVICES: All patient care departments.

POLICY: COMPLIANCE—KEY ELEMENTS

A. Category 1 and 2 devices are prohibited within six feet of all patients and in the following "cell phone prohibited" areas:

Any patient care area with operational electrical clinical equipment

Family Birth Place

ICU

Post Anesthesia Care Unit

Emergency Department

Operating Room

Med / Surg Rooms

Category 1 devices must be turned off within six feet of all patients and in the above cell phone prohibited areas.

Category 2 devices may be used in a 'listen only' mode in the 'cell phone prohibited' areas and / or within six feet of all patients. If there is a need to respond the user must step six feet away from the patient an/or leave the 'cell phone prohibited' area.

B. Category 3 devices can be used throughout the hospital.

C. Signage prohibiting the use of cellular phones and two-way communication devices will be posted in all 'cell phone prohibited' areas.

Signage designating 'cell phone safe' areas will be posted in designated areas.

D. Individuals using Category 1 or 2 devices in 'cell phone prohibited' areas will be directed to a 'cell phone safe' area.

PROCEDURE:

1. All staff members are to be informed of this policy and made aware of the possible EMI (electromagnetic interference) danger to medical equipment such as telemetry monitors, incubators/infant warmers, infusion pumps, and defibrillators.

2. Appropriate signage as described above will be posted throughout the facility.

3. The use of staff-owned cellular telephones and two-way communication devices is only allowed in the event of:

   a. An emergency/disaster.

   b. An employee working in a celling with another employee assisting on the ground; in such cases, if the work is being done in a patient care area, the staff must be informed that a cellular telephone or two-way communication device is in use and may cause EMI. If any trouble with medical equipment is reported, the cellular telephone or two-way communication device must be turned off immediately.

   In the event an equipment problem is noted, the user should step away from the patient or turn the device off immediately.

4. Areas where it is safe to use cell phones within the hospitals are: Lobby areas, Waiting Rooms, Cafeteria, as well as Business office areas, such as Admitting, Administration, PBO and Nursing Offices outside of Patient care areas.

5. Any patient care injuries resulting from the EMI should be reported immediately to the Risk Manager and/or Nursing Supervisor as per Administrative Policy

6. The use of cell phones for the purpose of transmitting digital pictures is prohibited in all areas of the hospital.

7. Avoid discussing or transmitting patient identifiable information that could give rise to allegations of breech of confidentiality.
8. Be aware of the potential for community transmissions that utilize these types of equipment to be overheard, listened in on, or even recorded.

Source: Courtesy of Tillamook County General Hospital, Tillamook, Oregon.

4-98 Equipment Management (Patient's Own Equipment Safety Check)

PURPOSE:

1. To ensure patient's electrical equipment that is brought in with them is basically safe for them to use during their hospital stay.
2. This evaluation needs to be done prior to use
3. Identify that this is a basic check; for intact electrical cords, no apparent danger identified

SPECIAL CONSIDERATIONS

1. Patients often elect to bring in their own personal care items such as hairdryers, curling irons, razors, etc.
2. Patients also may have their own medical equipment; ie: Bl-Pap machine, C-Pap machine, Ventilator, etc. Refer to Administrative Policy "Use of Patient Owned Medical Equipment (Ventilators)"

ELECTRICAL EQUIPMENT: PRIOR TO USE

1. Work Request
2. Medical Record: If the patient desires to keep a certain personal care item; or other electrical equip, document on the Admission form if present upon admission, or in the Clinical Notes if the equipment comes after Admission.

KEY WORDS/PHRASES	DIRECTIONS
PATIENT ADMISSION	

1. Explain that we would like all valuables to be sent home with the patient's family when possible.
2. Evaluate any concerns for the specific equipment and its safe use in the patient's environment; ie: radio, electronic games, other electronic equipment, etc.
3. Personal Care Equipment: In the event the patient desires to keep a certain piece of equipment for personal care such as a hairdryer, curling iron, electric razor, etc, and It is determined to be safe for their environment:
   a. Complete a Work Request.
   b. During business hours for Plant Services, call them and they will make this check a priority
   c. If not during business hours, call them in the AM.

Note: Personal Medical Equipment: In the event the patient needs or desires a certain piece of equipment for their medical/physical care; ie: such as Bl-Pap, C-Pap, or Ventilator, refer to Administrative Policy "Use of Patient Owned Medical Equipment (Ventilators)".

Source: Courtesy of Tillamook County General Hospital, Tillamook, Oregon.

4-99 Abduction, Infant and Child

POLICY SUMMARY/INTENT: To protect infants and children from removal from hospital by unauthorized persons.

Responsible Persons:

1. All Medical—Surgical Nursing Personnel
2. All Medical—Surgical Ancillary Personnel

KEY WORDS/PHRASES	DIRECTIONS

PREPARATION

1. On admission, infant or child will be placed in a room close to the nurses station.

IMPLEMENTATION

1. Identification band with patient name, age, physician, date of birth will be placed on ankle or wrist.
2. Parents are encouraged to stay with infants as much as possible.
3. Nursing staff will introduce self at beginning of shift.
4. Anyone carrying a baby (the patient) in the hallway will be questioned by Med/Surg staff.

EDUCATION

1. Upon hire, and yearly, staff will be Instructed on the above procedures.
2. Instruction will Include creating an awareness of the real risk of Infant/ child abduction and what to look for when observing activity on the unit; ie., individuals loitering, persons In piecemeal hospital garb without proper I.D. badges.
   a. Please note the "The typical Infant Abductor" on page two of this procedure.
   b. Supervise infant and children at all times. Be aware that a disturbance in another part of the hospital could be a diversion to draw attention away from the child.
   c. Report unidentified persons carrying infant or child from hospital.
3. Nursing Supervisor will be notified of questionable individuals or if suspicious behavior is observed.
4. Department Manager shall be notified If discrepancies In this procedure are observed In hospital staff.

COMMON CHARACTERISTICS OF THE TYPICAL INFANT ABDUCTOR

- Female, aged 15-44, often overweight
- Emotionally immature and compulsive
- Frequently has lost a baby or is incapable of having one
- Often married or cohabitating; companion's desire for a child may motivate the abduction
- Considers the baby her own once the abduction occurs
- Usually lives in community where abduction occurs
- Often visits nursery and asks detailed questions about hospital procedures and layout
- Usually plans abduction but does not necessarily target a particular infant
- Frequently impersonates nurse or other hospital personnel
- Often acquainted with hospital personnel or victim's parents

Source: Courtesy of Tillamook County General Hospital, Tillamook, Oregon.

4-100 Emergency Department Overcrowding

POLICY

It is the policy of Parkview Emergency Department that all patients be seen by the ER physician as soon as possible. Under no circumstances will a medical screening exam be delayed on the basis of insurance or ability to pay to facilitate ER flow during over crowding situations.

PURPOSE

To facilitate patient flow during patient over crowding. To ensure patient safety and crowd control in the Emergency Room.

Criteria

Meets more then 2 to 3 of the following criteria. The ER charge nurse will notify Director or Lead Clinical Nurse:
1. No beds available in the emergency room.
2. The charge nurse is using hall beds for patient.
3. Priority 2 patients waiting greater then 30 minutes.
4. Triage Holding and E-3 have been used as treatment and holding area.
5. Consider using Emergency Room Holding Area Criteria policy.

PROCEDURE

1. The charge nurse and ER physician determine ER Over Crowding policy needs to be implemented.
2. The charge notifies Director or LCN about staffing.
3. Rooms X1, X2, X3 used for priority 3 patients.
4. The charge nurse or designee assist with triage.
5. ER tech is placed in triage to assist with point of care and procedures.
6. Notify Radiology and Lab about patients and ordering.

Source: Courtesy of Parkview Medical Center, Pueblo, Colorado.

4-101 Fall Risk Assessment and Prevention

PURPOSE

To maintain a safe environment for all patients

To identify those at an increased risk of fall by a Fall Risk Assessment

EQUIPMENT

Computer or manual assessment initially.

Clinical Notes documentation

SIDE RAIL USAGE AND CRITERIA

1. The routine for side rail usage is for the upper two side rails to be up in order for the patient to assist with turning and positioning
2. The lower two side rails are down unless the patient meets one or more of the following criteria:
   a. Patient is sedated
   b. Patient is somnolent
   c. Patient is on life support equipment
   d. Patient requests the lower side rails to be up
   e. Physician Order to have the lower side rails up
3. The Total Care ICU beds have the controls on the lower rails; so one of the lower rails will remain up for convenience for the patient to access controls. The left or right rail may be up depending on the patient preference. If all side rails are raised, the restraint policy and procedure must be followed.

KEY WORDS/PHRASES	INSTRUCTIONS
GENERAL SAFETY MEASURES	
1.	Bed level is down
2.	Upper side rails up for assistance with turning and positioning
3.	Call light in place
4.	Family at bedside
5.	Post appropriate magnetic ambulation sign; Ambulatory, Semi-Ambulatory or Non-Ambulatory
6.	Take orthostatic vital signs with "dizziness with standing" symptoms
ADMISSION FALL RISK ASSESSMENT	
1.	Upon admission to the care units, the patient is assessed to determine their likelihood of falls. Screening includes:
a.	Age
1.	Less then 3 years
2.	70–79 years
3.	Greater than 80 years
b.	Needs assistance with toileting
c.	Is confined to chair or bed
d.	Experiences dizziness
e.	Has a history of falls within the past 6 months
1.	1-2 times
2.	greater then 2 times

f.   Has impaired hearing

g.   Has impaired vision

h.   Experiences incontinence

i.   Neuro Status Alteration due to CVA/Head injury

    1.   Decreased strength

    2.   Altered balance

    3.   Altered movement

Note: 100% of CVA patients are automatically placed on Fall Precautions

j.   Nocturia

k.   Medication:

    1.   Alcohol

    2.   Anesthetic

    3.   Antihistamine

    4.   Antihypertensive

    5.   Antiseizure/Antiepileptic

    6.   Benzodiazepine

    7.   Cathartic

    8.   Diuretic

    9.   Hypoglycemic

    10.   Narcotic

    11.   Psychotropic

    12.   Sedative

l.   Mental Status Alteration

    1.   Is oriented at all times

    2.   Has intermittent confusion

    3.   Confused at all times

    4.   Comatose

    5.   Climbs

    6.   Is forgetful

    7.   Experiences hypoxia

    8.   Has Sundowner's syndrome

m.   Multiple Diagnoses

n.   Orthostatic VS changes are significant

o.   Sleeplessness

p.   Incapable of Independent activity due to

    1.   Weakness

    2.   Unsteady gait

    3.   Prone to syncope

    4.   Other ____

q.   Inability to understand

r.   Uses assistive device such as walker or cane

2.   Based on nursing judgement, any one or combination of triggers may initiate Fall Precautions

FALL PRECAUTIONS

Fall Precautions include:

a. Educate to call, and how to call for help

b. Provide a room near the Nurses Station

c. Ensure call device is available, call light, bell, etc. Answer promptly.

d. Keep personal items, phone, bedside table and TV control within reach

e. Offer assistance for ambulation

f.   Ensure bed level is down any time patient care is not being directly delivered. This will enable the patient to sit on bed with his/her upper legs parallel to the floor. Ensure the knee gatch is flat.

g.   Ensure bed and wheelchair brakes are locked

h.   Provide antiskid footwear

i.   Keep environment free of clutter or spills

j.   Place walker and assistive devices near patient

k.   Utilize bedside commode if appropriate to gait

l.   Keep urinal within reach as appropriate

m.   Ensure Side Rails up ×2. (Upper side rails are up routinely; lower side rails are up only if the patient meets the above criteria). Exception for the ICU beds because of the patient controls.

n.   Place appropriate magnetic ambulation sign is posted; Ambulatory, Semi-ambulatory or Non-ambulatory. This alerts all healthcare providers of patient safety status.

o.   Ensure night light is on

p.   Anticipate patient needs and make frequent rounds and offer to assist to bathroom

q.   Toilet patients prior to sedative or diuretic and then make frequent rounds. Ensure other team members are aware of patient potential needs.

r.   Use Gait belts for transfers/ambulation as appropriate

s.   Encourage use of the Geri-Chair with tray or Orthopedic chair as appropriate

t.   Place Bed Alarm or TABS Unit as appropriate

u.   Place Fall Mats as appropriate

v.   Use restraint alternatives when needed.

w.   Use Restraints as a last choice for patient safety—acute-level medical and surgical care. The use of a restraint in this circumstance is necessary for the patient's well-being (to receive effective treatment) when less restrictive interventions, such as frequent rounds, family attendance, TABS alarm, etc., have been determined to be ineffective in providing adequate patient safety. There is an ongoing loop of assessment, intervention, evaluation, and reintervention.

x.   Monitor medications effects and side effects

y.   Observe for dehydration, perform orthostatic BP checks as indicated

z.   Observe and report "sundowner" effect

AGE SPECIFIC

Children age 2 and under shall have a crib available. The child shall be in the crib when unattended by parent or care provider. The crib sides shall be up at all times when patient is not directly attended.

The crib top shall be on if the child is able to climb up the side rail and has the potential to fall.

*A fall mat will be placed on the floor by the bed if the patient's parent or care giver takes the child out of the crib and uses the full size bed.

*NOTE: Recommendation by Quality Council 4/01 and Safety Committee 6/01

REFERRALS

Refer to Rehabilitation Services if the one or more of the following is met:
a. CVA
b. Recent Joint replacement
c. Neurological Disease
d. Need to learn to use assistive devices
e. Needing assistance with transfers and mobility
f. Physical barriers are present in living situation; ie: stairs, etc.
g. Unsafe with ambulation

PATIENT/FAMILY EDUCATION

a. Instruct patient/family/SO to ask for assistance when ambulating
b. Instruct patient/family/SO on prevention interventions—provide the Fall Risk Brochure to patient and family as appropriate
c. Reorient patient to time and place
d. Instruct patient that equipment in room, ie., IV poles, bedside table will not support weight and will roll.

REASSESSMENT

Patients are reassessed in an ongoing manner and may be placed on or taken off of Fall Precautions at any time, as determined appropriate

DOCUMENTATION

Clinical Record: Chart time, patient status at time of admission assessment, subsequent reassessments, Fall Precautions and safety measures implemented

Adapted Courtesy of Tillamook County General Hospital, Tillamook, Oregon.

4-102 Prohibited Abbreviations in Physician's Orders

POLICY

This nursing administrative policy and procedure outlines the steps for the Health Unit Coordinator (HUC) and the nurse to take when prohibited abbreviations appear in physician's orders. The procedure differs slightly for handwritten orders and Computerized Provider Order Entry (CPOE) medication orders. Other CPOE orders (non-medication orders) do not require clarification since they are not transcribed to other portions of the permanent medical record (this is a JCAHO time limited exception for computer systems).

The HCS Abbreviations Policy outlines prohibited abbreviations and the approved reference for other abbreviations. See for the list of prohibited abbreviations.

Handwritten Orders

HUCs and Nurses cannot accept or process any written orders containing prohibited abbreviations. Medication orders with prohibited abbreviations may not be transcribed to the Medication Administration Record (MAR). Orders containing prohibited abbreviations cannot be implemented until the orders are clarified and rewritten. Pharmacy is responsible for contacting physicians/providers for clarification of medication orders. Nurses are responsible for clarification of all other orders (non-medications). If a medication needs to be given immediately as with STAT orders or for patient care needs such as pain, then the RN must contact the physician/provider for medication order clarification.

CPOE Medication Orders

HUCs and nurses cannot accept CPOE medication orders with prohibited abbreviations. Medications orders with prohibited abbreviations cannot be transcribed to the MAR. Medications cannot be administered until the order is clarified by revision in CPOE. Most prohibited abbreviations will be found in comment lines or in free text orders. This only applies to medication orders. The nurse is responsible for contacting the physician about medication order revision in CPOE. Non-medication orders do not require clarification.

Areas with Unit Stock Medications and Pyxis Non-Profile Machines

In some clinical care areas, pharmacy does not review all medications orders prior to administration. The nurse directly accesses medication supplies in stock locations or Pyxis non-profile machines. In this situation the nurse is responsible for contacting the provider for medication order clarification. These nursing units and clinical care areas include: Emergency Department, Pediatric Urgent Care, Urgent Care Center, Labor & Delivery, Newborn Nursery, General Clinical Research Center, Main Operating Room (OR), Post Anesthesia Care Unit (PACU), Procedural Care Suites (PCS), Women's & Children's OR, Women's and Children's PACU, Women's and Children's PCS, ACC Day-Op, and most procedural areas and outpatient clinics.

Procedure

I. For Handwritten Physician's Orders:

A. **HUC or RN**

    1. Review orders for prohibited abbreviations. See example below.

DATE: **6/9/04**	TIME: **0800**	PM	ROOM NO. **9999**	University of North Carolina Hospitals Chapel Hill, NC 27514

Digoxin 0.25 mg po QD

Flush feeding tube with 25 cc free H2O q4h

				University of North Carolina
DATE: **6/9/04**	TIME: **0800**	PM	ROOM NO. **9999**	Hospitals Chapel Hill, NC 27514

P. Abbreviation, MD 999999 6/9/04		TRANSCRIBED BY:	CHECKED BY:

2. Highlight any orders containing prohibited abbreviations in yellow. In the example the digoxin contains the prohibited abbreviation "QD" and the flush order contains "cc".

				University of North Carolina
DATE: **6/9/04**	TIME: **0800**	PM	ROOM NO. **9999**	Hospitals Chapel Hill, NC 27514

Digoxin 0.25 mg po QD

Flush feeding tube with 25 cc free H2O q4h

P. Abbreviation, MD 999999 6/9/04		TRANSCRIBED BY:	CHECKED BY:

3. Notify the RN caring for the patient.

4. Make a note to the right of the order: "RN Notified".

				University of North Carolina
DATE: **6/9/04**	TIME: **0800**	PM	ROOM NO. **9999**	Hospitals Chapel Hill, NC 27514

Digoxin 0.25 mg po QD *RN Notified*

Flush feeding tube with 25 cc free H2O q4h *RN Notified*

P. Abbreviation, MD 999999 6/9/04		TRANSCRIBED BY:	CHECKED BY:

5. Transcribe other orders as usual. Highlighted orders are not transcribed.

6. Sign the "Transcribed By" box on the order sheet when complete.

B. **RN**

1. Notify the physician/provider for any non-medication orders containing a prohibited abbreviation. The physician/provider needs to rewrite the order for clarification. Orders cannot be implemented until rewritten. Make a note on the order sheet: "MD Notified."

2. For STAT or urgently needed medication orders, contact the physician/provider for order clarification prior to administering the medications. For other medication orders, pharmacy will contact the physician.

   Note: For nursing units or areas where pharmacy does not review all medication orders prior to administration, the nurse is responsible for contacting the physician/provider for medication order clarification.

3. The RN may need to take a verbal order to support patient care needs.

4. Verify all other orders.

514

5. Sign "Checked By" box on the order sheet when complete.

6. During Chart Checks (24 hour or 12 hour in ICUs) review the orders to see if all yellow highlighted orders have been revised. If needed, notify the physician/provider again.

II. <u>For CPOE Medication Orders:</u>

A. **HUC or RN**

1. Review orders for medication orders with prohibited abbreviations. See example below.

```
^&13G                                                      Page:    1

UNC HOSPITALS                          00001202001-2
CHAPEL HILL, NORTH CAROLINA 27514      BAGGINS ,FRODO T          M - 6
                                       02/14/1981   23
PHYSICIANS ORDERS                          1202001143        P   P
                                       8BT   8306P1
                                                         06/09/04

Medicare will only pay for services that it determines to be reasonable and
necessary under section 1862(a)(1) of the Medicare Law.  When ordering tests
for which Medicare reimbursement will be sought, physicians should order only
those individual tests that are necessary for the diagnosis and treatment of a
patient, rather than for screening purposes.
- - - - - - - - - - - - - - - - - - - - - - - - - - - - - - - - - - - - - - - -
ALLERGIES:
AMOXICILLIN
- - - - - - - - - - - - - - - - - - - - - - - - - - - - - - - - - - - - - - - -

ORDER#  DESCRIPTION                                  START / STOP

   4 ALUM/MAGN HYDROX + SIMETHICONE 30. CC PO ONCE DAILY    06/09/04 08:28
                                                            /  /     :

   5 DIGOXIN 250. MCG PO ONCE DAILY                         06/09/04 08:28
                                                            /  /     :
     HOLD IF PULSE LT 60        CHECK APICAL PULSE QD PRE DOSE
```

2. Highlight any medication orders containing prohibited abbreviations in yellow.

3. Notify the RN caring for the patient.

4. Make a note to the right of the order: "RN Notified"

5. Transcribe other orders as usual. Highlighted orders are not transcribed to the MAR.

6. Sign the "Transcribed By" line on the order sheet when complete.

B. **RN**

1. Notify the physician/provider that a medication order contains a prohibited abbreviation. The physician/provider needs to clarify the order by revising the order in CPOE. Make a note on the order sheet: "MD Notified."

2. Medications cannot be administered until the orders are clarified by revision in CPOE.

3. The RN may need to take a verbal order to support patient care needs.

4. Verify any remaining orders.

5. Sign "Checked By" line on the order sheet when complete.

6. During Chart Checks (24 hour or 12 hour in ICUs) review the orders to see if all yellow highlighted orders have been revised. If needed, notify the physician/provider again.

Source: Courtesy of UNC Health Care, Chapel Hill, North Carolina.

4-103 Elements of a Hospital Emergency Response Plan

This Emergency Response Plan is intended for hospitals involved in a community response to a hazardous substance incident. The plan should address the following elements:

- pre-emergency drills implementing the hospital's emergency response plan;
- practice sessions using the Incident Command System (ICS) with other local emergency response organizations;
- lines of authority and communication between the incident site and hospital personnel regarding hazards and potential contamination;
- designation of a decontamination team, including emergency department physicians, nurses, aides and support personnel;
- description of the hospital's system for immediately accessing information on toxic materials;
- designation of alternative facilities that could provide treatment in case of contamination of the hospital's Emergency Department;
- plan for managing emergency treatment of non-contaminated patients;
- decontamination procedures and designation of decontamination areas (either indoors or outdoors);
- hospital staff use of Personal Protective Equipment (PPE) based on routes of exposure, degree of contact, and each individual's specific tasks;
- prevention of cross-contamination of airborne substances via the hospital's ventilation system;
- air monitoring to ensure that the facility is safe for occupancy following treatment of contaminated patients; and
- post-emergency critique of the hospital's emergency response.

When a hospital has been designated by the Local Emergency Planning Committee (LEPC), it must prepare to fulfill its role in community emergency response. This is accomplished by engaging in emergency response planning activities that involve all segments of the community (i.e., employers, other emergency response organizations, local government, and the emergency medical community). With this in mind, the hospital should consider the following:

- The hospital must define its role in community emergency response by pre-planning and coordinating with other local emergency response organizations, such as the fire department. In particular, the hospital must be familiar with the ICS used by other local organizations during emergencies and should participate in training and practice sessions using the ICS.
- All hospital personnel who are expected to respond in emergencies where hazardous substances are released must be trained in handling contaminated patients and objects including body fluids.
- Training must be based on the duties and responsibilities of each employee.

516

- Hospitals should have a contingence plan for managing other patients in the emergency response system when contaminated patients are being treated.
- There should be communication between other members of the ICS, the incident site, and the hospital personnel regarding the hazards associated with potential contaminants.
- Hospitals should have access to a database that is compiled by the LEPC to provide immediate information to hospital staff on the hazards associated with exposure to toxic materials that may be used by local employers.

Source: *Hospitals and Community Emergency Response—What You Need to Know.* Emergency Response Safety Series. U.S. Department of Labor, Occupational Safety and Health Administration, Washington, DC. OSHA Publication No. 3152.

4-104 Alcohol-Based Hand Rub Solutions: CMS Fire Safety Requirements

This interim final rule adopts the substance of the April 15, 2004 temporary interim amendment (TIA) 00-1 (101), Alcohol Based Hand Rub (ABHR) Solutions, an amendment to the 2000 edition of the Life Safety Code, published by the National Fire Protection Association (NFPA). This amendment will allow certain health care facilities to place alcohol-based hand rub dispensers in egress corridors under specified conditions.

The benefits of using ABHRs have been well demonstrated. However, until a short time ago there were concerns about placing ABHR dispensers in egress corridors. The ABHRs are most commonly found in a gel form contained in a single use disposable bag that is inserted into a wall-mounted dispenser, similar in appearance to wall-mounted hand soap dispensers. The dispenser compresses the bag to operation and replacement, the dispenser remains a closed system, meaning that vapors are not released into the atmosphere. In addition, refilling is done using single-use disposable bags rather than large bulk containers. The relatively small quantity of gel in each dispenser combined with the absence of vapor release means that these dispensers, when properly installed and used, pose little fire risk in health care facilities.

CMS adopted the amendment to Chapters 18 and 19 of the 2000 edition of the Life Safety Code, specifically the changes to Chapters 18.3.2.7 and 19.3.2.7. Adopting the amended chapters will allow health care facilities to place ABHR dispensers in egress corridors. Chapters 18 and 19 will apply to hospitals, long-term care facilities, religious non-medical health care institutions, hospices, programs of all-inclusive care for the elderly, hospitals, intermediate care facilities for the mentally retarded, and critical access hospitals.

A health care facility will be viewed to be in compliance with the requirements if the placement of ABHR dispensers meets the specified conditions listed in Section II. A of this interim final rule.

The ABHR dispensers will also be required to meet the following criteria that are listed in chapters 18.3.2.7 and 19.3.2.7 of the 2000 edition of the LSC:
- Where dispensers are installed in a corridor, the corridor shall have a minimum width of 6 ft (1.8 m).
- The maximum individual dispenser fluid capacity shall be:
    —0.3 gallons (1.2 liters) for dispensers in rooms, corridors, and areas open to corridors.

—0.5 gallons (2.0 liters) for dispensers in suites of rooms.
- The dispensers shall have a minimum horizontal spacing of 4 feet (1.2 m) from each other.
- Not more than an aggregate 10 gallons (37.8 liters) of ABHR solution shall be in use in a single smoke compartment outside of a storage cabinet.
- Storage of quantities greater than 5 gallons (18.9 liters) in a single smoke compartment shall meet the requirements of NFPA 30, *Flammable and Combustible Liquids Code.*
- The dispensers shall not be installed over or directly adjacent to an ignition source.
- In locations with carpeted floor coverings, dispensers installed directly over carpeted surfaces shall be permitted only in sprinklered smoke compartments.

After careful and thorough consideration of the numerous studies and recommendations presented above, we believe that placing ABHR dispensers in all appropriate areas, including corridors, is safe and appropriate for patients and providers alike.

Specifically, we are adding a new provision that will allow these facilities to place ABHR dispensers in various locations, including egress corridors, if the facilities met the following conditions:

- The use of ABHR dispensers could not conflict with any State or local codes that prohibit or otherwise restrict the placement of ABHR dispensers in health care facilities. Allowing ABHR dispensers to be installed in egress corridors will be a significant lessening of restrictions. States and/or local jurisdictions may choose to retain stricter codes that prohibit or otherwise restrict the installation of ABHR dispensers in health care facilities. Facilities will still be required to comply with those stricter State and local codes. Therefore, facilities could only install ABHR dispensers if the dispensers were also permitted by State and local codes.
- The dispensers were installed in a manner that minimized leaks and spills that could lead to falls. Like soap, ABHRs are very slick. As such, it is more likely for someone to slip and fall on a surface that is covered by an ABHR solution than on a surface that is clean. The increased risk of falls posed by the presence of leaky or spilled ABHR dispensers might be compounded by the medical conditions of patients or residents. While a healthy individual may fall and only suffer a bruise, a frail individual may suffer a broken hip. It is the specific safety needs of the patient populations found in hospitals and other health care facilities that necessitates the requirement that facilities take extra steps to ensure that ABHR dispensers do not leak or spill. In addition to any extra steps such as additional hardware installation, facilities should follow all manufacturer maintenance recommendations for ABHR dispensers. Regular maintenance of dispensers in accordance with the directions of the manufacturer is a crucial step towards ensuring that the dispensers do not leak or spill.
- The dispensers were installed in a manner that adequately protected against access by vulnerable populations, such as residents in psychiatric units. There are certain patient or resident populations, such as residents of dementia wards, who may misuse ABHR solutions, which are both toxic and flammable. As a toxic substance, ABHR solutions are very dangerous if they are ingested, placed in the eyes, or otherwise misused. As a flammable substance, ABHR solutions could be used to start fires that endanger the lives of patients and destroy property. Due to disability or disease, some patients are more likely to harm themselves or others by misusing ABHR solutions. In order to avoid any and all dangerous situations, a facility will have to take all

appropriate precautions to secure the ABHR dispensers from misuse by these vulnerable populations.

- The dispensers were installed in accordance with Chapters 18.3.2.7 and 19.3.2.7 of the 2000 edition of the LSC. The revisions to the chapters were thoroughly examined by the NFPA's fire safety experts and are based on the fire modeling study conducted by Gage-Babcock for the ASHE. The study demonstrated that ABHR dispensers installed in egress corridors do not increase the risk of fire if certain conditions, as outlined in Chapters 18.3.2.7 and 19.3.2.7 of the 2000 edition of the LSC, are met. The study also showed that if those conditions are not met, there will be an increase in the risk of fire.

Source: Medicare and Medicaid Programs; Fire Safety Requirements for Certain Health-Care Facilities; Amendment. *Federal Register*, Vol. 70, No. 57, March 25, 2005. Rules and Regulations, pp. 15229-15233.

MANAGEMENT OF HUMAN RESOURCES

4-105 Rationale for Patient Care Staffing

1. _____ staffs patient care units based on patient acuity levels, unit census, scheduled appointments and established national guidelines.
2. Data related to census and acuity shall be collected and monitored at different intervals specific to the care area.
3. Managers respond to this data by adjusting staffing mixes at the appropriate interval.
4. Options to respond to staffing needs varies by service area. Each service area may respond to varying staffing needs for short term and long term solutions.
5. _____ utilizes appropriate solutions to varying staffing needs which include area-specific float pools, staff who have been trained to provide care in different areas, managers who may provide direct patient care, as well as the use of contract nursing when appropriate.
6. The Risk Management Root Cause Analysis Tool is used to assess for staffing related issues when as warranted.
7. Monitoring activities such as the Nursing Quality Report, Risk Management Reports and Patient Satisfaction data are used to monitor trends related to staffing.

A staffing variance is handled by a variety of methods:

- use of qualified float pool staff
- managers work with each other, floating of qualified staff
- incentive pay for staff, voluntary overtime is offered to staff
- management staff accept patient assignments
- use of case management staff
- pharmacy staff has assumed additional duties
- increased support by transportation
- delivery of supplies by disciplines other than nursing
- elective surgeries may be rescheduled
- patient beds may be closed

Source: Courtesy of Parkland Health & Hospital System, Dallas, Texas.

4-106 Delineation of Privileges: Department of Emergency Medicine

Name:

Please specify below all categories requested, and initial:

_____ Evaluation of patient health care needs and provision of such services as are indicated

_____ Performance of definitive treatment, as falls within my areas of competence, and when appropriate, referral to other physicians for definitive care

_____ Care of life-threatening situations, with the facilities and staff available until such time as another physician or facility assumes responsibility for the patient's care.

Requested	Privilege	Approved	Denied
	Emergency Care of all systemic diseases within my capabilities as an Emergency Physician, or under the direction of an attending physician		
	Burns: Emergency or Initial Care only		
	Initial patient stabilization and care in cases of major trauma		
	Other:		
	Anesthesia:		
	Local		
	Regional		
	Nerve Blocks		
	Sedation & Analgesia		
	Other:		
	Cardiac Management:		
	Defibrillation		
	External pacemaker		
	Intracardiac injection		
	Pericardiocentesis		
	Open/Closed chest massage		
	Advanced Cardiac Life Support (ACLS)		
	Pediatric Advanced Life Support (PALS)		
	Preparation/Administration of Thrombolytics in Acute MI		
	Control of Hemorrhage by:		
	Packing		
	Cautery		
	Suture		
	Silver nitrate		
	Delivery of Baby/Fetus		
	Delivery of placenta (does not include retained placenta)		
	Sexual Assault Evaluation & Treatment		

520

Requested	Privilege	Approved	Denied
	Advanced Trauma Life Support (ATLS)		
	Initial assessment & stabilization of psychiatric patients		
	SPECIAL STUDIES AND PROCEDURES:		
	Arterial puncture		
	Arterial catheterization		
	Arthrocentesis		
	Aspiration		
	Joint		
	Lymph node		
	Biopsy		
	Skin		
	Other:		
	Catheterization		
	CVP or Subclavian		
	Foley		
	Splint Application		
	Noncircular casting		
	Continuous Positive Airway Pressure		
	Cricothyroidotomy		
	EKG (with interpretation)		
	Excision of minor lesion/cyst		
	Excision of nail		
	Endotracheal intubation		
	Gastric Lavage		
	Incision (w/without drainage or FB removal)		
	Abscess/Cyst		
	Hematoma		
	Skin/subcutaneous tissue		
	Injection of dye for radiologic studies (IVP, CT scan)		
	Insertion of:		
	Arteriovenous dialysis fistula		
	Chest tube		
	Intubation (Endotracheal/nasotracheal)		
	Lumbar puncture		
	Pacemaker insertion—temporary		

Requested	Privilege	Approved	Denied
	Paracentesis		
	Pericardiocentesis		
	Peritoneal dialysis		
	Rapid sequence intubation		
	Reduction		
	Dislocation		
	Fracture (closed only)		
	Removal of foreign body (w/without incision)		
	Repair of simple laceration		
	Facial		
	Other sites:		
	Sedation: IV/Conscious		
	Splinting		
	Suprapublic cystostomy		
	Tracheostomy—temporary		
	Thoracotomy/thoracostomy		
	Thrombolytic agent administration		
	Venous cutdown		

I understand that the completion of these forms at the present time does not preclude me from requesting additional privileges in accordance with the medical staff bylaws.

I also understand that, in conjunction with such privileges, occasional consultations are suggested, particularly when unexpected complications develop, failure to respond as expected occurs, or unfamiliar features arise.

I understand that I shall be authorized to treat any medical disease or perform any medical or surgical procedures at the hospital in an emergency situation. For these purposes, an emergency is defined as any situation in which any delay in administering treatment would result in serious harm or an immediate threat to the life of the patient.

I have no mental or physical condition that would impair my ability to perform the above procedures, and I am proficient and qualified to perform all such procedures.

_____   _____
Date   Signature of Applicant

ACTION OF THE CHIEF OF EMERGENCY MEDICINE:

_____   Clinical Privileges Approved as requested

_____   Clinical Privileges Approved WITH THE FOLLOWING CHANGES:

_____

_____

Date   Signature of Chief

ACTION OF THE MEDICAL BOARD

____   Approved

____   Approved WITH THE FOLLOWING CHANGES:

_____

_____

Copy sent to physician Date: _____

Date _____   Signature of Chief of Staff: _____

Source: Adopted from Huntington Hospital, Huntington, New York.

4-107 LPN Competency Record

Name: ....

Date of Employment: ....

Dates of Orientation: ....

Date Record Initiated: ....

Assigned Preceptors: ....

....

Certifications

Title   Exp. Date

_____

_____

_____

_____

I. Purpose

The LPN Competency Record has been developed to

A. facilitate orientee self-assessment prior to orientation and promote his or her involvement in the learning process

B. facilitate the Staff Development process in providing an individualized orientation

C. provide a current and objective assessment of the nurse's performance in the delivery of patient care services

D. provide documentation of individual nurse competence, as necessary, for assigning clinical responsibilities

II. Policy

A. The LPN Competency Record will be initiated by staff development at the beginning of orientation.

B. The LPN orientee will complete the self-assessment section and collaborate with staff development in planning for specific orientation needs.

C. Asterisked competency statements require completion of the appropriate competency checklist.

Orientation Self Assessment			Skills & Competencies	END ORIENTATION		END PROBATION		YEAR____		YEAR____	
Competent	Needs Review	No Experience		Date	Init	Date	Init	Date	Init	Date	Init
			I. Maintenance of Safe, Effective Care Environment								
			A. Knowledge of Legal/Ethical Framework for Care								
			1. Verbalizes protocol for reporting child and elder abuse								
			2. Verbalizes knowledge of rape policy and kit location								
			B. Environment Safety								
			1. Describes the physical plan of the ED								
			2. Demonstrates awareness of ED Policy and procedure book								
			3. Verbalizes calling a code in the ED								
			4. Demonstrates location and correct use of adult and pediatric crashcart checklist and pediatric work cart								
			5. Demonstrates correct use of the Lifepak 6-S defibrillator Nihon Kohen monitors								
			6. Demonstrates correct use of IV fluid warmer								
			7. Demonstrates ability to set up and assist with specific procedures in the ED including, but not limited to, phlebotomy, paracentesis, peritoneal tap, thoracentesis, sigmoidoscopy, lumbar, puncture, and minor procedures as scheduled in ED								
			II. Maintenance of Physiologic Integrity								
			A. Medications/IV therapy								

continues

525

Orientation Self Assessment											
Competent	Needs Review	No Experience	Skills & Competencies	END ORIENTATION		END PROBATION		YEAR ___		YEAR ___	
				Date	Init	Date	Init	Date	Init	Date	Init
			1. Demonstrates ability to perform venipuncture for IV administration								
			2. Demonstrates ability to initiate IVPB medications as directed by RN								
			B. Application of Nursing Process for Emergent Patients								
			1. Applies general elements of nursing process for emergent patients								
			a. Verbalizes ED policy/procedure for triage								
			b. Discusses ED policy re initial and ongoing assessment of patient								
			c. States ED policy re: fast track methodology								
			d. Explains standing orders implementation								
			e. Verbalizes transfer policy and procedure								
			f. Verbalizes discharge policy and procedure								
			2. Uses nursing process to render care appropriate and specific to emergent patients with impairment of the INTEGEMENTARY SYSTEM								
			a. Assesses status of patient's skin								
			b. Demonstrates the ability to implement the emergency nursing protocol for patients presenting with surface trauma, as directed by RN, inclusive of, but not limited to								
			1. abrasions								
			2. avulsions								
			3. contusions								

continues

526

Competent	Needs	No Experience	Skills & Competencies	END ORIENTATION Date	Init	END PROBATION Date	Init	YEAR Date	Init	YEAR Date	Init
			Orientation Self Assessment								
			4. lacerations								
			5. puncture wounds								
			6. foreign body injury								
			7. traumatic amputation								
			8. human bites								
			9. animal bites								
			c. Demonstrates the ability to implement the emergency nursing protocol for patients presenting with thermal injuries								
			1. Verbalizes thermal injury protocol for patients presenting with thermal injuries								
			2. Implements nursing interventions appropriate to thermal injury classification as directed by RN								
			3. Implements protocol for transfer of major burns to burn treatment center as directed by RN								
			3. Uses nursing process to render care appropriate and specific to emergent patients with impairment of HEAD AND NECK/NEUROLOGICAL SYSTEM								
			a. Assesses status of emergent patients presenting with neurologic impairment including head, neck, and face								

continues

527

Orientation Self Assessment				END ORIENTATION		END PROBATION		YEAR ____		YEAR ____	
Competent	Needs Review	No Experience	Skills & Competencies	Date	Init	Date	Init	Date	Init	Date	Init
			b. Demonstrates the ability to assist in the implementation of the emergency nursing protocol for patients presenting with head, neck, and facial trauma inclusive of, but not limited to								
			1. CVA								
			2. Seizures/status epilepticus								
			3. Unconsciousness								
			4. Spinal cord and neck								
			4. Uses nursing process to render care appropriate and specific to emergent patients with impairment of the CARDIOVASCULAR SYSTEM.								
			a. Achieves a score of 70 or better in basic cardiology exam								
			b. Achieves and maintains ACLS certification								
			c. Assesses patient's cardiovascular status								
			d. Implements standing orders for patients presenting with chest pain as directed by RN								
			e. Demonstrates ability to implement the emergency nursing protocol for patients presenting with chest pain								
			1. Demonstrates ability to use Dinemapp								
			2. Demonstrates ability to analyze basic rhythm strips								
			3. Recognizes lethal dysrhythmias								

continues

528

Orientation Self Assessment			Skills & Competencies	END ORIENTATION		END PROBATION		YEAR _____		YEAR _____	
Competent	Needs Review	No Experience		Date	Init	Date	Init	Date	Init	Date	Init
			4. Demonstrates ability to apply monitor leads and set parameters for individual patients								
			5. Verbalizes protocol for transfer of patient to CCU or telemetry								
			6. Demonstrates ability to do an EKG								
			7. Assists in transport with orderly to 3E, CCU, ICU, as directed by RN								
			5. Uses nursing process to render care appropriate and specific to emergent patients with impairment of the PULMONARY SYSTEM								
			a. Assesses patient's pulmonary status								
			b. Demonstrates the ability to recognize and implement the emergency nursing protocol for patients presenting with a pulmonary emergency inclusive of, but not limited to								
			1. pulmonary edema								
			2. asthma/status asthmatics								
			3. emphysema								
			4. smoke inhalation								
			5. croup								
			6. Uses nursing process to render care appropriate and specific to emergent patients with impairment of the MUSCULOSKELETAL SYSTEM								
			a. Assesses status of patients presenting with musculoskeletal emergencies								

continues

Orientation Self Assessment										
Competent	Needs Review	No Experience	Skills & Competencies	END ORIENTATION		END PROBATION		YEAR ____		YEAR ____	
				Date	Init	Date	Init	Date	Init	Date	Init
			b. Demonstrates the ability to recognize and implement the emergency nursing protocol for patients presenting with musculoskeletal emergencies as directed by RN, inclusive of but not limited to								
			1. soft tissue injuries								
			a. strains								
			b. sprains								
			2. fractures: closed, open								
			a. extremities—arm, leg, shoulder								
			b. pelvis								
			c. hip								
			3. dislocations								
			4. assists with cast application								
			c. Provides nursing interventions, including patient education, related to								
			1. crutch walking								
			2. cervical collar								
			3. knee immobilizer								
			4. buddy-taping								
			5. ace bandage								
			6. cast care								
			7. arm sling								
			7. Demonstrates the ability to implement the emergency nursing protocol for patients presenting for conscious sedation								

continues

530

Orientation Self Assessment			Skills & Competencies	END ORIENTATION		END PROBATION		YEAR		YEAR	
Competent	Needs Review	No Experience		Date	Init	Date	Init	Date	Init	Date	Init
			a. Verbalizes the protocol for caring for a patient undergoing conscious sedation								
			8. Uses nursing process to render care appropriate and specific to emergent patients with impairment of the METABOLIC SYSTEM								
			a. Demonstrates the ability to recognize and implement the emergency nursing protocol for patients presenting with a potential or actual metabolic emergency as directed by RN, inclusive but not limited to								
			1. hypoglycemia								
			2. DKA								
			3. HHNKS								
			b. Demonstrate ability to perform BGM testing								
			9. Uses nursing process to render care appropriate and specific to emergent patients with impairment of the GENITOURINARY SYSTEM								
			a. Assesses status of patients with genitourinary emergencies								
			b. Demonstrates the ability to implement the emergency nursing protocol for patients presenting with genitourinary emergencies as directed by an RN, inclusive of, but not limited to								
			1. urethral trauma								
			2. urinary retention								
			3. hematuria								

continues

531

Orientation Self Assessment			Skills & Competencies	END ORIENTATION		END PROBATION		YEAR ____		YEAR ____	
Competent	Needs Review	No Experience		Date	Init	Date	Init	Date	Init	Date	Init
			4. cystitis								
			5. acute epididymitis								
			6. testicular Torsion								
			7. clotted graft in dialysis patients								
			10. Uses nursing process to render care appropriate and specific to emergent patients with impairment of the GYNECOLOGICAL/OBSTETRICAL SYSTEM								
			a. Assesses status of patients with gynecologic/ obstetrical emergencies.								
			b. Demonstrates ability to recognize and implement the emergency nursing protocol for patients presenting with obstetrical or gynecological emergencies as directed by RN, inclusive of, but not limited to								
			1. ectopic pregnancy								
			2. abruptio placenta								
			3. placenta previa								
			4. emergency delivery								
			5. post-partum hemorrhage								
			6. abortion								
			7. sexual assault								
			a. Implements nursing interventions appropriate for patient who has been sexually assaulted								

continues

532

Orientation Self Assessment			Skills & Competencies	END ORIENTATION		END PROBATION		YEAR ___		YEAR ___	
Competent	Needs Review	No Experience		Date	Init	Date	Init	Date	Init	Date	Init
			11. Uses nursing process to render care appropriate and specific to emergent patients with impairment of the EARS/NOSE/THROAT								
			a. Demonstrates the ability to implement the emergency nursing protocol for patients presenting with ear emergencies as directed by RN, inclusive of, but not limited to								
			1. FB ear								
			2. bleeding, discharge or wax in external canal								
			3. frostbite								
			b. Demonstrates ability to implement nursing interventions appropriate for ear emergencies as directed by RN, inclusive of, but not limited to								
			1. location and set up ENT tray and instruments								
			2. otoscope								
			3. ear syringe								
			4. tuning fork								
			5. controlling bleeding								
			c. Demonstrates the ability to implement the emergency nursing protocol for patients presenting with nose emergencies as directed by RN, inclusive of but not limited to								
			1. epistaxis								
			2. FB								

continues

533

Orientation Self Assessment				END ORIENTATION		END PROBATION		YEAR ___		YEAR ___	
Competent	Needs Review	No Experience	**Skills & Competencies**	Date	Init	Date	Init	Date	Init	Date	Init
			d. Assesses status of patient's throat								
			e. Demonstrates the ability to implement the emergency nursing protocol for patients presenting with throat emergencies								
			12. Uses nursing process to render care appropriate and specific to emergent patients with impairment of EYES								
			a. Assesses status of a patient's eyes								
			b. Tests for visual acuity								
			c. Demonstrates the ability to implement the emergency nursing protocol for patients presenting with eye emergencies as directed by RN								
			13. Uses nursing process to render care appropriate and specific to emergent patients with MULTIPLE SYSTEM TRAUMA								
			a. Assesses status of patients presenting with multiple system trauma as directed by RN								
			1. Verbalizes knowledge of primary trauma survey using ABC4. (airway, breathing, circulation, cervical spine, chest, consciousness)								
			2. Verbalizes knowledge of secondary survey								
			3. Verbalizes knowledge of general management following completion of systemic assessment								

continues

534

Orientation Self Assessment			Skills & Competencies	END ORIENTATION		END FROBATION		YEAR _____		YEAR _____	
Competent	Needs Review	No Experience		Date	Init	Date	Init	Date	Init	Date	Init
			4. Verbalizes knowledge of hospital medical policy for patients presenting with multiple trauma—surgeon on call is								
			14. Uses nursing process to render care appropriate and specific to emergent patients with INFECTIOUS DISEASE								
			a. Demonstrated ability to recognize and implement the emergency nursing protocol for patients presenting with a potential infectious disease as directed by RN								
			1. isolates for possible infectious disease, including rash.								
			2. labels room appropriately								
			3. demonstrates ability to implement and use								
			15. Uses nursing process to render care appropriate and specific to patients with TOXICOLOGIC emergencies								
			a. Assesses status of patients who present with a potential or actual toxicologic emergency								
			b. Demonstrates the ability to recognize and implement the emergency nursing protocol as directed by RN, with a toxicologic emergency inclusive of, but not limited to								
			1. acetaminophen								
			2. food poisoning								

continues

Orientation Self Assessment			Skills & Competencies	END ORIENTATION		END PROBATION		YEAR ___		YEAR ___	
Competent	Needs Review	No Experience		Date	Init	Date	Init	Date	Init	Date	Init
			3. Salicylates, NSAIDS								
			4. Narcotics								
			16. Uses nursing process to render care appropriate and specific to patients with PEDIATRIC emergencies								
			a. Assesses status of pediatric patients who present with a chronic or acute emergency, using the following criteria								
			1. visual assessment								
			2. level of activity								
			3. skin color								
			4. breathing pattern								
			5. rectal temperature								
			6. heart rate								
			7. respiratory rate								
			8. blood pressure (if over 4 years)								
			9. weight								
			b. Demonstrates the ability to implement the emergency nursing protocol for Pediatric patients as directed by RN, inclusive of but not limited to								
			1. hypoxia								
			2. nasopharyngeal obstruction								
			3. oropharyngeal obstruction								
			4. upper airway obstruction—(croup, FB)								

continues

Orientation Self Assessment											
Competent	Needs Review	No Experience	**Skills & Competencies**	END ORIENTATION		END PROBATION		YEAR ___		YEAR ___	
				Date	Init	Date	Init	Date	Init	Date	Init
			5. lower airway obstruction (asthma, bronchiolitis)								
			6. fevers								
			7. set up infant radiant warmer								
			III. Maintenance of Psychosocial Integrity								
			A. Assesses the general level of patients psychosocial adaptation								
			B. Demonstrates the ability to recognize and implement the emergency nursing protocol for patients presenting with a psychiatric emergency inclusive of, but not limited to								
			1. acute anxiety attack								
			2. acute depression								
			3. suicidal ideation								
			4. assaultive behavior								
			5. acute psychotic reactions								
			6. drug-related psychiatric emergencies								
			IV. Health Promotion/Maintenance								
			A. Provides special need referrals								
			1. emergency housing								
			2. Pederson-Krag Clinic								
			3. Family Service League								
			4. drug abuse hot line								

continues

537

Orientation Self Assessment			Skills & Competencies	END ORIENTATION		END PROBATION		YEAR ____		YEAR ____	
Competent	Needs Review	No Experience		Date	Init	Date	Init	Date	Init	Date	Init
			5. Alcohol abuse hot line								
			6. Department of Health								
			7. Haven House for Battered Women								
			8. Well Baby Clinic								
			B. Makes support group referrals								
			1. Victims Information Bureau								
			2. Alcoholics Anonymous								
			3. Drugs and Alcohol Withdrawal								
			4. Women's Coalition								
			C. Special Procedures								
			1. Maintains well stocked environment								
			2. Demonstrates ability to provide a sterile field								
			3. Assists with collection, accurate labeling, and delivery of specimens obtained during procedure to the lab								
			4. Obtains consent, site verification for procedure as indicated								
			5. Requests H & P from physicians as necessary								
			6. Documents pertinent information to charge nurse								
			7. Reports pertinent information to charge nurse								

continues

Orientation Self Assessment			Skills & Competencies	END ORIENTATION		END PROBATION		YEAR _____		YEAR _____	
Competent	Needs Review	No Experience		Date	Init	Date	Init	Date	Init	Date	Init
			8. Cleans instruments and sends back to central supply								

Source: Courtesy of Huntington Hospital, Huntington, New York.

4-108 Emergency Department Physician Assistant Orientation Checklist

INTRODUCTION

Purpose of Orientation
- ☐ Provide knowledge necessary to perform ED responsibilities.
- ☐ Meet Joint Commission requirements.
- ☐ Avoid potential pitfalls.
- ☐ Decrease medicolegal risk.

PA ADMINISTRATIVE RESPONSIBILITIES

Scheduling and Staffing
- ☐ Procedures for shift requests, including due dates and necessary materials
- ☐ Procedures for vacation requests, due dates and necessary materials
- ☐ Shift swapping, illness and other emergencies which impact a scheduled shift
- ☐ Sign-in sheet, double coverage provisions
- ☐ Punctuality

Credentialing
- ☐ Current medical license
- ☐ Recredentialling AAPA & EMSA requirements
- ☐ Other certifications (e.g., ACLS, ATLS, PALS)

General Performance Expectations
- ☐ Clinical expectations
- ☐ Appearance
- ☐ Meeting attendance

Medical Staff Relationships
- ☐ Referral of private patients to specialists
- ☐ Call list
- ☐ HMO: Department-specific policies including use of call list
- ☐ Disagreements about disposition: how to handle
- ☐ Importance of providing service to medical staff
- ☐ Social interaction with medical staff
- ☐ General conflict resolution guidelines

Nursing Relationships
- ☐ Nursing capabilities (RN, LPN, Aides, Techs)
- ☐ Standing orders
- ☐ Triage protocols on test ordering and order patient seen
- ☐ Triage out of ED and management of HMO patients
- ☐ Prompt response to nursing requests
- ☐ Conflict resolution
- ☐ Notifying nurses whenever PA leaves department
- ☐ Praise and constructive criticism: appropriate way
- ☐ Nurses are the greatest asset to success of the ED: efforts to ensure their operation

Patient Satisfaction
- ☐ We are in a service role.
- ☐ Empathetic attending behavior: appearance, name tag, identification, eye contact, touch
- ☐ Explanation of waiting times
- ☐ Pain relief
- ☐ Managing chronic pain patients
- ☐ Physician-Patient communication
- ☐ Communicating discharge instructions
- ☐ Dealing with problem patients

General Administrative Issues
- ☐ ED administration: Chain of command; names and telephone numbers
- ☐ Mail
- ☐ Reference books
- ☐ Long distance and private telephone use
- ☐ EMSA CME
- ☐ Employee health program
- ☐ Meal breaks

EMSA Employee Issues
- ☐ Interface with corporate office
- ☐ Bloodborne pathogen manual

CLINICAL PRACTICE

Introductions to Department Staff and Hospital Administration
- ☐ Highlights regarding key hospital administrative and medical staff leaders
- ☐ Tour of Facility

Patient Flow Overview
- ☐ Patient demographics
- ☐ Patient flow through department
- ☐ Problem solving (i.e., lab, X-ray)
- ☐ Direct admissions
- ☐ Visitors
- ☐ Triage

Charting Documentation
- ☐ ED Medical Record
- ☐ Flow of medical record
- ☐ Legibility
- ☐ Dictation capabilities
- ☐ Discharge instructions
- ☐ Patient consents
- ☐ Patient transfers
- ☐ Voice BillStat (intro to key parameters)

Nursing Orders
- ☐ Method of conveying orders to nursing and clerical staff

Radiology Services

- ☐ Availability of CT/MRI, ultrasound, IVP, nuclear medicine
- ☐ Daily coverage in-house, specific tests
- ☐ After-hour coverage, specific tests
- ☐ Obtaining radiologists' readings
- ☐ Completing temporary reports
- ☐ Receipt of review of radiology readings
- ☐ Follow-up of discordant X-ray readings

Laboratory Services

- ☐ Availability of various lab results
- ☐ Mechanism for ordering lab tests
- ☐ Procedure for managing lab tests or type specific blood on an emergent basis
- ☐ Follow-up on culture results and abnormal lab studies received after patient discharge
- ☐ Blood bank (indications for blood products)

Cardiopulmonary Services

- ☐ EKG, blood gases
- ☐ How to order
- ☐ Stat. vs. I Stat.

Specialty Services

- ☐ Poison control
- ☐ Social services
- ☐ Inpatient care units: types/availability
- ☐ Psychiatric

EMS

- ☐ System overview
- ☐ Emergency physicians medical control and/or interaction
- ☐ Standing orders
- ☐ Bypass procedures

Equipment and Supplies

- ☐ Mechanism for requesting new or different type of equipment
- ☐ Documenting deficiencies in equipment or supplies
- ☐ Formulary: medications available in ED and process for obtaining different medications

Technical Procedures and Protocols

- ☐ Equipment availability and location

Chest tubes	Arterial lines
CVP lines	Temporary pacing
Splinting	Suturing
Epistaxis	Laryngoscopy
Doppler	Slit lamp
Airway mngt.	Peritoneal lavage
Surgical trays	Deliveries
Spinal taps	

542

☐ Medical staff considerations
☐ Procedures not to be done in ED
☐ Clinical Protocols (i.e., thrombolytics)

Patient Disposition

☐ Philosophy on admission vs. discharge
☐ Admission orders process
☐ Transfers: procedures, consent, COBRA, state regulations, documentation, destination
☐ Patient holding and observation
☐ Discharges: procedures, discharge instructions, follow-up referrals
☐ Rechecks

Reimbursement

☐ Changing guidelines
☐ Documentation
☐ Site-specific considerations

Participation in Performance Improvement Program (PI)

☐ Discussion of indicators and thresholds
☐ Responsibilities in PI data collection and evaluation
☐ Attendance at PI peer-review meetings
☐ Hospital Integration with PI
☐ Recredentialing use of PI data

Participation in Risk Management Program

☐ Incident reporting to EMSA Risk Management
☐ 1-800-NOW-EMSA
☐ Risk management alerts and audiotapes

Policy and Procedure Issues

☐ Hospital policy and procedure manual
☐ ED policy and procedure manual
☐ Disaster manual
☐ Infection control manual
☐ Bloodborne pathogens

Physician Assistant Name: _____ **Date:** _____
Orientation Conducted by: _____ **Date:** _____

Source: Courtesy of Suburban Hospital, Inc., Bethesda, Maryland.

4-109 Emergency Department Physician Assistant Orientation: Minimum Standards of Care

PEDIATRICS

Subjective

- Interaction with parents/guardians, pre/post-natal course/PARA/PMD/last visit/allergies
- Appropriate interaction with environment based on age; onset of complaint (improved/status quo/worsening) fever/TMAX/how temperature was determined, i.e., PO/rectal/ear
- Response to treatment/home remedies
- Associates S/S/diarrhea/vomiting/number of wet diapers/able to cry
- Behavior changes
- Exposures
- Meningeal signs, responsiveness to parents/ambulatory
- Medications
- Allergies
- Growth/development

Objective

- Examine from least invasive (chest, arm) to most invasive (ENT)
- General—listen to parents, hydration, nasal flare, capillary refill, color vital signs
- Neuro—appropriateness, consolable, alert, smile, plays, good suck, ambulation
- Chest—retractions/abnormal sounds
- Lung—diminished, wheezes, cough, races, referred
- Heart sounds—rate, rub murmur
- Abdominal—bowel sounds, tone guarding, rebound, localized tenderness, organomegaly, masses
- Head fontalelles/deformities/asymmetry
- Ears—adjust auricle, do not force ophthalmoscope, tmS, Fb, cerument obstruction, cannals
- Eyes—perl, follows objects, discharge, injection
- Nose—foreign body, odor discharge
- Mouth—dentation, lesions, odor especially if ingestion is suspected
- Throat—lesions, nodes
- Neck—supple
- Skin—rashes, genitalia (sexual abuse/physical abuse)

Intervention

- Fever without a source, consider the following based on appearance of child: chest X-ray, urine, CBC, culture, SMA6
- In general—oxygenation, O_2 sat, hydration, teaching, parenting, pain relief

Common Drugs

- Tylenol—15 mg/kg for pain and fever (toxic is 150 mg/kg)
- Pediaprofen—10 mg/kg/tid
- Amoxicillin—40 mg/kg/tid
- Septra—10 kg = 5 mg bid

- Ceclor—40 mg/kg/bid/tid
- Augmentin—40 mg/kg (animal bites)
- Suprax—qd
- EES—3-50 mg/kg qid
- Pediazole—50 mg/kg 8 kg = 2.5 ml, 16 kg = 5 ml qid
- Rocephin—50 mg/kg IM (100 mg/kg if meningitis)
- Phenogran—.5 mg/lb q4-6
- Proventil Syrup—.1 mg/kg (2 mg = 5 ml) tid
- Nystatin Suspension—100,000 units/ml qid
- Duricef—30 mg/kg bid

MEDICAL ILLNESSES

Diabetes

Subjective
- Oral or Sub-Q insulin/last taken/duration of DM
- Pain/fever
- DKA (breath)—ABG/.9NSS
- Complications/risks/silent MI
- Neuropathy/foot problems
- Cellulitis/abscesses
- Abdominal pain
- New onset, polyuria, polydipsia, frequent abscesses, frequent yeast infections, family history

Objective
- Neurological (LOC and peripheral neuropathy)
- Breath
- HR, RR, adventitious sounds
- ABD-BS, point tenderness, rebound, guarding

Interventions
- IV .9NSS, SMA7, CBC, urine (CXR, EKG, amylase dependent upon history)
- Ketones dependent on urine dip
- Hypoglycemic reactions: oral vs. insulin

Seizure Disorder

Subjective
- Duration, time, type
- Injuries, preceding, after
- Etiology
- Complaint with medications
- Additional medical history
- Allergies

Objective
- Postical/injuries
- Head to toe assessment
- Hypoglycemia, hypothermia

- ETOH, drug abuse
- Medications

Sickle Cell

Subjective

- Onset, duration of pain, similar to previous crisis
- Pain medication used
- Caution if pregnancy or abdominal pain
- Is there a H/O drug seeking?

Objective

- Head to toe/often icteric
- Pain relief, CBC, Hgb, retic

ENT

Subjective

- Onset, duration of symptoms, associated malaise, fever, rash, H/O swimming or URI
- H/O trauma, nasal bleed
- Check risk factors/hypertension
- Anticoagulants
- Trauma
- If no risk factors, often infectious

Objective

- Ears—TMS, cannals, FB, auricle, lymphadenopathy
- Nose—septal hematoma, subcutaneous emphysema, discharge, bleeding
- Fractures
- Mouth—jaw, TMJ, dentition (number, pointing, abscess)
- Lesions, palate uvula, salivation, stridor, loose teeth (aspiration)
- Risk
- Throat—lesions, lymphadenopathy

Intervention

- Nosebleed—direct pressure, packing, if packing is done place on antistaph coverage
- Teaching—vaseline in nares
- Follow-up—in 24 hours for packing removal
- Pharyngitis vs. mono vs. lymphadenitis vs. AIDS
- History and appropriate F/U
- Able to handle secretions
- Medications
- Amox—250/500 tid
- Pen-VK—250/500 qid
- Cavities vs. abscess: pain relief vs. drug seek follow-up, antibiotics (teeth numbered when record)
- Foreign body ear—4 percent lidocaine and irrigate with WARM water or use alligators, cerumen spoon, operating head of ophthalmoscope

Dermatology

Subjective

- Onset duration, distribution and appearance when initiated, painful or pruritic, exacerbating, and relieving symptoms, associated symptoms, i.e., SOB. Self-treated?
- Prior history, medications, topics, and exposures

Objective

- Allergic reactions: check respiratory status, urticaria, angioedema, H1 or H2 inhibit (Atarax, Benadryl, or Cimetidine, if severe, steroids, epi) (check cardiovascular first)
- Cellulitis—warm, red, tender, check DM and fever, treat antibiotics (Duricef, Keflex)
- Chicken pox—respiratory S&S, 7-21 day incubation, dew drop on rose petal, vesicles, crusting, often initiate on trunk, crops of lesions
- Chronic discoid lupus erythematous
- Contact dermatitis—pruritic, exposed areas, linear, prevent with soap and water after exposure. Rx steroids (poison ivy)
- Corns—shoes, podiatry follow-up
- Cutaneous candidiasis—(check oral and anal area) keep dry, Lotrimin, if oral
- Nystatin or Mycelex (immunocompromised)
- Dandruff (seborrhea)—Sebulex or other shampoo
- Decubitis ulcers—positioning, dressings, debridement, infection
- Dyshidroses—sweat blisters
- Drug eruptions—onset, Atarax, Benadryl
- Eczema—history of steroids, cool compresses (atopic dermatitis)
- Erythema multiform
- Erysipelas
- Folliculitis—warm wash cloths, antibiotics, check nodes
- Fungal—tinea capitis, corporis, circinata, cruris, pedis…Lotrimin
- Furuncles (boils) and carbuncles
- Herpes simplex—cold sores
- Herpes zoster—shingles, painful, nerve distribution, ophthalmologist if near eyes, Acyclovir
- Impetigo—gold exudate…antibiotics p.o. or Bactroban
- Intertrigo—fat folds
- Insect bites—Td status and antihistamines, if infected—antibiotics
- Miliaria—"baby acne" hormonal change 4-12 weeks
- Pediculosis—K well, contacts
- Pityriasis rosea—viral, Christmas tree distribution, herald patch
- Psoriasis—steroids
- Skin tumors
- Tinea versicolor—Tegrin shampoo

Assessment

In general, wet needs, drying and vice versa. Although most rashes represent benign or self limiting problems, DO NOT think of them as minor. Some rashes represent diseases, meningitis, AIDS, renal failure, liver failure, syphillis, Rocky Mountain spotted fever, Lymes. Be aware of petechia (pinpoint flat, purplish red, caused by intradermal and submucous hernorrhage. ALWAYS check for bleeding disorders, liver, etc.)

Intervention

- Teaching, infection, spread, scratching (short nails, bandaids)
- Itching: cool compresses H1 or H2 inhibitor, steroid creams, consider oral steroids or Decadron, epinephrine .2 mg SC in adult, .01 mg/kg in child
- Referral to derm clinic; Refer to private derm

Wounds

Subjective

Mechanism, onset, tetanus status, foreign body

Objective

Shock, bleeding, size, depth, FB, function, N/V status, degree and body percentage if burns

Intervention

- Subungual hematomas use cautery
- Burns—major, treat shock first; if minor, pain relief—iced saline, narcotic, silvadene and dressing
- Puncture wounds—depth, foreign body; Teaching potential for infection or osteo, dimple cleaning. Consider X-ray or antibiotics.
- Suturing—Refer to text book anesthesia after N/V check. Palpate FB, fracture, plan closure. If unsure get help. Controversy about closing old wounds ... 8 hours or more on body, 24 hours or more on face. Ortho involvement if tendon or joint space involved. Be aware of all hand wounds. Consult hand surgery when indicated.
- Suture materials: Need to add gloves, suture, and anesthetic to tray.
  - A. Skin closure (usually nonabsorbable)
    - -Nylon (ethilon, Dermalon)
    - -Polybytestes (Novafil)
    - -Polypropelene (Prolene)
    - -Silk (rarely used—too much tissue reaction)
    - -Fast absorbing gut (absorbable) sometimes used on children's faces
  - B. Subcutaneous closure (usually absorbable); fascia, muscle sheath closure Vicryl, Dexon, Maxon, Gut
  - C. Other staples (for straight wounds)
- Knots—I general, simple interrupted sutures are best. Vertical mattress have fallen into disfavor (good subQ closure eliminates need). Tunning sutures for long straight wounds distribute tension. Horizontal mattress for "loose skin" dorsum of hand, eyelid. Bury the knot for subcutaneous, subcuticular.
- Suture/staple removal guidelines—
  - Face 5–7 days
  - Scalp 10–14 days
  - Trunk 10 days
  - Extremity 10–14 days (extensor surfaces—14 days)
- Topical anesthetic—Tetracaine (4% lidocaine)—4 cc
  - Adrenaline (1:1000 epinephrine)—2 cc
  - Cocaine 10 percent—4 cc

- Buffer: Lidocaine with bicarbonate (1:10)
- Close skin with a monofilament suture material

Intervention

Demonstrate simple closure, refer for suture removal to private or HMO unless you desire to see follow-up

Psych

Potential violent... decrease stimulation, restraints, position near door, call for security if needed, never jeopardize self.

Subjective

Suicidal, homicidal, auditory or visual hallucinations, medications, of no prior history, and > 35 look for metabolic cause.

Objective

Heart, lungs, abdomen, screening CBC, or SMA

Assessment

Commitment voluntary vs. involuntary, CIS consult.

Detox

Subjective

Type and amount of drug, last used, usual use, prior rehab, psych exam.

Objective

Heart, lungs, abdomen, chest pain, DT's.

Intervention

Consult, CIS.

Ophthalmology

Onset, mechanism, photophobia, visual acuity, Alcaine, Slit lamp, fluorescein, PERL without "A", irrigation of Morgan lens, patching, X-ray, tetanus, follow-up, to ophthalmologists

OB/Gyn

Subjective

Onset, duration, LMP, GPA, BC, GI, GU

Objective

Open vs. closed OS, cervical motion tenderness, cultural media viral vs. bacterial, results to PMD/HMO.

1. PID/vaginitis; all cultures need results to private doc, OPC, or health dept. Partners to be referred to health dept, "Safe Sex"

2. Suspect ectopic: check pallor, conjunctiva, VS, consider T&screen with CBC; 6 weeks from LMP is classic.
3. Dysfunctional uterine bleed: consider Provera or BCP depending on age, and last PAP.
4. Bartholin's
5. Miscarriage
6. Ultrasound

Intervention
Perform pelvic exam, do not contaminate, size of uterus

Ortho
Before calling Ortho consult, know your anatomy.

Subjective
Mechanism and PMH

Objective
Back pain, point tenderness, joint stability, ROM strength, sensation, joints above and below. Back pain—check straight leg raising, extremities, ask about bowel and bladder.

Intervention
Pain relief: consider Toradol, morphine esp if dislocation. Only good X-rays, comparison views, growth plates, casting... no circular, crutches, R.I.C.E., knees should follow-up in 24 hours, referrals know your anatomy, demonstrate splinting.
If snuff box tenderness is detected on exam with X-ray, the patient should be discharged with a thumb slicer splint or a wrist splint with additional thumb immobilization which should be worn until the patient is evaluated by an orthopedic physician in follow-up.
If an acute spinal cord injury presents, implement the high dose methylprednisolone protocol.
Immobilize and make non-weight bearing in most acute orthopedic injuries until the follow-up visit.

Surgery
Subjective
N/V, onset, last meal, fever, PMH

Objective
Abscess, cyst, may I&D, consider ethylene chlorid as well as xylocaine to numb. Abdomen appendicitis, gallbladder, cellulitis often staph, mark streaks, DVT-Dopler studies, DAA. If the patient presents with a complaint related to previous surgery within 30 days of the surgical procedure, the patient's surgeon should be consulted.

Asthma

COPD, pneumonia, bronchiolitis, asthma, protocols, O_2 saturation, peak flow, teaching. Use multiple respiratory treatments, steroids, check abdominal pain, N/V and tachypnea in children.

Headaches

Subjective

Onset, duration, trauma, similar to past, worst of life

Objective

Neurocranial II-XII, drift, reflexes, discs, muscle strength, gait, change from baseline mental status

Intervention

Consider relaxation, IV compazine 10 mg, Toradol IM 60 or 30 mg, Thorazine IV. Check with MD and consider CT if worst of life or focal findings or new onset seizure.

Urology

Obtain an IVP on every patient presenting with known or suspected urolithiasis. If there is an allergy to IVP dye, a sonogram should be performed.

Facial Trauma

Pay specific attention to air fluid levels in the facial sinuses which may indicate a blow-out facial fracture.

In general, HMO patients treated here should be given follow-up with their HMO, unless prearranged with the HMO authorizing agent.

For orthopedic/foot/surgery consultation: If HMO, contact the HMO.

Source: Courtesy of Suburban Hospital, Inc., Bethesda, Maryland.

4-110 Patients in Police Custody

Policy: Patients in Police Custody (Nonclinical Forensics Personnel)	**Manual:** Human Resources
Function: Management of the Environment of Care	**Policy Number:**
Effective:	**Page:** 1 of 2
Revised:	
Author: Security Work Group	**Distriction:** Systemwide

POLICY

It is the policy of this health system to ensure that patients under law enforcement custody receive proper medical treatment, while also providing a safe environment for its patients, visitors, and staff. The law enforcement officer requires an appropriate orientation to the organization, the procedures, and responses to emergency and disaster codes.

PROCEDURE

A. The Admissions Department or other department of entry into the system will notify Security or designee that a law enforcement officer or individual with a patient in custody is in the hospital. Security Officer or designee will then meet the law enforcement officer and review with them a Nonclinical Forensic Orientation Pamphlet and a Pocket Guide. Unit/department staff will also be available to the officers to answer questions and provide clarification on policy.

    1. Orientation Pamphlets and Pocket Guides will be available on individual units and in the Security or Administrative office at each facility.

    2. Officers will receive any necessary additional unit-specific orientation from the department manager or designated associate in charge.

B. The orientation will include, but not be limited to the following:

    1. fire safety

    2. safety/security

    3. right to know

    4. infection control

    5. hospital channels of communication

    6. patient rights.

C. The health system representative will confirm the identity of the officer and the patient and verify:

    1. name, badge, and agency of the officer,

    2. patient identity by name, date of birth, and patient number,

    3. patient is in legal custody by contacting the law enforcement agency if questions arise.

D. Upon admission, the health system representative will work with the Healthcare Access Department and unit staff to:

    1. Have patient placed in a private room as needed.

    2. Coordinate other law enforcement needs that arise.

E. Patient care units:

    1. The law enforcement officer will be solely responsible for guarding the patient while in a health system facility.

    2. All personal clothing and property will be removed by health system staff on the patient care unit and will be released to the officer.

    3. For law enforcement purposes, the officer will communicate with the medical team on the use of administrative restraints that do not interfere with medical care to ensure a safe environment.

    4. Medical restraints are applied according to the organization's administrative policy (Restraints and Seclusion).

F. Visitors:

    1. All visitors to patients in officer custody will require approval of the physician and the responsible officers. The officer assigned to the patient will screen visitors.

    2. The Healthcare Access Department will ensure that the Information desk card and other records are marked "Law Enforcement Custody." All inquiries should then be directed to the Security Department or the designated unit representative.

3. Phone service will not be extended to the patient's room without the approval of the officer responsible for the patient.

G. Outpatient transfer:
1. If a patient under custody is brought to the hospital for outpatient treatment, the department manager or associate in charge will immediately contact the Security Department.
2. Security will obtain proper identifying information as outlined in C above.
3. If a patient under custody is brought to a nonhospital health system facility for outpatient treatment, the department manager or the designated unit representative will obtain proper identifying information.
4. Security or the designated unit representative will coordinate with the responsible officer to provide a secluded area while awaiting treatment, if necessary, so as not to present a threat to other patients or Kennedy staff.

RESPONSIBILITIES

A. Healthcare Access or other department of entry.
1. Will notify Security of presence of a patient under custody in the hospital.
2. Healthcare Access will mark records as indicated in F above.
3. Nonhospital departments will designate a "unit representative" to identify the officer and the patient.
B. The Information desk will refer all inquiries for patients in custody to Security.
C. Department manager or designated unit representative will coordinate room placement, visitor contacts, etc. with Security.
D. Security will coordinate activities and responsibilities for hospital and nonhospital departments as outlined in this policy.

Source: Courtesy of Kennedy Health System, Voorhees, New Jersey.

4-111 Communication with Persons with Limited English Proficiency

PURPOSE

To efficiently and effectively serve patients with Limited English Proficiency and/or communication needs.

POLICY

No patient shall be denied effective access to health and social services based on their ability to communicate.

Limited English Proficiency (LEP) shall be defined as patients who cannot speak, read, write or understand the English language at a level that permits them to interact effectively with health care providers and social service agencies.

Language Assistance services shall be offered 24 hours per day, 7 days per week.

Onsite interpreters and/or telephone interpreting services shall offer Language Assistance services throughout the PHHS system.

Persons with Limited English Proficiency shall be offered interpreting services free of charge via onsite interpreters and/or telephone interpreting services.

Persons with hearing impairments shall be offered sign language interpreting services and/or use of a TTD/TTY machine free of charge.

Family members, friends, visitors shall not be used to assist with language assistance services unless specifically requested by the patient.

Children under 18 years of age shall not be used to provide/assist with language assistance.

Validation of competency shall be completed for all Language Assistant personnel throughout the hospital system via competency testing prior to employment.

PROCEDURE

Requesting Language Assistance
- Information required when making request for onsite interpreter *(regardless of location)*:
  - ☐ Patient name
  - ☐ Patient location
  - ☐ Specific language, dialect or other communication need
  - ☐ Service required *(i.e., consent, history and physical, psychosocial interview, etc.)*
  - ☐ Estimated length of time required
  - ☐ Requesting staff to contact and phone/pager number.

Availability
- Language Assistants are assigned to areas in the hospital and can be reached by their individual pagers or by calling the Patient Relations department.
- Onsite Spanish interpreters are available 24 hours a day, 7 days a week.
- Onsite Vietnamese, Chinese, Cambodian, Laotian interpreters are available Monday-Friday, day shift only.
- Telephone interpreting services are available 24 hours a day, 7 days a week.
- Verbal and written interpreting services are available.
- Onsite interpreting services for Women's & Children's Services *(except L&D)* are provided by Language Assistance staff in the Women's & Children's Division.
- Onsite interpreting for all other areas *(ESO, Medicine, Surgery, OPC, L&D, etc.)* are provided by Language Assistance staff in the Patient Relations department.
- TTD/TTY machines are available through the Patient Relations department.

Telephone Interpreting Services:
- Available 24 hours a day, 7 days a week throughout the hospital.
- Language Line can be accessed from any telephone. Reference the specific unit, HUC or call Patient Relations for directions on how to access.

- Cordless interpreter phones are available in designated areas; services through these phones are available 24 hours a day, 7 days a week; service is accessed by pressing the appropriate button on the hand-held speaker.
- Concerns regarding telephone interpreting services will be communicated to the Manager of Patient Relations and/or the Director of Social Services.

Documentation
- Language assistance services provided shall be documented in the patient's medical record
- Information to be documented shall include:
  - ☐ Date and time of services
  - ☐ Language
  - ☐ Health Care Provider involved *(i.e., name of physician, nurse, social worker, etc.)*
  - ☐ Type of service provided *(i.e., consent, H&P, patient teaching, etc.)*
  - ☐ Signature, title and ID# of Language Assistant providing interpreting services.

Use of Non-Language Assisant Staff for Interpreting:
- Family members, friends, visitors or other patients shall not be utilized to provide interpreting services unless the patient has specifically been offered free interpreting services and refused them as well as specifically requested a family member or friend be utilized to interpret.
- Children shall not be utilized to provide interpreting services.
- Incentive Pay staff shall be utilized for general, non-clinical, non-technical interpreting only *(i.e., directions, non-medical questions such as address, phone #, etc.)*.
- Bilingual Providers *(i.e., physician, nurse, dietitian, etc.)* may provide medical/health care services to patients in the patient's primary language providing they:
  - ☐ Are fluent in the patient's primary language including medical terminology
  - ☐ Document in the patient's medical record the services they provided were provided in the patient's primary language
  - ☐ Bilingual Providers who have limited fluency or no medical terminology in the patient's primary language shall use Language Assistance staff. (i.e., is provider is fluent conversationally but has no medical terminology training)
  - ☐ Do not act as interpreters for other staff.

Competency
- Competency for all Language Assistance (Language Assistant/Patient Representative L100 & L101) staff shall be validated prior to employment.
- On-going continuing education is the responsibility of each employee.
- Continuing education opportunities shall be offered jointly by Patient Relations, WCS and COPC.

Source: Adapted from Parkland Health and Hospital System, Dallas, Texas.

4-112 Patients With Limited English Proficiency, Civil Rights VI

The U.S. Department if Health & Human Services (HHS) has released new regulations for organizations that receive federal financial assistance regarding Language Assistance to Persons with Limited English Proficiency (LEP). We are obligated to follow these regulations just as we are for TDH, HCFA & JCAHO.

1. **Reason for New Regulations:**
   a) To ensure that persons with limited English skills (Spanish, Chinese, etc.) can effectively access health & social services. The regulations are part of Title VI of the Civil Rights Act of 1964 (Title VI).
   b) Title VI & its implementing regulations provide that no person shall be subjected to discrimination based on language. Title VI prohibits recipients of Federal financial assistance from denying LEP persons access to programs, on the basis of their national origin (language).

2. **Examples of LEP Violations:**
   a) Providing services to LEP persons that are more limited in scope or are lower in quality than those provided to other persons
   b) Subjecting LEP persons to unreasonable delays in the delivery of services
   c) Limiting participation in a program or activity on the basis of English proficiency
   d) Providing services to LEP persons that are not as effective as those provided to those who are proficient in English.

3. **What This Means & Steps To Comply:**
   a) Assess Current Practice:
   ___ Identify the non-English languages that are likely to be encountered in its program and by estimating the number of LEP persons that are eligible for services. (Determine non-English speaking languages & the approximate number of patients that speak that specific language)
   ___ Identify the language needs of each LEP patient & document this information in the medical record. (Directors to determine if this is performed in their assigned areas for non-English speaking patients)
   ___ Identify the points of contact in the organization or activity where language assistance is likely to be needed. (All areas of the organization including business/registration staff shall be educated & have the capability to access translation services as needed)
   ___ Identify the resources that will be needed to provide effective language assistance.
   ___ Identify the location and availability of these resources.
   ___ Identify the arrangements that must be made to access these resources in a timely fashion.
   b) Development of Comprehensive Written Policy on Language Access.
   c) Training of Staff:
   Performed by Translation Services. Directors to ensure staff attendance.
   d) Monitoring:
   (Patient Satisfaction Surveys, Patient Complaint/Grievance Data, Risk Identification Reports & other internal documents used for Performance Improvement)

Source: Adapted from Parkland Health and Hospital System, Dallas, Texas.

4-113 Nursing Direction in the Emergency Department

PURPOSE

To define the duties and organizational guidelines for the Director of Emergency Nursing and to provide an alternative plan for Nursing direction in the absence of the Director of Emergency Nursing.

POLICY

A designate registered nurse who is qualified by relevant training, experience, and current competence in emergency care will act as the Director of Emergency Nursing to supervise the care provided by all nursing services personnel within the Emergency Department. The Director of Emergency Nursing will participate in committee activities concerned with the emergency department.

In the absence of the Director of Emergency Nursing, the Lead Clinical or Triage Charge Nurse will be the nurse in charge and will make decisions regarding policy. An attempt to reach the Nursing Director or her designee by telephone should be made. In the event of an extended absence of the Nursing director, a designee will be appointed to carry on administrative duties. This nurse will be responsible for over-seeing nursing functions in the Department, until the Nursing Director returns to her regular duties.

Source: Courtesy of Parkview Medical Center, Pueblo, Colorado.

MANAGEMENT OF INFORMATION

4-114 Emergency Department Management

POLICY

The EDM system is used for the initial reception of patients, nursing and physician documentation, treatment and diagnostic ordering, and discharging of ER patients.

PURPOSE

To establish guidelines for the use of emergency department management EDM.

PROCEDURE

1. System Access
   a. Access to the EDM stations will be via a user ID combined with a password. A bar-coded badge will also be used to 'swipe' access into the system.
   b. The user ID will be the Meditech nemumonic.
   c. The user chooses confidential passwords. The bar-coded badge will be re-set every 90 days.
   d. Purposeful disclosure of system password is grounds for immediate termination of employment.

    e. Passwords are 6 alpha-numeric characters.

    f. Access privileges will be based on specific location and specific job titles.

    g. Passwords will have an expiration of 90 days. A user at anytime may change passwords. A user must change their password/swipe badge if there is a chance the confidentiality of the password has been compromised.

2. Reception

    a. The triage nurse or the nurse who receives the patient into the ER will fill out the reception screen, which puts the patient onto the active patient tracker.

3. Nursing/Physician Documentation

    a. The triage nurse will fill out the triage assessment screen as indicated.

    b. The primary nurse will fill out the following screens:
- Arrival History (required)
- Assessment (required)
- Outgoing disposition assessment (required)
- IV fluid flow sheet (as indicated)
- Medication/Vital signs flow sheet (as indicated)
- Ortho/Procedure flow sheet (as indicated)

    c. The physician will complete the Physician Chart (required).

4. Orders

    a. The ER physician, nurse, or unit clerk may enter orders into EDM.

    b. ER physicians will e-sign all orders entered by the unit clerk or nurse

    c. All orders entered by the nurse will be 'verbal' orders.

    d. The unit clerk will enter orders, which are written, on a physician order form. A hard copy of this physician order will be maintained with the patient record.

    e. Any orders entered by the ER unit clerk will be checked and noted by the ER RN.

    f. Outside physicians will give written orders and therefore e-signature will not be used.

5. Printing Reports

    a. Admitted patients will have their EDM record printed via the 'Reports' function and will be sent to the admitting unit at the time of transport to that unit.

    b. When private physicians, specialists, etc arrive to the ER to care for their patients, the ER unit clerk will print a copy of the EDM record as well as any diagnostic test results and the order summary for them to review.

6. Problem Solving

    a. A number of resource people are available to assist with problem solving on each shift.

    b. The EDM quick start manual is available.

    c. For problems unable to be resolved, contact the ER administrator on call or designee.

7. EDM Down Time

    a. Paper charts/forms will be kept on hand in the event that Meditech is unavailable for a period of time. These charts/forms will be stocked and kept in the ER triage area cabinets.

Source: Courtesy of Parkview Medical Center, Pueblo, Colorado.

4-115 Emergency Department Psychiatry Documentation Standard

POLICY

It is the policy of the psychiatry emergency department to document in the patient's medical record according to the following standards.

PURPOSE

To provide documentation standards to physicians and nurses assigned in the psychiatry emergency department.

PROCEDURE

Physician Documentation Responsibilities

1. Patient allergies
2. Time patient is examined
3. Patient history indicating chief complaint
4. Current patient medications
5. Physician assessment
6. Time seclusion or restraint orders activated
7. Diagnosis, discharge or admission
8. Patient disposition
9. Patient condition or discharge
10. Time and date of disposition
11. Signature

Registered Nurse Documentation Responsibilities

1. The following data will be documented:
   a. initial nursing assessment time/date
   b. mode of arrival to department
   c. patient allergies
   d. patient's chief complaint
   e. physical nursing assessment addressing chief complaint findings
   f. initial vital signs
   g. medical history
   h. current medications
   i. community resources/support groups
   j. initial treatment implemented
   k. signature/title
2. The RN will document the medications administered in the emergency department, including
   a. name of medications
   b. dosage
   c. route/site

    d. time

    e. initials

    f. signature

3. Documentation will be based on level of care, as follows:

Level of Care	Initial Assessment	Assessment and Documentation	Vital Signs
I	Immediately upon arrival	Every hour	Every hour
II	Immediately upon arrival	Every four hours	Every four hours
III	Within 30 minutes of arrival	Every four hours	Every four hours
IV	Within two hours of arrival	Upon discharge	Upon admission
V	Within two hours of arrival	Upon discharge	Upon admission

4. Any changes in the patient's condition will be documented and the physician will be notified.

5. Patient response to treatments, procedure, or medications administered will be documented.

6. Level of care IV and V—The patient's chief complaint will be reassessed at time of discharge and documented in the nursing notes.

7. Level of care I, II, and III—The plan of care will be reviewed and documented every four hours.

Source: Adapted from Parkland Memorial Hospital, Dallas, Texas.

4-116 Emergency Department Nurses' Notes

Bed # _ _ _ _ _ _ _ _

Time	Temp.	Pulse	Resp.	BP	Output	IVs and Meds.	Pain (1–10)	No change in status	Nursing Observations, Treatments and Signature

BELONGINGS LIST:	VALUABLES:		DISPOSITION OF BELONGINGS AND VALUABLES	Nurses' Signature Initial
__ Shirt/Blouse __ Trousers/Pants/ Shorts __ Dress/Skirt __ Shoes/Slippers __ Underwear __ Robe/Pajamas __ Coat/Sweater/ Gloves	__ Wallet/Purse __ Watch __ Ring __ Necklace/ Bracelet __ Earrings __ Money	__ Dentures __ Upper/Lower/ Partial __ Glasses/ Contacts __ Prosthesis __ Ambulatory Aid __ Other	__ With Patient __ With Family __ To Safe __ Other	— —

Source: Adapted from Johnston Memorial Hospital, Abingdon, Virginia.

4-117 Managers' HIPAA guide

Here's a quick guide to help you remember some of the most compelling things that should be going on to comply with HIPAA.

1. Notice of Privacy Practices is displayed in clinics, admissions, ER, and posted on the hospital's web site.
2. Give patients a copy of the Notice of Privacy Practices...and make good-faith efforts to obtain written acknowledgment of receipt.
3. Avoid verbal discussions of protected health information (PHI) on the phone, public areas, or in reception/waiting areas that are within earshot of people who don't have a need to know.
4. Don't leave sensitive information on telephone answering machines.
5. Limit or use minimum necessary PHI in announcements made in clinic waiting rooms.
6. You may share PHI with family, friends, personal representative identified by the patient as someone involved in their care.
7. Limit patient information on whiteboards, X-ray boxes, computer screens and other areas that may be visible to the public and others who don't need access to PHI.
8. Follow safeguards for PHI that is transmitted by fax or e-mail.
9. File away promptly and secure folders that contain patient medical records.
10. Make sure that computer/network security measures are in place (e.g., that screen-savers kick in quickly, passwords are not taped to the monitor, machines are turned off at night, and access from off site is carefully restricted).
11. Do not share passwords.
12. Make sure the physical plant is locked down at night, with windows closed and doors locked.
13. Remind people that only the "minimum necessary" PHI should be disclosed except for treatment purposes.
14. Make sure separated employees turn in their keys and building cards and terminate their network access.
15. Enter required disclosures of PHI in the Disclosure Tracking Database.
16. Make sure written authorizations to use and disclose PHI are received except for treatment, payment, operations, and exceptions permitted in the policy.
17. Make sure new and existing employees participate in HIPAA privacy training.
18. Make sure everyone is aware of the rights patients have to review (and get copies of) their records and what procedures will be followed.
19. Make sure everyone knows who patients should speak with if they have questions about their HIPAA privacy rights.
20. Be sure everyone in your work force knows who the privacy officer is and who they should contact with patient privacy questions or problems. The Privacy Officer is _____, extension _____.

Adapted courtesy of the University of California-Davis Compliance Department, Sacramento, California.

4-118 Sample Protected Health Information Policy and Procedure

POLICY

Protected health information (PHI) is individually identifiable health information that is transmitted or maintained by electronic media or any other form or medium, excluding information in educational records and inmate records. PHI will be used and disclosed in accordance with the Health Insurance Portability and Accountability Act (HIPAA) Privacy Standards and other applicable law; deidentified information is not subject to these regulations.

PROCEDURE

1. PHI includes oral, written, or otherwise recorded information that is created or received by [COVERED ENTITY].
2. PHI may relate to an individual's physical or mental health, payment, or health care services provided to an individual.
3. PHI may pertain to a health condition or payment in the past, present, or future, and the person who is the subject of the information may be alive or deceased.
4. PHI will be protected in any form, including, but not limited to, telephone conversations and voice mail, paper records, computers, transmissions over the Internet, dial-up lines, private networks, fax machines, electronic memory chips, magnetic tape, magnetic disk, CD-ROM.
5. Deidentified information is not subject to [COVERED ENTITY'S] privacy policies and procedures.
6. PHI may be deidentified by removing, coding, encrypting, or otherwise eliminating or concealing the information that makes the PHI individually identifiable, including the following identifiers of the individual or of relatives, employers, or household members of the individual: names, all geographic subdivisions smaller than a state (except for the initial three digits of a ZIP code if the total population in the ZIP code areas covered by such three digits of a ZIP code exceeds 20,000), all elements of date (except year), telephone numbers, fax numbers, electronic mail addresses, Social Security numbers, medical record numbers, health plan beneficiary numbers, account numbers, certificate/license numbers, vehicle identifiers and serial numbers, Web universal resource locators (URLs), Internet protocol (IP) address numbers, finger or voice prints, photographic images, and any other unique identifying numbers, characteristics, or codes regardless of whether the covered entity has actual knowledge that the information could identify an individual.

Source: Knag, Paul. *HIPAA: A Guide to Health Care Privacy and Security Law.* (Aspen Publishers 2004).

4-119 Disclosure Consent and Authorization Checklist

Review with your organization to determine whether these types of disclosures are made—also use as a guide as requests for disclosure occur.

Purpose of Disclosure	Consent or Authorization Requirement

Mandatory Disclosures

__ Individual requests own information
__ DHHS requests for compliance enforcement purposes

Treatment, Payment, or Health Care Operations:	**Consent Required**

__ Treatment
__ Payment
__ Operations (quality assessment, professional evaluations, insurance rating, medical audits, business planning, business management)

Certain Types of Public Purposes:	**Authorization Not Required**

__ Public health activities (public health authorities, child abuse reporting, FDA-regulated companies, persons at risk of communicable disease, employers for work-related injury, or medical surveillance of workplace)
__ Victims of abuse, neglect, or domestic violence (can disclose to authorized governmental authority if required by law or individual approves)
__ Health oversight purposes (audits, investigations, inspections, licensure, discipline)
__ Judicial and administrative proceedings (court order, subpoena—see law enforcement checklist if requesting party is law enforcement official)
__ Law enforcement purposes (see law enforcement checklist)
__ Decedents (coroners, medical examiners, funeral directors)
__ Cadaveric organ, eye, or tissue donation purposes
__ Research purposes (need waiver of authorization form approved by IRB or privacy board)
__ Avert a serious threat to health or safety (if imminent threat to individual or public health or safety)
__ Specialized government functions (military, veterans, national security, intelligence, medical suitability determinations, correctional institutions, government programs providing public benefits)
__ Workers' compensation

Special Cases

__ Facility directory	**Opportunity to Orally Agree/Object Required**
__ Person involved in care	**Opportunity to Orally Agree/Object Required**
__ Psychotherapy notes	
__ Research involving treatment	

Source: Knag, Paul. *HIPAA: A Guide to Health Care Privacy and Security Law.* Gaithersburg, MD: Aspen Law & Business, 2004.

4-120 Access to Medical Records by or on Behalf of a Patient

INFORMATION

While the medical record is the property of the hospital, the hospital recognizes an individual's right to examine and/or obtain a copy of their medical record.

The hospital also recognizes the right of an individual, or the individual's designee, to be provided with one free copy of their medical record.

INSTRUCTIONS

1. When a patient requests to examine or obtain copies of the medical records, designated medical records personnel will review the medical record.
2. In all cases in which the patient's request for access to the medical records is granted, the patient must complete an authorization for release of information form, or its equivalent, before he or she will be provided with copies of the record. The form and a record of the transaction will be filed in the medical record.
3. Medical records personnel will provide requested copies of medical records, prepared for mailing to or for pick-up by the requester, within 7 business days of the written request.

Charges for Copies of Medical Records

A patient or patient's designee is entitled to one free copy of the medical records; all additional copies cost $1.00 per page.

Note: Third-party payers are not considered first requesters and are charged in accordance with contractual agreements with the hospital.

Medical records will release the free copy of the medical record on a first-come, first-served basis. Patients, as well as third parties who hold a release signed by the patient and dated within sixty (60) days of the date of the request, may receive a free copy of the medical records by being the first requester.

Medical records are copied by service dates. Any part of a specific service date record that has been copied and released as the first free copy will be copied at a charge of $1.00 per page for additional copies. Those parts of a specific service date record that have not yet been provided as a first free copy will remain available to be requested as the first free copy.

Health care providers are not charged for copies of a medical record and will not be considered a first requester.

The department of disability determination pays $10.00 per request for copies of medical record and will not be considered a first requester.

Source: University of Kentucky Hospital, Lexington, Kentucky.

4-121 HIPAA Privacy and Disclosures in Emergency Situations

Persons who are displaced and in need of health care as a result of a severe disaster need ready access to health care and the means of contacting family and caregivers. We provide this bulletin to emphasize how the HIPAA Privacy Rule allows patient information to be shared to assist in disaster relief efforts, and to assist patients in receiving the care they need.

Providers and health plans covered by the HIPAA Privacy Rule can share patient information in all the following ways:

TREATMENT. *Health care providers can share patient information as necessary to provide treatment.*

- *Treatment* includes:
  - —sharing information with other providers (including hospitals and clinics),
  - —referring patients for treatment (including linking patients with available providers in areas where the patients have relocated), and
  - —coordinating patient care with others (such as emergency relief workers or others that can help in finding patients appropriate health services).
- Providers can also share patient information to the extent necessary to seek payment for these health care services.

NOTIFICATION. *Health care providers can share patient information as necessary to identify, locate and notify family members, guardians, or anyone else responsible for the individual's care of the individual's location, general condition, or death.*

- The health care provider should get verbal permission from individuals, when possible; but, if the individual is incapacitated or not available, providers may share information for these purposes if, in their professional judgment, doing so is in the patient's best interest.
  - —Thus, when necessary, the hospital may notify the police, the press, or the public at large to the extent necessary to help locate, identify or otherwise notify family members and others as to the location and general condition of their loved ones.
- In addition, when a health care provider is sharing information with disaster relief organizations that, like the American Red Cross, are authorized by law or by their charters to assist in disaster relief efforts, it is unnecessary to obtain a patient's permission to share the information if doing so would interfere with the organization's ability to respond to the emergency.

IMMINENT DANGER. Providers can share patient information with anyone as necessary to prevent or lessen a serious and imminent threat to the health and safety of a person or the public—consistent with applicable law and the provider's standards of ethical conduct.

FACILITY DIRECTORY. Health care facilities maintaining a directory of patients can tell people who call or ask about individuals whether the individual is at the facility, their location in the facility, and general condition.

Of course, the HIPAA Privacy Rule does not apply to disclosures if they are not made by entities covered by the Privacy Rule. Thus, for instance, the HIPAA Privacy Rule does not restrict the American Red Cross from sharing patient information.

Source: Hurricane Katrina Bulletin: HIPAA Privacy and Disclosure Bulletin. September 2, 2005. Director, U.S. Department of Health and Human Services Office for Civil Rights, Washington, DC.

4-122 Emergency Department Encounter Record

PATIENT NAME

TIME | LOGICARE C/O

TRIAGE NOTES

Police: _____ Animal Control: _____ ME: _____

Mode of Arrival: ❑ Wheelchair ❑ Ambulatory ❑ Carried ❑ FD

PTA | MEDS GIVEN:

❑ Backboard ❑ C-Collar ❑ CID ❑ IV ❑ Oxygen ❑ Splints ❑ Monitor

PAIN RATING: _____ 0-10 Numeric _____ 0-10 Faces _____ 0-10 FLACC (or)
Observed Behavior: _____

MEDICAL - SURGICAL HISTORY

INTERVENTIONS @ TRIAGE	SOURCE OF INFO	DATE/TIME OF ACCIDENT/ILLNESS

CURRENT MEDICATIONS

PRIORITY OF ADMISSION ❑ 1 ❑ 2 ❑ 3 ❑ 4 | VITAL SIGNS (Triage)

LMP	WEIGHT	HEIGHT	OFC	TET

Temp _____ P _____
R _____ BP _____

IMMUNIZATIONS REVIEWED
❑ UTD ❑ Not UTD, Information Given
❑ Developmental age is appropriate OR
❑ Developmental screening is required

PMD NAME

ALLERGIES

MD TIME		MD TIME		MD TIME		NURSE'S SIGNATURE
	CBC		UA		PORTABLE STRETCHER W/C	
	BMP		CCMS I/O		Skull	
	CMP		Wet Prep		Soft Tissue Neck	
	CP Profile		Gram Stain		C-Spine 1 2 3	
	Trauma Profile		GC Culture		T-Spine 1 2 3	
	CKMB		Chlamydia		LS-Spine 1 2 3	
	Troponin				CXR IV 2V	
	PT/PTT					
	Lipase				ABD KUB 2 V	
	Amylase		Monitor		Pelvis	
	ETOH		EKG		Extremity	
	Tylenol		O2 Liters		R L	
	ASA		PEFR		R L	
	Pregnancy Test		UABD		R L	
	Quant. HCG		2		R L	
	Urine HCG		3			
	Urine Drug Scr		Continuous			
			Pulse OX		IVP	
			Room Air Y or N		Sono	
					Sono	
			Blood Culture		CT	
			X1 X2		VQ Scan	
			Throat CS		Head	
			RSV Culture		Head Angio	
			Rapid Strep		Chest IV Contrast	
			Urine CS		Chest Angio	
					Abd IV Rectal PO	
					Pelvis IV Rectal PO	

TIME ORDERED	TREATMENTS / MEDICATIONS / PROCEDURES	TIME DONE	INITIALS

INITIALS	SIGNATURE - RN/TECH	INITIALS	SIGNATURE - RN/TECH

M.D. TIME	PHYSICIAN DOCUMENTATION

TIME ORDERED	ORDERS AT TIME OF DISCHARGE	TIME DONE	INITIALS

CLINICAL IMPRESSION

DISCHARGE INSTRUCTIONS: (Time Ordered: _____)
_____ F/U Physician ❑ PRN _____ day(s)
❑ Appointment in _____ day(s) ❑ And if not better, call in _____
❑ Return to ED in _____ day(s) or _____ hour(s) for _____

PHYSICIAN SIGNATURE

❑ Return to Work in _____ day(s) with _____ limitations.
Pain Management Plan: _____

CONDITION OF DISCHARGE: ❑ Stable _____ Time ❑ Home ❑ Nursing Home
❑ Admit - Rm. # _____ ❑ Other: _____ ❑ Transfer:
MEDS/OTHER/DISCHARGE TOPIC: _____

PAIN RATING: _____ 0-10 Numeric _____ 0-10 Faces _____ 0-10 FLACC (or)
Observed Behavior: _____

FORM #31800 (Rev. 5/02)   **1st COPY** - MEDICAL RECORDS   **2nd COPY** - DEPARTMENT   **3rd COPY** - QUEST CARE

Source: Courtesy of Medical Center of Plano, Plano, Texas.

568

4-123 Emergency Unit Nursing Record

BED #	TIME
MD/TIME	

AIRWAY: ❏ Patent ❏ Denies Sx ❏ Secretions/blood ❏ Stridor
❏ Obstruction:
Treatment: ❏ Airway: Oral / Nasal ❏ ETT# _____ Oral / Nasal
❏ Cricothyroidotomy ❏ Tracheostomy
Time: _____ , by _____

RESPIRATORY: ❏ Denies Sx ❏ Spontaneous ❏ Unlabored
❏ Labored ❏ Assisted ❏ Mechanical / BVM
Chest: ❏ Symmetrical Expansion ❏ Accessory Muscle Use
❏ Injury / Tenderness (See Diagram)
Breath Sounds: Right: ❏ Present ❏ Absent ❏ Clear ❏ Diminished
❏ Wheezes ❏ Crackles ❏ Rhonchi
Left: ❏ Present ❏ Absent ❏ Clear ❏ Diminished
❏ Wheezes ❏ Crackles ❏ Rhonchi
Treatment: ❏ O2 _____ L/min ❏ Nasal Cannula ❏ Non-rebreather
❏ Venti-mask _____ % ❏ Face mask ❏ Other: _____
TB Risk Assessment:
Possibly has Pneumonia with Bloody Sputum ❏ Yes ❏ No
❏ Notify M.D., Request Resp. Isolation and Notify Infection Control.

CARDIOVASCULAR: ❏ Denies Sx ❏ Palpitations
❏ Chest Pain Level: _____ (0-10)
Pulse: ❏ Regular ❏ Irregular ❏ Thready ❏ Diminished
❏ Absent (See CPR Record)
Rhythm:
Skin: ❏ Warm ❏ Hot ❏ Cool ❏ Dry ❏ Moist ❏ Diaphoretic
Color: ❏ WNL ❏ Pale ❏ Flushed ❏ Cyanotic

NEURO: ❏ AA&O X _____ ❏ Responds to verbal
❏ Responds to pain ❏ Unresponsive ❏ +LOC
❏ Pedi: ❏ Alert / Active / Playful ❏ Age appropriate
Pupils: Right: ❏ Reactive ❏ Sluggish ❏ Unreactive ❏ Size _____ mm
Left: ❏ Reactive ❏ Sluggish ❏ Unreactive ❏ Size _____ mm

GLASGOW COMA SCALE INFANT / TODDLER			GLASGOW COMA SCALE CHILDREN / ADULT			INITIAL	ONE HOUR
EYE OPENING	SPONTANEOUS	4	EYE OPENING	SPONTANEOUS	4		
	TO VOICE	3		TO VOICE	3		
	TO PAIN	2		TO PAIN	2		
	NONE	1		NONE	1		
BEST VERBAL RESPONSE	SMILES, INTERACTS	5	BEST VERBAL RESPONSE	ORIENTED	5		
	CONSOLABLE	4		CONFUSED	4		
	CRIES TO PAIN	3		INAPPROPRIATE WORDS	3		
	MOANS TO PAIN	2		INCOMPREHENSIBLE WORDS	2		
	NONE	1		NONE	1		
BEST MOTOR RESPONSE	NORMAL SPONT. MOVEMENTS	6	BEST MOTOR RESPONSE	OBEYS COMMAND	6		
	LOCALIZES PAIN	5		LOCALIZES PAIN	5		
	WITHDRAWS TO PAIN	4		WITHDRAWS (PAIN)	4		
	ABNORMAL FLEXION	3		FLEXION (PAIN)	3		
	ABNORMAL EXTENSION	2		EXTENSION (PAIN)	2		
	NONE	1		NONE	1		

ABDOMEN: ❏ Denies Sx ❏ C/O Pain: ❏ RUQ ❏ RLQ ❏ LUQ ❏ LLQ
Palpitation: ❏ Soft ❏ Distended ❏ Rigid ❏ Pregnant ❏ Non-Tender
❏ Tender: ❏ RUQ ❏ RLQ ❏ LUQ ❏ LLQ
Bowel Sounds: ❏ Active X 4 quads ❏ Hypoactive ❏ Hyperactive ❏ Absent
Symptoms: ❏ Nausea ❏ Vomit ❏ Diarrhea ❏ Hematemesis ❏ Melena

GYN: ❏ N/A
LMP: _____ Gravida _____ Para _____
Pregnant: ❏ N/A: Hyst / Tubal
❏ Neg ❏ Pos: _____ weeks
❏ Abd Cramping
Genitalia: ❏ Pain ❏ Discharge
❏ Itching
Vag Bleeding: ❏ None ❏ Spotting
❏ #/pads/hr: _____ ❏ Gross

GU: ❏ Denies Sx ❏ Pain
❏ Burning ❏ Discharge
❏ Odor ❏ Frequency/Urgency
❏ Retention ❏ Hematuria
❏ Dip UA: + / −
Genitalia (Male): ❏ Denies Sx
❏ Testicular Pain
❏ Sudden Onset

MUSCULOSKELETAL: ❏ Denies Sx
❏ Pain/Swelling/Deformity/Injury (See Diagram)
Extremities: ❏ Sensory Intact X 4 ❏ Deficit: ❏ RUE ❏ LUE ❏ RLE ❏ LLE
❏ Motor Intact X 4 ❏ Deficit: ❏ RUE ❏ LUE ❏ RLE ❏ LLE
❏ Equal Strength: ❏ Upper Ext ❏ Lower Ext
Pulses: Right: ❏ Carotid ❏ Radial ❏ Femoral ❏ Dorsalis Pedis
Left: ❏ Carotid ❏ Radial ❏ Femoral ❏ Dorsalis Pedis
Pelvis: ❏ Stable ❏ Unstable **Spine Precautions:** ❏ C-Collar ❏ Backboard

INITIALS	NURSE'S SIGNATURE

1. Abrasion
2. Amputation
3. Avulsion
4. Bite
5. Burn
6. Contusion
7. Crush
8. Deformity
9. Open Fracture
10. GSW
11. Hematoma
12. Laceration
13. Puncture
15. Stab Wound / Impalement
16. Swelling
17. Wound Unknown
18. Pain
20. Rash/Hives

EYES: ❏ Denies Sx ❏ Redness ❏ Vision Changes ❏ Drainage
❏ Foreign Body ❏ Trauma
Visual Acuity: Corrected: _____ OD _____ OS _____ OU ❏ N/A
Uncorrected: _____ OD _____ OS _____ OU

PSYCHOSOCIAL: | **REASSURANCE:**
❏ Cooperative ❏ Calm ❏ Combative | ❏ Patient ❏ Family
❏ Anxious ❏ Tearful ❏ Uncooperative

PAIN ASSESSMENT: PAIN RATING: _____ 0-10 Numeric _____ 0-10 Faces _____ 0-10 FLACC
(or) Observed Behavior: _____
Location: _____ Severity 0 1 2 3 4 5 6 7 8 9 10
Quality: ❏ Sharp ❏ Dull ❏ Stabbing ❏ Pressure ❏ Twisting ❏ Tearing
❏ Other _____ Onset: _____
Duration: ❏ Constant ❏ Intermittent
Worsened by: ❏ Cough ❏ Movement ❏ Deep Breath ❏ Pressure ❏ Other _____
Eased by: ❏ Nothing ❏ Rest ❏ Splinting ❏ Heat ❏ Cold ❏ Meds ❏ Other _____

NO PAIN						WORST PAIN
	0	2	4	6	8	10

INTERVENTIONS: ❏ Notify Phys. ❏ Monitor ❏ O2 ❏ Ice/Elevate
❏ Comfort Measures ❏ Safety ❏ Reassure
Siderails: ❏ Up x 2 ❏ Up x 1 **ID Band:** ❏ Yes ❏ No

DIAGNOSTIC	TIME	RADIOLOGY	TIME	RETURN
Blood Drawn		X-Rays		
UA		IVP		
EKG		CT		
ABG		Ultrasound		
RT Treatment		Nuclear Medicine		

IV FLUIDS						
TIME	IV #	SITE	GA.	SOLN.	LTC/TOTAL	INT
					/	
					/	
					/	

TOTAL INTAKE: _____ cc **TOTAL OUTPUT:** _____ cc

COMMENTS: _____
_____
_____

DISPOSITION: ❏ Home ❏ Admit ❏ Transfer ❏ Death ❏ AMA ❏ LWBS
MODE: ❏ Ambulatory ❏ Carried ❏ Stretcher ❏ Ambulance
D/C: ❏ Instructions given to: ❏ Patient ❏ Parent ❏ Other: _____
❏ Verbalizes Understanding
VITAL SIGNS: BP: _____ **PULSE:** _____
RESP: _____ **TEMP:** _____
PAIN RATING: _____ 0-10 Numeric _____ 0-10 Faces _____ 0-10 FLACC
(or) Observed Behavior: _____
TIME: _____ **SIGNATURE:** _____

Source: Courtesy of Medical Center of Plano, Plano, Texas.

4-124 Operative/Invasive Checklist Report

		LEFT SIDE PROCEDURES	ALL OTHER PROCEDURES	RIGHT-SIDED PROCEDURES
		(Complete Form on Left side)	(Complete In Center)	(Complete on the Right Side)
PRE-TESTING			Patient Identity Verified by NAME and DOB:	
			Scheduled Surgery/Procedure:	
			Consent for: Same as above: Y N If no:	
			* Orally verified procedure/site/side with whom: _____ if not verified, reason:	
			* * The side/site was initialed by: If not initialed, reason:	
Signature:			Date: Time:	
FLOOR / OSU / ICC / ENDO / ED (circle one)			Patient Identity Verified by NAME and DOB:	
			Scheduled Surgery/Procedure:	
			Consent for: Same as above: Y N If no:	
			* Orally verified procedure/site/side with whom: _____ if not verified, reason:	
			* * The side/site was initialed by: If not initialed, reason:	
Signature:			Date: Time:	
PRE-PROCEDURAL AREA			Unit or Area:	
			Patient Identity Verified by NAME and DOB:	
			Scheduled Surgery/Procedure:	
			Consent for: Same as above: Y N If no:	
			* Orally verified procedure/site/side with whom: _____ if not verified, reason:	
			* * The side/site was initialed by: If not initialed, reason:	
Signature:			Date: Time:	
PROCEDURAL AREA			**Final Verification ("TIME-OUT")**	
			Unit or Area:	
			TeamVerified Patient Identity by Name and DOB:	
			Procedure to be performed verified by team:	
			Procedure:	
			Side/Site Verified by Team:	
			Correct equipment/supplies/implants available:	
			Physician:	
			Anesthesia;	
			Nursing Staff Member(s):	
			Radiology Staff Member(s):	
Signature:			Date: Time:	

* Verify procedure/side/site, upon entry to facility and when care is transferred to another caregiver with patient awake and aware, if possible.
* *With patient awake and aware if possible, the person performing the procedure is to initial the procedural site in all cases involving laterality. multiple structures (fingers, toes, lesions), or multiple levels (spine). Initialing is to be done by the person doing the procedure. Initialing the procedural site on pediatric patients 2 years or younger is done at the discretion of the physician.

PATIENT IDENTIFICATION

GF-335A (Rev 7/04) MAC 844

☐ This side of form is waived for bedside procedures not involving the surgical team._____RN

	Exceptions noted by receiving unit:
ID Band: Y / N	
Allergy Band: Y / N	
Blood Band: Y / N / NA	
NPO after: _____	
H&P present: Y / N H&P current: Y / N	
Procedural consent complete: Y / N Blood Consent complete: Y / N	
Height: _____ Weight: _____	
Time: _____ Blood Pressure: _____ Pulse: _____	
Respirations: _____ Temperature: _____ O2 Sat: _____	
Lab Tests Done: Y / N / NA Current Labs Printed and on Chart: Y / N / NA	
X-Rays Done: Y / N / NA	
EKG Done: Y / N / NA	
Dentures Removed: Y / N / NA	
Disposition:_____	
Jewelry/Piercings Removed: Y / N / NA	
Disposition: _____	
Contact Lenses Removed: Y / N / NA	
Disposition: _____	
Hearing Aid(s) Removed: Y / N / NA	
Disposition: _____	
Glasses Removed: Y / N / NA	
Disposition: _____	
List patient cosmetic implants (e.g. breast, chin): ☐ None	
List patient implants that contain metal (e.g. metal plates, screws, total joints, etc): ☐ None	
Current MAR printed for in-house patients: Y / N / NA	
Special Needs/Comments (if none, write none): _____	
_____	
_____	
_____	
_____	
_____	
Significant others waiting: Y / N Location:_____	
EMERGENCY DEPARTMENT CONSIDERATIONS:	
X-Rays sent with patient: Y / N / NA	
If no, Radiology Notified: Y / N	
Signature of sender: Date: Time:	

PATIENT IDENTIFICATION

GF-335B (Rev 7/04) MAC 188

Source: Courtesy of Medical Center of Plano, Plano, Texas.

4-125 Post-Mortem Record

ROUTINE INQUIRY

On every death, contact Southwest Transplant Alliance (STA) at 1-800-201-0527 to determine what organs and/or tissues can be donated and discuss the family approach.

Name of STA contact person: _____ Confirmation # _____ Date/Time of Call: _____

☐ Patient/decedent was determined medically unsuitable for donation due to: (Please write reason for unsuitability): _____

☐ Patient/decedent was determined to be medically suitable candidate for donation.

Name of designated requestor who offered the option of donation to the family: _____

Name of relationship of family member who was approached for consent:

Name: _____ Relationship: _____

Did the family agree to donate? ☐ Yes ☐ No   If yes, then a consent form must be completed and placed in the patient's chart.

Name and Title of person completing routine inquiry: _____ Date/Time: _____

MEDICAL EXAMINER

Meets hospital criteria ☐ Yes ☐ No If no autopsy being done, explain why: _____

Meets Medical Examiner's Criteria* ☐ Yes ☐ No   Medical Examiner notified by: _____ at _____ ☐ AM ☐ PM

Body release by: _____

Medical Examiner postmortem ordered by: _____ Date: _____
* Listed on back of top Copy

CONSENT FOR GENETIC TESTING

Medical Center of Plano is authorized to remove tissue specimens and perform genetic testing on _____

who expired on _____ at _____ ☐ AM ☐ PM

Signature: X_____ Relationship: _____

Witness Signature: X_____ Date: _____

CONSENT FOR POSTMORTEM EXAMINATION

Postmortem Examination _____ Postmortem Examination Date: _____

I (we) being the next of kin of the decreased, hereby grant permission for the performance of a complete postmortem examination upon the body of the above patient by the staff pathologists. Authority is also granted for the preservation and study of any and all tissues that may be removed. This authority shall be limited only by the conditions expressly stated below:

_____

Signature: X_____ Relationship to deceased: _____

Witness Signature: X_____ Date: _____

RELEASE OF BODY

Medical Center of Plano is authorized to release the body of _____

who expired on _____ at _____ ☐ AM ☐ PM _____ Funeral Home.

Articles of clothing or valuables to accompany the body are (if none, write the word NONE): _____

_____ Date: _____ Time: _____ ☐ AM ☐ PM

Signature: X_____ Relationship to deceased: _____

(Signature and relationship of nearest relative of person authorized to release).

REMOVAL OF BODY

The body of the above named deceased person has been received by the undersigned person. Articles of clothing and/or valuables are to be disposed of as instructed by the person or persons authorizing the release of the body from Medical Center of Plano.

X			X	
SIGNATURE	DATE	TIME	NAME OF FUNERAL HOME	LICENSE NUMBER

PATIENT IDENTIFICATION

Medical Examiner Criteria

All duties of death investigation are the responsibility of the Collin County Medical Examiner. The following criteria are used to report hospital deaths:

1. All Emergency Department deaths.
2. All trauma deaths, obvious and suspected.
3. All deaths under anesthesia and the immediate post-anesthesia period.
4. All deaths within 24 hours of entry into the hospital.
5. All deaths occurring as a result of, during, or following a diagnostic procedure.
6. When the suspected cause of death is work-related, whether traumatic or natural.
7. All dead on arrival cases.
8. When the attending physician has no reasonable cause of death.
9. Stillbirths and instantiates if the delivery took place outside the hospital or if the delivery and/or death is related to, or suspected to be related to trauma.
10. Maternal deaths during or after delivery or where abortion is suspected.

If there is any doubt as to whether the death needs to be reported, call the Medical Examiner's Office. Don't guess or make a decision if you are not absolutely sure. Medical Examiner's Office 1-972-548-3775.

Hospital Autopsy Criteria

It is the responsibility of the attending physician to request and encourage the family of the deceased to permit an autopsy. The permit will be maintained in the permanent medical record. Indications for autopsy are as follows:

- Autopsy may help explain unknown or unanticipated complications;
- Cause of death is not known with certainty based on the clinical findings;
- Unexplained or unexpected death occurred during or following any medical or surgical diagnostic procedure or therapy;
- Unexplained or unexpected death that is apparently natural and not subject to a forensic medical jurisdiction;
- Death occurred during participation in a clinical trial of an investigational drug or device;
- Death occurred following an injury sustained while hospitalized;
- Death resulting from high-risk infectious and contagious diseases;
- Obstetrical death;
- Pediatric or neonatal death;
- Suspected illness may have bearing on survivors or recipients of transplant organs;
- Death known or suspected to have resulted from environmental or occupational hazards.

The attending physician's request and the family's permission or refusal for autopsy should be documented in the medical record. The attending physician will notify the Pathology Department of cases referred for autopsy.

PATIENT IDENTIFICATION

GF-070B (Rev 11/02) MAC 303

Source: Courtesy of Medical Center of Plano, Plano, Texas.

SURVEILLANCE, PREVENTION, AND CONTROL OF INFECTION
4-126 Infection Control Policies

I. Employees

A. All employees receive an introduction to infection control during their orientation. Both formal and informal inservice programs are provided thereafter.

B. Employees are required to report illnesses due to infection or contagious diseases to the Occupational Health Nurse. If an illness is due to infection or contagious disease, a physician's statement is required stating that the employee is non-infectious and is able to return to work.

C. Universal precautions are used for the care of all patients using appropriate protective equipment (gloves, gowns, masks, goggles, etc.) for contact with blood and body fluids. This equipment is readily accessible in the department.

D. Employees are to wash their hands before and after contact with patients and after contact with contaminated objects.

E. Attire:
    1. Emergency & Shock Trauma Center nursing personnel wear scrub uniforms in accordance with the departmental dress code.
    2. While acting as a member of the Trauma Team, the established Trauma Protocols are followed.

F. Communicable Disease Exposure
    1. The Occupational Health Section of the Infection Control Manual contains the appropriate procedures to be followed. An Employee Accident Report must be completed.
    2. The Infection Control Nurse/Nursing Supervisor are notified as per the protocol outlined in the Infection Control Manual.

G. All employees are offered and encouraged to receive the Hepatitis B vaccination. The Emergency Department is considered to be a high-risk area for exposure.

II. Care of Patients With Infectious Diseases/Conditions

A. Patients admitted to the Emergency Department who have a known or suspected infectious or communicable disease should be treated and released/admitted as soon as possible. Isolation policies and procedures as outlined in the Infection Control Manual shall be followed while the patient remains in the Emergency Department. Every attempt is made to separate the patient from other patients and visitors. Room 14 is used for isolation whenever possible.

B. Documentation on the patient's Emergency Department record should include specific isolation procedures followed while the patient is in the Emergency Department.

C. The Infection Control Nurse is notified on weekdays; the Nursing Supervisor, on weekends, nights, and evenings.

D. For patients being admitted, the Admitting Office will be notified of the type of isolation required so that an appropriate bed assignment can be made.

E. The department/nursing unit to which the patient is being admitted is notified of the type of isolation or precautions required.

F. When transporting patients on Strict of Respiratory Isolation, the patient will wear a surgical mask.

III. Physical Layout

A. Storage of clean and sterile supplies are separated from used or contaminated equipment in the appropriate utility room.

B. Only authorized personnel are admitted to the supply areas in order to minimize traffic.

C. The performance of incision and drainage of abscesses, wound irrigation's, etc., that could possible cause cross-contamination is done such that all materials used are contained at the bedside, and disposed of (or prepared for CSS reprocessing) as appropriate. The surrounding area is cleaned after use.

IV. Specimen Collection

A. All specimens are considered contaminated.

B. Appropriate precautions will be used as needed (gloves, mask, goggles, etc.) when collecting specimens. All specimens are placed in ziploc plastic bags prior to transport to the laboratory.

V. Instruments/Equipment

A. All reusable instruments or equipment will be returned to CSS for sterilization. Reusable instruments will be rinsed to remove any gross soilage and placed in red biohazard containers kept in dirty utility room to soak. CSS is responsible for picking up dirty instruments. Used laryngoscope blades are sent to CSS for exchange.

B. Electronic thermometers with disposable probe covers are used routinely. For patients on Strict Isolation or VRE Precautions, glass thermometers are used.

C. EKG machines, monitors, and cables are wiped off daily with the approved hospital disinfectant.

D. All stretchers/wheelchairs are wiped with the hospital approved disinfectant solution after use where soiling or contamination has occurred, and weekly per schedule.

E. IV Pumps/Controllers are wiped with disinfectant weekly.

VI. Linen

A. All dirty linen is placed in a fluid-resistant bag and sent to the Laundry via the laundry chute.

VII. Housekeeping

A. Daily cleaning of the department is provided according to a schedule provided by the Housekeeping Department.

B. Nursing staff will direct Housekeeping staff in required terminal cleaning procedures.

VIII. Communicable Disease Reporting

The Emergency Department physician who examines a patient with one of the communicable diseases listed, shall complete the "Maryland Confidential Morbidity Report" (DHMH-1140, 12–74). This form shall be mailed to the Montgomery County Health Department. Attached list of REPORTABLE DISEASES.

IX. A. Attached follow-up of Communicable Disease Exposure incidents occurring in the ER/Hospital Personnel.

1. The physician involved in the case shall consult with the Infection Control Nurse to discuss whether follow-up measures are indicated. Consultation will be sought from the Infection Control Committee Chairman when necessary.
2. Infection Control will coordinate employee follow-up with the Employee Health Service, and provide counseling to those concerned.
3. Any prophylactic medications recommended will be ordered by the ER physician or the Employee Health Nurse.

B. Follow-up of the Exposed persons not employed by the Hospital (medics, Police) or concerned community members.

ANY PUBLIC/PARAMEDICAL INQUIRIES FOR INFORMATION ON EXPOSURES SHALL BE DIRECTED TO INFECTION CONTROL, OR CONTACT THROUGH NURSING SUPERVISOR ON WEEKENDS OR OFF-SHIFTS.

1. The Infection Control notifies the appropriate facility where the exposed person is employed to explain the circumstances. Follow-up is conducted by that facility.
2. The Infection Control Nurse reports the case to the Health Department (if it is a reportable disease/condition).

Source: Adapted from Suburban Hospital, Inc., Bethesda, Maryland.

4-127 Employee/Occupational Health & Safety Exposure Control Plan

The goals of Employee/Occupational Health & Safety (E/OHS) include protection of the employee against exposure to blood or other potentially infectious body fluids by providing Hepatitis B immunizations and education regarding infectious pathogen transmission. Hepatitis B Vaccination is available to all employees, including those who have such potential occupational exposure. Evaluation and follow-up is provided for employees who experience actual exposures. E/OHS is responsible for recordkeeping of occupational exposures. This includes maintenance of exposure-related documentation of the incident, including lab results, the health care professional's written opinion regarding the exposure incident, and the need for Hepatitis B vaccination.

This plan includes a description of the procedure to be observed following a potential exposure, as well as the forms developed to comply with Occupational Safety and Health Administration (OSHA) regulations and hospital policies. This plan includes discussion of definitions related to occupational exposures; Hepatitis B vaccination; procedures to follow after an exposure; post-exposure prophylaxis and evaluation of illnesses; post-test counseling procedures; the written opinion; and medical recordkeeping requirements. E/OHS will follow the Hospital Infection Control Exposure Control Plan and guidelines regarding potential exposure tasks, engineering/work practice controls, personal protective equipment, methods of compliance, information and training, and other requirements of the plan.

DEFINITIONS

Occupational Exposure means reasonably anticipated skin, eye, mucous membrane, or parenteral contact with blood or other potentially infectious materials that may result from the performance of an employee's duties. This includes any fluid containing visible blood, semen, vaginal secretions, cerebral spinal fluid, synovial, amniotic, pleural, pericardial, or peritoneal fluids, and body fluids in situations where it is difficult to differentiate between body fluids. In addition, unfixed tissue or organ from a human, and human immunodeficiency virus (HIV)-containing cell/tissue/organ cultures or culture medium or solutions are considered potentially infectious materials in the hospital setting.

Parenteral means piercing mucous membranes or the skin barrier through such events as needlesticks, human bites, lacerations, and abrasions.

HEPATITIS B VACCINATION

The Hepatitis B vaccination series will be offered and recommended to all employees who work in areas with potential exposure to blood or body fluids, and to employees who have an occupational exposure and have not received the vaccine. New employees will sign the Hepatitis B Consent form at the time of their pre-employment health screening. New employees will be offered the vaccination within 10 working days of their initial assignment Current employees who have not declined to be immunized with the vaccine will be offered the vaccine at the time of their annual employee health screening. A declination statement is included in the consent form and must be signed for employees who refuse the vaccine.

Additional educational materials and time for questions regarding the vaccination are provided through E/OHS. Booster doses will be made available to the employee as recommended by the CDC. If the employee's AHBS (Hepatitis B surface antibody) is negative, the employee will be eligible for Hepatitis B booster doses up to a second complete series of 3. The vaccine is available at no cost to employees.

POST-EXPOSURE EVALUATION PROCEDURES

An employee who sustains an occupational exposure should wash hands and other exposed skin with soap and water, or flush mucous membranes with water immediately, or as soon as is possible following contact with blood or body fluids. The employee must report the incident to his supervisor and to Employee/Occupational Health & Safety. The Exposure Packet contains exposure instructions for the employee and the manager, as well as forms which must be completed by the employee and signed by the manager. These include the Potential Exposure Report and the Informed Consent and Agreement to HIV testing forms for employee and source patient. The employee must report to E/OHS as soon as is possible, or prior to the end of the shift A confidential medical evaluation and follow-up will be provided. This evaluation will include the following:

1. Documentation of route of exposure and circumstances under which the exposure occurred.
2. Identification and documentation of source individual if known,
3. Employee will be tested for HIV after consent is obtained and far Hepatitis B surface antibody and Hepatitis C.
4. HIV consent will be obtained from the source individual or authorized substitute. The source will then be tested for HIV. The source is also tested for Hepatitis B and Hepatitis C.

Lab testing for the employee and source patient will be done using confidential procedures. Lab testing and post-exposure medical evaluations will be provided at no charge.

Exposures on Evenings/Weekends

Initial post-exposure procedures for exposures occurring after office hours will be coordinated by the Hospital Nursing Supervisor. Both nursing and non-nursing employees must notify their immediate supervisor at the time of an exposure as well Nursing Supervisor. The Potential Exposure Report and HIV Consent form must be completed by the employee. The Nursing Supervisor will investigate and initiate exposure follow-up. The employee may also be evaluated and treated in the emergency department if directed by the Nursing Supervisor. All exposure related forms must be forwarded to E/OHS. Finally the employee should contact E/OHS the following business day for follow-up.

POST-EXPOSURE PROPHYLAXIS AND FOLLOW-UP

Post-exposure prophylaxis and follow-up will include the confidential medical evaluation, employee counseling, and evaluation of reported illnesses. The health care professional will review medical records relevant to the treatment of the employee, including vaccination status, and the results of the source individual's testing. The Hepatitis B vaccine will be offered if the employee has not received it and other immunizations will be offered if necessary (Hepatitis B Immune Globulin, immune globulin, and/or tetanus). For HIV positive source exposures the employee will read and be counseled on the Protocol for Occupational HIV Post-Exposure Chemoprophylaxis at which time they can choose or decline to take post exposure prophylactic medications in accordance with new CDC guidelines. Employee/Occupational Health & Safety will provide appropriate follow-up. If the employee elects to begin HIV Post-exposure Chemoprophylaxis, the employee should be seen immediately for counseling/treatment/Rx and baseline lab work. The employee will be advised of the follow-up schedule and is responsible for contacting Employee/Occupational Health & Safety for follow-up appointments.

POST-TEST COUNSELING

The employee will be notified of his/her own and the source individual's HIV and hepatitis test results. He/she must contact E/OHS to obtain these results. E/OHS will notify the source patient of test results if requested and/or if the source tests positive for HIV, Hepatitis B or Hepatitis C. E/OHS will review regulations with the employee regarding disclosure of identity and infectious status of the source. Specific counseling regarding HIV test results is outlined below.

Negative post-test counseling will include information that test result was negative; information regarding the meaning of a negative result; and schedule for repeat HIV testing for the exposed employee.

Indeterminate HIV results will be given in person, and include explanation of meaning; review of information regarding transmission and prevention of transmission of HIV;

recommendation that person return in 8 to 12 weeks for repeat HIV tests, and the recommendation that the person take precautions as if the person's HIV test result had been positive until the person retests negative.

Positive HIV post-test counseling will be performed in person, and include the test result; meaning of a positive test, discussion about notification of sexual and needle-sharing partners; prevention of transmission of HIV; and medical recommendations and implications of being HIV positive. Education will be given regarding how the local health department can assist with partner notification; and other assistance will be offered regarding partner notification. The individual will be referred to their primary physician or the local health department for medical follow-up. The individual will be provided with a copy of the "Information for HIV Infected Persons" card/sheet.

HEALTH CARE PROFESSIONAL'S WRITTEN OPINION

The employee will be provided with a copy of the health care professional's written opinion for Hepatitis B vaccination and post-exposure evaluation and follow-up within 15 days of completion of the evaluation. This shall be limited to the following:

1. Indications for Hepatitis B vaccination, and if employee has received same.
2. Statement that employee has been informed of results of evaluation.
3. Statement that employee has been told about any medical conditions resulting from exposure to blood/body fluids that require further evaluation or treatment.

All other findings or diagnoses shall remain confidential and shall not be included in the written opinion to the employee.

MEDICAL RECORD-KEEPING

Employee/Occupational Health & Safety will maintain records for employees with occupational exposures. Medical records will include the following:

1. Employee name, birth date and social security number.
2. Copy of Hepatitis B vaccination status, including dates of vaccination, and medical records relative to ability to receive vaccination.
3. Copy of results of examinations, medical testing, and follow-up procedures.
4. Copy of health care professional's written opinion.
5. Copy of information provided to the health care professional including the Exposure report with description of employee's duties as they relate to the exposure incident; route and circumstances of the exposure; results of source and employee blood testing; and medical records relevant to the appropriate treatment of the employee. Employee and source patient HIV Informed Consent forms will also be included.

Medical records will be kept confidential and are not disclosed or reported without the employee's written consent. Records shall be maintained for the duration of employment plus 30 years.

SUMMARY

In summary, this plan describes the procedures regarding follow-up after an occupational exposure incident and Hepatitis B vaccination. An Employee/Occupational

Health & Safety Nurse is a member of the Infection Control Committee and a designated trainer for hospital employees for OSHA Exposure Control training requirements. OSHA updates and new regulations are reviewed on an ongoing basis by the Infection Control Committee. In addition, this committee will meet periodically as new regulations or recommendations develop.

Source: Adapted from Suburban Hospital, Inc., Bethesda, Maryland.

4-128 Guidelines for Significant Blood/Body Fluid Exposures

A tetanus-diphtheria booster should be offered if the employee has not had one in 5 years. Immune Globulin, 0.06 ml/kg, gluteal muscle should be offered as soon as possible.

KNOWN SOURCE:

TEST	IF SOURCE NEGATIVE:	IF SOURCE POSITIVE:
HBSAG	• Employee's Employee Health Antibody Hepatitis B Surface Antigen (EHAHBS) will be tested as part of EH/PANEL. • No Rx. Offer vaccine to those who have not initiated series. Offer booster dose to those whose Hepatitis B Surface Antibody (AHBS) is negative and have previously been immunized (for up to a total of two complete series of three).	• Employee's EHAHBS will be tested as part of EH/PANEL. • Offer HBIG, 0.06 ml/kg, gluteal muscle, as soon as possible. • If employee has completed Hepatitis B vaccination series, and AHBS is positive, no further RX. • If employee has completed Hepatitis B vaccination series, and EHAHBS is negative, offer vaccination booster. • If employees has initiated Hepatitis B vaccination series, continue on series schedule. • If employee's EHAHBS is negative, employee's Hepatitis B Surface Antigen (HBSAG) will be tested at 3 months, 6 months, and 12 months.
HCVAB	• Employee's Employee Health Hepatitis C Virus Antibody (EHHCVAB) will be tested as part of EH/PANEL. • No Rx.	• Employee's EHHCVAB will be tested as part of EH/PANEL. • No Rx—according to the CDC there is no licensed tx or prophylaxis for Hepatitis C exposure. Employee EHHCVAB will be retested at 3 months, 6 months, 12 months.
HIV	• Employee's Employee Health HIV Antibody (EHHIVAB) will be tested as part of Employee Health series of tests (EH/PANEL). • In accordance with Maryland state law, Source EHHIVAB may not be baseline tested unless employee also agrees to be tested. • Retest employee EHHIVAB at 3 months and 6 months.	• (Know positive or confirmed by Western Blot) • Employee's baseline EHHIVAB will be tested as part of EH/PANEL. • Employee's EHHIVAB will be retested at 6 weeks, 3 months, 6 months and 12 months. See Protocol for Occupational HIV Post-Exposure Chemoprophylaxis.

UNKNOWN SOURCE:

- Employee will be baseline tested (EHHIVAB, EHAHBS, and EHHCVAB).
- If employee has not completed or initiated Hepatitis B vaccination series, it should be offered at this time.
- Retest employee's EHHIVAB at 3 months, 6 months, and 12 months.

Source: Courtesy of Suburban Hospital, Inc., Bethesda, Maryland.

4-129 Management of Occupational Blood Exposures

Provide immediate care to the exposure site.
- Wash wounds and skin with soap and water.
- Flush mucous membranes with water.

Determine risk associated with exposure by
- type of fluid (e.g., blood, visibly bloody fluid, other potentially infectious fluid or tissue, and concentrated virus) and

- type of exposure (i.e., percutaneous injury, mucous membrane or nonintact skin exposure, and bites resulting in blood exposure).

Evaluate exposure source.
- Assess the risk of infection using available information.
- Test known sources of HBsAg, anti-HCV, and HIV antibody (consider using rapid testing).
- For unknown sources, assess risk of exposure to HBV, HCV, or HIV infection.
- Do not test discarded needles or syringes for virus contamination.

Evaluate the exposed person.
- Assess immune status for HBV infection (i.e., by history of hepatitis B vaccination and vaccine response).

Give PEP for exposures posing risk of infection transmission.
- HBV
- HCV: PEP not recommended.
- HIV
  —Initiate PEP as soon as possible, preferably within hours of exposure.
  —Offer pregnancy testing to all women of childbearing age not known to be pregnant.
  —Seek expert consultation if viral resistance is suspected.
  —Administer PEP for 4 weeks if tolerated.

Perform follow-up testing and provide counseling.
- Advise exposed persons to seek medical evaluation for any acute illness occurring during follow-up.

HBV exposures
- Perform follow-up anti-HBs testing in persons who receive hepatitis B vaccine.
  —Test for anti-HBs 1–2 months after last dose of vaccine.
  —Anti-HBs response to vaccine cannot be ascertained if HBIG was received in the previous 3–4 months.

HCV exposures
- Perform baseline and follow-up testing for anti-HCV and alanine amino-transferase (ALT) 4–6 months after exposures.
- Perform HCV RNA at 4–6 weeks if earlier diagnosis of HCV infection desired.
- Confirm repeatedly reactive anti-HCV enzyme immunoassays (EIAs) with supplemental tests.

HIV exposures
- Perform HIV-antibody testing for at least 6 months postexposure (e.g., at baseline, 6 weeks, 3 months, and 6 months).
- Perform HIV antibody testing if illness compatible with an acute retroviral syndrome occurs.
- Advise exposed persons to use precautions to prevent secondary transmission during the follow-up period.
- Evaluate exposed persons taking PEP within 72 hours after exposure and monitor for drug toxicity for at least 2 weeks.

Source: Centers for Disease Control *MMWR Reports & Recommendations*, June 29, 2001/50(RR11);43-4. *http://www.cdc.gov/mmwr/previous/mmwrhtml/rr5011a2.htm.* Accessed 8/14/01.

4-130 Procedure for Employee Exposures (During Office Hours)

Contact Nursing Supervisor for evening/weekend/holiday exposures.

EMPLOYEE:
1) IMMEDIATELY AFTER CONTACT WITH BLOOD OR BODY FLUIDS:
   - Wash hands and any other affected skin area(s) with soap and water.
   or
   - Flush mucous membranes with water.
2) Notify immediate supervisor.
3) Notify Employee/Occupational Health & Safety immediately and report to Employee/Occupational Health & Safety before the end of shift.
4) Complete Potential Exposure Report.
5) Have blood drawn for baseline lab tests after reporting to Employee/Occupational Health & Safety.

MANAGER/SUPERVISOR:
1) Notify Employee/Occupational Health & Safety of exposure.
2) Obtain source HIV consent for medically determined exposures (applies to Nursing Managers/Charge Nurses).
3) Forward <u>ALL</u> exposure related forms to Employee Health.

HIV orders related to exposures should not be documented on patient chart.

Source: Courtesy of Suburban Hospital, Inc., Bethesda, Maryland.

4-131 Procedure for Employee Exposures (Evening/Weekends/Holidays)

1) IMMEDIATELY AFTER CONTACT WITH BLOOD OR BODY FLUIDS:
   - Wash hands and any other affected skin area with soup and water.
   or
   - Flush mucous membranes with water.
2) Notify immediate supervisor.
3) The employee contacts the Nursing Supervisor who will evaluate the incident to assess whether this is an actual exposure to source blood/body fluids. If the incident is an actual exposure, the employee completes the Potential Exposure Report.
4) The Nursing Supervisor will determine if the employee needs to be seen in the ER for a tetanus booster, Hepatitis B vaccine, H-BIG, immune globulin, human immunodeficiency virus (HIV) Post-Exposure Chemoprophylaxis, or other treatment.
5) The Nursing Supervisor will obtain source HIV consent

6) Nursing Supervisor:
   - Due to the fact that Employee/Occupational Health & Safety labwork is now irretrievable, the employee may now be admitted using their own name, SS#, date of birth, and address.
   - Admit source patient using the patient's own name, SS#, date of birth, and address.
7) Order the following labs:
   Employee: EH/PANEL
   Source: EHP/PANEL
8) Employee reports to Ambulatory Testing/Outpatient Lab (or the ER if they are closed) for blood work and calls Employee/Occupational Health & Safety the following day/Monday.
9) If the source is HIV+, the employee should read and be counseled on the Protocol for Occupational HIV Post-Exposure Chemoprophylaxis. If the employee elects to begin HIV Post-Exposure Chemoprophylaxis, the employee should be seen in the ER immediately for counseling, treatment, Rx, and baseline lab work. The following lab work should also be ordered EELR, ECBC, EHHEPPA.
10) Forward ALL exposure forms to Employee/Occupational Health & Safety.

If the employee is seen in the ER, the ER physician completes/signs The Statement of Medical Findings. The employee should follow up with Employee/Occupational Health & Safety the following day if not seen in the ER. If it is a Friday evening or Saturday, ER evaluation is recommended.

Source: Courtesy of Suburban Hospital, Inc., Bethesda, Maryland.

4-132 Potential Exposure Report

EXPOSURE DATE: ____/____/____

NAME: _____ SS#: _____ DEPT: _____

BIRTHDATE:___/___/___ TIME OF EXP: _____ LOCATION OF EXP: _____

DATE REPORTED:___/___/___ TO WHOM: _____ WITNESS: _____

SOURCE (PATIENT) NAME. _____ SS#: _____

SOURCE BIRTHDATE:___/___/___ ADDRESS: _____

Please check exposure type:

_____ Needle puncture

_____ Eye splash

_____ Mucous membrane contact

_____ Open wound contact (includes chapped skin)

_____ Contaminated Sharp

_____ Other (specify) _____

Describe incident in detail: (What employee was doing, how exposure occurred, exposure site)

_____

_____

_____

I request that efforts be made by _____ to seek the informed consent of the source to test his/her blood for the presence of HIV if there is a medically determined exposure. I agree to submit a sample of my blood to be tested for HIV.

_____   _____

Employee Signature   Date   Supervisor Signature   Date

STATEMENT OF MEDICAL FINDINGS

VACCINATION STATUS: Last tetanus date _____ (if applicable, i.e., puncture wound)

Hepatitis B Vaccinations? _____ yes _____ no Date completed: _____

NATURE OF EXPOSURE/TREATMENT/FOLLOW-UP:

_____

MEDICAL DETERMINATION OF EXPOSURE: (see exposure criteria)

_____ Massive Exposure

_____ Definite Exposure

_____ Probable Exposure

_____ Doubtful Exposure

_____

Examiner's signature

Source: Courtesy of Suburban Hospital, Inc., Bethesda, Maryland.

4-133 Exposure Criteria

MASSIVE EXPOSURE

- Transfusion of blood
- Injection of more than 1ml of blood/body fluids
- Parenteral exposure to lab specimens containing a high titer of virus

DEFINITE EXPOSURE

- Injection of blood/body fluids (less than 1ml)
- Deep intramuscular injury with a blood/body fluid contaminated needle
- Laceration or wound produced by a visibly blood/body fluid contaminated instrument which causes bleeding in the health care worker
- Laceration or fresh wound inoculated with blood/body fluids

PROBABLE EXPOSURE

- Subcutaneous (superficial) injury with blood/body fluid contaminated needle
- Wound produced by blood/body fluid contaminated instrument which does not cause spontaneous bleeding
- Prior wound/skin lesion contaminated with blood/body fluid
- Mucous membrane inoculation with blood/body fluid

DOUBTFUL EXPOSURE

- Subcutaneous (superficial) injury with a needle or device contaminated with non-infectious, non-bloody fluid (e.g., urine, feces, sweat, tears)
- Laceration produced by non-infectious body fluid contaminated instrument
- Prior wound/skin lesion contaminated with non-infectious body fluid
- Mucous membrane inoculation with non-infectious body fluid

Source: Courtesy of Suburban Hospital, Inc., Bethesda, Maryland.

4-134 Employee Consent for Treatment

- The recommendations for employees who experience a potential contaminated exposure have been explained to me. I have had the opportunity to ask questions about the risks associated with this exposure, and to request additional information.
- I understand the necessity for base-line lab tests for me and the source individual, and follow-up tests for myself. I understand that these tests will be done, and records will be maintained, using confidential practices.
- I understand that test results will not be given to me or to others over the phone. If the results so indicate, I will be informed of possible follow-up treatment.
- If the source patient is **known to be positive for human immunodeficiency virus (HIV),** I will read and be counseled on The Protocol For Occupational HIV Post-Exposure Chemoprophylaxis.
- Compliance with recommended follow-up is my responsibility.

I hereby agree:

_____ • to be tested for HIV, AHBS (Hepatitis B surface antibody), & Hepatitis C
(initial)

_____ • choose/decline/N/A (circle) HIV Post-Exposure Chemoprophylaxis, if the source patient is known to be positive for HIV.
(initial)

_____   _____
Employee Name (print)   Date   Employee Signature

_____
Witness Signature

Report the following symptoms to Employee Health:
   a) Infection—redness, swelling, pain, drainage from the site.
   b) Hepatitis—fever, malaise, anorexia, dark urine or jaundice.
   c) Acute viral symptoms within 6 weeks of exposure—fever, rash, lymph node inflammation.

Source: Courtesy of Suburban Hospital, Inc., Bethesda, Maryland.

4-135 Informed Consent and Agreement to HIV Testing

With my signature below I acknowledge that I have read (or have had read to me) and understand the following information:

Facts About HIV Testing

I HAVE BEEN TOLD THAT: (1) My blood or other body fluid or tissue sample will be tested for signs of an infection by the human immunodeficiency virus (HIV), the virus that causes acquired immunodeficiency syndrome (AIDS); (2) My consent to have my blood tested for HIV should be FREELY given; and (3) Every attempt will be made to keep the results of this test confidential, but that confidentiality cannot be guaranteed.

What a NEGATIVE Result Means:

A negative test means that the laboratory has not found evidence of HIV infection in my blood sample.

What a POSITIVE Test Result Means:

A. A positive HIV test means that I have HIV infection and can spread the virus to others by having sex or by sharing needles;

B. A positive HIV test DOES NOT mean that I have AIDS—other test are needed;

C. If my test result is positive, I may experience emotional discomfort and, if my test result becomes known to the community, I may experience discrimination in work, personal relationships, and insurance.

What Will Be Done for Me if My Test is Positive:

A. I will be given a copy of the Department of Health and Mental Hygiene's publication, "Information for HIV Infected Persons," which contains information about counseling services which may help me;

B. I will be told how to keep from spreading my HIV infection by; (1) Avoiding sexual intercourse, or practicing SAFER sex; (2) Not sharing drug needles—better still, getting off drugs; (3) Not donating or selling my blood, plasma, organs, or sperm; (4) Avoiding pregnancy; and (5) Not breastfeeding, or donating breast milk;

C. Unless my test is performed at a designated anonymous test site approved by the Department of Health and Mental Hygiene, my unique patient identifying number will be given to the local health department and, if I have signs or symptoms of HIV infection, my name will be reported to the local health department to assist me in obtaining services and help the health department understand and control the AIDS problem;

D. I know that my local health department or doctor may assist me in notifying and referring my partners for medical services—without giving my name to my partners;

E. If I refuse to notify my partners, my doctor may either notify them or have the local health department do so. In this case, my name will not be used. Where required by law, when a local health department knows of my partners, it must refer them for care, support, and treatment and

F. I have had a chance to have my questions about his test answered. My counselor has explained to me about the use of a portion of my Social Security number in the unique patient identifying number and I have indicated below whether or not a portion of my Social Security number can be used for this purpose.

___ YES, I allow the use of a portion of my Social Security number.

___ NO, I DO NOT allow the use of a portion of my Social Security number.

I hereby agree to have my blood drawn for an HIV test.

Name of Person Tested   Date

Signature of Patient or Authorized Substitute   Signature of Counselor

Source: Courtesy of Suburban Hospital, Inc., Bethesda, Maryland.

4-136 Potential Exposure to Hepatitis B

Vaccination and antibody response status of exposed workers*	Treatment		
	Source HBsAg[†] positive	Source HBsAg[†] negative	Source Unknown or not available for testing
Unvaccinated	HBIG × 1 and initiate HB vaccine series	Initiate HB vaccine series[¶]	Initiate HB vaccine series
Previously vaccinated			
Known responder**	No treatment		No treatment
Known nonresponder[††]	HBIG × 1 and initiate revaccination or HBIG × 2[§§]	No treatment	If known high risk source, treat as if source were HBSAg positive
Antibody response unknown	Test exposed person for anti-HBS[¶¶] 1. If adequate,** no treatment is necessary 2. If inadequate,[††] administer HBIG × and vaccine booster	No treatment	Test exposed person for anti-HBs 1. If adequate,[¶] no treatment is necessary 2. If inadequate,[¶] administer vaccine booster and recheck titer in 1–2 months

*Persons who have previously been infected with HBV are immune to reinfection and do not require postexposure prophylaxis.

[†]Hepatitis B surface antigen.

[§] Hepatitis B immune globulin; dose is 0.06 mL/kg intramuscularly.

[¶]Hepatitis B vaccine.

**A responder is a person with adequate levels of serum antibody to HBsAg (i.e., anti-HBs ≥ 10 mlU/mL).

[††]A nonresponder is a person with inadequate response to vaccination (i.e., serum anti-HBs < 10 mlU/mL).

[§§] The option of giving one dose of HBIG and reinitiating the vaccine series is preferred for nonresponders who have not completed a second 3-dose vaccine series. For persons who previously completed a second vaccine series but failed to respond, two doses of HBIG are preferred.

[¶¶]Antibody to HBsAg.

Source: Centers for Disease Control and Prevention. Updated U.S. Public Health Service Guidelines for the Management of Occupational Exposures to HBV, HCV, and HIV and Recommendations for Postexposure Prophylaxis. *MMWR* 2001;50(No RR-11):22.

4-137 Written Opinion Regarding Occupational Exposure

You have sustained an exposure to blood or body fluids which may require preventive immunizations or further evaluation or treatment. Indications for hepatitis B vaccination have been reviewed by your health care provider and are listed below:

_____ Your AHBS (hepatitis B antibody) is positive. Vaccination is not indicated.

_____ Hepatitis B vaccination is indicated. Please call our office at _____ to schedule this immediately.

_____ You have received one or two hepatitis vaccinations. Future immunization(s) are due on the following date(s): _____

Please call _____ to schedule appointment(s).

I acknowledge that I have been informed of the results of the evaluation regarding my exposure incident. I have been told about any medical conditions resulting from exposure to blood or other potentially infectious materials which may require further evaluation or treatment.

I realize that Employee/Occupational Health & Safety will contact me for follow-up. Remarks:

_____

_____

_____

_____

_____   _____
Employee Signature   Date

_____   _____
Print Name CLEARLY   Department

Source: Courtesy of Suburban Hospital, Inc., Bethesda, Maryland.

4-138 Decontamination Room Preparation and Use Policy and Procedure

SUBJECT:

Decontamination Room Preparation and Use

PRIMARY SERVICE:

Emergency

590

EFFECTIVE DATE:

CONTRIBUTING SERVICES:

PURPOSE

To outline the basic setup and use of the Decontamination Area for those patients who have been exposed to radiation and/or hazardous materials. The type of exposure will determine the type of care required. Further guidance and direction will be given by the Emergency Physician on duty and the Safety Officer.

POLICY

To ensure safe decontamination of hazardous materials the following procedure must be carefully followed.

PROCEDURE

1. For those patients with minor exposures to chemicals, the following are general steps to be followed:
   A. Admit to the Emergency Department. Designated area depends upon the type of chemical involved. Most patients will be treated in the main Emergency Department areas without the need for special decontamination procedures.
   B. Treat symptomatically for specific chemical, if known, including oxygen and observation.
   C. Admission depends on specific chemical, if known, and symptoms.
   D. Reassure all patients
   E. Body Surface Decontamination
      1. Attendant will gown and glove
      2. Clothing and dressing removal—place in appropriate labeled container (red bags)
      3. Wound irrigation and debridement
      4. Save all F.B. and tissue; place in appropriate labeled container (sterile cups)
      5. Washing techniques
         a. Type of solution, H_2O and/or soap and detergent
         b. Ambulatory; shower at 45 degree angle top to bottom
         c. Stretcher borne; washcloth top to bottom
2. Approach to the Radiation Exposed Patient
   A. If you have prior warning of radiation exposure event:
      1. Communication of event from accident site—possible prior decontamination;
      2. Check patient in ambulance;
      3. Treat life-threatening injuries;

591

4. Prevent contamination of facility by covering floor, emergency radiation area (ERA), equipment and supplies (see B below);
5. Rope off the Emergency Department Area (Decontamination Room);
6. Monitor patient and personnel;
7. Double gown personnel appropriately (caps, masks, gowns, foot covers, gloves);
8. Decontaminate body while protecting wounds from contamination, then decontaminate wounds;
9. Use shield, if necessary;
10. Consider short exposure periods for personnel and maintain distance if possible;
11. All patient's clothing and effects should be collected and placed in containers for surveillance and disposal;
12. Effluent should be collected in containers for surveillance and disposal whenever possible;
13. Patient should be treated for any injuries and when stabilized transferred to hospital setting with care being taken to protect the facility from contamination;
14. All attendant personnel should be monitored and decontaminated and their garments appropriately disposed of.

B. Site Preparation
1. Designate arrival triage area—separate entrance through Decontamination Room.
2. Establish radiation control zone
   a. Triage area
   b. Decontamination + Rx area
3. Establish buffer zone; backup clean Rx area
4. Prepare radiation control zone
   a. D/C air circulation
   b. Utilize radiation kit
   c. Rope off
   d. Plastic floor covering
   e. Close vents

3. Decontamination Procedures
A. Patient management—decontaminate
1. Triage assessment
   a. ABCs
   b. Hazard assessment
2. Patient transport to radiation control zone;
3. Repeat hazard assessment;
4. Historical assessment—It is important to differentiate the individual types of radiation accidents. There are three (3) main radiation accidents of significance:
   a. External contamination—external contamination complicated by wound/s;
      1. Wound/s necessitate that cross-contamination between the wound/s and surrounding tissue be avoided;

2. Cleanse wounds and surrounding tissue separately;
3. Irrigate all dirty tissue;
4. Debride early.

THIS IS A POTENTIAL HAZARD TO ALL ATTENDANTS, OTHER PATIENTS AND THE ENVIRONMENT. STRICT ISOLATION TECHNIQUE IS MANDATORY.

b. Internal contamination—This involves inhalation or ingestion. Treatment is basic-ally cleansing of the contaminated material deposited on the body surface during airborne exposure. Collection and retainment of body waste for measurement of nuclear isotopes is also done to determine the appropriate therapy.

THERE IS NO HAZARD TO ATTENDANTS OR OTHER PATIENTS OR THE ENVIRONMENT. HOWEVER, MAINTAIN ISOLATION TECHNIQUE.

c. External radiation—Whole or partial body involvement. There is no basic hazard to attendants or other patients or the environment.

HOWEVER, ALL THREE ARE TREATED WITH THE FOLLOWING DECON-TAMINATION PROCEDURE:

B. Decontamination
1. Clothing and dressing removal; place in appropriate labeled container;
2. Wound irrigation and debridement;
3. Save all F.B. and tissue; place in appropriate labeled container;
4. Washing technique
    a. Type of solution, H_2O and/or soap and detergent;
    b. Ambulatory; shower at 45 degree angle top to bottom;
    c. Stretcher borne; washcloth top to bottom; REMEMBER; H_2O with deter-gent removes 90% of contamination

SAVE ALL MATERIALS USED AND PLACE IN APPROPRIATE CONTAINERS "RADIOACTIVE DO NOT DISCARD."

5. Additional information can be obtained in the Safety Policies and Procedures #29 "Hazardous Materials and Waste Management."
6. The Hazardous Materials (Hazmat) Team may be contacted through the Emer-gency Operations Center (EOC) for guidance and/or assistance in caring for a contaminated patient or potential Hazmat situations.

Source: Courtesy of Suburban Hospital, Inc., Bethesda, Maryland.

4-139 Practice Recommendations for Health Care Facilities Implementing the U.S. Public Health Service Guidelines for Management of Occupational Exposures to Bloodborne Pathogens

Practice Recommendation	Implementation Checklist
Establish a bloodborne pathogen policy.	All institutions where health care personnel (HCP) might experience exposures should have a written policy for management of exposures. The policy should be based on the U.S. Public Health Service (PHS) guidelines. The policy should be reviewed periodically to ensure that it is consistent with PHS recommendations.
Implement management policies.	Health care facilities (HCF) should provide appropriate training to all personnel on the prevention of and response to occupational exposures. HCF should establish hepatitis B vaccination programs. HCF should establish exposure-reporting systems. HCF should have personnel who can manage an exposure readily available at all hours of the day. HCF should have ready access to postexposure prophylaxis (PEP) for use by exposed personnel as necessary.
Establish laboratory capacity for bloodborne pathogen testing.	HCF should provide prompt processing of exposed person and source person specimens to guide management of occupational exposures. Testing should be performed with appropriate counseling and consent.
Select and use appropriate PEP regimens.	HCF should develop a policy for the selection and use of PEP antiretroviral regimens for HIV exposures within their institution. Hepatitis B vaccine and HBIG should be available for timely administration. HCF should have access to resources with expertise in the selection and use of PEP.
Provide access to counseling for exposed HCP.	HCF should provide counseling for HCP who might need help dealing with the emotional effect of an exposure. HCF should provide medication adherence counseling to assist HCP in completing HIV PEP as necessary.
Monitor for adverse effects of PEP.	HCP taking antiretroviral PEP should be monitored periodically for adverse effects of PEP through baseline and testing (every 2 weeks) and clinical evaluation.
Monitor for seroconversion.	HCF should develop a system to encourage exposed HCP to return for follow-up testing. Exposed HCP should be tested for HCV and HIV.
Monitor exposure management programs.	HCF should develop a system to monitor reporting and management of occupational exposures to ensure timely and appropriate response.

594

Evaluate

- exposure reports for completeness and accuracy,
- access to care (i.e., the time of exposure to the time of evaluation), and
- laboratory result reporting time.

Review

- exposures to ensure that HCP exposed to sources not infected with bloodborne pathogens do not receive PEP or that PEP is stopped.

Monitor

- completion rates of HBV vaccination and HIV PEP and
- completion of exposure follow-up.

Source: Centers for Disease Control *MMWR Reports & Recommendations*, June 29, 2001/50(RR11);43-4. *www.cdc.gov/mmwr/preview/mmwrhtml/rr5011a2.htm.* Accessed 8/14/01.

**4-140 Guideline for Hand Hygiene in Health-Care Settings
Recommendations of the Healthcare Infection Control Practices Advisory
Committee and the HICPAC/SHEA/APIC/IDSA Hand Hygiene Task Force**

Prepared by John M. Boyce, M.D.1 Didier Pittet, M.D.2 *1 Hospital of Saint Raphael New Haven, Connecticut*
2 University of Geneva Geneva, Switzerland

Summary

The Guideline for Hand Hygiene in Health-Care Settings provides health-care workers (HCWs) with a review of data regarding handwashing and hand antisepsis in health-care settings. In addition, it provides specific recommendations to promote improved hand-hygiene practices and reduce transmission of pathogenic microorganisms to patients and personnel in health-care settings. This report reviews studies published since the 1985 CDC guideline (Garner JS, Favero MS. CDC guideline for handwashing and hospital environmental control, 1985. Infect Control 1986;7:231-43) and the 1995 APIC guideline (Larson EL, APIC Guidelines Committee. APIC guideline for handwashing and hand antisepsis in health care settings. Am J Infect Control 1995;23:251-69) were issued and provides an in-depth review of hand-hygiene practices of HCWs, levels of adherence of personnel to recommended handwashing practices, and factors adversely affecting adherence. New studies of the in vivo efficacy of alcohol-based hand rubs and the low incidence of dermatitis associated with their use are reviewed. Recent studies demonstrating the value of multidisciplinary hand-hygiene promotion programs and the potential role of alcohol-based hand rub in improving hand-hygiene practices are summarized. Recommendations concerning related issues (e.g., the use of surgical hand antiseptics, hand lotions or creams, and wearing of artificial fingernails) are also included.

Recommendations

Categories

These recommendations are designed to improve hand-hygiene practices of HCWs and to reduce transmission of pathogenic microorganisms to patients and personnel in health-care settings. This guideline and its recommendations are not intended for use in food processing or food-service establishments, and are not meant to replace guidance provided by FDA's Model Food Code.

As in previous CDC/HICPAC guidelines, each recommendation is categorized on the basis of existing scientific data, theoretical rationale, applicability, and economic impact. The CDC/HICPAC system for categorizing recommendations is as follows:

Category IA. Strongly recommended for implementation and strongly supported by well-designed experimental, clinical, or epidemiologic studies.

Category IB. Strongly recommended for implementation and supported by certain experimental, clinical, or epidemiologic studies and a strong theoretical rationale.

Category IC. Required for implementation, as mandated by federal or state regulation or standard.

Category II. Suggested for implementation and supported by suggestive clinical or epidemiologic studies or a theoretical rationale.

No recommendation. Unresolved issue. Practices for which insufficient evidence or no consensus regarding efficacy exist.

Recommendations:

1. Indications for handwashing and hand antisepsis

A. When hands are visibly dirty or contaminated with proteinaceous material or are visibly soiled with blood or other body fluids, wash hands with either a non-antimicrobial soap and water or an antimicrobial soap and water (IA).

B. If hands are not visibly soiled, use an alcohol-based hand rub for routinely decontaminating hands in all other clinical situations described in items 1C-J (IA). Alternatively, wash hands with an antimicrobial soap and water in all clinical situations described in items 1C-J (IB).

C. Decontaminate hands before having direct contact with patients (IB).

D. Decontaminate hands before donning sterile gloves when inserting a central intravascular catheter (IB).

E. Decontaminate hands before inserting indwelling urinary catheters, peripheral vascular catheters, or other invasive devices that do not require a surgical procedure (IB).

F. Decontaminate hands after contact with a patient's intact skin (e.g., when taking a pulse or blood pressure, and lifting a patient) (IB).

G. Decontaminate hands after contact with body fluids or excretions, mucous membranes, non-intact skin, and wound dressings if hands are not visibly soiled (IA).

H. Decontaminate hands if moving from a contaminated-body site to a clean-body site during patient care (II).

I. Decontaminate hands after contact with inanimate objects (including medical equipment) in the immediate vicinity of the patient (II).

J. Decontaminate hands after removing gloves (IB).

K. Before eating and after using a restroom, wash hands with a non-antimicrobial soap and water or with an antimicrobial soap and water (IB).

L. Antimicrobial-impregnated wipes (i.e., towelettes) may be considered as an alternative to washing hands with non-antimicrobial soap and water. Because they are not as effective as alcohol-based hand rubs or washing hands with an antimicrobial soap and water for reducing bacterial counts on the hands of HCWs, they are not a substitute for using an alcohol-based hand rub or antimicrobial soap (IB).

M. Wash hands with non-antimicrobial soap and water or with antimicrobial soap and water if exposure to *Bacillus anthracis* is suspected or proven. The physical action of washing and rinsing hands under such circumstances is recommended because alcohols, chlorhexidine, iodophors, and other antiseptic agents have poor activity against spores (II).

N. No recommendation can be made regarding the routine use of non-alcohol-based hand rubs for hand hygiene in health-care settings. Unresolved issue.

2. Hand-hygiene technique

A. When decontaminating hands with an alcohol-based hand rub, apply product to palm of one hand and rub hands together, covering all surfaces of hands and fingers, until hands are dry (IB). Follow the manufacturer's recommendations regarding the volume of product to use.

B. When washing hands with soap and water, wet hands first with water, apply an amount of product recommended by the manufacturer to hands, and rub hands together vigorously for at least 15 seconds, covering all surfaces of the hands and fingers. Rinse hands with water and dry thoroughly with a disposable towel. Use towel to turn off the faucet (IB). Avoid using hot water, because repeated exposure to hot water may increase the risk of dermatitis (IB).

C. Liquid, bar, leaflet or powdered forms of plain soap are acceptable when washing hands with a non-antimicrobial soap and water. When bar soap is used, soap racks that facilitate drainage and small bars of soap should be used (II).

D. Multiple-use cloth towels of the hanging or roll type are not recommended for use in health-care settings (II).

3. Surgical hand antisepsis

A. Remove rings, watches, and bracelets before beginning the surgical hand scrub (II).

B. Remove debris from underneath fingernails using a nail cleaner under running water (II).

C. Surgical hand antisepsis using either an antimicrobial soap or an alcohol-based hand rub with persistent activity is recommended before donning sterile gloves when performing surgical procedures (IB).

D. When performing surgical hand antisepsis using an antimicrobial soap, scrub hands and forearms for the length of time recommended by the manufacturer, usually 2-6 minutes. Long scrub times (e.g., 10 minutes) are not necessary (IB).

E. When using an alcohol-based surgical hand-scrub product with persistent activity, follow the manufacturer's instructions. Before applying the alcohol solution, prewash hands and forearms with a non-antimicrobial soap and dry hands and forearms completely. After application of the alcohol-based product as recommended, allow hands and forearms to dry thoroughly before donning sterile gloves (IB).

4. Selection of hand-hygiene agents

A. Provide personnel with efficacious hand-hygiene products that have low irritancy potential, particularly when these products are used multiple times per shift (IB). This recommendation applies to products used for hand antisepsis before and after patient care in clinical areas and to products used for surgical hand antisepsis by surgical personnel.

B. To maximize acceptance of hand-hygiene products by HCWs, solicit input from these employees regarding the feel, fragrance, and skin tolerance of any products under consideration. The cost of hand-hygiene products should not be the primary factor influencing product selection (IB).

C. When selecting non-antimicrobial soaps, antimicrobial soaps, or alcohol-based hand rubs, solicit information from manufacturers regarding any known interactions between products used to clean hands, skin care products, and the types of gloves used in the institution (II).

D. Before making purchasing decisions, evaluate the dispenser systems of various product manufacturers or distributors to ensure that dispensers function adequately and deliver an appropriate volume of product (II).

E. Do not add soap to a partially empty soap dispenser. This practice of "topping off" dispensers can lead to bacterial contamination of soap (IA).

5. Skin care

A. Provide HCWs with hand lotions or creams to minimize the occurrence of irritant contact dermatitis associated with hand antisepsis or handwashing (IA).

B. Solicit information from manufacturers regarding any effects that hand lotions, creams, or alcohol-based hand antiseptics may have on the persistent effects of antimicrobial soaps being used in the institution (IB).

6. Other Aspects of Hand Hygiene

A. Do not wear artificial fingernails or extenders when having direct contact with patients at high risk (e.g., those in intensive-care units or operating rooms) (IA).

B. Keep natural nails tips less than 1/4-inch long (II).

C. Wear gloves when contact with blood or other potentially infectious materials, mucous membranes, and nonintact skin could occur (IC).

D. Remove gloves after caring for a patient. Do not wear the same pair of gloves for the care of more than one patient, and do not wash gloves between uses with different patients (IB).

E. Change gloves during patient care if moving from a contaminated body site to a clean body site (II).

F. No recommendation can be made regarding wearing rings in health-care settings. Unresolved issue.

7. Health-care worker educational and motivational programs

A. As part of an overall program to improve hand-hygiene practices of HCWs, educate personnel regarding the types of patient-care activities that can result in hand contamination and the advantages and disadvantages of various methods used to clean their hands (II).

B. Monitor HCWs' adherence with recommended hand-hygiene practices and provide personnel with information regarding their performance (IA).

C. Encourage patients and their families to remind HCWs to decontaminate their hands (II).

8. Administrative measures

A. Make improved hand-hygiene adherence an institutional priority and provide appropriate administrative support and financial resources (IB).

B. Implement a multidisciplinary program designed to improve adherence of health personnel to recommended hand-hygiene practices (IB).

C. As part of a multidisciplinary program to improve hand-hygiene adherence, provide HCWs with a readily accessible alcohol-based hand-rub product (IA).

D. To improve hand-hygiene adherence among personnel who work in areas in which high workloads and high intensity of patient care are anticipated, make an alcohol-based hand rub available at the entrance to the patient's room or at the bedside, in other convenient locations, and in individual pocket-sized containers to be carried by HCWs (IA).

E. Store supplies of alcohol-based hand rubs in cabinets or areas approved for flammable materials (IC).

Performance Indicators

1. The following performance indicators are recommended for measuring improvements in HCWs' hand-hygiene adherence:

A. Periodically monitor and record adherence as the number of hand-hygiene episodes performed by personnel/number of hand-hygiene opportunities, by ward or by service. Provide feedback to personnel regarding their performance.

B. Monitor the volume of alcohol-based hand rub (or detergent used for handwashing or hand antisepsis) used per 1,000 patient-days.

C. Monitor adherence to policies dealing with wearing of artificial nails.

D. When outbreaks of infection occur, assess the adequacy of health-care worker hand hygiene.

Source: Centers for Disease Control and Prevention. Guideline for Hand Hygiene in Health-Care Settings: Recommendations of the Healthcare Infection Practices Advisory Committee and the HICPAC/SHEA/APIC/IDSA Hand Hygiene Task Force. *MMWR* 2002;51 (No. RR-16):31–34, 45.

4-141 Sharps-Safety and Needlestick-Prevention Device Assessment Form

Device: _____

Supplier/trade name: _____

Applications: _____

Reviewer: _____

Date: _____

For each question, circle the appropriate response for the protective device being evaluated.

Health care worker safety

1. A.	Does the protective device prevent needlesticks or other sharps injuries during use (i.e., before disposal)?	Yes	No
B.	Does it do so after use (i.e., does the safety mechanism remain activated through disposal of the protective device)?	Yes	No
2. A.	Does protective device provide protection in one of the following ways: either intrinsically or automatically? (Answer "No" if a specific action by the user is required to activate the safety mechanism.)	Yes	No
B.	If "No," is the mechanism activated in one of the following ways: either by a one-handed technique or by a two-handed technique accomplished as part of the usual procedure?	Yes	No
3.	During the use of protective device, do the user's hands remain behind the needle or sharp until activation of the safety mechanism is complete?	Yes	No
4.	Is the safety mechanism reliable when activated properly?	Yes	No
5.	Does the protective device minimize the risk of user exposure to the patient's blood?	Yes	No

Patient safety and comfort

6.	Does the protective device minimize the risk of infection to the patient (e.g., through cross-contamination)?	Yes	No
7.	Can the protective device be used without causing more patient discomfort than a conventional device?	Yes	No
8.	*For* intravenous (IV) protective devices: Does the protective device attach comfortably (i.e., without causing patient discomfort) at the catheter port or IV tubing)?	Yes	No

Ease of Use and Training

9.	Is device operation obvious? That is, can the device be used properly without extensive training?		Yes	No
10.	Can the protective device be used by a left-handed person as easily as by a right-handed person?		Yes	No
11.	Is the technique required for using the protective device the same as that for using a conventional device?		Yes	No
12.	Is it easy to identify the type and size of the product from the packaging?		Yes	No
13.	For IV catheters and blood collection needle sets: Does the protective device provide a visible blood flashback during initial insertion?		Yes	No
14.	Please rate the ease of using this protective device			
A.	Under normal conditions	Excellent	Good	Fair	Poor
B.	When using the device with wet gloves	Excellent	Good	Fair	Poor
15.	Please rate the quality of the in-service training	Excellent	Good	Fair	Poor

Compatibility

16.	Is the protective device compatible with devices (e.g., blood collection tubes) from a variety of suppliers?	Yes	No
17.	For IV protective devices:		
A.	Is the protective device compatible with intralipid solutions?	Yes	No

600

B.	Does the protective device attach securely at the catheter port?	Yes	No
C.	Does the protective device attach securely or lock at a Y-site (e.g. for piggybacking)?	Yes	No
18.	Is the protective device easy to dispose of in sharps containers of all sizes (if required)?	Yes	No
19.	Does using the protective device instead of a conventional device result in only a modest (if any) increase in sharps container waste volume? (Answer "No" if the protective device will increase waste volume significantly.)	Yes	No

Overall

20.	Would you recommend using this device?	Yes	No

Comments (e.g., describe problems, list incompatibilities)

_____

_____

_____

Source: © 2001 ECRI. Published in: *Sharps Safety and Needlestick Prevention*. Additional copies available through www.ecri.org/sharpssafety. This page may be reproduced.

4-142 Sample Sharps Injury Log

Please complete a Log for each employee exposure incident involving a sharp.
Fill in the one circle corresponding to the most appropriate answer. Use block print and avoid touching lines.

Institution: _____ Department: _____

Address: _____ Page # _____ of _____

City: _____ State: _____ ZIP code: _____

Date filled out: _____ by: _____ Phone number: ( ) _____

Facility Injury ID#: _____ Date of injury: _____ Time of injury: _____
month   day   year

Sex: ___ Male   Age_____
___ Female

Description of the exposure incident
_____
_____
_____
_____
_____

Job classification
___ MD   ___ Nurse
___ Medical assistant
___ Phlebotomist/lab tech
___ Housekeeper/Laundry
___ CNA/HHA
___ Student, type _____
___ Other _____

Department/Location
___ Patient room   ___ Emergency dept
___ Operating room   ___ Procedure room
___ CCU/ICU   ___ Home
___ Clinical laboratory
___ Medical/outpatient clinic
___ Service/utility area (disp rm./laundry)
___ Other _____

Procedure
___ Draw venous blood   ___ Heparin/saline flush
___ Draw arterial blood   ___ Cutting
___ Injection, through skin ___ Suturing
___ Start IV/set up heparin lock
___ Unknown/not applicable
___ Other _____

Did the exposure incident occur
___ During use of sharp   ___ Disassembling
___ Between steps of a multistep procedure
___ After use and before disposal of sharp
___ While putting sharp into disposal container
___ Sharp left, inappropriate place (table, bed, etc)
___ Other _____

Body part (check all that apply)
___ Finger   ___ Face/head
___ Hand   ___ Torso
___ Arm   ___ Leg
___ Other _____

Identify sharp involved (if known)
Type: _____
Brand: _____
Model: _____
e.g., 18g needle/ABC Medical/"no stick" syringe

Did the device being used have engineered sharps injury protection?
___ yes   ___ no   ___ don't know
Was the protective mechanism activated?
___ yes, fully   ___ yes, partially   ___ no
Did the exposure incident occur?
___ before? ___ during? ___ after activation?

Exposed employee: If sharp had no engineered sharps injury protection, do you have an opinion that such a mechanism could have prevented the injury? ___ yes ___ no
Explain: _____

Exposed employee: Do you have an opinion that any other engineering, administrative or work practice control could have prevented the injury? ___ yes ___ no
Explain: _____

Source: Sharps Injury Control Program (Sharps), Department of Health Services, Occupational Health Branch/University of California.

4-143 Model Exposure Control Plan

The following model for an Exposure Control Plan includes all elements required by the OSHA bloodborne pathogens standard (29 CFR 1910.1030). The intent of this model is to provide employers with an easy-to-use format that may be used as a template to develop a written exposure control plan tailored to the individual requirements of their establishments.

POLICY

The (Your facility name) is committed to providing a safe and healthful work environment for our entire staff. In pursuit of this goal, the following Exposure Control Plan (ECP) is provided to eliminate or minimize occupational exposure to bloodborne pathogens in accordance with OSHA standard 29 *CFR* 1910.1030, "Occupational Exposure to Bloodborne Pathogens."

The ECP is a key document to assist our organization in implementing and ensuring compliance with the standard, thereby protecting our employees. This ECP includes:

- Determination of employee exposure
- Implementation of various methods of exposure control, including:
  —Universal precautions
  —Engineering and work practice controls
  —Personal protective equipment
  —Housekeeping
- Hepatitis B vaccination
- Post-exposure evaluation and follow-up
- Communication of hazards to employees and training
- Recordkeeping
- Procedures for evaluating circumstances surrounding exposure incidents Implementation methods for these elements of the standard are discussed in the subsequent pages of this ECP.

PROGRAM ADMINISTRATION

- (Name of responsible person or department) is (are) responsible for implementation of the ECP. (Name of responsible person or department) will maintain, review, and update the ECP at least annually, and whenever necessary to include new or modified tasks and procedures. Contact location/phone number: _____.
- Those employees who are determined to have occupational exposure to blood or other potentially infectious materials (OPIM) must comply with the procedures and work practices outlined in this ECP.
- (Name of responsible person or department) will provide and maintain all necessary personal protective equipment (PPE), engineering controls (e.g., sharps containers), labels, and red bags as required by the standard.

- (Name of responsible person or department will ensure that adequate supplies of the aforementioned equipment are available in the appropriate sizes. Contact location/ phone number: _____.

- (Name of responsible person or department) will be responsible for ensuring that all medical actions required by the standard are performed and that appropriate employee health and OSHA records are maintained. Contact location/phone number: _____.

- (Name of responsible person or department) will be responsible for training, documentation of training, and making the written ECP available to employees, OSHA, and NIOSH representatives. Contact location/phone number: _____.

EMPLOYEE EXPOSURE DETERMINATION

The following is a list of all job classifications at our establishment in which all employees have occupational exposure:

Example:

Job Title　　　　　　　　　　　　　　　　*Department/Location*
Phlebotomists　　　　　　　　　　　　　　　Clinical Lab

(use as many lines as necessary)_____

The following is a list of job classifications in which some employees at our establishment have occupational exposure. Included is a list of tasks and procedures, or groups of closely related tasks and procedures, in which occupational exposure may occur for these individuals:

Example:

Job Title　　　　　　　　*Department/Location*　　　　　*Task/Procedure*
Housekeeper　　　　　　　Environmental Services　　　　　Handling Regulated Waste

(use as many lines as necessary)_____

NOTE: Part-time, temporary, contract, and per diem employees are covered by the bloodborne pathogens standard. The ECP should describe how the standard will be met for these employees.

METHODS OF IMPLEMENTATION AND CONTROL

Universal Precautions

All employees will utilize universal precautions.

Exposure Control Plan

Employees covered by the bloodborne pathogens standard receive an explanation of this ECP during their initial training session. It will also be reviewed in their annual refresher training. All employees can review this plan at any time during their work shifts by contacting (Name of responsible person or department). If requested, we will provide an employee with a copy of the ECP free of charge and within 15 days of the request.

(Name of responsible person or department) is responsible for reviewing and updating the ECP annually or more frequently if necessary to reflect any new or modified tasks and procedures that affect occupational exposure and to reflect new or revised employee positions with occupational exposure.

Engineering Controls and Work Practices
Engineering controls and work practice controls will be used to prevent or minimize exposure to bloodborne pathogens. The specific engineering controls and work practice controls used are listed below:

- (For example: non-glass capillary tubes, SESIPs, needleless systems)
- _____
- _____

Sharps disposal containers are inspected and maintained or replaced by (Name of responsible person or department) every (list frequency) or whenever necessary to prevent overfilling.

This facility identifies the need for changes in engineering controls and work practices through (Provide examples: Review of OSHA records, employee interviews, committee activities, etc.).

We evaluate new procedures and new products regularly by (Describe the process, literature reviewed, supplier info, products considered). _____.

Both front-line workers and management officials are involved in this process in the following manner: (Describe employees' involvement). (Name of responsible person or department) is responsible for ensuring that these recommendations are implemented.

Personal Protective Equipment (PPE)
PPE is provided to our employees at no cost to them. Training in the use of the appropriate PPE for specific tasks or procedures is provided by (Name of responsible person or department).

The types of PPE available to employees are as follows:
(gloves, eye protection, etc.)_____

_____

_____

PPE is located (List location) and may be obtained through (Name of responsible person or department). (Specify how employees will obtain PPE and who is responsible for ensuring that PPE is available.)

All employees using PPE must observe the following precautions:

- Wash hands immediately or as soon as feasible after removing gloves or other PPE.
- Remove PPE after it becomes contaminated and before leaving the work area.
- Used PPE may be disposed of in (List appropriate containers for storage, laundering, decontamination, or disposal.)
- Wear appropriate gloves when it is reasonably anticipated that there may be hand contact with blood or OPIM, and when handling or touching contaminated items or

surfaces; replace gloves if torn, punctured or contaminated, or if their ability to function as a barrier is compromised.

- Utility gloves may be decontaminated for reuse if their integrity is not compromised; discard utility gloves if they show signs of cracking, peeling, tearing, puncturing, or deterioration.
- Never wash or decontaminate disposable gloves for reuse.
- Wear appropriate face and eye protection when splashes, sprays, spatters, or droplets of blood or OPIM pose a hazard to the eye, nose, or mouth.
- Remove immediately or as soon as feasible any garment contaminated by blood or OPIM, in such a way as to avoid contact with the outer surface.

The procedure for handling used PPE is as follows:
(may refer to specific procedure by title or number and last date of review; include how and where to decontaminate face shields, eye protection, resuscitation equipment)

_____

_____

_____

Housekeeping

Regulated waste is placed in containers which are closable, constructed to contain all contents and prevent leakage, appropriately labeled or color-coded (see the following section "Labels"), and closed prior to removal to prevent spillage or protrusion of contents during handling.

The procedure for handling sharps disposal containers is:
(may refer to specific procedure by title or number and last date of review)

_____

_____

The procedure for handling other regulated waste is: *(may refer to specific procedure by title or number and last date of review)*

_____

_____

Contaminated sharps are discarded immediately or as soon as possible in containers that are closable, puncture-resistant, leak proof on sides and bottoms, and appropriately labeled or colorcoded.

Sharps disposal containers are available at (must be easily accessible and as close as feasible to the immediate area where sharps are used).

Bins and pails (e.g., wash or emesis basins) are cleaned and decontaminated as soon as feasible after visible contamination.

Broken glassware that may be contaminated is only picked up using mechanical means, such as a brush and dustpan.

Laundry

The following contaminated articles will be laundered by this company:

_____

_____

Laundering will be performed by (Name of responsible person or department) at (time and/or location).

The following laundering requirements must be met:

- handle contaminated laundry as little as possible, with minimal agitation
- place wet contaminated laundry in leak-proof, labeled or colorcoded containers before transport. Use (specify either red bags or bags marked with the biohazard symbol) for this purpose.
- wear the following PPE when handling and/or sorting contaminated laundry: (List appropriate PPE).

Labels

The following labeling methods are used in this facility:

Equipment to be Labeled (specimens, contaminated laundry, etc.)	Label Type (size, color) (red bag, biohazard label)

(Name of responsible person or department) is responsible for ensuring that warning labels are affixed or red bags are used as required if regulated waste or contaminated equipment is brought into the facility. Employees are to notify (Name of responsible person or department) if they discover regulated waste containers, refrigerators containing blood or OPIM, contaminated equipment, etc., without proper labels.

HEPATITIS B VACCINATION

(Name of responsible person or department) will provide training to employees on hepatitis B vaccinations, addressing safety, benefits, efficacy, methods of administration, and availability.

The hepatitis B vaccination series is available at no cost after initial employee training and within 10 days of initial assignment to all employees identified in the exposure determination section of this plan. Vaccination is encouraged unless: 1) documentation exists that the employee has previously received the series; 2) antibody testing reveals that the employee is immune; or 3) medical evaluation shows that vaccination is contraindicated.

However, if an employee declines the vaccination, the employee must sign a declination form. Employees who decline may request and obtain the vaccination at a later date at no cost. Documentation of refusal of the vaccination is kept at (List location). Vaccination will be provided by (List health care professional responsible for this part of the plan) at (location).

Following the medical evaluation, a copy of the health care professional's written opinion will be obtained and provided to the employee within 15 days of the completion of the evaluation. It will be limited to whether the employee requires the hepatitis vaccine and whether the vaccine was administered.

POST-EXPOSURE EVALUATION AND FOLLOW-UP

Should an exposure incident occur, contact (Name of responsible person) at the following number _____. An immediately available confidential medical evaluation and follow-up will be conducted by (name of licensed health care professional). Following initial first aid (clean the wound, flush eyes or other mucous membrane, etc.), the following activities will be performed:

- Document the routes of exposure and how the exposure occurred.
- Identify and document the source individual (unless the employer can establish that identification is infeasible or prohibited by state or local law).
- Obtain consent and make arrangements to have the source individual tested as soon as possible to determine HIV, HCV, and HBV infectivity; document that the source individual's test results were conveyed to the employee's health care provider.
- If the source individual is already known to be HIV, HCV and/or HBV positive, new testing need not be performed.
- Assure that the exposed employee is provided with the source individual's test results and with information about applicable disclosure laws and regulations concerning the identity and infectious status of the source individual (e.g., laws protecting confidentiality).
- After obtaining consent, collect exposed employee's blood as soon as feasible after exposure incident, and test blood for HBV and HIV serological status.
- If the employee does not give consent for HIV serological testing during collection of blood for baseline testing, preserve the baseline blood sample for at least 90 days; if the exposed employee elects to have the baseline sample tested during this waiting period, perform testing as soon as feasible.

ADMINISTRATION OF POST-EXPOSURE EVALUATION AND FOLLOW-UP

(Name of responsible person or department) ensures that health care professional(s) responsible for employee's hepatitis B vaccination and post-exposure evaluation and follow-up are given a copy of OSHA's bloodborne pathogens standard.

(Name of responsible person or department) ensures that the health care professional evaluating an employee after an exposure incident receives the following:

- a description of the employee's job duties relevant to the exposure incident
- route(s) of exposure
- circumstances of exposure
- if possible, results of the source individual's blood test
- relevant employee medical records, including vaccination status

(Name of responsible person or department) provides the employee with a copy of the evaluating health care professional's written opinion within 15 days after completion of the evaluation.

PROCEDURES FOR EVALUATING THE CIRCUMSTANCES SURROUNDING AN EXPOSURE INCIDENT

(Name of responsible person or department) will review the circumstances of all exposure incidents to determine:

- engineering controls in use at the time
- work practices followed
- a description of the device being used (including type and brand)

- protective equipment or clothing that was used at the time of the exposure incident (gloves, eye shields, etc.)
- location of the incident (O.R., E.R., patient room, etc.)
- procedure being performed when the incident occurred
- employee's training

(Name of Responsible Person) will record all percutaneous injuries from contaminated sharps in a Sharps Injury Log.

NOTE: If revisions to this ECP are necessary (Responsible person or department) will ensure that appropriate changes are made. (Changes may include an evaluation of safer devices, adding employees to the exposure determination list, etc.)

EMPLOYEE TRAINING

All employees who have occupational exposure to bloodborne pathogens receive initial and annual training conducted by (Name of responsible person or department). (Attach a brief description of their qualifications.)

All employees who have occupational exposure to bloodborne pathogens receive training on the epidemiology, symptoms, and transmission of bloodborne pathogen diseases. In addition, the training program covers, at a minimum, the following elements:

- a copy and explanation of the OSHA bloodborne pathogen standard
- an explanation of our ECP and how to obtain a copy
- an explanation of methods to recognize tasks and other activities that may involve exposure to blood and OPIM, including what constitutes an exposure incident
- an explanation of the use and limitations of engineering controls, work practices, and PPE
- an explanation of the types, uses, location, removal, handling, decontamination, and disposal of PPE
- an explanation of the basis for PPE selection
- information on the hepatitis B vaccine, including information on its efficacy, safety, method of administration, the benefits of being vaccinated, and that the vaccine will be offered free of charge
- information on the appropriate actions to take and persons to contact in an emergency involving blood or OPIM
- an explanation of the procedure to follow if an exposure incident occurs, including the method of reporting the incident and the medical follow-up that will be made available
- information on the post-exposure evaluation and follow-up that the employer is required to provide for the employee following an exposure incident
- an explanation of the signs and labels and/or color coding required by the standard and used at this facility
- an opportunity for interactive questions and answers with the person conducting the training session.

Training materials for this facility are available at (name location).

RECORDKEEPING

Training Records

Training records are completed for each employee upon completion of training. These documents will be kept for at least three years at (Location of records).
The training records include:

- the dates of the training sessions
- the contents or a summary of the training sessions
- the names and qualifications of persons conducting the training
- the names and job titles of all persons attending the training sessions

Employee training records are provided upon request to the employee or the employee's authorized representative within 15 working days. Such requests should be addressed to (Name of responsible person or department).

Medical Records

Medical records are maintained for each employee with occupational exposure in accordance with 29 *CFR* 1910.1020, "Access to Employee Exposure and Medical Records."

(Name of Responsible person or department) is responsible for maintenance of the required medical records. These confidential records are kept in (List location) for at least the duration of employment plus 30 years. Employee medical records are provided upon request of the employee or to anyone having written consent of the employee within 15 working days. Such requests should be sent to (Name of responsible person or department and address).

OSHA Recordkeeping

An exposure incident is evaluated to determine if the case meets OSHA's Recordkeeping Requirements (29 CFR 1904). This determination and the recording activities are done by (Name of responsible person or department).

Sharps Injury Log

In addition to the 1904 Recordkeeping Requirements, all percutaneous injuries from contaminated sharps are also recorded in a Sharps Injury Log. All incidences must include at least:

- date of the injury
- type and brand of the device involved (syringe, suture needle)
- department or work area where the incident occurred
- explanation of how the incident occurred.

This log is reviewed as part of the annual program evaluation and maintained for at least five years following the end of the calendar year covered. If a copy is requested by anyone, it must have any personal identifiers removed from the report.

HEPATITIS B VACCINE DECLINATION (MANDATORY)

I understand that due to my occupational exposure to blood or other potentially infectious materials I may be at risk of acquiring hepatitis B virus (HBV) infection. I have been given the opportunity to be vaccinated with hepatitis B vaccine, at no charge to myself.

However, I decline hepatitis B vaccination at this time. I understand that by declining this vaccine, I continue to be at risk of acquiring hepatitis B, a serious disease. If in the future I continue to have occupational exposure to blood or other potentially infectious materials and I want to be vaccinated with hepatitis B vaccine, I can receive the vaccination series at no charge to me.

Signed: (Employee Name)_____ Date:_____

Source: *Model Plans and Programs for the OSHA Bloodborne Pathogens and Hazard Communications Standards.* OSHA 3186-06N. 2003. Available online at: *http://www.osha.gov.*

PART 5

CMS and Joint Commission Standards Checklist

The following materials serve as examples. Hospitals should consult with counsel or other appropriate advisors before adapting the materials in this part to suit particular purposes.

INTRODUCTION

"Hospital Checklist: CMS and Joint Commission Standards" is a tool designed to references similarities and differences between CMS regulations and Joint Commission accreditation standards for hospital compliance. It is an invaluable tool for quality assurance nurses, directors of nursing, infection control nurses, medical records personnel, risk managers, and hospital administrators.

CMS regulations are cited in the Code of Federal Regulations (C.F.R.). The Hospital Conditions of Participation (COPs) at 42 C.F.R. Subpart E is cited as 42 C.F.R. 482. CMS expects the hospital, as part of its participation agreement, to implement a demonstrable process and system to produce the desired outcome for compliance with the regulations. Citations or Statements of Deficiency (SODs) are written when the hospital fails to maintain a system to produce the desired outcome or when the hospital fails to monitor and correct undesirable outcomes. CMS can take termination actions if the intent of the regulation is not objectively met by the hospital.

"Hospital Checklist: CMS and Joint Commission Standards" compares CMS regulations to Joint Commission accreditation standards in a table format. The table contains a section for the user to enter applicable state laws for a complete reference guide. Remember, the hospital's policies, procedures, and protocols (PPPs) must reflect the requirements of CMS, the Joint Commission, and the state to be in compliance, so it makes sense to include all of the requirements in one easy-to-use checklist.

This checklist is intended for use as a reference guide to aid the user in determining the most stringent requirements for compliance, so the user can formulate PPPs that meet or exceed the most restrictive requirement. It is not intended to be utilized as a complete set of regulations, conditions, standards, or laws governing hospitals or compliance.

Denise Atwood, Paralegal, RN, BSS, a teeny tiny corporation, dba C.A. Enterprises

Source: Copyright 2000, Denise Atwood and Rose Sparks.

AREAS OF ASSESSMENT

Requirement	CMS		Joint Commission	State
Compliance Federal, State, Local Laws	**482.11(a)** **482.11(c)**		**LD.1.20**—The hospital identifies how it is governed **LD.1.30**—Hospital complies with applicable law and regulation	
Governing Body (GB) Administration	**482.12**	Legally responsible for the conduct of the hospital **(a)** Appoint medical staff (MS) **(a)(4)** Approve MS bylaws and rules/regulations **(a)(5)** Ensure MS is accountable to the GB for quality of care provided **(c)** Patients under the care of a physician **(c)(2)** Patient admitted by licensed independent practitioner (LIP) **(d)** Plan and budget **(d)(6)** Revised/updated annually **(d)(7)** Plan prepared under the direction of the GB **(e)** Responsible for contracted services **(f)** Emergency services	**LD.1.20**—Governance responsibilities defined in writing, as applicable **LD.2.10**—Individual(s) responsible for operating hospital according to authority conferred by governance **HR.1.20**—Hospital has process to ensure person's qualifications are consistent with job responsibilities **LD.3.10**—Leaders engage in short- and long-term planning **LD.2.50**—develop and monitor annual operating budget **LD.3.50**—Services provided by contractual arrangements are provided safely and effectively	

Requirement	CMS		Joint Commission	State
Patients' Rights (PR)	482.13	Hospital must promote and protect each PR	**RI.2.10**—Hospital respects PR	
		(a)(1) Inform patient or representative of PR before furnishing or discontinuing care	**RI.2.20**—Patients receive information about PR	
		(a)(2) Establish a patient grievance process that is approved by the GB	**RI.2.120**—Hospital addresses the resolution of complaints	
		(b)(1) Patients have the right to participate in plan of care	**RI.2.30**—Patients involved in decisions about care	
		(b)(2) Patient or representative has the right to make informed decisions for care	**RI.2.40**—Informed consent obtained	
		(b)(3) Patient has the right to formulate advanced directives	**RI.2.80**—Hospital addresses wishes of patient for end-of-life issues	
		(c)(1) Right to personal privacy	**RI.2.130**—Hospital respects confidentiality, privacy and security	
		(c)(2) Right to receive care in a safe setting	**RI.2.150**—Right to be free from abuse, neglect, and exploitation	
		(c)(3) Right to be free from abuse or harassment	**PC.12.60**—Restraint or seclusion limited to emergencies where risk of patient harming self or others and nonphysical interventions ineffective	
		(d)(1) Right to confidentiality of medical records (MR)	**PC.12.50**—Nonphysical techniques are preferred	
		(e)(1) Right to be free from restraints (physical or chemical) not medically necessary	**PC.12.70**—LIP orders restraint/seclusion	
		(e)(2) Restraint used only to improve the patient's well-being	**PC.12.90**—LIP sees and evaluates patients in person	
		(e)(3) Use of a restraint must be	**PC.12.100**—Written or verbal orders for initial or continuing use are time limited	
		(e)(3)(i) used when less restrictive measures ineffective	**PC.13.70**—Behavior management conforms to treatment plan	
		(e)(3)(ii) in accordance with a physician's/LIP order. The order must	**PC.12.140**—Patients are monitored	
		(e)(3)(ii)(A) never be written as a standing or as needed order	**PC.12.110**—Regularly evaluated	
		(e)(3)(iii) according to written changes to patient's plan of care	**PC.12.30**—Staff is trained and competent	
		(e)(3)(iv) implemented in the least restrictive manner possible	**PC.12.150**—Discontinued when patient meets behavior criteria	
		(e)(3)(v) in accordance with safe restraining techniques	**PC.11.50**—Orders for initiation and renewing are consistent with PPP and patient condition	
		(e)(3)(vi) ended at earliest time	**PC.11.70**—Patients are monitored	
		(e)(4) Patient must be continually assessed, monitored, reevaluated	**PC.12.180**—Hospital collects data on use of restraint and seclusion	
		(e)(5) Direct patient care staff must have ongoing education and training in safe use of restraints		
		(f)(1) Patient has the right to be free from seclusion and restraint imposed as coercion or discipline		

Requirement	CMS		Joint Commission	State
		(f)(2) Only used in emergency situations **(f)(3)(ii)(C)** Practitioner must see and evaluate restraint/seclusion within 1 hour of intervention **(f)(3)(ii)(D)** Restraint or seclusion orders max: 4 hours adults, 2 hours age 9-17, 1 hour if under 9—for a total of 24 hours **(f)(4)(i)** Restraint *and* seclusion require continual face-to-face monitoring *OR* **(f)(4)(ii)** continuous video and audio monitoring **(f)(7)** Hospital must report to CMS any death that occurs while a patient is restrained or secluded		
Quality Assurance (QA)/ Performance Improvement (PI)	482.21	GB ensures there is an effective hospitalwide program **(a)** Written plan, ongoing activities **(a)(1)** Evaluation of contracted services **(a)(2)** Evaluation of infections and medication therapy **(a)(3)** Evaluation of medical and surgical services **(b)** Services meet medically related needs of patients. **(c)** Implementation of program and documentation of remedial actions and outcomes	**PI.1**—Organization wide approach to performance measurement, analysis and improvement **LD.3.5**—Services provided by contractual arrangements are provided safely and effectively **PI.1.10**—Hospital collects data to monitor performance **PI.2.10**—Data are systematically aggregated and analyzed **PI.3.10**—Information from data analysis used to make changes to improve performance and patient safety **PI.2.30**—Process to identify and manage sentinel events **PI.3.20**—Ongoing program for identifying and reducing adverse events **PC.11.20**—PI process identifies way to reduce risks associated with restraint use **LD.4.10**—Leaders use process to assess and improve the hospital's activities **LD.4.50**—PI organization priorities in response to unusual events **LD.4.60**—Resources for measuring, assessing and improving performance and safety **MS.3.10**—MS has leadership role in PI activities **MS.3.20**—MS participates in PI processes **ORYX specific requirements are not included in the scope of this manual.**	

Requirement	CMS		Joint Commission	State
Medical Staff (MS)	482.22	Organized MS responsible for the care of patients **(a)** Composition of MS **(a)(1)** Periodic peer review **(a)(2)** Credentialing **(b)** Accountable to the GB **(b)(2)** If MS has executive committee, majority of members are MDs or DOs **(b)(3)** Responsibility for the organization and conduct of MS assigned to an MD or DO **(c)** MS bylaws adopted and enforced **(c)(1)** Approved by the GB **(c)(2)** Statement of privileges of each category of MS **(c)(3)** Describe MS organization **(c)(4)** Describe qualifications for MS appointment **(c)(5)** History and physical (H&P) are completed 7 days before or 48 hours after admission by an MD, DO, or oromaxillofacial surgeon **(c)(6)** Criteria for determining privileges	**MS.2.10**—MS oversees quality of patient care, treatment, services **MS.1.10**—Organized, self-governing MS **MS.4.10**—MS has credentialing process **MS.4.40**—MS evaluates individuals for quality care **MS.1.20**—MS bylaws **MS.2.20**—Patient's care responsibility of practitioner with privileges **MS.2.30**—Process to monitor LIP **PC.2.130**—Initial assessments performed as defined by hospital **MS.4.20**—Process for clinical privileges	

Requirement	CMS		Joint Commission	State
Nursing Services	482.23	Organized, 24 hour NS under the supervision of an RN **(a)** Plan of administrative authority and delineation of responsibilities for patient care Director of Nursing (DON) must be an RN **(b)** Staffing and delivery of care ensures immediate availability of an RN for patient care **(b)(2)** Nurses must have valid, current licenses **(b)(3)** RN supervises/evaluates care for each patient **(b)(4)** Current nursing care plans for each patient **(b)(5)** RN makes patient care assignments **(b)(6)** Responsibility for nonemployee nurses (registry) **(c)** Preparation and administration of drugs and biologicals **(c)(2)** Orders for drugs and biologicals must be in writing and signed by the practitioner responsible for the patient's care **(c)(2)(i)** Telephone orders per PPP **(c)(3)** Blood transfusions and IV medications are administered per approved MS PPP **(c)(4)** Reporting transfusion and adverse drug reactions and errors in administration of drugs	**NR.2.10**—Nurse Executive is an RN **NR.1.10**—Nurse Executive directs nursing services **NR.3.10**—Nurse Executive establishes PPP **LD.2.20**—Each program, service, department has effective leadership **HR.1.20**—Hospital has a process to ensure a person is qualified **PC.4.10**—Development of plan of care **PC.2.130**—Initial assessments performed as defined by hospital **PC.2.150**—Patients are reassessed as needed **MM.5.10**—Medications are safely and accurately administered **IM.6.50**—Qualified personnel accept and transcribe verbal orders **MM.6.10**—Effects of medications are monitored **MM.6.20**—Actual or adverse drug events and medication errors	

Requirement	CMS		Joint Commission	State
Medical Records Services (MR)/ Information Management (IM)	**482.24**	MR must be maintained for every person evaluated or treated **(a)** Must employ personnel to ensure prompt completion, filing, and retrieval of records **(b)** Form and retention of MR: accurate, promptly filed, retained, and accessible and system of author identification that protects security of entries **(b)(1)** Retained at least 5 years **(b)(2)** Coding and indexing system **(b)(3)** Procedures for ensuring confidentiality and release **(c)** Content of MR: reason for admission, patient's progress, and response to treatment **(c)(1)** Legible, complete, and authenticated (name and discipline) and dated promptly **(c)(1)(ii)** Authentication: signatures, written initials, or computer entry **(c)(2)** MR must document the following: **(c)(2)(i)** H&P 7 days before or 48 hours after admission **(c)(2)(ii)** Admitting diagnosis **(c)(2)(v)** Properly executed informed consent forms **(c)(2)(vi)** Information necessary to monitor the patient's condition **(c)(2)(vii)** Discharge summary, outcome, and follow-up care **(c)(2)(viii)** MR completed in 30 days after discharge	**IM.6.10**—Complete and accurate MR for every patient assessed or treated **IM.6.60**—Access to all relevant information from MR **IM.2.10, 2.20 and 2.30**—Confidentiality, security, and integrity of data/information are maintained **IM.5.10**—Information resources readily available and current **IM.6.20**—Records contain information to care, treatment and services **PC.2.130**—Hospital defines in writing time frames for conduction initial assessment(s) **RI.2.40**—Informed consent obtained **IM.4.10**—IM system provides information for use in decision making **IM.6.40**—MR contains summary list diagnoses, procedures, drug allergies, medications **PC.2.130**—Initial assessments performed as defined by hospital **RI.2.40**—Informed consent obtained	

Requirement	CMS	Joint Commission	State
Pharmaceutical Services (PS) 482.25	PS to meet the needs of patients. MS is responsible for developing PPP that minimize drug errors **(a)** Pharmacy or drug storage is administered in accordance with professional principles **(a)(1)** Full-time, part-time, or consulting pharmacist is responsible for developing, supervising, and coordinating activities of PS **(a)(2)** Adequate number of personnel to ensure quality of PS **(a)(3)** Current, accurate records on receipt and disposition of all scheduled drugs **(b)(1)** Compounding, packaging, and dispensing under the supervision of a pharmacist **(b)(2)** Drugs and biologicals must be kept in a locked storage area **(b)(3)** Outdated, mislabeled, or unusable drugs and biologicals must not be available for patient use **(b)(4)** PPP for removing drugs when pharmacist is not available **(b)(5)** Protocol for automatic stop orders determined by the MS **(b)(6)** Drug administration errors, drug reactions, and incompatibilities reported immediately to physician **(b)(7)** Reporting of abuse and loss of controlled substances **(b)(9)** Established formulary	**MM.4.10**—review of prescriptions or orders **MM.4.20**—Medications prepared safely **MM.4.30**—Medications labeled appropriately **MM.4.40**—Medications dispensed safely **LD.2.20**—Each program, service, department has effective leadership **HR.1.20**—Hospital has a process to ensure a person is qualified **MM.2.30**—Emergency medications available, controlled and secured **MM.4.50**—System for safely providing medications to meet patient needs **MM.4.70**—Medications are retrieved when recalled or discontinued **MM.4.50**—System for safely providing medication when pharmacy is closed **MM.5.10**—Medications safely and accurately administered **MM.6.20**—Responds appropriately to actual or potential adverse drug events or medication errors	

Requirement	CMS		Joint Commission	State
Radiologic Services (RS)	482.26	**(a)** Hospitals must maintain, or have available, diagnostic RS **(b)** Must be free from hazards for patients and personnel **(b)(2)** Periodic equipment inspections must be done **(b)(3)** Use of exposure meters or badge tests **(b)(4)** Provided only on the order of practitioners with privileges **(c)(1)** Personnel: full-time, part-time, or consulting radiologist **(d)** Record of RS must be maintained **(d)(1)** Signed reports of interpretations **(d)(2)** Retained at least 5 years	**LD.2.20**—Each program, service, department has effective leadership **HR.1.20**—Hospital has a process to ensure a person is qualified **PS.3.230**—Diagnostic testing for determining patient's health care needs is performed	
Laboratory Services (LS)	482.27	**(a)** Hospitals must maintain, or have available, adequate LS **(b)(1)** Emergency LS must be available 24 hours a day **(b)(2)** Written description of LS must be available to the MS **(b)(4)** MS and a pathologist must determine tissue specimens that require macroscopic or macroscopic and microscopic examinations **(c)(1)** Potentially HIV infectious blood and blood products **(c)(2)** Services furnished by an outside blood bank **(c)(4)** Patient notification of administration of potentially HIV infectious blood or blood products **(c)(5)** Timeframe for notification **(c)(6)** Content of notification **(c)(7)** Policies and procedures for notification **CLIA (waived testing) specific requirements are not included in the scope of this manual. They can be found at 42 C.F.R. 493, Subpart P.**	**LD.3.30**—Hospital demonstrates a commitment to community by providing essential services in a timely manner **PC.16.30**—Staff performing tests have training and demonstrate competence **PC.16.40**—Approved PPP governing testing processes are current and available **PC.16.50**—Quality control checks, as defined by hospital, are conducted on each procedure **PC.16.60**—Quality control and test records are maintained	

Requirement	CMS		Joint Commission	State
Food and Dietetic Services (FDS) and Nutrition Care	482.28	Must have an organized FDS that is directed and staffed by adequate personnel **(a)(1)** Must have a full-time employee who— **(a)(1)(i)** serves as the director **(a)(1)(ii)** is responsible for the daily management of FDS **(a)(2)** There must be qualified dietitian, full-time, part-time, or consulting **(b)(1)** Therapeutic diets must be prescribed by the practitioner(s) responsible for the care of the patient **(b)(2)** Nutritional needs must be met in accordance with recognized dietary practices **(b)(3)** Therapeutic diet manual approved by the MS and dietitian and available to staff	**LD.2.20**—Each program, service, department has effective leadership **HR.1.20**—Hospital has a process to ensure a person is qualified **PC.7.10**—Process for preparing and/or distributing food and nutrition products **PC.2.120**—Initial assessments performed as defined by hospital	
Utilization Review (UR) or Continuum of Care	482.30	**(a)** This section applies except in the following circumstances: **(a)(1)** A PRO has assumed binding review for the hospital **(a)(2)** CMS has determined the UR procedures by the state under Title XIX of the Act are superior to the procedures required in this section **(b)** UR committee composition **(c)** Scope/frequency of review **(d)** Determination regarding admissions or continued stays **(e)** Extended stay review **(f)** Review of professional services	**PC.1.10**—Hospital accepts for care those patients whose needs it can meet **PC.5.60**—Hospital coordinates the care, treatment and services provided **PC.15.10**—Process addresses need for continuing care and services after discharge or transfer **PC.15.20**—Patient's transfer or discharge to another level of care is based on patient's assessed needs and hospital's capabilities **RI.1.40**—When care and services are subject to review resulting in denial of care or services, the hospital makes the decision regarding ongoing care and services	
		These sections are compared for total content only. DO NOT compare line by line.	**These sections are compared for total content only. DO NOT compare line by line.**	

Requirement	CMS		Joint Commission	State
Physical Environment (PE)	**"Life Safety Code"**			
	482.41	**(a)** PE must be constructed and maintained to ensure safety of patients **(a)(1)** There must be emergency power and lighting **(a)(2)** There must be facilities for emergency gas and water **(b)** Life safety from fire **(b)(2)** Must have procedures for the storage and disposal of trash **(b)(3)** Must have a written fire control plan **(b)(4)** Must maintain written evidence of inspection and approval of fire control agencies **(c)(2)** Facilities, supplies, and equipment must be maintained to ensure safety and quality **(c)(4)** Must be proper ventilation, light, and temperature controls in PS and FDS	**EC.5.50**—Hospital develops and implements activities to protect occupants when building does not meet Life Safety Code **EC.4.10**—Addresses emergency management **EC.7.20**—Provides emergency electrical power source **EC.1.10**—Manages safety risks **EC.1.20**—Maintains a safe environment **EC.3.10**—Manages hazardous materials and waste risks **EC.5.10**—Manages fire safety risks **EC.6.10**—Manages medical equipment risks **EC.7.10**—Manages utility risks **EC.5.40**—Maintains fire-safety equipment and building features	
Infection Control (IC)	482.42	The hospital must have an active program for the prevention, control, and investigation of infections and communicable diseases **(a)** Have designated infection control officer(s) develop and implement policies **(a)(1)** Infection control officer(s) must develop a system for identifying, reporting, investigating, and controlling infections and communicable diseases **(a)(2)** Must maintain a log of incidents related to infections and communicable diseases **(b)** The CEO, MS, and DON must— **(b)(1)** ensure hospitalwide QA and training programs address problems identified by infection control officer(s) **(b)(2)** be responsible for implementation of successful corrective action plans	**IC.1.10**—Hospitalwide infection control program **IC.2.10**—IC program identifies risks **IC.3.10**—Goals for preventing development of health care-associated infections **IC.5.50**—Evaluation of effectiveness of IC interventions **IC.7.10**—IC program is managed effectively **IC.9.10**—Hospital leaders allocate resources for IC program **IC.4.10**—Strategies implemented to achieve IC goals	

Requirement	CMS		Joint Commission	State
Discharge Planning (DP)	482.43	Must have DP policies and procedures that apply to all patients **(a)** Must identify all patients who are likely to suffer adverse health consequences on discharge if there is no DP **(b)(2)** An RN, social worker, or other qualified personnel must develop or supervise the DP evaluation **(b)(3)** Evaluation must include patient's need for post-hospital services and availability of services **(b)(4)** Evaluation must include patient's capacity for self-care or care in the environment from which they entered the hospital **(b)(5)** Evaluation must be completed in a timely manner, to avoid delays in discharge **(b)(6)** Evaluation must include discussion of the plan with the patient or the individual acting on the patient's behalf and must be in the MR **(c)(3)** Hospital must arrange for the initial implementation of the DP **(c)(4)** Hospital must re-assess DP if needs change	**PC.15.20**—Patient's transfer or discharge to another level of care is based on patient's assessed needs and hospital's capabilities **PC.6.10**—Patient receives education and training specific to needs **PC.2.120**—Initial assessments performed as defined by hospital **PC.2.20**—Hospital defines in writing data and information gathered during assessment and reassessment **PC.15.10**—Process addresses needs for continuing care and services after discharge or transfer **PC.15.30**—When patients transferred or discharged, information related to care and services is provided	

Requirement	CMS		Joint Commission	State
Organ, Tissue, and Eye Procurement (OTEP)	482.45	**(a)** Must have and implement written protocols **(a)(1)** Agreement with a designated organ procurement organization (OPO), which the hospital must notify in a timely manner of all deaths **(a)(2)** Agreement with at least one tissue bank and one eye bank **(a)(3)** Ensures families of potential donors are informed of donation options **(a)(4)** Use discretion and sensitivity with respect to potential donors **(a)(5)** Ensure that staff is educated on donation issues, death records are reviewed to improve identification of potential donors, and potential donors are maintained while testing and placement of organs is done **(b)(1)** A hospital where transplants are performed must be a member of the Organ Procurement and Transplantation Network (OPTN) and abide by its rules. **(b)(2)** "Organ" means human kidney, liver, heart, lung or pancreas **(b)(3)** A transplanting hospital must provide data to OPTN, the Scientific Registry, and the OPOs	**LD.3.110**—Implement policies and procedures, developed with MS participation, for procuring and donation of organs and tissues **RI.2.80**—Hospital addresses wishes of patient relating to end of life decisions	
		These sections are compared for total content only. DO NOT compare line by line.	**These sections are compared for total content only. DO NOT compare line by line.**	

Requirement	CMS		Joint Commission	State
Surgical Services (SS)	**482.51**	SS must be well organized and provided in accordance with acceptable standards of practice **(a)(1)** OR must be supervised by RN, MD, or DO **(a)(2)** LPNs and scrub techs work under the supervision of an RN **(a)(3)** RNs perform circulating duties **(a)(4)** SS must maintain a roster specifying surgical privileges **(b)** Must develop policies governing surgical care **(b)(1)** Must be an H&P in every patient's chart before surgery (except in emergencies) **(b)(2)** Properly executed informed consent form for the operation must be in every patient's chart before surgery (except in emergencies) **(b)(3)** Must have the following equipment: call system, cardiac monitor, resuscitator, defibrillator, aspirator and tracheotomy set **(b)(4)** Must have provisions for postoperative care **(b)(5)** OR register complete and must be up-to-date **(b)(6)** Operative report written or dictated immediately following surgery and signed by surgeon	**LD.2.20**—Each program, service, department has effective leadership **HR.1.20**—Hospital has a process to ensure a person is qualified **PC.13.20**—Procedures that require administration of moderate or deep sedation or anesthesia are planned **PC.13.30**—Patients are monitored during administration of moderate or deep sedation or anesthesia **PC.13.40**—Patients are monitored immediately after the administration of moderate or deep sedation or aesthesia **RI.2.40**—Informed consent is obtained **EC.4.10**—Hospital addresses emergency management **IM.6.30**—MR documents procedures use moderate or deep sedation or anesthesia	

Requirement	CMS		Joint Commission	State
Anesthesia Services (AS)	**482.52**	Must be provided in a well-organized manner under the supervision of a physician **(a)** Organization of AS must be appropriate to scope of services anesthesia administered by— **(a)(1)** A qualified anesthesiologist **(a)(2)** Doctor of medicine or osteopathy **(a)(4)** Certified RN anesthetist under the supervision of the operating practitioner or anesthesiologist who is immediately available **(a)(5)** Anesthesiology assistant **(b)** Policies on anesthesia procedures must include delineation of pre-anesthesia responsibilities. The policies must ensure the following are provided: **(b)(1)** Pre-anesthesia evaluation performed within 48 hours prior to surgery by an individual qualified to administer anesthesia **(b)(2)** Intraoperative record **(b)(3)** Post-anesthesia follow-up report written within 48 hours after surgery for inpatients **(b)(4)** Post-anesthesia follow-up evaluation for anesthesia recovery in accordance with PPP approved by MS for outpatient	**LD.2.20**—Each program, service, department has effective leadership **HR.1.20**—Hospital has a process to ensure a person is qualified **MS.4.20**—Process for clinical privileges **PC.13.20**—Procedures that require administration of moderate or deep sedation or anesthesia are planned **PC.13.30**—Patients are monitored during administration of moderate or deep sedation or anesthesia **PC.13.40**—Patients are monitored immediately after the administration of moderate or deep sedation or aesthesia **IM.6.30**—MR documents procedures use moderate or deep sedation or anesthesia	

Requirement	CMS		Joint Commission	State
Nuclear Medicine Services (NMS)	482.53	**(a)** Organization of NMS must be appropriate to scope of services **(a)(1)** Director must be a doctor of medicine or osteopathy qualified in nuclear medicine **(a)(2)** Qualifications, training, and responsibilities of NMS personnel must be approved by NMS director and MS **(b)** Radioactive materials are handled in accordance with acceptable standards of practice **(b)(1)** In-house preparation **(b)(2)** Storage and disposal **(b)(3)** Laboratory tests and quality control **(c)** The equipment must be— **(c)(1)** maintained in safe operating condition **(c)(2)** inspected, tested, and calibrated at least annually by qualified personnel **(d)(1)** NMS reports must be maintained for at least 5 years **(d)(2)** The practitioner approved by the MS to interpret diagnostic procedures must sign and date test interpretations **(d)(3)** Must maintain records of receipt and disposition of radiopharmaceuticals **(d)(4)** NMS is ordered only by a practitioner whose scope of licensure and defined privileges allow such referrals	**LD.3.30**—Hospital demonstrates a commitment to community by providing essential services in a timely manner **LD.2.20**—Each program, service, department has effective leadership **HR.1.20**—Hospital has a process to ensure a person is qualified **EC.3.10**—Hospital manages hazardous materials and waste	
Outpatient Services (OS)	482.54	**(a)** Must be organized and integrated with inpatient services **(b)(1)** Assign an individual to be responsible for the OS **(b)(2)** Have appropriate professional and nonprofessional personnel available	**IM.6.40**—Continuing ambulatory care services MR must contain summary list all significant information **LD.2.20**—Each program, service, department has effective leadership **HR.1.20**—Hospital has a process to ensure a person is qualified **MS.4.20**—Process for clinical privileges	

Requirement	CMS		Joint Commission	State
Emergency Services (ES)	482.55	**(a)(1)** Must be organized and under the direction of a qualified member of the MS and **(a)(2)** Services must be integrated with other hospital departments **(a)(3)** PPP governing medical care are established by and a continuing responsibility of the MS **(b)(2)** Must be adequate medical and nursing personnel qualified in emergency care to meet the needs of the facility **NOTE: THESE ARE NOT THE REQUIREMENTS FOR EMTALA. EMTALA is found at 42 C.F.R. 489.20 and 489.24.**	**LD.2.20**—Each program, service, department has effective leadership **HR.1.20**—Hospital has a process to ensure a person is qualified **MS.2.20**—Patient's care responsibility practitioner with privileges **LD.3.30**—Hospital demonstrates a commitment to community by providing essential services in a timely manner **LD.3.70**—Leaders define number of staff to provide care, treatment, and services	
Rehabilitation Services (RS)	482.56	**(a)** Organization of the RS must be appropriate to the scope of services offered **(a)(1)** The director of RS must have knowledge, experience, and capabilities to properly supervise and administer RS **(a)(2)** RS must be provided by staff who meet the qualifications specified by the MS consistent with state law **(b)** Services must be furnished in accordance with a written plan of treatment. RS must be given in accordance with medical staff orders, and the orders must be incorporated in the patient's record	**LD.2.20**—Each program, service, department has effective leadership **HR.1.20**—Hospital has a process to ensure a person is qualified	
Respiratory Care Services (RCS)	482.57	**(a)** Organization of RCS must be appropriate to the scope and complexity of services offered **(a)(1)** Director of RCS must be a doctor of medicine or osteopathy. The director may be full- or part-time **(b)** Services are delivered in accordance with MS directives **(b)(1)** Written procedures for personnel and supervision **(b)(2)** Blood gases or other clinical laboratory tests **(b)(3)** Services must be provided in accordance with doctor's orders	**LD.2.20**—Each program, service, department has effective leadership **HR.1.20**—Hospital has a process to ensure a person is qualified **MS.2.20**—Patient's care responsibility of practitioner with privileges **IM.6.50**—Qualified personnel accept and transcribe verbal orders	

Requirement	CMS	Joint Commission	State
Human Resources (HR)	No COP titled "Human Resources"	**LD.3.70**—Leaders define qualification and sufficient number qualified/competent persons to provide care *Planning* **HR.1.10** through **HR.1.30** *Orientation* **HR.2.10** through **HR.230** *Competence Assessment* **HR.3.10** through **HR.3.20**	
Environment of Care (EC)	No COP titled "Environment of Care"	*Planning and Implementation Activities* **EC.1.10** through **ED.8.80** *Measuring and Improving Activities* **EC.9.10** through **EC.9.30**	

DEEMED STATUS

Background

The Social Security Act §§ 1861(e) and 1865(a) permit for deemed status of hospitals. Deemed status means that institutions accredited as hospitals by the Joint Commission or the American Osteopathic Association (AOA) are deemed to meet all of the Medicare Conditions of Participation, except

- The requirement for utilization review as specified in § 1861(e)(6) of the Act in 42 C.F.R. 482.30
- The additional special requirements necessary for the provision of active treatment in psychiatric hospitals §§ 1861(f) of the Act and 42 C.F.R. 482.60
- Any requiremnts under § 1861(e) of the Act and implementing regulations that CMS, after consulting with the Joint Commission or AOA, identifies as being higher or more precise than the requirements for accreditation in § 1865(a)(4) of the Act.

Procedure

A hospital deemed to meet program requirements must authorize the accreditation organization to release to CMS, or the state agency responsible for licensing, a copy of the most current accreditation survey. The hospital must furnish the accreditation survey report to the government agency that processes the deemed status requests (CMS or the state agency).

Determination

CMS or the state agency will review the survey, and related survey information, and make a determination to grant or deny deemed status to the hospital.

If deemed status is granted, the hospital is considered in compliance with the Medicare Conditions of Participation for the period of time the accreditation is valid (usually a period of three years).

CMS may use a validation survey (42 C.F.R. 488.7) or an accreditation survey or any other survey information (such as Life Safety Code requirements) to determine that a hospital does not meet the Medicare Conditions of Participation. In this case, the hospital is not granted deemed status, and may be required to submit a Plan of Correction to CMS to maintain Medicare certification.

ADDITIONAL RESOURCES

www.jcaho.org
www.cms.hhs.gov
www.cdc.gov
www.cms.hhs.gov/quality/hospital
www.organdonor.gov
www.fda.gov
www.osha.gov

Source: Copyright 2000 Denise Atwood and Rose Sparks.